ABRAHAM LINCOLN

1809–1858

In Two Volumes

VOLUME I

Abraham Lincoln

ABRAHAM LINCOLN

1809–1858

BY

ALBERT J. BEVERIDGE

VOLUME I

BOSTON AND NEW YORK

HOUGHTON MIFFLIN COMPANY

The Riverside Press Cambridge

1928

The Riverside Press
CAMBRIDGE · MASSACHUSETTS
PRINTED IN THE U.S.A.

PREFACE

WHEN Mr. Beveridge had finished his *Life of John Marshall*, he already had in view writing a Life of Abraham Lincoln, to be, as he expressed it, a companion piece to the Marshall, continuing the institutional interpretation of America and weaving it about the life and career of Lincoln as he had tried to weave the first part of such an interpretation around the life and career of Marshall. In the two works he would have covered the subject from colonial days to the end of the War of Secession. The story told in the volumes now published is complete to November, 1858.

The methods used by Mr. Beveridge in gathering the material for this work were controlled by the true spirit of research. He made his own investigations, questioning what had been published by others and trusting no agent without duly verifying his work. He made journeys to the Lincoln country, sifted the many traditions which have grown wherever the family rested, and sought to see for himself how far the neighborhood could influence the man. He was tireless in reading collections of papers still unpublished, in carefully going through files of newspapers preserved in many and widely separated cities, seeking the fact and coloring of narrative he used so skilfully and convincingly. In his own words he stated the value he placed upon such minute research:

'Facts when justly arranged interpret themselves. They tell the story. For this purpose a little fact is as important as what is called a big fact. The picture may be well-nigh finished, but it remains vague for want of one more fact.

'When that missing fact is discovered all others become clear and distinct; it is like turning a light, properly shaded, upon a painting which but a moment before was a blur in the dimness.'

Having located and obtained what seemed of importance he would write the chapter in its first form, or draft. That was a preliminary stage, for he would work over his material again and again, rewriting the entire chapter many times — a single chapter in the second volume was rewritten fifteen times — until it had taken a shape which appeared to him fairly complete in contents, but still wanting the finish of a last revision. In that form he submitted it to recognized experts in the different phases of the history, asking, or rather urging them to correct misstatements of fact, or wrong inferences, or an unconscious bias of treatment.

The chapters of these volumes, except Chapter X in the second volume, are the result of the many recastings he gave to them. That last chapter is in the state of a first draft, admittedly unfinished, yet, dealing with a single situation, it is a sufficiently full summary of the debates with Douglas in the senatorial contest of 1858 in Illinois. Mr. Beveridge planned to devote a year to a final revision of the whole work. One familiar with his method would know that the process of revising would have been continued throughout the year, in the proof and even in the page form, about to go to press; for his active mind and trained sense of the power of the spoken sentence would suggest changes at every reading of manuscript or proof.

The text, then, was at the time of his death in substance what Mr. Beveridge had accepted as giving the sequence of the story, the principal features and the large drafts from the material he had so laboriously gathered from many sources. He had developed the main incidents of Lincoln's career and described the influences which had opened the opportunities to advance, in spite of serious rebuffs and downright defeat. He did not overload the narrative with the trivial and unessential, and rejected much which would have added to the picture; but he wished to show that as a politician, in its best as in its less laudable meaning, Lincoln was measured and judged in his generation and can only be rightly comprehended as such. From that aspect the story is complete. The narrative, as he left it, has not been modified or changed. Quotations and references in the text have been verified and obvious errors corrected. In form and substance the volumes are as Mr. Beveridge left them. His intention had been to end this first part of the 'Life' with Lincoln's inauguration in March, 1861, and nearly two years of intense political activity remained to be treated to round out the period. A sketch of those years has been appended, with no attempt to deal in detail with the many influences and situations they presented, or to cover them after the manner of Mr. Beveridge. It may be imagined how he would have revelled in the story, making a study in practical politics, in the decay and growth of parties, and in the tyranny of party, so near to his aim in writing and to his own experience in public life; but no other could accomplish the history as he would have done it, or even forecast the outline as he would have sketched it. That is the real tragedy of the interrupted task.

There remains the pleasurable duty of acknowledging the aid and encouragement given to him and those working after him. That the acknowledgment is not in his own words is a misfortune. A part of it may be found in the notes running through the two volumes; another part cannot be expressed, for it was known only to him; and still another may be overlooked or wrongly measured. What follows will indicate the greater debts of obligation and a wish to recognize their extent.

The largest and most important aid was derived from Mr. Beveridge's friend of long standing, Jesse W. Weik, of Greencastle, Indiana. The law partner of William H. Herndon, and inheritor of his unique collection of Lincoln material, Mr. Weik had throughout his life greatly added to it and increased its value. Unused by any writer since Lamon except by Herndon and Weik in their joint *Life of Lincoln*, this remarkable collection was placed unreservedly at the service of Mr. Beveridge. The zeal and honest purpose of the gatherers have provided essential matter for almost every chapter. When used by Messrs. Herndon and Weik in their *Life of Lincoln*, a work unappreciated at the time, it was not possible to prove the richness of the record.

Second in importance was the unrestricted access given to the collection of Lincolniana belonging to Mr. Oliver R. Barrett, of Chicago. His enthusiasm and opportunity have built up a collection of remarkable size and scope, rich in personal association. Mr. Barrett not only gave freely the use of his possessions, but also aided Mr. Beveridge in locating other manuscripts.

Judge Otis M. Mather, of Hodgenville, and Judge Lafayette S. Pence, of Lebanon, Ky., have both placed their expert knowledge on the Lincolns in Kentucky at Mr. Beveridge's service and have been as untiring as generous in searching the local records of that State and resolving the complicated problems that arose from tradition and imperfect knowledge on the subject.

Prof. Theodore C. Pease, of the University of Illinois, afforded special aid in making available the labors of others in the history of Illinois, in indicating where material for study could be found, and in reading the chapters as completed. Prof. Arthur C. Cole, of Ohio State University, performed many of the same services. From Mr. William L. Patton, of Springfield, Ill., were obtained many important documents and much information on Lincoln in Illinois. His willingness to answer questions was only matched by the accuracy of his replies. Mr. J. C. Thompson, of Springfield, has given time and thought to matters connected with the work on which his knowledge has proved its worth. Mr. Logan Hay, also of Springfield, has been helpful and obliging in his special knowledge of what relates to Springfield. Mr. Thomas D. Masters, of Springfield, freely gave of his time and coöperation. Documents and information have also been furnished by Judge Frank K. Dunn, of the Supreme Court of Illinois; Judge John J. Drennan, of Chicago; Mr. William K. Townsend, of Lexington, Ky.; Prof. Ulrich B. Phillips, of the University of Michigan; Miss Alice and Miss Fannie Fell, daughters of Jesse W. Fell; Dr. Charles L. Patton, of Springfield, possessor of the Lanphier MSS.; Mr. David Rankin Barbee, of Asheville, N.C.; Mr. Thomas C. Fisher, of Louisville, Ky.; and Mr. William Fortune, of Indianapolis, Ind.

Mr. Beveridge sent a draft of the chapters to a number of friends and experts in whose opinion he had confidence. He was thus specially indebted to Mr. Justice Oliver Wendell Holmes, of Washington, D.C.; Mr. John T. Morse, Jr., of Boston; Prof. Charles A. Beard, of New York; and Mr. Ellery Sedgwick, of Boston, who were most helpful in comment and in encouragement as the writing progressed. In their various interests the following also contributed their trained knowledge: Mr. J. Franklin Jameson, of the Carnegie Institution; Mr. Ferris Greenslet, of Boston; Prof. Chauncey S. Boucher, of the University of Illinois; Prof. Nathaniel W. Stephenson, of New

York; Prof. William O. Lynch, of Indiana University; Prof. Thomas M. Marshall, of Washington University, St. Louis; Prof. S. E. Morison, of Harvard University; the late Prof. John Spencer Bassett, of Smith College; Prof. James A. Woodburn, of Ann Arbor, Mich.; Prof. Frank L. Owsley, of Vanderbilt University, Nashville, Tenn.; Prof. Henry G. Pearson, of Boston; and Mr. H. J. Eckenrode, of Richmond, Va.

For their reading of certain chapters may be named Prof. Frank H. Hodder, of the University of Kansas, and Mr. William E. Connelley, of the Kansas State Historical Society, both of whom were liberal in aid and counsel; Prof. George R. Poage, of Illinois College; Prof. William W. Sweet, of DePauw University; Prof. Herbert E. Bolton, of the University of California; Prof. Eugene C. Barker, of the University of Texas; Mr. Robert L. O'Brien, of Boston; Hon. Jacob M. Dickinson, of Chicago; Judge Clarence R. Martin, of Indianapolis; the law office of Mr. George W. Wickersham; and Dean Henry M. Bates, of the Law School, University of Michigan.

From Mr. and Mrs. James W. Fesler, of Indianapolis, were received friendly criticism, comment, and encouragement. But of all who closely followed the preparation of the chapters no one had greater influence than Prof. Edward Channing, of Harvard University, whose scholarship and understanding of the history of the period were drawn upon heavily and can be only in part acknowledged in the notes.

Many special favors were obtained from many libraries. Among them may be named: the Library of Congress and its assistant librarians, the late Appleton P. C. Griffin and his successor Mr. Fred W. Ashley; the Illinois State Historical Society, its very capable librarian, the late Mrs. N. W. (Jessie Palmer) Weber, daughter of Gen. John M. Palmer, and her successor, Miss Grace L. Osborne; the Boston Public Library and Mr. Frank C. Blaisdell, of the circulation department; the Indiana State Library, the librarian of which, the late Dr. Demarchus C. Brown, was useful in many ways; the Massachusetts State Library, and its librarian, Mr. Edward Redstone; the Newberry Library, Chicago, and its librarian, Mr. George B. Utley; the Massachusetts Historical Society, the

Chicago Historical Society, and the American Antiquarian Society, Worcester, Mass., and their officers. The *Chicago Tribune*, through Mr. Tiffany Blake, gave access to their files.

Mr. Paul M. Angle, of Springfield, Ill., has particularly verified references to the Journals of the Illinois House of Representatives and extracts from Illinois newspapers, and Mr. Edward H. Bohne, at one time secretary to Mr. Beveridge, has done the same service for references to or extracts from the volumes quoted by Mr. Beveridge.

To Mrs. Walter Farwell thanks are given for permission to use the portrait of Mrs. Stephen A. Douglas; to Mrs. Vardry Echols McBee, daughter of Preston S. Brooks, and James Elliott Heath for permission to use the portrait of Preston S. Brooks; and to Frederick Hill Meserve, of New York, for freely contributing from his great collection what was desired.

CONTENTS

WORKS CITED IN THESE VOLUMES   xvii

I. KENTUCKY: BIRTH AND CHILDHOOD   1

The United States in 1809 — Birth of Abraham Lincoln — Thomas Lincoln — Lincolns in Virginia — Removal to Kentucky — Nancy Hanks — Marriage of Thomas Lincoln — Elizabethtown — Removal to Sinking Spring farm — To Knob Creek — Riney's and Hazel's schools — Early years of Abraham — War of 1812 — Influx of settlers — Migration to Indiana — Land suit.

II. INDIANA: BOYHOOD AND YOUTH   38

Forests of Indiana — Lincoln's tract — Removal of family — The half-faced camp — Arrival of the Sparrows and Dennis Hanks — Death of the Sparrows and of Nancy Lincoln — Elkin's visit — Manner of living — Schools and dialect — Crawford's school — Marriage of Thomas Lincoln and Sarah Bush Johnston — Her influence on the family — Dorsey's and Sweeney's schools — Abraham at school — Want of sympathy between father and son — Abraham's love of reading — Thomas joins the church — Abraham's religion — History and Scott's *Lessons* — Abraham's social qualities — Youthful speeches — *Quinn's Jests* — Sarah's marriage — Dispute on ferry — Gentry and journey to New Orleans — Death of Sarah — 'Chronicles of Reuben' — Removal to Illinois — Politics.

III. NEW SALEM: EARLY MANHOOD AND DEVELOPMENT   100

Webster's reply to Hayne — Migration to Illinois — Great snowstorm — Offut and New Orleans — Slavery — Abraham at New Salem — Election — Clary Grove Boys — Lincoln — Armstrong fight — Lincoln's address as candidate — Visit of the *Talisman* — Black Hawk War — Lincoln's service — Canvass and speech — Berry and Lincoln — Wreck of Radford's store — Nullification in South Carolina — Appointed postmaster — Studies surveying — Calhoun and Graham — Lincoln's reading — Again a candidate — Elected representative — Paine and Volney — Law readings — Attitude toward women — Mary Owens — Ann Rutledge and McNamar — Death of Ann Rutledge — Reëlected — Robert Allen — Mary Owens and Lincoln's explanation.

IV. LEGISLATURE AND SPRINGFIELD   160

Vandalia in 1834 — Lincoln's first session — His votes and labors — Bank charters — Bank of the United States — Special session — National politics — Removal of the State capital — Leading members of court and legislature — Stephen A. Douglas — Lincoln's news letters — Governor Duncan's message — Discussion on slavery — Resolutions of the Southern States — Replies from the North — Action of Illinois — Stone and Lincoln's protest — Internal improvements report — Location of the State capital — Lincoln's defence of the bank — Selection of Springfield as capital — The place in 1837 — Lincoln's arrival and law partnership with Stuart — Interest in politics — Controversy with General Adams — Sampson's Ghost letters — Elijah P. Lovejoy and the Alton riot — Wendell Phillips's first appearance — Outbreaks of mob violence — Lincoln's Lyceum address.

V. LAST YEARS IN THE LEGISLATURE   232

Panic of 1837 — Duncan's message — Lincoln and Ewing on Springfield — Bank and internal improvements — Messages of Governors Duncan and Carlin — A National Bank or Sub-Treasury — Lincoln's support of the State Banks — Vandalia and Springfield — Resolution on the Abolitionists — Liquor laws — Lincoln's proposal to purchase the public lands in the State — The 'Long Nine' — Stuart and Douglas election — Special session and internal improvements — Lincoln's Whig address on the National Bank — Fight over internal improvements policy and banks — Legislation on liquor — Harrison and Van Buren campaign — Lincoln's instructions to Whig workers — Democrats carry Illinois — Special session on debt situation — Question of adjournment — Lincoln's exploit from window — Financial discussion — Lincoln's votes — License Bill — Lincoln's absence from the House — Reply to Kitchell — Election of a public printer — Reorganization of Supreme Court — Question of the alien voter — End of session.

VI. YEARS OF DISCIPLINE   298

Lincoln at Springfield — Coming of Herndon — Lincoln's reading and memory — His literary style — Member of the Whig Junto — 'Madison' letters — Social position of Lincoln — Relations with women — The Edwards family — Mary Todd — Lincoln's attentions and engagement — His doubts — Fails on day set for marriage — Lincoln's apathy and gloom — Sarah Rickard — Lincoln's visit to the Speed house — Joshua Speed and Fanny Henning — Slaves on the *Lebanon* — Advises Speed on marriage — Lincoln's temperance address — Speed's wedding — Visit of Van Buren — Lincoln meets Mary Todd by aid of Mrs. Francis — Failure of the State Bank — Auditor Shields issues circular — The 'Rebecca' letters — Mary Todd and Julia Jayne take part — Shields learns of Lincoln's authorship — Challenge and Lincoln's conditions — Merryman and Whiteside — Duel avoided — Marriage of Mary Todd and Lincoln — Whig address — Congressional election and Lincoln's conduct — His defeat — Lincoln takes Herndon into partnership — The Clay-Polk campaign.

VII. CONGRESS AND DECLINE   370

Lincoln's candidacy for Congress — Contest with Hardin — Lincoln's nomination — War with Mexico — Illinois troops — Alamo, Goliad, San Jacinto — Peter Cartwright — Lincoln's election — Johnston and verses — Lincoln attends River and Harbor Convention at Chicago — Return of troops from Mexico — Rev. Albert Hale's prayer — The Matson slave case — Lincoln goes to Washington — The capital in 1848 — Lincoln's committee appointments — Leading members of the House — Polk's message and Whig attack — Causes of war with Mexico — Santa Anna — Benjamin Lundy — John Quincy Adams — Opposition to continuing the war — Lincoln on annexation and slavery — His 'spot' resolutions — Ashmun's resolution — Lincoln's speech — Reaction in Illinois — The Young Indians.

VIII. NATIONAL POLITICS AND COLLAPSE   434

Death of John Quincy Adams — Lincoln's votes — Letter to his wife — The *Pearl* incident — Mrs. Lincoln's plea — Lincoln favors candidacy of General Taylor — The Whig Convention — Meeting of the Free-Soilers — Lincoln instructs Herndon on politics — Corrects Greeley on boundary — Aids National Whig Committee — Suggestions to Taylor — Gossip of capital — Lincoln's speeches — Dedication of Washington Monument — Lincoln's stump speech in Congress — Letters on political prospects of party — Situation in Massachusetts — Charles Sumner

— The Free-Soil Party — Lincoln at Worcester, Mass. — His speech —
Entertained by Levi Lincoln — Lincoln hears Seward — His return to
Springfield — Demands of his father and Johnston — The short session
in Washington — Slavery in the District of Columbia — Address of the
Southern Delegates in Congress — Neglect of Lincoln by the new Administration — Patronage and the Land Office — Butterfield's appointment — Letter to Clayton — Oregon offices — Lincoln's sense of failure.

IX. LAW: LIFE: GROWTH   494

Growth of Springfield — Law office of Lincoln and Herndon — Lincoln's
neglect of personal concerns — The Lincoln house — Lincoln's domestic
habits — Described by Whitney — Lincoln's relations with his children
— Mrs. Lincoln — Death of Thomas Lincoln — Riding the circuit —
David Davis — Swett and Lamon — Naming the town of Lincoln —
Lincoln's reading — Opinion of biography — Lincoln's associates on circuit — His melancholy — Taste in poetry — 'Mortality' — Superstition and belief in destiny — Aids to young lawyers — Country roads
and taverns — Lincoln's humorous stories — His temperance — Liking
for shows — His moods not understood — Question of his religion —
Father Chiniquy's suit — Wide acquaintance of Lincoln and belief in his
honesty — Acts as judge — The Todd estate and claim against Lincoln
— Cases in which Lincoln appeared — His methods — Scores a judge —
Peachy Harrison — Ridicule.

X. LAST YEARS AT THE BAR   552

Lincoln's fees — The Wright pension case — Rebecca Daimwood —
Herndon's overcharge in the Scott case — Davis's rebuke of Lincoln —
The Duff Armstrong murder trial — Production of the *Almanac* — Lin-
coln explains the working of his mind — Railroad litigation — A slander
suit — The 'Reaper Case' — Lincoln retained — Harding and Stanton's
treatment of him — Effect of Harding's argument on Lincoln — Hard-
ing's vote in 1860 — Tax case of the Illinois Central Railroad Company
— Lincoln's wish for employment — His fee and resulting suit —
George B. McClellan — The Rock Island Bridge Company's case —
Lincoln's argument — Lincoln's enlarged house.

ILLUSTRATIONS

ABRAHAM LINCOLN   *Photogravure Frontispiece*
From an ambrotype made at Springfield, Illinois, August 13, 1860 (maker unknown)

MAP OF SANGAMON AND NEIGHBORING COUNTIES IN ILLINOIS, SHOWING SPRINGFIELD AND NEW SALEM   108

JOHN J. HARDIN   180
From a portrait in the possession of Mrs. Amelia M. D. Hardin

JOHN T. STUART   214
From a portrait in the office of Mr. Logan Hay

MARY TODD LINCOLN   308
From a print in the collection of Mr. Oliver R. Barrett

JOSHUA F. SPEED AND HIS WIFE   324
From a portrait by George P. A. Healy

JAMES SHIELDS   354

ABRAHAM LINCOLN ABOUT 1848   424
From a photograph of the daguerreotype formerly owned by Robert T. Lincoln, in the collection of Mr. Frederick H. Meserve

DAVID DAVIS   514

WORKS CITED IN THESE VOLUMES

ACKERMAN, WILLIAM KELLY. Illinois Central Railroad. Chicago, 1890.

ADAMS, JOHN QUINCY. Memoirs. Ed. by Charles Francis Adams. Phila., 1874–77.

AMBLER, CHARLES HENRY. Sectionalism in Virginia, 1776–1861. Chicago, 1910.

—— Thomas Ritchie: a Study in Virginia Politics. Richmond, 1913.

American Historical Association. Reports, 1889–1922.

American Historical Review, 1896–1927.

AMES, HERMAN VANDENBURG. State Documents on Federal Relations. Phila., 1900–06.

ANDREAS, ALFRED THEODORE. History of the State of Kansas. Chicago, 1883.

ARNOLD, ISAAC NEWTON. Life of Abraham Lincoln. Chicago, 1885.

—— History of Abraham Lincoln and the Overthrow of Slavery. Chicago, 1866.

BALDWIN, JOSEPH GLOVER. Flush Times in Alabama. New York, 1853.

BANCROFT, FREDERIC. Life of William Henry Seward. New York, 1900.

BARTON, WILLIAM ELEAZAR. The Paternity of Abraham Lincoln. New York, 1920.

—— Life of Abraham Lincoln. 2 vols. Indianapolis, 1925.

BAY, WILLIAM VAN NESS. Bench and Bar of Missouri. St. Louis, 1878.

BEECHER, EDWARD. Narrative of the Riots at Alton. Alton, 1838.

BEVERIDGE, ALBERT J. Life of John Marshall, 1755–1835. Boston, 1916–19.

BIRNEY, JAMES GILLESPIE. American Churches, the Bulwarks of American Slavery. 3d ed. Concord, 1885.

BLACKMAR, FRANK WILSON. Life of Charles Robinson. Topeka, 1902.

BLANCHARD, JONATHAN, and NATHAN LEWIS RICE. Debate on Slavery, . . . October, 1845, in the city of Cincinnati. Cincinnati, 1846.

BOONE, RICHARD GAUSE. History of Education in Indiana. New York, 1892.

BOURNE, GEORGE. Slavery illustrated in its Effects upon Women and Domestic Society. Boston, 1837.

—— The Book and Slavery Irreconcilable. Phila., 1816.

BOWERS, CLAUDE G. Party Battles of the Jackson Period. Boston, 1922.

BREMER, FREDRIKA. America of the Fifties: Letters. New York, 1924.

BROOKE, SAMUEL. Slavery and the Slaveholder's Religion. Cincinnati, 1846.

BROWN, GEORGE WASHINGTON. Reminiscences of Gov. Robert J. Walker. Rockford, Ill., 1902.

BROWNING, ORVILLE HICKMAN. Diary; edited by T. C. Pease and J. G. Randall. Vol. I. Springfield, 1925.

BRYAN, EDWARD B. The Rightful Remedy. Charleston, 1850.

BRYAN, WILHELMUS BOGART. History of the National Capital. New York, 1914–16.

BRYANT, WILLIAM CULLEN. Prose Writings. Ed. by Parke Godwin. New York, 1884.

BUCHANAN, JAMES. Works. Ed. by John Bassett Moore. Phila., 1908–11.
BUCKINGHAM, JAMES SILK. The Slave States of America. London [1842].
BURMEISTER, HERMANN. The Black Man. New York, 1853.
BUSEY, SAMUEL CLAGETT. Personal Reminiscences and Recollections. Washington, 1895.

CALHOUN, JOHN CALDWELL. Works. Ed. by Richard K. Crallé. New York, 1854–56.
CAMPBELL, OLIVE DAME, and CECILE JAMES SHARP. English Folk Songs from the Southern Appalachians. New York, 1917.
CARSON, HAMPTON LAWRENCE. The Supreme Court of the United States. Phila., 1891.
CARTWRIGHT, PETER. Autobiography. Ed. by W. P. Strickland. New York, 1857.
Case of Dred Scott in the Supreme Court of the United States. December Term, 1854.
CATON, JOHN DEAN. Early Bench and Bar of Illinois. Chicago, 1893.
CATTERALL, RALPH CHARLES HENRY. Second Bank of the United States. Chicago, 1903.
CHAMBERS, WILLIAM. American Slavery and Colour. London, 1857.
CHANNING, EDWARD. History of the United States. New York, 1905–25.
CHANNING, WILLIAM ELLERY. Address on Emancipation in the West Indies. Lenox, 1842.
CHASE, PHILANDER. Reminiscences; an Autobiography. Peoria, 1841–42.
CHEEVER, HENRY THEODORE. Tract for the Times. New York, 1859.
CHEVALIER, MICHAEL. Society, Manners and Politics in the United States. Boston, 1839.
Chicago River and Harbor Convention. Fergus' Historical Series.
CHILD, LYDIA MARIA. Anti-Slavery Catechism. Newburyport, 1836.
CLAY, HENRY. Works; Life, Correspondence and Speeches. Ed. by Calvin Colton. New York, 1897.
COCKRUM, WILLIAM MONROE. Pioneer History of Indiana. Oakland City, 1907.
COFFIN, JOSHUA. An Account of some of the Principal Slave Insurrections in the United States. New York, 1860.
COFFIN, LEVI. Reminiscences. London, 1876.
COLE, ARTHUR CHARLES. The Constitutional Debates of 1847. Springfield, 1919.
—— Centennial History of Illinois. III. Era of the Civil War. Springfield, 1919.
—— The Whig Party in the South. Washington, 1913.
COLEMAN, MRS. CHAPMAN. The Life of John J. Crittenden. Phila., 1871.
COLLINS, LEWIS. History of Kentucky; rev. by R. H. Collins. Covington, 1878.
CONDON, WILLIAM H. Life of Major General James Shields. Chicago, 1900.
Congressional Directory. Washington, 1848.
CONNELLEY, WILLIAM ELSEY. Provisional Government of Nebraska Territory. Lincoln, 1899.
—— Standard History of Kansas and the Kansans. Chicago, 1918.

—— An Appeal to the Record. Topeka, 1903.

CONNOR, HENRY GROVER. John Archibald Campbell. Boston, 1920.

The Constitution, a Pro-Slavery Compact. Edited by Wendell Phillips. Two editions. New York, 1856.

CORWIN, EDWARD SAMUEL. Doctrine of Judicial Review. Princeton, 1914.

COTTERILL, ROBERT SPENCER. History of Pioneer Kentucky. Cincinnati, 1917.

Covode Investigation. June 16, 1860. [36th Cong. 1st Sess., House Report, 648.]

CUNNINGHAM, JOSEPH OSCAR. History of Champaign County. Chicago, 1905.

CURTIS, BENJAMIN ROBBINS. Memoir of Benjamin Robbins Curtis. [Ed. by George Ticknor Curtis.] Boston, 1879.

CURTIS, GEORGE TICKNOR. Life of James Buchanan. New York, 1883.

CUTTS, JAMES MADISON. Brief Treatise upon Constitutional and Party Questions as I received it from the late Stephen A. Douglas. New York, 1866.

Jefferson Davis, Constitutionalist, his Letters, Papers and Speeches. Ed. by Dunbar Rowland. Jackson, 1923.

DAVIS, JOHN PATTERSON. The Union Pacific Railway. Chicago, 1894.

DAVIS, VARINA ANNE BANKS. Jefferson Davis, a Memoir. By his wife. New York [1890].

DeBow, JAMES DUNWOODY BROWNSON. Industrial Resources of the Southern and Western States. New Orleans, 1852–53.

—— DeBow's Review of the Southern and Western States. New Orleans, 1850–52.

DESMOND, HUMPHREY JOSEPH. Know Nothing Party. Washington, 1905.

DEW, THOMAS RODERICK. See Pro-Slavery Argument.

DEWEY, DAVIS RICH. Financial History of the United States. New York, 1903.

DIXON, MRS. ARCHIBALD (SUSAN BULLITT). True History of the Missouri Compromise and its Repeal. Cincinnati, 1899.

DOUGLAS, STEPHEN ARNOLD. Autobiography. Journal Ill. State Hist. Soc., v.

DRAKE, DANIEL. Pioneer Life in Kentucky. Ed. by C. D. Drake. Cincinnati, 1870.

DUDLEY, ROBERT, pseud. of James Baldwin. In my Youth. Indianapolis, 1914.

DUIS, ETZARD. Good Old Times in McLean County, Illinois. Bloomington, 1874.

DUNBAR, CHARLES FRANKLIN. Economic Essays. New York, 1904.

DUNCAN, ROBERT B. Old Settlers. Indianapolis, 1894.

ECKENRODE, HAMILTON JAMES. Jefferson Davis. New York, 1923.

EGGLESTON, EDWARD. The Circuit Rider. New York, 1874.

EGGLESTON, GEORGE CARY. The First of the Hoosiers. Phila., 1903.

ELLIOTT, ROBERT GASTON. Foot Notes on Kansas History. Lawrence, 1906.

ESAREY, LOGAN. History of Indiana. Indianapolis, 1915.

EWART, DAVID. A Scriptural View of the Moral Relations of African Slavery. Charleston, 1859.

FAIRFIELD, JOHN. Letters. Lewiston, 1922.

FAUX, WILLIAM. Memorable Days in America: being a Journal, 1823. In Early Western Travels: Thwaites, xi.

Federal and State Constitutions. Ed. Francis Newton Thorpe. Washington, 1909.

FEHLANDT, AUGUST F. A Century of Drink Reform. New York [1904].

FILSON, JOHN. Discovery, Settlement, and present State of Kentucke. Wilmington, 1784.

[FISHER, SIDNEY GEORGE.] The Laws of Race, as connected with Slavery. Phila., 1860.

FITZHUGH, GEORGE. Sociology of the South. Richmond, 1854.

FLINT, HENRY MARTYN. Life of Stephen A. Douglas. New York, 1860.

FLOWER, GEORGE. History of the English Settlement in Edwards Co., Ill. Chicago, 1882.

FORD, THOMAS. A History of Illinois. Chicago, 1854.

FORDHAM, ELIAS PYM. Personal Narrative of Travels in Virginia, etc. Ed. by Frederic A. Ogg. Cleveland, 1906.

FORTUNE, WILL. Warrick and its Prominent People. Evansville, 1881.

FOSTER, STEPHEN SYMONDS. Brotherhood of Thieves. Boston, 1844.

GARRISON, WENDELL PHILLIPS, and FRANCIS JACKSON GARRISON. William Lloyd Garrison, 1805–79. New York, 1885–89.

GIHON, JOHN H. Geary and Kansas. Phila., 1857.

GILDERSLEEVE, BASIL LANNEAU. Creed of the Old South, 1865–1915. Baltimore, 1915.

GILLESPIE, JOSEPH. Recollections of Early Illinois. Chicago, 1880.

GLADSTONE, THOMAS H. The Englishman in Kansas. New York, 1857.

GOBRIGHT, LAWRENCE AUGUSTUS. Recollections of Men and Things at Washington. Phila., 1869.

GOING, CHARLES BUXTON. David Wilmot, Free-Soiler. New York, 1924.

GOODELL, WILLIAM. Slavery and Anti-Slavery. New York, 1852.

GOUVERNEUR, MARIAN (CAMPBELL). As I remember; Recollections of American Society. New York, 1911.

GRAYSON, WILLIAM JOHN. The Hireling and the Slave. Charleston, 1855.

GREELEY, HORACE. Recollections of a Busy Life. New York, 1868.

GRUND, FRANCIS JOSEPH. Americans in their Moral, Social, and Political Relations. London, 1837.

HALE, EDWARD EVERETT. Kansas and Nebraska. Boston, 1854.

HALL, EDWARD HEPPLE. Springfield City Directory, and Sangamon County Advertiser, for 1855–6. First Publication. Springfield, 1855.

HALL, JAMES. Sketches of History, Life and Manners, in the West. Cincinnati, 1834.

HAMMOND, JAMES HENRY. See Pro-Slavery Argument.

HARPER, WILLIAM. See Pro-Slavery Argument.

HARRIS, BRANDON L. Some Recollections of my Boyhood.

HARRIS, THADDEUS MASON. Journal of a Tour, into the Territory Northwest of the Allegheny Mountains. In Early Western Travels: Thwaites, iii.

HARVEY, PETER. Reminiscences and Anecdotes of Daniel Webster. Boston, 1877.

HAYCRAFT, SAMUEL. History of Elizabethtown. Elizabethtown, 1921.

HENDERSON, ARCHIBALD. Conquest of the old Southwest. New York, 1920.

HENING, WILLIAM WALLER. Statutes at Large . . . Virginia. New York, etc., 1819–23.

HERNDON, WILLIAM HENRY, and JESSE WILLIAM WEIK. Herndon's Lincoln (3 vols.). Chicago [1889]. (Cited as Herndon.) Second edition (2 vols.). New York, 1892. (Cited as Herndon and Weik.)

HILDRETH, RICHARD. The Slave; or, Memoirs of Archy Moore. Boston, 1840.
—— The White Slave. Boston, 1852.

HILL, FREDERIC TREVOR. Lincoln the Lawyer. New York, 1906.

History of the Organization of the Methodist Episcopal Church, South, 1845.

History of Transportation in the United States before 1860. (Carnegie Institution.) Washington, 1917.

History of Warwick, Spencer and Perry Counties. Chicago, 1885.

HOBSON, JONATHAN TODD. Footprints of Abraham Lincoln. Dayton, 1909.

HOIT, TRUE WORTHY. Right of American Slavery. St. Louis, 1860.

HOLLOWAY, JOHN NELSON. History of Kansas. Lafayette, 1868.

Howard Committee. Congressional Investigating Committee on the Troubles in Kansas. Washington, 1856.

HOWELLS, WILLIAM COOPER. Recollections of Life in Ohio from 1813 to 1840. Cincinnati, 1895.

HULME, THOMAS. Journal, 1828. In Early Western Travels: Thwaites, x.

HUNDLEY, DANIEL ROBINSON. Social Relations in our Southern States. New York, 1860.

Illinois. House Journals, 1832–58.

INGRAHAM, JOSEPH HOLT. The Southwest, by a Yankee. New York, 1835.

IRELAN, JOHN ROBERT. The Republic. Chicago, 1886–88.

JAY, WILLIAM. An Examination of the Mosaic Laws of Servitude. New York, 1854.

JAYNE, WILLIAM. Abraham Lincoln. [Chicago, 1908?]

JOHNSON, ALLEN. Stephen A. Douglas: a Study in American Politics. New York, 1908.

JOHNSON, CHARLES BENEULYN. Illinois in the Fifties. Champaign, 1918.

JOHNSTON, RICHARD MALCOLM, and WILLIAM HAND BROWNE. Life of Alexander H. Stephens. Phila., 1878.

JONES, CHARLES COLCOCK. Religious Instruction of the Negroes in the United States. Savannah, 1842.

JULIAN, GEORGE WASHINGTON. Political Recollections, 1840–72. Chicago, 1884.

KEMBLE, FRANCES ANNE (MRS. BUTLER). Journal of a Residence on a Georgian Plantation. London, 1863.

Kentucky. Register of the Kentucky Historical Society. Louisville, 1903–26.

KOERNER, GUSTAVE. Memoirs, 1809–1896. Ed. by T. J. McCormack. Cedar Rapids, 1909.

KRAMER, JOHN THEOPHILUS. The Slave Auction. Boston, 1859.

LAMON, WARD HILL. Recollections of Abraham Lincoln, 1847–1865. Edited by Dorothy Lamon Teillard. Chicago, 1895.

—— Life of Abraham Lincoln; from his Birth to his Inauguration. Boston, 1872.

LATROBE, CHARLES JOSEPH. The Rambler in North America. 1832–33. London, 1835.

LEARNED, MARION DEXTER. Abraham Lincoln. An American Migration. Phila., 1909.

LEVERING, JULIA HENDERSON. Historic Indiana. New York, 1909.

LINCOLN, ABRAHAM. Complete Works. Biographical edition. New York [1905].

Lincoln-Douglas Debates of 1858. Ed. by Edwin Erle Sparks. Springfield, 1908.

Lincoln Centennial Association. Publications. Springfield, Ill., 1924–26.

LINCOLN, WALDO. History of the Lincoln Family. Worcester, 1923.

LINDER, USHER FERGUSON. Reminiscences of the Early Bench and Bar of Illinois. Chicago, 1879.

LORD, NATHAN. Letter of Inquiry to Ministers of the Gospel of all Denominations on Slavery. Boston, 1854.

—— A Northern Presbyter's Second Letters. Boston, 1855.

LOVEJOY, JOSEPH CAMMET, and OWEN LOVEJOY. Memoir of [Elijah Parish] Lovejoy. New York, 1838.

LUNDY, BENJAMIN. The War in Texas; a Crusade against Mexico. Phila., 1857.

LYELL, SIR CHARLES. Travels in North America in 1841–42. London, 1845.

—— A Second Visit to the United States, 1845–46. New York, 1849.

McCALL, GEORGE ARCHIBALD. Letters from the Frontier. Phila., 1868.

McCLELLAN, GEORGE BRINTON. Mexican War Diary. Ed. William Starr Myers. Princeton, 1917.

McCULLOCH, HUGH. Men and Measures of Half a Century. New York, 1888.

MACKAY, ALEXANDER. The Western World, or Travels in the United States. London, 1849.

McKEE, THOMAS HUDSON. National Conventions and Platforms of all Political Parties, 1789–1900. Baltimore, 1900.

McMASTER, JOHN BACH. History of the People of the United States; from the Revolution to the Civil War. New York, 1883–1913.

MADDEN, RICHARD ROBERT. Twelvemonth's Residence in the West Indies. London, 1835.

MARSHALL, THOMAS MAITLAND. History of the Western Boundary of the Louisiana Purchase. Berkeley, 1914.

MARTINEAU, HARRIET. Retrospect of Western Travel. London, 1838.

—— Society in America. London, 1837.

MATHESON, JAMES. See Andrew Reed.

MAY, SAMUEL JOSEPH. Some Recollections of our Anti-Slavery Conflicts. Boston, 1869.

MERRIAM, GEORGE SPRING. Life and Times of Samuel Bowles. New York, 1885.

Messages and Papers of the Presidents, 1789–1897. Comp. by James Daniel Richardson. Washington, 1896–99.

MICHAUX, FRANÇOIS ANDRÉ. Travels. In Early Western Travels: Thwaites, III.

MILLER, R. D. History of Menard and Mason Counties. Chicago, 1879.

MITCHELL, DAVID WILLIAM. Ten Years in the United States. London, 1862.

MITCHELL, SAMUEL AUGUSTUS. Illinois in 1837. Phila., 1837.

—— An Accompaniment to Mitchell's Map. Phila., 1838.

MOSES, JOHN. Illinois, Historical and Statistical. Chicago, 1889.

MURAT, NAPOLÉON ACHILLE. America and the Americans. New York, 1849.

NEWTON, JOSEPH FORT. Lincoln and Herndon. Cedar Rapids, 1910.

NICOLAY, JOHN GEORGE, and JOHN HAY. Abraham Lincoln. New York, 1890.

NORWOOD, JOHN NELSON. Schism in the Methodist Episcopal Church, 1844. Alfred, N.Y., 1923.

OGDEN, ROLLO, ed. Life and Letters of Edwin Lawrence Godkin. New York, 1907.

OLIVER, WILLIAM. Eight Months in Illinois. Newcastle-upon-Tyne, 1843.

OLMSTED, FREDERICK LAW. A Journey in the Seaboard Slave States. New York, 1856.

ONSTOT, THOMPSON GAINS. Pioneers of Menard and Mason Counties. Forest City, 1902.

PALMER, JOHN MCAULEY. Personal Recollections. Cincinnati, 1901.

PARKER, JOHN A. What led to the War, or the Secret History of the Kansas-Nebraska Bill. New York, 1880.

PARKER, THEODORE. Speeches, Addresses and Occasional Sermons. Boston, 1852.

PARRISH, JOHN. Remarks on the Slavery of the Black People. Phila., 1906.

PARSONS, CHARLES GRANDISON. Inside View of Slavery; or, a Tour among the Planters. Boston, 1855.

PAULDING, JAMES KIRKE. Slavery in the United States. New York, 1836.

PAXTON, WILLIAM MCCLUNG. Annals of Platte County, Mo. Kansas City, 1897.

PEASE, THEODORE CALVIN. The Frontier State, 1818–1848. Chicago, 1910.

—— Illinois Election Returns, 1818–48. Springfield, 1923.

PELZER, LOUIS. Cæsar Augustus Dodge. Iowa City, 1908.

PETERSON, CHARLES JACOBS (J. THORNTON RANDOLPH, pseud.). The Cabin, and the Parlor; or Slaves and Masters. Phila., 1852.

PHILLIPS, ISAAC NEWTON. Abraham Lincoln; a Short Study. Bloomington, 1901.

PHILLIPS, ULRICH BONNELL. American Negro Slavery. New York, 1918.

—— Plantation and Frontier, 1649–1863. 1910.

PHILLIPS, WENDELL. Speeches, Lectures and Addresses. Boston, 1863, 1891.

PIERCE, EDWARD LILLIE. Memoir and Letters of Charles Sumner. Boston, 1878–1894.

PIERPONT, JOHN. Anti-Slavery Poems. Boston, 1843.

PILLSBURY, PARKER. The Church as it is, or, the Forlorn Hope of Slavery. Boston, 1847.

Political History of Jackson Co., Mo. Kansas City, 1902.

POLK, JAMES KNOX. Diary during his Presidency, 1843–49. Ed. Milo M. Quaife. Chicago, 1910.

POOLEY, WILLIAM VIPOND. Settlement of Illinois from 1830 to 1850. Madison, 1908.

POORE, BENJAMIN PERLEY. Perley's Reminiscences of Sixty Years in the National Metropolis. Phila. [1886].

POWER, JOHN CARROLL, and MRS. E. A. (HARRIS) POWER. History of the Early Settlers of Sangamon County, Ill. Springfield, 1896.

[PRINGLE, EDWARD.] Slavery in the Southern States. Cambridge, 1852.

Pro-Slavery Argument. Charleston, 1852. Contains essays by Thomas Roderick Dew, James Henry Hammond, William Gilmore Simms and William Harper.

Protest against Slavery.

PRYOR, MRS. ROGER ATKINSON (SARA AGNES RICE). Reminiscences of Peace and War. New York, 1904.

PULSZKY, FERENCE AUREL (FRANCIS), and TERÉZ (THERESA) PULSZKY. White, Red, and Black; Sketches of American Society. New York, 1853.

RANDOLPH, J. THORNTON, pseud. of Charles Jacobs Peterson.

RAY, PERLEY ORMAN. Repeal of the Missouri Compromise. Cleveland, 1909.

REED, ANDREW, and JAMES MATHESON. Narrative of the Visit to the American Churches. London, 1835.

REED, THOMAS P. Lincoln at New Salem. Chicago, 1927.

Register of Debates in Congress. Washington, 1825–35.

—— Congressional Globe, 1833–1860. Washington, 1835–1860.

Reminiscences of Abraham Lincoln. Ed. Allen Thorndike Rice. N.Y. 1888. Washburne, Elihu Benjamin. Weldon, Lawrence.

REYNOLDS, JOHN. Pioneer History of Illinois. Belleville, 1848.

—— My Own Times. [Belleville] 1855.

RHODES, JAMES FORD. History of the United States from the Compromise of 1850. New York, 1893–1906.

RICE, NATHAN LEWIS. Ten Letters on the Subject of Slavery. St. Louis, 1855. See also Jonathan Blanchard.

RICHARDS, JOHN THOMAS. Abraham Lincoln: The Lawyer-Statesman. Boston, 1916.

RICHARDSON, ALBERT DEANE. Beyond the Mississippi. Hartford, 1866.

RICHARDSON, RICHARD HIGGINS. 'Wickedness in High Places.' A Discourse occasioned by the Bill for the Government of Kansas and Nebraska. Chicago, 1854.

RIDDLE, ALBERT GALLATIN. Life of Benjamin F. Wade. Cleveland, 1888.

RIVES, GEORGE LOCKHART. The United States and Mexico, 1821–1848. New York, 1913.

ROBERTSON, GEORGE. The American Party, its Principles, its Objects and its Hopes. Frankfort, 1855.

ROSS, FREDERICK AUGUSTUS. Slavery ordained of God. Phila., 1857.

ROSS, HARVEY LEE. Early Pioneers of Illinois. Chicago, 1899.

Ross, Robert W. Historical Souvenir of Vandalia. Effingham, Ill., 1904.

Rupp, Daniel. The Geographical Catechism of Pennsylvania and the Western States. Harrisburg, 1836.

Sawyer, George S. Southern Institutes; or, an Inquiry into . . . Slavery and the Slave-Trade. Phila., 1858.

Schaff, Phillip. Slavery and the Bible. Chambersburg, 1861.

Schmeckebier, Laurence Frederick. History of the Know Nothing Party in Maryland. Baltimore, 1899.

Schuckers, Jacob William. Life and Public Services of Salmon Portland Chase. New York, 1874.

Schurz, Carl. Reminiscences. Garden City, 1907–08.

Scisco, Louis Dow. Political Nativism in New York State. New York, 1901.

Scott, Franklin William. Newspapers and Periodicals of Illinois, 1814–1879. Springfield, 1910.

Seitz, Don Carlos. Horace Greeley. Indianapolis [1926].

Seward, William Henry. Life and Public Services of John Quincy Adams. Auburn, 1849.

—— Works. Boston, 1884.

Shaler, Nathaniel Southgate. Kentucky: A Pioneer Commonwealth. Boston, 1884.

Sheahan, James Washington. Life of Stephen A. Douglas. New York, 1860.

Simms, William Gilmore. See Pro-Slavery Argument.

Smith, Justin Harvey. The War with Mexico. New York, 1919.

—— The Annexation of Texas. New York, 1919.

Smith, Oliver Hampton. Early Indiana Trials and Sketches. Cincinnati, 1856.

Smith, Theodore Clarke. Liberty and the Free Soil Parties in the Northwest. New York, 1897.

Smith, William L. G. Life at the South, or Uncle Tom's Cabin as it is. 1852.

Sons of the Sires: A History . . . of the American Party. By an American. Phila., 1855.

South Vindicated from the Treason and Fanaticism of the Northern Abolitionists. Philadelphia, 1836.

Southern Literary Messenger. Richmond, 1834–64.

Spear, George L. History of Bement, Ill.

Speed, James. James Speed: a Personality . . . Louisville, 1914.

Speed, Joshua Fry. Reminiscences of Abraham Lincoln. Louisville, 1864.

Speer, John. Life of General James H. Lane. Garden City, Kas., 1896.

Spring, Leverett Wilson. Kansas. Boston, 1885.

Stanwood, Edward. History of the Presidency. Boston, 1898.

Starr, John William, Jr. Lincoln and the Railroads. New York, 1927.

Stearns, Edward Josiah. Notes on Uncle Tom's Cabin. Phila., 1853.

Stearns, Frank Preston. Life and Public Services of George Luther Stearns. Phila., 1907.

Steiner, Bernard. Life of Roger Brooke Taney. Baltimore, 1922.

Stephens, Alexander Hamilton. Constitutional View of the War between the States. Phila., 1868–70.

—— Recollections of A. H. Stephens. His Diary. Ed. Myrta Lockett Avary. New York, 1910.

STEPHENSON, NATHANIEL WRIGHT. Texas and the Mexican War. Chronicles of America, XXIV. New Haven, 1921.

STEVENS, FRANK EVERETT. Life of Stephen A. Douglas. Journal Ill. State Hist. Soc., XVI.

STILL, WILLIAM. Uncle Tom's Cabin Reviewed.

STOWE, CHARLES EDWARD. Life of Harriet Beecher Stowe. Boston, 1890.

—— Life and Letters of Harriet Beecher Stowe. Ed. by Annie Fields. Boston, 1897.

STOWE, HARRIET BEECHER. Uncle Tom's Cabin. Boston, 1852. Dred. Boston, 1856.

STRINGER, LAWRENCE BEAUMONT. History of Logan County, Ill. Chicago, 1911.

STRINGFELLOW, BENJAMIN FRANKLIN. Negro-Slavery, No Evil; or The North and the South: A Report made to the Platte County Self-Defensive Association. Boston, 1854.

STUART, JAMES. Three Years in North America. Edinburgh, 1833.

STUART, MOSES. Conscience and the Constitution. Boston, 1850.

STUART-WORTLEY, LADY EMMELINE. Travels in the United States during 1849 and 1850. London, 1851.

SUMNER, CHARLES. Works. Boston, 1870–83.

SUNDERLAND, LEROY. The Testimony of God against Slavery, or a Collection of Passages from the Bible. Boston, 1835.

SWEET, WILLIAM WARREN. The Methodist Episcopal Church and the Civil War. Cincinnati, 1912.

TANNER, HENRY. The Martyrdom of Lovejoy. Chicago, 1881.

THAYER, ELI. History of the Kansas Crusade. New York, 1889.

—— The New England Emigrant Aid Company. Worcester, 1887.

THWAITES, REUBEN GOLD. Daniel Boone. New York, 1902.

TILLSON, CHRISTIANA HOLMES. A Woman's Story of Pioneer Illinois. Chicago, 1919.

TOCQUEVILLE, ALEXIS DE. Democracy in America. Trans. by Henry Reeve. Ed. by Francis Bowen. Cambridge, 1862.

TOWNSEND, GEORGE ALFRED. Washington Outside and Inside. Hartford, 1871.

TOWNSEND, WILLIAM HENRY. Lincoln the Litigant. Boston, 1925.

—— Abraham Lincoln, Defendant. Boston, 1923.

TRACY, GILBERT AVERY. Uncollected Letters of Abraham Lincoln. Boston, 1917.

TUCKER, NATHANIEL BEVERLEY. The Partisan Leader. New York, 1856 [1836].

TURNER, NAT. Confessions of, Leader of the Late Insurrection. New York, 1861.

TURPIE, DAVID. Sketches of My Own Times. Indianapolis, 1903.

TYLER, SAMUEL. Memoir of Roger Brooke Taney. Baltimore, 1872.

Tyrant Paupers, 1843.

United States Census 1840, 1850, 1860.

Unjust Judge. A Memorial of Roger Brooke Taney. New York, 1865.

VILLARD, HENRY. Memoirs of Henry Villard. Boston, 1904.
VILLARD, OSWALD GARRISON. John Brown, 1800–1859. Boston, 1910.

WAKEFIELD, JOHN ALLEN. History of the Black Hawk War. Jacksonville, 1834.
WARDEN, ROBERT BRUCE. Private Life and Public Services of Salmon P. Chase. Cincinnati, 1874.
WARREN, CHARLES. The Supreme Court in United States History. Boston, 1922.
WARREN, LOUIS AUSTIN. Lincoln's Parentage and Childhood. New York [1926].
WASHBURNE, ELIHU BENJAMIN. See Reminiscences of Abraham Lincoln.
WAYLAND, JOHN WALTER. History of Rockingham County, Virginia. Dayton, Va., 1912.
WEBSTER, DANIEL. Writings and Speeches. Boston, 1903.
—— Private Correspondence. Ed. by Fletcher Webster, Boston, 1857.
WEIK, JESSE WILLIAM. The Real Lincoln. Boston, 1922. See William H. Herndon.
WEISS, JOHN. Life and Correspondence of Theodore Parker. New York, 1864.
WELBY, ADLARD. Visit to North America, 1821. In Early Western Travels: Thwaites, XII.
[WELD, THEODORE DWIGHT.] American Slavery as it is: The Testimony of 1000 Witnesses. New York, 1839.
WELDON, LAWRENCE. See Reminiscences of Abraham Lincoln.
WENTWORTH, JOHN. Reminiscences. Fergus' Historical Series, I. Nos. 7, 8.
WHARTON, ANNE HOLLINGSWORTH. Social Life in the Early Republic. Phila., 1903.
WHEAT, MARVIN T. Progress and Intelligence of Americans; Collateral Proof of Slavery . . . as founded on Organic Law. [n.p., 1865.]
WHIPPLE, CHARLES KING. Relations of Anti-Slavery to Religion. [New York, 1856.]
WHITE, CHARLES THOMAS. Lincoln and Prohibition. New York [1921].
WHITE, HORACE. Lincoln in 1854. Address before the Illinois State Historical Society, 1908.
—— Life of Lyman Trumbull. Boston, 1913.
WHITNEY, HENRY CLAY. Life of Lincoln. New York, 1908.
—— Life on the Circuit with Lincoln. Boston [1892].
WILDER, DANIEL WEBSTER. Annals of Kansas. Topeka, 1875.
WILSON, HENRY. History of the Rise and Fall of the Slave Power in America. Boston, 1872–77.
WILSON, JAMES HARRISON. Life of Charles Anderson Dana. New York, 1907.
WILSON, RUFUS ROCKWELL. Washington, the Capital City. Phila., 1901.
WINTHROP, ROBERT CHARLES. Addresses and Speeches. Boston, 1852.
WOOD, AARON. Sketches of Things and Peoples in Indiana. Indianapolis, 1883.
WOODS, JOHN. Two Years' Residence. In Early Western Travels: Thwaites, X.

WOOLLEY, JOHN G., and WILLIAM E. JOHNSON. Temperance Progress of the
    Century. London, 1903.
Worcester Society of Antiquities. Rugg, Arthur P. xxv, 226.
WRIGHT, ELIZUR, JR. The Sin of Slavery and its Remedy. New York, 1833.
WRIGHT, HENRY CLARKE. No Rights, No Duties. Boston, 1860.

YOAKUM, HENDERSON, and others. History of Texas. New York, 1856.

ABRAHAM LINCOLN

ABRAHAM LINCOLN

.·.

CHAPTER I

KENTUCKY: BIRTH AND CHILDHOOD

Biographies, as generally written, are not only misleading, but false. The author makes a wonderful hero of his subject. He magnifies his perfections, if he has any, and suppresses his imperfections. History is not history unless it is the truth. LINCOLN.

IN America, democracy was in control of Congress; and the popular idol, Thomas Jefferson, was enthroned in the Presidency. His choice of a successor had been ratified by the people, and James Madison was about to be inaugurated. The great radical and politician was soon to retire from office with such public acclaim as no President ever received.

In spite of grave mistakes, Jefferson had achieved this phenomenal favor with the masses chiefly by his sincere and expressed faith in the people, a faith they instinctively felt; also by his theoretical championship of States' rights and opposition to strong national government — an attitude then considered by the majority as best assuring individual liberty and preventing spoliation of the poor and the weak.

The Federalist party, first and most constructive of American political organizations, was fast dissolving. For five years, Hamilton, preëminent supporter of national power and the almost undisputed Federalist chieftain, had been in his grave. Notwithstanding the soundness of many Federalist policies, that party was disintegrating, principally because of its sharp and outspoken distrust of the people, but also by reason of its British partisanship, and its resistance to the westward advance of the Republic.

France and England were at war and, as the result of Jefferson's policy of prohibiting imports and abolishing foreign commerce, American trade on the sea had all but ceased and the American flag had well-nigh disappeared from the oceans. All

New England was tempestuous with wrath, and along her coasts the resistance to national law and authority, accompanied by talk of secession from the Union, swept like a winter hurricane. From the Supreme Bench of the United States was heard the voice of wisdom and statesmanship. Chief Justice Marshall, who was stoutly opposed to Jefferson's policy of commercial exclusion and non-resistance, nevertheless used stern language against acts 'destructive of the Union.'

While America was thus in convulsion, her commerce nearly extinct, her navy neglected and rotting, despised abroad and distracted at home, Europe was rocking with martial preparation. On the sea the British navy was triumphant and irresistible, but on the continent Napoleon still was master.

England, far-sighted, dexterous, implacable, had long since set in motion her traditional foreign policy and all Europe was now being combined against France. Napoleon, at the summit of his power, was not far distant from the downward road and yet pursued his destined course with a spirit, brilliancy, and dash not since equalled. Just as Jefferson's second term was closing, and the rumblings of disunion were sounding from New England, Napoleon was making ready to take the field once more, this time with an army of boys called to the colors two years in advance, four years in advance. With faith in his star still unshaken he exclaimed: 'I am starting for Vienna with my little conscripts, my name, and my long boots.'

While the foundations of the Union trembled and the Old World throbbed with armed activity and pulsed with intrigue; while, in the United States, democracy and virile government were antagonistic instead of harmonious; and while war made brilliant with uniform and pomp every capital of Europe; far from the turmoil, across the mountains, in a log cabin in the heart of Kentucky, on February 12, 1809, Abraham Lincoln was born.[1]

[1] Daniel Webster, then twenty-seven years of age, had not yet entered Congress; Henry Clay, at thirty-two, was already in the Senate and well started on his unprecedented and unequalled career; John C. Calhoun, also twenty-seven, was still in the Legislature of South Carolina; Lee was a child of two years; and Grant not yet born.

In Europe, February 12, 1809, was the birthday of another man who was destined profoundly to influence the thought of the world, Charles Darwin. Tennyson and

The earth was the floor of that shelter. The roof of rough slabs was held in place by poles and stones. In the log walls a small square opening, possibly covered with greased paper, let in a scant, dim light. Two long, broad slabs, fastened together and attached by hinges of wood or of hide to the side of a cut in the walls high enough for a man to pass through, served as a door.

At one end of this cabin was a rude fireplace of stone with a chimney of sticks and clay. In a corner opposite was a pallet or bed, the frame made by a crotched stick driven into the ground upon which the ends of a long and a short pole rested, the other ends thrust between the logs of the cabin. Across this frame were placed rough slats, and upon these bedding of some sort was spread.[1] The whole structure was of wood, no iron being available.[2]

This log hut stood on the edge of a tract of poor land, with few trees[3] and covered by tall, coarse grass. Immediately in front of the cabin the ground sloped sharply downward. A spring flowed from a horizontal cave-like channel of rock in the low hillside and, dropping abruptly into another but perpendicular opening of rock, disappeared. From this, the distinctive feature of the place, the land on which Thomas Lincoln and his family lived was then known as the 'Sinking Spring Farm.'

Yet farm it could hardly be called, so unproductive was it at that time. Nor was the spot attractive in other respects, save perhaps for the spring and three or four oaks that grew by it and

Gladstone, too, were born in that year. The period was productive of men of the first rank in letters and statesmanship. Victor Hugo and Cavour, and Disraeli, Dickens and Bright, Thackeray and Bismarck, were all born within the dozen years centering about 1809.

[1] 'He [Abraham Lincoln] was born . . . in an obscure back settlement of cane-brake society, in a hunter's hut not fit to be called a home.' Judge John B. Helm to W. H. Herndon, June 20, 1865. Weik MSS. The cabin in which Lincoln was born was torn down and the logs used for firewood by Henry Brother, who bought the Sinking Spring Farm in 1827 and lived in the cabin for some years. *Footprints of Abraham Lincoln:* J. T. Hobson, 15. The year of purchase is also given as 1835.

For methods of building cabins and bed frames, homes of more prosperous settlers, see *History of Elizabethtown:* Samuel Haycraft, 70–2. This history, first published in the *Elizabethtown News*, is a source book of repute.

[2] *Sketches of the West:* James Hall, ii, 67.

[3] 'It is rather poor land and at that . . . day not worth over $1. per acre.' E. R. Burba to Herndon, Hodgenville, Ky., March 31, 1866. Weik MSS.

in the gentle hollow. Half a mile distant flowed the South Fork of Nolin Creek. Along this watercourse small trees lifted their modest tops, among which dogwood here and there sent forth its blossoms in springtime. During the winter months, a more cheerless place than the cabin by the Sinking Spring did not exist in all Kentucky.

The farm was just within the border of 'the Barrens,' that curious tract which so impressed Michaux, the French traveller and scientist, when he rode over it not long before Thomas Lincoln took his wife and infant daughter to inhabit the log house by the Sinking Spring. This section, seventy miles long and sixty miles broad, was made treeless from long-continued successive fires started by the Indians for the purpose of opening a place where the buffalo could graze.[1] It contained many subterranean caverns and springs similar to that hard by the Lincoln cabin, but not so picturesque, and was barren of other vegetation than the tall grass and a scattering of small trees along the infrequent streams. Few people then lived in the region.[2]

The picture of Thomas Lincoln, the father of Abraham Lincoln, is distinct, clear-cut. Research has left no feature vague, except his stature.[3] He was compactly built, inclined to stoutness. His face was round, complexion swarthy, hair black and

'At the birth of Lincoln it was a barran waste so to speak, save some little patches on the creek bottom.' Burba to Herndon, May 25, 1866. Weik MSS.

Even to-day [1924] this land is estimated at only fifty dollars per acre. Judge O. M. Mather of Hodgenville, Ky., to author, July 14, 1924.

In references hereafter to be made, particular weight must be given to any statement of E. R. Burba, of Hodgenville, Ky., because of his extensive acquaintance and credibility. He was a hot advocate of Lincoln: 'I verily believe . . . he was the greatest man since . . . Washington.' Burba to Herndon, March 31, 1866. Weik MSS.

'He [Burba] was elected Clerk and served as such for many years. No man in the County had a wider acquaintance than he, and I think you may rely on what he says.' Judge O. M. Mather to author, July 17, 1924. Also 'History of Hodgenville,' O. M. Mather, in *LaRue County News*, April 22, 1920.

[1] *Kentucky: A Pioneer Commonwealth:* N. S. Shaler, 28–30. Prof. Shaler says that 'in another two hundred years the Indians would probably have reduced the larger part of the surface of Kentucky to the condition of the prairies.' And see *History of Pioneer Kentucky:* R. S. Cotterill, 2–3.

[2] 'On the road where the plantations are closest together we counted but eighteen in a space of sixty or seventy miles.' F. A. Michaux's *Travels:* Reuben Gold Thwaites, III, 220–1. See also *ib.*, 217–8.

[3] He 'was 5-10½ high very stoutly built and weighed 196 pounds. . . . He was a man of great strength . . . could stand fatigue for any length of time.' Dennis Hanks's second statement, June 13, 1865. Weik MSS.

coarse, eyes brown.[1] He was improvident,[2] yet in a slow and plodding way industrious. He was good-natured,[3] inoffensive, law-abiding, notably honest.[4] Without a vestige of book learning [5] he was able only to write his name in a painful scrawl; but he preferred to make his mark and usually did so, even in legal documents of importance to himself in the trivial litigation presently to be noted.[6] He had no use for books and, in languid fashion, despised all print.[7]

He was a carpenter of sorts,[8] and did well two or three jobs

'Thomas Lincoln was a large man, say 6 feet or a little less, strong and muscular.' Nathaniel Grigsby's statement, Sept. 12, 1865. Weik MSS.

'Thomas Lincoln . . . was rather a low heavy built clumsy honest man.' Samuel Haycraft to Judge John B. Helm, July 5, 1865. Weik MSS.

'He was a square, stout-built man of only ordinary height.' Haycraft to Herndon, no date, Weik MSS.

Like E. R. Burba, Samuel Haycraft of Elizabethtown, Ky., is a witness of the highest possible credibility. No more esteemed and trusted man lived in Hardin County, where he was clerk of both County and Circuit Courts from 1816 to 1857 inclusive, a member of the Kentucky State Senate and 'one of the most determined . . . supporters of the Union.' Haycraft knew personally those of whom he writes; and, like Burba, was a staunch friend of President Lincoln.

[1] Hanks's second Chicago statement. 'Darke hair Rather Corse Hazel Eye . . . Broder face than Abe Walked slow and Shore a Mity strought Man.' Hanks to Herndon, no date, Weik MSS.

[2] He 'was not a thrifty man of his class.' Helm to Herndon, June 20, 1865.

[3] In his two Chicago statements Dennis Hanks tells of a desperate fight without anger or malice between Thomas and some one, just to see which was the better man. Lincoln whipped his friendly antagonist 'in less than two minutes.' In these statements made within a week, he names two different men as having been Lincoln's discomfited opponent. Weik MSS.

This fight is probably one of Hanks's inventions, made because 'unless a man could boast of whipping somebody, he was not taken up in the best society.' Burba to Herndon, May 25, 1866. Weik MSS. Burba adds: 'I never heard of any of the Lincoln family thus engaged.' *Ib.*

Dennis Hanks is watchful in the extreme in exalting the Hanks and Lincoln families; but aside from his boastfulness ('Now William be Shore and have My Name very Conspikus.') and championship of his clan, his statements are accurate. Luckily, it is easy to distinguish between fact and imagination in his letters and interviews.

[4] 'Thomas Lincoln was considered to be a strictly honest hard working man.' Burba to Herndon, March 31, 1866. Weik MSS.

'He was a plain unpretending and scrupulously an honest man.' Haycraft to Herndon, Dec. 7, 1866. Weik MSS.

[5] 'When I first knew him in 1805 or 1806, he was a very illiterate man.' Haycraft to Helm, Elizabethtown, July 5, 1865. Weik MSS.

[6] See p. 22, *infra.*

[7] He 'looked upon bone and mussel sufficient to make the man and, that time spent in school as doubly wasted.' Helm to Herndon, June 20, 1865. Weik MSS.

[8] He was 'a tolerable country . . . carpenter, worked some on my father's house in

that were remembered. But his heaviest undertaking turned out unhappily; his employer, an important man in the community, was so dissatisfied that, as we shall see, payment was refused and two law-suits resulted.[1] He was a farmer in a desultory way, but he liked hunting more than anything else, delighted to roam the forests and kill such game as came within convenient range. Thus the meat was supplied upon which his wife and children chiefly subsisted.[2]

Thomas Lincoln was the youngest son of Abraham Lincoln who, about 1776, had gone to Kentucky to look over the country and had entered one thousand acres of land there. He lived in Rockingham County, Virginia, where he owned an excellent farm of two hundred and sixty-two acres on which his children were born, Thomas on January 6, 1778.[3] John Lincoln, father of Abraham, had come from Pennsylvania, in which State the family had settled in the course of several migrations. The genealogy of the Lincolns runs clear and unbroken to its source in England; all were upright persons of moderate substance and good reputations in the various communities where they lived; one or two rose to some prominence,[4] but none showed any quality that marked the subject of these volumes.

1805, and afterward did all the carpenter's work on Hardin Thomas house.' Haycraft to Helm, July 5, 1865. Weik MSS. Also Haycraft's *History of Elizabethtown*, 123. Also Haycraft to Herndon, no date, Weik MSS.

'The old man was a kind of rough carpenter and quite useful in that way. in those days the country was sparsely settled.' Burba to Herndon, March 31, 1866. Weik MSS.

[1] See p. 22, *infra*.

[2] He 'made his living by labor and hunting till game became scarce.' Helm to Herndon, June 20, 1865. Weik MSS.

'Thomas Lincoln . . . delighted in having a good hunt. . . . [It] was a great source of subsistance.' He 'could with propriety be classed with the "Hunters of Kentucky." he seldom failed of success.' Hanks's first Chicago statement. Weik MSS.

[3] These dates are taken from *History of the Lincoln Family*: Waldo Lincoln, 193–4, 333 — a comprehensive and trustworthy volume on the Lincoln Genealogy. Louis A. Warren, *Lincoln's Parentage and Childhood*, 40–2, cites the Tax Books of Washington and Hardin Counties for 1795–7 and asserts an earlier year of birth. In 1795 and 1796 Thomas was listed as between sixteen and twenty years and in 1797 as twenty-one or over. If he became of age in 1797 he was born in 1776, but this is not supported by the President's statement that Thomas was six years of age when his father Abraham was killed. It is possible that Thomas, for some reason, made himself to be older than he really was. The family Bible record — January 6, 1778 — is not final, as it is mutilated.

[4] The Lincoln migrations were first described by Professor Learned of the University of Pennsylvania, and his volume containing deeds, wills, and other documents is the

In Rockingham County, Virginia, then, we find the father of Thomas Lincoln in 1780, a well-to-do Virginia farmer, who, without the help of slaves, tilled his own fields. The soil of this county then was and it still remains of the richest in the United States. The county had been settled by Germans from Pennsylvania who had soon turned into a garden its fertile acres. No part of the Shenandoah Valley was or is more productive, or engaging to the eye, than the county of Rockingham.[1]

John Lincoln had given to Abraham two hundred and ten acres of this pleasing farm, and the son, by purchase, had added fifty-two acres.[2] Prosperous neighbors were plentiful and not distant; the population of Rockingham County then was not less than five thousand, consisting of the families of small farmers like Lincoln himself, most of whom possessed few if any slaves, the farm work being done by the owners of the soil and their sons.

The men of proper age who were drawn belonged to the militia and, at one time, Abraham was captain of his company.[3] He took no interest in the Revolution, however, and at the darkest hour of the War for Independence sold his Virginia fields for £5,000 in the then greatly depreciated Virginia currency,[4] and, like many others, plunged into the vast and dangerous wilderness beyond the mountains.

Why Abraham Lincoln should have decided to leave his agreeable surroundings in Virginia can only be conjectured. It would appear that many motives formed his resolution. Virginia was hard pressed to raise funds for carrying on the conflict with Great Britain and the Legislature was laying mountains of

most authoritative treatment of the subject. *Abraham Lincoln, An American Migration:* Marion Dexter Learned. *History of the United States:* Edward Channing, VI, 255.

[1] *History of Rockingham County:* John W. Wayland, chaps. I–IV.

[2] Waldo Lincoln, 193.

[3] *Ib.*

[4] Lincoln sold his Rockingham farm February 18, 1780, but his wife Bathsheba did not join in the deed until September 24, 1781. Waldo Lincoln, 193–4.

At the time of the sale the depreciation of Virginia currency had become so great that the Legislature established the rate of forty to one. *Statutes at Large:* W. W. Hening, x, 348. A year later the Legislature enacted that paper money theretofore issued by the state should no longer be legal tender and should be redeemed by exchange of loan office certificates at the rate of one thousand to one in specie; but provided that until October 1, 1782, warrants for unappropriated land 'at the price now established by

taxes on the people.[1] Soldiers, too, were continually being re-
cruited and conscription was talked of.[2] Continental currency
had become worthless and ceased to circulate; and that of the
Commonwealth was falling like a plummet in fresh water. In
1780 the prospects of the American cause were desperate.

Against this background of gloom and disaster appeared rosy
and inviting pictures of Kentucky, then a part of Virginia. A
distant relative by marriage of Abraham Lincoln,[3] Daniel
Boone and his little band of adventurers had brought back
from that region accounts of a land, lovely and opulent beyond
human dreams — 'a second paradise,' Boone called it;[4] and
went back himself with his family to live there.[5] Even more
weighty than these inducements to western migration were the
land laws passed by the Legislature of Virginia in 1779. By
these Acts the rights of actual settlers already on the ground were
defined and the confusion of land titles in Kentucky somewhat
untangled; a Land Office was established and methods provided
for making settlements, surveys, and to obtain certificates and
patents.[6]

law,' might be purchased by holders of depreciated Continental or state paper money
at its face value. Act of November, 1781. Hening, x, 456. Since the Legislature found
it necessary to fix as a matter of law such rates of depreciation, the actual value of
state currency was, of course, much less.

The following year the time of redemption at 1000 to 1 was extended to June 1,
1783, and the privilege of buying land warrants extended to the same date. *Ib.*, xi,
133. And see *History of American Currency:* Davis Rich Dewey, 39–55.

[1] As examples of these war time tax laws in 1779 see Hening, x, 165–72; 182–8;
189–91; in 1780, 241–54; 271–2; in 1781, 490–2; 501–17. (This act allowed payment
even of taxes on land at the rate of one to ten; and provided that other taxes might
be paid in tobacco, hemp, or flour. *Ib.*, 508.)

[2] A draft of every twenty-fifth man actually was enacted in 1778. Hening, ix, 589.
This failing, a more stringent law was enacted in 1779. *Ib.*, x, 82.

[3] Waldo Lincoln, 52.

[4] Boone's Autobiography in *The Discovery, Purchase and Settlement of Kentucky:*
John Filson, 54. Filson wrote Boone's autobiography which was widely circulated
and gave Boone his fame. Archibald Henderson describes him as 'that inaccurate and
frenzied amanuensis.' *Am. Hist. Rev.*, xx, 86, and Thwaites says that Filson's narrative
is untrustworthy. *Life of Daniel Boone:* Reuben Gold Thwaites, 153, 199.

Col. Richard Henderson founded Transylvania 'solely' because of Boone's description and persuasion (*ib.*, 114); and Henderson, after visiting Kentucky, also wrote
that the country was 'a paradise.' *Ib.*, 124. Also *Conquest of the Old Southwest:*
Archibald Henderson, 159.

[5] Boone surveyed many large tracts for himself, as for example: 'Aperel the 22 1785
on the Bank of Cantuckey Survayd for Dal Boone 5000 acres,' etc. *Boone:* Thwaites,
208–9.

[6] Hening, x, 35–65, and see *History of Kentucky:* Lewis Collins, i, 253–7.

Under the pressure of economic conditions of which these laws were an expression, the trickle of emigrants became a thin stream.[1] But stronger than the expelling force of taxes, military service and war burdens, stronger than the lure of romantic descriptions or persuasive laws, was that instinct for expansion which, from the first, has been an outstanding characteristic of the American people. This impulse to seek new lands, to occupy a far country, to invade and conquer forest and prairie was the compelling cause of pioneer advance; and it is the most important fact in the economic development of America. Through all other concrete and practical motives of Abraham Lincoln for leaving his comfortable Virginia farm ran, like living nerves, this yearning for the wilderness and distant places.[2]

Having chosen a tract in which to set up a new home in Kentucky, he brought his family from Virginia sometime between 1782 and 1784.[3] Upon Land Office warrants purchased with part of the currency received for his Rockingham farm,[4] he had entered three tracts of land aggregating twelve hundred acres, himself and sons surveying one by the crude and inaccurate methods of the time.[5] For these tracts patents were later issued, the first by Beverly Randolph, Lieutenant Governor of Virginia, May 17, 1787, for eight hundred acres on Green River in Lincoln County; the second by James Garrard, Governor of

[1] The western movement was almost wholly for new lands. By 1790, over 100,000 had gone West. Petitions for titles are full of the germs of squatter sovereignty. These settlers were intensely individualistic and fought land companies as fiercely as they fought Indians. See *Sectionalism in Virginia:* Charles Henry Ambler, 42–5.

Travellers at the time, however, attributed western migration to restlessness and daring. *Rambler in North America:* Charles Joseph Latrobe, 72–3.

The immigrants to Kentucky were almost exclusively from Virginia and North Carolina; there were 'none from Europe, and scarcely any from the eastern states.' These pioneers were, by nature and training, hunters and soldiers, fearless, daring, and thoroughly American. Hall, II, 95–7.

[2] Collins says that there was 'a flood of immigration' (Collins, I, 253); but in comparison with the later volume of settlers, the incoming pioneers of 1780–5 were not impressive in number.

[3] Waldo Lincoln, 194.

[4] These Land Office Warrants, dated March 4, 1780, were numbered 3333, 3334, and 3335, each for 400 acres, and for each Lincoln paid £160.

[5] The Floyd's Fork tract, the survey being made May 7, 1785. Many settlers did their own surveying; 'with a compass and chain, a few hours' work would suffice to mark the boundaries of a thousand-acre tract.' *Boone:* Thwaites, 119.

Kentucky, July 2, 1798, for four hundred acres on the Long Run of Floyd's Fork in Jefferson County.[1] Such were the moderate land holdings of Abraham Lincoln, fairly large for a small farmer, although inconsiderable compared to the estates of opulent planters which often ran into tens of thousands of acres.

Evidence exists that he lived for a time on his land on Green River, Lincoln County. In 1779, Jacob Gum and his brother-in-law, Oliver Dever, obtained eight hundred acres on Green River under the Virginia 'Occupancy Law' and, setting up an 'improver's cabin' on the tract, lived there, thus complying with the requirements of the law. Lincoln bought the two warrants from them in June, 1780, and the description of the land reads: '800 acres six miles below Green River Lick including an improvement [the cabin] made by Jacob Gum and Oliver Dever.' The description was imperfect, giving no county, and Lincoln filed in the clerk's office of Lincoln County a more correct description: '800 acres lying and being on Green River six miles below Green River Lick in the County of Lincoln.' Proper entry of the corrected description was made in the Surveyor's Book[2] and on Oct. 2, 1784, the land was surveyed for Lincoln by William Montgomery, assistant surveyor of the county, both Abraham and Hannaniah Lincoln being present. There can be no doubt of Lincoln's occupying the land and cabin, as he was bound to do under the Virginia law, then quite rigidly enforced.

Gum removed to Nolin Creek, Nelson County, in 1782 or 1783, as his deposition[3] of Oct. 2, 1787, in a suit on Miller's

[1] A tax return made by Mordecai Lincoln in 1796 listed the three tracts mentioned and also one of 1134½ acres on Green River, which stood in the name of John Reed but belonged to Abraham Lincoln. This last holding, represented by warrant No. 14487, was originally 2268 acres, but, it is claimed, Reed forged a release of one-half. Warren, 10, 11.

It appears that in December, 1782, Abraham entered, on Treasury Warrant No. 5994, five hundred acres in Campbell (now Pendleton) County, being a part of two entries of 1000 acres each noted in Boone's Survey Book as for 'Lincoln.' Draper MSS. This tract was not even surveyed until 1798, more than ten years after Lincoln's death, and the patent was not issued until June 30, 1799. Waldo Lincoln, 195–6. It was sold by Mordecai Lincoln June 8, 1808, and it may have been from his share of the proceeds that Thomas Lincoln got the money to buy the Sinking Spring farm. See p. 23, infra.

[2] Surveyor's Entry Book, vol. 2, Book E, 379, Lincoln County Court Records.

[3] Deposition Book B, 406. Records of Nelson County Quarter Sessions Court.

Big Spring, on Nolin Creek, shows, and that was in all probability the time when Abraham Lincoln brought his family to Green River. How long they remained there, before removing to land adjoining Hughes Station, Jefferson County, has not been determined.[1]

Sometime, within a few years after he had settled with his family in this new wild land, the father, while working a short distance from his cabin, was killed by an Indian.[2] The elder son,

[1] This important location of Abraham Lincoln in Lincoln County has been supplied by Judge L. S. Pence. From him also has been obtained the following description of Abraham Lincoln's land in Jefferson County: '1780, May 29, lying on Floyd's Fork, lying about 2 miles above [Powell's] trace ford crossing of Long Run.'

[2] The time and place of the pioneer Abraham's death were long in doubt. Family tradition gave 1784, and Judges Mather and Pence inferred from certain court records the spring of 1788 as the time and Nelson County as the place. Although the administrator of his estate was appointed Oct. 14, 1788, in Nelson County, Lincoln held no land in it. In a suit brought in 1797 by Mordecai Lincoln, heir at law of his father, he stated that his father died without a will May, 1786. His 'widow' remained on the farm certainly until Sept., 1786, for her name, so described, is among those of the vicinity who subscribed to an expedition against the Indians, her contribution being a gun. Warren, 297-8.

On Nov. 15, 1787, in the case of James Davis, Administrator, vs. Abraham Lincoln and Arvin Kilbreath, an alias was issued in Nelson County against the latter, living in Jefferson County, the summons having been executed on Abraham Lincoln, which indicates that he was then living in Nelson County. For this document I am indebted to Judge L. S. Pence, of Lebanon, Kentucky, who has made long and painstaking research, and who believes that Lincoln was wounded by an Indian in Jefferson County, 'wildly fled' to old man Richard Berry's — his brother-in-law — in Nelson County and lived for more than a year after the attack upon him. Judge Pence believes that Abraham died in Nelson County in April, 1788, as the above suit was discontinued, May 14, 1788, the first sitting of the court after the death of the resident defendant. L. S. Pence to author, May 20, 1924.

On the same day another suit, Aaron Colvin, Assignee, vs. Abraham and Hannaniah Lincoln, was also 'discontinued.' Order Book, Nelson County Court, 1788. Judge O. M. Mather, who furnishes this citation, believes that this suit was abated because of the death of the defendant, Abraham Lincoln. Mather to author, Aug. 11, 1924. Judges Mather and Pence agree that the only probable inference from these records is that Lincoln died in Nelson County in the spring of 1788.

In further evidence Judge Pence calls attention to an order of the court of Nelson County, Dec., 1786, appointing James Winn and William Allen to settle a boundary dispute with Jefferson County. The report of the agents has not been found, but the situation suggests that in Sept., 1785, when the first court was held at 'Bairdstown,' Lincoln's plantation and domicile were included in Nelson County, and the summons of 1787 and administration over his personal estate in 1788 would rest upon his being within the jurisdiction of Nelson County. Later the disputed boundary was set back into the original Jefferson County. Lincoln may have been shot in Jefferson County and fleeing to Nelson County lived there a sufficient time to create a legal jurisdictional status for administration of his estate. L. S. Pence to W. C. Ford, June 25, 1927.

Abraham's land adjoined that of Morgan Hughes (Hughes Station), was surveyed on the same day as Hughes' and both properties were in Jefferson County.

Mordecai, in turn shot the savage and rescued his brother Thomas who appears to have been with his father at the time.[1]

The widow with her children soon left for Nelson County [2] where the family lived for some years. It would seem that Mordecai, the most intelligent and energetic as well as the oldest son, took charge of his father's holdings by common consent, managed the family's affairs, selling the land when he liked and dividing the proceeds. The English law of descents had been abolished by Virginia, and inheritances went equally to the children of intestates.[3] So, as we shall see, Thomas got his share of the proceeds of his father's small estate when his perhaps more provident brother disposed of any part of it.

Thomas appears to have been held in small esteem by his brother and little attention would seem to have been given to him. While Mordecai acquired, in some way, a fair education for a pioneer farmer and could write well, no more ignorant boy than Thomas could be found in the backwoods. At any rate, after his sixteenth year he roved about, now here, now there, in this county and in that.[4] Once he journeyed through the woods to Tennessee, where he lived for some months with an uncle. By the time he was twenty-one years old, however, he seems to have settled down to what, for him, was a steady life in a given place.

On September 2, 1803, with money given him by Mordecai as Thomas's share of the proceeds of a sale of land inherited from the father,[5] he bought of John T. Slater for £118 two hundred and thirty-eight acres of land in Hardin County, about eight miles north of the prosperous and thriving village of Elizabethtown; [6] but it does not appear that Thomas ever tilled his soil,

---

[1] In 1782 Indian warfare became intense and lasted for several years. Collins (ed. 1874), i, 254–7. Between 1783 and 1790, 1500 Kentuckians were killed by the Indians. *Boone:* Thwaites, 205.

[2] Waldo Lincoln, 201–2. This book and all biographies say that the widow and her children went to Washington County; but that county was not created until 1792, when it was cut off from Nelson. Collins, ii, 748.

[3] Act of October, 1785, Hening, xii, 138–40; and see Clay *vs.* Cousins (1824): T. B. Monroe's (Ky.) *Reports*, i, 75–8.

[4] 'That Thomas was of a roving disposition cannot be denied.' Waldo Lincoln, 335.

[5] *The Paternity of Abraham Lincoln:* William E. Barton, ·267.

[6] Deed Book B, 253, Records Clerk of Hardin County, Ky.

or, indeed, that he even lived upon his farm. He remained in Hardin County, however, probably in Elizabethtown, for he served on juries four times, and guarded prisoners three times in 1803–04.[1] He owned a horse in 1804–05 and was taxed for it in those years.[2]

On March 25, 1805, the County Court appointed him and three other young men 'Patrolers in the northwardly district of this County,' with Christopher Bush as captain.[3] The law required patrollers to seize any slave strolling without permit or found at any unlawful assemblage and, 'at the discretion of the captain,' to administer not to exceed ten lashes on his or her bare back; and to do the same to any slave 'found in the possession of any article of property, without such writing.' [4] These officers had to patrol as many hours as the court directed, 'but not . . . less than twelve hours in each month,' the captain receiving four shillings and each assistant three shillings for every twelve hours of service, and being exempt from militia service during the term of appointment.[5]

Although Hardin County at that time was very large, being one hundred and forty miles long by fifty miles wide,[6] roughly speaking, there were comparatively few slaves in the whole extent of it, not more than four hundred at most.[7] These must have been very recalcitrant and dangerous to have required so many patrollers to keep them in hand; or, perhaps, the letter of the law was stretched, according to the free and easy frontier

[1] Hardin County Order Book, 1803–04.

[2] Tax records Hardin County, 1804–05.

[3] Order Book of Hardin County Court, March Term, 1805, 13. This Christopher Bush was the father of Sarah Bush, the second wife of Thomas Lincoln, and of Isaac Bush, from whom Lincoln bought the Sinking Spring Farm. See p. 24, *infra*.

[4] *Acts of Kentucky:* Nov. 29, 1799, chap. xiv, 36–8. If the slaves were taken before the court thirty-nine lashes might be inflicted.

[5] *Ib.*, and Hening, xi, 489.

[6] Haycraft, 21.

[7] According to the census of 1800, the total population of Hardin County was then 3653, of which the number of slaves was 325, and that would be about the number when Thomas Lincoln was patroller.

That part of Hardin County which is now LaRue, where Lincoln was born and where the family lived until they went to Indiana in 1816, was peopled almost exclusively by whites. 'There were very few slaves in the whole country round here then perhaps not 50 in what is now this County.' Burba to Herndon, March 31, 1866. Weik MSS.

methods of the time, and the duty of patrollers made to cover
white vagabonds and peace-disturbing wanderers who appear
to have infested Hardin County in unusual numbers during
those years.[1]

But Thomas Lincoln did not long continue official slave
supervisor, nor do the records show that he received anything
for his services. Five months after his appointment, nine other
patrollers were named for Elizabethtown exclusively, Thomas
Lincoln not being one of them.[2] In 1807 six patrollers were appointed for the northern part of Hardin County and again
Thomas Lincoln was not included.[3] It is clear, however, that in
1805 he had lived in Hardin County long enough, and had established a reputation good enough, to serve briefly as a peace
officer, albeit his strictly legal duties in that capacity were
solely the watching and whipping of obnoxious slaves.

In Elizabethtown there dwelt one Joseph Hanks, a carpenter
by trade, who must have been kept busy in that rapidly growing
frontier town. From him, Thomas Lincoln got his knowledge of
the craft.[4] Joseph Hanks had a niece, Nancy, the natural child
of his sister Lucy Hanks;[5] and this girl was destined to become

[1] Haycraft, 63–4.

[2] Hardin County Court Order Book, 58, Nov. 26, 1805. These patrollers agreed to
'make no charge . . . for their services.'

[3] *Ib.*, 180, Sept. 28, 1807. The appointment of so many slave supervisors of this
little town alone is curious. It would seem to indicate unusual lawlessness at the small
county-seat.

[4] Hanks's first Chicago statement. Weik MSS.

[5] On Nov. 24, 1789, the Grand Jury of Mercer County presented [indicted] Lucy
Hanks, the mother of Nancy, for some offence; but on May 25, 1790, the case was
'discontinued.' Records Mercer County, Harrodsburg, Ky., Order Book i, 415, 516.
This document was discovered by Barton, but for it I am indebted to Judge L. S.
Pence of Lebanon, Ky., who writes: 'Evidently Lucy was indicted, as we say, for
"unbecoming conduct." ' Letters to author, June 18 and June 21, 1924.

It would appear that such indictments were common; Collins chronicles that of
seventeen cases before the first session of the first court at Harrodsburg in the spring
of 1783, eight were for fornication. Collins, i, 258.

Mercer County was then a part of Lincoln County, one of the three counties into
which Kentucky was originally divided. See Collins, ii, under title 'Mercer County.'

Lucy Hanks was finally married to Henry Sparrow, April 3, 1791, in Mercer County,
Ky., Records in office Clerk of County Court, Mercer County.

The date of the birth of Nancy Hanks is unknown; but since she is supposed to
have been twenty-five or twenty-six years of age when she married Thomas Lincoln,
she probably was born in 1783 or 1784, six or seven years before her mother, Lucy
Hanks, married Henry Sparrow.

the mother of Abraham Lincoln. For some years she had made her home with an aunt, Betsy Hanks, who had married Thomas Sparrow. The father of Nancy Hanks is unknown, although, in an unwonted burst of confidence, Lincoln told his law partner that his maternal grandfather was 'a well bred Virginia planter'; and from this source flowed, as Lincoln believed, his noblest powers.[1]

The picture of Nancy Hanks is as uncertain and confused as that of Thomas Lincoln is fixed and clear. Dim as the dream of a shifting mirage, her face and figure waver through the mists of time and rumor. Those who knew her disagree even as to the color of her eyes, the shade of her hair, her physical build and

---

[1] *Herndon's Lincoln* (1st ed., Belford-Clarke & Co., 1890), I, 3–4; and *ib.*, in reprint by Herndon-Lincoln Publishing Co. This work was the joint product of William Henry Herndon and Jesse William Weik and will be cited in these notes as 'Herndon.' Also Herndon to Weik, Jan. 19, 1886. Weik MSS.

'Lincoln once told me that his mother ... was the illegitimate child of a Virginia planter; he told me never to tell it while he lived and this I have religiously kept and observed.' *Ib.*

That Nancy Hanks was a natural child was well-known; and the fact was talked of by neighbors and their children, even when living in Indiana and long after her death. See 'Lincoln in Indiana': Rev. J. Edward Murr, *Indiana Magazine of History*, XIII, 332–4. Mr. Murr rests his statement on interviews with members of his congregation who were boyhood friends of Lincoln.

'His [Lincoln's] mother was an illegitimate child. I have always understood that from what my mother said about it.' Statement of a natural son of Sophie Hanks to Arthur E. Morgan, *Atlantic Monthly*, cxxv, 218. Sophie Hanks was a daughter of Sarah or Polly Hanks who, 'though she never married, had six children.' *Ib.*, 208.

Another Nancy Hanks, sister of Lucy, was the mother of Dennis Hanks, who was also born out of wedlock: 'I am a Base Born Child My Mother was Nancy Hanks the Ant of A Lincolns Mother.' Hanks to Herndon, Feb. 22, 1866. Weik MSS.

The father of Dennis Friend Hanks was Charles Friend: 'My mother ... sayes your Grandfather was my father.' Hanks to Charles Friend as quoted in Friend to Herndon, Aug. 20, 1889. Weik MSS. 'My GrandFather Charles [Friend] is said to be the Father of D. F. H. The Old Man believed it himself.' Same to same, Feb. 22, 1866; also July 31, 1889; and Burba to Herndon, March 31, 1866. Weik MSS.

This Nancy Hanks afterwards lived with Levi Hall, probably as a 'common-law wife,' since no record of a marriage has been discovered. This couple followed the Lincolns to Indiana, where they died; and a son of theirs, Squire Hall, afterwards went with the Lincolns to Illinois.

In order to establish the regularity of the birth of Nancy Hanks, her cousin, Dennis, insisted that her name was Sparrow, daughter of Thomas Sparrow and Betsy (Hanks) Sparrow, with whom the child was left and made her home. Thomas and Betsy Sparrow married in 1796.

'He [Thomas Lincoln] married Miss Nancy Sparrow.' Hanks's first Chicago statement. Weik MSS. 'if you call hir Hanks you make hir a Base born child which is not treu. ... Now Billy this question is all gamon.' Hanks to Herndon, Feb. 10, 1866. Weik MSS. 'hir Madin Name Nancy Sparrow So what is the use of all this.' Same to same, Feb. 22, 1866. Weik MSS.

height.[1] She was absolutely illiterate. No signature of Nancy Hanks has yet been discovered; whenever she had to sign a legal document she made her mark. There is no evidence whatever that she could read. At the very best, she was simply an attractive young pioneer woman, and of a class [2] having the least and poorest opportunities for any kind of education such as the primitive schools of the time afforded.

But the qualities of her mind and character were impressed more distinctly than was her physical appearance. All remember that she was uncommonly intelligent; had 'Remarkable Keen perseption,' as Dennis Hanks put it.[3] Dennis waxes enthusiastic about the mind and heart of his maternal cousin with whom he had been brought up in the Sparrow sanctuary; [4] 'She was Keen, shrewd — smart,' he told Herndon; 'I do say highly intellectual by nature. Her memory was strong, her judgment . . . accurate. She was Spiritually and ideally inclined.' [5] Nathaniel Grigsby, too, declares that she was 'Known for the extraordinary strength of her mind . . . a brilliant woman . . . of great good sense and

---

[1] 'She was a woman of rather low stature, but heavy and well set.' Haycraft to Herndon, no date. Weik MSS.

Again: she 'was rather a heavy built Squatty woman.' Haycraft to Helm, July 5, 1865. Weik MSS.

On the other hand Dennis Hanks declares that she was 'Spare Made thin Visage . . . Lite hare and Blue Eyes.' Hanks to Herndon, Weik MSS.; but in his second Chicago statement Hanks says that Nancy's 'hair was dark — eyes blueish green,' that she was five feet eight inches tall and weighed 'one hundred and thirty pounds.'

She 'was a Medium Sized Woman, rather spare in her person, fair complexion, light Hair, Blue Eyes.' A. H. Chapman's statement, no date, Weik MSS.

'She had dark Hair Hazle Eyes, was 5 feet 7 inches high a spare delicate form, weighed about 120 pounds.' John Hanks to John Miles as quoted in Miles to Herndon, May 25, 1865. Weik MSS.

'Her hair was black . . . eyes . . . blue . . . rather above medium hight, more spare made than otherwise . . . rather coarse featured.' Brooner to David Turnham, as quoted in Turnham to Herndon, Nov. 19, 1866. Weik MSS.

'She was . . . of pale complexion, dark hair, sharp features, high forhead, bright keen gray or hazel Eyes.' Nathaniel Grigsby's statement, Sept. 12, 1865. Weik MSS. Grigsby was only seven years old when he first saw Nancy Hanks and but nine years of age when she died; and he made his statement from hearsay to Herndon forty-seven years later.

[2] 'She [Nancy Hanks] was very obscure.' Helm to Herndon, June 20, 1865. Weik MSS.

[3] Hanks to Herndon, no date, but 1865. Weik MSS.

[4] Friend to Herndon, Aug. 20, 1889. Weik MSS.

[5] Hanks's second Chicago statement. Weik MSS.

moral[i]ty.' [1] All testify that she was inordinately kind and affectionate.[2]

Thomas Lincoln, then at least twenty-eight years of age, had
been looking for a wife, it appears, and had asked Sarah Bush,
the daughter of his patroller captain, Christopher Bush, to
marry him; but she had refused.[3] Thomas next proposed to
Nancy Hanks who accepted; [4] and on June 12, 1806, they were
married by Jesse Head,[5] in the cabin of Richard Berry, close to
Beechland in Washington County. Only one account of the
wedding exists and that is extravagant and untrustworthy.[6] It
is reasonable to suppose, however, that the event was attended
and followed by that boisterous merriment with which such
ceremonies then were and, for half a century, continued to be
celebrated, particularly by those of the class to which Thomas
and Nancy belonged — the over-eating, over-drinking, violent
sports, coarse jests, rude fun.[7]

We next find husband and wife at Elizabethtown, seat of
Hardin County, where they set up housekeeping in a cabin fourteen feet square off the main pathway through the village which

[1] Grigsby's statement. Weik MSS. Grigsby gives this account from what the
neighbors said in Indiana in 1818–19. He himself could not have remembered her
qualities even if he had opportunities to observe them.

[2] Chapman's narrative. Weik MSS.

[3] Thomas Lincoln himself said that he first courted Sarah Bush, who declined his
proposal. Helm's statement, July 19, 1865. Weik MSS. Also Life of Lincoln: Henry
C. Whitney, I, 12. Sarah Bush immediately married Daniel Johnston, March 13,
1806.

[4] The account of a camp-meeting at Elizabethtown, where a girl of the name of
Hanks who was 'to be married next week' and a young man, went through emotional
performances ending in an embrace before the altar, given in Herndon, I, 14, 15, could
not have referred to Nancy Hanks, since in the Helm MS. from which the story is taken,
the incident is stated to have occurred in 1816, ten years after her marriage to Thomas
Lincoln.

[5] Head was a deacon in the Methodist Episcopal Church, ordained October 3,
1805, a Justice of the Peace, etc. For a careful account of Jesse Head see 'Life
of Rev. Jesse Head' by L. S. Pence in Lebanon (Ky.) Enterprise, April, 1921–June,
1922.

[6] That of Christopher Columbus Graham, who was nearly one hundred years old
when he made his statement, having been silent during the many years when the
controversy as to the marriage was raging. See Life of Abraham Lincoln: William E.
Barton, I, 17.

[7] Pioneer Life in Kentucky: Daniel Drake, 185–6. 'Weddings, commonly in the
daytime, were scenes of carousal, and of mirth and merriment of no very chastened
character.' The same occurred at the infare.

served as its principal street.[1] Although a frontier town, it was
then the scene of energy, even of ambition. While by far the
greatest number of the houses were still log cabins, yet many of
these were comparatively large and some were of hewn logs.[2]

Two or three frame structures had gone up, a large brick
residence, imposing for the time and place and not unworthy
even now, had been built;[3] another residence of brick, two
stories high, had 'marble steps' in front;[4] and there was another of wood, three stories in height with deep and massive
foundations and understructure of stone.[5] A stone jail, expensive even for that day, and a new court house of brick were
under construction;[6] and 'E-town,' as it was called, boasted a
brick yard, a tannery, a distillery, and three stores,[7] one of them
run by John J. Audubon, who later became the great ornitholo-
gist. There were three or four blacksmiths and gunsmiths;[8] a
tailor and a shoe maker;[9] but Joseph Hanks appears to have
been the only carpenter.

Several lawyers of signal ability and considerable learning had
been admitted to the bar of Hardin County and some of them

[1] Haycraft to Herndon (no date). Weik MSS. Haycraft says that the house was
'removed three times, being used twice as a slaughter house and now [1865] as a stable.'

[2] 'Hewed logs gradually took the place of round log houses, with shingled roofs' —
this before 1800. Haycraft, 74.

[3] This house, the residence of Major Ben Helm, was built in 1801-2. Haycraft's
description of it is helpful to an understanding of Elizabethtown when Thomas Lincoln
lived there: It was fifty by twenty-five feet, two stories high, the brick walls resting on
'huge stone' foundations with a 'deep cellar under the whole building.' The wainscoting
was of 'seasoned black walnut,' and the mantelpieces, 'curiously wrought,' were also
of black walnut. The plaster was 'more than one inch thick . . . and so well trowelled
that a man could almost see his face in it.' Seventy years afterward 'the blue ash
floors were nearly as perfect as when laid.' Ib., 76.

[4] That of Major James Crutcher, the merchant. Ib., 77.

[5] That of Samuel Haycraft, Sr. More than one hundred wagon loads of stone were
required for the foundation and chimney of Haycraft's house, which was fourteen
feet wide and forty feet high. It was built in 1798-9. At that time Elizabethtown had
about 150 people. Ib., 75.

[6] 'It was then considered to be a fine house, and the country flocked in to see it.'
This court house was in use seventy years later. Haycraft, 28-9.

[7] Haycraft, 75-6; 92-3; 168-9. The stores of James Crutcher (ib., 99-101), Blakely
and Montgomery (ib., 105), and Audubon & Rozier (ib., 108). Charles Helm and
Samuel Stevenson were early merchants in Elizabethtown and so were Major Ben
Helm and Duff Green (ib., 109), at one time a noted champion of Jackson and later
as strong an advocate of Calhoun.

[8] Ib., 165-6.   [9] Ib., 73-4.

lived at the county seat.[1] All judges and county justices were Calvinistic Baptists and every one of them was a large land owner.[2] So many lawyers practiced at Elizabethtown that the court made a rule in 1812 that no more than two attorneys should appear on one side unless by special permission of the judges;[3] and one Justice of the Peace was fined five pounds and costs for charging 'high blooded fees.'[4] Strict indeed was the administration of justice; in one case a new trial was asked because the jury ate, drank, and danced during an intermission in the trial.[5] A school had been started by a Methodist preacher, who also was an excellent maker of chairs.[6] There was only one doctor, attendance upon the sick being still in the hands of the women of the household, whose simple remedies of hot herb teas, blanketing and sweating generally sufficed to relieve most ills.[7]

Religion flourished in Elizabethtown and, indeed, throughout Severns Valley. From the first settlement Baptist communities were established;[8] and, as early as 1799, the town had a church building of hewn logs which also served as a schoolhouse; and in 1805 Samuel Haycraft, Sr., gave an acre for a church and burying ground. Services were also held in the brick Court House and in many private houses, the fine residence of Major Helm, with whom the preachers always stopped, being a favorite place of worship.[9] But while in Elizabethtown, neither Thomas nor Nancy Lincoln became a church member.

The vigorous people of Hardin County were as prolific as they were godly, the average family numbering twelve children.

---

[1] By 1806, twenty-two lawyers had been admitted to the Hardin County bar. (Haycraft, 33–55.) Among these were Felix Grundy, afterwards Senator from Tennessee, Ninian Edwards, afterwards Governor of Illinois, Thomas B. Reed, afterwards Senator from Mississippi, Henry P. Brodnax, John Rowan, John Pope, Gabriel Johnson, Worden Pope, and Robert Wickliffe. Haycraft observes of certain lawyers who practiced at Elizabethtown when Thomas Lincoln lived there: 'Either of these men was far ahead in legal knowledge, statesmanship and administrative capacity of some of our Presidents.'

It was at the house of John Rowan near Bardstown that the song 'My Old Kentucky Home' was written. Rowan finally removed to Louisville and became one of the foremost lawyers of his time.

[2] *Ib.*, 31.   [3] *Ib.*, 62.   [4] *Ib.*, 39.
[5] *Ib.*, 54.   [6] *Ib.*, 29.   [7] *Ib.*, 151.

[8] 'No other orthodox denomination had a representation on these waters for many years after.' *Ib.*, 38.

[9] *Ib.*, 82–3.

They were sticklers for regular living, the early grand juries frequently presenting men for swearing, drunkenness, selling liquor without license; and often presenting women for having children 'without the necessary appendage of a husband.' Imprisonment for debt was inflicted [1] and many were punished for other offences in the stocks and thus exhibited in public.

While conditions were hearty, cordial, and democratic, divisions in society had already appeared. Costumes of the frontier still prevailed; but here and there among buckskin leggings, hunting shirts, coon-skin caps, and moccasins, were to be seen beaver hats, short breeches, stockings, low shoes, and silver buckles at knee and ankle; [2] and one man of pride and fashion, a lawyer, rode in careful attire, his negro servant following at the prescribed distance.[3] Another lawyer wore his hair powdered and tied behind.[4] There was a dancing-master, too, who also wore knee-breeches.[5]

Lexington, ninety miles distant, with more than three thousand population,[6] had become a centre of culture not surpassed by any town west of the Alleghenies, and was an emporium for books as well as merchandise.[7] There Major Helm went to buy

[1] Haycraft, 34, 44, 69, 175.　　　[2] Ib., 37.

[3] James Furgeson. 'He was a fine dressed man and traveled with a servant, in the style of that day, the servant at a respectable distance behind with a large portmanteau on the crupper, a glazed hat in his hand and a brace of horseman's pistols at the pommel.' Ib., 58–9.

[4] Henry P. Brodnax, who dressed in 'white cassimere short breeches, silver knee buckles . . . and very fine cotton stockings,' and a long white ribbed dimity coat, the long skirts of which nearly touched the ground. Ib., 178–9.

[5] Ib., 74.

[6] Michaux: Thwaites, III, 199. Lexington then had tanyards, ropewalks, potteries, nail machines and powder mills, and there were many tailors, shoemakers, tinsmiths, masons and carpenters. Ib., 200–3.

[7] In the Kentucky Gazette, published at Lexington, Parker Brothers advertised, May 30, 1789, forty items of dry goods among which were Irish linens, Scotch shirting, 'silk for gowns,' lawn and cotton, 'silk and thread lace,' 'garters and stay laces,' etc.; as many items of household utensils, such as knives and forks and carving knives, 'leather, paper and brass inkstands,' razors, 'crooked combs,' 'sugar tongs and nutmeg graters,' pins, needles, and all kinds of articles for stable and farm.

A large assortment of groceries, too, were for sale, as well as Bibles, hymn books and Watts' psalms, English and Dutch testaments, spelling books and primers, writing paper and playing cards, window glass, mirrors, china cups and saucers, tumblers and wine glasses, together with 'delf dishes assorted,' etc., and 'a variety of other articles too tedious to mention.' And in same issue see the advertisement, equally extensive, of Wilson and Parker, another firm.

wrought nails for the woodwork in his pretentious dwelling,[1] and there too, we may be sure, books were purchased by those ambitious for improvement. As early as 1792 a surprising number of volumes were advertised by Lexington merchants.[2] Bailey's *Etymological Dictionary* seems to have made a wide appeal, for Mordecai Lincoln bought one almost as soon as the stock of books was received;[3] and we shall hear of this volume many years later.[4] But Thomas Lincoln felt no such impulse for intellectual improvement; and since, as we have seen, neither he nor his wife could read, nor, at that time, so far as can be found, had either any wish or will to learn, it is not likely that any book then found a place beneath his 'E-town' rooftree.[5]

During the year of his marriage to Nancy Hanks and perhaps for some months before, Thomas Lincoln worked hard and steadily; indeed it may be said that he then reached the peak of his sluggish energy. He had credit at the village grocery, once paid a doctor's bill,[6] bought a 'bason,' dish and plates at an administrator's sale, paying about six dollars; and at the same time he spent three dollars for a sword,[7] though what use he had for a sword does not appear.[8] He did the carpentry on one

---

[1] Haycraft, 76.

[2] William Leavy advertised one hundred and twenty-one different titles. Among these were Vattel's *Law of Nations*, Horace, Virgil, Sallust, Ovid, Savary's *Greece*, Savary's *Egypt*, Burke's *Works*, Pope's *Iliad*, *Junius' Letters*, Aristotle's *Works*, Chesterfield's *Letters*, Paine's *The Rights of Man*, Ferguson's *Astronomy*, Nicholson's *Philosophy*, Blackstone's *Commentaries* and many other law books, as well as religious works, Bibles, testaments, reading and spelling books. Four dictionaries were for sale including Bailey's. *Kentucky Gazette*, July 27, 1793.

[3] This volume is now in the possession of Mr. James A. McMillen, Librarian of Washington University, St. Louis, Mo.

[4] Levi Hall brought this book to Indiana in 1826 and Abraham Lincoln wrote his name in it. P. 73, *infra*.

[5] It appears that the Lincolns did not have even a Bible until after the death of Nancy. P. 70, *infra*.

[6] This probably was later for an operation on himself.

At an unknown date Thomas Lincoln was ill of the mumps which must have resulted in an operation. Burba to Herndon, March 31, 1866; Friend to same, July 31, 1889; Hanks's second Chicago statement. Weik MSS. It is possible that it was for this that he employed the physician.

[7] Will and Inventory Book of Hardin County, 297.

[8] It has been suggested that he made a hunting or shaving knife out of the sword. This was possible, although he could have bought a good knife for less money at any store in Elizabethtown.

residence, and so well did he perform that task that his work was in good condition sixty years afterward.[1]

About the same time, however, he undertook a labor which, for him, was heavy, and which required skill and accuracy. Denton Geoghegan, a wealthy farmer of high repute,[2] had determined to build a mill and employed Thomas Lincoln to hew the timbers. Geoghegan was sharply dissatisfied with Lincoln's performance of the job and refused to pay the full amount demanded, because, as he said, the work was not done in a workmanlike manner, the timbers being neither square nor of proper length.

Such were the allegations made by Geoghegan in a law suit that resulted, which, first brought and won by Lincoln before a Justice of the Peace, was appealed to the County tribunal which affirmed the judgment. But Geoghegan would not yield, and, in his turn, sued Lincoln in the Circuit Court. Months afterward the dispute was settled by agreement between the two and the suit dismissed at plaintiff's costs.[3]

So ended Thomas Lincoln's only period of sustained and constructive effort. After a year and a half in Elizabethtown, where meanwhile a daughter had been born to him,[4] he took wife, child and the small household belongings and left forever the bustle and stir of village or town. He lived thenceforth on farms. Why he quitted the attractive community of Elizabethtown does not appear. Perhaps the pretensions of its society annoyed him, for both Thomas and Nancy Lincoln were 'the most humble and obscure in this humble class of people;'[5] perhaps

---

[1] That of Hardin Thomas. Haycraft, 123.

[2] Denton Geoghegan came to Elizabethtown in 1806 with his father, Ambrose Geoghegan, a graduate of an Irish College, who 'possessed considerable means, was an accomplished engineer and surveyor, . . . an accomplished gentleman and of social disposition' and very popular. Immediately after coming to Hardin County the family purchased several adjoining farms. *Ib.*, 126–7.

Thomas Lincoln's employer and antagonist 'was a large farmer . . . a remarkably clear-headed man, strictly honorable in all his dealings, and noted for his punctuality,' declares Haycraft, who knew Denton Geoghegan well. He became a Justice of the Peace and served as such for many years. The Geoghegan family was one of the most important and influential in Hardin County. *Ib.*, 126–30.

[3] Warren, 308, 309, 333.

[4] Sarah, born February 10, 1807. Waldo Lincoln, 342.

[5] Helm to Herndon, June 20, 1865. Weik MSS.

the gossip about the parentage of his wife was repellent to both; perhaps the intellectual ferment of the little but sprightly County seat bewildered him; perhaps his business as a carpenter was ruined by Geoghegan's talk and suit, for the angry miller pursued Lincoln, suing him after he had left the County seat, the settlement not being made until after the birth of his first son.

At any rate, about May, 1808, he went to live on a farm, but not the Mill Creek farm which he still owned, a circumstance which never has been explained. Instead he bought, at sixty-six and two-thirds cents per acre, three hundred acres on which stood the cabin by the Sinking Spring. This farm was much poorer than his two hundred acres on Mill Creek. It was about three miles south of Hodgen's mill, where the family grist was ground. Yet Thomas Lincoln did not at once proceed to the Sinking Spring farm — indeed he did not buy it until December, 1808. Where he passed the interval is in doubt.[1]

In November or December, however, they occupied the cabin by the Sinking Spring, where on February 12 of the following year, Abraham Lincoln came into the world.[2] Here they remained for perhaps four years, Thomas tilling a few acres, hunting, doing carpentering for other farmers. He kept one or two horses and for two years he was taxed on three horses.[3] Then, quite suddenly, he abandoned the Sinking Spring farm, seemingly because of a curious and wholly unexplained incident.

On December 12, 1808, Thomas Lincoln, for two hundred

[1] It has been stated that late in May, 1808, Lincoln, his wife, and daughter turned their backs upon Elizabethtown and went to the farm of George Brownfield, about seventeen miles from Elizabethtown, where, in a 'plum orchard' near Brownfield's log house, they occupied for some months a cabin or hut made of poles, and Lincoln did odd jobs of carpentry or other work about the farm. Judge R. W. Creal, a well-informed man of the locality, who has served in the Kentucky Legislature and as Judge in LaRue County, states that his father, who was nine years older than Abraham Lincoln, told him of this stay on the Brownfield farm. The tax list of 1812 shows that Brownfield had no real estate whatever in the county, only a number of horses. He may have been living on the 'plum orchard' place in 1808, but evidently he did not own it. Interview of the author with Judge Creal and information from Judge Mather. See *Paternity:* Barton, 189.

[2] Haycraft to Helm, July 5, 1865; Friend to Herndon, March 19, 1866; Burba to same, March 31, 1866. Weik MSS.

[3] 1808, 1 horse; 1809–10, 2 horses; 1811, 1 horse; 1812, 3 horses; 1813, 2 horses; 1814, 3 horses, Hardin County Tax Records.

dollars, had bought the Sinking Spring farm from Isaac Bush [1] who, on November 2, 1805, had for the same amount purchased the land from David Vance. On May 1, 1805, Vance had bought it from Richard Mather, a man of much importance in Hardin County and the owner of a considerable holding of fifteen thousand acres, of which this tract was a part.

Vance had paid Mather all of the purchase price but fifteen pounds, twelve shillings, four pence; and for this sum he gave Mather his promissory note, dated May 1, 1805, and due eighteen months after date 'in good trade.' At the same time Mather gave Vance an agreement to execute and deliver to Vance a warranty deed for the farm, when the remainder of the purchase price, as evidenced by the note, should be paid.

Under this incumbrance, the farm came into the possession of Thomas Lincoln, who fully understood the obligation to Mather and his lien upon the land. But Vance had removed to Mississippi leaving his note unpaid. So on September 1, 1813, Mather filed against Vance, a bill in equity alleging that he was a non-resident without other property in Kentucky and praying that the land be sold for the payment of Vance's note. Mather also averred that Bush and Lincoln (who throughout the bill and in the summons is called Linkhorn) [2] had bought the land as stated, with full knowledge of the facts and that they took it subject to Mather's 'equitable claim,' and asked that both Bush and Lincoln be made defendants.

September 7, 1813, Lincoln answered, admitting that when he bought the land he knew that Mather had a lien upon it as claimed; but that Lincoln had been told that Vance had paid part of his note to Mather; that he had offered to pay Mather the remainder which Mather agreed to accept; but that Mather had brought suit before Lincoln could 'make arrangements.' Lincoln said that he believed Mather brought suit only to get

[1] Son of Christopher Bush, Captain of the patrollers of whom Thomas Lincoln was one, and brother of Sarah Bush, Lincoln's second wife.

[2] 'they wer called Linkhorn that proves nothing as the old settlers had a way of pronouncing names as they pleasd they called Medcalf, Cap., Kaster, they pronounced Custard etc.' Friend to Herndon, March 19, 1866. Weik MSS.

Thomas Lincoln 'was always called Linkhorn.' Haycraft to Helm, July 5, 1865; Haycraft to Herndon, no date; Helm to same, June 20, 1865. Weik MSS.

cash 'for the amount of his trade note' and prayed that he be compelled to make a deed and 'to receive his pay in good trade.' [1] Bush answered to the same effect.[2] In his replication, filed the same day with Bush's answer, Mather denied the statements of Lincoln and Bush 'so far as they contradict' statements in Mather's bill of complaint.

Without waiting for trial and judgment, Thomas Lincoln left the Sinking Spring farm and, with his family of three, moved to his next place of abode, the third within six years. Some three years later, on December 19, 1816, the farm on which Abraham Lincoln was born was, under decree of the Court rendered September 12, 1816, sold to John Welsh for $61.50, the remainder of the debt due Mather, together with interest and costs, amounting in all to $87.74.[3]

It is this sacrifice for so small a sum of a farm for which he had paid two hundred dollars, on which Thomas Lincoln had lived for over four years and where two of his children had been born, that would seem to defy rational explanation, especially since he expressed his willingness to pay the amount still due Mather, which was only $61.50, and since his sale of the Mill Creek farm brought him one hundred pounds at that very time.

For, in the midst of this litigation, on October 27, 1814,

---

[1] To this answer Thomas made his mark, as he did also to an amended answer.

[2] September 18.

[3] Records Hardin County, Equity Papers, H.C.C. Bundle 24. In the same decree, it was provided that Thomas Lincoln 'recover of Bush the purchase money with interest from the day of payment' and that Bush recover the same from Vance.

It appears that Bush did not pay Lincoln, for on November 11, 1816, he made oath, before Samuel Carpenter, Justice of the Peace for Nelson County, to a cross-bill against Bush filed in the Hardin County Court, January 21, 1817, alleging his payment of $200 to Bush for the Sinking Spring farm and praying for judgment for that amount and costs, paying, as Carpenter notes, '$2.50 to pay the printer.'

At the same time Bush filed a like cross-bill against Vance, but failed to answer the cross-bill of Lincoln; and during the September term of the Court, 1817, a decree was rendered confirming the former decree in favor of Mather, adjudging that the cross-bill of Lincoln against Bush be taken as confessed because not answered, and that Lincoln recover of Bush 'the sum of $200.00 with interest thereon at the rate of six per cent per annum from the first day of January, 1809, till paid, and also his costs by him in said suit expended.' Ib.

The records do not show whether Bush satisfied this judgment; but it is probable that he did. Two years later, soon after the death of his first wife, Thomas Lincoln returned to Elizabethtown and married Sarah Johnston, the sister of Isaac Bush. See p. 57, infra.

Thomas Lincoln sold to Charles Melton for one hundred pounds, two hundred acres of his Mill Creek farm, this tract to be taken out of the two hundred and thirty-eight acres 'where he thinks proper.' [1] Thereupon Lincoln again removed to another farm about ten miles to the northeastward.[2] How he got this tract of thirty acres or how much he paid for it, if anything, has not been discovered; but he probably took possession under what was then called a 'title bond,' which was a written promise to convey land, a kind of contract for the sale of the property. Such instruments were not always recorded and it was by means of them that most lands were sold at that time. Only an equitable right was given which did not become a title until deed was executed and delivered.[3]

The surroundings of this third cabin home of the Lincoln family deserve careful description, for it was there that the early boyhood of Abraham Lincoln was spent and first impressions were received.

Some seven or eight miles north and east from the Sinking Spring farm, a tremendous stone escarpment called Muldraugh's Hill, divides the Barrens from the lower and heavily timbered land to the northward.[4] This vast cliff is pierced by a valley four miles in length and from one fourth of a mile to two miles broad. High hills, abrupt, and mountainous in appearance, rise on either side. Lengthwise through the valley a deep and rapid stream, Knob Creek, hurries to the Rolling Fork, a large stream at the valley end; and the Rolling Fork, in turn, flows into Salt River which empties into the Ohio.

From the gorges of the lofty elevations on either side of the valley smaller streams feed Knob Creek which has its rise in the

---

[1] Deed Book E, 193, Records Clerk's Office, Hardin County, Ky. To this deed Nancy Lincoln made her mark.

[2] On Knob Creek. The land is in Thomas Lincoln's name on the commissioners' Tax List for 1815.

[3] Judge O. M. Mather to author, August 9, 1924.

[4] Michaux describes Muldraugh's Hill as 'a steep and lofty mountain that forms a kind of amphitheatre. From its summit the neighbouring country presents the aspect of an immense valley [of the Rolling Fork, not the small space through which Knob Creek runs], covered with forests of an imperceptible extent, whence, as far as the eye can reach, nothing but a gloomy verdant space is seen, formed by the tops of the close-connected trees, and through which not the vestige of a plantation can be discerned.' Michaux: Thwaites, III, 213; Collins, II, 540.

cliffs that separate the valley from the higher land of the Barrens. For five hundred feet this eminence sharply falls to land and streams below; and the abutting hills, stretching out from the parent cliff like gnarled and knotted arms of a giant, are almost as imposing.[1]

Formed as it is of the silt carried from the surface of the hills, the product of decomposing vegetation throughout ages of time, the soil of this valley is extremely rich and productive. Some of the little triangles of land that project from Knob Creek into the hills on either side are not surpassed in fertility — the mere dropping of seed with the slightest cultivation suffices to yield a crop. In 1813, when Thomas Lincoln moved to Knob Creek from his sterile farm on the edge of the Barrens, the main stream and tributaries teemed with fish and the surrounding hills were full of game. A more ideal spot for the winning of a livelihood with the least possible exertion could not be found.

At the end of such a hollow projecting from Knob Creek into the cliff-like hills, two and one half miles from the Rolling Fork,[2] Thomas Lincoln set up his new home;[3] and there 'in abject poverty,'[4] he and his family lived for perhaps three years until, because of several circumstances, he once more removed. Seven miles southwest of his Knob Creek cabin, was Hodgen's mill, where Thomas Lincoln took his corn to be ground, although other grist mills were nearer to his cabin. There were thirty acres in the hill-enclosed triangle that Lincoln occupied. Not all of the small farm could be cultivated, however, since part of the thirty acres ran up into the encompassing hills. Dennis Hanks thus describes Lincoln's Knob Creek holding: 'The 30 acre farm in K[entuck]y was Knotty — Knobby — as a piece of land could be, with deep hollows and ravines, cedar trees covering the . . . Knobs as thick as trees could grow.'[5] At least half of the farm was on the bottom, for Thomas tilled fourteen acres

[1] Hanks's Charleston statement, Weik MSS., and personal inspection.

[2] Hanks to Herndon, no date, Weik MSS.

[3] Haycraft to Herndon, no date, Weik MSS.; J. M. Atherton to O. M. Mather, June 20, 1924, and Mather to author, July 24, 1924.

[4] Atherton to Mather, and Mather to author, July 24, 1924. Mr. Atherton says that his 'information came direct from Austin Gollaher,' the boyhood companion of Lincoln.

[5] Hanks's second Chicago statement. Weik MSS.

'running up and down the branch about 40 feet on either side.' [1]
His cabin was much like the one by the Sinking Spring.[2]

This valley was comparatively well settled, and neighbors
were more numerous and not so distant as had been the case
in the region of the Sinking Spring.[3] Sometime during the sojourn of the Lincoln family on Knob Creek a school was opened
in the vicinity by one Zachariah Riney, a Catholic; [4] and Sarah
accompanied by her little brother went to this school for a few
weeks. Later another school, taught by one Caleb Hazel,[5] was
attended by the Lincoln children for an even briefer period.

'It was from that place [Knob Creek cabin],' writes Haycraft
to Herndon, 'that young Abraham commenced trugging his way
to school to Caleb Hazel with whom I was well acquainted and
could perhaps teach spelling, reading and indifferent writing and
perhaps could cypher to the Rule of three — but he had no
other qualification of a teacher except large size and bodily
strength to thrash any boy or youth that came to his School.' [6]

Humble indeed was the appearance of these children of the
poverty burdened pioneers, Abraham being clad in 'a one piece

[1] Hanks's Charleston statement. Weik MSS.

[2] 'I've been at the cabin in my boyhood which had then tumbled down. . . . Judging
by the ruins of the Knob Creek Lincoln cabin, it was about the size of the one he
[Abraham] was born in.' Atherton to Mather, June 20, 1924, and Mather to author,
July 24, 1924.

[3] This is the opinion of Judge O. M. Mather, who has made careful and extended
study of the early history of Hardin County, particularly of that part which is now
LaRue County. For an excellent account of Muldraugh's Hill and the settlement of the
adjacent country, see 'Explorers and Early Settlers South of Muldraugh's Hill,' by
Otis M. Mather, Hodgenville, Ky., in *Reg. Ky. Hist. Socy.*, XXII, No. 64, 19–39.

[4] This Riney was probably one of a colony of Catholic emigrants that settled on
Pottinger's Creek in 1785, some of whom joined the settlement on Cartwright's Creek.
See *Centenary of Catholicity in Kentucky:* Benjamin J. Webb, 80.

[5] 'He went to school . . . a short time to a man by the name of Riney and . . . to
another by the name of Caleb Hazle. The latter I think was some eight miles from
here [Hodgenville] where his father moved to near . . . Atherton's ferry [on Knob
Creek].' Burba to Herndon, March 31, 1866. Weik MSS.
'Mr. A. L. Went to Two School Masters Calib Hazle and one Riney. Hazle taught
on my Grand Father's farm and to get to the school House he had to go some 2½
miles.' Friend to Herndon, March 19, 1866. Weik MSS.

[6] Haycraft to Herndon, no date, Weik MSS. Hazel also kept an inn or 'ordinary'
at his house on Knob Creek. Hardin County Court Order Book. Prices of food and
lodging were fixed by the County Court. These were 7½ pence for ½ pint of whisky,
dinner 1 shilling 6 pence, lodging for one night 3 pence, stabling and hay 1 shilling six
pence, etc. Some taverns were authorized to sell half pints of whiskey for 6 pence.
Haycraft, 20.

long linsey shirt' without other garments, since school was held only in warm weather.[1] Three months, at best, was the extent of the instruction the girl and boy thus received.[2] These schools, like all others at that time, were subscription affairs, a very small charge being made for each child taught. But, admits Dennis Hanks, 'Abe had no books in Ky.' [3]

Abraham's experiences on Knob Creek were, however, of far greater value than any premature schooling could have been. Lovely and noble were his surroundings, perfect and healthful conditions. The steep and rocky heights that rose from the yard of the Lincoln cabin and all about the valley, were clad with majestic trees, mostly of cedar,[4] two and more feet in diameter, their crests from seventy to a hundred feet above the earth. Clear as light was the water of the streams — so clear that through them pebbles in deep pools could be seen as plainly as on the surface of the ground.[5]

There was no bustle of hurrying people, no noise, no tumult, no distraction. It was a place of peace, calm, silent, and serene. A still and tranquil grandeur was the most intimate companion with which destiny supplied Abraham Lincoln at the time of his first impressions of life and the world. Yet it does not appear that he sought solitude or was in any way peculiar. While recollections of him at that time are, of course, indistinct and to be received with caution, he was, by vague accounts, much like other boys.

One of his companions remembers that Abraham and he went hunting together and cornered a ground hog in a cliff whence young Lincoln was determined to dislodge him.[6] Another re-

[1] Austin Gollaher's statement to Atherton, by him to Judge O. M. Mather, June 20, 1924, and by Mather to author, July 24, 1924.

[2] 'Lincoln went to school about 3 mo[nths] — with his sister — all the Education he had in Ky.' Hanks's second Chicago statement. Weik MSS.

[3] Hanks's second Chicago statement. Weik MSS. Yet Dennis says at another place in the same statement that Lincoln's mother taught him and his sister their Abc's out of Webster's old spelling book and also taught him to read the Bible, although the Lincolns had no Bible until two years after their removal to Indiana.

[4] Hanks's second Chicago statement. Weik MSS.

[5] Knob Creek 'is one of the prettiest streams I ever Saw. You can see a pebble in 10 foot water.' Burba to Herndon, May 25, 1866. Weik MSS.

[6] Rev. John Duncan's account to Charles Friend; Friend to Herndon, March 19, 1866, Aug. 20, 1889. Weik MSS.

calls that he fished Abraham out of the creek where he had
fallen from a log. The boys 'had no settled games,' says this
narrator, but mostly spent their time climbing the precipitous
hills and high trees, though 'Lincoln took a delite in excelling'
in anything his companions did.[1] Dennis Hanks declares that:
'Abe used to go with me . . . to shoot fish in puddles and holes
washed by the water — killed a fawn — Abe was tickled to
death — Abe exhibited no special trait in K[entuck]y except a
good, kind somewhat wild nature.' [2]

All that the careful Burba could learn fifty years later was
that at school, Abraham was quiet, considerate, and 'the one to
adjust difficulties between Boys of his size;' had no fights although considered brave; and 'was rather noted for keeping his
clothes cleaner longer than any others,' not a difficult task, one
would think, since he had only a one-piece covering to care for.
He liked to fish and hunt 'with his dog and axe,' and 'when his
dog would run a Rabbit in a hollow tree he would chop it out.' [3]
Haycraft dimly recalls that 'Abraham was a tall spider of a boy
and had his due proportion of harmless mischief.' [4]

Boyish pranks were played, some of them unpleasing in the
extreme,[5] a circumstance not to be overlooked in view of the
curious inclination toward relating such things which became so
striking and inconsistent a feature of Lincoln's mature years.
But, hill, stream, forest were stamped indelibly on the boy's
mind. When President, he described the country of his birth
and boyhood [6] to Dr. J. H. Rodman of Hodgenville, inquired
after the neighbors of that time, named them — the Cessnas,

[1] Austin Gollaher's story to Friend, Friend to Herndon, March 19, 1866. Weik MSS.
The stories of both Duncan and Gollaher have been doubted, but they give the usual
experiences of boyhood.

[2] Hanks's Charleston statement, Weik MSS. It was here that Herndon got his first
warning as to the credibility of Dennis. On margin of Herndon's MS. is this note:
'Hon. O. B. Ficklin [Representative in Congress from Charleston] and others told me
to be careful about what Hanks said.'

[3] Burba to Herndon, March 31, 1866. Weik MSS.

[4] Haycraft to Herndon, Dec. 7, 1866. Weik MSS.

[5] One of these Lincoln, when President, recounting incidents in Knob Creek, told
with glee to Dr. J. H. Rodman. Friend to Herndon, August 20, 1889. Weik MSS.

[6] 'He [Lincoln] seemed to know more about the general topography of the County
than any person he ever saw, described e[ve]ry house and farm hill creek and family
that lived there when he was a boy.' Ib.

the Brownfields, the Friends, the Ashcrafts, the Kirkpatricks, and particularly about 'my old friend and playmate Austin Gollaher' whom I 'would rather see than any man living.' [1] He 'asked about an old stone house that stands on Nolin Creek about 1½ miles east of Hodgenville near a spring where the young people used to hold their dances.' [2] His recollection of the Kirkpatrick stone house shows that when living on Knob Creek the boy Abraham must have seen it often; and this is best explained on the theory that, young as he was, Abraham sometimes took the family grist to be ground at Hodgen's mill,[3] the road to which passes directly in front of this then noticeable residence.

Although Kentucky fairly blazed with martial spirit from before the beginning of our second conflict with Great Britain, and numbers of volunteers [4] surely trod the road in front of the Lincoln cabin, both on their way to the front and back home after the war was over, it would seem that little if any impression was made on Thomas or Nancy Lincoln; Abraham could remember the smallest things about Knob Creek and vicinity; but all that he could recall concerning the War of 1812 was that his mother told him to be good to a soldier and the boy accordingly gave him a fish.[5]

[1] It was of a prank of Gollaher and Lincoln that the President told Dr. Rodman.

[2] Friend to Herndon, August 20, 1889. Weik MSS. This stone house still stands, no humble structure even now; and near by a spring gushes conspicuously from the hillside. In Lincoln's boyhood, it was the home of Joseph Kirkpatrick, a wealthy farmer and member of the South Fork Baptist Church.

[3] Robert Hodgen then ran a saw mill as well as a grist mill, at a place in the present town of Hodgenville. An excellent account by O. M. Mather, of Robert Hodgen and the town that bears his name, will be found in the *LaRue County News*, April 1, 8, 15, 22, 1920.

[4] 'The popular passion for the war blazed with fury. . . . Seven thousand volunteers at once [upon declaration of war] offered their services.' Collins, I, 298. Hardin County was as hot for war as any part of Kentucky. John Thomas, Major General of the Kentucky Militia who enlisted for the New Orleans campaign, lived within four miles of the Sinking Spring cabin, where Thomas Lincoln was at the outbreak of hostilities. See Mather, *Reg. Ky. Hist. Socy.*, Jan., 1924, 34. Many of Lincoln's neighbors also enlisted. Mather to author, Sept. 1, 1924.

[5] Nicolay and Hay, I, 27. Yet Dennis Hanks says that when the soldiers came home from the war Thomas Lincoln 'fed and cared for them by companies.' He was able to do this because he lived in a 'double cabin with a passage . . . between.' Hanks's second Chicago statement, Weik MSS. Since Lincoln, although recalling the fish incident, could not remember anything about this lavish entertainment, and since the

In the autumn of 1816 Thomas Lincoln again sought another abiding place, this time beyond the Ohio. Financial chaos had stricken Kentucky,[1] but this could not have troubled Lincoln, since his small dealings were mostly by barter, 'good trade,' as the frontier expression was.[2] Yet in spite of the monetary derangement, the State was throbbing with civic activity. Roads were being made, bridges built,[3] and water transportation encouraged.[4] New counties were being formed from the old ones, courts established, legal procedure facilitated;[5] for population had swollen vastly since Thomas Lincoln had gone to Hardin County and especially since his marriage to Nancy Hanks.

The influx of settlers which so impressed observers from 1780 until 1790 was but an advance guard to the hosts that poured over the mountains after Aaron Burr's picturesque adventure in 1806 had advertised the 'Western Country'; and this became nothing less than a folk movement when the War of 1812 released the energies of the youthful and the daring. By 1816 full half a million people were in Kentucky and more were coming.[6]

cabin was a small one of one room, it is certain that Hanks was indulging his fancy. This is a good illustration of his inaccuracy when magnifying the Lincolns. Hanks also says in this statement that Lincoln was born in this Knob Creek cabin.

[1] Collins, I, 317-8. Money was poor as it was scarce, and, to help hard pressed debtors, relief laws were passed. Spanish milled dollars, which slowly succeeded coonskins and other articles as a medium of exchange, were still, in practical effect, the only specie. Kentucky merchants took them to Philadelphia and purchased goods with the product of recoinage. Ib., 246x. And see Haycraft, 98-9. Even cut silver was 'extremely scarce.' Michaux: Thwaites, III, 204-5.

A few years earlier (1802) Michaux records that 'I have seen convoys of this kind that consisted of fifteen or twenty horses.' Paper currency was so generally counterfeited, that the people often refused to take even bills of the Bank of the United States. Ib., 204.

[2] Even at Lexington as late as 1802 most business was done by barter. Ib., 203.

[3] Money for these was raised mostly by lotteries. See Acts of Kentucky: 1810, 36-7, 145-6, 153-4; 1811, 58-9; 1812, 21, 37, 41-2; 1814, 310-6, 307-8; 1815, 524-5, 529-31, 611.

[4] Acts of Kentucky, 1815, 607-10, 585-6. In 1816 a Steamboat Company was authorized. Ib., 538-41.

[5] At that time most of the laws were, of course, devoted to courts and legal rights, remedies of procedure. The legislation of the period was directed to the fundamentals of the establishment of regular methods and orderly society.

[6] 406,511 in 1810 and 564,317 in 1820. Compare this with 73,677 in 1790. Collins, II, 259. The land laws were modified in 1804, making easier terms of purchase and thus encouraging settlement.

Hardin County alone had between eight and ten thousand inhabitants.[1]

And this, to Thomas Lincoln, crowded population was demanding the improvements of civilized life. Everywhere schools
were being opened, seminaries and academies established.[2]
Library associations were being incorporated,[3] books thus being
brought within the reach of every seeker after knowledge. Here
and there authority to pave streets of ambitious towns was being
given by the Legislature,[4] and fire insurance companies were
chartered.[5] Altogether Kentucky was the scene of notable intellectual, moral, and commercial advancement in the autumn of
1816. Her vigorous, aggressive people were developing modern
society, building a state.

What effect all this had on Thomas Lincoln and his wife can
only be conjectured, although, in the light of their former movements and the one now to be made, it would seem to be reasonably certain that the civic and social ferment going on about
them was not to their liking. As elsewhere south of the Ohio
slavery had increased in Kentucky, but we now know that this
fact had nothing whatever to do with the family's removal from
that State. Not the faintest evidence has been found indicating
that slavery was so much as a contributing cause for their departure;[6] indeed it is doubtful whether that institution made
any impression, one way or another, on Thomas Lincoln's pallid
mind.

[1] 7,531 in 1810 and 10,498 in 1820. *Ib.*, 258.

[2] *Acts of Kentucky*, 1811, 61, 126–8; 1812, 64–6; 1813, 133–5, 145–6, 149–51, 182–3,
203–6; 1814, 282–5, 309. As early as 1806 a female academy, one of the first in the
United States, was established at Paris, Ky., and from the beginning had from 150 to
300 students. Kentucky Annals in Collins, I, 26.

[3] For examples, at Winchester, *Acts of Kentucky*, 1810, 12; at Washington, *ib.*, 136–9;
Washingtonian and Versailles, 128–34; Frankfort, *ib.*, 1811, 141–2; 1814, 285–8.

[4] *Acts of Kentucky*, 1812, 22; 1814, 258–9.

[5] *Ib.*, 1810, 107–11; 1811, 167; also *Statutes of Kentucky*, III, 25.

[6] 'It is said in the Biographies that Mr. Lincoln left the State of K[entuck]y because
... slavery was there. This is untrue. He moved to better his condition to a place where
he could buy land for his Children and others for $1.25 per acre. Slavery did not
operate on him. I know too well this whole matter.' Hanks's second Chicago statement; also Hanks to Herndon, March 7, 1866. Weik MSS.

'I have never heard that slavery was any cause of his leaving Ky — and think quite
likely it was not — for there were very few slaves in the whole country round here
[Hodgenville, then Hodgen's mill] then perhaps not 50 in what is now this County'

He had seen slaves all his life, had supervised them as patroller. But teeming population and all that went with it were new to husband and wife. Then too, his brother, Josiah, seems to have tired of changing conditions in Kentucky, for he had already gone to Harrison County, Indiana,[1] and there is a tradition that he influenced his younger brother to follow him. Doubtless Thomas would have done so in any case, seeking like his ancestors the rainbow's ever receding end.[2]

But another incident, more definite, more disturbing had stronger effect. Suits in ejectment were brought by non-residents of Kentucky claiming title to Kentucky lands, among which were the fertile acres of the Knob Creek Valley; and several of the small farmers of the region were made defendants, among them Thomas Lincoln.[3] Plain must have been such a case to have had the smallest chance of success, overwhelming and undisputed the proof. Not only the statutes of Kentucky favored the settlers who lived upon and worked their lands, but

[LaRue]. Burba to Herndon, March 31, 1866. Weik MSS. On the other hand the controversy on slavery in the South Fork Church, mentioned p. 37, *infra*, is not without significance.

Burba adds a view of his own as to the reason for the Lincolns leaving Kentucky: 'My own opinion is that, if it is true that the Hanks family were a little unfortunate, he [Thomas Lincoln] had no desire to remain where it was so well known and being of a stout hearty robust constitution broke out to try some unknown parts. This is my own conjecture.'

[1] Waldo Lincoln, 330.

[2] In 1860, forty-six years after the removal to Indiana, Abraham Lincoln said that the family left Kentucky partly because of slavery, but chiefly on account of the confusion in land titles. Autobiography. We now know that these were not the reasons for the migration.

[3] Order Book E, Hardin Circuit Court, 299. The suits were filed Feb. 12, 1816, by Thomas Stout, Hannah Rhodes and Abraham Sheridan against Thomas Lincoln, Isaac and Jesse LaFollette, William Brownfield, Clark Tucker, Peter Minges, Job Dye, William Ash, George Redman [or Redmond] and Ignatius Strange, 'tenants in possession.'

On June 11, 1816, George Lindsey (*ib.*, 336) and Thomas Lincoln (*ib.*, 361), by separate attorneys, made answer, joined issue and a jury was ordered.

By order of court (Order Book E, 367) the land was surveyed, and depositions taken (*ib.*, 387). Then came continuances and other survey orders (*ib.*, 450; Order Book F, 59, 92, 158, 255) — all continuances at cost of the plaintiffs. These proceedings ran into the summer of 1818 when, on June 9, the jury found for the defendant farmers with costs against plaintiffs (*ib.*, 301–2); which costs were, however, finally assessed against the defendants (*ib.*, 303, 328–34, 338). Only the Lincoln and Lindsey cases were tried in Hardin County; the other cases were transferred to Nelson County. The decrees for the defendants in the Hardin County cases controlled the other cases.

they had on their side the militant sympathy of juries, the favor of judges.[1] So, after many continuances, the defendants won.

At first, Thomas Lincoln resolved to defend his occupancy, his attorney being Worden Pope, than whom there then was 'no better "land lawyer" in that part of Kentucky.' [2] But very soon, even before depositions were taken, he sold his interest in the little Knob Creek farm, it is said, for a quantity of whisky,[3] resolving to leave forever Kentucky's contentious soil; and made off to find another dwelling place beyond the great river and in the crudest, loneliest spot then to be found within a week's journey. If consulted at all, Nancy Lincoln readily agreed to go. She appears to have accepted her lowly state in life as fixed and irrevocable,[4] and was very humble, unprotesting, thankful for a friendly word or act.[5] Indeed no family in all Kentucky was more obscure; those who lived near by took no notice of the Lincolns.[6]

Thomas Lincoln must suddenly have made up his mind to leave, for on May 13, 1816, he was ordered by the court to see that the short road through the Knob Creek Valley from Muldraugh's Hill to the Rolling Fork [7] was kept in repair. Perhaps

---

[1] Kentucky Courts disposed of these cases rapidly; 'perhaps fifty judgments would be rendered in one hour.' Haycraft, 64.

[2] Mather to author, July 24, 1924.

[3] Hanks's second Chicago statement. Weik MSS. 'Mr. Lincoln got $300 [for the farm of thirty acres] and took it in whiskey.' Ib.

If Hanks is at all right about the selling price, $300 would have purchased several barrels of whisky considering the low price of it, even at the greatly depreciated value of Kentucky currency at that time. The fact would seem to have been that Thomas Lincoln bartered his few acres in a hollow of the hills for what he could get for them. Whisky represented something of value, of small bulk, it was more easily transported, and it served as a medium of exchange.

[4] Lincoln: Whitney, I, 13.

[5] 'Mrs. Lincoln now and then visited the McDougals after the birth of Abe. She was always plainly clad and received any kindness with gratitude. This I heard from my McDougal kin.' Atherton to Mather, June 20, 1924.

[6] 'I knew several families ... who lived not far off where Abe was born ... and I never heard the name of Lincoln mentioned by these old people. Not until after he was nominated in 1860 did I hear the family referred to.' Ib.

'Had not the Boy turned out to be what he did ... his family record would scarce ever have been thought of here.' Burba to Herndon, March 31, 1866. Weik MSS.

'The Lincoln Family at that day cut no considerable figure.' Same to same, May 25, 1866. Weik MSS.

[7] The order was 'that Thomas Lincoln be and he is hereby appointed surveyor of that part of the road leading from Nolin to Bardstown which lies between the Bigg

the order of the court may have quickened his decision; he had no taste for public service, even the humblest; and while the duties of road 'surveyor,' as it was called, were slight and without pay, they would have laid some additional burden on Lincoln's reluctant shoulders.[1]

At sometime during this eventful year Thomas Lincoln became a member of a congregation of 'Separate' Baptists known as the Little Mount Church, and was baptised in Knob Creek by the Rev. William Downs,[2] probably during the summer or early fall. The church was about five miles distant from the Lincoln cabin. Thus spiritually equipped he made ready for his journey.

hill [Muldraugh's] and the Rolling Fork in place of George Redman and that all the hands that assisted said Redman to assist said Lincoln in keeping said road in repair.' Records in office of Hardin County.

[1] See *Statutes of Kentucky*, Act of February 16, 1808, 459. A road 'surveyor' was required to keep in order the road designated by the court, and for that purpose to notify persons living along the route to turn out and work the road. This legal requirement was continued in many states until long after the Civil War. It was a kind of tax, very unpopular and to be avoided, much like service on juries. The man ordered to oversee a road was considered unlucky.

The Kentucky law under which Thomas Lincoln was designated was rather severe. The sheriff was fined for failure to serve the order of the court on the road surveyor or even failure to execute the order; and the surveyor fined from $2.50 to $10 for failure 'to perform his duty agreeably to law.'

It is said that he then owned four horses, one a stallion. It does not appear what he could have done with so many horses on a thirty acre farm, part of which was steep cliffs and only fourteen acres of which were under cultivation; nor yet how he fed the horses under such circumstances during the winter months. There was another Thomas Lincoln, uncle of Thomas of Knob Creek, to whom the horses taxed under that name could have belonged. Certainly such equine opulence, even assuming that the money value of the animals was small, cannot be adjusted to the facts of Thomas Lincoln's condition then or thereafter.

[2] Thomas Lincoln 'joined the Free will Baptist Church in Hardin C[ount]y, Ky., in 1816, and was imersed by a preacher named William Downs in Knob Creek.' Chapman's second narrative. Weik MSS.

Thomas Lincoln and his wife 'belonged to the Little Mount Church . . . he was baptised in the Rolling Fork.' Friend to Herndon, March 19, 1866. Weik MSS.

Chapman is the better authority since he got his information directly from Thomas Lincoln.

Rev. William Downs was a 'Separate Baptist' and his congregation was doubtless of that order. The minutes of the South Fork Baptist Church, which was more 'regular,' show that Downs in 1812 was not to be invited to preach in the South Fork meeting house nor in the houses of members of the congregation. Judge Mather has found that Lincoln's teacher, Caleb Hazel, and Mary Stevens were married in Hardin County by William Downs, October 15, 1816, so that Downs was certainly a neighbor of the Lincolns.

[3] This belated joining church is one of the welter of strange incidents in Thomas

On the Rolling Fork, two and one half miles from his cabin, he built a rude flat-boat or raft of poplar logs [1] and taking his barrels of whisky, his tools and 'other effects' floated to Salt River and thence to the Ohio.[2] While on the first named stream the clumsy raft spilled whisky and tools, presumably near shore, for he managed to get on board again all the whisky, but lost most of the tools.[3] And so, he drifted across and down the Ohio to a landing on the Indiana bank, like a piece of human flotsam thrown forward by the surging tide of immigration, the black and prodigious depths of mighty woods before him.

Lincoln's life. When in Elizabethtown he could have become a Baptist. While on the Sinking Spring farm he could have joined the South Fork Baptist Church which was only about two miles from his cabin; or he could have become a member of the Nolin Baptist Church which was between three and four miles away.

Another curious circumstance is that some of the acquaintances and relatives of Thomas and Nancy Lincoln belonged to the nearby South Fork Church as shown by the records of that congregation. Isaac and Jesse Friend were members and so was 'Caty' Friend. Jesse Friend was the husband of Mary Hanks, whom he had married in Hardin County, December 16, 1795. In 1808–10 there was a schism in this church over the slavery question. I am indebted for these facts to Judge O. M. Mather of Hodgenville, Ky., who has the records of the South Fork Church.

[1] Hanks's second Chicago statement, and Friend to Herndon, March 19, 1866. Weik MSS.

[2] Hanks's second Chicago statement. Weik MSS.

[3] Hanks's second Chicago statement. Weik MSS. Not the Ohio, as generally stated.

CHAPTER II

INDIANA: BOYHOOD AND YOUTH

New birth of our new soil, the first American. LOWELL.

'WHEN, on the barren peak of some rocky hill, you catch a distant view, it generally is nothing but an undulating surface of impenetrable forest,' wrote Elias Pym Fordham in his diary, when making his way through southwestern Indiana, early in 1818. As was the case with all travellers, Fordham was depressed by the thick and sombre woods, for he complains that 'it is seldom that a view of two hundred yards in extent can be caught in Indiana,' because 'Indiana is a vast forest . . . just penetrated in places by backwoods settlers who are half hunters, half farmers.' [1]

Vast, forbidding, tremendous, this mighty forest stretched northward from the Ohio, its trees, like giant sentinels of nature, guarding the wilderness. Sycamore, oak, elm, willow, hackberry, poplar, sugar-maple, ash, sweet-gum, hickory, beech, walnut,[2] grew as thickly as their great size would permit. In 1819 Welby measured an oak in southwestern Indiana and found it to be twenty-four feet in circumference four feet above the ground; and he remarks that there were many others even larger.[3] Thick grapevines wove a net among the trees.[4]

Michaux records that, in southern Ohio a few years earlier, he measured a tulip poplar which was forty-seven feet in circumference. As late as 1833, Hugh McCulloch found Indianapolis to be a mere village 'in the heart of a magnificent forest,' and, on the road to Fort Wayne which was only an opening 'through the

[1] *Personal Narrative of Travels*, etc.: Elias Pym Fordham, 96, 152–3. Also see 'History of the English Settlement in Edwards Co. Ill.': George Flower, 52. *Chicago Hist. Socy. Coll.*, I.

[2] Dennis Hanks to Herndon, Jan. 6, 1866; Mrs. Elizabeth Crawford to same, May 3, 1866; J. W. Whartman to same, June, 1866. Weik MSS.

[3] 'A Visit to North America': Adlard Welby, Thwaites, XII, 230.

[4] 'The Journal of a Tour,' etc.: Thaddeus Mason Harris, Thwaites, III, 359. This traveller tells of grapevines 'nine inches in diameter' which 'spread a canopy over the summits of the highest trees.'

woods,' estimated that many of the trees were nearly one hundred feet in height. David Turpie records that in his boyhood the boles rose from fifty to eighty feet without a branch; and a Methodist circuit-rider testifies that in 1823 the woods in Ohio were so thick that sunlight could not get through the dense foliage.[1] As late as 1850 the country near Logansport, Indiana, as described by a resident, was 'nothing but woods, woods, woods, as far as the world extends!' [2]

In 1816 these forests were full of animals — raccoon, squirrel, opossum, skunk, deer, bear, wolf, wildcat, panther. Wild turkeys ran through underbrush filled with grouse and quail; wild ducks and geese flew overhead. Incredible numbers of pigeons hid the sun, 'darkening the air like a thick passing cloud' and, when settling for the night, broke down stout branches of trees. Swarms of mosquitoes rose from dank, stagnant pools and noisome swamps; large black and poisonous yellow flies abounded. Innumerable frogs rasped the stillness.[3]

The advancing tide of settlement had poured more than five hundred thousand people into Kentucky and nearly as many into Ohio; and the overflow had deposited in small and scattered communities, chiefly lying on the rivers, some sixty-four thousand persons. With this population Indiana was about to be admitted to the Union when Thomas Lincoln landed at the farm of Francis Posey.[4] Fewer people had penetrated this sec-

---

[1] Michaux: Thwaites, III, 175; *Men and Measures of Half a Century*, Hugh McCulloch, 70-1, 79; *Sketches of my Own Times:* David Turpie, 19. Also *Early Indiana Trials; Sketches:* O. H. Smith, 79; *Reminiscences of Levi Coffin*, 81-2. See especially *Pioneer History of Indiana*. William M. Cockrum; *A Western Pioneer:* Rev. Alfred Brunson, I, 276-8. See also *Some Recollections of my Boyhood:* Brandon L. Harris, 31-2.

[2] *In my Youth:* Robert Dudley, 8.

[3] Hanks to Herndon, March 22, 1866; David Turnham to same, Feb. 21, 1866. Also Hanks's Chicago and Charleston statements. Weik MSS. *Sketches of Things and People in Indiana:* Rev. Aaron Wood, 11; 'Two Years Residence': John Woods, Thwaites, x, 249; Faux's 'Journal,' Thwaites, XI, 236-7; Hulme's 'Journal,' July 5, 1819, near French Lick, Indiana, Thwaites, x, 63; Brunson, I, 276-8; Hanks to Herndon, May 4, 1866. Weik MSS. See especially Cockrum, 427-57, 504, 506.

[4] Francis Posey had, April 17, 1811, entered land in Township 5 S., Range 4 W. and section 29, a township later to be named Huff. A ferry from Kentucky to Anderson Creek, Indiana, is known to have been in existence before Lincoln's coming, and by that means the passage was made and probably up Anderson's Creek until Posey's place was reached. From Posey's farm the direction to Lincoln's land would be almost west.

tion than any other part of the southern quarter of the new
State — hardly more than one adult white man to every four
square miles, and, counting women and children and youths
under twenty-one, a little over one human being to each square
mile.[1]

Into this abode of gloom and solitude, Thomas Lincoln made
his slow and toilsome way in mid-autumn of 1816. Leaving his
whisky and remaining tools with some one at Posey's on the
river's bank [2] and taking only his axe and hunting-knife, he
struggled inward, cutting a way, now and then, through the
thick and tangled underbrush.

Sixteen miles he journeyed and, at last, having reached the
vicinity of a scattered cluster of other dwellers in the fast-
nesses,[3] chose a place to which to bring his family. Upon a
knoll surrounded by marshy land, culture fields of malaria,[4]
he decided to start life anew — his fourth venture since he
had married Nancy Hanks ten years before. 'I will jest Say
to you that it was the Brushes [brushiest] Cuntry that I have
Ever Seen in any New Cuntry, . . . all Kinds of under groth
Spice wo[o]d . . . Shewmake Dogwood grape Vines Matted to-
Geather So that as the old Saying goes you could Drive a
Butcher Knife up to the Handle in it,' wrote Dennis Hanks
who went there the following year.[5] Perchance the trees on
the little hill were fewer, as sometimes was the case with these
elevations.

A curious circumstance distinguished Thomas Lincoln's selection of his future home — strange because other settlers had
chosen tracts not greatly superior to his, but every one had

[1] In the region which now comprises Warrick, Spencer and Vanderburg counties,
Indiana, there were by the end of 1815, 285 'white males over twenty-one years of
age.' Including women and children, the total population was but 1415. Census of
Warrick County, Dec. 4, 1815, as given in *Warrick and its Prominent People:* Will
Fortune, 15.

[2] Hanks to Herndon, March 7, 1866. Weik MSS.

[3] Perhaps seven families. *Ib.* Six families, two or three miles apart, were considered
to be a good settlement as late as 1815. Cockrum, 459.

[4] Nicolay and Hay, I, 30. 'The country was . . . swampy.' Hanks's second Chicago
statement. Weik MSS.

[5] Hanks to Herndon, March 22, 1866. Also Jan. 6, 1866; and David Turnham to
Herndon, Feb. 21, 1866. Weik MSS. And see *Recollections:* Harris, 20-1.

built his cabin near a spring or stream. Water at hand was the first essential of the pioneer family.[1]

Lincoln overlooked this requisite, for the supply of drinking water nearest the knoll selected by him was a spring more than a mile away; and no brook ran closer. Little Pigeon Creek was slightly less distant,[2] but not so accessible as the spring; and the pools left by rains were as unhealthful as they were inconvenient. As wells were not successful on his land, seepage into holes dug for the purpose was the only other source of water for drinking and cooking, a fact that later caused Lincoln much labor and annoyance.[3]

Roughly marking by brush heaps the tract he proposed to occupy, Thomas Lincoln returned to Kentucky to bring his family to their new wilderness home.[4] Memory of the loss of the Sinking Spring farm, or rather, of the two hundred dollars which he had paid Isaac Bush for it, still dully smouldered within his breast, it appears; for, as we have seen, late as the season already was, he went to Nelson County and, on November 17, 1816, made oath to a cross bill against Bush, demanding judgment for the amount.

Not earlier, then, than the approach of December, 1816, the Lincoln family started for the Indiana solitudes. Two horses bore husband, wife, and children as well as household belongings. Upon one horse rode the father, his little son mounted behind him; on the other horse was Nancy Lincoln, with their nine-year old daughter.[5] How they carried through Kentucky on two horses thus laden articles needful in journey and forest abode,[6] does not appear; but it was managed in some fashion.

Thus Thomas Lincoln 'packed through,' as such methods of

[1] 'The pioneers made their location where there was plenty of good spring water.' Cockrum, 510.

'The pioneer located his home with little regard to anything but a supply of good water.' *History of Indiana*: Logan Esarey, 421.

[2] Hanks to Herndon, March 12, 1866. Weik MSS.

[3] Murr, *Indiana Magazine of History*, xiii, 319; *Life of Abraham Lincoln*: Ward Hill Lamon, 21–2.

[4] Hanks's second Chicago statement. Weik MSS.

[5] Hanks to Herndon, March 7, 1866. Weik MSS.

[6] Hanks in his second Chicago statement says that they carried feather beds, clothing, and other articles, which, of course, is absurd.

travel and conveyance were then called, to the Kentucky shore
of the Ohio. Their route lay through Elizabethtown [1] where,
however, it seems they did not tarry. In two days, the ferry was
reached, where, leaving the horses, the Lincoln family was taken
across the river to Posey's farm on the Indiana side.

There, it is said, Thomas Lincoln borrowed a wagon to take
wife, children, and household articles to Pigeon Creek. If he
went in a wagon, it is well-nigh certain that it was wholly of
wood, with solid wheels made from sections of great logs, since
few if any other kind of vehicles were used in the backwoods at
that time; [2] and it is probable that this clumsy contraption was
drawn by oxen.[3] But it is more likely that he used the common
conveyance of those days, a stout heavy sled, which generally
was employed for rough going, even in summer time.[4]

Two days, at the very least, it must have taken to reach the
knoll which the father had selected several weeks earlier; no road
whatever existed,[5] and only a trail, 'Blazed out part of the way
By a Man By the [name] of Jesse Hoskins,' served to guide
them. 'The Ballance of the way . . . Lincoln had to Cut his
way,' writes Dennis Hanks. So Thomas felled trees, cut underbrush and vines and made openings through which the oxen
could drag the sled or wagon forward. Over stumps and rocks,
across gullies, bogs, mounds, and soggy ground, they crept onward and, finally, reached the spot 'Rite in the Brush,' [6] where
Abraham Lincoln was to spend the next fourteen years.

Winter was at hand — it may be that the thin snow even then
was beginning to fly. Thomas hastily built a shelter for his
family. It was a 'half-faced camp,' such as hunters were wont

[1] Friend to Herndon, March 19, 1866. Weik MSS.

[2] 'We did not have wagons in those days.' Statement of Allen Brooner: Hobson, 19.

[3] Even in 1830, fourteen years later, in Wayne County, Ind., where the settlers were
unusually enterprising, the only wagons were of this kind and usually hauled by oxen.
Recollections: Harris, 22–4.
The first wagon of any kind in the State was brought by John Small in 1814, but
it is not described. Murr, *Indiana Magazine of History*, XIII, 320. And see *Historic
Indiana:* Julia H. Levering, 71–2.

[4] *Recollections:* Harris, 22–4. Such sleds are still used over difficult forest roads in
Maine and elsewhere during the summer months, since wagons are impracticable
because of destructive wrenching from rocks and roots or miring in sloughs.

[5] Grigsby's statement. Weik MSS.

[6] Hanks to Herndon, March 7, 1866. Weik MSS.

to throw up as a protection against the weather, not unlike that
sometimes found in sugar-camps at a later day.[1] A pole was laid
from branch to branch of two convenient trees; a few feet opposite these trees two stout saplings forked at the top, the bottom ends sharpened, were thrust into the ground; another pole,
parallel with the first, laid in the crotches; and the frame was
completed by still two other poles fixed upon the ends of those
already placed. On three sides poles were piled upon one another; and a roof was contrived of poles, brush, and leaves.

One side of this structure, which was only fourteen feet wide,[2]
was not enclosed; and before this open side, a fire, started by
steel and tinder,[3] was kept burning, upon which cooking was
done. The fire also furnished such heat as the inhabitants of the
half-faced camp could get, albeit sometimes accompanied by
smoke, according to the caprices of the wind. At night, too, the
blaze served to keep wild beasts from those who slept beneath
that roof of brush.[4] The loose, unhardened earth was the floor,
on which leaves were thickly strewn; and over these was spread
such bedding as had been brought, skins for the most part and
possibly a blanket.[5]

Within and about this camp of poles and brush existed Abraham Lincoln, then in his eighth year, together with his sister and
parents throughout the winter of 1816–17.[6] Hanks relates that
the second day after the family arrived, the boy killed a turkey
'with his farthers Riffle,' more by accident than skill, since

[1] Hanks's Chicago statements. Weik MSS.

[2] Hanks to Herndon, no date, but in 1866. Weik MSS.
'It was not a Cabin at all it was one of those half face camps a Bout 14 feet open in
front.' *Ib.*
In his second Chicago statement Hanks says that he helped build the half-face camp,
although he did not come to Indiana until a year later.

[3] This method continued until 1850. Dudley, 47. Often fire was borrowed, live coals
covered with ashes being carried in a kettle from one cabin to another. *Ib.*, 55. And
see Levering, 72.

[4] For a good description of this half-faced camp see Murr, *Indiana Magazine of
History*, XIII, 320–1. And see Esarey, 421–2; Cockrum, 161; *Boone*, Thwaites, 63–4.
As for Thomas Lincoln's hut, see Lamon, 22.

[5] This was not unusual. Many settlers, at first, had only brush and skins to sleep on.
Cockrum, 501–2.

[6] 'He lived quite on the level, if not below, that of thousands of slaves whom he
afterwards liberated.' Murr, *Indiana Magazine of History*, XIII, 321.

'Turkies two Numer[ous] to Mention.'[1] No other food but
game brought in by Thomas Lincoln was possible at first; and
water was to be had only by melting the snow, or by carrying in
a kettle from the distant spring. Luckily Thomas Lincoln did
not have far to go to get sustenance for his family, game filling
the thickets that surrounded the small hill on which the half-
faced camp was built. 'We did not have to go more than 4 or 5
hundred Yards to Kill deer, turkeys and other wild game,'
Dennis Hanks relates of the following year.[2]

At last came the spring of 1817. Wild rose, swamp lily, wild
honeysuckle, blue flag and yellow flag, Sweet William bloomed;
crab apple, wild plum, haw trees blossomed; grape clusters began
to form; abundant dogwood made spots of white among the
brush and trees.[3] The waters of Pigeon Creek rose in their banks
and, warmed by the season, invited those begrimed by winter's
unwashed months.

Thomas Lincoln went back to Kentucky for swine, animals
which all settlers kept, and on his return to Indiana was accom-
panied by Thomas Sparrow and Dennis Hanks. Dennis tells
that 'at the Same time he [Lincoln] Drove his stalk Hoggs to
Poseys and thare left them in the Beach Mast.' But alas for the
pigs and Lincoln's hope of pork! 'I and Sparrow,' writes Hanks,
'Started home [Kentucky] and we had Not Ben at home Not
More than a week tell here cum all the Hoggs A Bare had got a
Mung them [and] Killed one this was a Bout 80 miles the[y]
Cum.'[4]

In the autumn of 1817, Nancy Lincoln's heart was gladdened

[1] Hanks to Herndon, March 7 and 12, 1866. Also Hanks's second Chicago statement. Weik MSS.

[2] Hanks's second Chicago statement. Weik MSS.

[3] Hanks to Herndon, May 4, 1866; and Elizabeth Crawford to same, May 3, 1866.
Weik MSS.

[4] Hanks to Herndon, March 12, 1866. Also Hanks's Charleston statement. Weik
MSS. The hogs 'swam the Ohio' back to Kentucky. I 'saw them Knew them.' Ib.

Swine were kept in large numbers by the pioneers, the poorest settler always having
several hogs. They lived on mast and became very wild. Bear constantly attacked
them. See Cockrum, 470, 490–3.

'The bears, during the summer, are lean and hungry, and seize hogs and eat them
alive. It is no uncommon thing to see hogs escape home with the loss of a pound or
two of living flesh.' Faux: Thwaites, xi, 228, near Princeton, Ind., Nov. 7–8, 1819;
Recollections: Harris, 39–40; Michaux: Thwaites, iii, 246.

by the arrival of her aunt and uncle, Betsy and Thomas Sparrow, who with Dennis Hanks, now eighteen years of age,[1] had come to live permanently with the Lincolns.[2] 'Lincoln had Bilt another Cabin By this time,' says Hanks, 'and got in it a Bout 40 Rods apart' from the half-faced camp.[3] This cabin was of the usual type, round logs with the bark on [4] and roof of poles and slabs. It was larger than any the Lincoln family had lived in, being eighteen feet wide and twenty feet long; and it was high enough for a loft beneath the roof, reached by pegs driven in the log walls.[5]

But no floor was laid, no door contrived, no window; [6] even the roof was not finished when cold weather came. Nor did the approach of another winter quicken the domestic enterprise of Thomas Lincoln; and Hanks chronicles of this and later years, that 'we all hunted pretty much all the time, Especially So when we got tired of work — which was very often I will assure you.' [7]

In the uncompleted cabin Thomas, Nancy and their children spent the fall of 1817 and the following winter; Thomas and Betsy Sparrow with Dennis Hanks, occupying 'that Darne Little half face camp,' as Dennis called it,[8] near by. No dogs or cats cheered the Lincoln hut, no chickens, hogs or cows were about.[9] The only light was from hog fat.[10] For most of the day the two men roved with their rifles, they, Nancy, and the children, living well-nigh exclusively on wild animals and birds —

[1] Hanks was born in Hardin County, Ky., May 15, 1799. R. N. Chapman to Jesse W. Weik, March 22, 1904. Chapman was Hanks's grandson. Also Hanks's written statement, April 2, 1866. Weik MSS.

[2] Hanks to Herndon, March 12, 1866. Weik MSS.

[3] *Ib.* Hanks is badly confused as to the time of his arrival and of other events, but says, 'I cant tell Exactly Bout Dates.' Same to same, no date, but in 1866, and his second Chicago statement.

[4] Cabins of hewed logs were seldom built before 1830. *History of Warrick, Spencer and Perry Counties,* Ind., 411.

[5] Hanks's second Chicago statement. Weik MSS. Hanks thus describes the beds in the loft: 'Here were the beds. The floor of the loft was clap board and the beds lay on this. Here I and Abe slept and I was married there to Abes Step Sister, Miss Elizabeth Johnston.' *Ib.*

[6] *Ib.*; Nicolay and Hay, i, 29.

[7] Hanks's second Chicago statement. Weik MSS.

[8] Hanks to Herndon, March 12, 1866. Weik MSS.

[9] Hanks's second Chicago statement. Weik MSS.   [10] *Ib.*; Levering, 68–9.

'ate them as meat, water and bread,' as Hanks told Herndon.[1] Sometimes Lincoln and Hanks varied their hunting by search for wild honey and 'found bee trees all over the forest.' [2] In the autumn nuts and wild fruit added variety to their fare. Hanks records that 'the country was full of chesnuts, Paw paus, . . . wild-turky peas;' [3] and hickory-nuts, walnuts, hazel-nuts were plentiful.

Now and then, when not hunting, the men cleared a patch of about six acres; [4] and a little corn and other vegetables were raised. If any corn ripened, the kernels were broken by pounding with a stone or axe-head in a mortar made by hollowing a place on top of a hard-wood stump, as was done by most people of the backwoods.[5] No mill was nearer than seventeen miles on the banks of the Ohio 'close to Posey's;' and when we got there, laments Dennis Hanks, 'the mill was a poor concern . . . a little bit of a tread horse mill the ground meal of which a hound could Eat as fast as it was ground.' [6]

David Turnham describes the mill as one that 'would grind from ten to fifteen bushels of corn in a day;' even a better mill built later gave such scanty output that Turnham often had to go 'twice to git one grist.' [7] Yet even such a mill 'was a God Send.' [8] Thereafter, when small fields had been cleared and before other mills were built nearer to his cabin, Thomas Lincoln and others of the scattered settlement went to this mill to have their sacks of corn ground into coarse meal, as occasional variation from the grain broken in the stump mortars.[9]

---

[1] Hanks's Charleston statement. Weik MSS.

[2] Hanks's second Chicago statement. Weik MSS. And see Cockrum, 338.

[3] Hanks's Charleston statement. Weik MSS.

[4] Hanks's second Chicago statement. Weik MSS.

[5] This method was practised in Wayne County as late as 1833. *Recollections:* Harris, 9; Turpie, 21–2. And see Levering, 67.

[6] Hanks's second Chicago statement. Weik MSS.

[7] Turnham to Herndon, Feb. 21, 1866. Weik MSS.

[8] Hanks's second Chicago statement. Weik MSS.

Two years after this, in 1820, settlers in Wayne County, one of the richest parts of Indiana, went from ten to thirty miles to mill and often waited two or three days for their turns. Boys usually took a sack of corn on horseback and returned with the meal. *Recollections:* Harris, 9.

[9] The miller's toll was one fourth of the grain ground. Levering, 70. Wheat, oats.

It was more than a year after he had squatted on the land, that Thomas Lincoln bethought him of the necessity of entering it legally. So he made his way through the forests ninety miles to Vincennes where the land office then was, and, on October 15, 1817, entered the Southwest quarter of Section 32, Township 4 South, Range 5 West, paying the preliminary instalment of sixteen dollars, for which a receipt was given him.[1] This tract of one hundred and sixty acres, for half of which, as will appear, Thomas Lincoln finally succeeded in getting a patent, was at that time in Hurricane Township, Warrick County, which within a year became Carter Township, Spencer County. But four other entries of land had then been made in the whole township, each for an entire section or more.[2]

The following year, however, nine new settlers entered at the land office for tracts in Carter Township, all but two of the entries being for undivided sections.[3] Thus Lincoln acquired a sort of option on one hundred and sixty acres. In December he paid sixty-four dollars more, thus completing his first instalment of eighty dollars,[4] one fourth of the purchase price, the land being sold by the government for two dollars per acre. His right to a patent to the land when he should make the remaining payments thus being established, he rested content and the routine of farming, hunting, and carpentering continued.

Thus dragged along the slow dull weeks. Another winter went by, another spring and summer. Then in the autumn of 1818 a disease, mysterious as forest shadows, came suddenly upon Pigeon Creek. 'The milk sick' the settlers called it, because it attacked cattle and particularly milch cows as virulently as men and women. No cure was known and those seized generally died, and died quickly. The nearest doctor lived thirty-five miles from Pigeon Creek [5] and, if accessible, could have done no

and barley were thrashed with a flail and winnowed with a sheet. *Ib.* and 67. Faux found that one eighth was the miller's toll. Faux: Thwaites, xi, 199.

[1] No. 8499. General Land Office Records, Interior Department, Washington. In this receipt Lincoln's name is spelled Linkern.

[2] *Hist. W., S. & P. Cos.*, Ind., 272.   [3] *Ib.*

[4] Receipt No. 9205. General Land Office Records, Interior Department, Washington. Lincoln's name is here spelled Linkhorn.

[5] Hanks's second Chicago statement. Weik MSS.

good, since medical treatment proved wholly inadequate then, or for many years afterward.[1]

Betsy and Thomas Sparrow, who were known in the settlement as 'Mrs. Lincoln's father and mother,'[2] were stricken in the half-faced camp and there on skins and leaves covering the ground they died, about eighteen months after their coming.[3] A tree was felled, a log of right length cut and whip-sawed into rough, uneven boards. These Thomas Lincoln fashioned into rude boxes, fastening them together with wooden pegs driven into holes made by a small auger, for no nails were at hand.[4] Into these boxes the bodies were placed, and, upon a wooded hill some quarter mile distant, were buried.

To the sick old man and woman Nancy Lincoln had given all the help she could; she had visited, in her last illness, the wife of Peter Brooner, a hunter chiefly,[5] whose cabin was only half a mile away.[6] Mrs. Brooner died, too; and, at the same time, Nancy Lincoln fell sick. Neighbors attended her and one of them, William Wood, recalls that he 'sat up with her all one night.'[7] Thus 'she struggled on' for a week; and at the last, calling Sarah and Abraham to her side, told them to be good to their father, to each other, and to reverence God.[8] She died in October, 1818,[9] on the seventh day of her illness.

Thomas Lincoln made a coffin for his wife as he had for the others; and on a sled,[10] as the first pioneer woman in that region had been taken to her grave, the body of Nancy Lincoln was

---

[1] For the best account of the 'milk sickness,' see Cockrum, 401. Col. Cockrum, who wrote from personal observation and experience, says that whole towns were depopulated by the scourge; also a bilious fever, resembling yellow fever, was quite as deadly and more general than the milk sickness.

[2] William Wood's statement. Weik MSS.

[3] Hanks to Herndon, March 12, 1866. Weik MSS.

[4] 'There was not a nail in a hundred miles of them.' Cockrum, 161.

[5] Brooner, like Lincoln, had come from Kentucky and was 'a widely known bear hunter.' Hist. W., S. & P. Cos., Ind., 557.

[6] Statement of Henry Brooner: Hobson, 18.

[7] Wood's statement. Weik MSS.

[8] Hanks's second Chicago statement. Weik MSS.

[9] Grigsby's statement. Weik MSS. Grigsby does not name the day of the month, which is said to have been October 5, but there is no evidence as to the exact date of her death.

[10] Statement of Henry Brooner: Hobson, 18.

hauled to the knoll and buried by the side of her foster parents.[1] No stone or board was placed to mark where she lay, nor during the life-time of her husband or son was a monument of any kind erected over that neglected grave.[2]

Abraham was now nine years old, and there is no evidence that his emotions were unlike those of other children of similar age and in the same situation. Back to their doorless, window-less, floorless cabin, went Thomas Lincoln and his children; and there, with Dennis Hanks, they lived through the remainder of the winter, through the spring, the summer and the autumn of 1819. Sarah, now in her thirteenth year, did the cooking.[3]

The father and Dennis Hanks kept on hunting, between in-frequent intervals of work in the clearing and when Thomas was not doing some small job of carpentering for other settlers. 'We always hunted,' Dennis reiterates, 'it made no difference what came for we more or less depended on it for a living — nay for life.' Abraham brought water from the spring and creek, or from holes dug to catch the seepage from rains; but this device was 'a tempo[ra]ry affair.' [4]

Sometime after the death of Nancy Lincoln, an itinerant Bap-tist preacher, David Elkin, came from Kentucky on a visit to the Pigeon Creek settlement; and while there preached a sermon over the graves of Nancy Lincoln and those who had died from the plague during the fatal days of 1818.[5] Abraham and his sister were present of course, as were Thomas Lincoln and Dennis Hanks, and all who lived in the settlement, about twenty in number.[6] But Abraham had not written to Elkin

---

[1] Hanks to Herndon, April, 1866. Weik MSS.

The particular spot where each of these people is buried is, of course, unknown; but the location of the grave of Nancy Lincoln is approximately determined, since the graves are close together.

[2] Lamon, 29.   [3] Hanks's second Chicago statement. Weik MSS.   [4] *Ib.*

[5] Hanks to Herndon, Jan. 6, 1866. Weik MSS. Hanks says that Elkin came to visit the Lincoln family. 'David Elkins of Hardin County Ky. Cum to pay us a Visit and preacht hir furnel.' *Ib.* There was much visiting between the Indiana settlers and their Kentucky friends. Dennis Hanks went back and forth frequently. Hanks's second Chicago statement. Weik MSS.

[6] 'Next question how many people was at Mrs. Lincoln furnel at hir Beriel Thare was aBout 20 persons the hole Nabourhood.' Hanks to Herndon, Jan. 6, 1866. Weik MSS.

And see list of settlers in Carter township: *Hist. W., S. & P. Cos.,* Ind., 272. A year

asking him to come and preach a funeral sermon over his mother's grave, as legend has it; even if the boy had thought of such a ceremony, of which he then could have known little or nothing, he could not write at that time, nor indeed for five years thereafter, 'so that he could understand' what he wrote.

Other settlers were taking up claims in the region, cabins of unbarked logs were rising here and there, children multiplying, society forming. In common with most people of the Western country, those on and about Pigeon Creek were very ignorant, rough mannered, vividly superstitious. The waxing and waning of the moon marked for them, the times to plant and sow. The howling of a dog meant the certain coming of death among them; and if a shovel or edged tool was brought into a cabin there could be no doubt that a coffin would be taken out. Nothing must be begun on Friday; a bird alighting at the window or flying into the house meant coming sorrow. Ghosts visited earthly scenes and haunted the unworthy. Witches, too, were real beings of evil; dreams were forecasts of events to come. Faith doctors and charms were 'implicitly believed in.'[1]

The cabins of these wood folk were often ill-kept, dirty in the extreme, infested with vermin.[2] There was no sanitation. Bathing or washing the body in any way was seldom attempted, seldom thought of except, of course, during 'swimming time' in warm weather. It is hard to see how, from December to March inclusive, the clothes they wore could have been washed.[3] Food was mostly of flesh, with some corn or wheat

later, however, thirty-one men, all then living in the whole of Carter township, voted at an election held in the home of Jonathan Greathouse. *Ib.*

[1] Murr, *Indiana Magazine of History*, XIII, 335–9. Murr tells of these and other superstitions from personal observation. See also Cockrum, 339–41, and *The First of the Hoosiers:* George Cary Eggleston, 88.

[2] Welby: Thwaites, XII, 233–4.

[3] Lack of bathing and washing clothes was practically universal among the pioneers. A well-educated and carefully reared New England woman who went with her husband to live in Illinois about this time records that she could not wash clothes oftener than every three months. *A Woman's Story of Pioneer Illinois:* Christiana Holmes Tillson, 86. Mrs. Tillson was a New England woman who went with her husband to Illinois in 1822. The book consists of letters to her children and is one of the best sources on early Illinois.

Between Princeton and Vincennes Faux saw only two 'neat log houses' — all others

broken in stump mortars; and, generally, the cooking was poor and insufficient, frying in grease being a favorite method.

Cabins usually were packed, husband and wife, children, guests, relatives, and hired men living in a single small room — cooking, eating, and sleeping there,[1] a loft sometimes relieving the congestion. The sense of modesty was embryonic, and men took off their clothes before women without a thought by either of any impropriety.[2] Men and boys wore deerskin trousers and coats and coonskin caps; the clothing of women and girls was of linsey-woolsey, home-made from wool and flax.[3] Usually everybody went barefoot during spring and summer;[4] and when they did not, wore moccasins made of hide, until shoes appeared.

Incredible quantities of whisky were consumed,[5] everybody,

were 'miserable log holes ... and indolent, dirty, sickly, wild-looking inhabitants.' Faux: Thwaites, xi, 213.

[1] Travelers and others wrote many descriptions of cabins with numerous inmates, such as that of an early schoolmaster who boarded in a cabin sixteen feet square, where dwelt husband, wife, ten children, three dogs, two cats, and the teacher. Nicolay and Hay, i, 18.

'In a little log-hole ... belonging to Mr. Ferrel, who, with his family, some adults, male and female, in all ten souls, sleep in one room, fifteen by ten ... in three beds standing on a dirt floor.... The victuals are served up in a hand-bason; and thus one room serves for parlour, kitchen, hall, bed-room and pantry.' Faux: Thwaites, xi, 231. Nov. 9, 1819, near Princeton, Ind.

A Methodist circuit rider often found 'but one room to cook, eat, preach, pray, and sleep in for the whole family' and preacher. Brunson, i, 219.

[2] In one of the best cabins seen by William Faux, that of John Ingle in southwestern Indiana, 1819, the two men slept together next to 'six fine but dirty children,' while Mrs. Ingle and the hired girl slept in another bed. 'Males dress and undress before the females and nothing is thought of it. Shame or rather ... false shame, or delicacy, does not exist here. It is not unusual for a male and a female to sleep in the same room uncurtained, holding conversations while in bed.' Faux: Thwaites, xi, 226. Nov. 6, 1819; and Welby: Thwaites, xii, 229.

[3] Levering, 69.   [4] Esarey, 424.

[5] 'No difference if grain was scarce or dear, or times hard, or the people poor, they would make and drink whiskey. And the number of little distilleries was wonderful. Within two miles of where we lived there were three of them.... The custom was for every man to drink it, on all occasions that offered; and the women would take it, sweetened and reduced to toddy.' *Recollections of Life in Ohio from 1813 to 1840:* William Cooper Howells, 125–6.

At Princeton, in 1819, Faux noted 'excessive drinking seems the all-pervading, easily-besetting sin of this wild hunting country.' Faux: Thwaites, xi, 212–3, Nov. 2, 1819.

'Another failing in their character is drunkenness; and they are extremely quarrelsome when intoxicated.' Woods: Thwaites, x, 317. And see Fordham, 65.

In 1819 alone, three licenses were granted to retail liquor in Boonville, Warrick County, although that town then had a population fewer than one hundred; eleven

women and preachers included, drinking the fiery liquid.[1] A
bottle was in every cabin — to offer it was the first gesture of
welcome, to refuse unpardonable incivility.[2] All used tobacco,
chewing, smoking, snuffing; and corn-cob pipes in the mouths
of women were a not uncommon sight.[3] Men were quick to
fight and combats were brutal.[4] Profanity was general and emphatic.[5]

Yet an innate love of justice, truthfulness, and fair dealing
permeated every community, and generous and ready hospital-
ity was the highest ordinance. The desire that their children
should get 'learning' was well-nigh a passion, second only, indeed, to their respect for law and insistence upon that regular
procedure afforded by courts. The upright judge, was, by them,
the most respected of men; the capable lawyer, the most admired. Religion, too, was a vital part of their lives;[6] and
churches were organized as soon as there were settlers enough to

---

years later, 1830, but eighty-seven people lived there. *Hist. W., S. & P. Cos.*, Ind., 76.

An inn at Corydon, the State capital, a village of about one hundred cabins, adver-
tised that dinner for 'gentlemen' on the Fourth of July would include 'plenty of
Domestic Liquors,' all for '$1 per head.' *Indiana Gazette*, June 29, 1821, as quoted by
Charles Moores in *Indiana Magazine of History*, xiii, 37.

As late as 1833 the Sheriff of Perry County was fined for being so drunk during
court time that he could not perform his duties. *Hist. W., S. & P. Cos.*, Ind., 621.

[1] Grigsby's statement. Weik MSS.

[2] 'Whisky was invariably offered to a guest. The farmer who did not supply his
field-hands with liquor was considered too stingy to work for. . . . "Two" fips a gallon
was the price.' Levering, 74.

Faux found whisky, as well as bread and meat, to be considered 'common necessities.' Faux: Thwaites, xi, 177.

[3] 'We frequently saw women nursing their children with pipes in their mouths.'
Woods, Sept. 7, 1819: Thwaites, x, 247. Also Dudley, 15. 'The mother sat smoking
her pipe, fat and easy.' Faux: Thwaites, xi, 248.

[4] Levering, 184. The largest number of fines by Justices of the Peace was for fighting.
There were then so many cases of this kind in Spencer County that its historian calls
the period the 'Fist and Skull Age.' *Hist. W., S. & P. Cos.*, Ind., 400.

In Perry County at the fall term of court, 1815, there were sixteen indictments,
'mainly for assault and battery.' *Ib.*, 618.

'I saw a man this day with his face sadly disfigured. He had lost his nose, bitten
off close down to its root, in a fight with a nose-loving neighbour.' Faux: Thwaites,
xi, 22.

Fordham found that biting and gouging were common methods of fighting. Fordham, 65, 149.

[5] At the first Circuit Court in Perry County, April 3, 1815, twenty-five men were
indicted for profanity. *Hist. W., S. & P. Cos.*, Ind., 617.

[6] Levering, 86.

form small congregations. Preaching was crude, direct, vociferous; but it was an effective force for good.[1]

Schools were started [2] almost as soon as churches — in fact church and school were companion influences for decency, knowledge, and morality in pioneer life. And grave was the need of them. The drinking of whisky, the fighting and the swearing, were accompanied by repellent conditions of living. Men and boys told noisome anecdotes. Social relations were loose and undisciplined.[3]

A peculiar and distinctive dialect resulted from the untaught and unrestrained speech; and this dialect became common to the vast majority of people who had crossed the mountains to occupy the forests and prairies of the Western Country. If a man was feeble he was 'powerful weak,' and when he grew better he was 'fitter.' The word 'sot' meant sit, set, or sat. Nobody fought, they 'fit.' You did not stay awhile, but 'a spell.' How do you do, was expressed by the exclamation 'howdey.' You came 'outen,' not out of, the house, or field; and when there was much or many of anything there was a 'heap.' Wages were 'yearned,' not earned, and children always were called 'young uns.' When a person was persuaded or induced, he was 'hornswoggled.' Where was 'whar'; came 'kum'; heard 'hearn'; took 'tuck';

[1] Observers are unanimous in praise of these pioneer preachers. The Methodist 'circuit-rider' is especially commended. Smith, 97. *Ind. Hist. Soc. Pubs.*, I, 163.

For an excellent description of the appearance of these men see *The Circuit Rider:* Edward Eggleston, 88; and as to the matter and manner of their preaching see *ib.*, 103–9.

'Mr. Devan, when preaching at Mr. Ingle's, stripped at it, taking off coat, waistcoat, and cravat, unbuttoning his shirt collar, and wildly throwing about his arms. He made the maddest gesticulations for the space of two hours, ever seen in a man professing sanity.' Faux: Thwaites, XI, 285. Nov. 30, 1819, at 'The English Settlement' near Princeton, Ind.

Rev. Alexander Devan was a prosperous farmer, a member of the Indiana Constitutional Convention in 1816, and one of the first Baptist preachers in southwestern Indiana. *Ib.*

[2] The impulse for education in early Indiana is shown by the number of ambitious private schools established: a seminary at Corydon in 1816, Vincennes Academy 1817, Martin's Academy at Livonia 1819, New Albany School 1823, New Harmony Seminary 1826, Cambridge Academy at Lawrenceburg 1826, Hanover Academy 1827, and Eel River Seminary at Logansport 1829. *Hist. of Education in Indiana:* Richard G. Boone, 60. There was literary ambition too. In 1818 a Life of Napoleon, of unknown authorship, was printed in Salem, Ind., by Ebenezer Patrick and Beebe Booth — the first book printed in that town.

[3] At the first circuit court of Perry County, April 3, 1815, nearly all indictments were

care 'keer'; than 'nor'; because, 'kase.' Distance and direction were expressed by 'way back' or 'over yander.' When addressing the chairman of a public meeting the speaker said 'Misteer Cheermun.' [1] Many of these idioms and pronunciations Lincoln retained throughout life — he began his famous Cooper Union speech by saying, 'Mr. Cheerman.' [2] In addition to this dialect, plain, short words were used which now are avoided. In short, says Esarey, the language of the pioneers was that of the peasantry of the eighteenth century.[3]

The amusements of the people were so contrived as to get needed work done; but they were boisterous with rampant jollity. The felling of the splendid forests to make clearings left great quantities of logs that could not be used for cabins or stables; and these logs were burned. So at 'log rollings' everybody helped mightily, ate heavily, and drank much whisky; and robust was the play and rough the jests at meal-time or when the logs were gathered and set on fire. Much the same happened when neighbors came to help put up the frames of houses or build cabins, 'raisings,' as these events were called.[4]

'Corn shuckings' were the scenes of greatest enjoyment. Men and boys were chosen by two captains and thus divided into equal groups, each strove to husk the most corn. Songs were

for rape, divorce, bigamy, slander, assault and battery, and adultery. Several divorces were granted, 'usually for unfaithfulness to the marriage vows, and for desertion.' Six or seven slander and divorce cases were tried at nearly every term of court. *Hist. W., S. & P. Cos.*, Ind., 616–8.

It was the same in other counties. At Boonville, county seat of Warrick County, cases of divorce, slander, and the like 'were on the docket almost every term of court.' *Ib.*, 62–6.

The early court records of Spencer County were destroyed by fire in 1831, but they showed, of course, the same state of things as in the adjoining counties, for, at the court held in Rockport in 1833, there were two indictments for fornication and adultery. *Ib.*, 308–9.

There were comparatively few indictments for larceny, partly because 'thieving ... is here deemed worse than murder in consequence of the very great facility [difficulty] of living.' Faux: Thwaites, xi, 283. Nov. 29, 1819.

[1] These examples, with others, may be met in Tillson, 64–6, 79–82, 89, 96, 121–3; Dudley, 3, 45, 47, 53, 75, 141, 233; *Recollections of Early Illinois:* Joseph Gillespie, Fergus Historical Series, ii, No. 13, 10–1.

[2] Murr, *Indiana Magazine of History*, xiv, 15.   [3] Esarey, 418–9.

[4] *Recollections:* Harris, 263. In Wayne County, 1820–30, the meals on these occasions were boiled ham, cooked potatoes, boiled turnips, corn pone, and pumpkin pie. The men drank whisky and the women eggnog. Boys carried the whisky. *Ib.*

sung, stories told, jokes cracked; 'and pass the bottle around' was the order of the hour.[1] Sugar-boilings, wool-shearings, and hog-killings were scenes of similar festivities.[2]

'Quilting bees,' where women met to make coverings for beds, were times of scarcely less cheer; for the provisions were the same and the men had nothing to do but play and drink whisky, which was as freely offered at quiltings as at the other pioneer festivities.[3]

Such were the surroundings and the society in which Abraham Lincoln's formative years were to be spent; and we shall now witness his development under these conditions, from his tenth to his twenty-first year.

When there were enough children in the settlement to justify the starting of a school, Andrew Crawford opened one in a cabin of unhewn logs, two or three miles from the hut of Thomas Lincoln. Like all others of the time it was a subscription school,[4] the teacher taking his pay in skins or farm produce,[5] far more valuable than the 'wild-cat' paper, which then was the only form of money. Indeed Dennis Hanks testifies that throughout their sojourn in Indiana deerskins, 'Hogs and Venison hams was a Legal tender and Coon Skins all So.' [6]

The Lincoln children went to Andrew Crawford's school for

---

[1] *Recollections:* Harris, 34. And see *Pioneer Hist. of Ill.*: John Reynolds, 316–7. For favorable description of 'corn shuckings,' see *Circuit Rider:* Edward Eggleston, 20–9.

[2] Levering, 75–6. Also B. B. Lloyd's statement, no date. Weik MSS.

[3] Drake, 186. Dr. Drake says that all these gatherings were occasions for drinking, profanity, fighting, and indecency. *Ib.*, 184.

[4] 'Schools were then supported wholly by subscription.' *Hist. W., S. & P. Cos.*, Ind., 409.

[5] Joab Hungate, a teacher of a similar school in Spencer County at that time, was paid eight dollars a month which 'was taken partly in grain.' *Ib.* At Rockport parents paid as high as from $1.00 to $2.00 a quarter for each child. *Ib.*, 399.

[6] Hanks to Herndon, Jan. 6 and March 22, 1866. Weik MSS.
Cash was asked only for powder, shot, whisky, and salt. Levering, 82–3.
Groceries, and other provisions were traded for skins, feathers, produce, etc., which, at stated season, 'the merchant shipped off to market, and then laid in a new stock.' *Hist. W., S. & P. Cos.*, Ind., 263–4.
J. W. Lamar, who lived at Troy, says that the settlers 'took their deer and bear hides, venison hams and other game' to that village and exchanged them for powder and shot, coffee, sugar, and clothing. Hobson, 23–4.
Barter was everywhere used. For many years afterward and in so opulent a settlement as the first to be made in Wayne County 'store goods' were bought by barter. *Recollections:* Harris, 59.

a while during the winter of 1818–19.[1] The school was held in 'a rude pole cabin with huge fire-place, rude floor of puncheons and seats of same, and a window made by leaving out a log on the side to admit the light, often covered with greased paper to keep out the wind.'[2] Spelling, reading, writing, and 'ciphering to single rule of 3 no further' were taught in the haphazard manner of the period and region.[3] It was a 'blab' or 'loud school,' the children studying vocally. Punishment was administered by whipping or making the child wear the 'dunce cap.'[4] 'When we went to Crawford he tried to learn us manners,' relates Nathaniel Grigsby, showing the pupils how to enter a room, the formalities of introduction and the like.[5]

But the teacher gave up after one season, it appears, as frontier school promoters sometimes did. Thereafter Andrew Crawford disappears from the chronicles of Pigeon Creek pedagogy.[6] Lincoln was then in his tenth year and he did not again go to school until 'he was about 14 or 15.'[7] What he learned from Crawford we do not know; a little simple reading, perhaps, and how to form words with a quill pen — certainly not much more, since he could not write well until four or five years later.[8]

Back and forth during the winter months of 1818–19, went the Lincoln children from the log schoolhouse in the woods to the unfinished cabin on the knoll. Thomas Lincoln and Dennis

---

[1] Grigsby's statement, Sept. 12, 1865. Weik MSS.

[2] *Hist. W., S. & P. Cos.*, Ind., 413. Even three years later at Rockport, the County seat of Spencer County, the school was held in this kind of a cabin of 'round logs' — not hewed logs (*ib.*, 398–9); and this was the best schoolhouse in the County.

For an excellent description of these pioneer schools see Cockrum, 459–63. Panthers and bears sometimes attacked these school cabins. *Ib.*, 464–5.

[3] Mrs. Allen Gentry's statement. Also Hanks's first Chicago statement. Weik MSS.

[4] *Recollections:* Harris, 12–3. And see the *First of the Hoosiers*, Eggleston, 32–43.

[5] Grigsby's statement. Weik MSS. Grigsby is clear and positive as to the order in which Lincoln went to school in Indiana — first to Crawford, second to Dorsey, and third to Swaney, *ib.* The biographies usually give Dorsey as the first teacher.

[6] In May, 1818, Andrew Crawford was made a Justice of the Peace. *Hist. W., S. & P. Cos.*, Ind., 294.

[7] Grigsby's statement. Weik MSS.

[8] 'Abraham learned to write So that we could understand it in 1821.' Hanks's second Chicago statement. Weik MSS. With characteristic bragging, Hanks claimed that it was he who taught Lincoln to read and write: 'I taught Abe his first lesson in spelling, reading and writing. I taught Abe to write with a buzzards quill.' *Ib.*

Hanks were the providers, protectors, mentors. Hanks complains that they had 'to work Very hard Clair ground for to Keep Sole and Body to Geather and Every Spare time that We had we picked up our Rifle and feched in a fine Deer or turkey and in the winter time we went a Coon Hunting;' but Dennis seems to have included in this description of their toil all the years spent in Indiana.[1]

Imagination must picture the situation and manner of existence of these two men living with the girl and boy in that hut in the brush throughout the year 1819. From trustworthy accounts of better conditioned families in the same wilderness, it can only be believed that for the Lincolns 1819 was a year of squalor — mostly flesh for food, unfit water, wretched cooking, no knives or forks, bare feet, bodies partly clad, filthy beds of leaves and skins.[2]

A time came when even Thomas Lincoln could stand it no longer. So back to Kentucky he journeyed for another wife. He knew where to go, it appears, for he went directly to Elizabethtown where the woman he had first courted, Sarah Bush, still lived. She was now a widow, her first husband, Daniel Johnston, having died of the 'cold plague' in 1814,[3] leaving three children

[1] Hanks to Herndon, March 22, 1866. Weik MSS.

[2] Lamon, 26, 31.

'There are several English families living without bread, butter, milk, tea or coffee, for months. . . . Some three families cook and bake in one iron skillet, called the cook-all.' Faux: Thwaites, xi, 287–8, Dec. 9, 1819, at 'the English Settlement,' near Princeton, Ind. 'A spider skillet with lid and an earthen pot were more than the average cooking utensils possessed by a family.' Esarey, 422–3. It was with these that little Sarah Lincoln cooked for four persons for more than a year.

Faux describes the manner of life of two brothers, English immigrants in about this part of the county, though across the line in Illinois, 'living without any female, and fast barbarizing, in a most miserable log-cabin, not mudded, having only one room, no furniture of any kind, save a miserable, filthy, ragged bed. . . . Both were more filthy, stinking, ragged, and repelling, than any English stroller or beggar ever seen; garments rotting off, linen unwashed, face unshaven and unwashed, for, I should think, a month. . . . He [the elder brother] expects his sisters and [other] brothers into this miserable abode.' Ib., 268, Nov. 26, 1819.

'This morning Mr. Ingle, in descending a ladder from his cock-loft bed-room, into which sun, moon, and stars peep, and all the winds and storms of heaven blow upon us, was left suspended by his arms to the chamber-floor, while the ladder fell from under him. Such are the miserable shifts to which people here submit without grumbling.' Ib., 286, Dec. 1, 1819, at 'the English Settlement,' near Princeton, Ind.

[3] Haycraft to Helm, July 5, 1865. They were married March 13, 1806. The date of births of the children are not known, and Elizabeth is sometimes given as the second daughter, as, indeed, Dennis Hanks, who married her, does in one instance. See p. 45 n, supra.

for Sarah to care for, John D., Sarah [Elizabeth], and Matilda.
Immediately on coming to Hardin County, Lincoln must have
seen Sarah's brother, Isaac Bush, and collected from him at least
part of the money which he had paid Isaac for the Sinking
Spring farm eleven years before.[1] If so, it is but natural that the
two men should have talked of the plight of widow and widower
and the good sense of their marriage.

Certainly Lincoln made quick work of the business when he
saw Sarah in Elizabethtown, and as certainly he was in funds.
As related by Samuel Haycraft, then deputy clerk of Hardin
County Court, Thomas Lincoln, on December 1, 1819, went to
the house of Sarah Johnston in Elizabethtown, reminded her of
their mutual bereavement and proposed that they get married
'right off.' The widow said she could not 'right off as she owed
some little debts which she wanted to pay first.' Lincoln asked
for a list of the debts 'got the list paid them off that evening.
Next Morning I issued the license and they were marr[i]ed . . .
right off.' [2]

Without delay Thomas and Sarah, with her three children,
started for Indiana. They took with them the household goods
and furniture which had been gathered by the thrifty Sarah
during the lifetime of her first husband. In comparison with the
store taken by Thomas and Nancy Lincoln in the winter of
1816, Sarah Lincoln's domestic effects must have been opulent;
for it took a wagon and team of four horses, borrowed from
Ralph Crume, a brother-in-law of Lincoln, to haul the load to
the Ohio.[3] Pots, pans, skillets, blankets, covers, a feather bed,
a bureau which 'cost 45 dollars in K[entuck]y,' [4] were among the
things piled in the wagon.[5]

So, in mid-winter 1819–20, came Thomas and Sarah Lincoln

[1] See p. 23, *supra*.

[2] Haycraft to Herndon, Dec. 7, 1866. Weik MSS. Thomas Lincoln and Sarah Johnston were married, Dec. 2, 1819. Records Hardin County Court.

[3] Nicolay and Hay, I, 32. Thomas Lincoln's sister, Mary, married Ralph Crume,
Aug. 5, 1801. Waldo Lincoln, 202.
'The Last time the time Mrs. Johnston cum . . . he cum in a wagon . . . a 4 horse
team Belonging to his Broth[er]-in-law Ralph Crumes of Brackinridge County Ky.'
Hanks to Herndon, March 12, 1866. Weik MSS.

[4] Statement of Mrs. Thomas Lincoln, Sept. 8, 1865. Weik MSS.

[5] Herndon, I, 30, 31.

to the dirty, unkempt cabin near Pigeon Creek, where his neglected children and the vagrant Dennis Hanks were maintaining a bare existence. So, too, began a new and distinct period in the life of Abraham Lincoln. Sarah Lincoln was blessed with energy and sense, was a good housekeeper, prudent, systematic, and with a passion for cleanliness. She was, says her grand-daughter, 'a very tall Woman, Straight as an Indian, fair Complection and was when I first remember her, very handsome, Sprightly talkative and proud, Wore her Hair curled till Gray, Is Kind hearted and very Charitable and also very industrious.'[1]

No more hunting for Thomas Lincoln and Dennis Hanks until they had split and smoothed puncheons and made a floor, finished the roof, put in a door, cut a place for greased paper to let in the light.[2] The children were washed, combed and 'dressed ... up' so as to look 'more human'; the cabin cleansed, decent bedding put on the 'bedsteads made ... of poles and clapboards.'[3] The fire-place was overhauled, ample cooking utensils installed; and Thomas was stirred into making a proper table, better stools and, perchance, a hickory chair or two.[4] The change was so pronounced that, nearly thirty-five years afterward, Lincoln remembered and described it.[5]

Eight persons, three adults and five children, now inhabited the Lincoln cabin.[6] Three or four years later, in 1823, John Hanks, the half-brother of Dennis Hanks, joined the Lincoln family and lived with them for four years,[7] thus making nine who dwelt within those crowded walls. But, under Sarah Lincoln's guidance, there were comparative order and harmony. The increased size of the family required more food and clothing of course, but this was easily managed by the efficient housewife. The burden of supplying provisions was chiefly upon Thomas Lincoln and Dennis Hanks; this did not trouble them greatly.

[1] Harriet A. Chapman to Herndon, Dec. 17, 1865. Weik MSS.
[2] Lamon, 31-2.   [3] Mrs. Lincoln's statement. Weik MSS.
[4] Herndon, I, 31; Nicolay and Hay, I, 32.
[5] A. H. Chapman to Herndon, Oct. 8, 1865. Weik MSS.
[6] Thomas and Sarah Lincoln, Dennis Hanks, two Lincoln and three Johnston children.
[7] John Hanks to Herndon, June 13, 1865.

Without heavy exertion they produced sufficient vegetables, relying for the most part, however, upon game; for 'the Country was wild and desolate.' [1] The impulse to work which Sarah Lincoln brought into the life of her husband never spurred him to produce a surplus — he 'Jest Raised a Nuff for his own use,' not 'Mor than Bought his Shugar and Coffee and Such Like,' declares Dennis Hanks, adding that Lincoln 'was a very pore Man.' After awhile, indeed, when brush and trees had been cut from a few more acres, there were bigger crops of corn, and even 'Sum wheat a Nuf for a cake [on] a Sundy morning.' [2]

But often the family larder was allowed to run very low, it seems. Once all they had to eat was potatoes, which led Abraham to remark, when his father asked 'the blessing,' that they were 'very poor blessings.' [3] Food little concerned the boy, however, for 'Abe was a moderate eater,' his stepmother assures us. 'He ate what was set before him, making no complaint; he seemed carless about this. I cooked his meals for nearly 15 years.' And Mrs. Lincoln adds that 'he always had good health.' [4]

Thomas Lincoln varied his occupations of hunting and farming by working as carpenter. Some thought, indeed, that he preferred such work to labor on the farm, and 'relied upon it for a living' rather than upon agriculture.[5] 'Often and at various

[1] Mrs. Lincoln's statement, Sept. 8, 1865. Weik MSS.

Faux records that, in the fall of 1819, Major Hooker 'killed fourteen deer and one bear. . . Cook also met a fine bear.' Faux: Thwaites, xi, 286. At 'the English Settlement' near Princeton, Ind., Dec. 1, 1819

'Partridges, or quails, are here so tame that, at noon-day, a man may kill them by throwing a stick into the covey.' Ib., 299. Dec. 25, 1819.

Even thirty years afterward deer, wild turkey, otter and the like were still abundant in the forests of Spencer County. As late as 1848 Samuel Graham killed six deer 'in one day, besides three wild turkeys;' and on another day he 'killed nine otters, and on still another day sixty-seven muskrats;' and this chronicler observes of the times of Thomas Lincoln and Dennis Hanks, that 'the earlier hunters had higher sport with larger and fiercer animals.' Hist. W., S. & P. Cos., Ind., 260.

In 1820 Robert Harding, while in his canoe at night on White River near the present site of Indianapolis, killed nine deer in the space of five miles; and thirty-seven turkeys out of a single flock were killed on a spot that is now the heart of the city. Old Settlers: Robert B. Duncan, Ind. Hist. Soc. Pubs., ii, 387–8.

[2] Hanks to Herndon, Jan. 26, 1866. Weik MSS.

[3] Harriet A. Chapman to Herndon, Dec. 10, [1866]. Weik MSS.

[4] Mrs. Lincoln's statement. Weik MSS.

[5] John Romine's statement, Sept. 14, 1865. Weik MSS.

times,' says William Wood, a settler living near the Lincolns, 'he worked for me — made cupboards and other household furniture for me. He built my house . . . did all the inside work;' and Wood relates that 'Abe would come to my house with his father and play and romp with my children.'[1] Thomas Lincoln made furniture for other cabins too, such as that of Josiah Crawford which had one low room fifteen feet square.[2] Sometimes Abraham helped the father in his carpentering, although he disliked hammer and drawing-knife even more, if possible, than he did the plough and hoe. Once the two built a wagon for James Gentry, we are told, constructing the vehicle 'entirely out of wood, even to the hickory rims to the wheels.'[3]

From the first Thomas Lincoln had been hard put to get water, and this defect was sharply noted by Sarah Lincoln as soon as she was on the ground. Her daughter, then a very little girl, writes that 'My Earliest recellection of Abe is . . . carrying water about one mile' — a pet cat following him to the spring.[4] To get water nearer to his cabin Thomas Lincoln sunk many holes, but without result. He 'dug his hill to find water with a hand comb as it were — wanted water badly,'[5] Dennis Hanks told Herndon. Seemingly he did not succeed and believed that no water could be found by digging; for he refused to hire 'a Yankee' to discover water by a 'driving rod.' 'Do you suppose,' said he, 'that I am going to give you $5 for a pig in a poke?'[6]

[1] Wood's statement. Weik MSS.

[2] Statement of Elizabeth Crawford. Weik MSS. Josiah Crawford came to Indiana from Kentucky in 1824, five years after the second marriage of Thomas Lincoln. Also see Hobson, 22.

[3] Statement of J. W. Lamar. Weik MSS. Also Hobson, 24.

[4] Mrs. Moore's statement, Sept. 8, 1865. Weik MSS. Since there were no cats before Sarah Lincoln came, it is reasonably certain that this cat was brought by her.

[5] Hanks's Charleston statement, Sept. 8, 1865. Weik MSS.

[6] Ib. Detection by means of a 'driving [divining] rod,' of water beneath the surface of the soil then was, and for decades continued to be, a favorite method of determining spots for the digging of wells. The 'water finder' would cut a forked switch and, with an end in either hand, the butt straight forward, would walk slowly over the ground where water was sought. It was believed that when a point was reached where water was not far underground, the butt of the rod would turn sharply downward. Many had faith in this device and 'water finders' charged heavily for their discoveries. The sum asked of Thomas Lincoln, for instance, was extortionate for the time and place, especially since there was practically no currency, and the wizard usually required cash payment in advance.

When Abraham was old enough, he was sent to the mill with a bag of corn, and these journeys left upon his mind the most pleasing recollections of his boyhood. Thomas Lincoln had acquired a horse or two, and trips to the mill were made bareback with the sack of grain or meal carried in front of the rider. After young Lincoln had learned to read he poured into the ears of companions on these mill rides everything he had read.[1]

A year or two after the coming of Sarah Lincoln, another school, about four miles away, was started by one Azel W. Dorsey.[2] It was exactly like that of Andrew Crawford except that Dorsey did not try to 'learn manners' to the children. Abraham went to this school for a short time.[3] A schoolmate tells us that he was 'long and tall . . . wore low shoes, short socks and his britches made of buckskin' were so short that they left bare and naked 6 or more inches of Abe Lincoln's shin bone.' [4] The school books from which the teacher gave out his lessons were the Bible, Webster's or Dilworth's *Spelling Book*, Pike's *Arithmetic* and a song book.[5]

It was at Dorsey's school that he perfected that clear, distinct chirography, so like that of Washington and Jefferson; and here too he learned to spell with that accuracy which was to become a tradition in the neighborhood. He did all the writing for the family and indeed for everybody in the settlement.[6] Even more important to his avid mind was the fact that he learned to read with ease and fluency.

So ended the education of Abraham Lincoln in schools, except

[1] Statement of Henry Brooner: Hobson, 19.

[2] The Christian name of this teacher is given in most biographies of Lincoln as 'Hazel'; but it was Azel W. The cause of this error was that in the letters and statements made by old settlers, acquaintances of the Lincolns, the name 'Hazel' Dorsey is given. This well illustrates the corruption of names and words by the pioneers. Dorsey was the first coroner of Spencer County. *Hist. W., S. & P. Cos.*, Ind., 278. He was one of nine men to contribute $250 for the building of a bridge near Rockport. *Ib.*, 279.

[3] John Hanks to Herndon, June 13, 1865. Also Grigsby's statement. Weik MSS.

[4] Grigsby's statement, Sept. 12, 1865. Weik MSS. Grigsby says that all children were thus dressed: 'This was our school dress, our Sunday dress and every day dress.'

[5] *Ib.*, and Mrs. Moore's [Matilda Johnston] statement. Weik MSS.

[6] Mentor Graham to Herndon, July 15, 1865. Weik MSS. Also *Campaign Life of Lincoln*: John C. Scripps, 2.

This took little time, since mails were infrequent and expensive, the postage for a letter often amounting to forty cents. The pens were of goose-quill, and pokeberry juice served as ink. Levering, 83.

for a short and broken attendance in 1826 at a similar school taught by William Sweeney.[1] Including the two schools in Kentucky the boy went to school for less than a year. 'His father has offten told me,' relates John Hanks, that Abraham 'had not gone to School one year in all his life;' [2] and Lincoln himself, long afterward said the same thing.[3] Nathaniel Grigsby thinks that Lincoln went to the Indiana schools for not less than eighteen months, altogether; [4] but Dennis Hanks insists that 'he got about Six Months Schooling while he lived in Indiana,' [5] and this estimate is probably the more accurate.

There was, indeed, no reason for him to go longer to these backwoods teachers — they 'could do him no further good; he went to school no more.' [6]

In the Indiana schools he excelled, it appears, particularly in spelling and could 'spell down' the whole class when, at the close of the school every Friday,[7] the older children were placed in line against the log wall for a contest in spelling.[8] He was unselfish with his proficiency. One day he showed a girl schoolmate, Anna C. Roby, the proper letter in the word 'defied,' by covertly placing a finger on his eye.[9]

He was notably studious in everything [10] — 'head and Shoulders above us all,' confesses Dennis Hanks.[11] He would help the other pupils, 'would learn us get our cip[h]ers.' [12] His stepmother tells us that, when at home, Abraham 'cyphered on

---

[1] *Hist. W., S. & P. Cos.*, Ind., 413. This is another example of mispronunciation. The settlers called Sweeney, 'Swaney' and so gave the name to Herndon. The biographies, following his MSS., have said that William Swaney was the third teacher of Lincoln in Indiana.

[2] John Hanks to Herndon, June 13, 1865. Weik MSS.

[3] Autobiography, 2.   [4] Grigsby's statement. Weik MSS.

[5] Hanks's first Chicago statement. Weik MSS.

[6] Mrs. Allen Gentry's statement, Sept. 17, 1865. Weik MSS. Mrs. Gentry was a schoolmate of Lincoln and of the same age. Her maiden name was Anna C. Roby. *Hist. W., S. & P. Cos.*, Ind., 452.

[7] John Hoskins' statement, Sept. 16, 1865. Weik MSS.

[8] Hanks to Herndon, March 22, 1866. Weik MSS. And see George Cary Eggleston, 44–5.

[9] Mrs. Gentry's statement. Weik MSS.

[10] Grigsby's statement. Weik MSS.

[11] Hanks's Charleston statement. Weik MSS.

[12] *Ib.*

boards when he had no paper or no slate and when the board would get too black he would Shave it off with a drawing Knife and go on again: When he had paper he put his sums down on it.'[1] He made a copy-book by sewing together blank sheets which Dennis Hanks gave him: 'I bought the paper [and] gave it to Abe.'[2] In this he did his work in arithmetic, scribbling at three places this legend:

'Abraham Lincoln, his hand and pen
he will be good but God knows when.'[3]

He early showed that kindness of heart which distinguished him throughout life. At Crawford's school the boy reproved other children for cruelty to animals, particularly the placing of glowing coals on backs of turtles; and, even then, wrote 'short sentences' against it.[4] While at Dorsey's school he wrote poetry. 'Abe took it up of his own accord,' relates Grigsby. He kept this up at Sweeney's too, and at both schools also wrote 'compositions against Cruelty to animals,' which barbarity seems to have been a favorite practice of his schoolmates, and young Lincoln's particular aversion. Indeed, revulsion at brutality, sympathy for the suffering, animals as well as humans, constituted the dominant note of his character, even in boyhood. He always came to school good humored and laughing and 'he scarcely ever quarreled.'[5]

He continued to write poetry as well as prose compositions long after his school days were over, it appears, and took his pieces 'straight' to the interested neighbor, William Wood, for comment and criticism. Even thirty-seven or thirty-eight years afterward, Wood could remember that one of Abraham's compositions was 'a poem' entitled 'The Neighborhood broil.'[6] The copy-book in which his school figuring was done, contains these lines in his youthful hand:

[1] Mrs. Lincoln's and Grigsby's statements. Weik MSS.

[2] Hanks's Charleston statement. Weik MSS.

[3] A leaf of this book is among the Weik MSS. The same inscription is in the Mordecai Lincoln copy of Bailey's *Dictionary*, 'Mordecai' being in place of 'Abraham' and 'you' in place of 'God.'

[4] Mrs. Lincoln's and Grigsby's statements. Weik MSS.

[5] Grigsby's statement. Weik MSS.   [6] Wood's statement. Weik MSS.

'Time what an empty vapor tis
And days, how swift they are
Swift as an Indian arrow
Fly on like a shooting star
The present moment just, is here
Then slides away in haste
That we can never say they're ours
But only say they're past.' [1]

The ability to read meant more to him, however, at this period of his development than did all else acquired at school. It opened to him the world of books — a world hitherto closed to him, well-nigh unknown, indeed. From this time forward, reading was the passion of the youth and, as will be seen, continued for more than twenty years to be the passion of the man.

About the time he learned to read, the boy was big enough to do work upon the ungracious farm, and to labor for others, his earnings going to the father, a legal right which Thomas Lincoln exacted rigidly until Abraham reached the full age of twenty-one. He worked for several of the small farmers of the settlement, for Romine, for Wood, for Taylor, for Crawford, for Turnham, ploughing, making rails, 'daubing' with mud the chinks between the logs of the cabins.[2]

By 1824 Lincoln and Hanks had 'a Bout 10 acres of corn and a Bout 5 acres of wheat 2 acres of oates one acre of medow;' and there was 'Very Little Change to 1830' in this proportion, says Hanks, who asserts that 'I No Exacly for I helped Do it.' [3] They kept some live stock too, but made little in that way. 'We Raised Sheep and Cattle But they Did not fecth Much Cows and Calfes was onely worth 6 Dollars Corn 10 cts wheat 25 [cents] at that time.' [4] So there was need for Abraham to work for other farmers or for anybody who would employ him.

Between Thomas Lincoln and his son, so different in intellect, character and appearance, there was little sympathy or understanding; and for some reason the father treated Abraham

[1] A. H. Chapman to Herndon, Oct. 8, 1865. Weik MSS.; also in Barrett Collection.
[2] Statements of Wood, Mrs. Crawford and Green B. Taylor. Weik MSS.; J. W. Lamar: Hobson, 22.
[3] Hanks to Herndon, Jan. 26, 1866. Weik MSS.
[4] Hanks to Herndon, Jan. 6, 1866. Weik MSS.

roughly. Sometimes a blow from the old man's fist would hurl the boy 'a rod.' [1] 'I have Seen his father Nock him Down of the fence when a Stranger would call for Information to NeighBour house,' testifies Dennis Hanks, who adds that 'the Old Man Loved his Childern.' [2] Thomas Lincoln also thrashed the lad, who took his punishment in silence, tears the only outward sign of what he felt and thought.[3]

All this led Dennis Hanks to doubt whether 'Abe Loved his farther Very well or Not,' and to conclude that 'I Dont think he Did.' For that matter Dennis was not certain of Abraham's affection for any of his relatives, then or thereafter. 'When he was with us he Seemed to think a great Deal of us But I thought Sum times it was hipocritical But I am Not Shore.' But Hanks is sure about the father. He 'Loved his Relitives Do anything for them he could No Better Man than Old Tom Lincoln.' [4] A. H. Chapman, son-in-law of Dennis Hanks, says: 'Thos. Lincoln never showed by his actions that he thought much of his son Abraham when a boy. He treated him rather unkindly than otherwise, always appeared to think much more of his stepson John D. Johnston than he did of his own son Abraham.' [5]

The father's ill-treatment of the son seems the more extraordinary in view of Abraham's remarkably good nature; for he was conspicuously obliging, eager to please everybody, his parents most of all. 'Abe was a good boy . . . the best boy I ever saw,' declares his stepmother. 'I can say,' she continues, 'what scarcely one woman, a mother can say in a thousand . . . Abe never gave me a cross word or look and never refused . . . to do anything I requested [of] him. I never gave him a cross word in all my life. . . . His mind and mine, what little I had, seemed to run together — move in the same channel.' [6] Abraham's devotion to Sarah Lincoln, whom he always called 'mama,' is

[1] Hanks's second Chicago statement. Weik MSS.

[2] Hanks to Herndon, Jan. 26, 1866. Weik MSS.

[3] Hanks's second Chicago statement. Weik MSS.

[4] Hanks to Herndon, Jan. 26, 1866. Weik MSS.

[5] A. H. Chapman to Herndon, Sept. 28, 1865. Weik MSS. Chapman adds: 'But after Abe was grown up and had made his mark in the world the old man appeared to be very proud of him.'

[6] Mrs. Lincoln's statement. Weik MSS.

striking. Many years later he told Chapman of 'the encouragement he always had received from his Step Mother' and declared
that 'she had been his best Friend in this world and that no Son
could love a Mother more than he loved her.' [1]

It cannot be too often stated that cheerful friendliness was
the most striking feature of his personality — so striking, that
it is noted with emphasis in all accounts given by acquaintances
and observers of Abraham Lincoln in those days. He was
'Kindly disposed toward Everybody and Everything,' asserts
Nathaniel Grigsby; [2] and his step-sister, Matilda Johnston,
testifies that he was 'good to me, good to all. . . . Abe seemed to
love Everybody and Everything; he loved us all and Especially
mother.' [3] Once he picked up a drunken man whom he saw
sleeping in the snow and carried him home,[4] a noteworthy performance since, usually, no attention was then paid to such not
infrequent cases.

The mystery of the father's attitude towards Abraham is
deepened by the unanimous and positive testimony to the placid
character of Thomas Lincoln. Dennis Hanks, who was devoted
to him, describes him as a 'good humored, sociable man who
took the world easy, loving everybody and everything.' [5]
Dennis Hanks's son-in-law declares that Thomas Lincoln was
'remarkable peaceable . . . good natured;' [6] John Hanks says
that 'happiness was the end of life with him,' [7] and Nathaniel
Grigsby recalls that he was 'happy, lived Easy and contented.' [8]

Yet from his point of view, Thomas Lincoln was, perhaps,
not without some excuse for his harshness; for certain it is that
Abraham was so absorbed with books that he showed no love
for work with his hands, and was not quick to take up any
physical task. 'Farming, grubbing, hoeing, making fences,' as
John Hanks describes the boy's work,[9] had no attraction for
him. He would carry a book with him when he had to go

[1] Chapman to Herndon, Oct. 8, 1865. Weik MSS.
[2] Grigsby's statement. Weik MSS.   [3] Mrs. Moore's statement. Weik MSS.
[4] John Hanks to Herndon, June 13, 1865. Weik MSS.
[5] Hanks's Chicago statements. Weik MSS.
[6] Chapman's narrative. Weik MSS.   [7] Lamon, 15.
[8] Grigsby's statement. Weik MSS.
[9] John Hanks to Herndon, June 13, 1865. Weik MSS.

to work, and over its pages he would pore when rest time came.[1]

Even the alertly partial Dennis Hanks admits that Abraham 'was lazy — a very lazy man. He was always reading, Scribbling, writing, ciphering, writing Poetry,' etc.[2] This too is the testimony of his step-sister: 'Abe was not energetic except in one thing — he was active and persistent in learning — read everything he could — ciphered on boards, on the walls.' [3] The son-in-law of Dennis Hanks declares that 'Lincoln was not industrious as a worker on the farm or at any kind of manual labor' and that 'he only showed industry in the attainment of knowledge.' [4]

Of young Lincoln's dislike of work John Romine, a neighbor, asserts: 'He worked for me, [but] was always reading and thinking, I used to get mad at him. . . . I say Abe was awful lazy. he would laugh and talk and crack jokes and tell stories all the time didn't love work but did dearly love his pay. . . . Lincoln said to me one day that his father taught him to work but never learned him to love it.' [5] 'He was no hand to pitch in at work like killing snakes,' says Mrs. Josiah Crawford, 'but he would take hold of his work as camely [calmly] and pleasant as his manner was other ways.' [6]

The distasteful toil in field and wood was lightened by Abraham's fun and wit; and, although he had no voice for singing, he would join the other hands in shouting the songs of the time and place — in the language of Dennis Hanks, 'Hail Collumbia Hap[py] Land if you aint Broke I will Be Damned,' or 'the turbentuck [turbaned Turk] that Scorns the world and Struts aBout with his whiskers curld for No other Man But himSelf to see and all Such as this.' [7] Other and rougher songs there were. Nathaniel Grigsby tells us that: 'we sung what is called carnel Songs and love songs. i cannot repeat any of them at this time

[1] Grigsby's statement. Weik MSS.
[2] Hanks's Charleston statement. Weik MSS.
[3] Mrs. Moore's statement. Weik MSS.
[4] Chapman's narrative. Weik MSS.   [5] Romine's statement. Weik MSS.
[6] Mrs. Crawford to Herndon, Sept. 7, 1866. Weik MSS.
[7] Hanks to Herndon, Dec. 24, 1865. Weik MSS.

we sung a song called Barbra allen also we sung the Silk Merchant daughter and others.' [1]

Hanks recalls that, 'Abe gaust [used] to try to sing pore old Ned But he Never could Sing Much;' [2] but Mrs. Crawford, who had an uncommonly strong memory,[3] says that Lincoln 'use to sing one was cauled John adconsons [Anderson's] lementation and one that was cauled William riley and one that was made about gineral Jackson and John adams . . . though I can't memorise but verry little of any of them he sang but verry little when he was about the house.' [4] Mrs. Crawford dwells upon John Anderson's Lamentation and insists that it was the song which Abraham sang most frequently. It was a commonplace and badly written jingle about the death of Anderson's wife, his condemnation to be hanged, the destitution of his children, all due to 'much intoxication.'

So the tall, bony youth, with a coonskin cap on his head and clad in deerskin shirt and homemade trousers [5] which were still always far too short, exposing many inches of 'sharp, blue and narrow' shins,[6] went about the countryside doing, in languid fashion, the jobs he was hired to do, or working reluctantly on his father's stumpy farm; but always cracking jokes, telling stories, joining, though poorly, in the songs of the other workers; and, whenever his father or employer was not about, making speeches to his fellows. Strangely enough Abraham did not care for fishing or hunting,[7] rarely joining the pursuit of even coon and turkey,[8] although, boasts Dennis Hanks, 'we sure were excellent bow shots — a squirrel couldnt escape.' [9]

Reading, however, was the outstanding phase of Lincoln's

---

[1] Grigsby to Herndon, Jan. 21, 1866. Weik MSS. Versions of Barbara Allen and The Silk Merchant's Daughter are in *English Folk Songs from the Southern Appalachians:* Campbell and Clark, 90, 186.

[2] Hanks to Herndon, Dec. 24, 1865. Weik MSS.

[3] It was she who gave Herndon, from memory, the exact wording of the 'Chronicles of Reuben,' thirty-six years after that satire was written. See p. 92, *infra.*

[4] Elizabeth Crawford to Herndon, Feb. 21, 1866. Weik MSS. 'William Riley' was a well-known ballad of English origin, but 'John Anderson' is not to be confused with Burns' verses of the same title, nor with George J. Bennet's 'John Anderson's gane.'

[5] Hobson, 22.   [6] Romine's statement. Weik MSS.

[7] Chapman's narrative. Weik MSS.   [8] Grigsby's statement. Weik MSS.

[9] Hanks's Charleston statement. Weik MSS.

life at this time. Much as he loved pranks with other youths, he would forego their jollity and lose himself in some new volume upon which he chanced. 'Whilst other boys were idling away their time,' says a schoolmate and companion, 'Lincoln was studying his books. . . . He read and thoroughly read his books whilst we played.' [1] But there was little if any studying by the wavering light from logs in the fireplace or from the dim glow of turnip candle. On the contrary, he studied in the daytime, says his stepmother; 'didn't after night much, went to bed early, got up early and then read.' [2]

Thus he consumed the scanty store of books brought to the Lincoln cabin by his stepmother, when she came to Pigeon Creek near Christmas time, 1819, wrought in cabin and surroundings the miracle we have witnessed, and rescued the children from the dirt accumulated since their mother died a year before. There had been a few books in her Kentucky household and, although Sarah Lincoln could not read, she knew the value of them, it seems, and brought them with her. There were but four or five volumes — *Robinson Crusoe*, *Pilgrim's Progress*, *Sinbad the Sailor*, *Æsop's Fables*.[3] It appears that this was the first time a Bible found a place in the cabin, for Hanks records that 'Thomas Lincoln brought the Bible in 1818 or 19.' [4]

On March 2, 1821, Congress extended the time for making payments on government land bought by settlers under the Act of 1800, and on September 12, Thomas Lincoln claimed his right under that act.[5] There the matter rested for six years. As the summer opened the Lincoln cabin was cheered by a wedding within the family. Dennis Hanks married Elizabeth Johnston [6] who, if she was the eldest of Sarah Lincoln's children, could not

[1] Mrs. Chapman's statement; Grigsby's statement. Weik MSS.

[2] Mrs. Lincoln's statement, Sept. 8, 1865. Weik MSS.

[3] This was a fairly large library for a pioneer cabin. As late as 1833 in a richer and more advanced part of the state, a large library consisted of *Pilgrim's Progress*, *Robinson Crusoe*, Weems's *Washington*, Weems's *Marion*, a *History of the United States*, an abridged *English History*, Cowper's *Poems* and the Bible. Turpie, 20.

[4] Hanks's Charleston statement. Weik MSS.

[5] Declaration No. 1964. Lincoln signed his name to this paper. General Land Office Records, Interior Department, Washington.

[6] June 9, 1821. Marriage Register, Spencer Co., Indiana.

possibly have been more than fifteen years of age.[1] It is well-nigh certain that they continued to live with the Lincolns, since the husband makes no mention of their having gone elsewhere.

In 1823, seven years after Thomas Lincoln came to Indiana and four years after his marriage to Sarah Johnston, he joined, by letter, the Pigeon Creek Baptist Church,[2] a congregation of Primitive Baptists,[3] the log house for which, one mile south of his cabin, he had helped to build in 1819.[4] He made the window frames, door casings and pulpit, we are told. This church house seems to have been a most pretentious building. In size it was twenty-six by thirty feet,[5] built of hewed logs, with fireplace and chimney of brick made by David Turnham, the mold for which was fashioned by Thomas Lincoln without a particle of iron, only wooden pegs being used.

To this church, after 1823, the family went when a preacher of that sect came to Pigeon Creek. When Abraham was in his fifteenth year, he would repeat to his companions and others, almost verbatim, the sermons he heard,[6] imitating the delivery of the preacher, for he was an excellent mimic.[7] His stepmother declares that 'he would hear sermons preached, come home, take the children out, get on a stump or log and almost repeat it word for word.'[8]

Although others of the family became members of the Pigeon Creek congregation, Abraham did not then or afterwards 'join church.' His stepmother explains that 'Abe had no particular religion — didn't think of that question at that time, if he ever did. He never talked about it.'[9] 'i cannot tel you what his notions of the bible were,' wrote Nathaniel Grigsby to Herndon; 'he talked about religion as other persons did but i do not now

---

[1] Her parents were married March 13, 1806.

[2] Records of Little Pigeon Creek Baptist Church, in possession of Samuel Alley of Buffaloville, Ind.

[3] Hanks to Herndon, no date, but 1866. Weik MSS.   [4] Hobson, 22.

[5] Murr: Indiana Magazine of History, XIII, 342.

[6] Statements of Mrs. Moore and Dennis Hanks. Weik MSS.

[7] Chapman's statement. Weik MSS., and Lamon, 55.

[8] Mrs. Lincoln's statement; and Hanks to Herndon, no date, but 1866. Weik MSS.

[9] Mrs. Lincoln's statement. Weik MSS,

his view on religion he never made any profession while in Ind[iana] that i now of.'[1] Mrs. Josiah Crawford, who knew all the Lincoln family well, in answer to a direct question writes: that she 'never heard of his ever making any such pretensions. I dont think he ever did though he seemed to be A well wisher he went to meeting some times and was well behaved.'[2] And Dennis Hanks avers that 'as to his perticlur views in Religion I cant tell But I Dont think he held any Views Very Strong.' But, Dennis adds, 'when he went to church he allways could tell the tex.'[3]

There is sharp dispute as to the extent of his reading of the Bible, Dennis Hanks asserting that 'Lincoln didnt read the Bible half as much as [is] said,' and that although 'he did read it, I though[t] he never believed it and think so still.'[4] Mrs. Lincoln confirms Hanks's testimony: 'Abe read the bible some, though not as much as said.'[5] On the other hand Grigsby declares that 'he was a great talker on the scriptures and read it a great deal;'[6] and Grigsby is supported by Lincoln's later literary style.

But, reports Dennis Hanks, 'He Never would Sing any Religious Songs it apered to me that it Did not Souit him.'[7] These songs were 'lined out' to the congregation by the preacher from Dupuy's[8] *Song Book*, the favorites being 'Oh when shall I see Jesus,' 'How tedious and tasteless the hours,' 'Jesus my all to heaven has gone' and 'Come thou fount of every blessing.'[9]

The books at home exhausted, he ranged the countryside in search of more, an intellectual prowler for the sustenance of the printed page. His step-mother asserts that 'Abe read all the

[1] Grigsby to Herndon, Jan. 21, 1866. Weik MSS.

[2] Mrs. Crawford to Herndon, Feb. 21, 1866. Weik MSS.

[3] Hanks to Herndon, no date. Weik MSS.

[4] Hanks's Charleston statement. Weik MSS.

[5] Mrs. Lincoln's statement. Weik MSS.

[6] Grigsby to Herndon, Jan. 21, 1866. Weik MSS.

[7] Hanks to Herndon, 'Aprail' 2, 1866. Weik MSS.

[8] The letters and statements of the pioneers to Herndon uniformly give the title of this volume as Dupree's *Song Book* — another example of slovenly pronunciation.

[9] Hanks to Herndon, 'Aprail' 2, 1866; and Grigsby to Herndon, Jan. 21, 1866. Weik MSS.

books he could lay his hands on.'[1] In 1823 when Abraham was fourteen years of age, Levi Hall who had married Nancy Hanks, aunt of Nancy Lincoln and mother without marriage of Dennis Hanks, came with his family to the Pigeon Creek settlement.[2] They brought the copy of Bailey's *Etymological Dictionary*,[3] which Mordecai Lincoln had bought in 1793. The fact that this dictionary was at his hand must be borne in mind while considering the books read by Lincoln during the years that he remained in Indiana.[4]

Several books were discovered by the eager youth and made his intellectual property; for, as we shall presently see, Lincoln remembered all he read. Only six of these volumes will here be noted, however, since the influence of these was determinative.

From some source and in some way he got hold of a copy of Grimshaw's *History of the United States*.[5] Of all the American histories in one volume published at that time none had such peculiar qualities as that by William Grimshaw.[6] The first chapter explains the advances made in astronomy, geography, and navigation; and, thus, the reader has before him at the start the existing condition of the world. Then follows the account

[1] Mrs. Lincoln's statement; Graham to Herndon, July 15, 1865. Weik MSS.

[2] Hanks to Herndon, March 12, 1866. Weik MSS.
Levi Hall and his wife Nancy, mother of Dennis Hanks, died while in Indiana and were buried close to the grave of Nancy Lincoln and Betsy Sparrow. 'The woman was Side by Side Abes mother in the Midle first my ant which was Thomas Sparrows wife on one Side of Abes mother and my mother on the othe[r] Side Levy Hall on the Side of his wife which wa[s] my mother and Thomas Sparrow on the Side of his wife which was my ant [and] the 5 togeather.' Hanks to Herndon, no date. Weik MSS.

[3] 'Hall brought the Dictionary to Indiana.' Hanks's Charleston statement. Weik MSS.

[4] On the inside cover of this volume is written in Lincoln's early handwriting, 'Abraham Lincoln his book, bought in the year of our Lord 1795.' Mordecai Lincoln has signed his name in four places. See p. 21, *supra*. Bailey's *Dictionary*, first published in 1721, was very popular and at least twenty-five editions were printed. It is said that Pitt the younger studied this dictionary word for word. It included all English words without regard to their vogue or repute, and is much superior to Johnson's *Dictionary*, published in 1755. Indeed, Johnson used an interleaved copy of Bailey in the preparation of his own work.

[5] 'Abe read I think Grimshaws History of the U[nited] S[tates].' Mrs. Moore's statement. Weik MSS.

[6] There were no less than fifteen *Histories of the United States*, each in one volume, and by different authors, published up to 1825; and there were three of two or more volumes. Grimshaw's *History* was published in Philadelphia and ran through fifteen large editions.

of the discovery of America and the development of the colonies.

Quickly the author reaches the subject of slavery, bitterly condemning it. 'What a climax of human cupidity and turpitude! . . . The colonists . . . place the last rivet to the chains!' Throughout the little volume the student is not permitted to lose sight of the shackle and the lash. The early New England persecutions are set forth in wrathful terms and an earnest plea made against intolerance. The causes of the Revolution are stated clearly, the patriot writings named, the War for Independence and later events described. The book ends with the cession of Florida to the United States; and, as a climax, the progress of literature, science and art is described.

The very last paragraph reads: 'Let us not only declare by words, but demonstrate by our actions, that "all men are created equal; that they are endowed by their creator, with the same inalienable rights: that among these are life, liberty and the pursuit of happiness." Let us venerate the instruction of that great and amiable man to whom, chiefly, under Providence, the United States are indebted for their liberties; the world for a common hero: "That there exists an indissoluble union between virtue and happiness, between duty and advantage."'

Abraham had worked for David Turnham, who lived near Grandview on the Ohio. Turnham, six years older than Lincoln, was a prosperous farmer, a Justice of the Peace and a man of uncommon ability.[1] As will presently appear, he had much influence on Lincoln's life. He owned the *Revised Laws of Indiana;* and sometime before he left the State, Lincoln borrowed this formidable volume of nearly five hundred long pages and read it repeatedly and with care. This was the first law book he ever read.[2] It contains the Declaration, the Constitution, the first twelve Amendments, the Virginia Act of cession of the Northwest Territory, the Ordinance of 1787, the Act admitting Indiana, and the first State Constitution. Then follow about four

[1] David Turnham was born Aug. 2, 1803, near Lebanon, Tenn., and came to Spencer County about 1818, settling near Grandview and 'becoming one of the foremost men of the county, and also a public official.' *Hist. W., S. & P. Cos.*, Ind., 562.

[2] Grigsby to Herndon, Oct. 25, 1865, Weik MSS.; Turnham to Herndon, Oct. 12, 1865; *Lincoln the Litigant:* William H. Townsend, 40.

hundred pages of laws on every subject which then required legislation — rights and remedies, crimes and punishments, courts and procedure, offices and fees, and all the machinery of civil government. Through this volume Lincoln acquired a fair understanding of the elements of law and government.

During this period, too, he read another book which had more and greater qualities making for general culture than any one volume he is positively known to have read. This volume was popularly called 'Scott's Lessons.' [1] Its formal title was *Lessons in Elocution, or Selections of Pieces in Prose and Verse for the Improvement of Youth in Reading and Speaking*, by William Scott, of Edinburgh. The book opens with short essays upon public speaking, the object of which should be to convey a 'precise idea.' Scott urges simplicity and intelligence of gesture, distinctness of enunciation, right placing of emphasis, pausing at the end of one sentence before beginning the next, and other items of the technique of delivery.

Then come what the compiler calls 'Lessons in Reading,' beginning with five pages of maxims. Brief selections from the classics follow, mostly fables and parables, but including essays on points of character and conduct, with sketches of Alfred, Catiline, Cæsar, Elizabeth, and other historic characters. Excerpts from many poems are next; and then a good selection of pieces for recitation, including parts of speeches by the Earl of Chatham, Lord Mansfield, Cicero, and Demosthenes, as well as the imaginary addresses of Hannibal and other commanders to their armies. Hamlet's advice to the players is printed as prose, as is the appeal of Brutus after Cæsar's death, Hotspur's soliloquy, and Falstaff's praise of sack. Antony's Oration, Hamlet's analysis of death, and the exhortations of Henry V before Harfleur and Agincourt, are given. Short and pointed quotations are made illustrative of various forms of speech — antithesis, climax, enunciation, query, and the like.

Lincoln is known to have studied the *Kentucky Preceptor*, a compilation by an unknown hand and not unlike Scott's *Lessons* in general contents. It contained short essays on Credulity, Haughtiness, Industry, and Indulgence; one on Liberty and

[1] Lamon, 37.

Slavery, but without reference to negro slavery as then found in the United States; anecdotes of Indians; Gouverneur Morris's Funeral Oration 'over the corpse' of General Hamilton, and also Eliphalet Nott's oration on Hamilton; Nott's Baccalaureate Sermon in Union College, May 1, 1805; Jefferson's inaugural speech, 1801; and scenes lifted from English playwrights and poets — all without indicating the author, except in one instance, where Thompson, the poet, is named. It was a school reader belonging to Josiah Crawford, of whom Lincoln borrowed it, and Mrs. Crawford, in giving the book to Herndon, stated that out of it 'Lincoln learned his speaches.' [1]

The other two books worthy of note, which are known to have been read by Lincoln while in Indiana, are Weems's *Life of Washington* and the same writer's *Life of Franklin*.[2] It has not been discovered where he got the *Life of Franklin*, but he borrowed Weems's *Washington* from Josiah Crawford, a young farmer of the neighborhood, who had brought the book with him from Kentucky. Abraham worked for Crawford, at times, having 'daubed' his fifteen feet square log cabin when the Crawfords arrived in 1824.[3] It seems that the youth left the book where rain injured it, a calamity of which he promptly told Crawford, who gave him the volume and he 'pulled fodder a day or two for it.' [4]

Just when Lincoln read these six books cannot be positively determined. Mrs. Josiah Crawford says that he read Weems's *Washington* in 1829, when he was twenty years of age,[5] and the likelihood is strong that he studied all the books named during his last four years in Indiana.

[1] This volume is in the collection of Oliver R. Barrett, of Chicago, with Herndon's note on its history. Herndon gave it, sometime before 1887, to J. E. Remsburg, of Oak Mills, Kan. It is the third edition published at Lexington, Ky., 1812, by Maccoun, Tilford & Company.

[2] Statement of Wesley Hall to J. Edward Murr, in his 'Lincoln in Indiana,' *Indiana Magazine of History*, XIII, 325.

[3] Elizabeth Crawford's statement. Weik MSS.

[4] *Ib.* In 1865, thirty-six years after Lincoln borrowed Weems's *Washington*, the Crawford library had grown to twelve or fifteen volumes, including two Bibles, four hymn books, *Great Events of America*, *Pioneers of the New West*, *Grace Truman*, and a small Webster's *Dictionary*. Herndon's account of his interview with Elizabeth Crawford, Sept. 16, 1865. Weik MSS.

[5] Elizabeth Crawford's statement. Weik MSS.

Such were the volumes, each of which it should be remembered Lincoln read so thoroughly that he could repeat, word for word, parts that best pleased him. 'When he came across a passage that struck him he would write it down on boards if he had no paper and keep it there till he did get paper, then he would rewrite it, look at it, repeat it. He had a copy-book, a kind of scrap-book in which he put down all things and thus preserved them.' [1]

At Rockport, where Abraham often went, he made the acquaintance of John Pitcher, the first resident attorney of Rockport, who afterwards became prosecuting attorney for Spencer County.[2] Pitcher had a good library which, as he declared sixty years later, included the 'standard works of that day,' as well as law books; and the use of this library was given to young Lincoln.[3] The youth also went to Boonville, some twelve or fourteen miles distant from the Lincoln cabin, and there saw the prosecuting attorney for Warrick County, John A. Brackenridge, who is said to have had an immense library for the time and place, consisting of at least four hundred and fifty-seven volumes.[4] Inference has been made that Lincoln borrowed many of these volumes and frequently visited the house of Brackenridge to read his books and take counsel of him; but no evidence is adduced to support these speculations or to show that the lawyer even knew the backwoods youth.[5]

Along with the pleasing fiction of midnight study by the log fire, we must dismiss the unhappy legend that Thomas Lincoln

---

[1] Mrs. Lincoln's statement. Weik MSS.

The Act creating Spencer County provided that ten per cent from the sale of town lots should be used for the establishment and maintenance of a county library. But if this was done while Lincoln lived in Indiana it would appear that he never heard of such a store of books; for, says the historian of Spencer County, 'after 1820 Spencer County had, at Rockport, a public library of several hundred volumes of the standard works of the day. The name Lincoln does not once appear on the records as [a] borrower.' *Hist. W., S. & P. Cos.*, Ind., 273.

[2] *Ib.*, 307.

[3] Pitcher's statement in O. C. Terry to Jesse W. Weik, July, 1888. Weik MSS.

[4] 'Lincoln's Boyhood in Indiana:' Roscoe Kiper, *Proceedings of Fourth Annual Conference on Indiana History*, 59–60. The size and importance of these libraries are the more striking, since lawyers in other parts of the State then relied wholly upon Espinasse's *Nisi Prius* and Peake's *Evidence*, which they carried with them when 'riding the circuit.' Smith, 19.

[5] See pages 90–1, *infra*.

interfered with Abraham's incessant reading. The father yielded to the influence of Sarah Lincoln, it appears, and did not disturb his son's devotion to books. 'As a usual thing,' says his wife, 'Mr. Lincoln never made Abe quit reading to do anything if he could avoid it. He would do it himself first . . . he himself felt the uses and necessities of education [and wanted] his boy Abraham to learn and he encouraged him to do it in all ways he could.' [1]

Sarah Lincoln makes the best case she can for her husband; but after Abraham had left the family in Illinois, the father's contempt for the studious habits of his son seems to have returned. 'I suppose Abe is still fooling hisself with eddication,' he complained to William G. Greene who chanced by what Greene calls the 'wretched abode' where Thomas and his wife lived in Coles County. 'I tried to stop it, but he has got that fool idea in his head, and can't be got out. Now I hain't got no eddication, but I get along far better than if I had;' and Thomas showed his visitor how he kept an account by making straight marks with a coal on a rafter and rubbing them out with a dish-rag: 'that thar's a heap better'n yer eddication.' [2] In Indiana, however, a boyhood companion of Lincoln, Wesley Hall, relates that, 'Old Tom couldn't read himself, but he wuz proud that Abe could, and many a time he'd brag about how smart Abe wuz to the folks around about.' [3]

Young Lincoln liked to tell what he knew — insisted on telling it. In fact, self-expression was indispensable to the youth, and he became a very geyser of loquacity, talking incessantly to all who would listen — and most were eager to hear him. For he never bored anybody. His talk was informing, to be sure; but it was witty too and full of humor. Nobody could resist his funny

[1] Mrs. Lincoln's statement. Weik MSS.   [2] Whitney, I, 74–5.

[3] Hall's statement to Murr: *Indiana Magazine of History*, XIII, 325.

Hall's statement is somewhat dramatic, including a picturesque account of his having been lost in a snow-storm while riding home from mill, his chancing on the Lincoln cabin where he was warmly welcomed and stayed all night, Abraham reading, at his father's request, until bedtime and by the light of the log fire, the *Life of Franklin*. Hall gave this description to Mr. Murr more than sixty years after the incident happened, and when Hall was over eighty years old. Murr sets down the narrative exactly as he received it. While it is, obviously, strongly colored by Hall's imagination, as are most stories of the kind, there can be no reasonable doubt that something of the sort happened and that Lincoln surely did read a *Life of Franklin*.

stories, and he was as fond of jokes as he was of reading. Yet Mrs. Lincoln relates that when neighbors came to visit her: 'Abe ... was a silent and attentive observer, never speaking or asking questions till they were gone and then he must understand everything — even to the smallest thing, minutely and exactly: he would then repeat it over to himself again and again, sometimes in one form and then in another and when it was fixed in his mind to suit him he became easy and he never lost that fact or his understanding of it. Sometimes he seemed pestered to give expression to his views and got mad almost at one who couldn't explain plainly what he wanted to convey.' [1] Dennis Hanks recalls that Abraham was 'a good listener to his superiors, bad to his inferiors — that is he couldn't endure jabber.' [2]

He was abnormally gregarious and, when not lost in the pages of some book, made shift to be where other people were, the larger the number the better he was pleased. Yet he did not seek crowds — indeed he shunned them, another of those contradictions of character which so often perplex the student of Lincoln, as they perplexed those who came in contact with him throughout his perplexing life.

Still he went to all the social gatherings — 'alway attended house raisings, log rolling corn shucking and workings of all kinds.' [3] There was a small prairie on the South Fork of Pigeon Creek and there members of the local militia gathered for muster.[4] Lincoln was always on hand at these jolly assemblages. And no other person in the now comparatively well populated settlement was so welcome everywhere, for he always was cheerful and tried to make others happy too.[5] No situation was too gloomy for his fun-making, no man so sour that Lincoln

[1] Mrs. Lincoln's statement. Weik MSS. It is obvious that there is much more of Herndon than there is of Sarah Lincoln in this interview. Herndon notes on the MS. that, at first, he had great difficulty in getting her to talk. The gossip of neighbors could have given the boy little food for questioning or thought, being, as such talk always was, chiefly about crops or hunting.

[2] Hanks's Charleston statement. Weik MSS.

[3] Grigsby to Herndon, Oct. 25, 1865. Weik MSS.

[4] Hanks to Herndon, April, 1866. Weik MSS. And see Welby: Thwaites, xii, 272; Turpie, 31.

[5] Grigsby to Herndon, Oct. 25, 1865; and Hanks's Charleston statement. Weik MSS.

could not make him laugh. Once with his father, he took produce to Troy in the all-wood wagon they had made for James Gentry. Heavy rain came on, the creek was swollen; drenched and cold, they staid all night at the house of J. W. Lamar. During the night wolves took nearly all the venison hams; but Abraham poked fun at the predicament and kept Lamar, who 'scarcely ever smiled,' rocking with laughter.[1]

Always he was surrounded by men and boys shouting with glee at his drollery, held by his charm, instructed by his information, interested in his reasoning. 'When he appeared in Company the boys would gather and cluster around him to hear him talk,' says Grigsby. 'He made fun and cracked his jokes making all happy.' Then, too, he 'naturally assumed the leadership of the boys.' But he was never dogmatic, it appears, never aggressive in his views, never turbulent or offensive in stating them, never insistent that others should think as he thought. 'He wounded no man's feelings' and even his jokes 'were at no man's expense.'[2] He was so good-natured that, coming on some boys stealing watermelons which Lincoln had raised, he 'sat down with us,' relates one of the culprits, 'cracked jokes, told stories and helped to eat the melons.'[3] All testify to Lincoln's honesty, too, and his absolute truthfulness. 'Men would swear on his simple word,' declares Joseph C. Richardson.

But 'Abe did not go much with the girls . . . didnt like girls much, too frivolous,' says Mrs. Allen Gentry, then Anna C. Roby, who saw as much of Lincoln at that time as any girl in the settlement except, of course, his sister and step-sisters.[4] His step-mother confirms Mrs. Gentry's opinion, saying: 'He was not very fond of girls.'[5] Joseph C. Richardson also relates that Abraham 'never seemed to care for the girls;'[6] and David Turnham bears witness that 'he did not seem to seek the company of the girls and when with them was rather backward.'[7] The girls liked him, however, because he was 'friendly, somewhat sociable,

---

[1] Hobson, 24. [2] Grigsby's statement. Weik MSS.
[3] Richardson's statement, Sept. 14, 1865. Weik MSS.
[4] Mrs. Gentry's statement. Weik MSS.
[5] Mrs. Lincoln's statement. Weik MSS.
[6] Richardson's statement. Weik MSS.
[7] Turnham to Herndon, Dec. 17, 1866. Weik MSS.

not so much so as we wanted him.' Certainly there was nothing attractive in Abraham's appearance, for he was 'a long, thin, leggy, gawky boy dried up and shriveled.' [1] Even by his sixteenth year he was '6 feet high' and 'bony and raw, dark skinned.' [2]

Lincoln began to make speeches as early as his fifteenth year.[3] He would mount a tree stump, or stand upon a fence and talk to his fellow workers, who would leave their jobs in fields or woods to listen. 'His father would come and make him quit, send him to work,' says his step-sister who saw and heard these incidents.[4] Her mother tells us the same thing. 'His father had to make him quit sometimes, as he would quit his own work to speak and made the other children as well as the men quit their work.' [5]

Of greater moment, however, than the fact that he made them at all, was the arrangement of his speeches and the style of his delivery. Considering the examples of exclamatory and emotional oratory furnished by preachers, lawyers, and candidates to whom he listened, the most reasonable explanation of young Lincoln's method and manner of speaking, is that he had taken Scott's *Lessons* seriously and that the advice of the Scotch schoolmaster was in harmony with his own thoughts on the subject. For all who heard him make these backwoods speeches, lay emphasis on the logical clearness of them and Lincoln's composure in delivery.

'He was calm, logical and clear alw[a]ys,' Dennis Hanks told Herndon.[6] Grigsby says the same thing; and adds that he 'was figurative in his Speeches, talk and conversation. He argued much from analogy and explained things hard for us to understand by stories, maxims, tales and figures. He would almost always point the lesson or idea by some story that was plain and near us that we might instantly see the force and bearing of what he said.' [7]

[1] Mrs. Gentry's statement. Weik MSS.
[2] Richardson's statement. Weik MSS.
[3] John Hanks to Herndon, June 13, 1865; and Mrs. Moore's statement. Weik MSS.
[4] Mrs. Moore's statement. Weik MSS.
[5] Mrs. Lincoln's statement. Weik MSS.
[6] Hanks's Charleston statement. Weik MSS.
[7] Grigsby's statement. Weik MSS.

The clearness and simplicity of these youthful speeches, so striking that all made note of and remembered those qualities, were partly the result of his writing and rewriting what he read and thought. Sometimes he wrote essays on weighty subjects. William Wood, then about forty-five years of age,[1] relates that one such paper, written in 1827 or 1828, was on 'national politics,' saying that 'the American government was the best form of Government in the world for an intelligent people, that it ought to be kept sacred and preserved forever; that general education should [be] fostered and carried all over the country; that the constitution should be [held] sacred, the union perpetuated, and the laws revered, respected and enforced.'[2]

Wood was so impressed by the essay that he gave it to the leading lawyer of Spencer County. 'I showed it to John Pitcher who was travelling over the circuit on law business and stopped at my house one night: he read it carefully and asked me where I got it. I told him that one of my neighbor boys wrote it: he couldn't believe it until I told him that Abe did write it. . . . Pitcher said to me "the world cant beat it." He begged for it — gave it to him and it was published.'[3]

Wood was a member of the United Brethren Church and a foe of hard drinking.[4] He was a subscriber for a temperance paper published in Ohio; and 'Abe used to borrow it, take it home and read it and talk it over with me. . . . One day Abe wrote a piece on Temperance and brought it to my house. I read it carefully over and over and the piece excelled for sound sense anything that my paper contained. I gave the article to one Aaron Farmer, a Baptist Preacher: He read it, it struck him: he said he wanted it to send to a Temperance paper in Ohio for publication: it was sent and published. I saw the printed piece, read it . . . over and over again.'[5]

One outstanding fact of Lincoln's life at this time is that, although his associates, and indeed everybody, drank a great deal of whisky, Abraham seldom touched liquor. To be sure he 'did drink his dram as well as all others did, preachers and Christians

[1] Wood died Dec. 28, 1867. Hobson, 52.   [2] Wood's statement. Weik MSS.
[3] Ib. Unfortunately Wood could not remember 'what paper it got into.'
[4] Hobson, 51–2.   [5] Wood's statement. Weik MSS.

included,' testifies Grigsby; [1] and his devoted friend and mentor, William Wood, reluctantly admits that 'Abe once drank as all people did here at that time.' [2] But this slight and casual drinking seems to have been entirely for the sake of comradeship and Lincoln's strong dislike of offending anybody.[3] Equally striking is the fact that, although profanity was general and intense, Lincoln never fell into that habit. 'I never knew him to swear,' testifies Wood; 'he would say to . . . other boys, leave off your boyish ways and be more like men.' Wood explains this attitude by concluding that 'Abe was always a man though a boy.' [4]

Yet, as we have seen, he was no prig; instead he was inordinately sociable, even familiar, and had faults extremely human, such as his love of a certain type of anecdote — a taste which he never overcame and the expression of which, as will appear, was so marked a feature of his manhood and so shocking to the eminent men among whom he did his historic work. Some of his boyhood companions got hold of a joke book; and, relates Nathaniel Grigsby, Abraham 'would read it to us out in the woods on Sunday.' Answering the question as to the title Grigsby says: '[I remember it] mighty well. It was the King's Jester — it was a book of funny stories.' [5] This little volume, *Quinn's Jests*, contained the stories and repartee of the English actor, James Quinn. The humor is heavy, the so-called jests

[1] Grigsby's statement. Weik MSS.   [2] Wood's statement. Weik MSS.

[3] Lamon, 57.   [4] Wood's statement. Weik MSS.

[5] Statement of Nathaniel Grigsby to William Fortune and General James C. Veatch in 1881, and by Mr. Fortune to the author, August 13, 1924.

Mr. Fortune, then a youth, had written a history of Warrick County, and accompanied General Veatch from Rockport, Ind., to Gentryville, to gather material for a book on Lincoln in Indiana, which General Veatch was preparing to write.

They talked with Nathaniel Grigsby, among others, who, after naming the books read by Lincoln as given in the biographies, said: 'There was another book that we boys got a lot of fun out of,' and in answer to questions, gave the account set out in the text.

Careful and prolonged search failed to discover such a book as 'The Kings Jester.' Among the books of jests in the British Museum was found, *Quinn's Jests or the Facetious Man's Pocket Companion, Containing every species of Wit, Humor and Repartee, with a Complete Collection of Epigrams, Bonmots, etc.*, published in London in 1766.

In the opinion of J. Christian Bay, of the John Crerar Library, Chicago, and of other experts, this is the book read by Lincoln to his boyhood companions in the woods of Spencer County, Indiana. J. Christian Bay to William Fortune, Nov. 5, 1922.

The conversion of *Quinn's Jests* into the 'King's Jester' is still another illustration of that careless pronunciation which prevailed among the pioneers.

often indecent and sometimes so filthy that they cannot now be reproduced.

In his seventeenth year his sister Sarah, then aged nineteen, married Aaron Grigsby,[1] son of a farmer and one of the important men in the settlement. Even then social distinctions were sharply drawn and upon the lines of property; and the Grigsbys were of the aristocracy of the backwoods. Abraham composed some doggerel in verse, which, it is said, was sung at the wedding by 'the Lincoln family.' It was a clumsy rhyme, telling, in eight verses, the story of the creation and marriage of Adam and Eve.

This bridal hymn of Sarah Lincoln argued that since woman was not made of man's feet he must not abuse her; nor should she 'rule him,' not having been taken from his head; but that he must protect her because 'she was taken from under Adam's arm.'[2] At the noisy wedding or thereafter, the Grigsby family did or said something which was strongly offensive to Lincoln. Thus was laid the materials of a feud, which was to be set blazing by a harsh circumstance two years later.

But in the meantime he adventured far, though briefly, into the world beyond the fifty-mile circuit of the Pigeon Creek settlement. He had seen something of river life, having been hired in 1825 by one James Taylor to help run a ferry boat across the Ohio from near the mouth of Anderson Creek.[3] Taylor had a farm, too, and when Lincoln was not taking travellers across the river, he ploughed, made fences, ground corn on the hand mill, and at 'hog killing time,' helped nearby farmers

[1] Grigsby's statement. Weik MSS. Also Hobson, 21. She was married in August, 1826. Chapman's Narrative. Weik MSS. The records of Spencer Co. show that the day was August 2.

On Sept. 13, 1826 (Marriage Register, Spencer Co., Ind.), 'Squire' Hall, married Mrs. Lincoln's youngest daughter, Matilda Johnston, and lived thenceforth in the Lincoln cabin. 'Squire' Hall, or Levi, Jr., was the son of Levi Hall and Nancy Hanks, mother of Dennis Hanks.

[2] Herndon, I, 48–9. This song and the account of it as stated in the text, were given in 1866 by Mrs. Josiah Crawford, who was at Sarah Lincoln's wedding. She says that Lincoln used to sing it and that it was 'sung at abrahams sisters wedding. I do not Know a linkern composed this song or not the first that I ever heard it was the linkern family sung it I rather think A L composed it him self but I am not certain. I know that he was in the habit of makeing songs and singing of them.' Elizabeth Crawford to Herndon, May 3, 1866. Weik MSS.

[3] Green B. Taylor's statement, Sept. 16, 1865; and that of Richardson, Weik MSS. Also Herndon, I, 60.

as well as Taylor — wielding the club, sousing the dead swine in barrels of scalding water, scraping the bristles and other incidents in the process.[1] As ferryman and farmer Abraham was paid six dollars a month, and as hog killer thirty-one cents a day in addition.[2]

Lincoln also built for himself a scow in which he would take travellers to passing steamers hailed in midstream. Another ferryman, John T. Dill, a Kentuckian, angered by this competition, haled Lincoln before a Kentucky Justice of the Peace, Samuel Pate, for running a ferry without a license. Lincoln said that he did not know that it was against the law to take passengers to steamboats in midstream, especially when the ferryboat was on the other side and the steamers would not land or wait. The plaintiff pointed out, however, that the jurisdiction of Kentucky ran to low water mark on the Indiana shore. But 'Squire' Pate decided that taking persons to passenger craft in midstream, was not 'setting them over' the river and, therefore, that Lincoln had not violated the statute. Abraham was deeply impressed and, thereafter, went to this rural court when cases were heard and decided. In such fashion began Lincoln's interest in the study and practice of the law.[3]

But running a ferryboat now and then, across the Ohio, taking an infrequent traveller to a steamer, ploughing, splitting rails and killing hogs for Taylor and others, gave Lincoln little more experience of human activities than Pigeon Creek had afforded. Heavy toil was the only lasting impression made upon him, for long years afterward, when one of the leaders of the Illinois Bar, he told Herndon that it 'was the roughest work a young man could be made to do.'[4] The boisterous life of the keel boatmen did not appeal to him — their heavy and continuous drinking of raw whisky, their loud and picturesque boasting made good by reckless and bloody fighting, even their fiddling and clamorous, hearty good cheer[5] did not attract him.

<hr />

[1] Taylor's statement. Weik MSS. And see *First of the Hoosiers:* George Cary Eggleston, 54–5.

[2] Taylor's statement. Weik MSS.

[3] *Litigant:* Townsend, 34–9.   [4] Herndon, I, 61.

[5] For excellent description by an eye witness of the Ohio keel boatmen see 'Historical

In his nineteenth year, however, the chance was offered to make a far journey; and the opportunity came as the result of Lincoln's good fellowship and integrity, and the friendship and confidence inspired by these qualities. The richest man in Carter Township was James Gentry, a native of North Carolina who in April, 1818, had come from Kentucky with his young wife to the Pigeon Creek settlement. He entered a thousand acres of land and afterward bought several hundred acres more. He had a large family, two of whom married into the family of another wealthy man, Gideon W. Romine.[1] Gentry soon began to keep a small stock of goods for sale at his farm house;[2] thus began the town of Gentryville.[3] Soon William David, a blacksmith, came[4] and in time a few cabins were built near by. Gentryville became the social as well as the trading centre of the countryside.

Gentryville was less than a mile and a half from the Lincoln cabin; and to the backwoods hamlet young Lincoln would speed like a homing pigeon when work was done for the day. For there gathered other youth and men who craved companionship and the story-telling, talk, and discussion which took place in country stores. About this time, one, William Jones, came from Vincennes[5] and opened a little store. Soon he and Lincoln became fast friends and Jones hired the boy to help him. But it was the village blacksmith who was 'Abes pertickler friend.'[6] Gentry and Jones formed a partnership, with Abraham sometimes assisting as man of all work.

As long as Gentry or Jones would keep the candles lighted and the log fire burning, Abraham would remain, talking, forever talking, relating his jokes, telling his rude and often unsavory

Writings of Judge Samuel Wilkeson:' *Pubs. Buffalo Hist. Socy.*, v, 179–81. See also Woods: Thwaites, x, 255. Sept. 18, 1821.

[1] *Hist. W., S. & P. Cos.*, Ind., 452, 558.

[2] In 1827 Gentry, who was very illiterate (Hobson, 24–5), took in as partners Gideon W. and Benjamin Romine, and opened a store at a crossing of the roads. 'Gentry started a cotton gin about 1824 . . . receiving patronage from a radius of thirty miles. Considerable cotton was raised. It grew well on new land.' *Hist. W., S. & P. Cos.*, Ind., 365–6.

[3] *Ib.*, 366. It was not entered of record as a town, however, until 1854.

[4] *Hist. W., S. & P. Cos.*, Ind., 366.

[5] Hanks to Herndon, no date, Weik MSS.

[6] *Ib.*, and Hanks to Herndon, March 22, 1866.

tales; flashing his kindly repartee, propounding his theories about everything. 'He was so odd, original and humorous and witty that all the People in town would gather around him,' Dennis Hanks told Herndon. 'He would Keep them there till midnight or longer telling Stories [and] cracking jokes. . . . I would get tired, want to go home, cuss Abe most heartily.' [1] And 'Sumtimes we Spent a Little time at grog piching waits,' says Dennis.[2]

Lincoln had great physical strength, so great that tales of his performances are well-nigh unbelievable. Long afterward one elderly person recalled that the young Hercules of Pigeon Creek bore away easily heavy posts which 'some of the men' were preparing to carry by means of bars.[3] 'Abe could sink an axe deeper in wood . . . He could strike with a mall a heavier blow than any man I ever saw,' testifies William Wood.[4] Stature, physical power, good humor, intellect, integrity, are the outstanding features of the picture of Abraham Lincoln during these years.

In April, 1828, James Gentry hired this strong, capable, and trustworthy youth to go with his son, Allen, on a flatboat loaded with produce to New Orleans, then the best market for such things as the upper Mississippi country had to sell.[5] The boat started from Gentry's landing on the Ohio, about three quarters of a mile from Rockport.[6] Lincoln acted as a bow hand, 'working the foremost oar and was paid eight dollars per month from the time of starting to his returning home.'[7] It was no ignorant lout but a fairly well-informed young person of grasping and absorbing mind, who, with quip and quiddity, droll story and quaint common sense, enlivened the hours, as Gentry's flatboat floated down the Ohio and Mississippi to the great Southern mart.

---

[1] Hanks's Charleston statement. Weik MSS.

[2] Hanks to Herndon, March 22, 1866. Weik MSS.

[3] Richardson's statement. Weik MSS.   [4] Wood's statement. Weik MSS.

[5] These boats, made of the trunks of big poplar trees, were from sixty to eighty feet in length. Meat, corn, flour and the like made up the cargoes. Cockrum, 508–10. Allen Gentry was two years older than Lincoln.

[6] Mrs. Allen Gentry's statement. Weik MSS

[7] Grigsby's statement. Weik MSS.

Nothing happened, it seems, to disturb that placid voyage until one night, when tied to the shore at the plantation of a Madame Duchesne, not far from New Orleans, a company of negroes armed with hickory clubs and bent on plunder, came upon the flatboat when the occupants were asleep. Aroused by the noise, Lincoln seized a club and furiously attacked the marauders. He knocked several into the river and the others fled, Lincoln and Gentry in hot pursuit. They, too, were wounded, it appears, for they were bleeding when they got on board again. Also they feared that the negroes would return; so they 'hastily swung into the stream and floated down the river till daylight.' [1]

So came Abraham Lincoln to New Orleans, the first city and the first place bigger than the Boonville or Rockport, Indiana, of 1828, he had ever seen. It was then a remarkable city of narrow streets, foreign-built houses, with colored stuccoes and iron railings, broad avenues lined by handsome houses, a cathedral, and immense warehouses for receiving, pressing, and storing cotton. From the levee, a much used causeway, could be seen nearly two miles of various descriptions of vessels, arks and flatboats from the north, steamboats still giving a sense of novelty, three-masters for foreign trade, with their broadsides to the shore — expressing the growing commerce of the river and people and offering 'one of the most singularly beautiful' sights that could be conceived.

At the market, the common place of meeting, could be found nuts and fruits of the tropics; fish from lake and gulf; sugar, grain, and meats. Lincoln saw and heard the bustle and heaving labor on the river front, sea-going vessels made ready, crews of strange speech. He could note the medley of people and dress — French, Spanish, Mexicans, Creoles, even Indians, and slaves, from the full negro through many degrees of mixed blood.[2] It all gave a new experience to the two youths from the backwoods of Indiana, but there is no evidence of the impression made upon Lincoln by this, his second contact with slavery.

[1] Nicolay and Hay, I, 44; Herndon, I, 63; Hobson, 25; also Mrs. Gentry's statement. Weik MSS.
'Lincoln was attacked by the Negroes — no doubt of this — Abe told me so.' Romine's statement. Weik MSS.
[2] Latrobe, II, 330–4.

The cargo sold, the young men returned to their Indiana homes in June,[1] making the journey up stream on one of the big and sumptuous steamboats of the time, the elder Gentry paying the fare. On Pigeon Creek Lincoln took up again the old routine, unchanged in speech or manner by his trip to the metropolis of the South. He was still the avid reader of books, the incessant talker, the bubbling fountain of good cheer.

But Gentryville no longer satisfied him; he had caught a glimpse of the world beyond Pigeon Creek, beyond Rockport and Boonville. The spell of the river had stolen over him; he wanted to be 'a steamboat man' on a big river craft like the one on which he had returned from New Orleans. In 1829, relates William Wood, 'Abe came to my house one day, and stood round about timid and shy. I knew he wanted something. I said to him, "Abe what is your care?" Abe replied, "Uncle, I want you to go to the River (the Ohio) and give me some recommendation to some boat." I remarked, "Abe, your age is against you. You are not 21 yet." "I know that, but I want a start," said Abe. I concluded not to go for the boys good.'[2]

So he stayed on at the Pigeon Creek cabin, doing the familiar work of the backwoods farm, felling trees, splitting rails, ploughing fields, helping Thomas Lincoln now and then in his casual carpentering. But he read and wrote more than ever, and lost no opportunity to hear speeches, especially legal arguments. When court was held in Rockport on the Ohio or at Boonville, county seats of Spencer and Warrick counties respectively, Lincoln would go,[3] making careful notes of all that was said and done.

These towns were mere villages, Boonville having some twenty cabins in which dwelt, perhaps, ninety or one hundred men, women, and children; and Rockport was but little larger. Evansville was then scarcely more important. The roads were well-nigh impassable except on foot or horseback, being mere open-

---

[1] Mrs. Gentry's statement. Weik MSS.
  It took about two months to make the trip. Romine's statement. Weik MSS.
[2] Wood's statement. Weik MSS.
[3] Hanks's Charleston statement. Weik MSS.

ings through the woods.[1] Business before the courts at these county seats consisted mostly, as we have seen, of criminal and divorce cases. Suits for debt or on contract were trifling; but they were contested stoutly with much argument by the lawyers, some of whom wore queues tied in eelskins.[2] Lincoln listened to the wrangling and speeches of these legal combatants and attracted the notice of at least two of them.

As we have seen, one of these was John Pitcher of Rockport, with whom, according to Pitcher, the youth wanted to study law; but 'his father was too poor to spare him away from the farm and the mill.'[3] Near Boonville lived John A. Brackenridge

[1] In southern Indiana the roads were so indistinct that travellers often were lost. Esarey, 246.

The road through Indiana to Cincinnati was too bad for ordinary travel. Fordham, 152.

As late as 1823 even between Richmond and Indianapolis, the road was little more than a trail. Coffin, 81.

In 1826 there were only Indian trails through the forests from Randolph County to Fort Wayne. O. H. Smith, 81 (*infra*).

Even as late as 1847, the roads in Wayne County, perhaps the best in the State, were 'almost impassable.' Coffin, 50. And see Welby: Thwaites, xii, 213. Near New Harmony, Welby found roads impassable in the spring. *Ib.*, 267.

As late as 1835 a Methodist circuit-rider describes the road from Ohio to Indianapolis as 'terrible.' Brunson: *Wis. Hist. Coll.*, xv, 270–1.

[2] Smith, 6, 130.

Examples of litigation at that time, as given by Judge Smith in his *Early Indiana Trials and Sketches*, are stealing a log chain, hog stealing, slander, assault, libel, murder, malpractice and the like. There were few cases for debt, but those were fought long and hard.

At Connersville, Ind., in 1820, Isaac Jones sued Edward Harper for twenty-five cents, the price of some beef Harper had bought from Jones. In the court of the Justice of the Peace several juries disagreed. When, after many trials, a jury agreed, appeal was taken to the Circuit Court, where again there were several 'hung juries.'

At the final trial, all Fayette County turned out en masse. Jones had four lawyers, Harper three; and the argument lasted two days. The jury was out all night and in the morning returned a verdict for Harper because the beef had made his family sick. The costs now amounted to $1100, to pay which Jones sold his farm; and the payment of Harper's lawyers bankrupted that stubborn litigant. *Ib.*, 11.

The people were extraordinarily litigious: 'I have known a lawsuit brought for a piggin or pail, of the value of 25 cents.' Woods: Thwaites, x, 317.

Attending court was a principal means of diversion; and the settlers gathered in throngs at trials which, sometimes, were conducted as much to please the hearers as to try the case. 'If the court please,' began a lawyer at a trial, when he was stopped by the presiding judge who gravely answered, 'Yes, we do please. . . . The people have come in to hear the lawyers plead.' Smith, 7.

In a suit for slander between two doctors, one an Allopathic and the other a 'root doctor,' there were five lawyers on each side and the trial lasted more than a week. *Ib.*, 12–3.

[3] Pitcher's statement to O. C. Terry, in Terry to Jesse W. Weik, July, 1888. Weik

who is said to have been an advocate of unusual brilliancy. In 1828 at a trial of note when Brackenridge was prosecutor of Warrick County, young Lincoln was present, and paid such 'calm intelligent attention' to the proceedings that Brackenridge observed it. When the trial was over Abraham went up to the lawyer, praised his speech to the jury as a 'clear, logical and powerful effort;' but Brackenridge, who won the case,[1] merely 'looked at the shabby boy.'[2]

Thus by reading, listening, absorbing, Abraham's knowledge grew. 'How did Lincoln and yourself learn so much in Indiana under such disadvantages?' Herndon diplomatically asked Dennis Hanks. The answer is the best explanation yet given. 'We learned by sight, scent and hearing. We heard all that was said and talked over and over the questions heard, wore them slick, greasy and threadbare.'[3] This fact must be borne in mind as we follow Lincoln through his remaining years in Indiana.

January 20, 1828, Sarah Grigsby died in child-birth,[4] and Abraham, grieving sorely, blamed Aaron Grigsby and the Grigsby family for his sister's death, which, declares J. W.

MSS. Pitcher says that Thomas Lincoln had built and ran a horse mill for the grinding of corn; but since those who knew the Lincoln family and lived near their cabin make no mention of such a mill and there is no other account of it, the probabilities are that Pitcher's recollection of it is inaccurate. He made the statement to Terry in the summer of 1888, at least sixty years after Abraham Lincoln came to his office in Rockport. At that time Pitcher was old and very deaf.

[1] It was not easy to secure convictions for murder, and when culprits were found guilty the people often petitioned for pardons. Smith, 8–9, 23.

[2] Statement of S. T. Johnson, Sept. 14, 1865. Weik MSS. Johnson was present at this trial and saw and heard what he relates. He says that he often saw Lincoln at the Warrick County Court at Boonville. Johnson is also the authority for the statement that, when Brackenridge saw Lincoln at Washington in 1862, the President 'instantly recognized' the lawyer whom he had not seen for thirty-four years, and assured him that it was at the Boonville trial that Lincoln 'formed a fixed determination to study the law and make that his profession;' and that the President told Brackenridge that his speech at the murder trial 'was the best speech that I, up to that time, ever heard. If I could, as I then thought make as good a speech as that, that my soul would be satisfied.' *Ib.*

Presumably Johnson had this story from Brackenridge, though in what way we are not informed. Brackenridge moved to Texas in 1852 or 1853. See 'John A. Brackenridge': Raleigh, in *Proceedings Southwestern Indiana Historical Socy.*, Oct., 1922, 60. Johnson also says that the trial was of a 'murder case'; but the court records of Warrick County show that no such case was tried in 1828.

[3] Hanks's Charleston statement. Weik MSS.

[4] The baby was stillborn. Chapman's narrative. Weik MSS.

Lamar, 'Abe always thought was due to neglect.' [1] Thus was ignited the antagonism which, it seems, had been slowly though silently accumulated since Sarah's marriage two years before.

In the spring of 1829 [2] two sons of Reuben Grigsby, Reuben, Jr., and Charles, were married. Lincoln was not invited to the wedding, nor yet to the infare which was held at the mansion of the elder Grigsby, a house of two stories built of hewed logs.[3] In hot resentment, he contrived through a confederate a confusion of brides and grooms after the festivities, to be corrected the moment the joke was known to the guests.[4]

With this incident for a text, he wrote a scurrilous description of it, entitling the screed 'The Chronicles of Reuben.' This he dropped at a place on the road 'carelessly, lost it as it were' and it was found by one of the Grigsby family.[5] It was anonymous, of course, but everybody knew who wrote it — nobody in the neighborhood but Lincoln could have written it. It was done in imitation of Old Testament narrative, and described the wedding and infare of the Grigsby boys, ending with a bold picture of the mix-up at the close of the merriment.

'The Chronicles' made a tremendous hit throughout the neighborhood.[6] Gossip on swift wings, carried the story of the marital misadventure all over the countryside. Coarse though the satire was, everybody talked about the salacious description; some committed the whole of it to memory and were able to repeat it as long as they lived.[7] Joseph C. Richardson proudly

---

[1] Lamar's statement: Hobson, 24. Rhoda M. Coffin records that, even in the best-conditioned families and in the most highly educated communities women frequently were badly injured by ignorant treatment at child-birth and thereafter 'blistered ... causing indescribable suffering.' Coffin, 61.

[2] April 15 or 16, 1829. [3] Hobson, 26.

[4] Richardson's statement. Weik MSS. [5] Ib. [6] Hobson, 28–9.

[7] Herndon, I, 51–4. Herndon got the 'Chronicles of Reuben' in 1865 from the wife of Josiah Crawford. She repeated it from memory to her son, S. A. Crawford, who wrote it out for Herndon. S. A. Crawford to Herndon, Jan. 4, 1866. Weik MSS.

Nathaniel Grigsby wrote Herndon that the copy Herndon secured was 'correctly writen.' Grigsby to Herndon, Oct. 25, 1865. Weik MSS. And see Hobson, 28–9.

'Lincoln did write what is called the book of chronicles, a satire on the Grigsbys.' Grigsby's statement. Weik MSS.

'The thing happened about as Mr. Herndon heard it. My father-in-law told the story to me and my wife often. My wifes father was a brother to the old lady Grigsby, and was at the infair when the thing happened.' John W. Lamar to J. W. Whartmann of Evansville, Jan. 3, 1887. Weik MSS.

relates that 'this poem . . . is remembered here in Indiana in Scraps better than the Bible, better than Watts hymns . . . this [was] the first production that I know of that made us feel that Abe was truly and really *game*. This called the attention of the People to Abe intellectually.' [1]

But the success of his trick and Hudibrastic lines did not satisfy Lincoln — he must further castigate the Grigsbys, although they and their friends were already 'fighting mad.' [2] Lincoln wrote a rhyme about another brother, William Grigsby, who appears to have been bald-headed, very ugly, and, judging from Lincoln's verses, was the butt of rude chaffing. This repellent rhyme was read and repeated as widely as 'The Chronicles of Reuben.' The meaning could be fully understood only by those who knew the incidents described.[3]

A fist fight was the only possible outcome of these attacks and such a fight took place; but Abraham did no fighting, except, perhaps, in the mêlée that followed. The details of the arrangement of this now famous contest are obscure and confused. All that is certainly known is that John D. Johnston, step-brother of Lincoln, had a savage fight with the outraged William Grigsby, and was soundly thrashed. It is said that Lincoln refused to meet Grigsby because the young giant was so much stronger than his offended opponent; and put Johnston forward in his place, an arrangement to which Grigsby agreed.[4] Another ver-

---

[1] Richardson's statement. Weik MSS.

[2] This incident is made harder to understand by the attempt, long after the Herndon investigations, to lay upon John D. Johnston the blame for the matrimonial contretemps after the infare; and by the assertion that, almost immediately thereafter, Lincoln was on friendly terms with the elder Grigsby. Hobson, 27.

[3] Mrs. Crawford's statement; also Romine's statement. Weik MSS.
Herndon, I, 55, prints two verses, but not as they came to him, and Romine gives others, which are not worth repeating.

[4] Many years after Grigsby, Taylor, Elizabeth Crawford, and others wrote to and were interviewed by Herndon, a new version of the fight was given to Rev. J. Edward Murr by James and Joseph Gentry, Redmond Grigsby, and Wesley Hall, who said that Lincoln and William Grigsby quarrelled over the ownership of a spotted pup. Grigsby dared Lincoln to fight it out, Lincoln refused because he could 'lick' Grigsby and put up his step-brother instead, the winner to get the pup. Grigsby was beating Johnston badly when Lincoln 'bodily hurled him over the heads of the crowd,' daring 'the entire Grigsby crowd to come into him.' But they were afraid, and the incident ended with Lincoln 'laughing and joking.'
According to this tale it was thereafter, and because of this fight, that Lincoln was

sion is that, although there were 'seconds' for each combatant and general agreement that the ring about the fighters should not be broken, Lincoln burst through, dragged Grigsby off Johnston, threw him 'some feet' away, 'waved a bottle of whisky over his head and said he was the big buck of the lick' — whereupon this 'being a general invitation for a general fight they all pitched in and had quite a general fight.' [1] However, it was a notable fight and everybody came. Lincoln was undoubtedly present because it was his quarrel.[2]

As to what happened afterward, however, we have William Grigsby's own account as given directly to his brother Nathaniel Grigsby who, in a letter, repeated it to Herndon: 'my old brother W[illia]m Grigsby tells me some things that past betwin himself and Abraham Lincoln which i wil rite . . . after the fite betwen Wm. Grigsby and John D. Johnson Abraham told Wm. Grigsby that he had whiped Johnson but i can whip you but Wm told him that he did not dispute that but if he Lincoln would give him Grigsby a fair c[h]ance he would fite him he Lincoln wish to now how he wish to fite, Grigsby told Lincoln he would fite him a duel Lincoln told Grigsby that he Lincoln was not a going to fool his life away with one shot, so the mater stoped.' [3]

In the autumn of 1829 Thomas Lincoln resolved to leave Indiana for Illinois. After staying with the Lincolns in Indiana for four years, John Hanks had gone back to Kentucky and thence in 1828 to Macon County, Illinois.[4] He sent back to Thomas Lincoln and Dennis Hanks the usual reports of a new country.[5] Also the 'milk sickness' had come again or was ex-

not invited to the Grigsby wedding and infare which caused him to devise the prank described in the text and to write the 'Chronicles of Reuben.' By this later account, Lincoln is made to apologize to the Grigsbys, stating that he meant only to have some fun, and to deliver to them the manuscript of the 'Chronicles.' Murr, *Indiana Magazine of History*, xiv, 38–41.

[1] Taylor's and John Hoskins' statements. Weik MSS. Taylor was the son of James Taylor, who hired Lincoln to run the ferryboat across the Ohio and who acted as the 'second' to John D. Johnston in his fight with Grigsby. *Ib.*

[2] Grigsby's statement. Weik MSS.

[3] Grigsby to Herndon, Oct. 25, 1865. Weik MSS.

[4] John Hanks to Herndon, June 13, 1865. Weik MSS.

[5] *Decatur* (Ill.) *Republican*, July 13, 1890.

pected.[1] So Thomas and Sarah Lincoln sold the Johnston lot in Elizabethtown, Kentucky, for one hundred and twenty-three dollars to Thomas J. Wathen,[2] going to Elizabethtown to execute the deed and get the money. After their return to Indiana they spent the winter of 1829–30 in making ready for the journey. Two years earlier Thomas Lincoln had succeeded in getting a patent for half of the one hundred and sixty acres which he originally had entered.[3] This eighty acres he now sold to James Gentry.[4] During the winter of 1829–30 Lincoln also sold what live-stock he had, and bought two yoke of oxen and a stout wagon for his journey westward.

Nor did the pious Thomas neglect to equip himself with a certification of church membership and regularity, although, seem-

[1] Hanks to Herndon, March 7, 1866. Weik MSS. Dennis gives different reasons for leaving Indiana: 'Thomas Lincoln hearing of the rich Prairies of Illinois already cleared up and prepared for the plow decided to go.' Hanks's first Chicago statement. Weik MSS. On the other hand, says Hanks: 'The Reson is this we war perplext By a Disese cald Milk Sick my Self Being the oldest I was Determed to Leve and hunt a Cuntry whare the milk was not I maried his oldest Step Daughter I Sold out and they concluded to gow with me . . . My wifs mother could not think of parting with hir and we Riped up Stakes and Started to Illinois.' Hanks to Herndon, March 7, 1866. Weik MSS.

[2] Records Hardin County, Deed Book C, 219.

[3] The patent, signed by J. Q. Adams, then President, for eighty acres, is dated June 6, 1827. Records Land Office, Interior Department. The patent was secured by releases and application of payments, a method often adopted by poor settlers. The Act of July 21, 1821, extending time for payments granted a discount of thirty-seven and one-half per cent when full payment was promptly made; but Lincoln could not get the money. December 22, 1818, one Charles Whiting had entered eighty acres in Posey County, Ind., paying the first installment of $80; and he assigned his interest to the heirs of one Memorial Forrest, whose guardian, James McCrery, got an order of court, April 2, 1827, to sell this interest. Three days later, at Vincennes, McCrery assigned it to Thomas Lincoln who, April 30, 1827, relinquished it to the government, and was allowed credit for the $80 that Whiting had paid on it.

At the same time Lincoln sold by relinquishment, the east half of the 160 acres he had entered in 1817, to James Gentry, who promptly paid the government cash for the remainder of the purchase price. How much Gentry paid Lincoln is unknown. The money which he had paid on this half ten years before was promptly credited to the balance due on the remaining eighty acres. Thus, full payment for half of his original entry having been made, Lincoln received his patent. Gen. Land Office Records, Interior Department. A brochure on this transaction has been prepared by George R. Wickham, Assistant Commissioner of the General Land Office, upon which, as well as upon the official records, I have relied.

This is the most extensive and complicated transaction in which Thomas Lincoln ever was engaged, and it suggests the resourceful business mind of James Gentry.

[4] The records of Spencer County having been destroyed in 1831, the amount paid Lincoln for the unproductive little farm is unknown, but probably was somewhat more than the $80 Lincoln paid the government for it.

ingly, as sour fruitage of Abe's feud with the Grigsbys, there was difficulty in obtaining it. On December 12, 1829, Little Pigeon Creek Church granted a 'letter of dismission' to Lincoln and his wife, which was recalled on the objection of Mrs. Nancy Grigsby that they were unworthy of such credential. The row must have been settled between the parties for, a month later, January 10, 1830, Thomas was appointed on a committee to settle a quarrel between two sisters of the congregation. Since this, the only distinction ever accorded him, was just before he left Indiana forever, it would seem to have been a sort of churchly emollient and farewell. However, Lincoln had been a generous contributor, having once given twenty-four pounds of meal to church support.[1]

During the last two years spent in Indiana a change of far-reaching results began to come over Abraham Lincoln. Although most people in Carter township were National Republicans and supporters of Henry Clay,[2] Thomas Lincoln and his family were Democrats and followers of Andrew Jackson[3] as, indeed, were most poor people.[4] Abraham, too, was a Jackson man — a 'Jackson Democrat,' as Dennis Hanks asserts with emphasis.[5] Political campaigns had invaded Spencer and Warrick Counties, and, by 1828, had become heated.[6] For some years political handbills had been scattered through the settlements and, recently, stump speakers had enlivened backwoods gatherings.

[1] Records Little Pigeon Creek Baptist Church, MS. March 10, 1828.

[2] The earliest records are for the Presidential election of 1832 when thirteen votes were cast for Jackson in Carter township and eighteen for Clay; in 1836, fourteen votes were cast for Van Buren, Democrat, and twenty for Harrison, Whig; in 1840, thirty-five for Harrison and six for Van Buren. The township continued strongly Whig and Republican until 1876 when Tilden carried it by three votes. In 1856 the American (anti-foreign) party cast fifty-four votes to twenty-five for the Republicans and sixty-five for the Democrats. In 1860 the vote was one hundred twenty-four for Lincoln, seventy-six for Douglas, eighteen for Bell and Everett and one for Breckinridge. *Hist. W., S. & P. Cos.*, Ind., 299–305.

[3] Hanks's Charleston statement. Weik MSS.

[4] Yet Nathaniel Grigsby says that 'we were all Jackson boys and men at that time in Indiana;' and the Grigsbys were comparatively rich. Grigsby's statement. Weik MSS.

[5] Such men were violently intolerant, voting for or against local candidates solely because those candidates supported or opposed Jackson. Smith, 81.

[6] As illustrative of the habits of the time, it is of interest to note that, even in com-

Lincoln's friend, William Jones, the store-keeper in Gentryville, who was a staunch Republican, took the *Louisville Journal*
and, perhaps, one or two other newspapers.[1] William Wood, too,
was a Republican, and, as we have seen, he also took newspapers published at Cincinnati.[2] In these newspapers the
speeches of Clay and other public men were printed, and able
editorial comment made upon them as well as upon all the
questions of the day. Much was reproduced from the Eastern
press also, particularly that of New England and Philadelphia.
The *Louisville Journal* was violently opposed to Jackson and
fervently supported Clay.

Lincoln read these papers[3] to as much purpose as he read
books. 'Abe read the newspapers . . . at least such as I took,'
Wood told Herndon; frequently borrowed the *Telescope*, which
Wood took from 1825 to 1830.[4] From 1824 to 1830, says Mrs.
Lincoln, 'newspapers were [to be] had' and 'Abe was a constant
reader of them. I am sure of this for the years of 1827-28-29-
30.'[5] To everybody he met and wherever he went, he told all
he read; he became 'a kind of newsboy' of the vicinity, says
Hanks.[6]

In the Presidential campaign of 1828 the National Republican
candidate was John Quincy Adams, then President; the Democratic candidate was Andrew Jackson. The outstanding issues
were Jackson's wrongs in 1824, when the House of Representatives elected Adams, internal improvements, a protective tariff
— 'the American system,' as Henry Clay called it — and the
Bank of the United States as fiscal agent of the government and
the supervisor of a stable currency. Discussion of these ques-

muuities priding themselves on superior morality, candidates who were successful at
elections had to treat everybody to whisky. *Recollections:* Harris, 63–4.

[1] William Jones was born at Vincennes, Ind., Jan. 5, 1800, and lived there until, in
his twenty-seventh year, he went to Gentryville. He had much influence on Lincoln's
early life. He enlisted as a Union soldier at the outbreak of the Civil War, rose to be
Colonel of his regiment, the 53rd Indiana Volunteer Infantry, and was killed in action
at Atlanta, Georgia, July 22, 1864. Hobson, 34. The *Louisville Journal*, founded in
1831 by George D. Prentice, was the leading paper in the West.

[2] Wood's statement. Weik MSS.   [3] Hobson, 34.

[4] Wood's statement. Weik MSS. *The Telescope* was a religious weekly, published in
New York City from 1824 to 1830, and perhaps later, and edited by W. Beach.

[5] Mrs. Lincoln's statement. Weik MSS.

[6] Hanks in Charleston statement. Weik MSS.

tions on the stump and in the newspapers was forthright and
within the range of popular understanding and credibility.[1]
Ratliff Boone was a candidate for Representative in Congress
from that district and made speeches which Lincoln undoubtedly heard; but since Boone was an ardent Democrat and aggressive supporter of Jackson, it would appear that he did not
greatly influence Lincoln.[2]

We 'went to political and other speeches and gatherings. . . .
We would hear all sides and opinions talk them over, discuss
them agreeing or disagreeing,' relates Dennis Hanks, and con-
tinues in disgust: 'Abe turned Whig in 1827–8 [3] — think Col.
Jones made him a Whig dont know it . . . I opposed Abe in
Politics when . . . he became Whig.' [4] Worst of all, laments
Dennis, he 'allways Loved Hen Clay's Speeches I think was the
Cause Mostly' of Lincoln's drifting away from Jacksonian
Democracy.[5]

Certainly the Republican position in 1828–30 was supported
by what Lincoln had experienced throughout his life — the necessity for means of communication, the worthlessness of the
local currency, so uncertain in value that he never knew the
purchasing power of his trifling wages.[6] Internal improvements

[1] Judge O. H. Smith says that 'stump speaking' began in Indiana about 1826. As
an example of popular ignorance, and intolerance of what was considered extravagant
statements by speakers, he relates that Judge John Test, a Representative in Congress
from the eastern district of Indiana, told an audience that the speed of railway trains
in England was thirty miles an hour. The crowd jeered and roared with laughter; and
one cried out 'you are crazy, or do you think we are fools; a man could not live a
moment [when going] at that speed.' For his assertion, Judge Test was defeated for re-
election. Smith, 80.

[2] Boone was, perhaps, the most active politician in Southwestern Indiana. He was
twice Lieutenant Governor and was six times elected to Congress. A life of this pioneer
politician and legislator is now being written by Hon. John E. Iglehart of Evansville,
Ind.

[3] Hanks's Charleston statement. Weik MSS. Whig is used for National Republican.
But David Turnham says he was still a Democrat when he left Indiana. Turnham
to Herndon, Sept. 29, 1866. Weik MSS.
Dennis Hanks, who declares twice in his Charleston statement that Lincoln turned
'Whig' in 1828–9, says in a letter to Herndon that he did not 'Turn Whig' until 'After
He cum to Illinois aBout 1830.' Hanks to Herndon, March 12, 1866. Weik MSS.

[4] Ib.; Hanks's Charleston statement. Weik MSS.

[5] Ib.; Hanks to Herndon, March 12, 1866. Weik MSS.

[6] See Cockrum, 403–4. The only specie was cut coin. Ib. At Vincennes in 1818
Faux 'passed away my twenty dollar note of the rotten bank of Harmony, Pennsylvania, for five dollars only.' Faux: Thwaites, XI, 207, Oct. 30. Even in Cincinnati

and stable money meant something tangible to Abraham Lincoln. Then too the men he knew best and most respected, William Jones, David Turnham, William Wood, were National Republicans and ardent champions of Henry Clay, the brilliant leader of that party.

Whatever the cause, it appears to be reasonably certain that it was at this period that Lincoln cut loose from the political faith of his fathers.[1] He said little about it, however, at the time, as was the case twenty-four years later when he left the Whig party. With that strange mingling of caution, secretiveness and craft which so confounded his opponents and puzzled his supporters in after years, Lincoln, in 1828–30, kept to himself his changed or changing conviction and his purposes. Indeed, Elizabeth Crawford recalls that in the Adams–Jackson campaign of 1828 she heard Abraham singing a Democratic campaign jingle.[2]

But though he may still have hurrahed for Old Hickory, the forces had been set in motion within his mind which revolutionized his political ideas and shaped his political career. When Abraham Lincoln left Indiana in 1830, he was a Whig at heart and ready to enlist, as he quickly did, under the banner of gallant, dashing 'Harry of the West.'

notes of the local banks were from thirty to forty per cent below those of the United States Bank; and outside the city they were practically worthless. *Ib.*, 171. Between Louisville and Vincennes in 1820 the difference in the value of bank notes was twenty-five per cent. Welby: Thwaites, xii, 270.

[1] It is worthy of note that all the Lincolns continued to be Democrats, none of them voting for Lincoln in 1860 or even enlisting in the Union Army. This, too, is true of the Hanks family, excepting only John Hanks, who became a Republican in 1860 and was later a Union soldier.

[2] Mrs. Crawford to Herndon, Feb. 21, 1866. Weik MSS.

CHAPTER III

NEW SALEM: EARLY MANHOOD AND DEVELOPMENT

One of the people! born to be
Their curious epitome. STODDARD.

I desire to live, and I desire place and distinction as a politician. LINCOLN.

IN the little semi-circular chamber where met the Senate of the United States,[1] every seat was filled and the small gallery was crowded. At his place stood a man little above medium height but broad-shouldered and compactly built, with remarkably large, dark eyes and cliff-like brow. He was dressed with careful regard to fashion, claw-hammer coat of blue broadcloth, the breast adorned by large polished brass buttons, a figured waistcoat and buff trousers. A high stock was around his neck and frills of a fine linen shirt protruded from his bosom. He was closing one of the greatest of speeches.

About him sat a company of men, historic in their eminence. One of these Senators, a young man of thirty-eight, with wide, intelligent gray eyes almost spiritual in appearance, and a face of striking manly beauty, leaned slightly forward in his chair. The composure of even Robert Y. Hayne of South Carolina was disturbed.

'Sir,' said Daniel Webster, his voice deep and compelling as the tones of a golden bell, 'Sir, I have not allowed myself to look beyond the Union, to see what might lie hidden in the dark recess behind. . . . While the Union lasts, we have high . . . prospects spread out before us, for us and our children. Beyond that I seek not to penetrate the veil. God grant that in my day, at least, that curtain may not rise! . . . When my eyes shall be turned to behold for the last time the sun in heaven, may I not see him shining on the broken and dishonored fragments of a once glorious Union; on States dissevered, discordant, belligerent; on a land rent with civil feuds, or drenched, it may be, in fraternal blood! Let their last feeble and lingering glance rather behold the gorgeous ensign of the republic, now known and

[1] The room where the Supreme Court now sits.

honored throughout the earth, still full high advanced, its arms and trophies streaming in their original lustre, not a stripe erased or polluted, nor a single star obscured, bearing for its motto, no such miserable interrogatory as "What is all this worth?" nor those other words of delusion and folly, "Liberty first and Union afterwards;" but everywhere, spread all over in characters of living light, blazing on all its ample folds, as they float over the sea and over the land, and in every wind under the whole heavens, that other sentiment, dear to every true American heart — Liberty *and* Union, now and for ever, one and inseparable!' [1]

With the echo of these words in the ears of the hearers, the Senate adjourned late in the afternoon of January 27, 1830. Since the convening of Congress in December the debate on the Foot Resolution [2] had been under way and for nearly three months more it was to continue. It had ranged throughout well-nigh every phase of the subject of free government; but, from the first, the supreme issue had thrust itself to the front and held the lead throughout the controversy — the issue of the right of a State to nullify national law as against the right of the Nation to suppress such opposition by force if necessary. Since the adoption of the Constitution this basic question had troubled all thoughtful Americans.

Only fifteen years before New England had been on fire with the spirit of separation and, in the midst of war, had contemplated withdrawing from the Union.[3] And now angered by the tariff of 1828, South Carolina had brought the question to a head. But not the gifted Hayne, not the mighty Webster was to lead the forces that finally battled for the antagonistic theories of government so powerfully set forth by these two men and their associates in that historic discussion.

[1] *Writings and Speeches of Daniel Webster* (National edition), vi, 75. *Register of Debates*, 21st Cong. 1st Sess., Part I, vi, 58–80. Webster began his speech Jan. 26 and concluded it the next day. He revised it later, and there are changes in style and phraseology between the speech as it appears in Webster's *Works* and in the *Register of Debates*.

[2] This resolution, offered by Senator Samuel Augustus Foot of Connecticut, provided for an enquiry 'into the expediency of limiting ... the sales of the public lands.' *Ib.*, 21st Cong. 1st Sess., 11.

[3] For a condensed account, see *Life of John Marshall:* Albert J. Beveridge, iv, 15, 27, 51–3.

At the time of this fateful parliamentary contest and about three weeks after the delivery of Webster's speech, a big, clumsy wagon drawn by two yoke of oxen moved out of the backwoods hamlet of Gentryville, Indiana. In the wagon three women and four children found room among the entire household effects of three families. In front or behind were five men, one riding a horse and another, a young giant of a man, six feet four inches in height, angular and awkward as he was tall, drove with gentle goad the slow and sleepy oxen.[1] A dog walked by his side.

Thus, in the middle of February, 1830, strode Abraham Lincoln toward his destiny. The Lincoln-Hanks-Hall clan were moving to Illinois. Of all in that company of migrants, he alone knew of the debate then raging in the Senate, and he alone heard of Webster's exposition of that philosophy which was to become his own political religion. Abraham had read Webster's speech published in the *Louisville Journal* at least two weeks before the Lincoln exodus from Indiana. But he had said nothing about it to any one of that dull, ignorant, indifferent company. Why should he? None of them could have understood, none cared to understand.

Perhaps Lincoln himself hardly realized the meaning of that conflict of reason and eloquence, coming from afar like sullen thunder sounding beyond the horizon. Yet he had heard it, that distant booming; and again, and soon, the unmistakable sound was to come to his ears, and thereafter again and yet again.

Thomas Lincoln, as we have seen, had sold everything he owned in Indiana; so had Dennis Hanks and so had 'Squire' Hall. The four oxen, the wagon, the goods in it and a horse,[2] represented all the property accumulated during their years in Indiana by the Lincolns, father and son, by Hanks, Hall and John D. Johnston, by Sarah Lincoln and her two daughters now

---

[1] Chapman's Narrative. Weik MSS.

[2] 'This is positively the first waggon he [Thomas Lincoln] ever owned.' *Ib.*

'He brought to Ill[inoi]s with him some stock cattle [the oxen], one Horse, 3 Beds and Beddings, 1 Bureau, 1 Table, 1 Clothes chest, 1 set of chairs, cooking utensils, clothings and so forth.' *Ib.*

married.[1] Among them they had little cash [2] save the 'shin-plasters,' notes of local Indiana banks, of such uncertain value as to be of small worth.

Northward, over the hills and through the forests of Indiana, they made their way to Vincennes, where they stopped for a while to see the wonders of that town, still the largest in the State. Crossing the Wabash above Vincennes, the crowded wagon with its motley escort crept over the 'black dismal prairie,' [3] still bleak and chill from departing winter. The grass which in summer time grew taller than a man, lay withered on the flat surface. No smoke from settler's cabin in the open cheered the landscape; and few if any such habitations greeted the travellers, even when they passed groves or clumps of trees.[4] At night they camped, wherever they chanced to be.

The frozen ground yielded a little to the sun and this thawing earth in which the wagon wheels sank caused the lumbering oxen to go more slowly even than their leisurely wont. There were no bridges and ice forming at night was a source of danger and delay; when fording streams the oxen 'would break through a square yard of thin ice at every step.' Once Lincoln's dog was left behind on the banks of a stream. Against protests from the other men who wanted to leave the distressed animal, Abraham

---

[1] Elizabeth to Dennis Hanks, June 9, 1821, and Matilda to 'Squire' Levi Hall, Sept. 13, 1826, son of Levi Hall and Nancy Hanks the aunt of Nancy Lincoln.

Dennis thus enumerates those who went to Illinois: 'There was 13 in the three familys Thos Lincoln wife Abe J. D. Johnston Squir Hall wife sun Dennis F. Hanks wife 3 Daughters one Sun John Hanks Sarah J Hanks Nancy M Hanks Hariet A. Hanks John Talbott Hanks.' Hanks to Herndon, April —, 1866. Wcik MSS. The eldest of these children could not have been more than eight years old.

Dennis includes John Hanks, thus making the number fourteen, which would indicate that John had probably joined the party on the road and accompanied the movers back to the place he had chosen for them in Illinois.

[2] Hanks says that he had some money. Hanks to Herndon, March 7, 1866. Such money as Thomas Lincoln had came from the sale to Gentry of Lincoln's eighty-acre farm and the sale of his hogs, etc.

[3] Tillson, 69.

[4] From Canton, through Peoria and Ottawa to Chicago, a traveller in 1827 did not see a single white person except in those small towns (*Early Pioneers*, etc. *of Illinois*: Harvey Lee Ross, 36); and from Blooming Grove [Bloomington] to Lake Michigan there were no houses at all; *Good Old Times in McLean Co., Ills.*: E. Duis, 1–2. North-east and west of Galena the whole country was an uninhabited wilderness. *History of Illinois*: Thomas Ford, 102–3.

Travelling from Terre Haute to Sangamon River in 1823 a Methodist preacher went six days without seeing a human being or human habitation. Coffin, 92.

took off his shoes, waded the icy water, and carried the shivering pet across, the dog giving 'frantic leaps of joy' when on solid earth again.[1]

For more than two weeks the band continued their journey; and, finally, early in March reached the place which John Hanks had selected for them in Macon County on a bluff overlooking the Sangamon River, about eight miles southwest of Decatur. The spot was well wooded and the five men soon built a cabin in which, it would appear, the Lincoln, Hanks and Hall families, spent the spring, summer, and fall of 1830 and the bitter winter that followed. Fifteen acres were broken and Abraham helped cut trees and split rails to fence it.[2] This task finished, he did odd jobs for other settlers.

Then for months he is hid from our view, as if behind the thick white smother that, in the winter of 1830–31, concealed all Illinois from the sight of man. On Christmas day the snow began to fall over the whole State and kept falling steadily for most of the winter. Men not far from home when the storm began, making fast for shelter, were blinded and lost. For weeks nobody ventured from cabin refuge except for firewood near at hand.[3] Even in the woods the snow lay a foot deep on the earth, then two feet, three feet, four feet; on the prairie drifts mounted to fifteen feet, and where the snow was level 'the tops of corn shocks could just be seen.'[4] The cold was intense, often ten to twenty degrees below zero.[5] Cattle died; deer and turkey which had been numerous were nearly exterminated.[6] Of wild animals, only the wolves survived, and even they suffered for food. A slight rain fell and a thick crust formed six feet above the roads.[7] All winter the settlers confined in the snow-bound cabins had nothing to eat but boiled corn and pounded meal.[8] How the Lincolns fared in the crowded log hut during this desperate sea-

[1] Lincoln's account to Herndon. Herndon, i, 68 n.

[2] The exact location was on the N.E. quarter of the S.W. quarter of Sec. 28, Township 16, N., Range 1, E., in what is now Harristown Township. It lies about two and a half miles south and seven and a half miles west of Decatur, Macon County. Information from J. C. Thompson and Mrs. Inez J. Bender.

[3] Duis, 9–10, 178–9.

[4] *Pioneers of Menard and Mason Co.*: T. G. Onstot, 134; Duis, 10.

[5] Ross, 51.   [6] Duis, 9.   [7] Onstot, 21–35.   [8] Duis, 192.

son can only be imagined. No chronicle of them at that time exists.

With the coming of spring the whole land was covered with water.[1] Creeks and rivers overflowed and, for a time, rude boats were the only means of getting about. The fame of John Hanks as a skilled Mississippi flatboatman who had made several trips to New Orleans [2] had spread throughout the region round about, and had come to the ears of one Denton Offut, a brisk, imaginative little man, full of mercantile projects. Offut had also heard, it seems, of Lincoln's southern journey on the Mississippi. At any rate that active promoter communicated in some fashion with these river navigators and hired them for sixteen and twenty dollars a month,[3] to take a flatboat laden with provisions to New Orleans from the landing-place of a straggling village containing five hundred and seventy people [4] called Springfield, four miles from Sangamon River.

So, taking John D. Johnston with them, John Hanks and Lincoln went in a canoe,[5] down the river from Decatur, to the place from which the expedition was to start. Upon their arrival no boat awaited them. Having failed to get one Offut set them to work on making a craft. On government land some distance above the mouth of Spring Creek the three men cut and hewed timber and floated it down to Sangamo Town, seven miles northwest of Springfield. At a nearby mill planks were sawn and finally the boat, eighty feet long and eighteen feet wide, was constructed.[6]

The work took six weeks, during which time the men camped in a shanty, hastily thrown together on the river bank. Abraham did the cooking; [7] but sometimes, 'when he felt like it,' he

[1] Duis, 10.   [2] Ib.

[3] Hanks had made a number of voyages to New Orleans. *Decatur* (Ill.) *Republican*, July 13, 1890; and John Hanks to Herndon, June 13, 1865. Weik MSS.

[4] *Settlement of Illinois:* William Vipond Pooley, 325. Seven years earlier a Methodist preacher described Springfield as 'a little cluster of cabins . . . all "squatters" on government land.' Coffin, 94.

[5] John Hanks to Herndon, June 13, 1865. Weik MSS. Canoes in Illinois at that time were made by hollowing out and shaping logs from cottonwood trees. They were much used to carry grain, supplies, and even hogs, as well as for travel. Harvey Lee Ross, 2.

[6] John Hanks to Herndon, June 13, 1865; John Hanks's statement. Weik MSS.

[7] *Ib.*

went to the cabin of Caleb Carman who lived not far away, for his own noonday meal. At first Carman thought Lincoln 'a Green horn tho after half hours Conversation with him I found Him no Green Horn.' For the first time since learning to read Lincoln was without a book, and at night he joined the others at cards, the game being seven-up, which he played uncommonly well. Clad in light blue jeans coat, very short, and trousers also short, and wearing a broad brimmed hat and low shoes, he attracted attention by his stature and sparkling humor.[1]

At work or play, he talked, told stories, perpetrated jokes; quoted poetry and declaimed fragments of orations learned from books in Indiana or from newspapers, all to the astonishment of bystanders and the delight and pride of Hanks and Johnston. Abraham discussed politics, too, with Caleb Carman and others, showing remarkable familiarity with that confused but engaging subject.[2] Finally Offut's vessel was finished and, on May 1, loaded with bacon, corn, and hogs, the southward journey began, with the owner in charge and Hanks, Lincoln and Johnston doing all the work.[3] Some miles on their way, the boat stranded on a mill-dam at the foot of the river bluff on which stood a few log cabins. The place was called New Salem.

Everybody in the hamlet came down to the river to see the trouble. Another boat was borrowed and part of the cargo transferred. Lincoln bored a hole in the end of Offut's craft through which the water in the boat ran out when the lower end was lifted [4] — an inventive feat which heightened Offut's growing admiration of his talents. At last the dam was passed, the provisions reloaded and the voyage continued. Throughout the incident Abraham was conspicuous because of his great height, his long legs wading about in the river accentuating his stature.

Only one thing of note happened on the journey to New Orleans. Five miles below New Salem lived 'Squire' Russell B. Godbey, from whom Offut bought several hogs which were very wild and refused to be driven onto the flatboat.[5] Somebody hit

---

[1] Carman's statement; Caleb Carman to Herndon, Nov. 30, 1866. Weik MSS.

[2] *Ib.*　　[3] John Hanks to Herndon, June 13, 1865. Weik MSS.　　[4] *Ib.*

[5] *Lincoln and New Salem*, 19. This is a carefully prepared pamphlet compiled and published by the Old Salem Lincoln League of Petersburg, Ill.

Coleman Smoot says that the hogs were bought from Henry Onstot, who owned a distillery. Smoot to Herndon, May 7, 1866. Weik MSS.

upon the expedient of sewing up the eyes of the swine and thus getting them on board. The eyelids of the pigs were stitched, but it is not certain whether the device produced the desired result. In the various accounts of witnesses to this incident, given more than thirty-five years afterward, there is irreconcilable confusion as to the part Lincoln took. One says that Lincoln suggested sewing up the eyes of the hogs; [1] another that he refused to wield the needle but held the pigs while the sewing was done; [2] still another that a farm hand near by offered to sew the eyelids if Lincoln would plough for him during the operation. [3] His love of animals, however, makes it improbable that Abraham took part in the brutality.

His second river trip to New Orleans, made when he was twenty-one years of age, was like the first, except that there was no attack by negroes. Thirty years later, at a political convention, John Hanks recalled that Lincoln and his companions went to the slave market and saw a handsome mulatto girl sold at auction; whereupon, said Hanks, 'the iron entered his soul' and he swore that, if ever he got a chance, he would hit slavery and 'hit it hard.' Hanks, however, does not make mention of this circumstance in his signed statement, [4] nor, except to Herndon, did Lincoln himself ever speak of it publicly or privately. Two decades were to pass before Lincoln showed much if any concern about slavery. Never the apostle of a cause, he was to become the perfect interpreter of public thought and feeling and so the instrument of events.

Offut's business transacted, the party came up the Mississippi on a steamboat, as Lincoln and Allen Gentry had done

---

[1] In *Lincoln and New Salem*, 19, it is stated that 'local tradition has it,' that Lincoln suggested the sewing of the hogs' eyes. R. D. Miller in his *History of Menard Co.*, 204, says the same thing.

[2] John Hanks to Herndon, June 13, 1865. 'Abe said I can't sew the eyes up. He held the heads of [the] hogs whilst Offutt did sew up their eyes.'

[3] Smoot to Herndon, May 7, 1866. Weik MSS. The simpler method of tying the legs of the hogs seems to have been overlooked, not to speak of the hogs already on the boat.

[4] John Hanks could not write and signed by making his mark.

In his Autobiography (1860) Lincoln says: 'Hanks had not gone to New Orleans, but having a family, and being likely to be detained from home longer than at first expected, had turned back from St. Louis.' *Works*, VI, 30.

three years before.[1] Lincoln had planned to stay in the south
and cut wood, but Hanks and Johnston fell ill and he returned
with them.[2] From St. Louis, where Johnston remained for a
time, Lincoln and Hanks walked to Edwardsville, whence Lincoln went to visit his father in Coles County.[3] Offut, captivated
by his tall, sensible, fun-making boatman, had engaged Lincoln
to help him keep a store which he planned to open at New
Salem as soon as he could buy and transport a stock of groceries
and dry goods.

For New Salem, then, Lincoln started in late July, 1831,[4] after
saying good-bye to his father and step-mother whom he was not
again to see for many a long year. Across the prairies he made
his way, his head and shoulders showing above the tall grass
which hid from view horses, cattle and men of average height.[5]
Only in the woods along watercourses had settlers built cabins
and the interminable open stretches were still practically unbroken.[6] He was now twenty-two years of age, and free to do as
he liked.

When he reached New Salem, a hamlet of fifteen log cabins,[7]
an election was about to be held.[8] Offut had not appeared, there

---

[1] John Hanks to Herndon, June 13, 1865. Weik MSS.

[2] J. R. Herndon to Herndon, May 28, 1865. Weik MSS.

[3] Thomas and Sarah Lincoln moved three times in less than two years: first from
Macon County to Buck Grove in Coles County in 1831, where they remained one year;
next to Muddy Point in the same county, staying at that place but a few months;
and finally to Goose Nest Prairie, also in Coles, where they continued to live. Chapman's Narrative. Weik MSS.

William G. Greene who in 1840, nine years later, stopped at the Lincoln cabin on
Goose Nest Prairie, says that it was 'the most wretched hovel he had encountered
in his journey. It was without a stable, outhouse of any kind, and not a shrub or
tree was in sight.' Whitney, I, 74–5.

[4] Lincoln and New Salem, 19.

[5] In the lowlands the grass was six to eight feet high. Duis, 1.

The prairie was most impressive; even the ocean did not excel it 'in beauty
and grandeur.' Travellers rose from their seats in wagons to see it. Brunson,
II, 31.

[6] There were only 157,447 people in the entire State when Lincoln made this trip.
Ford, 102.

In 1836, settlements were so scattered that the boundaries of the Methodist Conference were five hundred miles in length and seventy miles in breadth. Brunson, 31.

[7] R. B. Rutledge to Herndon, no date, but 1866. Weik MSS.

[8] The election was for Governor and members of Congress. The candidates for the

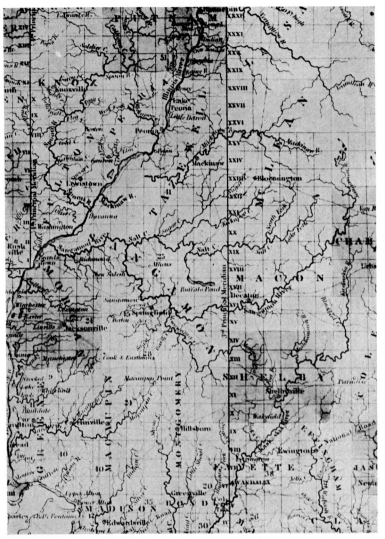

MAP OF SANGAMON AND NEIGHBORING COUNTIES IN ILLINOIS
Showing Springfield and (northwest of it) New Salem

was nothing for Lincoln to do and he went to a cabin where some men were gathered. There the voting was to be done. One of the election clerks, a young merchant, John McNamar, was ill; and the other, Mentor Graham, school teacher for the neighborhood, learning on inquiry that Lincoln could write, asked him to take McNamar's place. Lincoln did so,[1] and thus from the very beginning, took part in the politics of New Salem and Sangamon County.

As the tiresome hours wore on, broken only by voters announcing their preferences, which the clerks recorded, Lincoln brightened the time by telling stories, and thus from the outset, pleased and entertained those among whom he had come to live. Until Offut came, he did nothing but get acquainted,[2] boarding with the family of John M. Cameron,[3] who, with James Rutledge,[4] had built the mill and dam which had stopped Offut's flatboat three months earlier.[5] They were the founders of New Salem, too, important men in the little settlement.[6] Both belonged to the Cumberland Presbyterian Church and Cameron sometimes varied his milling and farming by preaching.[7] While still awaiting Offut, Lincoln earned a small sum from Dr. Nelson, by piloting from New Salem to Beardstown a raft upon which were the Doctor, his family, and belongings.[8]

Finally Offut arrived with his merchandise and opened his store in a small log house on a lot costing ten dollars, situated at the edge of the bluff just above the mill.[9] Lincoln proved himself a good clerk and swiftly grew in his employer's already inflated regard. Garrulous, boastful, restless, a 'wild, harumscarum kind of a man,' as New Salem folk termed him,[10] Offut

governorship were John Reynolds and William Kinney, both Democrats and strong Jackson men. Ford, 103.

[1] *Lincoln and New Salem*, 19, 20.   [2] *Ib.*, 19.

[3] R. B. Rutledge to Herndon, no date, but 1866. Weik MSS.

[4] Rutledge was born in South Carolina, May 11, 1781. *Ib.* Also 'Memoirs of the Rutledge family of New Salem:' J. E. Hamand, MS., 5.

[5] Statement of Mentor Graham, no date, but in 1866. Weik MSS.

[6] R. B. Rutledge to Herndon, no date, but 1866. Weik MSS.

[7] John McNamar to Herndon, June 4, 1866. Weik MSS.; Hamand, 2.

[8] *Lincoln and New Salem*, 21.

[9] Rutledge to Herndon, no date, but 1866. Weik MSS.

[10] James Short to Herndon, July 7, 1865. Weik MSS.

was forever bragging about the superiority of his assistant, physical as well as mental. But fate spoke by the wagging tongue of the strutting little merchant. A provoking challenge from him, brought about an incident which gave Lincoln a very human force that helped decisively to lift him into his political career.

Less than three miles [1] from New Salem was a grove, named after John Clary,[2] the first settler to build a cabin among its trees. Clary's sons and those of other farmers in the settlement, some twenty-five or more in number, were the best fighters in all that part of Sangamon County; indeed there was no 'harder set' in the entire State and they took part in all the 'rowdyism or revelry in a circuit of twenty miles.' No band of young roughs could cope with the 'Clary Grove Boys,' as the youthful warriors from the Clary settlement were called. Between them and 'the River timber boys' a feud existed [3] which seemingly was ended by the prowess of the Clary battlers. Led by a stalwart, pugnacious youth, Jack Armstrong, they could drink more whisky, swear more lustily, wrestle better, and fight harder than those from Sand Ridge, Indian Point, Concord, or any other group that gathered at New Salem, where everybody came on Saturdays to trade, gossip, wrestle, raffle, pitch horseshoes, run races, get drunk, maul one another with their fists, and indulge, generally, in frontier happiness,[4] as a relief from the week's monotonous drudgery on the raw and difficult farms.

With all their physical exuberance and prankish deviltry the Clary Grove Boys had fine elements of character. They were generous, sympathetic, frank, truthful, honest. Physical courage and strength were their ideals of masculine perfection; but they were as loyal to a friend as they were implacable to an enemy, and for the helpless and weak they were considerate and protective. They were hero worshippers, as untamed human

---

[1] Royal A. Clary's statement. Weik MSS.

[2] *Lincoln and New Salem*, 13. 　　　 [3] Miller, 208.

[4] Onstot, 53, 72, 132. An example of these curious and senseless fights is given by Onstot, whose book is largely his personal recollections. One Saturday, when the young men had mounted their horses to leave the village for their homes, one of them said to another, 'I can tear your hide,' whereupon all dismounted and the two fought heartily. There were no rules, kicking, biting, gouging being practised as well as striking with the fist. *Ib.*, 71–2.

beings usually are — the type of men that conquerors have used to fashion invincible armies and politicians to shape formidable followings.[1]

On a Saturday gala day, loudly proclaiming the manly prowess of his clerk, Offut offered to bet as much as five dollars [2] that Lincoln could throw anybody who would wrestle with him. John Clary's brother, William, who, for the moment, was running another 'store' in New Salem,[3] took the bet and produced as his champion Jack Armstrong. Jack had thrown or whipped every man who had wrestled or fought with him and was considered 'the best fighter' in all the countryside.[4] The contest was a notable affair, everybody attended, and bets of jack-knives, whisky, and even money were as numerous as the onlookers.[5]

Three or four accounts of the wrestling match between him and Lincoln agree only that it ended in such fashion as to win the friendship of Armstrong and the allegiance of his band. Probably the most accurate story of what took place is that of Rowan Herndon, an eye-witness, who says that after striving a long time without either man prevailing, Lincoln said: 'Jack, let's quit. I cant throw you — you cant throw me.' [6] Armstrong agreed and the matter was ended in fun. This, indeed, was but natural; for, as one of the band declared, Lincoln's good humor, wit, and flashing but friendly repartee, had already drawn 'him into our notice.' [7] Whatever happened, the Clary Grove Boys and their leader became, from that moment, warm friends of Lincoln and their friendship grew more ardent as time passed.[8]

[1] Herndon, i, 82. And see especially *Lincoln and New Salem*, 25–6. The analysis of the character of the Clary Grove Boys in this brochure is made from first-hand information obtained on the ground where these vigorous young men lived. The description of them in Nicolay and Hay (i, 79–80) as merely brutal creatures is pure imagination.

[2] Short to Herndon, July 7, 1865. Weik MSS.

[3] *Lincoln and New Salem*, 13. Clary's store was in reality a saloon and was about thirty steps from Offut's store. *Ib.*, 23.

[4] Rutledge to Herndon, no date, but 1866. Weik MSS.

[5] *Lincoln and New Salem*, 23.

[6] Henry McHenry's statement, Oct. 10, 1866. Weik MSS.

[7] Clary's statement. Weik MSS.

[8] Rutledge to Herndon, no date, but 1866. Weik MSS. Also *Lincoln and New Salem*, 25.

It would be hard to place too much emphasis upon the devotion to Lincoln of these hearty young ruffians. He 'so managed ... as to obtain complete control over them,' testifies Dr. Jason Duncan, one of the two physicians in New Salem, a warm friend of Lincoln, who watched his conduct with curious but cordial interest.[1] So great was his influence with his 'gang,' that at his command they would give up their most cherished project. One day Lincoln stopped them from rolling down hill in a barrel an old man who, for a gallon of whisky, had agreed to be thus handled.[2] Time and again he gave them proof that he was the strongest man New Salem ever had known; in wrestling bouts or the lifting of tremendous weights,[3] in running, jumping, and all manner of sport, Lincoln beat every one.[4] He was particularly fond of wrestling [5] and, in jumping contests, would wait till the last and then jump further than the best, bounding astonishing distances.[6] He was fearless, too, yet peaceable; and he sought, usually with success, to compose quarrels and stop fist fights.[7] Lincoln's interference with these combats was not rough, admonitory, self-assertive. 'Let's stop it,' he would say to an onlooker, and the two would separate the fighters, Lincoln laughing and joking while doing so. 'We never failed,' narrates one who thus helped him.[8] Yet sometimes, when a fight was arranged according to the custom of the time, Lincoln would act as 'second' for one of the antagonists.[9]

[1] Statement of Jason Duncan, no date. Weik MSS.

[2] Clary's statement. Short to Herndon, July 7, 1865, says Lincoln was not concerned in the affair. Weik MSS.

[3] 'I have seen him frequently take a barrel of whiskey by the chimes and lift it up to his face as if to drink out of the bung hole' — and he did this 'with the greatest ease.' R. B. Rutledge to Herndon, no date, but 1866. Weik MSS.

James Short says that he saw Lincoln lift '1000 pounds of shot by main strength.' Short to Herndon, July 7, 1865. Weik MSS.

J. Rowan Herndon testifies that Lincoln was 'By fare the stoutest man that i ever took hold of i was a mear child in his hands and i Considered myself as good a man as there was in the Cuntry untill he come about i saw him Lift Betwen 1000 and 1300 lbs of Rock waid in a Box.' J. R. Herndon to Herndon, May 28, 1865. Weik MSS.

[4] Clary's statement. Weik MSS.

[5] N. W. Branson to Herndon, Aug. 3, 1865. Weik MSS.

[6] Duncan's statement. Weik MSS.

[7] Ib. Also J. R. Herndon to Herndon, Aug. 6, 1865. Weik MSS.

[8] Russell B. Godbey's statement. Weik MSS.

[9] Such fights 'were conducted with as much ceremony and punctiliousness as ever

Most astonishing to his militant admirers Lincoln could read, an accomplishment only of the elect beyond their world. Then, too, he was the best fun-maker they had ever met and kept them laughing at jokes and shouting over roaring tales, not too delicate or subtle for their understanding. Yet he was no 'hail-fellow-well-met,' never familiar, although not aloof, and always respected the opinions of others.[1] Stranger still: while the Clary Grove Boys drank prodigiously and swore crashingly, and while Lincoln neither swore nor drank, he did not rebuke his boisterous, rollicking, aggressive associates.

Above all, they found that Lincoln was scrupulously truthful, and honest to well-nigh painful exactitude. What he said could be depended upon absolutely; and Lincoln's name became a synonym for fair dealing. Indeed precise truthfulness and meticulous honesty were his most striking characteristics.[2] So just was he that, on the regular Saturday holidays, Lincoln always was agreed upon as judge of contests of every kind and his decision accepted without question.[3] Finally, and not least in the eyes of the Clary Grove Boys, he stood by his friends — and with force if force were necessary. Lincoln became their hero, as much beloved as he was admired.

Presently Offut enlarged his enterprises by renting the mill on the river below his store;[4] and Lincoln ran from store to mill. His principal work at the mill was to unload, measure, and settle for sacks of grain brought in by farmers.[5] Offut also re-

graced the duelling ground.' A notable fight of this kind was that between Henry Clark and Ben Wilcox, in which Lincoln acted as second for Clark who was badly whipped. The seconds took the combatants to the river to wash and help dress them. Wilcox's second, who was a very small man said: 'Well Abe, my man has whipped yours, and I can whip you.' Lincoln agreed, provided the other would 'chalk out his size on Mr. Lincoln's person, and every blow struck outside of that mark should be counted [as a] foul.' Thereupon everybody burst into laughter and the matter ended in boisterous good humor. Rutledge to Herndon, no date, but 1866. Weik MSS. And see *Lincoln and New Salem*, 28.

[1] Duncan's statement. Weik MSS.   [2] *Ib.*

[3] Rutledge's statement. Weik MSS. Also Onstot, 54. One of these sports, 'gander pulling,' was particularly brutal. A live gander was hung by the legs from the limb of a tree, the contestants riding at utmost speed beneath the bird and snatching at its greased head. The rider who succeeded in pulling off the head, won the 'match.' *Ib.*, 53.

[4] *Lincoln and New Salem*, 22.

[5] Duncan's statement. Weik MSS. The mill was a saw-mill as well as grist-mill and supplied the vicinity with meal, flour and lumber. R. B. Rutledge's statement.

solved to navigate the Sangamon. The fact that the river was frozen in winter and shallow in summer troubled him not at all. He would put runners under the boat for ice and rollers in dry seasons; [1] and, with Lincoln in charge, 'By thunder! she'd have to go!' [2]

But the promoter's business soon languished and finally stopped altogether — 'petered out,' as Lincoln put it, and the little man suddenly disappeared.[3] Early in 1832, then, Lincoln found himself without a job or any means of earning a livelihood, for no work offered. He planned another trip to New Orleans and spent the winter preparing timber for a flatboat; [4] but a diversion more to his liking was presented to him. The extreme honesty of Offut's clerk had already won for him the appellation of 'Honest Abe,' [5] the political value of which was evident and basic. It was 'the height of ambition,' relates an Illinois politician of the period, of all aspiring men 'to get to the legislature.' [6] Lincoln was yearning for the distinction, and told Rowan Herndon that if he had been in New Salem instead of on Offut's flatboat trip to New Orleans, he would have run for the Legislature at that time.[7] Members of the General Assembly were to be elected in mid-summer, and Lincoln determined to become a candidate.[8]

The little community, and, indeed, all Illinois then seethed with politics. Political parties, as that term is now understood, did not exist; and while, roughly speaking, men were called Republicans or Democrats, such political alignments as existed were rather by groups attached to leaders. There were Jackson men and Clay men and followers of other conspicuous personages. In Illinois there were factions, rather than parties. No formal nominations of candidates were made and those who wished to stand for office merely announced their candidacies with a statement of the things they advocated; although, before

---

[1] Smoot to Herndon, May 7, 1866. Weik MSS.   [2] Herndon, I, 74.

[3] Short to Herndon, July 7, 1865. Weik MSS. Also *Lincoln and New Salem*, 34, 38.

[4] J. R. Herndon to Herndon, May 28, 1865. Weik MSS.

[5] *Lincoln and New Salem*, 35–6.

[6] Ford, 103.   [7] J. R. Herndon to Herndon, May 28, 1865. Weik MSS.

[8] It has been said that friends urged Lincoln to run, but no evidence of this has been discovered.

announcement, the most prudent office-seekers always consulted a caucus of friends.[1]

Local and state campaigns were almost wholly personal — visiting voters and their families, forming friendships, sometimes making speeches. Candidates ran on local hobbies.[2] Voting was influenced, well-nigh exclusively, by personal motives; and success at elections depended almost wholly upon individual friendships the candidate had made.[3] However, attachment to great national figures, such as Jackson or Clay, was a background from which local and state candidates had to work. Illinois was, at that time, overwhelmingly and combatively for Jackson and in Sangamon County the President was then strong,[4] his warfare on the Bank of the United States having brought to his standard most poor people and those of only moderate means.[5] Bold was the office-seeker who did not declare allegiance to Jackson.[6]

But Lincoln was a Clay man and said so; and at the Presidential election in November his first vote for President was cast for his hero, Henry Clay.[7] He was not offensive about his partiality for the Kentucky statesman, however, nor even aggressive. In friendly fashion he merely told his friends of his views. Still, since Clay was only second to Jackson in popularity among the people of Illinois,[8] he did not lose much by his preference for the great leader. Such were his situation and attitude when, on March 9, 1832, Lincoln issued an 'address to the people of Sangamon County' in support of his candidacy for the legislature, formally announced in the address. It was his first public utterance and he had toiled over it painfully, John McNamar

---

[1] Ford, 55, 201.   [2] McNamar to Herndon, June 4, 1866. Weik MSS.

[3] Ford, 88-9.

[4] Duncan's statement. Weik MSS.; *Lincoln and New Salem*, 41-2.

[5] Ford, 200. Ford says that all who were opposed to wealth rallied to Jackson.

[6] *Ib.*, 103. For a detailed yet condensed treatment of politics in Illinois from 1830 to 1834, see *The Frontier State*, 1818-1848: Theodore Calvin Pease, 136-49.

[7] Duncan's statement. Weik MSS. Lincoln was 'the Great admirer of Henry Clay.' J. R. Herndon to Herndon, Aug. 6, 1865. Weik MSS.

[8] *My Own Times:* Gov. John Reynolds, 161. Clay 'stood extremely well with the masses. He was the second choice of the State, and was my second choice also.'
   Although a Jackson champion, Gov. Reynolds was an enthusiastic admirer of Clay whom he calls the great leader of the Whig party. *Ib.*, 292.

the merchant,[1] Mentor Graham the school teacher and perhaps other friends, helping him.

The address was long, for Lincoln had not yet learned the art of condensation of which, in time, he was to become the master. 'In accordance with an established custom and the principles of true Republicanism,' he pompously says, it is his 'duty' to tell the people what he thinks of local affairs. No controversy for Abraham Lincoln over national questions! Most people were against him on those matters; so why arouse antagonism and lose votes unnecessarily!

But he is for internal improvements — the 'poorest and most thinly populated countries' needed 'good roads [and] navigable streams.' 'No person will deny' that. Who can object to railroads and canals — 'provided they cost nothing.' Paying for them is the rub. However Sangamon County must have a railroad and Lincoln wants it clearly understood that he emphatically favors the newly agitated project of a railroad from the Illinois River through Jacksonville to Springfield — but not now.

Think of the cost, $290,000! It is 'heart-appalling'! Better improve the Sangamon. It can be made navigable six months at least every year for vessels of from twenty-five to thirty tons and others of 'much greater burden a part of the time.' Lincoln knows what he is talking about, he says, having given 'particular attention' to the subject; and he reminds voters of his flatboat and other experiences on the Sangamon.

Lenders of money had been and were charging excessive interest; Lincoln is for a law fixing rates on loans. He denounces usury — that 'baneful and corroding system' by which what amounted to a 'direct tax' is laid on 'each county for the benefit of a few individuals only.' It can be stopped 'without materially injuring any class of people;' for, of course, 'in cases of extreme necessity, there could always be means found to cheat the law.'

Lincoln is strong for education, too, the 'most important' subject of all. Indeed it is 'vital' that everybody shall be able

---

[1] 'I corrected at his request some of the Grammatical errors in his ferst addres to the voters of Sangamon Co. his principal Hoby being the navigation of the Sangamon river.' McNamar to Geo. U. Miles, May 5, 1866. Weik MSS.

'to read the histories of his own and other countries, by which he may duly appreciate the value of our free institutions, . . . to say nothing of . . . all being able to read the Scriptures, and other works both of a religious and moral nature.' Still, Lincoln will not presume 'to dictate any plan or system' of education; but he is for education generally, for will it not advance 'morality, sobriety, enterprise, and industry?'

Then there are defects in existing laws. 'Many respectable men have suggested' that several statutes 'require alterations.' But Lincoln reminds voters that he had not first suggested the matter; that had been done by others. It is likely that 'the framers of those laws were wiser than myself' and, therefore, he will not lead an assault upon them; but if they 'are first attacked by others . . . I should feel it both a privilege and a duty to take that stand which, in my view, might tend most to the advancement of justice.' He is hesitant as to particular reforms, but bold for 'justice' as a general proposition.

Lincoln concludes by apologizing for having been 'more presuming than becomes me . . . considering the great degree of modesty which should always attend youth.' Only because he must disclose his mind fully has he been so specific in his address. 'I have spoken as I have thought.' True he may be wrong, but since 'it is better only sometimes to be right than at all times to be wrong,' he will abandon his opinions as soon as he finds them 'to be erroneous.'

The address ends by an appeal to the sympathy of the community; Lincoln's greatest ambition, he says, is 'that of being truly esteemed by my fellow-men, by rendering myself worthy of their esteem.' He is young; many do not know him. 'I was born, and have ever remained, in the most humble walks of life. I have no wealthy or popular relations or friends to recommend me. . . . My case is thrown exclusively upon the independent voters of the country' and, if they elect him, he will work hard to repay them. 'But, if the good people in their wisdom shall see fit to keep me in the background, I have been too familiar with disappointments to be very much chagrined.' [1]

Thus, at twenty-three years of age and within seven months

[1] *Works*, i, 1–9.

of his coming to New Salem, we find Lincoln a candidate for office; and we see in the vagueness and dexterity of his first public utterance the characteristics of the natural politician, a type of which he was to become, excepting only Jefferson, the supreme example. We observe, too, that cleverness and caution which distinguished his every public manœuver, and discomfited the most skilled antagonists.

No sooner was Lincoln's appeal to the voters issued, than two incidents occurred which greatly strengthened him politically. For three years the navigation of the Sangamon had been the one great subject of local discussion. Captain Vincent Bogue of Springfield firmly believed that a steamboat could ascend the river as far as that town. In January, 1832, he wrote from Cincinnati that, as soon as the ice broke up, he would bring such a vessel from there to Springfield. In due course a glowing advertisement appeared in the *Sangamo Journal* announcing the imminent departure from the Ohio city of 'the splendid, upper-cabin steamer *Talisman*.' Prodigious was the sensation. At last the optimists were to be vindicated, the scoffers put to rout.

The boat reached Beardstown where, as requested by Captain Bogue in his first announcement, it was met by several men, Lincoln among them, equipped with poles and long-handled axes to cut and push away overhanging branches and other obstructions. Lincoln took charge, and brought this craft of hope and promise triumphantly to the landing place near Springfield.[1] As the vessel moved upstream, several boys on horseback kept pace with it on shore, among them one of twelve, whose admiration of the bold and skilful navigator was intense, and years later was to develop into devotion and well-nigh worship. Thus William H. Herndon first saw Lincoln,[2] into whose life and career his own was to be so intimately woven.

The arrival of the *Talisman* set all Springfield frantic with joy. At the courthouse the steamboat Captain whom Bogue had employed — 'a vainly dressed fellow from the East'[3] — and his crew were given an ardent reception. There were dancing and festivity, whisky flowed, the gaudy commander of the *Talisman* and a woman who accompanied him as his wife, but was not,

[1] Bogue's Mill. Herndon, i, 88.   [2] *Ib.*, 87.   [3] *Ib.*, 88.

got drunk, the *Sangamo Journal* printed rhymed ecstasies.[1] Receding water warned the owner and his Captain that the return voyage must be made at once. Lincoln and Rowan Herndon were employed for forty dollars each to pilot the craft as far as Beardstown.[2] Four miles a day [3] the vessel crept down the Sangamon, the falling current barely floating her. At New Salem the mill dam had to be partly torn out, causing a night's delay. But all difficulties were overcome at last, and Lincoln safely brought the *Talisman* to Beardstown, from which place he walked back to New Salem,[4] the celebrity of the hour.[5]

Then followed an event still more advantageous to his political fortunes. Lincoln himself passed around his candidate's address in the form of a handbill, the favorite method of public appeal; [6] but before much campaigning could be done, everybody was startled by the news that Black Hawk and his braves were on the war-path, pillaging settlements, murdering settlers, and spreading terror along Rock River. The old Chieftain and his young men had returned to their ancestral lands which, by some sort of treaty, the government had acquired in 1804,[7] and which, after a stern show of military force by national and state troops in 1831 and a largess of corn, Black Hawk had agreed not to attempt to occupy again.[8]

Although a large number of soldiers and others of the regular army were on the ground soon after the Indians came, reinforce-

[1] Verses written by a lawyer, E. P. Oliphant, are printed in Herndon, i, 68, and frequently reprinted.

[2] J. R. Herndon to Herndon, June 11, 1865. Weik MSS.   [3] Herndon, i, 89.

[4] J. R. Herndon to Herndon, June 11, 1865.

[5] Out of this venture grew the first civil action against Lincoln in the Sangamon Circuit Court. With Nelson Alley he gave, October 30, 1832, a note for $104.87½, for the benefit of the creditors of V. A. Bogue. The exact nature of the transaction is not known, but Alley defaulted and in September, 1833, a default judgment was entered against Lincoln. The records show that he paid in full, March 17, 1834. *Litigant:* Townsend, 46–54. George Forquer was attorney for the plaintiff.

[6] Reynolds, 189.

[7] Black Hawk stoutly denied that the lands ever had been sold. McCall to father, June 17, 1831. *Letters from the Frontier:* George A. McCall, 230.

[8] General Atkinson in command of the National troops in 1831 gave Black Hawk 60,000 bushels of corn which then cost five cents the bushel; and some thought that it was to get another such subsidy, that the old Chief again brought his warriors across the Mississippi. 'Early Times at Fort Winnebago:' Satterlee Clark, *Wis. Hist. Coll.*, viii, 312.

ments were thought necessary. Governor John Reynolds called
for volunteers from the militia of northwestern Illinois.[1] So
great was the fear of the Indians, that nearly all men of fighting
age responded. Candidates and those ambitious for political
advancement quickly seized the opportunity; and, one of them,
Thomas Ford, who later became Governor of the State, declares
in his frank *History of Illinois* that the Black Hawk War created
many political careers. 'Jack Falstaff never slew as many men in
buckram as each and every one of these Illinois politicians did,'
chronicles a politician of the time.[2]

Lincoln was a member of the militia to which all men between
the ages of eighteen and forty-five were, by law, compelled to
belong,[3] and had been made captain of the local company.[4] Out
of work, penniless, a candidate for office, he promptly volunteered for thirty days' service [5] against the 'British band,' as
Black Hawk and his warriors were universally called.[6] To
voters, however, Lincoln's prompt enlistment was an exhibition
of pure patriotism. In the language of the place and time, as
expressed by a comrade and friend, he 'volunteered to Serve his
Cuntry with the Ballance of the Patriotick Boys to Defend the
frontier sett[l]ers . . . from the Savages tomihack and skelping

[1] Reynolds, 224.

[2] 'Reminiscences of Early Chicago:' Wentworth, Fergus Hist. Series I, No. 8, 26.

[3] Act, Jan. 25, 1826; *Laws of Illinois*, 1826, 1–44. This law was comprehensive and
well drawn. It required the enrolment of 'all free male white inhabitants' of the age
stated; that each militiaman 'provide himself with a good musket, fusee or rifle, with
proper accoutrements;' and that commissioned officers 'shall be armed with a sword
and pair of pistols.'

If any officer or private refused to serve 'either by himself or a substitute,' he was
liable to be punished as a deserter and provision was made for drafting, exemptions,
and substitutes. Only persons physically unfit and those 'conscientiously scrupulous
of bearing arms' could be exempted in peace time by paying one dollar and fifty cents
annually (reduced to seventy-five cents in 1830, *Laws*, 96); and in case of invasion, etc.,
only by furnishing a substitute.

Captains were elected by the men after five days' notice. The Sangamon County
militia belonged to the first division of the State forces.

[4] *Lincoln and New Salem*, 38.

[5] Clary's statement. Weik MSS.

[6] George A. McCall to his father, June 16, 1831. McCall, 225. Black Hawk's name
was Mucatah Muhicatah. He was a Chief of the Sacs, born about 1767, and was a
staunch adherent of the British, for whom he fought in the War of 1812, and who
always befriended him. Duis, 97–8.

For a good account of the Black Hawk War from the settlers' point of view, see
Ford, 109, *et seq.*

Knife.'[1] With others, Lincoln was enrolled, April 21, 1832, at Richland,[2] a village not far from New Salem. Among those who enlisted were his friends from Clary's Grove, who brought about Lincoln's election as captain of his company,[3] which, as William Miller, another soldier in that conflict testifies, 'was the hardest set of men he ever saw.'[4] One of Lincoln's comrades, J. R. Herndon, says that they made him captain 'By a unamis [unanimous] vote.'[5] Jack Armstrong was made sergeant[6] and Bill Kirkpatrick quartermaster.[7]

At Beardstown, where all troops met, Lincoln's company was attached to a mounted command.[8] Little of note occurred during the month for which the men had enlisted. There was some uncomfortable marching and, at one time, food was scarce for three or four days. While everybody, Lincoln most of all, was eager to meet the enemy,[9] they never came in sight of the Indians, although they reached the place of Stillman's defeat soon after that disaster.[10]

[1] J. R. Herndon to Herndon, May 28, 1865. Weik MSS.

[2] Muster Roll, Records War Dept. It would seem that the men were compelled to go. Roil [Royal] A. Clary says that he was 'drafted' twice (Clary's statement. Weik MSS.), and T. H. Onstot records that his father, Henry Onstot, hired a substitute, John Hillis, for thirty dollars and a rifle. Onstot, 17.

[3] *Lincoln and New Salem*, 38–40.

[4] B. F. Irwin to Herndon, Sept. 22, 1866. Weik MSS.

[5] J. R. Herndon to Herndon, May 28, 1865. Weik MSS.

[6] *Lincoln and New Salem*, 40.   [7] Clary's statement. Weik MSS.

[8] 'We were all mounted men.' *Ib.* Also Muster Roll, Records War Dept.

[9] B. F. Irwin to Herndon, Sept. 22, 1866. Weik MSS. Irwin says that Lincoln wanted to get into a fight with the Indians just to see how his company 'would meet Powder and Lead.'

[10] Clary's statement. Weik MSS.

One private in Lincoln's company relates that, when in camp at the mouth of Henderson River on the Mississippi, the captain was arrested and his sword taken from him for a day, because he had violated an order not to discharge any firearm within fifty steps of the camp; and that, at another time, when on Rock River, Lincoln was again arrested and made to carry a wooden sword for two days, as punishment for his company's having gotten drunk on liquor stolen from the officers and being unable to march. D. H. Pantier to Herndon, July 21, 1865. Weik MSS.

These tales are improbable, since no mention is made of the incidents by any other soldier or by any officer in the army, or by Lincoln himself. Pantier told these stories nearly thirty years afterwards. He admits, however, that Lincoln knew nothing of the theft of the wine, whisky, and brandy, or of the carousal that followed.

Another of Lincoln's men declares that an Indian came into camp or was captured and that 'our boys thought he was a spy,' and were about to shoot him; but that Lincoln 'jumped between our men and the Indian' and saved him. When somebody

William Cullen Bryant, then thirty-eight years of age, editor of the *New York Evening Post*, was making a tour of Illinois at that time, saw the troops, and thus describes them: 'They were a hard-looking set of men, unkempt and unshaved, wearing shirts of dark calico, and sometimes calico capotes;' and he adds that 'some of the settlers complained that they [the soldiers] made war upon the pigs and chickens.' The author of 'Thanatopsis' met Captain Lincoln, 'a raw youth, in whose quaint and pleasant talk' the poet and editor was greatly interested.[1]

When not on the march, the men lolled in the shade of trees by day, or gathered around camp fires at night, singing, telling stories, playing cards, cutting pranks.[2] Lincoln told more and better stories than anybody,[3] often spinning yarns 'until the lights were ordered out.'[4] Indeed, daily events supplied him with materials for new stories which he used throughout his career.[5] Then, too, the genial Captain jumped, ran, boxed, and wrestled better than any man in the expedition.[6] At Beardstown, however, where the troops gathered immediately after enlistment, Lorenzo D. Thompson of St. Clair County, in a wrestling bout, threw Lincoln at the first test; but Lincoln then threw Thompson twice.[7] When the thirty days were up, Lincoln was easily the most popular man in the whole army.[8]

Governor Reynolds, who was with the troops when the term of enlistment of Lincoln's company expired,[9] appealed to the

---

murmured, thinking Lincoln cowardly, he said: 'If any one doubts my courage Let him try it.' Clary's statement. Weik MSS.

This, too, may be imaginary, nobody else who was present having ever said anything about such a dramatic circumstance.

[1] *Prose Writings of William Cullen Bryant*, edited by Parke Godwin, II, 20.

[2] George M. Harrison (of Lincoln's company) to Herndon, Dec. 20, 1866; Clary's statement. Weik MSS.

[3] J. R. Herndon to Herndon, May 28, 1865. Weik MSS.

[4] Duis, 123.

[5] 'Mr. Lincoln had an inexhaustible supply of stories based upon his experiences in this war.' Wentworth, 27.

[6] J. R. Herndon to Herndon, May 28, 1865. Weik MSS.

[7] Rutledge to Herndon, no date, but 1866. Weik MSS.

[8] Harrison to Herndon, Dec. 20, 1866; J. R. Herndon to same, May 28, 1865. Weik MSS. A member of his company testifies that he 'Loved all of them as they Loved him.' *Ib.* 'He was decidedly the most popular man in the army.' Duis, 123.

[9] General McCall, then a captain in the Regular Army, thus describes the appearance

men to stay for twenty days more. Most of them went home,
but Lincoln and some others remained.[1] 'I was out of work and,
there being no danger of more fighting, I could do nothing
better than enlist again,' he explained many years afterward.[2]
So on May 27, 1832, we find him enrolled in the company of
Captain Elijah Iles[3] which was attached to a force called 'the
spy batallion.'[4] He was mustered in by a young Lieutenant of
the regular army, who nearly thirty years later was to be the
dramatic figure of the opening act of the Civil War, Robert
Anderson, 2nd Lieutenant of the 3rd U.S. Artillery. When his
twenty days were up Lincoln enlisted for the third time, June
16, in the company of Captain Jacob M. Early for thirty days
more.[5]

Although he saw no fighting Lincoln witnessed the results of
the skirmish at Kellogg's Grove, June 25, and helped bury five
men whom the Indians had scalped. 'I remember just how
those men looked as we rode up the little hill where their camp
was,' said he, when describing the incident long afterwards.
'The red light of the morning sun was streaming upon them as
they lay heads towards us on the ground. And every man had
a round, red spot on top of his head, about as big as a dollar
where the redskins had taken his scalp. It was frightful, but
it was grotesque, and the red sunlight seemed to paint everything all over. I remember that one man had on buckskin
breeches.'[6]

On July 16, 1832, Lincoln was mustered out[7] at Black River,

of Governor Reynolds at the front. General Gaines sent his aid, Captain McCall, to
invite the Governor to breakfast. McCall found Reynolds in a cart with leather
curtains: 'There, *Jupiter tonans!* there lay his linsey-woolsey Excellency, coiled upon
a truss of tarnished straw;' he declined breakfast because he had had 'chills and fever'
for three days. McCall to his father, July 1, 1831. McCall, 238.

[1] Clary's statement. Weik MSS. Also Muster Roll, Records War Dept.; and *Lincoln
and New Salem*, 40.

[2] Lincoln's statement to Herndon, Herndon, i, 100. Also see *Lincoln and New Salem*,
41.

[3] Muster Roll, Records War Dept.

[4] *History Black Hawk War:* Wakefield, 203, note 6; 207, note 5.

[5] Records War Dept. Early was in 1836 representative from Sangamon County in
the State Legislature.

[6] *Lincoln and New Salem*, 41.

[7] Muster Roll, Records War Dept. This Muster Roll is dated 'Black River.'

Wisconsin.[1] As his horse had been stolen the night before, he returned on foot and by canoe to New Salem.[2]

Thus Lincoln tided over three otherwise destitute months from April to July, 1832. At home once more, with cash in his pocket, he took up his candidacy, which had not suffered from his martial adventure. The boys who had returned several weeks before were his ardent champions. About the camp fires he had told them of his ambition and, as one of the men of his squad relates, 'the mess immediately pitched upon him as our standard-bearer, and he accepted.'

Dressed in his 'mixed jeans coat,' the 'clawhammer' tails of which were so short that he could not sit upon them, 'flax and tow-linen pantaloons and a straw hat' and wearing 'pot-metal boots,'[3] Lincoln went about soliciting votes. Frank and open in manner, always tactful and conciliatory, he avoided controversy and tried, successfully, to make people like him.[4] He made speeches whenever he could find a crowd; and the first of these is worthy of quotation as suggesting the method of the young politician before pioneer hearers and because of an incident at the time which got him more votes than any speech could possibly have secured.[5]

'The Speach hee made was at Paps Vill,' relates a hearer; 'thar was a large gathering thar on account of a sale of goods hee was the only candadate thar and was call on to make a Speach.'[6] Just before he began his first speech as a candidate, a fight broke out and soon became general, as usually was the case. One of his friends, Rowan Herndon, who had whipped Jesse Dodson, was set upon by Dodson's friends and was being badly mauled;

---

[1] Among other officers of the regular army who served in the Black Hawk War were Colonel Zachary Taylor, Lieutenant Albert Sidney Johnson, Lieutenant Jefferson Davis, and Lieutenant Robert Anderson; among the Illinois volunteers were E. D. Baker, John T. Stuart, and Lincoln. Duis, 121–3.

For a recent, accurate and condensed account of the Black Hawk War, see *The Frontier State*: Pease, 150–72.

[2] Harrison to Herndon, Dec. 20, 1866. Weik MSS. Also *Lincoln and New Salem*, 40.

[3] A. Y. Ellis to Herndon, June 5, 1866; Herndon, i, 104.

[4] Duncan's statement. Weik MSS.

[5] J. R. Herndon to Herndon, June 21, 1865. Weik MSS.

[6] James A. Herndon to Herndon, May 29, 1865; J. R. Herndon to same, May 28, 1865. Weik MSS.

Lincoln jumped down from the platform or wagon, and, seizing Herndon's principal assailant by neck and trouser seat, threw him 'twelve feet' — which, it appears, stopped the conflict.[1] Rowan Herndon's own statement is that he was attacked by 'a set of Ruffings and they atempted to shoe foul play he [Lincoln] piched in and Piched them out Like they ware Boys and told them his friend Could whip the whole of them one at a time that ended the fus.' [2]

Returning to the speaking place, Lincoln is said thus to have addressed the quieted gathering: 'Fellow Citizens, I presume you all know who I am — I am humble Abraham Lincoln. I have been solicited by many friends to become a candidate for the Legislature. My politics are short and sweet, like the old woman's dance. I am in favor of a national bank. I am in favor of the internal improvement system and a high protective tariff. These are my sentiments and political principles. If elected I shall be thankful; if not it will be all the same.' [3]

This was the only time, so far as recorded, that Lincoln made reference to national issues in his first political campaign. For the most part, he stuck to the advocacy of improving the Sangamon River. In the few days remaining before the election, he busily went from cabin to cabin, from one meeting place to another, making friends and delivering short speeches,[4] but, in order to offend nobody, never talking politics.[5] This, indeed, was the common practice of the time; candidates, says a participant in these early campaigns, usually 'agreed with all opinions, and promised everything.' [6] Lincoln's gift for anecdote was his favorite and most effective means of appeal. To a crowd at Island Grove, his address consisted largely of stories of a kind that drew the boys after him.[7] Whisky was plentiful at all meetings,[8] but Lincoln never indulged in it.

[1] J. R. Herndon to Herndon, May 28, and June 21, 1865; also James A. Herndon's statement, no date. Weik MSS.

[2] J. R. Herndon to Herndon, May 28, 1865. Weik MSS.

[3] As written from memory in 1865 by A. Y. Ellis who was present at the Pappsville meeting in 1832. Herndon, i, 104.

[4] J. R. Herndon to Herndon, May 28, 1865. Weik MSS.

[5] Onstot, 54.   [6] Ford, 202.

[7] A. Y. Ellis to Herndon: Herndon, i, 104. Ellis through 'modesty and veneration' refused to repeat these tales, although he remembered them well.   [8] Ross, 31–2.

Whenever they could, the Clary Grove Boys went with Lincoln, ready to fight anybody who criticised their chief.[1] At election time they were at the polls in New Salem eager to vote for Lincoln, whose local popularity was so great, however, that their combative support was neither needed nor displayed. So warm was the friendship for him that violent Democrats supported Lincoln, Clay man as he was, as ardently as they did Jackson himself.[2] Still, it was to the Clary Grove Boys that Lincoln owed his principal support.[3] At that time, voting was done by word of mouth, the voter speaking the name of the candidate he preferred. Of two hundred and eight preferences thus expressed at New Salem, all but three were for Lincoln.[4] In the county as a whole, however, he was beaten, although receiving a good vote, much larger indeed than several other candidates. But the period of his citizenship of Sangamon County was too brief to secure the acquaintance and reputation necessary for a successful candidacy for office. As will presently appear, this defect was speedily remedied.

The fires of political ambition had been lighted in Lincoln's breast, never to die out. Rather they had been fanned anew, for they had been burning long before. He disliked physical labor and wanted only to read and meet people. Work in a store gave him these opportunities. There were three stores in New Salem, one owned by Samuel Hill, the postmaster, who had, as silent partner, John McNamar, the most prudent and enterprising man of business in the whole community; another by Reuben Radford; the third by two brothers, James and Rowan Herndon, who opened their store in 1832.[5] But none of these trading places needed a clerk; for a time, Lincoln did nothing.

James Herndon 'didn't like' New Salem and promptly sold his share to William F. Berry;[6] and not long afterwards, Rowan

---

[1] *Lincoln and New Salem,* 41-2.

This was an election for Congress, with Joseph Duncan and Jonathan H. Pugh as candidates.

[2] Duncan's statement. Weik MSS. Squire Godbey was one such Democratic supporter of Lincoln. Godbey's statement. Weik MSS.

[3] *Lincoln and New Salem,* 27-8.   [4] Herndon, i, 105.

[5] *Lincoln and New Salem,* 43-5; statement of James A. Herndon, no date. Weik MSS.

[6] *Ib.*

Herndon, in whose cabin Lincoln was boarding, also wanted to quit the business. Herndon liked and trusted him, and sold his part of the store to his boarder [1] who gave a note for the purchase price; and thus was formed the partnership of Berry and Lincoln.[2] Lincoln hired a youth of eighteen, William G. Greene, who knew every person who came to New Salem, to help him in the store, William's principal duty being to tell his employer whether purchasers could safely be given credit.[3]

For some reason the Clary Grove Boys hated Reuben Radford, who appears to have defied them in such fashion as to arouse their spirit of destructive mischief. One day they came to his store in his absence, drank his whisky, and tumbled his goods about until the place seemed to be in ruins. Radford, in terror and disgust, impulsively offered to sell his stock to anybody who would pay him four hundred dollars for it. Young Greene who was standing by took Radford's offer, giving his note to the disconsolate merchant. For the same amount, Greene offered his bargain to Lincoln who accepted; but, finding upon making an inventory, that the goods were worth more, he insisted on paying his friend and assistant, two hundred and fifty dollars additional, giving Greene the note of Berry and Lincoln for the entire amount. James Rutledge, the tavern keeper, also had some merchandise and this, too, Berry and Lincoln bought.[4] Thus the new firm became the only competitor of Hill's store for the trade of the whole vicinity about New Salem.[5]

Whether Berry drank too much of the firm's whisky, or Lin-

---

[1] Statement of James A. Herndon, no date; J. R. Herndon to Herndon, May 28, 1865. Weik MSS.

[2] 'Durin that Summ[e]r J. R. H. and myself moove A Stack of Goods to Salam after Mr. Lincoln was beeting for office him and Wm Barry bought out our stock.' James A. Herndon to Herndon, May 29, 1865. Weik MSS.

[3] *Lincoln and New Salem*, 22.

[4] R. B. Rutledge to Herndon, no date, but 1866. Weik MSS.

[5] The goods sold in these New Salem stores included tea, coffee, sugar, salt, whisky, blue calico, brown muslin, cotton chain and straw hats, women's hats and the like. *Lincoln and New Salem*, 13.

The 'store' was a common grocery where whisky was sold by the drink. W. McNeely to Herndon, Nov. 12, 1866. Weik MSS. This was the understanding of McNeely's father who lived in or near New Salem at the time.

Most of the 'goods bought by Berry and Lincoln were liquors.' *Lincoln and New Salem*, 45. In most towns there were no drug stores, and medicines were kept by ordinary stores. *Pioneers:* Ross, 81.

coln was too negligent and generous in measurements, or too intent on reading, gossiping, and telling stories, the business did not prosper. In a few months they sold their groceries, dry goods, and liquors to two brothers of the name of Trent who gave Berry and Lincoln a note. Before the date of payment, Trent and Trent abandoned the store and fled the county. Then Berry died and Lincoln was left burdened with accumulated debts as the sole financial result of his business experience. Not for almost twenty years was he able to make full payment.[1]

Ever since he had come to New Salem, Lincoln had read the *Sangamo Journal* published at Springfield, the *National Intelligencer*, published at Washington, the *Missouri Republican*,[2] and the *Louisville Journal*,[3] which papers came to the post-office at the little hamlet on the Sangamon. Every Saturday, as he had done in Indiana,[4] he would read the news to all who wished to hear. Thus Lincoln kept posted on what was happening in State and Nation.

So it was that in the winter of 1832 Lincoln heard again the far-off tumult of that combat in which, eventually, he was to take the leading and decisive part. On November 24, 1832, the State Convention of South Carolina adopted the historic Ordinance of Nullification, which declared the Tariff Acts of 1828 and 1832 to be 'null, void and no law,' directed the State Legislature to provide for armed resistance, declaring that 'the people of South Carolina . . . will not submit to the application of force, on the part of the Federal Government, to reduce this state to obedience,' and that if force was employed South Carolina would withdraw from the Union and organize a 'separate government, and do all other acts and things which sovereign and independent States may of right do.'[5]

---

[1] J. R. Herndon to Herndon, May 28, 1865. Weik MSS. These debts aggregated $1100. *Lincoln and New Salem*, 52.

[2] Branson to Herndon, Aug. 3, 1865; Chapman's Narrative, Weik MSS. Chapman says that Lincoln was a 'warm admirer' of the *National Intelligencer*. It was the organ of the National Republican party and stood for 'vested rights and sober usages.' Reynolds, 288–9.

[3] J. R. Herndon to Herndon, Aug. 6, 1865. Weik MSS. J. R. Herndon says that he also read the *Congressional Debates* and *Acts of Congress*.

[4] J. R. Herndon to Herndon, May 28 and Aug. 6, 1865. Weik MSS.

[5] *Statutes at Large of South Carolina:* Thomas Cooper, I, 329–31.

The issues debated by Hayne and Webster two years before, were taking concrete, militant form. Governor John Reynolds was about to deliver his message to the Legislature of Illinois when the news of South Carolina's defiance came, and he added a paragraph denouncing 'nullification' which must be 'firmly and promptly resisted, and prostrated by public opinion. This happy Union ought, and, I hope in God, will be sustained at all hazards.' [1]

Six days later, December 10, 1832, came Jackson's Proclamation. Attributed to Edward Livingston, Secretary of State, it was and to this day remains one of the foremost of state papers; [2] and it was to be the model used by Lincoln twenty-eight years later, when composing his First Inaugural. All arguments that ever had or have since been advanced for national supremacy and against secession, were presented in Jackson's Proclamation, and stated, too, with a moderation and kindly appeal that added to their compelling power. Thus in his twenty-fourth year Lincoln was given a supreme example of the force of calm but strong method in public discussion, even on the gravest of subjects and in the most perilous of crises.

The newspapers read by Lincoln published in full South Carolina's Ordinance of Secession and Jackson's Proclamation. Indeed these papers had printed news of the secession movement before the Convention met. The *Sangamo Journal* reproduced letters of South Carolina Unionists against Nullification and, declaring editorially that the Union was in 'imminent danger,' called upon every 'good citizen to rally around the holy banner of our Constitution.' It praised Governor Reynolds for his stand, published a picturesque letter from a New York man in Charleston describing the thrilling scenes there — the Unionists were the 'respectable' people, the 'nullies are the rabble' — and news of the sending of troops and munitions to Fort Moultrie. The *Journal* printed extracts from the appeal of Edward Everett of Massachusetts, to preserve the bulwark of the Constitution, [3] and from Southern men and Northern papers on the 'worth of

[1] Reynolds, 269.

[2] *Messages and Papers of the Presidents:* Richardson, ii, 640–56.

[3] Nov. 17, 24, Dec. 8, 15, 1832. Everett's address was made in Charlestown, Mass.

the Union.' Editorially the paper declared that the only possible outcome, if nullification prevailed, was 'anarchy' and 'civil war.'

With the full Ordinance of Nullification the *Sangamo Journal* published [1] half a column from a correspondent at Charleston describing the Convention. The dramatic close of the address of that State was printed together with an editorial argument that if South Carolina seceded, Illinois could and would take from the national government her public lands. Then on December 30, appeared an 'Extra' edition of the Springfield paper with Jackson's Proclamation.

From the *Missouri Republican* Lincoln got both sides, for that paper printed extracts from journals which advocated as well as from those which opposed nullification. It published, also, two addresses of Governor Dunklin of Missouri, in support of South Carolina's action, and the inaugural address of Governor Hayne of that State. But the *Republican* contained many more speeches, articles and letters in maintenance of national authority — the great oration of Webster in Boston, part of the powerful message of Governor Marcy of New York, accounts of Union meetings all over the country, including the immense demonstration at Tammany Hall.[2] Editorially it again and again [3] denounced in words of fire the 'treasonable' conduct, 'traitorous designs,' and 'phrenzied violence' of the nullifiers, demanding that the Union 'be preserved at every hazard.' The *National Intelligencer* and *Louisville Journal* were even more emphatic and wrathful.

What effect all this had on the young politician, is unknown. Lincoln was silent then and for long afterward, although from the moment of South Carolina's action, Illinois like the rest of the country was deeply and increasingly stirred.[4] We know only that he read all that appeared in the papers taken at New Salem. The distant thunder, louder now, swelling from Charles-

---

[1] Dec. 22, 29, 1832.

[2] Dec. 4, 1832; Jan. 1, 8, 15, 29, 1833.

[3] Dec. 18, 25, 1832; Jan. 1, 8, 15, 22, 1833.

[4] Reynolds, 269. Gov. Reynolds says that Jackson's Proclamation was hailed by the people of Illinois as 'a kind of Godsend,' and the Legislature of the State formally approved it.

ton and the Nation's capital, and rolling across the mountains, forests and prairies, had reached him amid the log cabins on the bluffs of the Sangamon.

Out of business, loaded with debt and so depressed that his friends were much worried about him,[1] Lincoln was concerned with the immediate problem of making a livelihood. He would say nothing to cause bitterness in New Salem, whose citizens were not of one mind on South Carolina's action. One of these, the tavern keeper, James Rutledge, was a native of that State, and to the Rutledge inn Lincoln went to board in the spring of 1833,[2] his friend Rowan Herndon, at whose cabin he had been living, having moved to a farm. Before the close of the year, however, Rutledge gave up the inn which he had built in 1830, and the tavern was taken by Henry Onstot,[3] who also had a cooper shop.

To get money to pay for meals and lodging, Lincoln did all kinds of jobs, split rails, husked corn,[4] helped a young merchant, A. Y. Ellis, in running a new store, took whatever work could be found. His friends, sympathizing with Lincoln in his predicament, resolved to have him made postmaster, and, headed by Dr. Duncan, took very practical steps to secure the place for their favorite. Samuel Hill, the storekeeper, had been postmaster for the first year or two after a post office was established at New Salem. He was succeeded by another small merchant, Isaac P. Chrisman, who soon left the village, and Hill once more took the place.[5] Nobody liked him, and Lincoln's friends filed charges against him with the Department at Washington. Lincoln objected because he did not want Hill displaced for his benefit; but his supporters were obdurate and, finally, on May 7, 1833, Lincoln was made the village postmaster.[6] Thus he came into this small compensation which he

---

[1] Duncan's statement. Weik MSS.

[2] R. B. Rutledge to Herndon, no date, but 1866. Weik MSS.

[3] Onstot, 150.

[4] Short to Herndon, July 7, 1865. Short says that Lincoln was the best corn husker he ever saw: 'I used to consider myself very good but he would gather two loads to my one.'

[5] *Lincoln and New Salem*, 13, 50.

[6] Duncan's statement. Weik MSS. Also Records Post Office Department. In

continued to receive during the three years more that he lived in New Salem.

Soon other lucrative employment came to him. The County Surveyor was John Calhoun, one of the few New Englanders then in Sangamon. The country was now being rapidly settled,[1] demand for surveying was great and increasing, and Calhoun needed an assistant. A friend of Lincoln recommended him for the place and he was appointed.[2] Lincoln went to board at the cabin of Mentor Graham, the school teacher, who, at night, helped him to master a volume on surveying, given Lincoln by his employer.

Absorbed in calculations the two would often work until after midnight; for Lincoln had no aptitude for figures and had to labor hard and long to understand the intricacies of surveying. But within six weeks [3] he succeeded and, equipped for his task, began his work under Calhoun. This took Lincoln all over Sangamon County, broadened his acquaintance, multiplied his supporters. For he made 'hosts of friends wherever he went,' testifies Coleman Smoot, the rich man of the neighborhood, at whose house the young surveyor often stayed. Not only did his wit, kindliness, and knowledge attract the people, but his strange clothes and uncouth awkwardness advertised him, the shortness of his trousers causing particular remark and amuse-

Lincoln and New Salem, 50, it is said that Lincoln owed his appointment to the agitation of the women whose wrath was aroused because Hill would make them wait for their mail while he sold liquor and other goods. As a result a petition for the removal of Hill and the appointment of Lincoln was circulated and so numerously signed that the change was effected.

By 1833 New Salem had ceased to grow. A settlement two miles lower down the river — Petersburg — was regarded as the coming town, to be the seat of a new county — Menard — formed from Sangamon County. Yet Petersburg was a town only in name, having in the autumn of 1835 no more than two stores, two houses, and a cobbler's shop. Letter of Matthew S. Marsh, New Salem, Sept. 17, 1835, in the Barrett Collection.

[1] Duis, 138–9. Heavy immigration began in 1834.
Accounts of the Black Hawk War had tremendously advertised Illinois. Wentworth, 27–8; Reynolds, 268–9.

[2] The compensation depended upon the work done. For establishing a quarter section of land the fee was two dollars and a half; for a town lot when under forty in number, thirty-seven and a half cents, etc., and two dollars a day were allowed to the surveyor for travelling expenses when in discharge of his duties. *Laws of Illinois*, revised, 1833, 296.

[3] *Ib.*

ment.   Soon   the   name,   'Abe   Lincoln,'   became   a   household
word.[1]

Calhoun was a Democrat and an ardent follower of Jackson,
but this did not prevent his admiration and liking for his
deputy. He was a very handsome man of fine character and uncommon ability, had studied law in the East and was well versed
in general literature. He had found school teaching more to his
liking and perhaps more remunerative than practice at the bar,
and had taught at the county seat before he became surveyor.
John T. Stuart, a Major in the Black Hawk War, had met Lincoln during his service, and, like everybody else captivated by
his talents and charm, had urged him to study law. Calhoun
now gave his assistant the same advice and Lincoln resolved to
become a lawyer.

From the day he came to New Salem, he read more vora-
ciously than ever.[2] Mentor Graham had told him that a thorough knowledge of grammar was indispensable to one who
wished to advance politically or to appear well in society. Asked
where such a treasure could be found, the school teacher told
Lincoln that a farmer, John Vance, who lived about six miles
distant, owned a copy of Kirkham's *Grammar*. Thereupon Abraham, who was then boarding with Graham, rose from the breakfast table, walked to Vance's cabin, and returned with the book.

Under Graham's guidance he studied so hard and well that
in an incredibly short time he knew Kirkham's rules by heart
and observed them. Three decades afterward Graham declared
that, having then taught for forty-five years, he never had seen
any one so apt and quick at learning grammar as Lincoln was.[3]
Indeed, says Graham, he was the 'most studious, diligent strait
forward young man in the pursuit of a knowledge and literature
than any among the five thousand I have taught in schools.'
In his educational efforts Lincoln made use of his friends and

[1] Smoot to Herndon, May 7, 1866. Weik MSS.

[2] R. B. Rutledge to Herndon, Nov. 30, 1866. Weik MSS. Rutledge says that Lincoln
studied Kirkham's *Grammar* and books on surveying and law; and that he read history,
astronomy, philosophy, chemistry, and newspapers. Lincoln, in his Autobiography,
states that he studied Flint and Gibson on surveying, 'a little.'

[3] Graham to Herndon, July 15, 1865. Weik MSS. And Rutledge to same, Nov. 30,
1866. Weik MSS.

had one of them, the boy William G. Greene, hold Kirkham, while he answered questions which Greene asked him from the volume.[1] Dr. Jason Duncan helped him, too, and relates that Lincoln mastered grammar 'in a most astonishing manner.'[2] But his greatest debt was to Mentor Graham. 'I know of my own knowledge,' writes R. B. Rutledge, that Graham did more than all others to educate Lincoln.[3]

There were many books in and around New Salem and few escaped the enquiring and insatiable Lincoln who read them, not casually and in haste, but with infinite care and thoroughness, often writing out what he read, to be sure that he understood. 'I have,' states a credible witness, 'known him to write a proposition in three different forms in order to state the meaning as clearly and simply as possible — and to spend half a day doing so.'

In his reading and study Lincoln was a very miser of time, never wasting a moment. At the store customers found him absorbed in some book, which he would instantly take up again, when he had served them.[4] Often he would stretch himself on the counter the better to pore over the pages, oblivious to all else. When going to his meals a few steps distant, or walking through the dust or mud of New Salem's street, or strolling out into the country, always an open book was in his hand or closed beneath his arm, while he murmured to himself what he had just read. Even when he chanced to be with women and girls, whom he would try to amuse, Lincoln would take a book with him and read between jokes. When passing from one group of men to another, he would read as he walked, closing the volume as he joined the company.[5]

Whether sitting, lying down, or walking, he was usually reading.[6] He read until late at night and rose at daylight to read.[7]

---

[1] *Lincoln and New Salem*, 29–31.   [2] Duncan's statement. Weik MSS.

[3] Rutledge to Herndon, Nov. 18, 1866. Weik MSS.

[4] Same to same, Nov. 30, 1866. Weik MSS.

[5] J. R. Herndon to Herndon, Aug. 6, 1865; Rutledge to same, Nov. 30, 1866. Weik MSS.

[6] Carman to Herndon, Nov. 30, 1866.

[7] Branson to Herndon, August 3, 1865; J. R. Herndon to same, Aug. 6, 1865, and Rutledge to same, Nov. 30, 1866; James A. Herndon's statement. Weik MSS. James A.

Dressed in 'blue cotton round about coat, stoga shoes, and pale blue casinet pantaloons which failed to make the connection with either coat or socks, coming about three inches below the former and an inch or two above the latter,' [1] he went about New Salem, reading, thinking, talking to himself, seldom entirely conscious of his surroundings.

Lincoln took infinite pains to understand and remember all he read, recited poetry and history, and wrote down whole pages of books and conned them over and over.[2] So he forgot nothing.[3] While in partnership with Berry, Lincoln read Gibbon's *Decline and Fall of the Roman Empire*, Rollin's *Ancient History*, and a novel or two owned by A. Y. Ellis.[4] He read Burns and Shakespeare[5] which he probably found in the cabin of Jack Kelso, where Lincoln boarded for a short time;[6] and he spent much time over a volume on American Military Biography.[7] Frequently he would read aloud.[8] He talked a great deal about what he read, and, says Caleb Carman, would often 'Refer to that Great man Shakespeare allso Lord Byron as being a great men and Burns and of Burns Poems and Lord Nellson as being a Great Admarall and Naval Commander and Adams and He[n]ry Clay Jackson George Washington was the Greatest of all of them and was his Great favorite.' [9]

Herndon says that he often saw Lincoln at night in an open cooper's shop, 'gather up shavens and stick and feed the flame' by which he read.

[1] Short to Herndon, July 7, 1865. Weik MSS.

[2] Rutledge to Herndon, Dec. 4, 1866; J. R. Herndon to Herndon, July 6, 1865. Weik MSS.

[3] J. R. Herndon to Herndon, May 28, 1865. Weik MSS.

[4] Herndon, I, 113.

[5] Carman to Herndon, Nov. 30, 1866. Weik MSS.

[6] Kelso was an idle fellow of 'the village philosopher' type which always attracted Lincoln. Kelso lived in half of a double log cabin owned by Joshua Miller, and it was Kelso's wife who 'kept borders.' *Lincoln and New Salem*, 15. Kelso 'could catch fish when no man could get a bite' (Royal A. Clary's statement; Short to Herndon, July 7, 1865. Weik MSS.); and was called 'the champion hunter and fisherman of the village.' *Lincoln and New Salem*, 15. Kelso appears to have been utterly worthless; but it is said that he could 'recite Shakespeare and Burns by the hour.' *Ib.*, 54–5.

[7] This volume, and Rollin and Gibbon probably were in the cabin of Bennett Abell, who had 'a good Lot of history,' although McNamar, Hill, and other merchants had books. Rowan Herndon owned Lives of Washington, Jefferson, Clay, and Webster. J. R. Herndon to Herndon, Aug. 6, 1865. Weik MSS.

[8] Branson to Herndon, Aug. 3, 1865. Weik MSS.

[9] Carman to Herndon, Dec. 8, 1866. Weik MSS.

In 1833, a circus came to Springfield. It was an historic event — never before had the county seat been thus favored. All Sangamon County flocked to the attraction; thousands had never seen a circus. Among them was Lincoln who then displayed that fondness for such amusements which he never outgrew. The crowd was immense, whisky plentiful, excitement high, fun and fights marking the holiday spirit. Through it all moved Lincoln, entering into the mood and amusement of the day, and, under the tent, enjoying as much as any child the performances of acrobat and antics of clown.[1]

Indeed, next to his honesty and truthfulness which, increasingly, were the outstanding features of his character, Lincoln's love of fun and amusement was and always continued to be, most prominently displayed. His aptitude for story telling and his delight in it were given unbridled freedom in New Salem, and the tales he told, 'allways verry mery and full of fun,' were suited to the taste of his hearers. His fondness for jokes was intense, well-nigh abnormal,[2] and he even would turn his tuneless, singsong, nasal voice into an instrument of jollity. Young men and women were set into gales of laughter by Lincoln's rendering of a song called 'Legacy' in which, with ludicrous effect he substituted certain words.[3] He liked doggerel and, when a clerk or storekeeper, would convulse with applauding merriment the crowds that would fill the room evenings, by singing grotesque jingles, some of which he may have written himself.[4] His New Salem songs were of the same order as those he had been wont to shrill in Gentryville, Indiana, such, relates one who heard them, as 'Oald Oald Suckey bleuskin and the Woodpecker taping on the hollow Beach tree and a great many others that was Funny.'[5]

Yet reading, study, and meditation so absorbed him, that it would almost seem that he plunged into mirth from sheer

---

[1] Onstot, 47–50. Onstot tells, in great detail, the story of this circus, which, he says, caused as much excitement as the removal of the capital to Springfield.

[2] Caleb Carman to Herndon, Nov. 30, 1866. Weik MSS.

[3] R. B. Rutledge to Herndon, no date, Weik MSS.; *Lincoln and New Salem*, 32.

[4] Herndon, I, 114, 115.

[5] Carman to Herndon, Nov. 30, 1866. Weik MSS. 'The Woodpecker' by Thomas Moore can hardly be counted as a 'funny' song.

reaction, so inconsistent are these phases of his New Salem life.

When Lincoln became deputy surveyor his reading was, of course, interrupted. But his work took him among the people and all who met him liked the friendly, jovial, obliging young man. Never by any chance did he quarrel; on the contrary, says the wife of Jack Armstrong, he would 'do anything to accommodate anybody.' [1] His personal popularity widened until it covered Sangamon County. So many Democrats favored him that the leaders of that party, among them Bowling Green,[2] the Justice of the Peace at New Salem and most influential man in the township, proposed to make him their candidate for the Legislature in 1834. His friends, says Rowan Herndon, insisted that Lincoln should run; 'Claming that they had a Wright to a member from that Part of the County he was urged By Both Political Partys to Run.' [3]

Before closing with the Democratic offer, Lincoln consulted John T. Stuart of Springfield, leader of the Republicans, who advised him to accept. Lincoln promptly did so, and under this arrangement [4] again sought election as a Representative in the General Assembly. Although 'Clay was his favorite . . . he all but worshiped his name,' [5] it would appear that no mention of the great leader was made by Lincoln during this campaign.

He issued no formal written address as he had done two years before, nor does any account exist of the speeches he made. He seems to have gone quietly about, meeting everybody he could, telling stories, cracking jokes, taking part in any work or sport that would commend him to voters. Finding a farmer and his men harvesting and being told by them that he would have to show them that he could do farm work, Lincoln said: 'boys if that is all I am shure of your votes,' and taking up the cradle

[1] Mrs. Jack (Hannah) Armstrong's statement. Weik MSS.

[2] Green was the Democratic leader in New Salem. Duncan's statement. Weik MSS. In 1830, Gov. Reynolds appointed him to be one of the Canal Commissioners of Illinois. Reynolds, 203.

[3] J. R. Herndon to Herndon, May 28, 1865. Weik MSS.

[4] Statement of Ninian W. Edwards, brother-in-law of Lincoln, Sept. 22, 1865. Weik MSS. The district was 'profoundly Democratic.' R. B. Rutledge to Herndon, no date, but 1866. Weik MSS.

[5] J. R. Herndon to Herndon, May 28, 1865. Weik MSS.

led the way all around the field.[1] He went to every gathering, making short talks, as all candidates then did,[2] accompanied, whenever possible, by the faithful Clary Grove Boys, still fighting in his behalf.[3] The support of the Democrats amply accounts for his failure to put out the customary declaration of principles or to say anything that was remembered. At Mechanicsburg, however, in one of those general fights which then were a universal practice throughout the Western country, Lincoln jumped in and compelled fair play,[4] a more effective campaign device than any speech could be. On August 4, when the votes were counted, Lincoln had received only fourteen votes less than John Dawson and was elected a representative.[5]

After the election, his life in New Salem went on as before, surveying, distributing mail, mingling with people, and reading — incessantly and forever reading. Of general literature, Lincoln liked best works on philosophy. The French political theorists had again come into vogue in America [6] and some of their writings reached New Salem. When he was about twenty-six years of age Lincoln read in them,[7] and this fact cannot be overlooked in any just appraisement of his intellectual development.

The *Age of Reason*, partly written in a French prison by Thomas Paine, and reprinted in America under the encouragement of Thomas Jefferson, had wide circulation in the United States. At the time Lincoln read it religious sentiment in the Western country, except for the scepticism among the intelligent, which so alarmed Bishop Chase, was intense, uninformed, and savagely intolerant. Any one who did not accept every word in the Bible as literal truth, or ascribe to the Deity good

[1] J. R. Herndon to Herndon, May 28, 1865. Weik MSS.

[2] Ford, 201–2.

[3] *Lincoln and New Salem*, 27–8.

[4] Statement of James Gourley, no date, but in 1866. Weik MSS.

[5] The votes stood 1390 for John Dawson, 1376 for Lincoln, 1170 for William Carpenter, and 1164 for John T. Stuart. *Illinois Election Returns:* Pease, 275.

[6] Bishop Philander Chase, who was stationed in Illinois about this time, was gravely concerned: 'Infidelity and sin stalk fearlessly abroad wherever I travel.' Chase to his son, April 14, 1837, from 'Robin's Nest,' Peoria, Ill. *Reminiscences of Bishop Chase*, II, 380.

[7] Herndon, I, 125, mentions Paine, Volney, and Voltaire; *Lincoln and New Salem*, 56.

and bad fortune, was denounced as an infidel, then the blackest of epithets. Since the *Age of Reason* assailed much of the Biblical narrative, pointing out inconsistencies and questioning the good sense and morality of many teachings, the volume was furiously denounced.[1] But frontier orthodoxy in Illinois in 1835 made no distinction between doubt of the accuracy of ecclesiastical interpretation of the scriptures on the one hand, and disbelief in God on the other.

The *Ruins* by Constantine de Volney appeared about the same time as the *Age of Reason*. The Frenchman so combined calmness of statement with dramatic method that his philosophical pages are most engaging. The author pays imaginary visits to the ancient ruins of cities and nations, and there talks to an Apparition or Phantom, who is the Genius of History and Wisdom. By this device Volney examines government, religion, nature, and the human mind. Throughout the small volume everything is tested by reason.

The book begins: 'Hail, solitary ruins, holy sepulchres and silent walls! you I invoke; to you I address my prayer. . . . Oh Ruins! to your school I will return! I will seek again the calm of your solitudes; and there, far from the afflicting spectacle of the passions, I will cherish . . . the love of man . . . and build my own happiness on the promotion of his.' Pestilence, disease, death, ruin of cities, fall of nations caused by the wrath of a vindictive God! Absurd, says Volney.

The fact that anybody would even read such books was quite enough to taint the reader with the suspicion of infidelity, and Lincoln was thought to be thus afflicted. But he was so kind, gentle, considerate, and helpful to everybody, and so beloved by the whole community, that his non-conformity to the dogmas of the time did not, in the least, affect his popularity. Now and then some extreme religionist or opposing politician used against Lincoln the report that he was an infidel, but without avail. One Snodgrass tried to get that staunch Democrat, Squire Godbey, to vote against Lincoln because Lincoln 'was a Deist'; but Godbey voted for him in spite of that fact and also,

---

[1] No less than twenty answers were published; and it is said that 1,500,000 copies of the *Age of Reason* were sold in England alone.

as we have seen, against the Squire's own political convictions.[1]

Moreover, as with his political views, Lincoln did not press his religious opinions upon others, nor did he conceal them from his intimates, of whom, friendly as he was, he had but one or two. 'I think that when I first knew Mr. L. he was skeptical as to the great truths of the Christian Religion,' [2] says Joshua Speed, the closest of Lincoln's friends, whose association with him began a year or two after Lincoln had read these free thinkers.

Although he mastered most books with astonishing ease and rapidity, he found law books more difficult and he studied them with a sort of passionate determination. He borrowed them from John T. Stuart, then practising law in Springfield,[3] and at an auction in that town bought Blackstone's *Commentaries*.[4] These volumes he read incessantly, and with such concentration that he often was oblivious of his surroundings. Even when at work chopping he would stop, and, sitting on the wood pile, lose himself in a law book, to the amazement of observers. 'I think,' testifies R. B. Rutledge, 'that he never avoided men until he commenced the study of law.' [5]

Excessive reading and study began to impair his health. He became so pale, emaciated and abstracted that New Salem feared that his mind was breaking. So came the first indication of that mental peculiarity which we are to observe more than once in the years that quickly follow.

Even before reading Blackstone or the law books which Stuart loaned him, Lincoln began, in embryonic fashion, to

---

[1] Godbey's statement. Weik MSS. It has been stated that, at this time, Lincoln wrote an essay against Christianity (Herndon to Weik, Feb. 11, 1887. Weik MSS.), but, considering Lincoln's extreme caution and his dislike of offending anybody unnecessarily, this is unlikely. Few eminent men in our history have been less polemical than Lincoln.

[2] Joshua F. Speed to Herndon, Jan. 12, 1866. Weik MSS.

[3] J. R. Herndon to Herndon, May 28, 1865. Weik MSS. Some witnesses say that Lincoln walked to Springfield to borrow books from Stuart (Gourley's statement. Weik MSS.), while others insist that he always rode in the wagons of farmers who chanced to be going to town.

[4] Duncan's statement. Weik MSS. Also *Life of Lincoln:* Isaac N. Arnold, 40. Dr. Duncan says it was when Lincoln bought Blackstone that he resolved to become a lawyer.

[5] R. B. Rutledge to Herndon, Nov. 30, 1866. Weik MSS.

practice law in New Salem, arguing a case now and then before
Bowling Green who became more and more impressed by his
ability. At first Squire Green allowed Lincoln to speak in his
court because he was so funny. Green, who was 'an enormously
fat man weighing . . . three hundred pounds and given to
mirth,' would shake with laughter at Lincoln's droll humor.
But soon the Squire became deeply impressed by the mind and
the legal knowledge of the shabby young practitioner.[1] Lincoln,
towering six feet and four inches, his long, bony finger pointed
at the Justice of the Peace, who was clad only in shirt and
trousers held up 'by one linen suspender over the shoulder,'
would reason with immense dignity,[2] and then convulse the
Squire with some ludicrous tale.

In these early attempts he relied wholly on the *Revised Laws
of Illinois*, from which, says Dr. Duncan, Lincoln 'drew all his
legal knowledge.' This is an over-statement, since he read
thoroughly such legal volumes as Squire Green possessed.[3] He
bought a book of forms, and, from it, wrote out deeds, mortgages, and other contracts for those in need of such documents,
never charging anything for these small services or for his efforts before Squire Green.[4] Thus his popularity was further and
permanently strengthened while he was learning the use of the
simpler tools of his intended profession.

In like manner Lincoln's care of the scanty mail that came to
New Salem endeared him to everybody. So few were the letters
that he would carry them in his hat, a practice that he never
stopped, disposing of legal and other papers in the same way in
after years. The community sharply noted the difference between the treatment it received from Lincoln and the service
given by those whom Lincoln left in charge of the post office,
when he was absent on surveying trips, campaigning, or at the
Legislature — Hill, Onstot, Carman. For Lincoln strove to
please and accommodate — his substitutes merely gave out

---

[1] Duncan's statement. Weik MSS.; Onstot, 74. Green died of apoplexy.

[2] Duncan's statement. Weik MSS.

[3] *Lincoln and New Salem*, 54. Besides the *Statutes of Illinois*, Green had a few other
law books.

[4] William G. Greene's statement and Duncan's statement. Weik MSS.

mail when it was called for. But when Lincoln thought that some one urgently wanted a letter, he would walk miles to deliver it.[1] Accounts of such incidents spread over the countryside and confirmed the good opinion of and affection for Lincoln which everybody was coming to entertain. Mentor Graham bears testimony that not only was he called 'Honest Abe' because of his rectitude, but that all loved him because he was one of 'the most *companionable* persons you will ever see in this world.'[2]

We have a glimpse of him as postmaster in a letter of a settler in New Salem, Matthew S. Marsh: 'The Post Master [Lincoln] is very careless about leaving his office open and unlocked during the day — half the time I go in and get my papers, etc., without any one being there, as was the case yesterday. The letter was only marked 25, and even if he had been there and known it was double, he would not [have] charged me any more — luckily he is a very clever fellow and a particular friend of mine. If he is there when I carry this to the office, I will get him to "Frank it."'[3] Such was the favorable opinion held of him by a fellow townsman.

Then, too, his love of children, which he showed constantly and in various ways, endeared him to everybody. He would even stop his beloved reading to play marbles with little boys, one of whom declares that Lincoln was a 'great marble player' and 'kept us small boys running in all directions gathering up the marbles he would scatter.'[4] Once he found a barefooted boy, Ab Trent, chopping wood to get money to buy shoes; Lincoln did the work for the urchin.[5] He was, indeed, a kind of elder brother to the children of New Salem, who, barefooted and clad only in a tow-linen shirt during summer and usually without shoes even in winter,[6] clustered about Lincoln whenever he appeared, fairly worshipping him. Wherever he went he had a child with him; and he did helpful kindnesses to widows and

---

[1] *Lincoln and New Salem*, 50.

[2] Graham to Herndon, July 15, 1865. Weik MSS.

[3] Letter of Matthew S. Marsh, Sept. 17, 1835, in the Barrett Collection.

[4] Onstot, 25, 74.   [5] R. B. Rutledge's statement. Weik MSS.

[6] Onstot, 220–1. Onstot says that even as to men and women, 'boots were a luxury that few indulged in.' He, himself, never had boots until he was twelve years old and

poor people, such as gathering and chopping wood for them.[1] Lincoln's care for animals, so conspicuous in boyhood and youth, was displayed in New Salem. He was especially fond of cats, would take on his lap two kittens of Caleb Carman, play with them, compare their heads and decide that 'Jane had a beter countanance than Susan;' and when he started for Vandalia to attend the Legislature he left strict orders that the cats should have careful attention.[2]

Calhoun's term as County Surveyor expired in 1835, and his successor, Thomas M. Neale, at once reappointed Lincoln as his assistant. Thus Lincoln held and continued to hold as long as he lived in New Salem, three offices — postmaster, deputy surveyor, and Representative in the General Assembly of Illinois. Moreover, the combined fees and salaries he received were not only considerable in comparison with any amount he had ever made before; they were paid in the best money then in circulation,[3] although for surveying, Lincoln sometimes took buckskin for making trousers.[4] But he saved nothing and, failing to pay one of the notes he had so heedlessly given when trying to be a merchant, his horse and surveying instruments were taken on a judgment. James Short, at whose house Lincoln spent much time, paid the debt and restored his property.[5]

he was the first boy in Petersburg who wore such foot gear. In winter buckskin trousers, moccasins, and sometimes blue jean coats, were worn.

[1] J. R. Herndon to Herndon, May 28, 1865. Weik MSS.

[2] Carman to Herndon, Dec. 8, 1866. Weik MSS.

[3] Financial conditions were bad everywhere. In the bustling little town of Chicago, in 1835, money was so scant and poor that 'nearly every man . . . doing business was issuing his individual scrip, and the city abounded with little tickets, such as "Good in our store for ten cents," "Good for a loaf of bread," "Good for a shave," "Good for a drink."' Wentworth, Fergus, No. 7, 27.

Throughout the West specie was at a premium of from fifty to one hundred per cent. *Ib.*, 30.

[4] Godbey's statement. Weik MSS.

[5] This was the note of Berry & Lincoln for $400 which Lincoln had given to Greene who assigned it to Reuben Radford, from whom it was purchased by Peter Van Bergen. Lincoln took up this note by giving Van Bergen another note signed by himself and Greene. Van Bergen got judgment against both men. Short to Herndon, July 7, 1865. Weik MSS.

Lincoln repaid Short after he became a practising lawyer in Springfield. *Ib.*

Greene's horse, saddle, bridle and $125 in cash were also taken to satisfy the judgment; but Lincoln, considering this a debt of honor, discharged it fully in later years. *Ib.* See also *Litigant:* Townsend, 63–70.

Throughout all this time he kept at his books; only when on surveying trips did he suspend for a moment his intense study and reading. Not in after years did he acquire more knowledge in the same space of time. Indeed it is doubtful whether he ever again thought more deeply on fundamentals than during these years at New Salem.

In the midst of his studies, romance intruded, albeit with halting and uncertain footsteps. The mingling of admiration, indifference, and concern which Lincoln showed towards women is a most curious phase of his inexplicable character. Again at New Salem, that shyness appeared which caused him to shun the company of girls in Indiana.[1] As a clerk and storekeeper he disliked serving women and, in general, seemed to hold himself aloof from them; yet, acquaintance formed with particular women, Lincoln sought their society and indulged in 'innocent mischief' toward them. To women whom he knew especially well, he would 'prove . . . a complete hectorer.'[2] He was fond of the wife of Jack Armstrong, at whose house, four miles from New Salem, he would stay two or three weeks at a time when surveying; and Mrs. Armstrong made shirts for him and patched his trousers.[3] That she could not read and there were no books in the Armstrong cabin did not shorten his visits. He often went there, bringing candy for the children, and would rock a cradle while Mrs. Armstrong 'got him Abe something to eat.' Many years later he was to show his regard by defending without pay her son who was indicted and tried for murder — the boy whose cradle he rocked when a baby.[4] He liked Mrs. Bennett Abell, too, and often visited the Abell cabin, and the wife of Bowling Green had been of help to Lincoln when he was deeply troubled. But, until in his twenty-fifth year, he showed no sentiment for any individual woman, and even then only in doubtful and clouded fashion.

In 1833, Mary Owens, a cousin of Mentor Graham,[5] came

---

[1] Duncan's statement. Weik MSS.

[2] *Ib.*

[3] Statements of Mrs. Armstrong and Squire Godbey. Weik MSS.

[4] Statements of James Short, April 3, 1866, and of Mrs. Armstrong. Weik MSS. We didnt think about books papers — we worked.'

[5] Graham's second statement, no date. Weik MSS.

from Kentucky to New Salem on a visit to her sister, the wife of Bennett Abell. Miss Owens was vivacious, witty, spirited, and a girl of unusual good sense. She was, writes another cousin, Johnson G. Green, 'the most intellectual woman I ever saw.' She belonged to an excellent family in Kentucky, her father being a man of substance and standing in his community.[1] Mary had been well brought up and given a good education. Acquaintances relate that she was handsome rather than pretty, with dark blue eyes, black hair, and of generous figure — 'portly,' as one observer describes her. She dressed better than most young women in New Salem.[2] Lincoln met her at the Abell cabin, and, thereafter, called upon her several times But if there was any love-making, nothing came of it. At least there is no evidence of an engagement until her next visit, some three years afterward.

At the time of Miss Owens' first visit, Lincoln was boarding at the tavern kept by James Rutledge who, as we have seen, gave up the inn soon after Lincoln came and took his family to a farm owned by John McNamar. The Rutledge tavern was a log house with two rooms of medium size below and two above in a kind of half-loft. There were eleven persons in the Rutledge family, nine of them children.[3] The third of these was a girl, Ann, who, when Lincoln boarded at the inn, was twenty years of age.

The picture of Ann Rutledge is clear and vivid. She was about five feet two inches tall, plump rather than slender, her weight, as reported by friends, being from one hundred and twenty to

[1] J. G. Green's statement. Weik MSS.

[2] Graham's second statement, no date. Weik MSS. Graham says that Miss Owens was extremely good natured, 'very intellectual,' and that mirthfulness was the predominant element in her disposition. His description of her physically is as given in the text, except that he says her eyes were black, her face symmetrical but 'roundish' and that she had 'beautiful even teeth.'

Green describes her as having dark blue eyes, brown hair, light complexion and weighing one hundred and sixty pounds. J. G. Green's statement. Weik MSS.

[3] Jane O., born Nov. 23, 1808; John Miller, born Nov. 29, 1810; Ann Mayes, Jan. 17, 1813 — all in Kentucky; David Ham, Aug. 15, 1817; Robert Brannon, Feb. 23, 1819; Nancy Cameron, Feb. 10, 1821; Margaret Armstrong, June 21, 1823 — all in White Co., Ill.; William Blackburn, Nov. 28, 1826; (Mary Anderson, born June 5, died July 25, 1827); and Sarah F., Oct. 20, 1829 — all in New Salem. Rutledge Memoirs: Hamand, 52.

one hundred and thirty pounds. Her hair was so light that some observers called it golden. She had large, blue eyes, rosy but delicate complexion, and very red lips. Her disposition was sweet and friendly and her brother declares that she was 'the brightest mind of the family,' although she had only a moderate education. She dressed simply, but 'exceedingly neat' though she 'was poor.'[1] She was a notably good housekeeper, too, an important accomplishment, when we consider that the numerous Rutledge family and several boarders ate and some of the latter, Lincoln among them, slept in the not over-large log house.[2] Ann was in charge of the tavern, it seems, her mother having gone to Sand Ridge to keep house for a young farmer, then unmarried, by the name of James Short.[3]

Ann appears to have been the most attractive girl in New Salem and was courted by the two most prominent and prosperous young men of the village, Samuel Hill and John McNamar. McNamar was her favorite and she became engaged to the thrifty young financier with whom, it would appear, she was very much in love.[4] Lincoln, too, 'had great partialities' for her, but McNamar stood in his way.[5] More than thirty years later McNamar said that, for the reasons which follow, 'I think

[1] Mrs. Hardin Bale in Herndon, i, 131.

Mentor Graham describes her as having blue eyes, fair complexion, auburn hair, round face, good teeth, beautiful mouth, medium chin. She was vigorous, amiable, kind, and a 'tolerably good schollar in all the common branches.' Everybody loved her and she loved everybody. Graham's statement. Weik MSS.

She had 'light hair and blue eyes.' R. B. Rutledge to Herndon, no date, but in 1866. Weik MSS.

John McNamar says that 'Miss Ann was a gentle Amiable Maiden without any of the airs of your city Belles but winsome and comly withal a blond in complection with golden hair cherry red Lips and a bonny Blue Eye.' John McNamar to G. U. Miles, May 5, 1865. Weik MSS.

See also Onstot, 22; Short to Herndon, July 7, 1865. Weik MSS.

[2] *Ib.* There were no cooking or other stoves, the entire equipment being a 'flat oven,' a long-handled skillet and a teakettle. The food was chiefly meat fried over the coals in the skillet, corn dodgers baked in the flat oven, and lye hominy. Meat was often fried in the same skillet in which corn dodgers were baked. The best furnished kitchens sometimes had a coffee pot also. 'Sugar was unknown except where the sugar trees abounded.' Onstot, 219–20; Miller, 214–5.

[3] Short to Herndon, July 7, 1865. Weik MSS.

[4] R. B. Rutledge to Herndon, Nov. 21, 1866; William McNeely to same, Nov. 12, 1866; and B. F. Irwin to same, Aug. 27, 1866. Weik MSS.

[5] Duncan's statement. Weik MSS.

Neither Mr. Lincon nor myself were in a situation [1832–35] to enter into what Mr. Seward would call "Entangling Alliances."' [1]

McNamar and Lincoln were friends and the young merchant did not know that Lincoln was 'paying any particular attention to any of the Young Ladies of my acquaintance,' [2] as, indeed, he was not at that time. On her part, Ann was not then 'favorably impressed' with Lincoln, who was 'young poor and awkward' and without prospects, while both Hill and McNamar were 'up in the world.' [3]

McNamar came of a good family in the State of New York and was well educated.[4] When still a young man, McNamar's father lost his property and became heavily involved in debt. Saying nothing of his purposes, John left home for the Western country resolved to make enough money to pay his father's debts,[5] return to New York and bring the family to a new home.[6] At Cincinnati, he and Samuel Hill bought a stock of goods, shipped them to St. Louis, 'whence,' says McNamar, 'I set out on a voyage of Discovery on the praries of Illinois.' [7]

As the place to make his fortune, he quickly chose New Salem, arriving there in 1830, the year before Lincoln came, and, in order that his parents or relatives should not follow or interrupt him, he took the name of John McNiel by which he was known locally. McNamar, says the brother of Ann Rutledge, left home 'clandestinely, and in order to avoid pursuit by his parents, changed his name. His conduct was strictly high-toned, honest and moral.' [8] By sagacity and sharp attention, he soon accumulated property. He dealt in land, acquired a farm, was a partner in Hill's store, the only prosperous one in the vil-

---

[1] McNamar to Herndon, June 4, 1866. Weik MSS.

[2] McNamar to Miles, May 5, 1866. Weik MSS.

[3] B. F. Irwin to Herndon, Sept. 22, 1866, from inquiries made by Irwin of acquaintances and friends of Lincoln and Ann Rutledge. Weik MSS.

[4] *Lincoln and New Salem*, 48–50.

[5] R. B. Rutledge to Herndon, no date. Also McNamar to Miles, May 5, 1866. Weik MSS. 'my coming west being principally to obtain the means.'

[6] *Lincoln and New Salem*, 49–50.

[7] McNamar to Herndon, June 4, 1866. Weik MSS. McNamar claimed to be the discoverer of New Salem 'as a business point.' *Ib.*

[8] Rutledge to Herndon, no date. Weik MSS.

lage or country roundabout. Alert, diligent, reserved, John McNamar went quietly about his affairs, with steadily increasing success.

About the time that Lincoln went to board at the Rutledge tavern where McNamar also lived, the young business man had reached the mark to which he steadily had worked and was worth, in cash and property, some thousands of dollars.[1] At once he took the next step in his plan of returning to New York, paying off his father's debts and bringing his family to New Salem, after which he would marry Ann Rutledge. He told Ann of his plans, change of name and the reasons for it;[2] and then, in the summer of 1832,[3] started upon his eastward journey. They had agreed to be married on his return. Seemingly as a family arrangement, McNamar on July 26 of the previous year had bought half of Rutledge's eighty-acre farm, paying for the forty acres the sum of fifty dollars.[4] To this farm James Rutledge took his family about the time his prospective son-in-law departed for New York.[5]

So off across the prairies of Illinois and into the forests of Indiana and Ohio, rode John McNamar on 'Old Andy,' a horse that had been ridden by a New Salem volunteer in the Black Hawk disturbance. In Ohio he fell sick of fever and, for several weeks, was dangerously ill, part of the time delirious. When he re-

[1] *Lincoln and New Salem*, 49; Herndon, I, 132.
[2] R. B. Rutledge to Herndon, no date. Weik MSS.
[3] McNamar to Geo. U. Miles, May 5, 1866. Weik MSS.
[4] Transcript Record A, 183, Menard Co., Ill. The acknowledgment of this deed was before Bowling Green, J. P.
On February 8, 1828, James Rutledge entered the E. half S.W. quarter, Sect. 7, N. Range 7 W. in Sangamon County. General Land Office Records, Interior Dept. It was half of this that McNamar bought.
[5] R. B. Rutledge to Herndon, Nov. 21, 1866. Weik MSS.; John McNamar to Herndon, June 4, 1866; and Mrs. Bowling Green's statement in Miles to Herndon, March 23, 1866. Weik MSS.
McNamar's farm, which he had bought from Cameron, the partner of Rutledge, adjoined Rutledge's farm of which McNamar had bought half. On Jan. 20, 1833, James Rutledge and wife sold the remaining forty acres of his farm to John Jones, for $300. Transcript Record A, page 239, Menard Co., Ill. So that when Ann and her father died, James Rutledge owned no real estate. The entire eighty acres, entered by him in 1828, is rather poor farming land, and is now estimated by the present owner at $100 the acre. I am indebted for this data to G. E. Nelson, of Petersburg, Ill.
Lincoln had surveyed both farms. McNamar to Herndon, June 4, 1866. Weik MSS.

covered, he went on to New York, where he found his father very feeble and the financial condition of the family worse than ever.[1] He had written Ann of his illness and delay from Ohio and again from New York and she had answered his letters.[2] But mails were then slow, uncertain and expensive,[3] McNamar was harried by his father's creditors, worried by his father's declining health; gradually the correspondence seems to have languished and finally to have ceased. McNamar did not come back at once, as he had expected to do; 'perhaps,' writes Ann's brother, 'circumstances of the family prevented his immediate return.' McNamar's father died, the young man, in time, straightened out the tangled affairs of his family, paid the old debts and prepared to leave for New Salem and Ann Rutledge.[4]

Troubled that letters from her betrothed no longer came, Ann told her parents of McNamar's change of name. Suspicion instantly sprang up and quickly possessed the Rutledge family. Rumor of the circumstances soon ran from cabin to cabin in the little hamlet; gossip made the worst of the situation. McNamar must be a bad person, perhaps an escaped criminal, doubtless he had another wife.[5] In any case, Ann had been abandoned. Incessantly such talk fell upon the girl's ears; everybody pitied her, condemned the faithless lover. Ann became despondent and distracted.

So stood matters when Lincoln, through whose hands her correspondence with McNamar had passed,[6] began his courtship, the nature and course of which are misty. No positive and definite engagement resulted, although it seems that there was a tentative agreement to marry, 'conditional,' however, asserts Ann's brother, 'to an honorable release from the contract with McNamar.' Indeed, when urged by her younger brother, David, to marry Lincoln, Ann refused until she could see McNamar

---

[1] R. B. Rutledge to Herndon, no date. Weik MSS.

[2] Statement of Mrs. William Rutledge in Miles to Herndon, March 23, 1866. Weik MSS.

[3] In 1835 it cost twenty-five cents to send a letter from Chicago to New York, by the quickest and cheapest route. Wentworth, Fergus, 7, 27.

[4] R. B. Rutledge to Herndon, no date. Weik MSS.

[5] *Lincoln and New Salem*, 50-2.   [6] *Ib.*, 50.

again and 'inform him of the change.'[1] On Lincoln's part marriage was not to take place until Abraham had finished his study of the law and established himself in the practice of it.[2]

Neither Ann nor Abraham, it would seem, displayed any precipitancy of passion. James Short, who lived within half a mile of McNamar's farm while the Rutledge family lived there and whom Lincoln 'came to see . . . every day or two,' knew nothing of love-making, much less of an engagement.[3] Thus the affair wore on until the summer of 1835, when Ann Rutledge had 'brain fever.'[4] She grew steadily worse and, realizing that she would die, asked to see Lincoln and her brother David, then a student in Illinois College at Jacksonville[5] which had been established not long before. On August 25, she died in the farmhouse of her absent lover, and there, too, three months later, her father, James Rutledge, died of the same disease.[6]

Soon afterward, into New Salem drove John McNamar, his mother, brothers, and sisters in the wagon with him, the young man expecting to claim his bride, as he had planned to do.[7]

When Lincoln came from the bedside of the dying girl, observers noted that he was despondent and, when she died, he appeared gloomy and dejected. Again, in the village, 'old people' wagged their heads, and said that he was mentally unbalanced, this time because of sorrow.[8] 'But various opinions obtained as

[1] R. B. Rutledge to Herndon, no date. Weik MSS. Lincoln told Graham that they were engaged and Ann 'intimated' the same thing to him. Graham's statement. Weik MSS.

[2] R. B. Rutledge to Herndon, Nov. 21, 1866. Weik MSS.

[3] Short to Herndon, July 7, 1865. Weik MSS.

[4] R. B. Rutledge to Herndon, Nov. 21, 1866. Weik MSS. The term was applied to cases of typhoid fever.

[5] A. M. Prewitt, grandson of Jane Rutledge, to J. E. Hamand, Nov. 7, 1921. Hamand, 19.

Lincoln had entered into a bond with David Rutledge and William Green, January 31, 1833, for $150, the proceeds of which are supposed to have enabled the two younger men to enter Illinois College. In August suit was brought against the three. *Litigant:* Townsend, 55.

[6] Dec. 3, 1835, when fifty-four years of age. R. B. Rutledge's statement. Weik MSS.

[7] Herndon, i, 141.

[8] McNeely to Herndon, Nov. 12, 1866; Mrs. Bowling Green's statement in Miles to Herndon, March 23, 1866; B. F. Irwin to same, Aug. 27, and Sept. 22, 1866, and John Jones's statement attached to Rutledge to Herndon, no date, but 1866.

'Mother remembers . . . how sad his face was when he came out of the room where Ann lay dying.' A. M. Prewitt to J. E. Hamand, Nov. 7, 1921. Hamand, 19.

Mentor Graham says that Lincoln told him that he felt like committing suicide;

to the cause of his change, some thought it was an increased application to his *Law studies*, others that it was deep anguish of Soul (as he was all soul) over the Loss of Miss R.' [1] He must have shown distress, for James Short concluded that Lincoln's melancholy was due to love or an engagement, although he had heard of neither.[2] It was said in after years, that Lincoln refused to eat because of the death of Ann Rutledge, but Short flatly denies this story.[3] However, the effect on Lincoln of Ann's death, says her brother, was 'terrible' and because of it friends feared that he would become insane.[4]

Bowling Green, who lived about a mile from New Salem, took Lincoln to his cabin, where, in a fortnight, the care of Mrs. Green restored the sufferer. Mrs. Green's opinion was that Ann 'thought . . . as much of [McNamar] as she did of Lincoln to appearances.' [5] The wife of William Rutledge, one of Ann's brothers, went further and declared that if she 'had lived [she] would have married McNamar or rather . . . that . . . Ann liked him a little the best though McNamar had ben absent . . . for Near two years at the time of her death.' [6]

Lincoln came back to his study and surveying, boarding at the tavern, now kept by Henry Onstot. He talked to McNamar for whom he wrote a deed and who 'thought that he had lost some of his former vivacity.' [7] Neither then nor ever afterward did he show unfriendliness to his rival.[8] It would appear, indeed, that nobody told McNamar of a love affair between Lincoln and Ann. 'I never heard any person say that Mr. Lincoln

but Graham assured Lincoln that 'God's higher purpose' was working and Lincoln told Graham that he, too, 'thought so somehow — couldn't tell how.' Graham's statement, no date. Weik MSS.

[1] Henry McHenry in B. F. Farley to Herndon, Jan. 8, 1866. Weik MSS.

[2] Short to Herndon, July 7, 1865. Weik MSS.

[3] 'James Short "says it is not so about Lincolns Refusing to Eat on the account of the death of Miss Rutledge."' Caleb Carman to Herndon, Nov. 30, 1866. Weik MSS.

[4] R. B. Rutledge to Herndon, no date. Weik MSS.

[5] Mrs. Green's statement in George U. Miles to Herndon, March 23, 1866. Weik MSS.

[6] Statement of Mrs. William Rutledge in Miles to Herndon, March 23, 1866. Weik MSS.

[7] McNamar to Miles, May 5, 1866. Weik MSS.

[8] Twenty-three years after, in the Douglas campaign, Lincoln greeted McNamar 'cordially,' calling him by name. McNamar to Herndon, June 4, 1866. Weik MSS.

addressed Miss Ann Rutledge in terms of courtship neither her own family nor my acquaintances otherwise. I heard simply,' continues McNamar, 'from two prominent Gentlemen of my acquaintance and Personal friends that Mr. Lincoln was Grieved very much at her death.' [1]

A few months later, in 1836, Lincoln became a candidate to succeed himself in the Legislature. A President was to be elected; Van Buren was the Democratic candidate, the Whigs of the West and Southwest supported Senator Hugh L. White of Tennessee.[2] This time there was no fusion with the Democrats and Lincoln again published a statement of his political opinions. A piece in the *Sangamo Journal*, signed 'Many Voters,' demanded that all candidates for the Legislature 'show their hands.' 'Agreed,' wrote Lincoln to that newspaper. 'Here's mine. I go for all sharing the privileges of the government who assist in bearing its burdens;' so he favors the suffrage for 'all whites . . . who pay taxes or bear arms (by no means excluding females).'

If elected Lincoln will serve all the people, he says, 'as well those that oppose as those that support me.' He will be 'governed by their will,' when he knows what their will is; otherwise 'I shall do what my own judgment teaches me will best advance their interests.' On one issue he is positive: 'whether elected or not,' he favors 'distributing the proceeds of the sales of the public lands to the several States, to enable our State . . . to dig canals and construct railroads without borrowing money and paying the interest on it.' As to the Presidential campaign then in progress, he will vote for Hugh L. White for President.[3]

Some acrimony appears to have crept into this, Lincoln's third campaign. Robert Allen, a Colonel in the Black Hawk

[1] McNamar to Geo. U. Miles, May 5, 1866. Weik MSS.

Arnold in his *Life of Lincoln*, 42–3, says: 'Gossip and imagination have represented this early romance as casting a shadow over his whole after life, and as having produced something bordering upon insanity. The picture has been somewhat too highly colored, and the story made rather too tragic'; and dryly adds: 'In his recollections of her, there was a poetry of sentiment, which might possibly have been lessened had she lived, by the prosaic realities of life.'

[2] Michigan and Arkansas were admitted to the Union in 1836, thus continuing and strengthening the custom of bringing in slave and free states at the same time.

[3] *Works*, I, 14–5. June 13, 1836

War, started a report, damaging to Lincoln and a fellow candidate, Ninian W. Edwards of Springfield, one of the leaders of the little aristocracy of that town, whose sister-in-law Lincoln was to marry before long. When passing through New Salem, Colonel Allen had said that he knew facts which, if made public, would destroy the chances for election of Lincoln and Edwards, but that, for friendship's sake, Allen would not tell what he knew.

Lincoln instantly wrote Allen demanding that he make public any facts derogatory to Edwards or himself. If Lincoln has done anything to forfeit the confidence of the people, 'he that knows of that thing, and conceals it, is a traitor to his country's interest.' Since 'the public interest' is supreme, 'let the worst come.' But no matter how bad it may be, or 'however low it may sink me,' the revelation 'shall never break the tie of personal friendship between us.' Lincoln desires an answer and Allen is 'at liberty to publish both' letters.[1]

With this exception, the campaign was like those preceding except that Lincoln made more speeches. The Clary Grove Boys had sounded his praise long and loud and his fame as a speaker had reached Springfield. In the courthouse at the County seat, just before the election, the New Salem candidate made a speech of such 'great power and originality' that it 'produced a profound impression' even at that centre of oratory and learning. 'The crowd was with him,' Lincoln's friends exultant, the opposition dejected. A leading lawyer, George Forquer,[2] 'one of the champions of the former Republican party,' had recently become a Democrat and, 'almost simultaneous[ly],' received, from President Jackson, the appointment of Register of the Land Office. He had a fine new house; 'the best then in Springfield,' equipped with a lightning rod, the only one in town. Lincoln had made particular note of this device, since it was the first lightning rod he had ever seen.

Forquer answered Lincoln's speech, and at the beginning said that 'the young man would have to be taken down.' When the Democratic office-holder finished, Lincoln replied. At the close

[1] *Works*, I, 15–6. June 21, 1836.
[2] Who had filed the suit against Lincoln in 1833, p. 119 *n.*, *supra.*

of his remarks, Lincoln, turning to Forquer, made mention of Forquer's opening about taking him down, and, quickly facing the crowd exclaimed: 'It is for you not for me to say whether I am up or down! The gentleman has alluded to my being a young man. I am older in years than I am in the tricks and trades of politicians. I desire to live, and I desire place and distinction as a politician. But I would rather die now than, like the gentleman, live to see the day that I would have to erect a lightning rod to protect a guilty conscience from an offended God.' Lincoln's followers shouted in triumph and declared that his speech was the greatest ever made in Springfield. 'I have heard him often since in court and before the people,' relates the teller of this story, 'but never saw him appear so well as on that occasion.' [1]

When the campaign was over and the votes registered, Lincoln was again elected, and he led the ticket as he had not done two years before when running as a bi-partisan candidate, and his legislative career continued.[2] He was now firmly established, politically, in Sangamon County and his power and influence were steadily and rapidly growing.

In the midst of these rising fortunes, Mary Owens paid another visit to her sister, Mrs. Bennett Abell. The Abell cabin was only a mile from New Salem [3] and Lincoln often went to see her.[4] He afterward said that he had promised Mrs. Abell to marry her sister, but repented his 'rashness.' The matter is sadly confused, although those on the ground believed that 'Mr. Lincoln again fell in love.' Observers were sharply watching, for Ann Rutledge had been in her grave but a few months, and Mary Owens, 'dressed much finer than any lady who lived about New Salem,' attracted notice. She even had a 'fashionable silk dress' which the village thought 'in striking contrast with the calico dress . . . that Ann had worn.' [5]

---

[1] Narrative of Joshua F. Speed, no date. Weik MSS.

[2] He received 1716 votes, and the six other successful candidates ranked as follows: William F. Elkin, 1694; Ninian W. Edwards, 1659; John Dawson, 1641; Daniel Stone, 1438; Robert L. Wilson, 1353; Andrew McCormick, 1306. Pease, 299.

[3] Johnson G. Green's statement, no date. Weik MSS.

[4] Mrs. Bowling Green in Miles to Herndon, March 23, 1866. Weik MSS.

[5] Onstot, 24

At any rate the talk spread from cabin to cabin that Lincoln and Miss Owens were engaged. After her first visit he had boasted that 'if ever that girl comes back to New Salem I am going to marry her.'[1] But there was much sparring, and the lack of harmony between them steadily grew. Once Lincoln was away on a surveying trip, near McNamar's farm where the Rutledges were then living, and Miss Owens seems to have resented his failing to call upon her during that time; and Lincoln was equally offended, when, upon his return, Mary did not eagerly welcome him.[2] The village gossips had a story that when Abe and Mary were going with Mrs. Bowling Green to her cabin, Mrs. Green, who was carrying a very fat baby, had a hard time climbing a hill with the heavy child in her arms; and when Lincoln took no notice of it, Miss Owens laughingly said to him: 'You would not make a good husband, Abe.'[3] This tale she denied thirty years afterward.[4] Some young men and women, Lincoln and Mary among them, went on horseback to a party at Bowling Green's. When crossing a deep stream the other girls were carefully assisted by their escorts, but Lincoln rode across leaving Miss Owens without any attention; and, when she made mention of the neglect, told her with a laugh, that he knew she could take care of herself.[5] In such fashion ran this strange courtship.

Lincoln's state of mind is best expressed in letters to Miss Owens, and in a remarkable explanation of them made to Mrs. O. H. Browning. Since this is Lincoln's only love affair of which there is documentary evidence written by himself, and in view of his comments upon it then, and his version of the origin of the entanglement, these letters require particular attention. From Vandalia, where he was attending the Legislature, he wrote 'Mary' the gloomiest letter imaginable; he is sick and blue, he says, and wants her to cheer him up. His letter is 'dull and stupid,' he adds — as, indeed, it was. From the matrimonial

[1] Onstot, 24.

[2] Mrs. Bowling Green in Miles to Herndon, March 23, 1866; J. G. Green's statement, no date. Weik MSS.

[3] Johnson G. Green's statement. Weik MSS.

[4] Mary S. Vineyard (née Owens) to Herndon, July 22, 1866. Herndon, I, 149–50.

[5] Ib.

point of view, about which, however, he says nothing, the letter is most discouraging.[1]

Again Lincoln wrote 'Friend Mary' from Springfield, where, as we shall presently see, he had gone to live, a disconsolate letter. She would never like it there, no woman speaks to him, he has not gone to church and shall not because he would not know how to behave himself, he would be happier with her, but not if she would be discontented; he will 'most positively abide by' what he has said to her provided she wishes it, but Mary 'had better not do it.'[2]

Still he went out to New Salem to see the young woman, and immediately after one such visit — 'the same day on which we parted' — once more wrote her in terms still more depressing. He wants, says Lincoln, 'in all cases to do right, and most particularly so in all cases with women;' he would let Mary alone if he 'knew it would be doing right;' he 'rather suspect[s] that course is best' and she can 'drop the subject . . . forever . . . without calling forth one accusing murmur' from him. In short Lincoln will 'release' her if she desires, although he is willing and even anxious to bind her 'faster.' He is thinking only of her happiness, upon which his own depends; so if she does not answer, then 'farewell. A long life and a merry one attend you.'[3]

Then Lincoln, in writing, confides the whole affair to another woman, wife of O. H. Browning, who, years afterwards, was to play so important a rôle in Lincoln's career. He had formed the acquaintance of Mrs. Browning at Vandalia when attending the Legislature and she was, perhaps, the first woman of social position and political importance he had ever met. At all events he lays bare his heart to her, with jubilant and quizzical, albeit inept, pen.

Lincoln tells Mrs. Browning — 'between you and me' — that it was Miss Owens' sister, Mrs. Bennett Abell, who had trapped him; that she had 'proposed to' him that she would bring Mary back from Kentucky where Mrs. Abell was going on a visit, if he

---

[1] Lincoln to Mary Owens, Dec. 13, 1836. *Works*, I, 17–8.

[2] Same to same, May 7, 1837. *Ib.*, 52–4.

[3] Lincoln to Mary Owens, Aug. 16, 1837. *Works*, I, 55–7.

would marry the girl forthwith; and that Lincoln 'accepted the proposal.' How could he 'have done otherwise'? Besides, he was then 'most confoundedly well pleased with the project.' Why not? He 'had seen the said sister some three years before,' and thought it all right to go 'plodding through life hand in hand with her.'

So 'sure enough,' says Lincoln, when Mrs. Abell returned, she brought Mary with her. This puzzled Lincoln — it showed that 'she was a trifle too willing.' But when he saw Miss Owens! 'I knew she was oversize, but now she appeared a fair match for Falstaff.' No wonder she had been called an 'old maid.' Nobody could have 'reached her present bulk in less than thirty-five or forty years.' Then too she made Lincoln think of his mother, 'not from withered features — for her skin was too full of fat to permit of its contracting into wrinkles — but from her want of teeth, weather-beaten appearance in general.'

Lincoln explains to Mrs. Browning that, 'fairly convinced that no other man on earth would have her,' he resolved to 'stick to my word,' since to do so is, with him, 'a point of honor and conscience in all things.' He taught himself to think of Mary as his wife and searched for 'perfections in her which might be fairly set off against her defects.' At Vandalia he received letters from her, which confirmed his suspicions; and although 'fixed "firm as the surge-repelling rock" in my resolution,' he was 'continually repenting the rashness which had led me to make it.' Never in his life, he says, did he so much wish to be free from the 'thraldom' of any 'bondage, either real or imaginary.' He planned how he 'might get along in life after' marriage and how he 'might procrastinate the evil day ... which I really dreaded as much, perhaps more, than an Irishman does the halter.'

And here he is, at last, 'wholly, unexpectedly, completely out of the "scrape,"' without 'violation of word, honor, or conscience!' Miraculous! How does Mrs. Browning think he managed to escape? She never can guess, so Lincoln will tell her. 'I mustered my resolution and made the proposal to her direct; but, shocking to relate, she answered, No.' Again he made the attempt, again Mary 'repelled it with greater firm-

ness than before.' He tried it again and again with the same
result.

So, 'vanity deeply wounded' and 'mortified almost beyond
endurance,' he gave up. But alas! 'I then for the first time began to suspect that I was really a little in love with her. But let
it all go! I'll try and outlive it. Others have been made fools of
by the girls, but this can never with truth be said of me. I most
emphatically, in this instance, made a fool of myself. I have
now come to the conclusion never again to think of marrying,
and for this reason — I can never be satisfied with any one who
would be blockhead enough to have me.'

Lincoln needs distraction, it appears; when Mrs. Browning
gets his letter she must write him 'a long yarn about something
to amuse' him.[1]

This epistle, written in his twenty-ninth year, requires much
comment or none. Even after the affair had thus ended, Lincoln
told Mrs. Abell, whom he saw in Springfield one day, to 'tell
your sister that I think she was a great fool because she did not
stay here and marry me.'[2]

Twenty-eight years afterwards, Mary Owens, who soon married happily and well, gave Herndon her account, although reluctantly and as the result of much urging. She had never
heard, of course, of Lincoln's revelation to Mrs. Browning, nor
does it appear that his version had ever crept into the gossip of
New Salem. But Herndon by tenacious enquiry had learned
fragments of the facts and she felt, therefore, that the whole of
them should be stated. She writes frankly, yet with dignity and
reserve.

Referring to the report that she rebuffed Lincoln because of
his boast that he would marry her if she ever again came to
Illinois, Mrs. Vineyard writes that this is untrue. She did say to
her sister, 'who was very anxious for us to be married,' that she
'thought Mr. Lincoln was deficient in those little links which
make up the chain of woman's happiness — at least it was so in
my case.' Yet she did not attribute this deficiency to 'lack of
goodness of heart,' but to 'his training' which had been 'dif-

[1] Lincoln to Mrs. O. H. Browning, April 1, 1838. *Works*, i, 87–92.
[2] Mary S. Vineyard to Herndon, July 22, 1866. Herndon, i, 149–50.

ferent' from hers, so that 'there was not that congeniality which would otherwise have existed.' His letters to her showed that 'his heart and hand were at my disposal,' but she did not care enough 'to have the matter consummated.' When she left Illinois in 1838 her acquaintance and correspondence with Lincoln 'ceased without ever again being renewed.' [1]

No longer encumbered by the 'thraldom' of Miss Owens, Lincoln, with unburdened mind, could now practise law, which mildly interested him, mingle in the society of Springfield, which puzzled and attracted him, and, best of all, engage in politics, which fascinated and absorbed him. With the life of the Hankses, the Lincolns, and the Halls far behind him, out of New Salem which expired almost the moment he left it, free from sentimental ties with rural maidens, with even the Clary Grove Boys, now grown older and settled, only a fond but fast vanishing memory, Lincoln rapidly emerges upon his public career. Soon he is to move forward, sometimes halted by political misfortune, sometimes weighed down by domestic troubles, but onward in spite of all, and, on the whole, with ever increasing speed. Upon this journey, where the personal grows ever smaller and the public element ever larger, we shall now accompany Lincoln, taking as the first point of departure the Legislature at Vandalia.

[1] Mary S. Vineyard to Herndon, May 22, 1866. Herndon, I, 148.

CHAPTER IV
LEGISLATURE AND SPRINGFIELD

I am opposed to encouraging that lawless and mobocratic spirit . . . which is already abroad in the land. LINCOLN.

UPON the west bluff of the Kaskaskia River, sixty feet above high water, stood in 1834, perhaps a hundred buildings. All but two were of wood, some of them frame structures, but most of them log cabins. A little frame Presbyterian church house, without a steeple, nestled on a side street, while a still smaller building served for all other religious denominations as well as for school purposes and public gatherings. A comparatively large Methodist church was in process of construction.[1] Five or six of the bigger houses were taverns or boarding places, two of them would accommodate thirty or forty persons, though they were not entirely finished.[2] A watch and clock mender had a shop,[3] and three or four stores and groceries, the latter heavily stocked with all kinds of liquors,[4] supplied the wants of the town and countryside. A jail had just been finished.

[1] It was forty feet square and sixteen feet high. *Illinois Advocate*, Vandalia, Aug. 24, 1833.

The full title of this newspaper was at this time the *Illinois Advocate and State Register*. On April 15, 1835, it became the *Illinois Advocate* and so continued until March 8, 1836, when for about three months it was the *Illinois State Register and Illinois Advocate*. On June 24, 1836, it appeared as the *Illinois State Register and People's Advocate*, a name it retained until its removal in August, 1839, to the new capital, Springfield, where it dropped half its name and was from that time the *Illinois State Register*. The shorter titles — *Illinois Advocate* and *Illinois State Register* — are used in these notes.

[2] Carter's tavern was forty-four feet long by forty feet wide. *Ib.*, Feb. 9, 1833.

The National Hotel advertised a fine table and 'choicest wines and wholesome liquors.' *Ib.*, March 15, 1834.

'The House of Entertainment at the Sign of the Green Tree' assured customers that its 'Bar will be furnished with the choicest liquors of every kind.' *Ib.*, Dec. 16, 1835.

One tavern was called the 'New White House.' *Ib.*, Jan. 14, 1834.

The Vandalia Inn advertised that its dining room was forty-four by twenty feet and that it had thirteen bed-rooms. *Ib.*, Sept. 24, 1834.

[3] *Ib.*, Jan. 14, 1834.

[4] One of these advertised 'Groceries of all kinds, the most choice Liquors such as the best French Brandy, Holland Gin, Whisky, wines, etc.' *Ib.*, Feb. 4, 1835.

The most pretentious structure in the place was a brick building of two stories, in which met the General Assembly of Illinois when in session, members of the House in the lower story and those of the Senate in the upper story. On a street near by, a smaller brick building originally meant for a bank, was divided into a few rooms occupied by public officials. Two weekly newspapers, one Democratic and the other Whig, were published; and there was a school for 'Lads and Young Gentlemen.'[1]

About eight hundred people, including children, lived in the town[2] and the adjacent country was scantily settled; but marriages were frequent.[3] For the most part the surrounding land was heavily timbered, but to the north and west rolling prairies stretched into the horizon. The river bottoms were covered thickly with great trees, vines and all manner of rank vegetation; and from this valley came at the seasonable time clouds of mosquitoes.[4]

The streets of the village were eighty feet in width, deep with mud or dust according to the weather. There were no sidewalks. Two main roads ran through the place, one the National Road, scarcely opened as yet in this section,[5] from Washington seven hundred and eighty-one miles distant to St. Louis eighty-two miles to the southwest. Mails from Philadelphia and other Eastern cities were between two and three weeks on the way.[6]

[1] *The Illinois Advocate and State Register* and *The Vandalia Whig and Illinois Intelligencer.*
'Orthography, History, Rhetoric, Natural philosophy, Bookkeeping and Surveying,' as well as reading, writing, grammar, geography, and arithmetic were taught. *Illinois Advocate*, Sept. 14, 1833.

[2] *Illinois in 1837:* S. A. Mitchell, 129–30, states that the population of Vandalia was 850; but in *An Accompaniment to Mitchell's Map* published in 1838, 221, the population is given as 500; and *The Geographical Catechism:* Daniel Rupp, I, 357, says 750.

[3] In a single issue of the *Illinois Advocate* five marriage notices appeared, of one of which the editor observes: 'another of our young men has . . . stepped into the sea of connubial bliss, to be wafted by the gentle gales of domestic felicity, safely over the storms of life. . . . Let us go and do likewise.' *Illinois Advocate*, Dec. 7, 1833; Aug. 24 and Oct. 12, 1833.

[4] 'Bilious fever prevailed here. . . . There is a very extensive morass on the river bottom opposite the town . . . Vandalia cannot be a healthy place with this dismal swamp on the one side, and some very low wet prairies on the other.' *Eight Months in Illinois:* William Oliver, 99–100.

[5] 'This road is nothing more than a track.' *Ib.*, 99–100.

[6] This was especially true in the months of winter. The *Illinois Advocate* in January,

Another road, even more important at that time, led from Tennessee and Kentucky and traversed the whole of Illinois from
the southeast to the northwest corners of the State. This
thoroughfare passed through Springfield.[1]

Such was Vandalia [2] when on a winter day late in November,
1834, the regular stage coach was driven into the capital of
Illinois. Among the passengers was Abraham Lincoln, one of the
newly elected representatives from Sangamon County.[3]

He wore a new suit which, made by a tailor in Springfield, had
cost him sixty dollars. Lincoln had borrowed from Coleman
Smoot two hundred dollars in order properly to equip himself
and pay his expenses while away from New Salem on his first
legislative adventure. The loan was, whimsically declared Lincoln, when asking Smoot for the money, a kind of penalty upon
Smoot for having voted for him.[4] He was better attired and had
more clothes than ever before in his life.

It is reasonable to suppose that, upon this his initial journey
to the capital as a legislator, Lincoln accompanied John T.
Stuart and other members of the Sangamon delegation, and
that he put up at the same tavern where they boarded. Soon
the little town was thronged with law-makers, attorneys in attendance upon the Supreme Court of the State, and, more
numerous than all, those who wished the Legislature to adopt
various schemes. The gathering was 'unusually large.' [5] The
flow of whisky swelled in proportion to the increase of the tem-

1834, reported on the 23d that its 'latest dates from Washington are only of the 7th,'
and the interval might extend to seven weeks — Dec. 11 to Feb. 1 — as happened in
the winter of 1833-4. *Ib.*, Feb. 1, 1834.

[1] On Tanner's map of Illinois and Missouri, 1827, this road starts at Shawneetown
and runs through Mount Vernon, Washington, Edwardsville, Springfield, and Peoria
to Chicago on Lake Michigan.

[2] For descriptions of Vandalia in 1834 see *Historical Souvenir of Vandalia:* R. W.
Ross, 11–9; *Illinois Monthly Magazine*, II, 172–6 (Jan. 1832); Mitchell, 129–30; Oliver,
99–100; *Three Years in North America:* James Stuart, II, 397–408; *Illinois Advocate*,
Oct. 29, 1834.

The site of Vandalia was selected by a commission appointed under the Act of
March 30, 1819, as the place for the capital of the new state until 1840. The name was
probably reminiscent of the Vandalia Land Company of 1769.

[3] The stage left Springfield at six o'clock every Thursday morning and arrived in
Vandalia at two P.M. Friday. *Illinois Advocate*, Feb. 23, 1833; Herndon, I, 162.

[4] Smoot to Herndon, May 7, 1866. Weik MSS.

[5] The *Illinois Advocate*, Dec. 3, 1834.

porary sojourners in Vandalia and the popping of corks drawn from bottles was a familiar sound at candle-light. Lincoln found himself in a busy, joyous company, buoyant with the confidence of hope, thrilling with great projects and eager expectations.

During sessions of the Legislature, Vandalia was also the social centre of Illinois. The fashion and beauty of the State assembled at the capital at such times; wives of opulent members accompanied their husbands, and dancing and social gaiety enlivened the little town. Small and crude as Vandalia was, life there when the General Assembly met was in brilliant contrast with that of New Salem. All was planned and, as far as possible, conducted — manners, deportment, and dress — on the pattern of the capitals of the older states. More interesting still, and of first importance in the development of Lincoln's career, men of wealth and enterprise from all over Illinois, and even from other states, gathered at Vandalia during law-making season.

When on Monday, December 1, 1834,[1] Lincoln with his colleagues entered the State House, he found himself in a building, which, although erected but ten years earlier, was not far from the point of collapse. In places the brick walls were bulging, plaster had fallen from the ceiling, and dilapidation was conspicuous and menacing.[2] In his address to the Legislature Lieutenant-Governor William Lee D. Ewing [3] urged reform of the criminal code, that 'sanguinary body of criminal law;' but nothing was done to ameliorate its severity. Slave laws were drastic and cruel; yet nobody so much as suggested their amendment or repeal.[4] Advertisements of runaway slaves appeared frequently in the newspapers. On the third day of the session

[1] *House Journal*, Sess. 1834–5, 4.

[2] The condition of the State House was so bad that Governor Ewing in his message to the Legislature declared that the building 'is manifestly inconvenient for the transaction of public business' and that its 'appearance . . . is not calculated to add either character or credit to the State.' *Ib.*, 17.

The first State House, a frame structure, burned in the winter of 1823. During the following summer the citizens of Vandalia built the brick house described in the text, at a cost of $15,000, all but $3,000 of which was paid by the State. Robert W. Ross, 12–3.

[3] Gov. John Reynolds resigned, Nov. 17, 1834, and Lieutenant Governor Ewing thus became Governor until the inauguration of Governor-elect Joseph Duncan, Dec. 3. *Ib.*, 8, 24–5.

[4] No negro or mulatto 'held as a slave within this state' shall 'try his right to freedom,

three such advertisements with cuts were printed, giving particular descriptions of the escaping slaves.[1]

At this session Lincoln cast no vote of historical importance. With few exceptions, his name is recorded on calls of ayes and noes with that of John T. Stuart, leader of the Whigs in Sangamon County and, indeed, in the State. Stuart was also a member of the powerful Committee on the Judiciary.[2] As a new member, Lincoln was placed on the unimportant Committee on Public Accounts and Expenditures.[3] During the session he was appointed on two select committees, one to examine a bill to increase the number of election precincts in Morgan County and the other on the duties of the Attorney General.[4] He introduced a bill for a private toll-bridge across Salt Creek in Sangamon County which passed in due course.[5] The room in the State House used by the Council of Revision was not fit for occupancy; but Lincoln and two other members voted against renting a better office.[6]

The disposition of public lands belonging to the United States was a matter of first importance to the people of Illinois and for a number of years the Journals of the House and Senate contain many resolutions upon that subject. Midway in the session of the Legislature of 1834–35, Lincoln tried his hand at a solution of the problem. On January 10, 1835, he offered a resolution: 'that our Senators be instructed, and our Representatives requested, to use their whole influence in the Con-

---

or be discharged from slavery' by habeas corpus. Act, Jan. 22, 1827. *Revised Laws of Illinois*, 1827, 241. No negro or mulatto could settle in Illinois without a certificate of freedom and unless bond of $1000 was given that such colored person would not become a public charge as a poor person, and would 'demean himself or herself in strict conformity with the laws,' etc. Act, Jan. 17, 1829. 'Every black or mulatto person' without a certificate of freedom was 'deemed a runaway slave' whom anybody could arrest and take before a Justice of the Peace to be handed over to the Sheriff and, upon advertisement, hired out for one year. *Ib.*, 109–11. For an admirable summary of the 'black code,' see Ford, 33–4.

[1] *Illinois Advocate*, Dec. 3, 1834. These advertisements began to appear in large numbers just before Lincoln entered the Legislature. *Ib.*, Jan. 5, June 8, July 27, Aug. 31, Nov. 2, 1833, and March 1, May 3, Sept. 3, 10, 1834; and they continued throughout his entire legislative career. *Ib.*, Jan. 2, 6, 1836, Aug. 11, 14, 25, Sept. 1, 1837, etc. Often two or three slaves were described in a single advertisement.

[2] *House Journal*, Sess. 1834–5, 41.   [3] *Ib.*, 42.

[4] *Ib.*, 80, 453. Morgan County adjoined Sangamon.

[5] *Ib.*, 86, 141, 222, 245.   [6] *Ib.*, 86.

gress, of the United States, to procure the passage of a law relative to the public lands, by the operation of which the State of Illinois, would be entitled to receive annually, a sum of money not less in amount than twenty per cent upon the amount annually paid into the Treasury of the United States, for public lands lying within the limits of the said State of Illinois.' But the resolution was promptly laid on the table, without roll-call,[1] and Lincoln did not again press it.

In the election of State officers there was much trading, party lines not yet being so rigid as they speedily became. Lincoln supported his friends. Thus he voted for Ninian W. Edwards, a determined Whig, for Attorney General; but upon the resignation of Edwards, Lincoln voted for Jesse B. Thomas, an equally stubborn Democrat.[2] Lincoln voted for John J. Hardin, a fellow Whig, and against Stephen A. Douglas, Democrat, both of Morgan County, for State's Attorney of the First Judicial District; but he voted for William A. Richardson, an aggressive Democrat, and against a staunch and able Whig, O. H. Browning, for State's Attorney for the Fifth Judicial District.[3] Even in the election of a United States Senator, partisanship was not yet strictly observed. While Lincoln voted for Richard M. Young, then Whiggishly inclined, John M. Robinson, a forthright Democrat, was elected to succeed himself.[4]

---

[1] *House Journal*, Sess. 1834–5, 269. Mention of Lincoln's proposed amendment was made in the *Sangamo Journal* at Springfield, Jan. 24, 1835.

[2] Edwards was elected on the first ballot, receiving thirty-nine votes to thirty-six cast for Jesse B. Thomas, and on the second ballot forty-four to thirty-three for Thomas. *Ib.*, 196–7.

Thomas was elected, receiving fifty-five votes to thirteen for A. P. Dunbar and three for Seth T. Sawyer. *Ib.*, 521, Feb. 10, 1835.

[3] Douglas was elected, receiving thirty-eight votes to thirty-four for Hardin. *Ib.*, 522.

Richardson received fifty-seven votes to eleven for Browning. *Ib.*, 523–4. He was to become the chief lieutenant of Douglas in Congress, while Browning was to develop into one of Lincoln's most trusted agents in the United States Senate.

[4] Robinson, forty-seven, Young, thirty. *House Journal*, 142–3. Examples of Lincoln's other votes are: against a memorial to Congress praying that when public lands were sold they should be made subject to taxation (*ib.*, 69); against extending jurisdiction of Justices of the Peace (*ib.*, 73); for organizing agricultural societies (*ib.*, 101); that the House meet at nine instead of ten o'clock (*ib.*, 144); against making public prosecutors liable for costs in criminal suits not sustained in any court (*ib.*, 163); for the Public Roads Act (*ib.*, 171, 207); for the organization of circuit courts (*ib.*, 184); for election by the people of County Recorders and Surveyors (*ib.*, 129, 283, 284); for incorporation of Jacksonville Female Academy (*ib.*, 307, 326–7); and against making

Such are examples of Lincoln's votes and labors during his first experience as a legislator, such the nature of the business transacted by the General Assembly of Illinois at the session of 1834–35. In the end, an average amount of legislation was enacted. One law was of much importance and weighty influence on Lincoln's approaching career as a lawyer and legislator; of great effect, too, in the development of his economic and political opinions. This was the law, for which Lincoln voted, incorporating a new State Bank to be located at Springfield, an institution of which he was soon to become the stoutest champion and defender.[1] Also the charter of the Bank of Illinois at Shawneetown was extended;[2] and several acts, creating new judicial districts, directing the election of judges by the Legislature, providing for appeals and times of holding court, were passed.[3]

But, vital and pressing as were State problems and necessities, national politics also deeply interested the legislators. From the foundation of the Government a National Bank had been a source of sharp dispute among statesmen; and the people had divided on the issue, the commercial classes ardently favoring such an institution, while the farming and laboring classes were unfriendly to it. The first Bank of the United States, ably and honestly conducted as the fiscal agent of the Government, had been denied a recharter in 1811, partly because of Jefferson's hostility to it, but chiefly by the opposition of those who wished to establish and operate state banks without competition; and the second Bank of the United States, chartered in 1816, had had a stormy and variegated career. After a period of

the trustees of the Academy liable for contracts (*ib.*, 326); against the reapportionment of the State (*ib.*, 342); against reducing fees and salaries of Auditor and Treasurer (*ib.*, 219–20). He seldom was absent, missed scarcely a roll-call, and cast scores of votes, mostly on technical motions and unimportant matters.

[1] *House Journal*, Sess. 1834–5, 504–5, 511–2. Act, Feb. 12, *Laws of Illinois*, 1835, 7–14.

The bill was passed by a majority of only one and was the result of log-rolling. The 'making of a State's attorney made a State bank.' Ford, 171–2.

All Whigs were for the National Bank and most of them voted for this State institution. *Ib.*, 170. Ford says that there was no necessity for a State bank at that time. *Ib.*, 172–7; see especially, *Frontier State:* Pease, 304–5.

[2] Act, Feb. 12, 1835. *Laws of Illinois*, 1835, 21–2.

[3] Acts, Jan. 7, 17, and Feb. 13, 1835. *Ib.*, 150, 153, 167–72.

bad management, it, too, was successful and business had come to depend upon it for a trustworthy currency and the maintenance of stable conditions.

Soon after the election of Andrew Jackson, however, differences between the Bank and the President developed which speedily grew into hostility on both sides. The Bank was accused of subsidizing the press, buying influential politicians, corrupting Congress — worse still, of manipulating credits for its own advantage.

But the Bank was supported by the business interests of the country and Clay, Webster, and other powerful men in the National Senate and House were its determined champions. Influenced by hatred of the administration as much as by devotion to the Bank, these men had induced the Bank to apply formally to Congress in 1832 for a renewal of its charter which was to expire in 1836. This maladroit gesture was interpreted by Jackson as a move against him, the President accepted the challenge, and thus the Presidential campaign of 1832 had been fought largely on the issue of Bank or no Bank.

The popular voice was thunderous against the dread 'money power' of the East, and in support of 'the people's champion.' Jackson was re-elected,[1] and, thus sustained and heartened, he ordered that no more public funds be deposited with the Bank and was about to remove government money already there. Thereupon the Senate denounced Jackson's course as lawless, and the President replied by a protest which the Senate refused to enter on its Journal — a situation which aroused deep anger on both sides.

Of necessity, the Bank began to call its loans, and to the discerning signs were already apparent of the financial storm and business disaster which soon were to sweep over the land.[2] The Whigs denounced Jackson more bitterly than ever and the Democrats rallied to the cause of the 'Old Hero' with fiery enthusiasm. Clay and other anti-Jackson Senators were mere

[1] Clay was humiliatingly beaten, receiving forty-nine electoral votes to two hundred and nineteen for Jackson, eighteen being cast for other candidates.

[2] This business cataclysm was not wholly due to Jackson's attack on the Bank since the economic depression was world-wide in extent. See Channing, v, 455–8.

attorneys of the oppressive corporation and 'Menetekel is already written upon the Marble Palace,' declared the *Illinois Advocate*, voicing popular sentiment.[1]

So came the one notable political contest that took place in the Legislature of Illinois during the session of 1834–35, on a question which most concerned Lincoln for more than a decade. Those fundamental principles of national power under the Constitution, which Lincoln had already adopted and of which he was to become the greatest practical exponent, were the very crux of the Bank controversy.

On Monday, January 5, 1835, Jesse B. Thomas of Madison County introduced resolutions, with a long preamble, stating with vigor and ability the Democratic position on the Bank, stoutly supporting the course of President Jackson, and particularly approving the Administration's course toward France in relation to American claims upon that nation.[2]

Soon the matter came to a head [3] and the votes cast by Lincoln are of interest, showing his early views upon the grave constitutional and other questions involved in the Bank controversy. He voted against a motion to lay the resolutions on the table [4] and for a Whig amendment declaring 'a National Bank to be both useful and expedient.'[5] Lincoln then voted against the preamble and against every resolution, except that condemning the Senate for refusing to enter Jackson's protest upon its Journal and two others of a formal nature.[6] The next day the

[1] Jan. 18, 1834. 'The Marble Palace' was the popular name for the United States Bank at Philadelphia. See *Second Bank of the United States:* Ralph C. H. Catterall; Channing, v, 434–54; *Party Battles of the Jackson Period:* Claude Bowers, 287–385; *Life of Andrew Jackson:* John Spencer Bassett; and Beveridge, iv, 168–208, 288–9, 529–35.

[2] *House Journal*, Sess. 1834–5, 213–6. Thomas's resolutions and preamble were published in full in the Democratic organ, the *Illinois Advocate*, Jan. 21, 1835. The *Advocate* called the attention of Eastern Whig papers to the adoption of these resolutions by the Senate and observed, 'We hope the Whigs will make no further calculations on Illinois.'

[3] *House Journal*, Sess. 1834–5, 216–7.

[4] Defeated, forty-two nays to eight ayes, Lincoln voting nay. *Ib.*, 258.

[5] *Ib.*, 258–9. The amendment was beaten by a majority of nine.

[6] *Ib.*, 259–63. These other resolutions approved the Illinois delegation for supporting Jackson's administration and directed the Governor to transmit the resolutions.

These ballotings are important as showing the temper of the Legislature and the fluctuations in voting. The votes on the resolution condemning the Bank for mis-

Senate adopted similar resolutions by a vote of seventeen ayes to nine nays.[1]

But the friends of the Bank would not acknowledge defeat. Twelve days later the Bank resolutions were again considered, amended and adopted, Lincoln voting for them.[2] Still the matter was not settled. The vote was immediately reconsidered, and the fight renewed. After debate and a mass of parliamentary thrusts and parries, the resolutions as amended were again adopted, Lincoln once more voting aye.[3] Seemingly his views were not clear, though favorable to the Bank.

Heated debates in the House were supplemented by continuous discussion in the lobby which was a place almost equal to the House itself in influencing legislative opinion. Indeed, this third House may have been more effective on members.[4] After adjournment, especially at night, the lobby was always thronged, speeches made, and debates held without parliamentary restraints. Thus for nearly three weeks Lincoln heard what was said on all phases of the National Bank and the currency; but it does not appear that he took part in the controversy.

Finally, by the dim light of candles, the General Assembly finished its work and, sometime before midnight, February 13, 1835, adjourned *sine die*.[5] His first legislative experience thus ended, Lincoln went back to New Salem and again took up his surveying and handling of the scanty mail. The sum of his sojourn in Vandalia had been the making of friends, lessons in legislative procedure and manipulation, and the acquiring of

conduct and against recharter were ayes thirty-seven, nays fourteen; on approving Jackson's removal of deposits, ayes thirty-five, nays fifteen; on condemning the Senate for refusing to receive Jackson's protest, ayes forty-six, nays five; on instructing Illinois Senators and Representatives to oppose recharter and restoration of deposits, ayes forty-three, nays eight; on approving Jackson's course on the French claims, ayes twenty-nine, nays twenty-two; on approving the Illinois delegation for supporting Jackson's administration, ayes forty-four, nays seven; and on requesting the Governor to transmit, ayes forty-five, nays five.

[1] *Illinois Advocate*, Jan. 21, 1835.   [2] *House Journal*, Sess. 1834–5, 355–7.

[3] Thirty-one ayes to twenty-four nays. *Ib.*, 358–9.

[4] The lobby was the object of much good humored badinage. Once a satirical notice was published, signed 'Coke, Speaker' and 'Littleton, Clerk,' calling the lobby to assemble and take charge of legislation. *Illinois State Register*, June 17, 1837. The lobby was made up of important men. Herndon, i, 163.

[5] *House Journal*, Sess. 1834–5, 572–4.

knowledge of basic constitutional principles. He had heard great questions discussed by able and informed men. He had met cultivated women, too, and, in short, had visited a new world. Small wonder that, when he reached New Salem, he plunged into study with such abandon that his health suffered and friends thought him mentally affected. Henceforth the log-cabin hamlet on the Sangamon held little or nothing that was attractive to the aspiring young Lincoln.

So much remained to be done and so generally desired was a reapportionment of the State, that Governor Duncan called an extra session of the Legislature. It met December 7, 1835, and, from the beginning,[1] Lincoln took active and frequent part in the proceedings.[2] On the third day he moved to lay on the table a resolution for the reapportionment of the State.[3]

In an effort to amend the law incorporating the State Bank, there were much debate and some curious balloting. Lincoln voted to reserve to the State 'the right to repeal this section [the one then being enacted], whenever the public interest may require the same;'[4] yet he moved to strike out this very reservation and to add, instead, a new section providing that the Bank should report to every general session of the Legislature 'the amounts of debts due *from* said corporation, the amount of debts due *to* the same; the amount of specie in its vaults, and an account of all lands then owned by the same, and the amount for which such lands have been taken; and, moreover, if said corporation shall at any time neglect or refuse to submit its books,

[1] The *Sangamo Journal* (Dec. 5, 1835) anticipated a lively winter for its readers: Congress, Legislature, 'politics, the War in Texas, the threatened war with France,' etc., etc.

[2] For example: road petition (*House Journal*, Spl. Sess. 1835–6, 28); notice of a bill supplementary to the insolvent debtor law of 1829 (*ib.*, 32); memberships of select committees (*ib.*, 33, 34, 66); demand for ayes and noes on the convention system (*ib.*, 27); an important amendment to the State Bank bill (*ib.*, 124).

[3] *Ib.*, 28. This motion meant merely that the subject should be taken up later. Since the apportionment involved partisan politics, this motion indicates that Lincoln was becoming one of the Whig floor leaders.

[4] *Ib.*, 108. Lincoln merely voted for the bill after the reservation had been adopted by general consent. Reservation to Legislatures of the power to repeal or amend charters and other corporate privileges was the method adopted by State Legislatures when granting franchises, to avoid the decision of the Supreme Court of the United States in the Dartmouth College case, 1819, that a franchise is a contract and cannot be impaired. See Beveridge, IV, 220–81.

papers, and all and everything necessary to a full and fair examination of its affairs, to any person or persons appointed by the General Assembly, for the purpose of making such examination, the said corporation shall forfeit its charter.' [1]

The House *Journal* indicates that a flurry arose over Lincoln's motion, but, without roll-call, the House refused to strike out and by a vote of thirty-four to fifteen rejected his amendment. In his turn, he voted against an amendment for a heavy penalty on the State Bank for extending the time of redeeming its notes; and the bill finally passed by consent.[2] He also steadily upheld measures for the building of the Illinois and Michigan Canal.[3]

Echoes of the storm raging in Washington over the Bank of the United States again sounded in the tumble-down brick capitol of Illinois. After several days of debate the Senate, by a vote of fifteen to ten,[4] sent to the House for concurrence a joint resolution demanding that the National Senate expunge from its *Journal* the now famous resolutions of that body censuring Jackson for the removal of deposits from the Bank of the United States. Lincoln and fifteen other Whigs voted against this resolution which was adopted, however, by a vote of more than two to one. Several Whigs even supported it.[5]

Indeed national politics continually intruded on the work of the General Assembly. A Democratic Convention was held in Vandalia, December 7, 1835, and issued an address to the people in behalf of Van Buren,[6] and plans were laid to put through the House strong resolutions designed to aid the party in the ensuing Presidential campaign.[7] Early in the session the Senate, Whig

---

[1] *House Journal*, Spl. Sess. 1835–6, 124–5.   [2] *Ib.*, 125–6.

[3] *Ib.*, 39–40, 46, 54, 69, 71, 119.

[4] *Sangamo Journal*, Dec. 19, 1835.

[5] *House Journal*, Spl. Sess. 1835–6, 44, 62–3. The Vandalia correspondent of the *Sangamo Journal*, who almost certainly was Lincoln, predicted that if the Senate resolution passed the House at all, 'the majority will be small.' *Sangamo Journal*, Dec. 19, 1835.

[6] *Ib.*, Dec. 5, 1835. *Illinois Advocate*, Feb. 17, 1836. This campaign document filled three and one half columns of the Democratic organ and was signed by six leading Democrats, including Douglas, who probably wrote it. Much time and care were expended upon it, and it was not finished until Dec. 31, 1835, more than three weeks after the date of the Convention. *Ib.*

[7] *Life of Stephen A. Douglas:* Frank E. Stevens, *Journal Ill. State Hist. Soc.*, XVI, 295.

by a majority of one, passed a resolution nominating for President, Hugh L. White, United States Senator from Tennessee. Immediately the Democratic minority filed a vigorous protest which was printed in the Democratic organ.[1]

Thus State and National politics became intertwined. The party convention as a method of nominating candidates was not new as applied to states. In Illinois Stephen A. Douglas advocated and the Democrats had adopted it.[2] Already a Democratic National Convention at Baltimore, under orders from Jackson, had nominated Martin Van Buren of New York and Richard M. Johnson of Kentucky, as the Democratic candidates for President and Vice President in the campaign of the following year.

From the first the Whigs looked with disfavor upon this Democratic device and the Illinois Whigs were particularly antagonistic to it,[3] albeit their leader and idol, Henry Clay, had been nominated by a national convention in 1832. Democratic irritation was further inflamed by the anti-Jackson men taking the name of Whig.

Soon after the nomination of White for the presidency by the Whig majority of the Illinois Senate, a blazing Democratic resolution was introduced into the House denouncing 'the false and arrogant claims of the Webster, White, and Harrison party to the exclusive use of the ancient and honorable name of *Whig*,' endorsing the nomination by the Baltimore Convention of Van Buren and Johnson, approving the convention system, viewing with alarm the spurious Whig efforts to divide the Democratic party, exalting Jackson and assailing his foes.[4] These pronouncements, with an almost incoherent preamble,[5] were adopted by a strict party vote,[6] Lincoln voting nay.

[1] *Illinois Advocate*, Dec. 23, 1835; Feb. 17, 1836.

[2] *Frontier State:* Pease, 251–7; Ford, 203. See Ford's admirable description of a convention. Ford, 205–6. And see pre-convention editorial denouncing the Whig position in *Illinois State Register*, May 6, 1836. Douglas was then only twenty-three years old.

[3] Ford, 203.　　　　[4] *House Journal*, Spl. Sess. 1835–6, 211–2.

[5] This preamble declared that: 'Whereas, During the late War with England in 1812; and during the great political struggles of 1798–1812–1824 and 1828, the people

[6] Thirty-one ayes to twenty nays. *House Journal*, Spl. Sess. 1835–6, 233. About the year 1833 those opposed to Jackson began to call themselves Whigs.

The enraged Whigs fought hard. Lincoln's colleague from Sangamon, John Dawson, moved an amendment that such resolutions were beyond the duties of 'the Representatives of a free people;' and Stuart asked for debate by referring the entire matter to the Committee of the whole House.[1] The Democrats refused. Whig resolutions against the convention system were quickly offered, again the Whigs asked for debate, again the Democrats peremptorily declined. Lincoln voted for the Whig resolution condemning party conventions which, however, was defeated by a vote of thirty-two to nineteen; for one asserting that every man 'has an undeniable right to become a candidate ... without the sanction of a caucus or convention,' which was carried almost unanimously; for that declaring that 'the convention system ought not to receive encouragement or approbation from Legislative bodies,' which was defeated by only one vote; and for the resolution declaring that public officers should not attempt to influence elections, which only seven members had the temerity to oppose.[2]

Then the House again voted on the Democratic resolutions. Lincoln demanded a division of the question, and the wild preamble, together with each of the resolutions already described, was finally adopted, Lincoln voting against every one of them.[3] Influential Democrats from all over the State were in Vandalia watchful of their party's welfare, while prominent Whigs, on a similar mission, were absent. 'There are no White men here from a distance,' laments the Vandalia correspondent of the

of New York, Pennsylvania, Virginia, and the Southern and Western States, a great majority of whom are now supporting the election of Martin Van Buren, and Richard M. Johnson, and opposed to the election of Hugh L. White, were of the Democratic Party; and as the Federalists of the New England States, who are now supporting Webster for President; and opposed Madison the War President, and Democratic candidate in 1814; when the success of the war depended upon the democratic party, and opposed General Jackson in 1824, and voted against him in Congress in 1825 — the People's candidate — opposed to Executive Patronage; and as the State of South Carolina, now supporting Hugh L. White, has taken the lead in the measures of Nullification. Therefore Resolved, etc.'

[1] When the House went into Committee of the Whole it was for the purpose of preliminary debate and amendment. House Rules 38 and 39. *House Journal*, Spl. Sess. 1835-6, 58.

Dawson had been elected as a Democrat, but became a Whig about this time, as did many other Democrats.

[2] *Ib.*, 233-4.   [3] *Ib.*, 238-40.

Sangamo Journal, 'while the hotels are lined with the ruffle-shirted Vannies.[1] There is no one here whose sole business it is to puff Judge White; consequently I seldom hear his name except when I go among *the people,* where (God be praised!) I hear nothing else.' [2]

Stuart and Lincoln, with an eye to the contest in the next Legislature over the removal of the State capital to Springfield, seem to have cast their votes with foresight when the granting of favors, even appropriations of State money to particular counties, was brought to decision by roll-call.[3] They also supported a popular resolution that Congress grant to the State the right to enter not more than half a million acres of government land at a dollar and a quarter an acre upon ten years credit, to aid Illinois in making internal improvements.[4]

Necessary legislation for starting work on the Illinois and Michigan Canal was enacted,[5] the State reapportioned and, in response to the demand for internal improvements, several railway companies incorporated,[6] all but one of little or no importance. These, however, were but a small beginning of the riot of improvement laws that were to make the next Legislature one of the most notable in the history of Illinois. The movement for State construction and ownership which so powerfully moulded the legislation of the following year, was already under way. On Saturday forenoon, February 7, 1836, the extra session of the House was adjourned.[7]

In such fashion went forward Lincoln's training in legislation and the ways of public men. Back to New Salem he journeyed,

---

[1] Supporters of Hugh L. White or Martin Van Buren.

[2] *Sangamo Journal,* Dec. 19, 1835.

[3] For example $300 to Edgar County and $400 to Jefferson County to be expended by the County Commissioners 'for the improvement of the public roads therein.' *House Journal,* Spl. Sess. 1835–6, 292.

[4] *Ib.,* 360–1.

[5] *Laws of Illinois,* 2 Sess. 1835–6, 145–54. The plans for the canal involved a cost of $9,000,000, 'a mere nothing' to this Legislature, observes Gov. Ford. Ford, 197.

[6] Of the Illinois Central, the *Illinois Advocate* declared that it was 'a noble enterprise ... the backbone of the State,' and predicted that it would be extended to Nashville to meet at that city the railroads from Charleston and New Orleans. *Illinois Advocate,* Feb. 24, 1836. The history of the Illinois Central is related in *History of Transportation in the United States before* 1860 (Carnegie Institution): Victor S. Clark, 513–47.

[7] *House Journal,* Spl. Sess. 1835–6, 409, 414.

with increased distaste for the rough pleasures and placid joys of that hamlet which he was soon to abandon — but not before he should again be elected to the Legislature.

Party discipline had now become so strict that the Democrats, even of New Salem, did not again offer to Lincoln their organized support; but Sangamon County turned strongly Whig in the ensuing election and, as we have seen, Lincoln once more received a big majority. At the opening of the session of the General Assembly Monday, December 5, 1836, Stuart no longer being a member,[1] Lincoln was the Whig floor leader, recognized on all hands as a clever parliamentary tactician and likely to become the manager in the House. Only adroit and skilful persons — 'sleek men,' as Governor Ford calls them [2] — succeeded, Lincoln had observed; and since the one great contest of his life thus far — a contest the outcome of which was to have strong and directive influence on his career — was at hand, he was prepared to meet and overcome all the craft and guile that should oppose him. His supreme purpose now was to secure the removal of the capital to Springfield; upon the achievement of that design he concentrated every faculty during the next three months.

In 1833 the Legislature had provided that at the general election held the following year, the people should vote for a place at which the capital should be permanently established, but no majority was given for any location. Alton led with 7511, Vandalia followed with 7148, Springfield was third with 7044, Jacksonville, Peoria and 'The Geographical Centre,' dividing 1532 votes among them.[3] The Alton interest was very powerful

[1] Stuart was not a candidate for the Legislature in 1836, having run for Congress instead. But he was in Vandalia as a lobbyist for the removal of the State Capital to Springfield. See p. 178, *infra*. The Stuart whose name appears on the roll-calls during this session was Robert Stuart of Tazewell Co. *House Journal*, Sess. 1836–7, 4.

[2] Ford, 103.

[3] Springfield stoutly maintained that the law for this election was unfair. 'It was designed to divide the vote of the north, so that by artful management . . . a majority of votes, or at least a large plurality, could be obtained for Alton;' four places near Springfield had been named for which electors could vote, and thus the Northern men divided; some counties did not vote at all. At the same election 33,239 votes were cast for Governor and only 23,255 for all capital locations; it was sheer trickery, but for which Springfield would have received at least 14,000 votes and beaten Vandalia and Alton badly. *Sangamo Journal*, Sept. 27, 1834.

and either that town or Vandalia preferred the other over Springfield.

By the reapportionment of 1835 Sangamon County, with 17,571 white population, had seven representatives and two senators, the largest delegation in the Legislature. All were trained men, most of them having had legislative experience. Because of the great height of these men, they were given the nickname of the 'Long Nine.' They acted together and voted on all questions so as to promote the interests of Springfield.[1]

Vandalia had tried to impress the legislators.[2] The old State House was about to fall and a new frame building had been erected which, however, was unfinished — the plastering being so damp and the rooms so cold, that 'additional stoves' had to be put in.[3] But the town had increased in population and enterprise since Lincoln's first sojourn at the capital. There were two or three more stores, one of them advertising, among other things, 'Kid pumps,' another all kinds of shirtings, prints, flannels, cassimeres, 'ladies boots and shoes,' and men's fur, wool and palm leaf hats, while a grocery announced the arrival of three pipes of champagne, French and American brandy, and eight barrels of whisky;[4] and, before the Legislature met and during its sessions, a big advertisement appeared of a bookstore, with a long list of volumes, including law books, Bulwer's novels, as well as *Godey's Lady's Book* and other magazines.[5] A saddle and harness shop had been opened,[6] and the town had at least three doctors who published their professional cards in the press,

---

[1] Robert L. Wilson to Herndon, Feb. 10, 1866. Weik MSS.

[2] Two years earlier a committee of its citizens had issued a long and careful statement setting forth the advantages of the town, the injustice of the capital law, nay, its unconstitutionality. *Illinois Advocate*, July 19, 1834.

[3] Senate Resolutions, Feb. 3, 1837 (*House Journal*, Sess. 1836–7, 471); and Report of Select Committee (*ib.*, 479–80). The structure cost $16,378.22½ of which $5550 was paid by the State officers, out of the contingent fund and $450 by individual subscriptions, leaving $10,378.22½ unpaid. *Illinois State Register*, Dec. 16, 1836.

[4] *Illinois Advocate*, Jan. 20; *Illinois State Register*, July 29, Aug. 26, 1836.

[5] *Ib.*, Dec. 23, 1836. Also *Illinois Advocate*, Feb. 18, 1835, advertising school books and 'medical, historical and miscellaneous' standard works. A later advertisement included Vattel's *Law of Nations*, Blackstone, Zoller's *Law of Executors*, Jefferson's *Works*, 4 vols., Franklin's *Works*, 2 vols., Robertson's *America* and *Charles V*, Marshall's *Life of Washington*, etc. *Ib.*, Jan. 2, 1836.

[6] *Illinois Advocate*, Dec. 23, 1835.

as was the custom of the time.[1] In short, Vandalia was a place of comparative comfort and culture, energy and good cheer, during the winter of 1836–37.

This Legislature was remarkable not only in what was done but in the quality of its members. There was a strange mingling of vision and blindness, of fine ability bloated with unreasoning optimism; and through all ran the poisonous filaments of the politician's deals and trades. Of the more than one hundred members of House and Senate, not one had been born in Illinois; and this was true, too, of the three members of the Supreme Court, the many lawyers in attendance upon it, and the throng of lobbyists who came to Vandalia whenever the General Assembly met, and who, since great enterprises were at hand, were especially numerous during this session.

Most conspicuous were the members of the Supreme Court — William Wilson, Chief Justice, able and learned; Samuel D. Lockwood, highly educated and a fine lawyer; Thomas C. Brown, 'the Falstaff of the bench,' who never refused nor offered a drink, and made up for his total ignorance of the law by a quick, audacious wit and friendly good nature.[2] All three Justices were ardent Whigs.

Among the attorneys at Vandalia, the most prominent was Justin Butterfield of Chicago, who was attending the Supreme Court, a good lawyer and a cultivated man of sparkling humor,[3] and Josiah Lamborn who was afterwards elected Attorney-General.[4] Gurdon S. Hubbard was an example of the lobbyists. Born in New England, he had become an Indian trader in Illinois, spoke several Indian dialects perfectly, and during the ses-

---

[1] *Illinois Advocate*, March 16, 1836.

[2] *Reminiscences:* by Usher F. Linder, 73, 264–5. Also *Early Bench and Bar of Illinois:* John Dean Caton, 173. 'If he ever read a law book it was so long ago that he must have forgotten it. . . . He never wrote an opinion.' *Ib.* Judge Caton served with Brown as Justice of the Supreme Court, was an uncommonly able lawyer and became one of the foremost men of the State. He was a Democrat and an ardent supporter of Douglas.

[3] Linder, 87–8; Ford, 295. Twelve years later Butterfield beat Lincoln for Commissioner of the Land Office. See p. 489, *infra.* He was a native of New York, opposed the War of 1812 and came to Chicago to make a new start. It was Butterfield who, although a staunch Whig, said of the Mexican War when his party was opposing it: 'No, by G—d, . . . I opposed one war, and it ruined me, and henceforth I am for *War, Pestilence, and Famine.*' Linder, 87.

[4] *Ib.*, 258–9.

sion, with others scarcely less qualified, performed an Indian war-dance for the amusement of the legislators.[1] Former Governor John Reynolds, the 'Old Ranger,' was there, too,[2] cordial and grave, with the mingled reserve and heartiness of the frontier.

Of all those in Vandalia during that memorable winter, John T. Stuart was the best known. He was over six feet tall, the 'handsomest man in Illinois,' an able, and resourceful lawyer, deferential in manner, benignant of countenance and, for years to come, an influential man in the State.[3] But he was known as a plotter and manipulator — 'Jerry Sly,'[4] his political enemies called this closest associate of Lincoln. The reverse of Stuart in appearance and method was Rev. John Hogan of Alton, of Irish birth, once a Methodist preacher, florid of face, boisterous of manner, bold and outspoken, an incessant talker, frequently in debate, aggressively optimistic, looking at all things through rose-colored spectacles.[5]

Ninian W. Edwards of Springfield, who was 'naturally and constitutionally an aristocrat, and . . . hated democracy . . . as the devil is said to hate holy water,' was an example of the class-conscious higher orders of society. With a manner lofty and aloof, vain, proud of his name and family, he was unpopular.[6] His attire was of the best material, made in the latest mode of fashion. In the State Senate was Cyrus Edwards of Madison County, uncle of Ninian W. Edwards, and his equal in apparel and conduct. 'The great Edwards family' was well represented in the General Assembly of 1836–37.[7] Into this family Lincoln was to marry within five years.

Of the same type was another Whig, Edwin B. Webb of White County, born in Kentucky, of an old Virginia family, refined,

---

[1] Linder, 333–4. Hubbard had been a member of a preceding Legislature and introduced the first railroad bill to defeat the Illinois & Michigan Canal scheme. It passed the House and was beaten in the Senate by only one vote.

[2] Ib., 148–51.   [3] Ib., 347–9; Duis, 122.   [4] Linder, 347–9.

[5] Ib., 59–60; 371–3. Hogan was one of those who sought to compose the quarrel between Elijah Lovejoy and the citizens of Alton in 1837. Linder, then Attorney General of the State, strove to avert the collision and, failing to make peace, took with Hogan the side of the citizens against Lovejoy.

[6] Ib., 279–81.

[7] Ib., 353–5. Cyrus Edwards was six feet four inches tall, the exact stature of Lincoln.

undersized, alert. He was devoted to Lincoln, who returned his affection.[1] Another friend of Lincoln in the House whose adherence grew ever closer through the years, was 'a slim, handsome young man, with auburn hair, sky-blue eyes, with the elegant manners of a Frenchman,' Jesse K. Dubois of Lawrence County.[2] John A. McClernand, then of Shawneetown and a fighting Democrat who, twenty-five years later, was to bear so gallant and distinguished a part in the Civil War, was also a member of the House. He was only twenty-four years old, was uncommonly able, a fluent speaker,[3] and quickly developed into one of the Democratic leaders.

The Speaker, James Semple, originally a tanner but now a lawyer, was a Democrat of outstanding note and influence, strong-willed, domineering, but highly capable, though neither eloquent nor learned.[4] Orlando B. Ficklin of Wabash County was also a member of the House, well-informed, resourceful and, like Lincoln, a notable mimic, wag, and story teller.[5] One of the most popular members was a slender young man of twenty-six but already a veteran, having been dangerously wounded while serving as a soldier in Florida, James Shields, with whom, in a few years, Lincoln was to have a serious personal difficulty. Shields spoke and wrote French, was a hard student,[6] generous, frank, engaging, and utterly without physical fear. He was a thorough-going Democrat, and was thrice to become a Senator of the United States from three different States and to hold more offices, civil and military, than almost any other man in American history.

More of Lincoln's mould was Archibald Williams of Adams County, over six feet tall, angular and uncouth. He and Lincoln sat near to each other in the southeast corner of the House and were friends and confidants. So striking was their ungainly appearance that a stranger asked, 'Who in the hell are those two ugly men?' Years afterward Lincoln declared that Williams was 'the strongest-minded and clearest headed man he ever

[1] Linder, 266–7.

[2] *Ib.*, 68–9; Dubois named one of his sons for Lincoln, Major Lincoln Dubois of Hinsdale, Ill.

[3] *Ib.*, 71–2.   [4] *Ib.*, 218–9.   [5] *Ib.*, 110–2.

[6] *Life of James A. Shields:* W. M. Condon, 219.

saw.'[1] One of the most picturesque figures in the House and a member of power and influence was Usher F. Linder, who, many years later, wrote descriptions of his fellow members in this historic session. He, too, was more than six feet in stature, slender, raw-boned, and as awkward as Lincoln. He was born in Kentucky a few weeks after the birth of Lincoln and in the same county.[2] He was well-educated, a good lawyer, almost irresistible before a jury, a vigorous partisan, formidable in debate, and a 'terror on the stump.'

At this session appeared a young representative from Morgan County who, soon thereafter, pressed Lincoln hard for the Whig leadership of the House and within five years passed him in political career. He was a college graduate and a lawyer, able, combative, and courageous, but without Lincoln's adroitness and political cleverness. Tall, well-dressed, with dark eyes, thick black hair and bold, determined, intellectual face, John J. Hardin was an attractive, manly figure.[3] His father was Martin D. Hardin, Secretary of State of Kentucky, where the son was born. In exactly a decade after Hardin entered the Legislature of Illinois, it was to be his fortune to be killed in battle while leading his regiment at Buena Vista.

With Cyrus Edwards in the State Senate, was Orville H. Browning of Quincy, a stalwart Whig. He was a finely educated man, a careful and successful lawyer, a good politician, stately and courteous, always dressed with scrupulous care. He was to become one of the founders of the Republican party and, during the War, Lincoln's mouthpiece in the United States Senate. His wife was with him and Linder makes particular mention of her as 'an elegant and accomplished lady.'[4] It was she to whom Lincoln wrote the account of his escape from the matrimonial 'bondage' to Mary Owens.[5] In the Senate also was William H.

---

[1] Linder, 238–43.

[2] *Ib.*, 21. Linder was a Democrat in 1836–7, but became a Whig in 1838–9 and remained such until, as he declares, the Whigs were merged in the Abolitionists whom Linder, like most men of the time, greatly disliked. *Ib.*, 281.

[3] Daguerreotype of Hardin of a few years later.

[4] Linder, 83. She was Eliza Caldwell, of a Kentucky family, and married Browning Feb. 25, 1836.

[5] See p. 156, *supra.*

JOHN J. HARDIN

Davidson of White County, a brother-in-law of Chief Justice
Wilson, a handsome man, well educated, wealthy, of the old
Virginia school, and, of course, an unyielding Whig.[1]

Of all members of the General Assembly, however, the most
curious in appearance was a newly elected Democratic member
from Morgan County, Stephen A. Douglas, who, from the first,
attracted more attention than any other person in Vandalia.
Only slightly more than five feet tall, he seemed a dwarf among
the stalwart men about him — 'looked like a boy,' his colleagues said.[2] A mighty head covered with a great mass of
thickly growing dark brown hair, powerful neck and shoulders
and deep chest, made more conspicuous his short stature. His
voice was a deep barytone — some said a vibrant bass. Strong,
aggressive jaws and chin added to the impression of singular
force, even bellicosity, given by his whole physical make-up; but
the friendly, generous mouth softened the severity of his appearance.

If, aside from his small height, one feature was more striking
than others, it was his eyes of deepest blue, which were uncommonly large, intelligent, bold, alert, and so brilliant that a newspaper correspondent describes them as 'shooting out electric
fires.'[3] He was, if possible, more ambitious than Lincoln, an
incessant talker, fecund in plan, adroit in management. With
the vision of the statesman he was already an adept in the tricks
of the politician. As ingratiating as he was combative, he
made friends quickly and on every hand, and these friends stuck
to him through thick and thin.

Born in Vermont, April 23, 1813, he was twenty-three years
of age. His father was a physician, and tradition says his grandfather had been one of Washington's soldiers at Valley Forge.
Educated in the common schools of his native State and at
Brandon Academy, he had also learned the trade of cabinet-
making. He studied law in New York and thence went to Illinois to practise his profession. He arrived, practically destitute,
at Winchester, Morgan County, where at first he taught school
for a living. He soon removed to Jacksonville, opened a law

[1] Linder, 272-3.   [2] Ib., 78.
[3] Correspondent of New York Times, as quoted in Life of Douglas: H. M. Flint, 14.

office, and quickly growing in popularity, took active and vigorous part in politics. A local quarrel resulted in his election as
State's Attorney, which office he resigned when elected to the
Legislature. Because of an effective speech at a Democratic
meeting at Jacksonville in 1834 when all others in his party were
disheartened and despondent, he had been given the title of
'The Little Giant' — a title which his work in the Legislature
was to confirm and establish permanently. Stephen A. Douglas
was now to make his first appearance as a law-maker, and, on a
larger stage than his county, as a politician and a statesman.[1]

Such in general was the Legislature, the lobby and the surroundings in the midst of which Lincoln found himself in his
third session of the General Assembly. There was so much
drinking during those winter months that even Linder makes
mention of it — 'a little too convivial most of us were in early
times,' he observes.[2] Now and then, indeed, a member was too
drunk to debate well.[3] Duels were sometimes fought, and chal-
lenges expected when sufficient offence was given. Although
advertisements of runaway slaves were conspicuous in the
Vandalia newspapers and appeared with increasing frequency,[4]
no one did or said anything about the matter.

After organization on Monday, December 5, the House again
chose James Semple speaker. Immediately Lincoln, as Whig
floor leader, moved that the House proceed to the election of a
principal clerk.[5] Soon afterward Douglas, from the Committee
on Petitions, submitted a report and bill for the organization of

---

[1] 'Autobiography of Stephen A. Douglas,' *Journal Ill. State Hist. Socy.*, v, 323–42;
'Life of Stephen A. Douglas,' Frank E. Stevens, *ib.*, xvi, 247–86; *Stephen A. Douglas:
A Study in American Politics*, Allen Johnson, 3–22; *Life of Stephen A. Douglas:* James
W. Sheahan, 1–27.

'During that session Douglass made himself known all over the State.' John Wentworth to Herndon, Feb. 4, 1866. Weik MSS.

[2] Linder, 74–5, 228.

[3] *Ib.*, 52–3. Midway in this session a Vandalia grocery advertised an astonishing
variety of groceries and liquors, including champagne, six kinds of brandy in pipes and
barrels, Holland and American gin, several barrels of Irish and Monongahela whisky,
six barrels of beer, Burgundy, Madeira, Sherry, claret, and two brands of Port wines.
Also 'bottles assorted, pint and half pint flasks.' *Illinois State Register*, Jan. 19, 1837.

[4] In the *Illinois State Register* of Dec. 23, 1836, there were four such advertisements.
And see *ib.*, Jan. 6, March 9, 16, April 1, 8, 1836.

[5] *House Journal*, Sess. 1836–7, 5–8.

a new county to be formed of a part of Sangamon County. A minority report against the division of Sangamon County was offered, and Lincoln moved that it be spread on the Journal of the House in order 'that his constituents might see that report.'[1] Linder objected and a lively interchange between him and Lincoln ensued. Lincoln thought it 'uncourteous and a departure from the rules of etiquette' for Linder to meddle in the matter at all. Linder sarcastically thanked Lincoln for 'the lesson which he had read to the House on etiquette;' but if his constituents wanted the minority report 'let them print it out of their own pockets. They are rich enough, God knows: they hold the bag like Judas, and with as little merit as he.' For reasons soon to be stated Lincoln made no reply, and his motion was beaten by a vote of nearly two to one.[2]

Early in the session Richard M. Young was elected Senator of the United States, Lincoln voting for his friend Archibald Williams on each of the three ballots. As was the custom of the time, Senator-elect Young gave a banquet to his adherents at which much whisky and champagne were consumed and riotous merriment abounded. Douglas and Shields, as the smallest, lightest, and most agile of the banqueters, finally mounted the table, dancing together back and forth upon it amid shouts of approval and to such destruction of glasses, bottles, and other tableware that Young had to pay six hundred dollars for the damage done.[3]

Throughout the session, news-letters concerning the proceedings of the Legislature appeared in the Whig paper at Springfield, the *Sangamo Journal*, and some appear to have been written by Lincoln. While in New Salem he had begun to write pieces for the *Journal*[4] and the style of those from Vandalia strongly suggests him.[5] His authorship was suspected, it seems. A quaint letter dated Vandalia, December 30, 1836, relates that

[1] *House Journal*, Sess. 1836-7, 82-3, 86.

[2] Forty-four nays to twenty-four ayes. *Illinois State Register*, Jan. 12, 1837, reporting House proceedings of Dec. 21, 1836.

[3] Stevens, 299.

[4] Statement J. H. Matheny, no date. Weik MSS.

[5] For example, a one column letter in the *Journal*, Jan. 16, 1836, dated Vandalia, Jan. 6.

certain persons, offended by one of these reports in the *Journal* from the State capital, and 'believing ... that your correspondent was one of your county delegation,' took underhand measures against Sangamon County.[1]

Although the two subjects of first importance before the Legislature were internal improvements and the location of the State capital, national politics displaced them at first and, indeed, throughout the session continued to absorb members who sometimes were aroused to fighting pitch.

In his message to the Legislature, Governor Duncan violently denounced President Jackson for his hostility to the Bank of the United States. Unless Jackson's course was rebuked and checked, 'we shall ... have established a despotism more absolute than that of any civilized government in the world.' Upon the attitude of State legislatures depended 'the fate and future destiny of our *free republican* government.' [2]

The Whigs were jubilant, the Democrats furious. Their rage was the hotter because of what they considered to have been the Governor's apostasy from his party.[3] His message was a 'firebrand,' cried the Democratic organ.[4] A select Committee [5] replied to the Governor's assault on the President. The Committee's report, written and presented by McClernand, was able, restrained, impressive. The President's constitutional right of dismissal and appointment of officials 'results necessarily from the nature of the presidential office,' and had been

[1] *Sangamo Journal*, Jan. 6, 1837. The satire of this letter, in which pretence is made that the *Journal* correspondent was formerly on the staff of the *National Intelligencer* at Washington, where he could not make a living and that now, 'with almost murdered conscience,' is forced to write utterly false reports, is in Lincoln's best vein at that time of his life.

[2] *House Journal*, Sess. 1836-7, 19-26.

[3] Duncan had been sent to Congress as a Democrat and Jackson man, but had become hostile to the Administration while in Washington. This change was not known to the people generally when he was elected Governor in 1834. Ford, 168.

'Gov. Duncan was the last man in the State from whom an attack on Gen. Jackson should come; for he cannot but remember that he owes his present exaltation in the political scale, by rising on the popularity of the very man against whom he has now turned his weapons. Ingratitude — "How sharper than a serpents tooth it is."' *Illinois State Register*, Dec. 23, 1836.

[4] *Ib.*

[5] Douglas was on this Committee. *House Journal*, Sess. 1836-7, 29. *Illinois State Register*, Jan. 6, 1837.

practised by every previous President. Jackson was also sound in protesting against the resolution of the Senate condemning his course toward the Bank as unconstitutional and lawless; the Senate alone, cannot 'accuse and condemn' the President 'of an impeachable offence.' Impeachment was the business of the House, not the Senate.

The removal by the President of public money from the Bank of the United States, was clearly within his constitutional power. The only question was that of policy; but Jackson had often and emphatically declared that there were ample grounds for his action, and the people had sustained him — that was conclusive as to Jackson's policy. Also, the supervisory control by the President 'over the public money, as over other public property' had been exercised by all former Chief Executives. With brilliant ability the Committee stoutly defends the appointment to office of members of Congress. The expenditure of unusual sums of money — 'extravagance,' as Duncan had branded it — is explained by giving specific items of extraordinary but absolutely necessary outlay.[1]

So the Committee could see no reason for the concurrence of the Legislature in the Governor's 'charges'; but the Committee could not help seeing a 'perplexing and inscrutable mystery' in the 'emanation of so grave charges from such a source'—from Joseph Duncan, who had been sent to Congress four times by the Democrats of Illinois as an avowed Jackson man, and who had been a supporter of the Administration when many of the things he now denounced were done. The Committee, therefore, proposed resolutions approving Jackson's Administration and rejecting 'the correctness of the charges' preferred by Governor Duncan.[2]

Instantly, John J. Hardin of Morgan County, who, sneeringly

---

[1] The extinguishment of Indian titles, the increase of Indian annuities, the Seminole War, 'the protection of our Southern frontier from the violence of the War now raging between Mexico and Texas.' Contrast all this, said the Committee's report, with the more than eighty-five thousand dollars 'expended during the winter of 1835 by the Senate of the United States, for the printing of public documents, many of which were fraught with the most inflammatory tirades against President Jackson.' The Committee clinches its answer to Duncan's assertion of extravagance, by giving the annual expenditures of the National Government from 1817 to 1834 inclusive.

[2] *House Journal*, Sess. 1836–7, 102–14.

observes the Democratic organ, 'seems to have an itching to see his name in print,' [1] was on his feet. The Whigs had had enough of the fight against the Administration, and Hardin proposed to strike out the Democratic resolutions and adopt a Whig substitute that, in view of the legislation required and expected by the people concerning internal improvements and common schools, it was a waste of time and money to discuss national politics. But, by a vote of fifty-seven nays to twenty-four ayes, Lincoln voting aye,[2] the House refused to strike out the Democratic resolutions. Heated debate consumed the day.[3] Douglas, his deep voice booming through the hall, championed his hero, Jackson, and furiously assailed the Whigs. Duncan's purpose, he thundered, was to rally 'the sinking fortunes of a desperate political faction.' [4]

Great excitement prevailed. There were motions to adjourn, calls of the House, demands for the previous question.[5] The triumphant Democrats pressed their advantage; the desperate Whigs could not escape. The most stubborn of them, including Lincoln, voted that the main question should not be put, and were again badly beaten; [6] the Democratic resolution sustaining Jackson's Administration was adopted by the smashing vote of sixty-four ayes to eighteen nays, Lincoln voting nay; [7] and the resolution of rebuke to Duncan was carried by more than two to one, Lincoln once more voting nay.[8] The House then adjourned over Christmas, until Tuesday, December 27.

[1] *Illinois State Register*, Jan. 24, 1837.

[2] *House Journal*, Sess. 1836–7, 115.   [3] *Sangamo Journal*, Dec. 31, 1836.

[4] Stevens, 300–3. Douglas was frequently in debate, speaking for Jackson, for his own wise and practicable plan for two railroads and the Illinois & Michigan Canal, for his idea of voting by printed ballots instead of word of mouth, against granting divorces by personal bills in the Legislature, and for a general divorce law under which Courts alone could grant divorces, etc. See *ib.*, 300–4; and see *Illinois State Register*, Dec. 29, 1836. 'In all the proceedings of this legislature Douglas was active.' Stevens, 306.

[5] 'Every device which the tact of the Opposition party [Whigs] suggested, allowed by the rules of the House, was resorted to by them to defeat the resolutions.' *Illinois State Register*, Dec. 26, 1836.

[6] Fifty-three ayes to twenty-nine nays, Lincoln voting nay. *House Journal*, Sess. 1836–7, 116.

[7] *Ib.*, 117.

[8] Fifty-seven ayes to twenty-five nays. *House Journal*, Sess. 1836–7, 117. 3500 copies of the Democratic report and resolutions 'and the vote thereupon' were ordered to be printed, a most unusual proceeding, and plainly a method of getting a campaign

Thus Lincoln participated in one of those political discussions that were then taking place in State Legislatures throughout the country. McClernand's report was so well done that it amounted to a state paper of no mean rank; and the debate over it in the lobby more even than in the House, the discussion of it in conversations at taverns and wherever men met, afforded instruction in constitutional principles as thorough, perhaps, as Lincoln could have received at any college or university. The powers and duties of the President, the authority of Congress, the nature and disposition of patronage — well-nigh every practical subject with which he would have to deal one day, was examined with sense and learning, though spoiled by partisan heat and prejudice.

Soon another political explosion followed, the effect of which on Lincoln's future was far stronger. Again came the sound of that thunder which he had heard twice before; but now it was nearer and startlingly distinct. This time, indeed, disunion and civil war seemed not vague and distant theories, but concrete and impending probabilities, and this time not from an issue so easily remediable as the tariff which threatened the secession of South Carolina in 1832, but from the profound and complicated facts of slavery and the structure of society throughout half the Nation, together with the militant emotions of those who believed slavery to be a moral crime.

During the decade following the tacit agreement in 1820, that no more slave States should be admitted north of 36° 30′, some amelioration took place in the condition of the slaves; it was generally taken for granted that the vexed question was settled, and North and South were tranquil and harmonious. Generally, but not altogether. Here and there were men and women whose sense of the wrong of slavery would not be appeased by compromise or the slow processes of time and evolution.

On January 1, 1831, one of the great dates in human history, these devoted enthusiasts of freedom found a champion to give voice to their convictions. The publication of the *Liberator* began in Boston. 'I am in earnest, I will not equivocate, I will

document at public expense. The Whigs were obviously in a panic and tried to escape the publication of their names and votes, but the Democrats prevented. *Ib.*, 117–9.

not excuse, I will not retreat a single inch, and I WILL BE HEARD,'
exclaimed William Lloyd Garrison, and he cried aloud for immediate and unconditional emancipation. Abolition societies
were formed and proclaimed their cause with the ardor of
crusaders. During the spring and summer of 1835, these societies sent their pamphlets and pictures broadcast throughout the
country, many of them into the slave-holding States.

Peace and quiet were no more. The South was enraged, the
North disturbed, yet, for the most part, sympathetic with the
South.¹ Having ever in mind the ghastly results of the negro uprising and negro rule in Santo Domingo and with actual or suspected slave insurrections at home to remind them freshly of
that horror, Southern men and women felt the abolition propaganda to be an attack on Southern institutions. They firmly
believed that the safety of their homes, their very lives, even the
continuance of white supremacy were in deadly and imminent
peril.

And, indeed, some of the abolition pamphlets were well calculated to terrify and madden the Southern people. Slavery was
a 'sin,' slave-holders were 'robbers'; let them beware lest the
slaves give 'terrific proof' that they were men. Santo Domingo!
It was a 'blazing beacon' of liberty. Instant emancipation,
then, or 'human nature must be left to right itself by physical
force.' ²

Such publications, and pictures even more inflammatory,
drove Southern men to something like frenzy. During the winter of 1835–36 the matter was debated in the Senate, the
Southern Senators declaring that, because of the abolition
crusade, the South was facing 'an awful calamity.' They com-

¹ See Channing, v, 152–4.

² *The Sin of Slavery and its Remedy*, by Elizur Wright, Jr., N.Y., 1833. Another
abolition pamphlet, *The Testimony of God against Slavery, or a Collection of Passages
from the Bible*, by Rev. Le Roy Sunderland, Boston, 1835, was even more irritating.
The author compares the slaves to the children of Israel, whose God would deliver
them from the Egyptians. Most quotations are from the Old Testament.

An address by William Lloyd Garrison delivered to Free People of Color in several
northern cities in June, 1831, begins, 'I am ashamed of my own color;' and after sound
practical advice, admirably expressed, as to their self-improvement, tells the freedmen
that they are still the victims of 'unconstitutional enactments.' As to the slave-holders,
if the same force that annihilated the slave-trade 'descends again, they on whom its
crash shall fall will not be destroyed before I have warned them.'

pared the Abolitionists to 'madmen approaching their neighbors
house with a torch.' Even such able and moderate men as
Senator Felix Grundy of Tennessee gave earnest warning of certain catastrophe. Benton, in hot wrath, showed incendiary pictures and 'diabolical publications' which he had himself received.
The Abolitionists had turned back the clock of emancipation
'for fifty years,' he said. Grave and sincere charges were made
that the 'northern fanatics' were destroying the Union.[1]

Such were conditions when, in the spring of 1836, the Southern
States passed resolutions on the subject and transmitted them
to their sister States in the North, some of which responded
sympathetically, others were silent, and none were hostile. On
December 29, 1836, Governor Duncan sent to the Legislature
of Illinois a few of these reports, memorials and resolutions, for
its consideration.[2]

Virginia asserted that her exclusive right to deal with slavery
within her borders — a right given by the Constitution — 'will
be maintained at all hazards;' and she asks other States to suppress and punish societies under their jurisdictions which are
sending inflammatory pamphlets among the slaves tending to
incite them to 'insurrection and revolt.' Virginia's safety is at
stake; . . . and she feels that her sister States will not fail her in
view of those 'principles of the Union, enforced by the sympathies of common dangers, sufferings and triumphs, which ought
to bind us together in fraternal concord. . . . Congress has no
constitutional power to abolish slavery in the district of Columbia, or in the territories,' and Virginia would consider such action 'as affording just cause of alarm to the slaveholding States,
and bringing the Union into imminent peril.' [3]

Kentucky was out-spoken, determined. The Abolitionists
were inciting, through print and pictures, 'insubordination . . .
perhaps insurrection' of the slaves. 'For this institution
[slavery], the people of Kentucky hold themselves responsible
to no earthly tribunal, but will refer their cause to Him alone,
through the mysterious dispensations of whose providence, dominion has been given to the white man over the black. He,

[1] *Register of Debates*, xii, Pt. i, 71–810; Adams, ix, 251,
[2] *House Journal*, Sess. 1836–7, 134.   [3] Virginia Resolutions, Feb. 16, 1836,

alone, may judge of its compatibility with His will; and of its political expediency, we who witness its practical operation, are best competent to speak.' Kentucky, 'so long as she remains a sovereign member of this confederacy, can never permit *another State* to assail her local institutions, much less a combination of private individuals.' The Abolitionists, individually and as societies, are trying to do what the States themselves cannot do. All history proves that organized zealots can work 'irreparable mischief . . . especially when [they] . . . imagine themselves the special executors of the divine will.' If they become sufficiently numerous 'the history of the American Union, with all the high and glowing visions which now gladden the heart of the patriot, will have been written.' Freedom of speech and press! What 'grosser prostitution of the freedom of the press' could be conceived than 'the effort of the abolitionists to stir up a portion of the population of eleven States . . . to rebellion and bloodshed?'

If, as she fears, all appeal to Northern justice proves to be in vain, then 'certain and tremendous consequences' will ensue; then Kentucky will 'look to her condition,' and 'declare to the world her determined resolution to maintain inviolate, her domestic institution;' and she assures her sister slave-holding States of her 'earnest coöperation . . . to resist, at all hazards, every effort to interfere with that subject, either by Congress, any State, or combination of private persons.' [1]

In her memorial to the other States Alabama, 'with that confidence and good will which should characterize sisters of the same family,' said: 'The dark, deep and malignant design of the abolitionists . . . amongst you, in sending to our country their agents and incendiary pamphlets and publications, lighting up fires of discord in the bosom of our slave population, have never for a moment alienated our affections from the great mass of your citizens — and we have believed and still believe — that when you were fully apprised of the evils which this unholy band of cowardly assassins was bringing upon us,' their fell efforts would be stopped.

'The abolitionists are not numerous, but they are wealthy, ardent and talented. They . . . issue millions of essays, pam-

[1] Kentucky Resolutions, March 1, 1836.

phlets, and pictures, and scatter them amongst our slave population, calculated to urge them to deluge our country in blood.
This cannot be tolerated.' So Alabama asks her sister States to
prevent the 'malignant deeds of the abolitionists calculated to
destroy our peace, and sever this Union,' declares that abolition
of slavery in the District of Columbia, 'unless by the desire of
its own citizens,' would be a 'violation of the rights of that
district . . . and as the commencement of a scheme of usurpation and flagrant injustice.' [1]

The Mississippi resolutions were brief and defiant: 'We urge
upon our brethern of the non-slaveholding States . . . as they
value the harmony and safety of the Union,' that they suppress
by penal laws those who are 'plotting . . . to undermine, disturb
or abolish our institutions of domestic slavery, in any manner
or by any means, and under any pretext whatever.' [2]

In response to the Southern appeals, Connecticut declared
that slavery was a State institution and protected by the Constitution; denounced abolition societies as 'improper, unjustifiable, and dangerous,' and destructive of 'the harmony of
the Union;' expressed 'sympathy . . . for the inhabitants of the
slaveholding States;' and condemned abolition of slavery in the
District of Columbia as 'unjust and impolitic so long as slavery
exists in Maryland and Virginia.' But Connecticut thought it
unnecessary to enact laws restrictive of the press: 'Truth and
Justice have nothing to fear from a free Press in an enlightened
community.'

Undoubtedly, continued the Connecticut declaration, the
efforts of Abolitionists had 'tended to check the . . . improvements which were taking place in the condition of the slave
population . . . whilst they have occasioned much alarm and
anxiety to the whites. . . . Public opinion in this country is the
supreme law, and whatever may be the legal rights of slave pro-
prietors, they have been restricted and modified by public
sentiment.' [3]

The New York resolutions merely endorsed the message of

[1] Alabama Resolutions, Jan. 9, 1836.
[2] Mississippi Resolutions, Feb. 27, 1836.
[3] Connecticut Resolutions, May, 1836.

Governor William L. Marcy condemning abolition societies
and the abolition agitation. The people of New York, regardless of party or sect, had, with unexampled 'unanimity,' expressed disapproval of 'the whole system' of the Abolitionists,
and 'affection for their brethren of the south.' New York recognizes the right of each State to control, continue or abolish
slavery within its limits and gives that right her 'cordial concurrence.' [1]

When these papers were laid before the Illinois Legislature,
seven members of the House were appointed on a Joint Committee of the General Assembly, including McClernand, and
Lincoln's colleague from Sangamon County, Dan Stone.[2] For
two weeks this able Committee worked on the reply which
Illinois should make. On Thursday, January 12, 1837, the
chairman, James H. Ralston of Adams County, soon to be
elected Judge of the Fifth Judicial Circuit,[3] made the Committee's report.

They 'fully appreciate,' they declare, the 'anxiety and alarm
... produced in the slaveholding states, by the misguided and
incendiary movements of the abolitionists.' The Committee
'unanimously concur' that the purposes of the Abolitionists are
'reprehensible' and dangerous to 'every portion of our Union.'
Moreover, abolition activities 'have been and will continue to
be, disastrous to the slaves.' No 'true friend of the black man
can hope to benefit him' through abolition societies.

'Before their organization, changes were rapidly making in
public opinion' toward ameliorating the conditions of the slaves;
'they had already been elevated in morality and intelligence far
above the low estate of their fathers and kindred in their native
land;' and 'christian freemen' were looking forward to the moral
redemption of Africa from 'Pagan darkness' through American
slaves freed and sent back with the consent of their owners, to
their ancestral land, by the efforts of colonization societies, all in

[1] Report and Resolutions New York, May 18, 19, 1836.

[2] *House Journal*, Sess. 1836–7, 134. Stone was a lawyer of Springfield who gave
intelligent attention to other things as well as to law and politics, for instance, to the
cultivation of catalpa trees, on which he wrote with sense and knowledge. *Sangamo
Journal*, Jan. 11, 1834; Aug. 13, 1836.

[3] *House Journal*, Sess. 1836–7, 506–7.

the 'inscrutable wisdom' of Providence. How much better for the slaves such a mission than the fate of emancipated negroes in America! — witness the 'miserable abodes of wretchedness and squalled [*sic*] want' in which such unfortunates now exist.

But where now are the hopes of the philanthropist? Where the gladdening prospects of the slave? Where the energies of those associations which, in reality and not seeming, 'promised release from his manacles'? Abolition societies is the ready 'answer to all.'

Abolition societies 'have forged new irons for the black man and added an hundred fold to the rigors of slavery.

'They have scattered the fire brands of discord and disunion among the . . . States.

'They have excited the most rancorous and embittered feelings of [in] the same community.

'They have aroused the turbulent passions of the monster mob, whose actings are marked by every deed of atrocity' and undiscriminating 'fury.'

'They have . . . pertinaciously insisted on doctrines which . . . would deluge our common country in blood, rend the Union asunder, and bring desolation on all that was won by the valor and hallowed by the blood of our fathers.'

But public opinion, the true corrective, will administer the rebuke 'so richly merited, and allay all further cause of alarm and anxiety.' Citizens of slave States are no more to blame for slavery than citizens of free States; 'it was introduced by our common ancestry and came from them to us with the inviolable charter of our liberty, as a part of our heritage.'

The Constitution, child of 'mutual deference and concession, . . . guarantees to the States where it does exist, its continuance without interference by the National Government; rights . . . not surrendered by the States at the formation of the constitution cannot now be wrested from them.'

The people of Illinois will not submit to the open violation of our national compact, 'have a deep regard and affection for our brethren of the South,' and, upon any proper occasion, 'would fly to their assistance;' but since there are few, if any, abolition societies in Illinois,[1] 'a decided expression of public opinion is all that is at this time demanded.'

So the Committee recommends the adoption of resolutions that the General Assembly of Illinois 'highly disapprove the formation of abolition societies, and of the doctrines promulgated by them;' that 'the right of property in slaves, is [made] sacred to the slave-holding States by the Federal Constitution,' of which right 'they cannot be deprived . . . without their consent;' that 'the General Government cannot abolish slavery in the District of Columbia, against the consent of the citizens of said District without a manifest breach of faith.' [2]

After debate and much parliamentary manœuvering, the whole subject was referred to a select Committee of five with McClernand as Chairman, who, after several days, reported the resolutions with amendments; and to that against abolition in the District of Columbia, Lincoln moved to add 'unless the people of the said District petition for the same,' which was rejected without roll-call, neither Lincoln nor anybody else demanding the ayes and noes. On Friday, January 20, 1837, the resolutions as amended, were finally adopted by more than twelve to one, seventy-seven members voting aye and only six voting no, Lincoln among them.[3]

Not until six weeks later, Friday, March 3, 1837, was a protest against the passage of these resolutions presented. It was signed by Dan Stone and A. Lincoln, and, without comment, was spread upon the Journal of the House. They declared that 'they believe that the institution of slavery is founded on both injustice and bad policy, but that the promulgation of abolition doctrines tends rather to increase than abate its evils; . . . [that] Congress . . . has no power under the constitution to interfere with the institution of slavery in the different States,' but does have 'the power, under the constitution, to abolish slavery in the District of Columbia,' which power, however, 'ought not to be exercised, unless at the request of the people of the District;' and that 'difference between these opinions and those

---

[1] In 1835 an anti-slavery society was formed in Putnam County.

[2] *House Journal*, Sess. 1836–7, 241–4.

[3] *Ib.*, 244, 248–9, 309, 311.

contained in the said resolutions is their reason for entering this protest.' [1]

Thus when Lincoln was scarcely twenty-eight years old, the entire subject of slavery came directly before him, and was debated thoroughly by men of high standing. He studied the Southern view as presented by memorials and resolutions drawn with utmost care by the ablest men in various slave-holding States — the crisp demand of Virginia, the appealing request of Alabama, the spirited statement of Kentucky, the peremptory call of Mississippi. He pored over the well-written reply of Connecticut, the evasive answer of New York, the curious response of Illinois.

The origin and development of slavery, the unhappy effect of abolition propaganda on the improving condition of the slaves, the nature and extent of free speech and press, the constitutional powers of Congress — all were, maturely and with leisurely deliberation, considered by Lincoln during the winter of 1837, and he finally stated his conclusions, from which he did not vary for more than a quarter of a century. The only real point of difference between his views and those of the majority of the House was moral — the 'injustice' of slavery. As to the Abolitionists, no member disapproved of them more strongly than he.

If Lincoln and Stone held the opinions expressed in their protest before the belated time they filed it, they were not without reasons of practical politics for their delay. They were intent upon securing the permanent location of the State capital at Springfield. Nothing must interfere with that supreme purpose, no member be offended unnecessarily, no risk hazarded of losing a single vote without urgent cause. Not until after that matter had been settled, did they submit their views on the slavery question. It cannot be stated too often, that Lincoln subordinated everything to Springfield's interest.[2]

While these discussions on national affairs, so vital to Lincoln's political development, were in progress, the Legislature

---

[1] *House Journal*, Sess. 1836–7, 817–8; Lincoln, *Works*, I, 51.

[2] 'He declined to antagonize men or measures and thus it is we can see nothing striking in his protest against the abolition resolutions which makes a statement and then, as though afraid of it, he backs off like the crab.' Stevens, 306–7.

was also busy with the expansive project of internal improvements. Early in the session Douglas had presented a plan for a great central railroad through the whole length of the State from north to south, two other roads from east to west, together with the immediate construction of the canal from Lake Michigan to the Illinois River, all to be 'constructed and owned by the State exclusively;' and providing for the making of surveys and estimates of other works.[1] But the clamor for internal improvements which, by now, was sweeping the whole State, was not stilled by undertakings so limited; and, even before the questions of slavery, free press, and abolition were disposed of, petitions began to pour into the Legislature, demanding that a general improvement system be provided by law.

An Internal Improvement State Convention had been held in Vandalia at the beginning of the session.[2] Indeed this 'convention,' which was more like an organized lobby, had met in the hall of the House immediately after its first adjournment. Delegates from nearly all counties in the State were there. Thomas Mather, President of the State Bank at Springfield, was chosen President of the convention, which 'after two days' debate and deliberation passed resolutions instructing the Legislature to pass a comprehensive system of internal improvements, involving the building of innumerable roads and deepening and widening of countless streams; and, to accomplish all this, to issue and sell ten million dollars of State bonds.[3] Pressure from a numerous lobby was insistent and effective.[4]

On January 9, 1837, the Committee on Internal Improvements made an elaborate report ardently supporting the plan —

[1] *House Journal*, Sess. 1836–7, 36. *Illinois State Register*, Dec. 23, 1836, reporting House proceedings of Dec. 14. And see *Douglas:* Johnson, 31.

[2] *House Journal*, Sess. 1836–7, 134, 204. The *Sangamo Journal*, Nov. 19, 1836, strongly urged the holding of this convention. A big meeting to insist on an internal improvement law was held in Springfield, Nov. 19, and feverish letters demanding the adoption of the scheme were published. *Ib.*, and Dec. 3, 1836.

[3] Robert L. Wilson to Herndon, Feb. 10, 1866. Weik MSS. Wilson was a representative from Sangamon County in this Legislature. He lived at Athens not far from New Salem and was closely associated with Lincoln.

Mather's State Bank was the fiscal agent of the State and, of course, would handle the sale of the State bonds.

[4] On his return from Congress in 1836 Governor John Reynolds had found the 'people perfectly *insane* on the subject of improvements.' Reynolds, 324.

the people demand it, the nation expects it, immigration will stop if it is not adopted. Prior survey and estimate of costs are unnecessary in view of the topography of the State, its water courses, its level and boundless prairies. Let eight million dollars at once be borrowed on the credit of Illinois; and let work be started without delay on the larger rivers, and the two great railways advocated by Douglas. All this will increase population, add value to property, induce prosperity. Look at Pennsylvania, New York, Indiana.[1]

But the House was not content with the bill which the Committee presented with its report. Public meetings were being held throughout the State; [2] soon counties in increasing numbers began to insist upon their share of the improvements — 'every member wanted a road to his county town;' [3] and, to get votes of members from counties where such work was manifestly impossible, the convenient device was adopted of paying each of such counties two hundred thousand dollars in cash. In such fashion was enacted the Illinois Internal Improvement law of 1837.

The expense caused no apprehension to these optimists. John Hogan of Alton scoffed at the few doubting members. 'Our bonds would go like hot cakes, and be sought for by the Rothschilds and Baring Brothers, and others of that stamp,' at a premium of from fifty to one hundred per cent; the premium alone will construct most of the great works, the principal will go into the treasury and 'leave the people free from taxation for years to come.' [4] With the impatience of confidence, the Vandalia press insisted on immediate action.[5]

'I have heard it proved,' relates Governor Ford, 'by an ingenius orator in the lobby, that the State could well afford to borrow a hundred millions of dollars, and expend it in making internal improvements.' It was supposed, of course, that the bonds of Illinois would bring a premium of at least ten per cent.[6] Yet some obstinate members would not be satisfied. Alpheus

---

[1] *House Journal*, Sess. 1836–7, 202–15; Ford, 187; Reynolds, 324.

[2] *Illinois State Register*, Jan. 6, 1837.

[3] Linder, 59.   [4] *Ib.*, 59–60.

[5] *Illinois State Register*, Jan. 20, 1837.   [6] Ford, 185, 190.

Wheeler of Pike County insisted upon counting the cost; it was
fantastic, this building of railroads upon imagination, this making of waterways 'where nature never attempted it;' how senseless to tax people who cannot, as yet, even support their families.[1] But protests, warnings, black prophesies were unheeded.

Debate was unceasing. McClernand spoke ably for Douglas's
plan,[2] and for the Alton-Shawneetown railroad.[3] But Lincoln
would take no part; with one exception, he spoke on purely
local matters.[4] The Sangamon delegation, testifies one of Lincoln's colleagues, voted on every proposition in exchange for
promises of support in the fight over the removal of the capital.[5]
The session became one of barter and deal, a debauch of log-
rolling. Nor was this practice confined to efforts of the 'Long
Nine' to get votes for Springfield: 'members often support
measures that they would not otherwise vote for, to obtain another member's vote for a friend,' wrote John J. Hardin of
Morgan County.[6]

The capital of the State Bank at Springfield was increased by
two million dollars, that at Shawneetown by one million, the
stock to be taken by the State.[7] Members were eager for places
on boards and commissions which they themselves were creating. The people along the canal were threatened with the loss of
it, if other parts of the State were denied improvements. Alton
was given three railroads to get her powerful support. No pledge,
no threat, no manner of manipulation was overlooked. Through
this maze, the 'Long Nine' made their sure and skilful way, to
the one objective they were determined to reach.[8]

At last the Internal Improvement Act was passed,[9] providing
not only for the Illinois Central Railway and for the great canal,

[1] *Illinois State Register*, Jan. 12, 1837.

[2] *Semi-Weekly Illinois Register*, Jan. 24, 1837.

[3] *Ib.*, March 17, 1837.　　[4] Linder, 58.

[5] Robert L. Wilson to Herndon, Feb. 10, 1866. Weik MSS.

[6] Hardin to *Jacksonville Patriot* as quoted in *Illinois State Register*, Dec. 29, 1836.

[7] *Frontier State:* Pease, 306.

[8] For a vivid and accurate account of this curious event, see Ford, 184–7.

[9] *House Journal*, Sess. 1836–7, 674–6. Lincoln demanded the ayes and noes. The
vote was sixty-two ayes to twenty-two nays, Lincoln voting aye.

Douglas voted for this 'omnibus bill' with great reluctance (Johnson, 31–2) and only
under instructions from his County. *Autobiography*, 21.

but also for a multitude of short railways from and to places of no importance,[1] for the dredging and deepening of shallow rivers and creeks, all without connection or any sort of system. The jubilant lobby loudly applauded the passage of the bill.[2] In the streets of Vandalia bonfires blazed, fire-balls were thrown, windows illuminated, huzzahs resounded.[3] The press glowed with optimistic editorials. 'If the present Legislature had done no more they would have deserved the thanks of the People for the passage of this law.'[4] Thus the whole State, declares Governor Ford, writing from personal observation and first-hand knowledge, was 'bought up and bribed, to approve the most senseless and disastrous policy which ever crippled the energies of a growing country.'[5]

Governor Duncan and the Counsel of Revision disapproved the reckless measure. Futile precaution! The bill was contemptuously passed over their veto.[6] Lincoln's ardent friend, Edwin B. Webb of White County, and his colleague, John McCown, filed a long, bitter, and very able protest which was published in the Vandalia papers.[7] But the deed was done, the foresighted and prudent were in disfavor; and Lincoln, with votes pledged for Springfield, went happily to the contest over the location of the State capital, for which struggle he was now, for the first time, prepared.

Several times during the session the subject had arisen and much heat had been shown. Silent as he was on other matters, the discussion of which by him might have alienated possible votes for Springfield, Lincoln was quick to assail those who

[1] Only one of these roads was built. Ford, 189; Reynolds, 325.

[2] *Illinois State Register*, Feb. 2, 1837.   [3] *Sangamo Journal*, March 4, 1837.

[4] *Illinois State Register*, March 6, 1837.

[5] Ford, 187. Just before the final votes on the Internal Improvement bill, Lincoln reported from the Finance Committee, as required by a House Resolution, the receipts and estimates of the State government: 'amount receivable from all sources, $57,895.15; and amount required, $55,151.95,' to which should be added $15,000 for an increase of the contingent fund, or $70,151.97 (*sic*) as the total State budget for 1837, leaving a deficit of $12,256.82. *House Journal*, Sess. 1836–7, 603–4.

[6] *Ib.*, 720–1, 724. The vote was fifty-three ayes, twenty noes, Lincoln voting aye. And see Ford, 189; Reynolds, 324.

[7] *House Journal*, Sess. 1836–7, 680–3; *Illinois State Register*, March 1, 1837. John J. Hardin also opposed this internal improvement scheme and, at the time of its adoption, foretold its certain collapse. Linder, 61.

sought, in any way, to disparage that town. Thus is partly
explained his remarkable speech against the investigation of the
State Bank which had been located at the place where Lincoln
was about to go to practise law and politics. On January 7,
Linder offered sweeping resolutions for a legislative examination
of the Bank's conduct and affairs, in well-nigh every conceivable
particular. The resolutions were aggressively hostile to the
Bank, its officers and agents.[1] Four days later the subject was
taken up, Lincoln twice voting against considering it.[2]

Lincoln led the defence of the Bank. The Bank was constitutional, he said; the Supreme Court of the State had so decided.
Even if it were not constitutional, an investigating committee
could not remedy that fatal defect. One third of Linder's resolutions related to the distribution of Bank stock by the State
Commission; but the only question which could arise from that
was one 'between capitalists in regard to the ownership of
stock.' Ought the Legislature to 'squander thousands of the
people's money,' to settle such a controversy?

Suppose the Bank has made business connections with banks
in other States, is there any harm in it? The Bank's charter
contemplated that very thing. And suppose the Bank's employees did take an oath of secrecy? What of it? No honest man
cares? Such an oath was not forbidden by the Bank's by-laws.
'Does not every merchant have his secret mark? and who is ever
silly enough to complain of it?'

As to the charge that the conduct of the Bank had injured the
people, it was strange that the people 'are not sensible of it.' Let
them request an investigation, 'and I shall ever stand ready to
respond to the call.' The Bank had doubled the prices of
farmers' products, 'filled their pockets with a sound circulating
medium,' and the attack upon the Bank was 'exclusively the
work of politicians; a set of men who have interests aside from
the interests of the people, and who, to say the most of them,
are, taken as a mass, at least one long step removed from honest
men.' Lincoln meant nothing personal, he added, 'being a
politician myself.'

Suppose the Bank had 'loaned money at usurious rates of

[1] *House Journal*, Sess. 1836-7, 195-8.   [2] *Ib.*, 235-6.

interest?' Could the Committee 'redress the injured individuals?' His remedy was in the courts; let him look to 'the laws of the land.' Usury was 'much more frequent and enormous,' before than since the Bank was established. If the Bank had refused specie payments, it had violated its charter; but that could not be, since nobody had sued the Bank for the damages which the law provided in such a case. Dared any man say that the Commissioners had been bribed? and would it be easier to bribe them — 'twenty-four of the most respectable men in the State' — than to bribe '*any* seven members' of the House, constituting an investigating committee? — a point which Lincoln thrice repeats, with particularly severe reference to Linder.

The Legislature had as much right 'to compel the Bank to bring its coffers to this hall and to pour their contents upon this floor, as to compel it to submit to this examination. . . . I am by no means the special advocate of the Bank;' he had long thought that it should 'report its condition to the General Assembly,' and, at the last session he offered such an amendment to the Bank bill, but the House had rejected it.

Of course 'cases might occur when an examination might be proper;' but no such case had occurred, and, if it had, 'I should still be opposed to making an examination without legal authority. I am opposed to encouraging that lawless and mobocratic spirit, whether in relation to the Bank or anything else, which is already abroad in the land, and is spreading with rapid and fearful impetuosity to the ultimate overthrow of every institution, of even [every] moral principle, in which persons and property have hitherto found security.'

Even if the House had authority, what good can come from an investigation of the Bank? None at all. So 'why spend the public money in such employment?' To be sure the credit of the Bank would be injured. But whom would that hurt? The stock holders? No, for 'they are men of wealth . . . and consequently, beyond the power of malice.' Only the 'honest and unsuspecting farmer and mechanic' will suffer by depreciation of the Bank's paper, which they have innocently taken.[1]

[1] *Works*, I, 19–34.
Soon after Lincoln's speech, Linder was elected by the Legislature Attorney General

The president, officers, agents, and attorneys of the Bank were on the ground, and also the 'twenty-four most respectable men in the State' who had apportioned the Bank stock, and whom Lincoln had named personally when paying tribute to them.[1] Not only were they highly regarded but they were the most energetic, resourceful, and substantial men in Illinois. And all of them were Whigs, indeed the Bank was popularly known as the Whig concern.[2] In no possible manner could the young representative from Sangamon, and soon-to-be-lawyer at Springfield, have more quickly secured the approval, confidence, and attachment of these financial leaders, as well as of all business men of substance and standing in the State, than by his adroit but bold attack upon the proposed legislative investigation of the Bank of Illinois.

The Democratic organ denounced the Bank lobby: Its movements from the first day of the session were 'more than suspicious. The President of the Bank . . . and a large body of the officers and stockholders . . . have been hovering around the Legislature for the last three or four weeks; and when the searching investigation proposed by Mr. Linder was under consideration, every means which ingenuity could devise were used to defeat it in the House. These means were successful. If such be the conduct and power of this institution in the green tree, what will it be in the dry? Its officers and stockholders, although the Bank has not existed two years, already form a powerful body in the Legislature, and . . . the period is not distant when it must have possession of the Legislature. Are the People prepared to give up the temple of their power into the keeping of a monied aristocracy?'[3]

Springfield appreciated Lincoln's efforts in behalf of her pet institution. Lincoln carefully wrote out his speech and sent it to the *Sangamo Journal* which, of course, published it in full, with this editorial tribute: 'Mr. Lincoln's remarks on Mr. Linder's

of Illinois. *House Journal*, Sess. 1836–7, 273–5. He resigned as a member of the House, Feb. 11, 1837. *Ib.*, 589.

[1] *Illinois State Register*, Jan. 24, 1837. Several months before the Legislature convened, the State Bank of Illinois (the Springfield institution) had opened a branch at Vandalia. *Illinois Advocate*, Jan. 16, 1836.

[2] Ford, 178–9.   [3] *Illinois State Register*, Jan. 24, 1837.

Bank resolution, in this paper, are quite to the point. Our friend carries the true Kentucky rifle, and when he fires seldom fails of sending the shot home.'[1] Soon he was to fire another shot, which, while not verbal, was to bring down far bigger game to be carried to Springfield by him in much greater triumph.

Finally Linder offered a substitute to his prolix and drag-net resolutions, that a committee of the House examine 'the affairs and condition' of the Bank and its branches. To this Hardin moved an amendment that a joint committee inquire whether the Bank had forfeited its charter or abused its privileges, and whether the Bank was constitutional and a safe depository of public funds. Lincoln voted for Hardin's amendment, which, however, was rejected. Lincoln then moved to strike from Linder's substitute authority to inquire into the 'organization' of the Bank. The motion was lost by a vote of forty-four to thirty-four.[2]

On motions to adjourn, calls of the House and divisions of the question, Lincoln voted with friends of the Bank of whom, clearly, he was a leader. But when, at last, a vote was forced, Linder's substitute was adopted by a vote of sixty-six ayes to twenty-one nays, Lincoln voting nay.[3] Within five years the Bank of Illinois, with a circulation of three millions, was to fail,

---

[1] Sangamo Journal, Jan. 28, 1837.   [2] House Journal, Sess. 1836–7, 288–91.

[3] Ib., 294. The next day, Thursday, Jan. 19, the House received a Senate resolution for a joint committee 'to examine into the condition and financial concerns of the State Bank of Illinois and whether the Bank has violated its charter ... with a view of ascertaining whether the said Bank would be a safe and proper depository for the public moneys of this State,' etc. Ib., 296.

The Senate resolution was much like Hardin's amendment; and knowledge that the Senate had adopted it undoubtedly led Linder to offer his substitute.

Almost immediately after the House received the Senate resolutions, Linder's resolution and substitute were laid on the table, by a vote of fifty-five ayes to twenty-eight nays, Lincoln voting nay. Ib., 299–300.

The Senate resolutions were so amended that no officer, agent, attorney, or stockholders of the Bank should be on the investigating committee, Lincoln voting aye; that the investigation include the Bank's officers, Lincoln voting nay; and the branches of the Bank, Lincoln voting nay. Ib., 303–4.

As thus amended the Senate resolutions were adopted by two separate votes, that on the Springfield bank by seventy to ten, Lincoln voting nay; and that on the Shawneetown bank by forty-four to thirty-five, Lincoln again voting nay. Ib., 305–6.

Throughout this contest Douglas voted as steadily against the Bank as Lincoln voted for it.

The Joint Committee promptly examined the Bank and, a month later, made a long and careful report. The Committee said that they 'were satisfied of the soundness

causing profound and widespread distress among the people.[1] Governor Ford denounced the investigations of the two State Banks as mere farces, and one of the Committee to examine the bank at Shawneetown declared that he saw nothing but 'plenty of good liquor in the bank, and sugar to sweeten it with.'[2]

Although Lincoln and the Springfield partisans, of whom he was in command,[3] strove to delay final action on the location of the capital until the passage of the Internal Improvement bill, they could not prevent frequent consideration of that irritating and dangerous subject. Sometimes they were on the very edge of defeat, twice they actually were beaten. His colleagues were despondent, hopeless; but Lincoln never despaired. In the darkest hours he called the 'Long Nine' to his room in the tavern, heartened them, and devised plans for victory.[4]

Seldom has the management of legislative suffrage been cleverer than that of Lincoln in this notable and superheated contest.[5] The Legislature was Democratic, and Whig Springfield was in terror lest partisan politics should defeat her cherished ambition. The *Sangamo Journal*, in a long editorial, insisted that so trivial a thing should not affect a project so noble.[6] It did not — Lincoln had seen to that.

The Senate first passed the bill for the location of the capital by the present Legislature. This was met in the House by volleys of motions to amend, postpone, adjourn, and the like, all of

and safety of the condition of the State Bank;' that the Bank had not violated its charter, had not charged usurious interest, and had 'instantly' redeemed its paper when presented; that the Bank's officers had committed no impropriety, and that the Bank's investments were sound and profitable. 2500 copies of the report were ordered to be printed. *House Journal*, Sess. 1836–7, 616–35.

As it turned out, this report was as careless as it was prolix. When the Bank failed in 1842, it was found that very bad management for a long time was one cause of the collapse, and that some of the biggest and worst loans had been made about the time of this investigation.

[1] Ford, 222–3.

[2] *Ib.*, 197.   [3] Stevens, 308.

[4] *House Journal*, Sess. 1836–7, 612–3. *Illinois State Register*, Feb. 10, 1837. Also Robert L. Wilson to Herndon, Feb. 10, 1866. Weik MSS.

[5] Even an amendment to the bill for a repeal of the law was conceded by Lincoln (*Illinois State Register*, July 28, 1837), undoubtedly as one of the manœuvers necessary to get the capital bill passed.

[6] *Sangamo Journal*, Jan. 21, 1837.

which were defeated. So, in the end, the Senate bill was passed,[1] providing that, before adjournment, the Legislature should select, by ballot, the place at which the seat of government should be situated.

On February 28, 1837, six days before adjournment, after three months of management, bargaining, and intrigue, after the passage of the Internal Improvement bill with its clusters of improvident building, impossible improvements of impracticable streams, and appropriations of cash to importunate counties, the General Assembly in joint session chose Springfield as the permanent site of the State capital. On the first ballot she received thirty-five votes — more than twice as many as her next highest competitor, Vandalia; on the second ballot, forty-three votes; on the third, fifty-three votes; on the fourth and last, seventy-three votes, or a majority of all.[2]

The husbandry of the 'Long Nine' in the fields of vote-trading had yielded its harvest. Writing a few years later, just after the collapse of the Internal Improvement scheme, in explanation of the methods used to secure it and the location of the capital, Governor Thomas Ford bitterly concludes: 'Thus it was made to cost the State about six millions of dollars to remove the seat of government from Vandalia to Springfield, half which sum would have purchased all the real estate in that town at three prices.' [3] As we shall presently see, the resentment of this impartial observer was cherished by many others.

[1] *House Journal*, Sess. 136–7, 569–70; 592–4; 608–10; 612–4; 661–6.

Act, Feb. 25, 1837. *Laws*, 1837, 321–2. Among other concessions which Lincoln had to make to get the bill through was a requirement that the citizens of Springfield should donate $50,000 by May, 1837, for the building of the new State House — a concession that caused him some trouble thereafter.

[2] *House Journal*, Sess. 1836–7, 752–8. Examples of Lincoln's other votes at this session are: not to give the Legislature power to repeal or amend the act incorporating Quincy Academy (*ib.*, 147); to refer a divorce bill to the Committee on Petitions (*ib.*, 53); indefinitely to postpone a report of said Committee that Courts and not the Legislature should grant divorces (*ib.*, 62); indefinitely to postpone joint resolutions calling a Convention to amend the Constitution so as to prevent slavery in Illinois (*ib.*, 684–5); and against any Constitutional Convention (*ib.*, 685–6). Also for numerous internal improvement propositions.

Again legislative news in Lincoln's style, as letters from Vandalia, were printed in the *Sangamo Journal*. One of these ridiculing 'Paddy Shields' — James A. Shields, to whom Lincoln had taken a dislike — was almost certainly written by Lincoln. *Sangamo Journal*, Dec. 24, 1836.

[3] Ford, 187.

Five days after he had secured the capital for Springfield and six days after the Internal Improvement law was approved, Lincoln and Stone filed their protest against the slavery resolutions which had been adopted six weeks before.

But Lincoln had won his fight, the greatest of his life thus far, and one decisively influential on his whole future career. For he had determined to live in the new-made capital, city of his dreams, his aspirations, and his hopes. Before this session of the Legislature began Lincoln, on September 9, 1836, applied for a license to practise law; and on March 1, 1837, the very next day after his victory for Springfield in the General Assembly, he procured from the Supreme Court at Vandalia, a certificate of admission to the bar of Illinois and was formally enrolled as an attorney.[1]

Great was the rejoicing in Springfield, when glad tidings of the vote reached town. Not since the arrival of the *Talisman* had there been such jollification. And Lincoln was the hero of the hour. A long editorial in the *Sangamo Journal* [2] praised the Sangamon delegation for having secured the capital; and immediately after the Legislature adjourned, the 'Long Nine' went to Springfield to receive the plaudits of the people. They were welcomed by dinners, speeches, songs, hilarious congratulations. In all these expressions of public gladness Lincoln took part and leading citizens urged him to come to Springfield to live.[3] After the celebration he went out to the cabin hamlet on the Sangamon bluffs, to settle his small affairs and say good-bye to those among whom he had lived for seven years.

The ambitious little town of Springfield throbbed with enterprise. Her victory gave 'new life and energy to our citizens,' proudly declared the *Sangamo Journal*. All knew that they owed their good fortune to the representative from New Salem more than to anybody else. And he was coming to live among

---

[1] Roll of attorneys admitted by Sup. Ct., Central Grand Division, MSS. Office Clerk Sup. Ct. Ill., Springfield. The date of Lincoln's license is Sept. 9, 1836.

In the Records of the Circuit Court of Sangamon County there is an entry, March 24, 1836, stating that 'It is Ordered by the Court that it be certified that Abraham Lincoln is a person of good moral character.' In July of that year he filed papers in the first suit with which he had connection. *The Real Lincoln.* Jesse W. Weik, 134-8.

[2] March 9, 1837.

[3] Herndon, I, 180.

them. Seldom has a young man gone to any town to make his way, with so many friends awaiting him, as Lincoln found when on an April day in 1837 he rode into Springfield.

'The Empire County' of Illinois, as Sangamon was called because of its great extent and natural wealth, had a population of nearly twenty thousand,[1] and this was speedily increasing. The county seat and prospective capital was only fifteen years old, and for the first decade of its existence had consisted of 'only a few scattered log cabins.'[2] In the last five or six years, however, Springfield had grown prodigiously and, when Lincoln came there to live in the spring of 1837, had well-nigh fifteen hundred people within its limits. It was situated about four miles south of the Sangamon River, on the edge of broad and fertile prairie 'stretching away to the blue line of distant forest;' and this expanse was already filled with well cultivated farms. To the south and west great woods covered the bottoms.

While there were still many log cabins, frame houses, most of them small though some comparatively large, were far more numerous. Six church buildings lifted unassuming spires, two for Presbyterians and Baptists, and one each for Methodists and Episcopalians; and all had resident ministers and 're-spectable congregations.' Springfield had schools, too, and boasted an academy. The town spread out from a public square, in the centre of which stood a courthouse and a market, both brick buildings, surrounded by 'a green pleasant lawn inclosed by a railing.' There was also a jail.

The sides of the public square were 'lined with handsome edifices;' and in these or adjacent structures were nineteen dry-goods stores, one wholesale and six retail groceries, four drug stores, two clothing stores and one book-store. Springfield had four hotels, one an extensive three-story brick tavern house, and a casting foundry and four wool-carding machines were the

---

[1] 17,573 in 1835, State Census, 1835. *House Journal*, Sess. 1835-6, 86; and in 1840, 14,716, U.S. *Census*.

[2] Mitchell, 129. Five years before Lincoln went to Springfield, William Cullen Bryant, who visited the place, described it as being uncommonly poor and unkempt, even for a pioneer village, 'the whole town having an appearance of dirt and discomfort.' It was worse than Jacksonville, which was then a 'horribly ugly village.' Bryant, ii, 13-4.

beginnings of industries. Eighteen doctors ministered to the ailing and eleven lawyers served the litigious. Two papers, the *Illinois Republican* and the *Sangamo Journal*, one Democratic, the other Whig and both bitterly partisan, supplied the news and nourished the political prejudices of their readers.[1]

The broad streets were unpaved, no sidewalks led from residences to stores, churches, or schools and in rainy seasons shingles, chunks of wood, and sometimes a stray plank were made use of to prevent walkers from sinking to their shoe-tops in the mire. During wet seasons the wheels of heavily laden wagons went down to their axles in the mud; and in periods of drought the streets were scarcely less deep with dust. There was no street lighting and on moonless nights the town was in darkness, save for the vague radiance of candles shining dimly through windows.

Yet there were in the Springfield of 1837, gaiety and cheer, rich dressing and fine carriages,[2] social activities and creature comforts, literary interests and political aspirings, and all the expressions of cultivated as well as of frontier life. A number of the intellectually active had, long since, formed the Sangamon County Lyceum and debated at its meetings all manner of questions.[3] At the Springfield High School, Latin, Greek, Spanish, and French were taught among other of the higher branches of learning, the charge being '$200 per annum, $50 in advance.'[4]

Such was Springfield when Lincoln went there to live. He came to town riding a horse which he had borrowed. His entire possessions were in two saddle-bags. He engaged a rough bedstead from a cabinet-maker, but had no money for bed furnishings. His poverty depressed him, it seems, in spite of his laurels and bright prospects. 'I never saw so gloomy and melancholy a face in my life,' reports Joshua F. Speed, to whom Lincoln told his financial predicament. So Speed asked Lincoln to share his room over his store — it was a big room with a large double

---

[1] Mitchell, 129.

[2] 'There is a great deal of flourishing about in carriages here.' Lincoln to Mary Owens, May 7, 1837. *Works*, i, 53.

[3] An advertisement in the *Sangamo Journal*, March 29, 1834, shows that the Springfield Lyceum was in existence at that time.

[4] *Sangamo Journal*, May 6, 1837.

bed.[1] Another good Samaritan, William Butler, Clerk of the Sangamon Circuit Court,[2] who greatly liked and admired the young politician, also observed Lincoln's despondency and took him to his house for meals, making no mention of pay.[3] Thus were arranged his living conditions, which continued for more than four years without a dollar of expense.[4]

Lincoln at once went to the law office of Stuart and Dummer, where he had so often visited on his trips from New Salem to Springfield. As we have seen, he had applied for a license to practise law months before he came to live in Springfield, and he had secured his license immediately after winning the fight for the location of the capital. Obviously details of the partnership had been arranged by Stuart, for, in the paper of April 15, 1837, appeared a formal notice of the dissolution of the partnership between Stuart and Henry E. Dummer, and a new professional card: 'J. T. Stuart & A. Lincoln, Attorneys and Counsellors at Law, will practice, conjointly, in the Courts of this Judicial Circuit. Office No. 4 Hoffman's Row, upstairs, Springfield, April 12, 1837.'[5] The office was above a room in which the circuit court was held, and contained 'a small dirty bed, one buffalo robe, a chair and a bench,'[6] and a small bookcase containing a few legal volumes.[7]

Here, then, was Lincoln, but twenty-eight years old, leader of his party in the House of Representatives, winner of the fight for Springfield as the State capital, most talked of and best liked of all the Whigs of Sangamon County, and now partner of one of the ablest lawyers in Illinois and the foremost Whig in the State. Astounding progress! But yesterday pottering about New Salem in contact only with little things and crude surroundings, heavily in debt and with dim prospects for advancement; to-day starting on the high road of ambition and achievement!

---

[1] Speed's statement. Herndon, I, 184–5.

[2] Butler had been appointed in 1836, to succeed James H. Matheny, resigned. *Sangamo Journal*, Feb. 6, 1836.

[3] Herndon to Weik, Jan. 15, 1886. Weik MSS. [4] Herndon, I, 185–6.

[5] *Sangamo Journal*, April 15, 1837.

[6] Statement James H. Matheny, May 3, 1866. Weik MSS.

[7] Herndon, I, 184. Hoffman's Row was on the west side of the present North Fifth Street near Washington Street.

For Lincoln, the year was full of notable incidents. During the summer, Daniel Webster, whom he greatly admired,[1] made a tour of the West and about the middle of June came to Springfield. A mounted company with Captain Merryman as Marshal rode out many miles to meet the great orator and escorted him into the prospective capital. Whigs gathered from all over the County, a barbecue was held in the grove near town, a toast drunk to Webster, who then addressed the throng 'for an hour and a half . . . in a cool, dispassionate and able manner.' He was fair but forthright — never would he support a 'Treasury Bank;' to that experiment was due the present distress of the country. Webster's peroration — stand by the Constitution! — was so impressive that 'the multitude who listened to his appeal,' never forgot it.[2]

Talk of Webster's visit and speech had not subsided before another circumstance happened even more attractive to Springfield, and bringing Lincoln again into the foreground of the town's affections. On July 27, 1837, 'several members of the State Legislature and other distinguished men passing through our town' were given a big dinner as 'a proper tribute of respect' for what had been done for Springfield. The 'sumptuous' banquet, attended by sixty or seventy men, was held at the Rural Hotel and Colonel Spotswood was the host. 'The cloth having been removed, the following toasts were . . . received with great glee:' to Illinois, destined to be 'fairest and tallest among the sisters of this great Republic;' to the Legislature, whose 'duty has been nobly done;' to O. H. Browning,[3] whose monument will be the new capitol; to 'the "Long Nine of Old Sangamon" — well done good and faithful servants;' to Archibald Williams, 'clear in head and firm in purpose;' to Springfield, 'favorite of our State;' to McClernand, to Southern Illinois,

---

[1] Joseph Gillespie to Herndon, Jan. 31, 1866. Weik MSS.

[2] *Sangamo Journal*, June 24, 1837, reporting the meeting held on the previous Monday. Dr. Arnold Naudain, recently United States Senator from Delaware, arrived from the East on the same day. He, too, made a speech — his high expectations of Illinois had been surpassed by the reality and he probably would come there to live (cheers). Webster left Springfield the next morning 'for the north' and returned home by way of the Lakes.

[3] Browning had introduced the seat of Government bill.

to Northern Illinois, to the people of Illinois, to Internal Improvements, to everybody and everything, and particularly 'to our absent friends . . . who stood by us in our time of need.' Music and cheers greeted the toasts to Browning and Williams; and, responding, Browning said that the Sangamon delegation deserved credit for Springfield's victory.

Finally, when the twenty-two regular toasts had been drunk, many volunteer toasts were offered, of which the reporter could remember only a dozen. One among them was by Lincoln: 'All our friends — they are too numerous to be now named individually, while there is no one of them who is not too dear to be forgotten or neglected.' [1]

Thus merrily sped Lincoln's first months in Springfield, song and cheer and great occasion pleasingly interrupting the no less engaging game of politics which, from the first, he played incessantly and joyously. Stuart's whole thought was given to his ambition to go to Congress. He was determined to win next year and no detail must be overlooked in the ensuing months. Lincoln attended to practically all the business of the firm. Lucky for him that board and lodging cost him nothing, for the fees were few and trifling. The account book, kept by Lincoln, a provident habit which he abandoned as soon as possible, shows only five fees from April, 1837, to October, 1838, one for two dollars and fifty cents, two for five dollars, one for ten dollars and one, a 'chancery case' of fifty dollars, fifteen dollars of which was paid by furnishing a coat for Stuart.[2] The infrequency and smallness of these fees are striking in view of the fact that Stuart and Lincoln had more cases of record in the Circuit Court of Sangamon County than any other lawyer or firm of lawyers.[3]

[1] Douglas also proposed one of the remembered toasts: 'The last winter's Legislation — may its results prove no less beneficial to the whole State than they have to our town.' Stephen T. Logan gave by far the most sensible toast of the day, although it could not have been popular on that occasion or anywhere at that time: 'The System of Internal Improvements adopted by the late Legislature — the best mode of rearing it to perfection would be a liberal pruning of the superfluous branches.' One by Col. Spotswood was prophetic: 'Com. Alex. J. Dallas. He possesses every characteristic of the American officer. He has humbled the priest-ridden Government of Mexico, and she cries "peccavi."' *Sangamo Journal*, July 29, 1837.

[2] One page of this account book is owned by Jesse W. Weik of Greencastle, Ind.

[3] In the July term, 1837, Stuart and Lincoln had nineteen common law cases on the

In addition to this local business, Lincoln immediately began to attend court in the other counties of the circuit.[1]

But, like his partner, Lincoln was more interested in politics than in law, and he found it hard to confine himself to the firm's office. His real headquarters were the room where the *Sangamo Journal* was written and printed. He knew Simeon Francis, the editor, better, perhaps, than anybody else in Springfield except Speed and Stuart; and during the years that he had contributed to the *Journal*, Francis had become fond of him. Now that he was acknowledged to be one of the cleverest politicians in the General Assembly, high in the counsels of the party, regarded by his colleagues to be a coming man, and, above all, partner of the great Stuart, the editor of the Whig organ trusted Lincoln more than ever. In time Lincoln became so influential with Francis that he was said to have controlled the columns of the *Journal*. Douglas, then Register of the Land Office at Springfield, was equally constant in attendance at the office of the Democratic paper, the *Illinois Republican*, and as dominant over its policy.

Hardly had Lincoln become settled in Springfield when he got into a quarrel which, before it was finished, attracted the amused attention of the whole State. Since it involved the first law case of general interest he ever had and is connected with the longest political newspaper controversy he ever personally

docket of the Sangamon Circuit Court mostly in assumpsit, the amounts involved ranging from $20.50 to $1000 with an average of $500; while Logan and Baker represented ten, the next highest number of common law cases. Stuart and Lincoln had seven chancery cases at the same term and Logan and Baker had only one. Docket Book I, Circuit Court, Sangamon Co., Ill.

At the October term, 1837, Stuart and Lincoln had twenty common law cases and Logan and Baker eleven; and five chancery cases; while Logan and Baker had none. *Ib.*

In the March term, 1838, Stuart and Lincoln had thirty-three common law cases and Logan and Baker twenty-three; in chancery seven to four. *Ib.*

The proportion of cases of these two firms continues practically unchanged until 1839, when Logan and Baker passed their competitor. But in the July term, 1839, Stuart and Lincoln's common law cases rose to thirty-four to fourteen for Logan and Baker. *Ib.*

Treat sprang to the front almost immediately after he came to Springfield, having twenty-three common law cases at the March term, 1838, twenty-four at the July term and forty-six at the October term of 1838, together with twenty-three more as associate of Campbell. *Ib.*

[1] In Bloomington, 1837. Statement of David Davis, no date. Weik MSS.

engaged in, a brief statement of this strange tangle of incidents cannot be avoided.

In May, 1837, Mary Anderson and her son Richard, widow and son of Joseph Anderson deceased, came to Springfield from Fulton County where they lived, to get possession of and sell ten acres of land near Springfield which they claimed belonged to them as heirs of the deceased husband and father. They found the land occupied by the former attorney of Anderson, General James Adams, who claimed title to it through deeds and other documents of record. He refused, of course, to give the land to the Anderson heirs.

Mrs. Anderson and her son then asked Lincoln to recover the land for them. The young attorney examined the records, and finding features of them which aroused his suspicions, sent the Recorder, Benjamin Talbott, to Adams' house for the original deeds which were delivered to Talbott by Adams' son. The Recorder compared them with the copies in his office and found that the copyist had made the mistake observed by Lincoln, the originals being regular and perfect. This fact Talbott reported to Lincoln, who again unfolded the deeds for re-examination, when, as he asserted, a paper fell out, which appeared to be an assignment by Anderson to Adams of a judgment; but, according to Lincoln, this document, which Anderson had signed by his mark, was dated several months before the judgment and was, moreover, in the handwriting of Adams and freshly written.[1]

This and other circumstances convinced Lincoln, he said, that the assignment, upon which the title of Adams ultimately rested, was a forgery, and he agreed to bring suit for the recovery of the land. He engaged Stephen T. Logan, leader of the Sangamon County bar and later to become his partner, to assist in the litigation. He then wrote out a contract for a contingent fee, which on May 26, 1837, the widow and her son signed, Mrs. Anderson by her mark:

'Whereas the heirs of Joseph Anderson deceased are about to commence an action in chancery in the Sangamon Circuit Court, for the recovery of a certain piece of ground (describing the land

[1] *Works*, I, 58–64.

in controversy); and whereas, Stephen T. Logan, John T. Stuart and A. Lincoln have engaged to prosecute the suit as attorneys for the said heirs, we, the subscribers, being the widow and one of the sons of the said Anderson deceased, agree to give to said Logan, Stuart and Lincoln one-half of the said piece of ground for their services, provided they recover the same; but are not bound to pay anything unless the said piece of ground be recovered.' [1]

Thereupon, June 22, 1837, Lincoln and Stuart, together with Logan and Baker, filed suit against Adams for the recovery of the land, averring that it was now worth two thousand dollars and alleging that his title had been procured by fraud.[2] Adams promptly filed his sworn answer stating the manner in which he had acquired the land and asserting that the charges of fraud against him were 'little less than a tissue of misrepresentations.' Later Adams filed with the court what he claimed to be the original assignment to him by Anderson of the judgment, to which assignment Anderson's name was signed in writing.[3]

Here this celebrated case rested until October 17, when Lincoln and Logan filed a replication.[4] Meanwhile, a curious newspaper warfare, in which politics and the law suit were inextricably blended, had begun and for a long time continued to be waged between Lincoln and Adams, Lincoln being the aggressor.

---

[1] Lincoln MSS., Illinois State Historical Society.

[2] The land was worth but $30 in 1827 and the value of $2000 stated in the bill was the not uncommon exaggeration of the pleader. The ten-acre plot was 'a rough, untillable piece of timber, lying almost two miles from the State House in the hills upon which Oak Ridge Cemetery was subsequently located,' and the report of the Executors of Adams filed April 5, 1854, states that this specific ten acres was sold for $100 to one, Lewis, who, a year later, sold it for $175. In 1860 it was sold for $2400 and a slaughter house built upon it. Wm. L. Patton to author, March 18, 1925, citing Court and Deed records, Springfield, Ill.

It is curious that the bill itself is in three separate and distinct handwritings of which but six and one half lines — the description of the land by metes and bounds — are that of Lincoln, although there are eight pages of the bill. The signatures of the four solicitors for the complainant, obviously written by the same hand, are somewhat like that of Lincoln, but much bolder. Wright *et al. vs.* Adams. MS. Files Clerk Circuit Court, Sangamon County.

The bill shows that it was the composite product of three lawyers working together at the same time. In view of the political features of the case and of the outcome of the litigation, the inference cannot be avoided that local party politics had much to do with it.

[3] July 5, 1837. Record C, 421. [4] *Ib.*, 497.

JOHN T. STUART

Indeed the newspaper attack upon Adams began before the suit was brought against him.

A special election for certain county officers was to be held in August, and Adams was the Democratic candidate for Probate Judge, Dr. A. G. Henry, being the Whig candidate. The whole campaign appears to have centred about the contest for this office, and the Whigs were plainly alarmed at the popular strength of the Democratic candidate. Adams was one of the oldest settlers of Springfield, a frontier lawyer and very popular.[1] For three months the usual political charges and countercharges had been made by the organs of the two parties.

At this point Lincoln gave rein to his gift for writing anonymous letters to the press, which five years afterwards was to get him into serious trouble. On June 24, two days after Lincoln filed in court the suit against Adams, the *Sangamo Journal* printed a letter from 'Fork Prairie' signed 'Sampson's Ghost,' asking Adams to 'just tell the people' how he got the land in Springfield on which he was living. Vague insinuation was made that his title rested on a forged document, the inference being that the heirs of Sampson's Ghost were the rightful owners.[2]

The day after the suit was brought against Adams, another Sampson's Ghost letter appeared in the *Journal*, intimating that Adams had been disloyal in the War of 1812, and again asking

---

[1] Adams was fifty-four years old at this time, having been born in Hartford, Conn., Jan. 24, 1783. He had been Justice of the Peace at Springfield since 1823 and was a veteran of the Winnebago and Black Hawk Wars of 1827, 1831, and 1832. *Early Settlers of Sangamon County:* John Carroll Power, 76.

Just before the period of partisanship, in the *Sangamo Journal*, June 14, 1834, 'Many Voters' endorsed Adams as a candidate for Governor, and he immediately published a card, accepting the suggestion. *Ib.*, June 21, 1834. However, Adams' candidacy appears not to have gone beyond Sangamon County; but see *Illinois Election Returns:* Pease, under Adams.

[2] *Sangamo Journal*, June 24, 1837. This land was not the same tract for the recovery of which Lincoln, as attorney for the Anderson heirs, sued Adams; but the Sampson's Ghost charges are interwoven with the Anderson suit by identity of time, and by direct reference to that litigation.

Sampson's Ghost was not the restless spirit of the departed Anderson, however, but of one, Sampson, deceased, who seems to have once owned another piece of land in the town itself on which Adams lived. Adams' title to the Sampson land appears to have been a matter of speculation. Lincoln seized upon that fact in his newspaper attacks on Adams.

Sampson's sister lived in Philadelphia, and more than four years after the Ghost letters were published, William Primrose, an attorney of that city, wrote Logan and

about the title to the land.[1] Adams had answered the first
Sampson's Ghost letter declaring that his title was 'of record,
open to all persons;' but, said the Ghost in reply, would records
disclose forgery? If Adams would explain his title and the
people should then elect him, 'I will acknowledge that Sampson
never owned one foot of ground in Springfield.'[2]

In such fashion Sampson's Ghost rose to attack Adams again
and again in the Whig newspaper, and Adams replied in the
Democratic newspaper,[3] charging that a group of Whig lawyers
at Springfield had conspired to ruin him. Just before the election, an unsigned handbill, written by Lincoln, was circulated
giving a precise account of the discovery of Adams' alleged
fraud and explaining how the case against him had come into
the hands of Stuart and Lincoln.[4]

Adams won at the polls, however, by a majority of almost two
to one, and in the places where Lincoln's attacks were expected
to hurt Adams most he overwhelmed the Whig candidate, New
Salem going for Adams by a majority of nearly five to one and
Petersburg casting but eight votes for Henry to one hundred
and sixteen for Adams.[5] The Democratic organ was exultant, the
Whig paper angry and humiliated.[6] Then Adams published in

Lincoln to settle with Adams for half the value of the property, or to bring suit against
him for the recovery of it. Primrose to Stephen T. Logan and A. Lincoln, Phila., Sept. 1,
1841. MS. in possession of Logan Hay, Springfield, Ill. Logan and Lincoln did not
answer and Primrose wrote them again, Jan. 8, 1842 (*ib.*); but nothing whatever was
done in the matter. Seemingly Lincoln wanted no further trouble with Adams after
his encounter in the Court with that stubborn fighter.

[1] In his subsequent newspaper controversy with Adams, in which Lincoln signs his
own name, he says that: 'Gen. Adams himself, in reply to the Sampson's Ghost story,
was the *first man* that raised the cry of *toryism* and it was only by way of set off, and
never in seriousness that it was banded back to him.' Lincoln's reply to Adams, Sept. 9,
1837. *Works*, I, 65–75.

Even if this admission that he wrote the Sampson's Ghost letters had not been made,
Lincoln's authorship of them is established by conclusive circumstantial evidence. The
style of the letters is unmistakably that of Lincoln at that time in his life; the letters appeared immediately before and after he filed the suit against Adams, made reference to
points in it, and were continued until the election.

[2] *Sangamo Journal*, July 8, 1837.

[3] Three more Sampson's Ghost letters, an editorial and another anonymous letter,
dated '1st Monday in August,' were published before the election (*ib.*, July 15, 22, 29,
1837), all of them obviously written by Lincoln. Only in the last Sampson's Ghost
letter is mention made of the suit filed against Adams by Lincoln's clients.

[4] *Works*, I, 58–64.　　　　　　　　　　[5] *Sangamo Journal*, Aug. 12, 1837.

[6] *Ib.*

the *Journal*, his answer to Lincoln's pre-election unsigned handbill; and, in the same issue, just below Adams' reply, the
Journal printed the handbill with the statement that Lincoln
was the author of it.[1]

For months after the election, the warfare raged in the press,
Adams voluminously stating his side in the *Republican* and
Lincoln, over his own signature, replying at length and minutely
in the *Journal* — Adams' statements are 'false as hell,' his son
Lucian swears to a 'falsehood,' Miller, a witness, and a party to
the extensive transaction, has been 'tampered with' and testifies to an untruth, the charge of toryism in the Sampson's Ghost
letters had merely been 'banded back' to Adams.[2] Adams vehemently denied any wrongdoing and fiercely asserted that if
Lincoln and his friends had ever seen such a paper as the assignment described by Lincoln, it was a forgery gotten up by them
to beat Adams at the polls, win their wicked law suit, get his
land, and break down his reputation. Meanwhile other anonymous attacks upon Adams, signed 'An Old Settler,' were published in the *Journal*, plainly written by Lincoln.[3] Finally
even Stephen T. Logan got into the papers because, in one of
his answers to Lincoln, Adams had attacked Logan. After a
hot rejoinder, Logan announced that he would sue Adams for
libel.[4]

So filled were the Whig and Democratic papers of Springfield
with the Lincoln-Adams quarrel, that the matter got into State

[1] *Works*, I, 57–64, Aug. 19, 1837. In the various editions of Lincoln's *Works* no mention is made of this letter by Adams in reply to the handbill and printed with it in
the *Journal*. Four affidavits sustaining Lincoln's contention are also printed in the
same issue just below Adams' letter.

[2] *Ib.*, 65–76, Sept. 9; 76–87, Oct. 28, 1837.

[3] *Sangamo Journal*, Sept. 30, Oct. 7, Oct. 14, 1837. In one of these is printed a letter
of Elijah Iles recounting the circumstances of Adams' wrong-doing toward Iles in
another land transaction. Old Settler closes his letter by saying that Adams' 'duplicity
shall not be covered over by the mantle of religion.'

[4] *Sangamo Journal*, Oct. 28, 1837. Benj. Talbott, the County Recorder, also published a long letter against Adams. *Ib.*, Nov. 4, 1837.

Logan filed his complaint in the Sangamon Circuit Court, but on July 7, 1837, it
was removed to Schuyler County on motion of Adams based on the prejudice of the
judge. The case was finally dismissed by agreement at Adams' costs, April 5, 1841,
upon Adams' statement of record that 'he never intended to charge the plaintiff with
forgery, etc.' Records Schuyler County Cir. Ct., April, 1841. Douglas was Judge of
the Court in these proceedings.

politics.[1] The *Journal* was 'caused some pain' by the political attacks upon it, and in self-defence secured a transcript of an indictment for forgery against Adams when he lived in Oswego County, New York.[2] Adams, said the *Journal*, had left that State 'while an indictment for forgery was hanging over his head.'[3] So let the Democrats cease their scoffing, ridicule, and abuse.

In the end nothing came of this political and legal controversy. Adams was twice re-elected Probate Judge and died in office, August 11, 1843.[4] The suit against him brought by Lincoln was transferred to Schuyler County, whence it was remanded to Sangamon by Judge Stephen A. Douglas, because he had been 'of counsel' for Adams; depositions were taken, the material part of which was favorable to Adams' title to the land, but the case never was brought to trial; and, on a suggestion of the defendant's death, the suit was abated by the Court, November 29, 1843.[5] So the widow and heirs of James Adams received the land. It would appear, however, that Lincoln was not without grounds for his estimate of Adams' character, though the partisan motive for the entire controversy is undeniable.

While Lincoln was thus unmasking a dishonest man, as he must have believed, though at the same time creating public sentiment favorable to his side of a law suit and weakening an opposing politician, an event came to pass not far away, of

[1] 'A considerable portion of the People of this State are aware of the controversy.' *Sangamo Journal*, Nov. 25, 1837.

'Several of the Van Buren papers in other parts of the State, have united with the party paper here, and have endeavored to turn the current of public opinion against the *Journal*.' *Ib.*

'The Chicago *Democrat* again taunts us with the election of General Adams.' *Ib.*, Dec. 23, 1837.

[2] *Sangamo Journal*, Nov. 25, 1837.

[3] *Ib.*, Dec. 23, 1837.

[4] Power, 76.

[5] Record H., 219. This litigation was very complicated, but the main facts are these: The ten acres involved were entered Nov. 17, 1823, by Joseph Dixon and by him were conveyed to one —— Thomas, Nov. 29, 1825. On Sept. 17, 1825, Joseph Miller gave his promissory note for $27 to Joseph Anderson for this same land, Anderson agreeing to procure Thomas to convey it to Miller, which was done. Deed Book J., Recorder's office, 33–4.

A credit of $1.50 was made on the note, and, by confession, before Adams as Justice of the Peace, Sept. 14, 1826, Anderson secured a judgment against Joseph Miller for $23.67½, with $2 costs; and Adams, on Oct. 14, 1826, issued an execution against Ander-

mighty influence on the destiny of the nation. Once more that thunder rolled over the land which Lincoln had heard three times before; but now the crash was at Alton, Illinois, only sixty miles from Springfield.

When, in 1833, the tide of Southern alarm and resentment and Northern disapproval of Abolition methods and activities was rising, a young Presbyterian minister thirty-two years of age, Elijah Parish Lovejoy, went from Massachusetts to St. Louis and started a religious paper, called the *Observer*. At first he declared against '*immediate and unconditional emancipation*' and criticised the Abolitionists, although he denounced 'slave-drivers.' [1] But he soon grew bolder and, proposing gradual emancipation his subscribers requested him not to discuss slavery in the then excited state of the public mind.[2] Lovejoy grew defiant. He attacked the Catholic Church, also, not because of any connection of that institution with slavery, but as a

son in the Circuit Court of Sangamon County to enjoin the enforcement of this execution; and the injunction was ordered.

October 1, 1827, Adams, as attorney for Anderson, filed an answer, signed and sworn to by Anderson, to Miller's suit for injunction, alleging that he had procured a deed to be executed by Thomas conveying the land to Miller, which deed should be held in escrow by Adams, until Miller paid the judgment. On Oct. 6, 1827, the Court, 'after an inspection of the papers,' dissolved the injunction at Miller's cost. Records Circuit Court, Sangamon County, Book A, 323.

The records do not show any judgment in the Circuit Court against Miller for $25, May 10, 1827, which, with the assignment thereof by Anderson to Adams, Lincoln charged to be a forgery.

On Oct. 1, 1832, Miller conveyed the land to Adams (Deed Book J., Recorder's office, 35) in consideration of the satisfaction of Anderson's judgment against him, which, as Adams claimed, Anderson had assigned to Adams in discharge of a debt that Anderson owed Adams. Adams thus came into the possession of the three deeds — from Dixon to Thomas, Thomas to Miller, and Miller to Adams — but did not file any of them for record until June 18, 1836, when all were recorded. *Ib.*, 33–5.

Lincoln charged that both assignments of the judgment — the one discovered by him signed by Anderson's mark and the one alleged by Adams to be the only and original assignment in writing by Anderson — were forgeries by Adams; while Adams as vehemently asserted that he never heard of such a paper as Lincoln said he discovered and, Adams insisted, it was itself a forgery.

Curiously enough the bill in chancery against Adams filed by Lincoln and Stuart, and Logan and Baker as attorneys for the heirs of Anderson, does not make mention of either of these assignments about which the newspaper warfare raged, but merely charges that, by fraudulent collusion between Adams with Miller, Adams got Miller to convey the land to him. Wright Admr. *et al. vs.* Adams. MSS. Files Clk. Cir. Court, Sangamon Co.

[1] *Memoir of Lovejoy*, by his brothers, Joseph C. and Owen Lovejoy, 122–6.

[2] *Ib.*, 127–38.

part of his general crusade against whatever he disapproved. An editorial entitled 'Nunneries,' full of unsavory suggestions — well-nigh charges — of grave misdoings, was of a nature to enrage Catholic men and women.[1] In short the young editor, in his passionate and all-inclusive championship of 'righteousness,' as he saw it, made himself as offensive to as many people as possible.

Meetings of protest against abolition 'incendiarism,' were then being held all over the country and particularly in the South, and one of these was held in St. Louis. A free mulatto of evil repute named McIntosh, while resisting arrest, stabbed an officer and murdered a prominent citizen in the sight of large numbers of people, and had been burned by a mob, a thing that seldom happened in those days.[2] This tragedy added heat to the anti-abolition meeting. Resolutions that the Abolitionists were inciting anarchy and endangering the Union were adopted.[3]

Lovejoy earnestly protested against any interference with free speech, and offered himself a 'willing sacrifice' if popular vengeance needs a victim.[4] He furiously assailed the mob and castigated a Judge for charging the Grand Jury that it could not indict for the McIntosh lynching if the deed was done by 'congregated thousands' whose names could not be ascertained.[5] To Lovejoy's delight, another mob promptly attacked the office of the *Observer*;[6] and so hostile became the public temper,[7] that he removed to Alton, Illinois, with his press, where some unknown men threw it into the Mississippi River soon after it was put on shore.[8]

Alton was then at the climax of a remarkable period of prosper-

---

[1] Lovejoy, 105–16.

[2] *Ib.*, 168–71. 'In the name of Goodness, what is our country coming to.' *Illinois State Register*, May 6, 1836, editorial on the burning of McIntosh.

[3] Lovejoy, 138–40.

[4] *Observer*, Nov. 5, 1835; Lovejoy, 140–54.   [5] *Ib.*, 174–8.

[6] 'I have had the honour of being *mobbed* at last.' Lovejoy to his brother, July 30, 1836. *Ib.*, 181–3.

[7] *Ib.*, 181. The Presbyterian Synod at Marion, Mo., voted against Abolition. 'Two members from New England voted against us. . . . Eastern men when they go over constitute the most ultra-defenders of Slavery.' Lovejoy to his brother, Jan., 1836. *Ib.*, 160–2.

[8] *Ib.*, 180.

ity and was ambitious to take the place of St. Louis as a distributing point and centre of trade. Its principal commerce was with the South, especially New Orleans. In the then inflamed state of Southern feeling, fired by abolition activities, Alton wished to take no chance of offending its one great source of profitable business.[1] It was by far the wealthiest and most enterprising town in Illinois. Practically all its business men and most of its population were from New England, New York, and, in less numbers, from Virginia. Not only did Alton justly boast of her extraordinary material progress, but the rich little city was particularly proud of the religious, moral, and educational activity of her people.[2]

The citizens of this thriving community, indignant at the destruction of Lovejoy's press, immediately held a meeting, denounced those who had committed the outrage, 'unanimously' pledged themselves to buy another press for the unlucky editor, but disapproved Abolitionists and their methods; while Lovejoy, on his part, announced that although 'the uncompromising enemy of Slavery,' he was not an Abolitionist and had come to Alton to publish a religious, not an abolition paper.[3] The people of Alton and, indeed, of the State, understood that he pledged himself not to advocate or discuss abolition.[4] So a new press was bought for him and by August, 1837, the *Observer* had secured two thousand subscribers.

Not for long could Lovejoy subdue the fire burning within him. In a singularly inept editorial he charged the financial disaster of 1837, particularly severe in Alton, to over-specula-

---

[1] 'The citizens of Alton at the beginning presumed an abolition journal at their place, so near the State of Missouri, a slave State, would do the city of Alton a serious injury, and prevent the growth of the place. This was, as far as I understand, one reason the citizens urged against the establishment of such a paper at Alton.' Reynolds, 321.

The Bank of Illinois was helping Alton in its ambition to surpass St. Louis. Ford, 176–7.

[2] Mitchell, 113–5.

[3] Lovejoy to his brother, July 30, 1836. Lovejoy, 181–3. The *Alton Observer* merely said on the destruction of Lovejoy's first Alton press by mob: 'Its course is not such as we approve.' *Sangamo Journal*, July 30, 1836, condemned the mob severely and stood up for Lovejoy's constitutional rights.

[4] Reynolds, 318; Ford, 235. 'Upon this condition he was permitted to set up the *Alton Observer* without opposition.'

tion caused by the love of gain — that 'earth-born, grovelling propensity' — and also the source of slavery and the only thing that maintained it.[1] Other editorials appeared, each more denunciatory than the one before. In a heated controversy with a religious paper, the *Christian Mirror*, published at Cincinnati, Lovejoy was even more offensive than he had been in his anti-Catholic editorials in St. Louis.[2] Soon he began to advocate the formation of Abolition societies,[3] savagely attacked slavery and branded the Vice-President of the United States as the father of slaves.[4] The flag itself was made of material raised by slaves.[5]

So plunged Lovejoy toward his doom. Again his press was thrown into the river; but Abolitionists in Ohio bought another for him and the *Observer* continued its pugnacious and irritating course. The citizens of Alton held meetings of protest against the violation of Lovejoy's 'solemn pledge,' and committees labored with him.[6] The obdurate editor took his stand squarely on the freedom of the press, declaring, however, that he would discuss slavery 'with the meekness of a Christian.' Another public meeting assembled, Lovejoy grew more belligerent;[7] and finally, for the third time a mob threw his press into the river.[8]

The Abolitionists of the whole State were now aroused and a convention of 'all opposed to slavery and in favor of free discus-

---

[1] *Observer*, May 25, 1837. Lovejoy, 188–92. The *Baptist Banner* charged the Abolitionists with 'advocating amalgamation; that is, the intermarriage of whites and blacks' (*ib.*, 200); and Lovejoy wrote the editor of the *Christian Mirror*, Rev. Asa Cummings, a blistering letter, castigating preachers for not condemning slavery. *Ib.*, 192–200.

[2] 'I never said there was "not a chaste female in the [Catholic] church;" I said as a *general truth* there was not, and I repeat it.' *Observer*, May 25, 1837; Lovejoy, 202–4.

[3] *Observer*, June 29, July 6, 1837; Lovejoy, 212–6.

[4] *Observer*, July 20, 1837. Lovejoy, 234–44. This had been one of the Whig campaign charges against Richard M. Johnson of Kentucky, candidate for Vice-President with Van Buren in the campaign of 1836. Johnson was very popular in Illinois, because of his support of a liberal public land policy.

[5] Editorial, 4th July, 1837; *Martyrdom of Lovejoy*: Henry Tanner, 106.

[6] Lovejoy, 216–20. Resolutions by this committee were also adopted expressive of abhorrence of slavery, disapproval of abolition, and endorsement of such gradual emancipation as would be '*agreeable to the slave holding states.' Ib.*

[7] Lovejoy to the Committee, July 26, 1837. *Ib.*, 227–9. Governor Ford says that at this meeting Lovejoy denied that he made any pledge, which denial 'of what hundreds had heard him declare, increased the rage of the people.' Ford, 236.

[8] Ford, who wrote from information secured at the time, says: 'The people assembled and quietly took the press and types and threw them into the Mississippi.' *Ib.*

sion' was called to meet in Upper Alton,[1] October 26, 1837.
Many attended. Attempt was made to exclude everybody except Abolitionists, but the trustees of the Presbyterian Church
where the convention was to assemble, would not permit it to be
held in the Church unless all who 'opposed slavery' were admitted. Rev. Edward Beecher, President of Illinois College at
Jacksonville and a radical Abolitionist, delivered a sermon
which hearers considered a violent speech for immediate emancipation — 'for his part, he did not sanction the Constitution.'[2]
Other fiery abolition speeches were made, and Usher F. Linder,
then Attorney General, and Rev. John Hogan answered them.[3]

An Abolition society was formed, but not one of the first to
be organized in Illinois. Once more his Ohio friends had bought
a new press for Lovejoy; and the Abolitionists, now armed, organized and under the command of officers, went to Alton to
protect the press when it should arrive, announcing that they
were prepared to defend it by force and to the death.

Beecher came, too, and delivered an abolition lecture in a
church, attended by men with guns in their hands. Public excitement began to rise. Efforts at conciliation were made by the
more moderate citizens, but these attempts at adjustment came
to nothing. While Lovejoy seemed willing to compromise,
Beecher was adamant. 'Had they made the least concession,'
testifies Governor Ford, the tragedy that followed would have
been averted.[4]

Another public meeting proved futile. Resolutions offered by
Cyrus Edwards, Alton's member of the Legislature, while de-
precating violence and counselling law and order, declared that
matters had come to such a pass that, for the peace of Alton,

---

[1] A small town adjacent to Alton.

[2] Ford, 238; but see Beecher's account in *The Alton Riots:* Edward Beecher, 45–50.

Edward Beecher was a son of Lyman Beecher and brother of Henry Ward Beecher
and Harriet Beecher Stowe, author of *Uncle Tom's Cabin.* The Beecher family is one
of the most eminent in American history, nearly all of the thirteen children of Lyman
Beecher having attained distinction in literature or theology. Edward Beecher was
born in East Hampton, Long Island, Aug. 27, 1803. He was a graduate of Yale and
studied theology at Andover. Before his election as President of Illinois College, he
was pastor of the Park Street Congregational Church in Boston. He returned to the
ministry in 1844 and, upon his retirement in 1872, became the editor of the *Con-
gregationalist.*

[3] Ford, 238.   [4] *Ib.,* 240; Beecher, 84–98.

Lovejoy should 'be no longer identified with any newspaper' in the town. Many speeches were made, many resolutions adopted, all against forcible measures but in reproof of Lovejoy. Judges and preachers joined in the discussion. The editor spoke twice: he asked only his rights, he said; let the people mob him, he would not be driven away. 'If I die, I have determined to make my grave in Alton.' He denied that he had given any pledge and during his second speech 'burst into tears.' [1]

Ever higher rose public feeling. Business was suspended. The only talk on the streets was of the Abolitionists, their militant attitude, their military preparations. At last the press arrived and was hurried to a big stone warehouse where an armed company of sixty men stood guard over it. About ten o'clock at night, November 7, 1837, a mob gathered and demanded the press. Upon peremptory refusal accompanied by avowals that the press would be protected by powder and lead, stones were hurled at the building and the mob tried to storm it. Shots were fired and a young man named Bishop in the crowd outside the warehouse fell dead. The mob retired but soon returned, many inflamed by drink, and renewed the assault. The bells of the city were rung, horns blown, and large numbers of citizens hurried to the scene, some counselling quiet, others urging vengeance.

The roof of the warehouse was set on fire and extinguished, then set on fire again. Twice Lovejoy came out without being recognized, and fired at the mob. A third time he appeared at the door, was seen by the frenzied crowd and, before he could shoot again, was instantly killed by bullets from the muskets in the hands of the rioters. The defenders then surrendered, and for the fourth time the abolition press was thrown into the Mississippi.[2]

[1] Lovejoy, 271–82.

[2] In a few days, both sides were indicted and all acquitted, thus making the record show, sarcastically observes Governor Ford, 'that in fact the Abolitionists had not provoked an assault, that there had been no mob, and that no one had been killed or wounded.' Ford, 245.

Because of the profound prejudice of those who took part in this affair, it is difficult to determine the exact truth of the details, although all agree as to the principal features and incidents of it. While, on the whole, condemning the Abolitionists, perhaps the account of Governor Ford is the most unbiased and accurate.

About four years after Ford wrote his *History of Illinois*, Gov. John Reynolds wrote his reminiscences, *My Own Times*. Reynolds also disapproved of the abolition agitation,

Throughout the country the wrath of the Abolitionists flamed to the skies, and their newspapers and orators denounced in scorching language, the 'infamy' of Alton. Here, said they, was the hideous spirit of slavery, unmasked at last, and openly doing its devilish work even in a free State. Garrison's *Liberator*, with broad funeral border on each page, announced that an 'awful sensation' of 'shuddering horror pervades the land.' [1] The Boston *Wanderer* declared that 'the disenthralled spirit of Lovejoy is hovering around us . . . and a voice from his tomb cries, ONWARD! THE TIME IS COME!' [2] Abolition societies held fiery meetings and passed blazing resolutions. Public assemblages in many cities denounced the Alton mobs and their attack on the freedom of the press.[3]

One such gathering became historic. At Faneuil Hall, Boston, December 8, 1837, a great crowd came to a meeting, called by Rev. William Ellery Channing, to protest against the Alton outrage. Most of the audience, however, were opposed to abolition and unsympathetic with Lovejoy. After speeches from the platform, the Attorney General of Massachusetts, James T. Austin,[4] rose in the gallery and, in a loud voice trembling with passion, defended the Alton mob for throwing Lovejoy's press into the river: their spirit, he said, was the same as that of those who spilled the British tea into Boston harbor. As to Lovejoy, he had 'died as the fool dieth.' The 'storm of applause and hisses was deafening.' [5] Then a very young man of singular

and he wrote in 1854 that 'the public agitation . . . of slavery . . . should be avoided.' *Ib.*, 146. For Reynolds' account of Alton and Lovejoy see *ib.*, 317–21.

Two versions by Lovejoy's friends who were on the ground were written, one by Beecher, *The Alton Riots*, within a short time; and another by Henry Tanner, *Martyrdom of Lovejoy*, forty-three years afterward.

[1] However, Garrison, sternly true to his pacific principles, 'solemnly protested' against the use of 'carnal weapons under any pretext or in any extremity whatever.' *Liberator*, Nov. 24, 1837.

[2] Lovejoy, 331. For extracts from editorials of all papers thus denouncing the killing of Lovejoy see *ib.*, 222–37.

[3] *Ib.*, 314–22.

[4] Austin was then fifty-three years old. He had been Attorney General for five years and continued in that office for six years longer. He was a son-in-law of Elbridge Gerry and a pronounced, outspoken opponent of abolition methods, as were nearly all Boston professional and business men at that time.

[5] Commenting on Austin's speech, the *Boston Atlas* said that it was 'most able and triumphant.'

physical beauty and 'radiant of face' took the platform. Few at the meeting knew who he was, and the crowd did not want to hear him. When, finally, he was permitted to speak, he denounced Austin. In a voice quiet and attractive, yet 'thrilling with emotion,' he exclaimed: 'Sir, when I heard the gentleman lay down principles which place the murderers of Alton side by side with Otis and Hancock, with Quincy and Adams, I thought those pictured lips [pointing to the portraits in the Hall] would have broken into voice to rebuke the recreant American — the slanderer of the dead.' Wendell Phillips had begun his career; abolition had found its golden trumpet.[1]

Thus, from the moment of the killing of Lovejoy to that of the hanging of John Brown, 'The Martyrdom of Lovejoy' became a battle cry of Abolitionists;[2] and the Alton catastrophe did more to increase their numbers and inflame their feelings, than their warfare upon slavery itself.

For the most part, however, the press of the country was quiet, except for expressions of disapproval of mobs generally and insistence upon the freedom of the press. In Illinois, especially, general sentiment ran against Lovejoy, but one paper in the State, the *Peoria Register*, was outspoken and severe.[3] All, however, condemned mob violence. 'In the supremacy of the laws *ALONE* is security. The first duty of every citizen is to maintain that supremacy, whatever may oppose it, or whatever may be the hazard,' asserted one editor,[4] thus voicing the general sentiment to which Lincoln was soon to give expression. The Springfield papers merely printed, without comment, the formal statement of the Mayor of Alton giving the bare facts of the event.[5] But at Jacksonville, thirty miles

---

[1] *Speeches and Lectures of Wendell Phillips*, 3.

Phillips was then twenty-six years old, a graduate of Harvard and of Harvard Law School. He was tall, slender, an aristocrat of old Boston, strikingly handsome and his voice, though gentle and sweet, was strangely compelling and had remarkable carrying power. The Faneuil Hall speech gave him his first fame and he came to be recognized as a great orator.

[2] 'The burst of indignation from all parts of the land, as the result of this murder, was hardly exceeded by that which followed the battle of Lexington, in 1775.' Tanner, 158.

[3] Tanner, 166-7.   [4] *Illinois State Register*, editorial, Nov. 20, 1837.

[5] *Sangamo Journal*, Nov. 19, 1837. Other papers did the same. *Illinois State Re-*

from Springfield, Illinois College, the foremost educational institution of the State, seethed with anger. Its faculty were as outspoken as President Beecher himself.

Soon after the killing of Lovejoy, another mob at Vicksburg, Mississippi, hanged three white men, professional gamblers.[1] Indeed a wave of mob violence, chiefly directed at Abolitionists, had been sweeping over the land for four or five years.[2] In this state of things and about eleven weeks after the Alton affair, Lincoln delivered before the Lyceum in Springfield, a speech of capital importance. Although his theme was the danger and wickedness of mobs and the vital necessity of maintaining law and order, and although Lincoln specifically and at length spoke of the St. Louis and Vicksburg mobs and the burning of McIntosh, he made no mention of Lovejoy or Alton by name, but only a casual reference to the incident. The speech shows that it had been prepared with much thought and care; and this fact, together with the subject treated and the time and circumstances of its delivery, makes it the most notable of his life thus far and, in fact, for many years thereafter.

Here we Americans were, he said, with the most extensive and richest country in the world and blessed by institutions more conducive to civil and religious liberty than any of which history made record — all this 'bequeathed us' by noble ancestors. Our task and duty were to transmit this heritage 'to the latest generation that fate shall permit the world to know.'

So we must guard against danger to our country and institutions. Whence may we expect the approach of peril? From foreign military attacks? 'Never! All the armies of Europe, Asia, and Africa combined, with all the treasure of earth (our own excepted) in their military chest, with a Bonaparte for a commander, could not by force take a drink from the Ohio

gister, Nov. 24, 1837. The Mayor's statement was reproduced from the *Alton Spectator.*

[1] *Illinois State Register*, Nov. 24, 1837.

[2] Channing, v, 152–9; *Illinois Advocate*, Sept. 3, 24, 1834.

There was much lawless disturbance even in Springfield. In June, 1837, the Sheriff and a crowd broke into the office of the Democratic paper and, afterward, the Sheriff assaulted the editor with a loaded whip. *Illinois State Register*, June 30, 1837. Editorial on 'Mob Law.' This incident may have had something to do with the Lincoln-Adams quarrel.

or make a track on the Blue Ridge in a trial of a thousand years.'

Any real menace could come only from ourselves; and signs of doom had already appeared. Witness 'the increasing disregard for law,' the substitution of 'wild and furious passions in lieu of the sober judgment of courts, . . . the worse than savage mobs' rather than the officers of law. All this was apparent on every side — 'outrages committed by mobs form the every-day news of the times.' Mobs were not peculiar to any section; they prevailed in free and slave States alike. North and South, the mob spirit was 'common to the whole country.'

The worst were the Mississippi mobs that hanged 'the regular gamblers,' then hanged slaves suspected of plotting insurrection, then white men 'supposed to be leagued with the negroes, and finally strangers in Mississippi on business; and the St. Louis mob which burned the mulatto McIntosh, a barbarity 'the most highly tragic . . . ever . . . witnessed in real life.' The hanging of the gamblers in Vicksburg 'was of but little consequence' except for the fearful example it gave. So, too, of the burning of McIntosh in St. Louis. 'He had forfeited his life by the perpetration of an outrageous murder upon one of the most worthy and respectable citizens of the city, and had he not died as he did, he must have died by the sentence of the law in a very short time afterward. As to him alone, it was as well the way it was as it could otherwise have been.' Still, it afforded a 'fearful' example.

Such things encouraged 'the lawless in spirit,' and, besides, mobs in their blind fury were apt to hang or burn the innocent as well as the guilty. In short, the 'mobocratic spirit which all must admit is now abroad in the land,' might break down the people's 'attachment' to their government.

If this happened, if 'the vicious portion of population shall be permitted to gather in bands of hundreds and thousands, and burn churches, ravage and rob provision-stores, throw printing-presses into rivers, shoot editors, and hang and burn obnoxious persons at pleasure and with impunity, depend on it, this government cannot last.' Such was Lincoln's only comment on the Alton riots and the killing of Lovejoy.

Should this continue, he went on, some able and ambitious man would overturn the 'fair fabric' of our government, that 'fondest hope of the lovers of freedom throughout the world.' What, then, must be done? 'Let every American . . . swear by the blood of the Revolution never to violate . . . the laws, . . . and never to tolerate their violation by others.' To do so 'is to trample on the blood of his father, and to tear the charter of his own and his children's liberty.' Let reverence for and observance of law 'become the political religion of the nation.'

Of course there were bad laws, and 'grievances' for the redress of which no law existed; but, while bad laws ought to be speedily repealed, they should be obeyed, 'for the sake of example,' while they are on the statute books. Offences not provided for by law should be 'borne with, if not too intolerable,' until an appropriate law could be enacted, which should be done 'with the least possible delay.'

Take mobs: 'There is no grievance that is a fit object of redress by mob law. In any case that may arise, as, for instance, the promulgation of abolitionism, one of two positions is necessarily true: that is, the thing is right within itself, and therefore deserves the protection of all law and all good citizens, or it is wrong, and therefore proper to be prohibited by legal enactments; and in neither case is the interposition of mob law either necessary, justifiable, or excusable.'

If asked why, since we have preserved our institutions for fifty years, 'may we not for fifty times as long,' the answer is that there 'are now, and will hereafter be, many causes, dangerous in their tendency, which have not existed heretofore.' No wonder our government has lasted until the present time — 'it had many props to support it . . . which now are decayed and crumbled away.'

For example, the government 'was felt by all to be an undecided experiment,' and all persons with ambitions expected to gratify them by 'the success of that experiment;' but now that experiment was successful. No longer would the aspiring, energetic, and daring, be content with nothing more than 'a seat in Congress, a gubernatorial or a presidential chair.' To be sure, great and good men always can be found who would wish for nothing more; 'but such belong not to the family of the lion, or the tribe of the eagle.'

'What! think you these places would satisfy an Alexander, a Cæsar, or a Napoleon? Never! Towering genius disdains a beaten path. . . . It sees no distinction in adding story to story upon the monuments of fame erected to the memory of others. . . . It scorns to tread in the footsteps of any predecessor, however illustrious.'

Such genius 'burns for distinction; and if possible, it will have it, whether at the expense of emancipating slaves or enslaving freemen.' Sometime a man of 'the loftiest genius . . . will . . . spring up among us;' and, when he does, it will require an intelligent and united people, devoted to 'the government and laws, . . . to successfully frustrate his designs.'

Until lately the soldiers of the Revolution had furnished a 'living history' of that pure and heroic period, but they had departed. They had constituted a 'fortress of strength' to American institutions, but 'the silent artillery of time' had razed that fortress. They had been a 'forest' of giant oaks, but now they were prostrate; 'pillars of the temple of liberty,' but now they had crumbled away. So 'other pillars, hewn from the solid quarry of sober reason,' must be set up. 'Cold, calculating, unimpassioned reason — must furnish all the materials for our future support and defense.'

Then 'let those materials be moulded into general intelligence, sound morality, and, in particular, a reverence for the Constitution, and laws,[1] . . . Upon these let the proud fabric of freedom rest, as the rock of its basis; and as truly as has been said of the only greater institution, "the gates of hell shall not prevail against it!"'[2]

[1] At this point an apostrophe to Washington is so badly mangled by the printer that, as it appears in Lincoln's *Works*, it is unintelligible and therefore omitted in this summary of the speech.

[2] *Works*, I, 35–50. This and other editions of Lincoln's *Works* give the 'Lyceum Address' as having been delivered at Springfield, Jan. 27, 1837, although printed in the *Sangamo Journal*, Feb. 3, 1838. Lincoln was in Vandalia, Jan. 27, 1837. *House Journal.* The Vicksburg and Alton riots referred to in the speech did not take place until the summer and autumn of that year, and the address was made on Saturday, Jan. 27, 1838, as stated in the text. The error in Lincoln's *Works* is doubtless due to the not unusual circumstance that, by careless typesetting, the *Sangamo Journal* of Jan. 27, 1838, containing the notice of the Lyceum meeting bears the date of 1837 inside the paper.

Thus, with tremendous national issues and grave events mingling in Lincoln's experience with local quarrels, small town politics, daily cheer and casual law business, he was called to an extra session of the Legislature in the summer of 1838, made necessary by the deplorable financial condition of the State. For the last time but one, Lincoln again went to Vandalia to face a situation which he had done so much to create.

CHAPTER V

LAST YEARS IN THE LEGISLATURE

This was the first time that I began to conceive a very high opinion of the talents and personal courage of Abraham Lincoln. LINDER.

WHILE Lincoln was filling the columns of his party newspaper in Springfield with articles, letters, and editorials against James Adams, and accurately reflecting public sentiment in Illinois as to mobs, Lovejoy, and abolition, one of the worst financial panics of recent decades was sweeping around the world. The result of extravagance, speculation, and over-trading, it was very severe in America, and in the Western States it approached a catastrophe.

The Whigs declared that the hard times were the direct and certain result of Democratic mismanagement of the Nation's finances. See what had come of Jackson's warfare on the Bank of the United States, they said. Had they not warned the people what would happen?

The removal of government funds from the Bank, the refusal of Congress, under the direction of the President, to renew the charter of that powerful institution which was the keystone of American business, the consequent withdrawal of its credits and retirement of its bills, together with the resulting exclusive reliance upon fluctuating currency provided by State and private banking concerns — all this, asserted the Whigs, had caused the general economic breakdown from which the country was suffering. There was, indeed, much truth in the Whig charges and they fervently believed the disaster to be the natural fruit of the Democratic onslaught upon the commercial interests of the country. For the most part none knew of the business collapse in Europe or did not, at least, connect it with the American disaster.

Among other public misfortunes which accompanied the panic of 1837 was the inability of Illinois to obtain the loans required by her grandiose scheme of Internal Improvements. Worse still, her newly chartered State Banks suddenly found themselves in desperate case. In the spring they had suspended specie payments, as had all banks in the country; but the State Banks of Illinois held large deposits of State money.[1] So a special session of the Legislature was called to meet July 10, 1837, and Lincoln discontinued his newspaper controversy with Adams, while he attended that doleful and quarrelsome assembly of puzzled and resentful law-makers.

In his message, Governor Duncan struck forcibly the chord of despair. Everybody was happy and prosperous when the Legislature last met, he said, although, even then he was apprehensive; but 'no human forecast could have anticipated, so sudden a calamity as has been brought upon the country by the action of the Federal Government upon its currency.' When Jackson began his war on the Bank of the United States, 'there never was a sounder currency, or a more healthy state of things in any government in the world.' Now, we have 'a depraved and worthless currency,' made up of 'enormous issues of irredeemable paper' put out by 'hundreds of new banks.'

The present emergency rendered it an 'immediate and imperative duty' to consider the condition of the two State Banks of Illinois. All told, more than seven hundred thousand dollars of public money were deposited in their vaults and they had assumed large obligations of the State. Their charters were forfeit when they suspended specie payments, yet they had been forced to do so because of the general suspension by banks throughout the country.

'Immediate legislative action' must be taken to protect the interests of the State and save the State Banks from utter collapse. The desperate situation was fortunate in one respect. It afforded an opportunity 'to escape from the perils of that system of Internal Improvement adopted last winter, which . . . is so fraught with evil.'

Government construction, ownership, and operation were fundamentally wrong, said the Governor; individual enterprise, not government inefficiency, should undertake such work. And think of the wretched plight of national affairs, due to the usurpation of that autocrat, Andrew Jackson. The country is decay-

[1] Ford, 191.

ing, liberty perishing! Witness the last eight years! Once more Duncan made a ferocious attack upon the President's policies: 'may God in his infinite wisdom and mercy avert' the consequences of them.[1] Again the Democrats were furious at Duncan. 'We have never read a paper, from an official source,' so full of lies, so false to republican doctrines, declared the Democratic organ.[2]

The Governor's message, with which Lincoln heartily agreed, accurately gauged the heated feeling that pervaded the Legislature. Immediately a memorial of the State Bank of Illinois at Springfield praying a suspension of forfeiture of its charter was presented. Duncan and the Supreme Court were invited to sit with the House during the session,[3] and the short but gloomy proceedings began.

The questions which the Legislature had been called to consider related to the State Banks and to Internal Improvements; but friends of other projects could not be restrained. Earnest, almost wrathful effort was made to undo Lincoln's victory in securing the State capital for Springfield, and again his resourcefulness and courage were put to the test.[4] He was prepared, however; the Sangamo Journal had sounded the alarm. 'We are summoned to renew the same struggle. . . . Vandalia is wide awake, she has her strong man, General W. Lee D. Ewing [who] is a candidate for the Legislature. She is calling through her newspapers for a repeal of the law. All her energies are called into action.'[5]

Sure enough Ewing was elected to the House in place of John Dement, for the express purpose of securing the repeal of the State capital law.[6] He had held many important offices, had just finished an unexpired term in the Senate of the United States,[7] was one of the prominent men of Illinois, and very popular. He was an experienced politician, an excellent de-

[1] House Journal, Spl. Sess. 1837, 9–15.   [2] Illinois State Register, July 15, 1837.
[3] House Journal, Spl. Sess. 1837, 15, 17.
[4] Many country newspapers were violently opposed to Springfield. Illinois State Register, Dec. 9, 1837.
[5] Sangamo Journal, July 1, 1837; and Illinois State Register, June 10, 1837.
[6] Linder, 62.
[7] That of Elias K. Kane, to which Ewing was elected, Dec. 29, 1835.

bater, well educated, combative, and noted for his physical courage.[1] On the third day of the session he gave notice that he would presently introduce a bill to repeal the seat of government act, and he soon did so.[2]

Midway in the session a sharp engagement took place over the measure. Ewing made savage onslaught on Springfield. 'The arrogance of Springfield, its presumption in claiming the seat of government, was not to be endured; . . . the law had been passed by chicanery and trickery; . . . the Springfield delegation had sold out to the internal improvement men, and had promised their support to every measure that would gain them a vote to the law removing the seat of government.' Thus Ewing raged.[3]

Lincoln replied with even greater heat, denouncing Ewing fiercely for his charge of corruption 'and paying back with usury all that Ewing had said.' Ewing was furious. Speaking directly to the Sangamon delegation, all of whom sat together, Ewing exclaimed: 'Gentlemen, have you no other champion than this coarse and vulgar fellow to bring into the lists against me? Do you suppose that I will condescend to break a lance with your low and obscure colleague?'

Everybody expected a challenge; for Ewing was a fighting man and it was the day of duelling. But mutual friends interposed and the quarrel was settled without a fight. 'This was the first time,' declares Linder, who witnessed the encounter and relates the story of it, 'that I began to conceive a very high opinion of the talents and personal courage of Abraham Lincoln.'[4]

A lively parliamentary scrimmage followed, Lincoln winning on every roll-call; a bill on the subject favored by him was ultimately passed and for this session Springfield was secure.[5]

On the third day of the session, Lincoln's Committee on Finance, reported a Bank bill [6] authorizing suspension of specie

---

[1] Linder, 62.   [2] *House Journal*, Spl. Sess. 1837, 21, 48.

[3] Linder, 62. See also *Illinois State Register*, July 21, 28, 1837.   [4] Linder, 62–3.

[5] *House Journal*, Spl. Sess. 1837, 104–6, 119, 140. Lincoln was a member of the committee that reported the bill. The Senate did not act upon it, however, and so no law was enacted on the subject, which was what Lincoln and Springfield wanted.

[6] *Ib.*, 18, 28.

payments for a limited time and under careful restrictions; and next day James Shields moved to substitute a comprehensive bill of his own [1] which became the basis of the law finally enacted.[2] Most of the session was taken up with the consideration of this legislation — resolutions, motions, amendments, rollcalls, constant debate.[3] Excitement was high. 'The Bank question is, at present, the all absorbing topic,' declared the *Illinois State Register* in an editorial on the Legislature.[4]

Throughout these long and involved proceedings, Lincoln steadily voted favorably to the Bank, at one time going so far as to oppose an amendment reserving to the Legislature the right to repeal or modify the Act of 1835 incorporating the Bank, and requiring the Bank to consent to such reservation [5] — this, of course, in consideration of the passage of the suspension law now asked by the Bank. This vote, and, indeed, Lincoln's whole attitude and conduct in the Bank controversy were strongly conservative and in firm support of vested interests and the conduct of business, unmolested as far as possible, by legislative or any kind of governmental interference.

Yet he voted for the proposition that, in case the Bank act was violated during the suspension of specie payments, stockholders should be personally liable for the redemption of the notes of the Bank 'in proportion to their stock;' for an inquiry as to whether any members of the House were officers of the Bank or indebted to it; and then voted against the whole Bank bill as amended.[6]

In spite of well-nigh hopeless financial conditions, the Legislature could not muster up courage to abandon the Internal Improvement scheme, and a bill to repeal it was promptly killed by a heavy majority, Lincoln voting nay.[7] Douglas went to Vandalia and urged that work on internal improvements be sus-

---

[1] *House Journal*, Spl. Sess. 1837, 29–31.   [2] *Laws of Illinois*, Spl. Sess. 1837, 6–7.

[3] *House Journal*, Spl. Sess. 1837, 52–3, 70–2, 83–6, 90–1, 98–102, 132–6, 152–3.

[4] *Illinois State Register*, July 15, 1837. See also speech of William W. Happy of Morgan County against the Bank (*ib.*, July 28) and that of James A. Shields of Randolph County for the Bank. *Ib.*, Aug. 4, 1837.

[5] *House Journal*, Spl. Sess. 1837, 100–1.   [6] *Ib.*, 85–6, 152–3.

[7] *Ib.*, 74–5. 'Here ends we hope forever, the opposition to our noble system of Improvement.' *Illinois State Register*, July 15, 1837.

pended until a more favorable season; but even his support of the Whig Governor's request was unavailing.[1] After languid discussion the Legislature finally passed a brief act, Lincoln voting aye,[2] requiring the Commissioners of Public Works as soon as practicable 'to proceed to the survey, location and construction of several routes of railroads, and other public improvements.'[3] He opposed the calling of a Convention to make a new State Constitution,[4] secured the passage of an act extending the corporate powers of Springfield,[5] and was active in legislation concerning the location of roads.[6]

At this session was a member of the House who, thereafter, was to be intimately associated with Lincoln's early political activities. Edward D. Baker, born in England, was then twenty-six years old, strikingly handsome, gifted with an eloquence surpassed only by the great orators, and endowed with a rare and noble gallantry of spirit. He had been chosen at a special election as one of the representatives from Sangamon County to succeed Daniel Stone, who had resigned. He was soon to win greater popular favor than Lincoln himself and to have one of the most worthy and picturesque careers among those of the lesser figures in American history. Like Hardin, he was fated to die on the battle field.[7]

Upon adjournment, July 22, 1837, Lincoln went back to

[1] Stevens, 312. Douglas had been appointed Register of the Land Office upon the recommendation of members of the Legislature, vice George Forquer. *Sangamo Journal*, Feb. 11, 1837.

[2] *House Journal*, Spl. Sess. 1837, 139.

[3] *Laws of Illinois*, 1837, 45. A long report was also adopted militantly supporting the internal improvement law passed by the previous Legislature and rebuking Duncan. As to private rather than public construction and operation of railroads and canals, the report observes: 'If the mighty energies of this great State, should be trammelled by a connection with incorporated companies, managed and controlled by the moneyed interests of other States and countries, it could not fail soon to become a source of unavailing regret to her citizens.' *House Journal*, Spl. Sess. 1837, 177–81.

[4] *Ib.*, 62–3. The resolution passed the House, but was rejected by the Senate. *Ib.*, 115.

[5] *Ib.*, 88. This bill failed in the Senate.

[6] *Ib.* One of these road laws brings the flavor of New Salem. Lincoln procured an amendment authorizing Bowling Green, Bennett Abell, and John Bennett to relocate the part of the State road between Petersburg and New Salem. *Ib.*, 123; *Works*, I, 55.

[7] Power, 87–9. Stone resigned because he had been elected Judge of the Galena Circuit and he soon removed to that town.

Springfield, his already high reputation in that town still further enhanced and his popularity increased. His bellicosity expanded and continued to grow until deflated by a dramatic but unhappy incident that gave him his second and badly needed lesson in discipline.

When, for the last time, the General Assembly of Illinois met at Vandalia, December 3, 1838, Lincoln as undisputed leader of his party in the House was, of course, the Whig candidate for Speaker. He received his full party strength, but William Lee D. Ewing was elected by a vote of forty-three to thirty-eight for Lincoln.[1] The fine personal appearance of the members of the Legislature, of which mention has been made, was again noted by onlookers, one of whom declared that, having seen the Legislatures of several other States, none in this respect surpassed that of Illinois in 1838.[2]

The Governor's message outlined the work of the General Assembly. The big problem, he said, was how to get rid of the internal improvement incubus 'without too great a sacrifice of public or private interests.' Much money had been 'squandered' on useless projects, and sometimes to 'the detriment of the public interest.' Officers and employees of the improvement system had had members in the last Legislature and will have them in this one, to support or oppose any bill affecting their jobs. Government should have nothing to do with such projects; they should be 'left in the hands of the citizens ... or corporations.' Government ownership and operation meant not only waste and corruption, but through 'numerous officers and dependents' the influencing of elections and legislation. So Duncan urged the enactment of a general incorporation law; and, if the Legislature insisted on retaining the Internal Improvement system, at least let the survey of roads be subjected to revision by the Board of Public Works.

The Governor could not keep his hands off national politics, in which Lincoln was interested even more keenly than he. The Presidency had 'become a mere ... electioneering establishment, to furnish places, out of which their partisan friends can

[1] *House Journal*, Sess. 1838-9, 5-6.
[2] *Sangamo Journal*, Dec. 15, 1838, reporting legislative proceedings of Dec. 5.

make fortunes.' Congress was corrupted by patronage, which was also 'notoriously used to influence State elections.' Everybody knew that 'subordinate collectors ... have squandered the public money, with the perfect knowledge of the Executive.' If this keeps on liberty is doomed; already freedom languishes! [1]

With these words of admonition and foreboding Joseph Duncan went out of office. To take the place of the defunct National Bank, Van Buren had devised the Independent Treasury through which the Government could collect, keep and disburse the public revenues. The Whigs furiously assailed it. Here, they thundered, was a specific and compelling cause of the hard times that lately had ground the faces of the people. The Democrats of Illinois were stricken with panic.[2] So the newly elected Democratic Governor, Thomas Carlin, who was immediately inaugurated, delivered a message glowing with cheer and hope, in striking contrast with Duncan's melancholy words. The Democrats must be heartened.

Carlin buoyantly declared that 'the mismanagement and overaction' of the Banks of the country had caused the financial depression. See how quickly the nation had recovered. The progress of other States had been checked, but not that of Illinois — she had 'kept steadily on in the march of improvement.' Think of her growth in population, wealth, prosperity. 'Her prospects are truly bright and flattering;' soon Illinois would be second to no State in the Union.

Let Illinois attend chiefly to the education of her children. Of course banking required attention, too — sharp attention. Penal laws should be enacted to compel State Banks to observe their charters strictly; and the Legislature should frequently examine them. Government construction and ownership of internal improvements were much better than private. The system adopted by the Legislature of 1836–37 was, perhaps, too ambitious; but 'near two millions of dollars have been expended' upon it and 'the character and credit of the State forbid its abandonment.'

The Jackson-Van Buren policies were sound, wholesome, beneficent. The issue now was a National Bank or an Independ-

[1] *House Journal*, Sess. 1838-9, 10–17. [2] Stevens, 311–2.

ent Treasury; 'under these opposite measures, the two great political parties of the country have ranged themselves.' A National Bank was 'unconstitutional, irrepublican and dangerous;' an Independent Treasury would 'dissolve the connection between the Government and Banks,' collect and disburse the public revenue in specie, safeguard the public funds, 'insure a circulating and sound uniform medium,' and promote the general welfare.[1]

Thus were stated the creeds of the political parties of the day, one of which Lincoln championed with all the aggressive vigor of youth. He was now fairly within that period of partisanship from which, after a dozen years, he was to emerge disillusioned and chastened.

The belligerent Whigs promptly took up Governor Carlin's challenge. In less than a fortnight, Lincoln's personal friend and intimate, and his associate on the Committee on Finance, Archibald Williams of Adams County, presented from that Committee a remarkable report, obviously intended and admirably adapted to be a Whig campaign document. As a member of the Committee, Lincoln helped to formulate it, and the probability is almost conclusive that he wrote most or all of it. The style and method of reasoning are distinctly those of Lincoln.

A succinct history of banks in relation to the Government was given. They had been used as fiscal agents from and including the administration of Washington to that of Van Buren now in power, with two brief lapses.[2] During this long period our prosperity had been 'beyond all parallel in the previous annals of the world.' A financial system under which such happy wonders occurred, could not 'in itself be "*radically and fundamentally defective.*"' Then followed a rapid summary of the unsuccessful efforts to break down the system of banks as fiscal agents of the Government, and an examination of Van Buren's plan to substitute for that old and tested system, the 'new and untried' device of a Sub-treasury, which Congress had twice rejected, many

[1] *House Journal*, Sess. 1838-9, 26–30.

[2] One from 1811, when the charter of the first Bank of the United States expired, until 1816, when the Second Bank of the United States was chartered; and the other 'from the removal of the deposites from the latter bank in 1833,' by Jackson until the end of his term of office. *Ib.*, 98.

of the strongest Democrats in the National House and Senate having voted against it.

The fact that European nations had adopted similar methods to the Independent Treasury proposed by Van Buren was no reason that America should do so. Is there 'any thing in the character of their governments, or the condition of their subjects, which should excite the envy or challenge the imitation of the American people? . . . A divorce of Bank and State! . . . An Independent Treasury!' Independent of whom? Independent of the people, indeed, but 'dependent upon the President, the Secretary of the Treasury and thousands of subordinate officers, who hold their appointments at the discretion of the President,' including 'numerous secret agents who . . . may be sent into every part of the Union to operate upon elections.'

The 'declamation' that the public funds were not safe in Banks was answered by testimony to the contrary in the report of 1834–35 of Levi Woodbury, Secretary of the Treasury. The Committee quoted, too, President Van Buren's recent tribute to the Banks for their 'honorable course' during the late panic.[1] Against these Democratic testimonials consider 'the frequent and extensive defalcations of "individual agents of the United States;" . . . the surprising list of defaulters among the collectors and receivers of the public moneys' presented in the last report of the Secretary of the Treasury; 'and, very recently, the enormous defalcation of the collector at New York [Swartwout] amounting (as reported) to one million two hundred thousand dollars.'

So the Committee submitted resolutions that a Sub-treasury was bad; that the Illinois delegation be instructed to vote against that system 'in any form whatever;' and to 'use all their efforts to prevent . . . the chartering of a National Bank of any kind.'[2]

Thus the Illinois Whigs astutely opposed the Administration plan, while playing into the hands of all State Banks among which the national funds had been distributed. In the Whig report Lincoln's political cleverness is manifested no less than his literary skill.

[1] In his message of Dec. 3, 1838. *Messages:* Richardson, iii, 483–505.

[2] *House Journal*, Sess. 1838-9, 98–103.

At once the Democrats on the Finance Committee filed a minority report stating the position of their party. The Whig report having taken the National Bank out of the controversy, the Democrats were driven to an attack on State Banks, especially as public depositories, a most hazardous political manœuver. They strove to get out of the dilemma by excepting the State Banks of Illinois from their general indictment of State Banks. Banks were not safe — witness the numerous failures of State Banks which twice had thrown the General Government 'on the verge of bankruptcy;' the public funds would not be available in case of emergency, such as war; 'an unnatural and unholy alliance between the General Government and the State Banks' would be that 'union of the purse and the sword,' so abhorred 'in all countries, and at all times.'

How much better and safer an Independent Treasury by which public funds would slowly and gradually be withdrawn in specie from the State Banks, until 'no other currency shall be received or disbursed, but that known to the constitution . . . in the words of Daniel Webster, "a gold and silver currency, the law of the land at home, and the law of the world abroad."' Thus the money of the Government would always be safe, always sound, always available.[1]

The Whigs then struck their next blow by Senate Resolutions bitterly condemning the National Administration for its 'partiality' in depositing in Missouri State Banks funds collected in Illinois, especially from the sales of public lands situated in Illinois, and insisting that such revenue should be deposited in Illinois banks. John Calhoun, the Democratic member from Sangamon, countered with a resolution that, in view of the Act of Congress requiring State Banks to comply with certain conditions in order to become government depositories, the Presidents of the two Illinois State Banks be required to inform the House whether they had done so.[2]

Harvey T. Pace of Jefferson County moved to strike out the word 'partiality' from the Senate resolutions. Lincoln, in charge of them, objected. He would agree to omit the word if he 'thought it was not true.' He then summed up the arguments

[1] House Journal, Sess. 1838–9, 103–8.   [2] Ib., 172–4.

made by members on Pace's motion and showed 'that the
Government had been partial.' A Democratic member, Newton
Walker of Fulton County, had said that the Senate resolutions
struck at Lincoln's 'own party friends.' 'Well,' answered Lincoln, 'we are willing to go it;' let Walker 'do the same with his
party friends.' As to investigation before passing the resolutions, Lincoln 'had heard similar arguments often made to put
off trial in court.'[1] But he could not hold his full party strength,
and the motion was adopted by an overwhelming majority.[2]

Time and again the question of depositing government funds
in the State Banks was debated, amendments were offered and,
finally, Lincoln moved to dispose of the matter by laying the
whole on the table until July 4, which was done by a vote of
forty-six ayes to forty-two nays, Lincoln voting aye.[3] But when
that stubborn Whig, John Henry of Morgan County, resur-
rected the subject by offering resolutions against Van Buren's
Sub-treasury and specie plan, Lincoln voted against exactly the
same motion that he himself had made; for resolutions against a
recharter of any National Bank; against a flamboyant Democratic resolution which quoted Jefferson's famous words about
the probability that a National Bank might, in emergencies,
overthrow the Government; and once more against ending the
whole matter by laying it on the table until July 4.[4] 'There was
a regular pitched battle between the Locos and the Whigs the
remainder of the day.'[5] Finally discussion was cut off by the
previous question and Lincoln voted for all the Whig bank
resolutions which were adopted and sent to the Senate for concurrence.[6]

But the fight was not over. Next day James Copeland of
Johnson County, who had voted with the Democrats, asked to
change his vote on one amendment; and Revill W. English of
Greene County moved that the Senate be requested to return
the resolutions 'reported to them this morning, in relation to the

---

[1] *Illinois State Register*, Jan. 18, 1839, reporting proceedings of Jan. 17.

[2] Fifty-four ayes to thirty-four nays, Lincoln voting nay. *House Journal*, Sess.
1838–9, 231.

[3] *Ib.*, 231–2.   [4] *Ib.*, 257–60.

[5] *Sangamo Journal*, Feb. 9, 1839, reporting proceedings of Jan. 30.

[6] *House Journal*, Sess. 1838–9, 260–4.

Sub-treasury system.' English's motion was rejected, Lincoln voting nay, and the Whig Senate promptly concurred in the House resolutions.[1]

The Democrats were sadly confused. Thirty-eight of them signed a paper, seemingly designed to be secret for the time being, advising the Illinois delegation not to obey the Whig resolutions against the Sub-treasury; but one of the signers, not understanding the party plan, thought the document a protest, and moved that it be entered on the Journal of the House. To the chagrin of his party associates, this was done and the plot exposed. Thereupon one member asked to withdraw his name.[2]

As the Whig floor leader, Lincoln was suave but merciless. He would permit the withdrawal, he said; but he declared that statements in the document were false and, at the proper time, he would demand a retraction. He would hold the signers responsible to the people, but if any of them 'was ashamed of it, he hoped the house would permit them to withdraw their names.' To the infinite disgust of the Whigs, the Speaker finally allowed the 'Protest' to be withdrawn altogether.[3]

For the moment the struggle ended by the adoption of resolutions for the deposit in the Illinois State Banks of funds of the General Government collected in Illinois, Lincoln voting aye. But so keen was the interest in the party conflict that the Senate rejected a House resolution against further discussion of national politics. After a shower of motions and roll-calls, the House agreed with the Senate, Lincoln voting aye, and the party battle went on. Resolutions and counter-resolutions, motions to table and to adjourn, amendments, and amendments to amendments spouted from eager partisans, the Whigs, under Lincoln as their leader, always firmly in control.[4] Then came a Senate resolution against establishing a National Bank 'on any terms,' because 'the recent policy of the States, in the establishment of State Banks, and connecting them with the various systems of inter-

[1] House Journal, Sess. 1888-9, 264, 299.

[2] Sangamo Journal, March 2, 1839.

[3] Ib., March 9, 1839. This amusing paper does not appear, therefore, in the Journal.

[4] House Journal, Sess. 1838-9, 288-93, 299-300, 310-2, 330-4.

nal improvements in the several States, requires at the hands of
this State an uncompromising hostility to a United States'
Bank;' and thus the conflict ended.[1]

Suspicion of the State Banks, however, persisted. Richard
Murphy of Cook County offered a resolution of inquiry whether
they were doing mercantile business, particularly by the purchase of lead at Galena and the sale of it through bank agents
'in our Atlantic cities.' Sixty-eight members voted for this
significant resolution; only thirteen members, Lincoln among
them, voted against it.[2] There was a sharp contest over a bill
reported by Lincoln's Committee on Finance, to increase the
capital of the State Bank at Springfield, Lincoln voting for the
measure which was finally defeated by the narrow margin of one
vote;[3] and he voted against restricting the Bank from issuing
notes of less than five dollars, a proposition that came from his
own Committee.[4] He had cast the same vote earlier in the session on a separate bill which, however, was passed by more than
three to one, Lincoln voting nay.[5] In short, Lincoln was the
trustworthy supporter of the State Bank at Springfield.

Although as her friends thought, the selection of Springfield
as the State capital had been settled forever, although contracts
for the building of the new State House had been let and work
was actually in progress,[6] the smouldering wrath of the opponents of Springfield again burst into flame. On January 7, 1839,
Lincoln moved to take up the appropriation bill 'for the completion and furnishing' of that structure.[7] Instantly Orlando B.
Ficklin of Coles County moved amendments that the act should

[1] *House Journal*, Sess. 1838–9, 340. This resolution shows that the Whigs were now
in open alliance with the two Illinois State Banks, an alliance not admitted when
Lincoln made his vigorous resistance to an investigation of the State Bank at Springfield in the preceding Legislature.

[2] *Ib.*, 305–6.

[3] Thirty-eight ayes to thirty-nine nays. *Ib.*, 556–8.

[4] *Ib.*, 486. The restriction was refused by forty ayes to thirty-six nays, Lincoln
voting aye. *Ib.*

[5] Sixty-three to twenty. *Ib.*, 253–4.

[6] The contract for removing the courthouse from the public square upon which the
Capitol was to be built, was given to Reuben Radford, who had such melancholy experience with the Clary Grove Boys in New Salem; and the contract for brick was
awarded to Milton Hay, uncle of Lincoln's future secretary. *Ib.*, 140–1.

[7] *Ib.*, 181.

not be operative unless one hundred and twenty-eight thousand dollars, the amount of the proposed appropriation, were 'donated' by individuals and 'secured by bonds,' for the building of the State House; and, moreover, that at the ensuing election the electors of Illinois should 'have the privilege of voting for or against the removal of the seat of Government to Springfield.' If the majority favored that town, the State should reimburse the donors for all monies expended. Futile effort. After a volley of motions to adjourn, Ficklin's amendment was overwhelmingly defeated.[1]

But Vandalia would not yield. Immediately William J. Hankins of Fayette County (of which Vandalia was the county seat) moved an elaborate amendment that the Governor reconvey to Springfield the Public Square; and that at the next election the voters of the State should express at the polls their preference for the places where the new capital should be established.[2]

Obviously the Springfield men were alarmed. Two motions to adjourn were beaten and a third carried. Next morning Lincoln moved another adjournment which was refused, and the Vandalia amendment taken up; but after some confusion the House adjourned without doing any business whatever for that day.[3] On the following day, however, Springfield once more won decisively.[4] Still her opponents would not give up. A motion to kill Lincoln's capitol appropriation bill was beaten without roll-call; another very long amendment by the obstinate Hankins was rejected by a vote of nearly three to one; still another amendment that the people should vote on Lincoln's appropria-

[1] Twenty-six ayes to sixty-two nays, Lincoln voting nay. *House Journal*, Sess. 1838–9, 182–3.

[2] If no one place received a majority, voters at another election were to choose among the five places which had received most at the first election; and at succeeding elections, the contest was to be progressively narrowed until only two places remained and a final election was to settle the matter. *Ib.*, 183–4.

Hankins was only obeying the instructions of his constituents. On July 7, 1838, a public meeting had been held at Vandalia to protest against the removal of the capital and to demand the repeal of the capital law of 1837. That law was unconstitutional — the people of Vandalia had acquired vested rights under the original act. Moreover, every voter in Illinois in 1840 would have the right to express his preference at the ballot-box. *Illinois State Register*, July 6, 1838.

[3] *House Journal*, Sess. 1838–9, 184–5.

[4] Fifty-eight nays to twenty-four ayes, Lincoln voting nay, on Hankins' motion to reconvey to Springfield the Public Square, etc. *Ib.*, 185.

tion was defeated by an even greater majority; and his bill passed at last by a smaller but heavy margin.[1]

After the killing of Lovejoy at Alton, the Illinois Abolition Society made some headway and petitions against slavery began to reach the Legislature.[2] The Governors of Georgia and Maine had exchanged angry letters over the refusal of Maine to deliver two citizens of that State to the Georgia authorities, for having abducted a slave from Savannah; and this correspondence, sent to other States by the Governor of Georgia, was referred to the Legislature of Illinois by Governor Carlin. On January 5, 1839, the House Committee on the Judiciary, members of which included those brilliant and aspiring young Whigs, John J. Hardin and Edward D. Baker, made a careful and unanimous report.

The Committee expressed 'deep regret' that citizens of free States should interfere 'in any manner' with the rights of citizens of slave States. 'Said committee consider the holding of slaves as a constitutional privilege,' and any interference therewith 'a violation of a right which ought to be held as sacred as any other portion of the Constitution.'

'The cause of the abolitionists,' the Committee charged, was conducted with 'the intemperate zeal of misguided philanthropists,' the practical effect of which was to harden rather than to ameliorate the condition of the slaves. It was too bad that 'such questions should be agitated to distract the peace and quiet of the nation.' Until the Governor of Maine explains his course, the Committee hesitates to condemn that State as 'willing and disposed to encourage a policy [abolition] which ought to be viewed as a moral and political pestilence' and which, if encouraged, would finally 'spread devastation and ruin over the land.'

So, to prevent 'undue excitement of the people of the south,' by the conduct of 'misguided fanatics of the North' in defiance of 'sound policy ... honest patriotism, and ... the principles of constitutional law,' the Committee presented resolutions that the refusal by one State to deliver those charged with crime in another State was not only dangerous to the whole American

[1] Fifty-six ayes to twenty-six nays, Lincoln voting aye. *House Journal*, Sess. 1838-9, 185-9, 199, 434.

[2] *Ib.*, 213, 301.

people, 'but clearly and directly in violation of the plain letter of the Constitution;' and that no free State or its citizens ought to 'interfere with the property of slave-holding States ... guarantied unto them by the Constitution of the United States, and without which guaranty this Union, perhaps, would never have been formed.' [1]

Against this report and these resolutions Lincoln made no protest; indeed they stated his views with exactitude, albeit he took no part in the heated debate that again arose over the subject. The abolition petitions to the Legislature, however, aroused Lincoln's Democratic colleague and former employer, John Calhoun of Springfield; and, midway in the session, he offered, as an amendment to a Senate resolution on another matter, sharp resolutions against the Abolitionists — 'certain citizens, males and females,' who have petitioned the Legislature 'to act upon the subject of slavery, and the slave-trade in the United States.'

Calhoun's resolutions recognized the right of petition, however, and in response to the abolition appeals declared that the National Government cannot do indirectly what it is prohibited from doing directly; that, since abolition of slavery in the District of Columbia — the avowed purpose of the Abolitionists as a first step toward abolition in the States — would be doing indirectly what is forbidden to be done directly, Congress ought not to abolish slavery in the District of Columbia or the Territories or prohibit the slave trade between the States; that the Legislature 'do not "protest"' against the admission of slave States, nor 'against the annexation of Texas to the United States,' and that it is not only 'unconstitutional, but improper, inexpedient and unwise "to repeal all laws existing on the statutes of this State, which graduate the right of the citizens by the color of the skin."' [2]

These resolutions were laid on the table by a majority of eight, Lincoln voting against them.[3] Thus the more moderate resolutions of the Judiciary Committee, stronger in condemnation of the Abolitionists than the resolutions of Calhoun, were left as the final opinion of the House on the slavery question.

[1] *House Journal*, Sess. 1838–9. 170–1.   [2] *Ib.*, 322–3.   [3] *Ib.*, 329.

Throughout this heated controversy no word appears to have been spoken on Lovejoy and the Alton riots, no intimation given that anybody had ever heard of that tragedy.

Petitions against the sale of intoxicating liquor had also begun to trickle into the General Assembly.[1] Lincoln, himself, presented that of '631 citizens of Sangamon county, praying the repeal of all laws authorizing the retailing of intoxicating liquors.'[2] A great temperance agitation throughout the country was then beginning, and temperance speakers were holding meetings everywhere. The House granted the use of its hall to one of these orators, Timothy Turner, agent of the Illinois Temperance Society, for the purpose of delivering a lecture on temperance, Sunday evening, February 3, 1839.[3]

These petitions were referred to the Judiciary Committee. On January 26, 1839, John J. Hardin of Morgan County brought in from this Committee a lengthy report, accompanied by a bill 'to regulate the granting of tavern license,' and, without objection, one hundred and fifty copies of the bill and five thousand copies of the report were ordered to be printed, a most unusual proceeding.[4] Before the House could act, the Senate passed a

---

[1] For example: That of 'sundry citizens of Athens, Sangamon county,' for the repeal of the law granting tavern license (*House Journal*, Sess. 1838-9, 163); that of 140 ladies and gentlemen, citizens of Schuyler County, praying for 'An Act prohibiting the retailing of intoxicating liquors' (*ib.*, 206); that of 'twenty-six male and twenty-four female petitioners, praying the repeal of all laws authorizing the licensing of retailers of ardent spirits' (*ib.*, 301); that of '150 ladies and gentlemen of the county of Fulton,' praying to the same effect (*ib.*, 375); and from Greene, Henry and Macoupin Counties came like prayers (*ib.*, 128).

[2] *Ib.*, 319.   [3] *Ib.*, 329.

[4] *Ib.*, 287. The criminal code prescribed a fine of $100, forfeiture of license and denial of re-license to those permitting lewdness, public indecency, or gambling in their taverns. *Laws of Illinois*, Revised, 1839, 222.

Hardin's report declared that the Illinois liquor laws as 'interpreted . . . not only permit, but rather invite to the retail of intoxicating liquors.' Most crime, pauperism and insanity were caused by excessive drinking. Among laborers on the canal, the vice was intolerable, causing loss to the State. The number of groceries [saloons] had increased alarmingly. For instance, Galena had thirty saloons for 3000 people. In fifty counties there was an average of twenty saloons; and not less than 1,220 licensed grog shops in the State. Only one county, Montgomery, was free of them.

The Committee admits 'that there is but one effectual remedy for this evil, and that is, the total repeal of all laws permitting the retail of intoxicating liquors, and then imposing a severe penalty on those who may treat at elections,' as had been done in Maine, Massachusetts, Tennessee, and other States; but the 'Committee have not the evidence . . . that the majority of the people of this State call for the enactment of

similar measure, and the two bills were thereafter considered together [1] and extensively discussed.

On the final roll-call, Lincoln voted against the House temperance bill, thus killing that measure, which was lost because of an equal number of ayes and noes.[2] When the Senate license bill was taken up, an amendment that sales of 'spirituous liquors by the dram or drink' be prohibited was rejected without roll-call, and the bill was ordered to the third reading by an almost two to one majority, Lincoln withholding his vote; [3] immediately thereafter, he voted to strike out the provision of the bill authorizing Justices of the Peace to grant licenses, which motion was lost by practically the same vote.[4] The Senate temperance bill, with amendments, then passed by a vote of forty-three ayes to twenty-seven nays, Lincoln voting nay.[5]

such laws.' When public sentiment demanded, the Legislature should 'boldly grapple with the enemy, and banish it from the State.'

Meanwhile the existing liquor law should be strengthened and broadened. The trustees of incorporated towns should have the power to grant or refuse licenses, since their citizens suffered most, instead of County Commissioners' Courts having sole power over licenses, as the present law provided. Committee Report, Jan. 26, 1839.

Hardin's bill prohibited the retail by anybody, of any intoxicating beverage in less quantities than one gallon to be taken from the premises, 'unless he is first licensed to keep a tavern' — penalty $10 to $100; that County Commissioners should grant licenses, except in incorporated towns where the town trustees should have that power; that license fees should be raised to not less than $50 to not more than $300; that an applicant for license must prove that he had 'sufficient meat and provisions, and comfortable lodgings for at least four persons' besides his family; that liquor should not be retailed 'by a less quantity than one gallon, in any other house' than his own tavern; that no license should be granted except on the petition of at least twenty householders of the vicinity; that an applicant must give bond in a sum not to exceed $500 that he would keep an orderly house; that, upon conviction, for keeping a disorderly house, the penalty provided by the criminal code should be increased by forfeiture of the license; that any retailer without license should be fined $10 for each offence; that licenses should be granted only during regular sessions of town trustees and Commissioners Courts and never in vacation; that laws and parts of laws inconsistent with the proposed law be repealed.

[1] *House Journal*, Sess. 1838–9, 318, 341, 433–4, 522.

[2] *Ib.*, 527–8. John J. Hardin voted for the bill, showing that it probably was the anti-liquor measure which he had reported from the Judiciary Committee. *Ib.*, 287.

[3] The vote was forty-three ayes to twenty-four nays. *Ib.*, 535.

[4] Twenty-five to forty-one, Lincoln voting aye. *Ib.*, 535–6.

[5] *Ib.*, 536. This new law repealed the old law, authorizing county Commissioners' Courts to grant the necessary licenses; and providing that disorderly houses should be 'suppressed' by the County Commissioners' Court; that the cost of licenses should not exceed $12; that no license should be issued unless the applicant gave bond, if required, in the sum of $300 to 'be of good behavior, and observe all laws and ordi-

As we have seen, no one member of the General Assembly had done more than Lincoln to fasten upon the State the Internal Improvement scheme, and, now that it was beginning to crumble, he came forward with a plan to strengthen and continue it. His idea was that Illinois should buy from the General Government all public lands in the State for twenty-five cents an acre, sell them to settlers and other purchasers for one dollar and twenty-five cents an acre [1] and thus create a fund to pay interest on the Internal Improvement debt.

On January 17, 1839, Lincoln presented from the Finance Committee a report and resolutions, all of which he had written.[2] Lincoln began by saying that purchase by the State 'on reasonable terms' would give the State control of all land within its boundary and also increase the State's revenue, both of which consummations would decidedly and favorably affect the Internal Improvement system.

'We are now so far advanced' in this, that we cannot abandon

nances . . . relating to tavern keepers.' The law was very severe against selling liquor to slaves and minors. Act, Feb. 27, 1819, *Laws of Illinois*, Revised, 1839, 673–5. By Act of Feb. 12, 1835, the limit of license fees was raised from $12 to $50. *Ib.*, 675.

The Act of 1839, against which Lincoln voted, provided, in lieu of the old laws which it repealed, that County Commissioners' Courts might grant licenses 'to keep groceries,' the applicant to pay therefor not more than $300 nor less than $25, in the discretion of the Court, and give bond for $500 that he 'will keep an orderly house'; that the license might be revoked when the grocer abused the privileges granted or violated the law; that the license should not authorize the holder to sell liquor in more than one place to be specifically described in the license; that 'a grocery shall be deemed to include all houses and places where spirituous or vinous liquors are retailed by less quantities than one gallon;' that 'the president and trustees of incorporated towns shall have the exclusive privilege of granting licenses to groceries within their incorporated limits;' all license fees to be paid to the County, and no license granted, if 'a majority of the legal voters,' in any county, town or ward in any city petitioned against the retailing of liquors, unless a majority should petition that such license be granted. Act of March 2, 1839. *Laws of Illinois*, 1838–9, 71–2. While not stringent, the act of 1839 was far more severe than the old laws. In some respects it was stronger than the Committee's bill.

[1] The minimum price at which the Government then sold public lands.

[2] 'I send you a copy of my Land Resolutions, which passed both branches of our legislature last winter.' Lincoln to Stuart, Jan. 1, 1840. *Works*, I, 140.

While the MS. of this important paper has not been discovered there can be no doubt of Lincoln's authorship of it. Aside from Lincoln's statement to Stuart, the peculiar style and reasoning of this important document are unmistakably those of Lincoln. Even his habit of underscoring words and phrases appears in the Committee's report.

The copy inclosed in the letter to Stuart was in Lincoln's writing but has no words underscored. The original Stuart letter and inclosure are in the possession of Logan Hay of Springfield, Ill.

it 'without disgrace and great loss.' Our improvement of the country enhanced the value of the government land as well as all other real property in the State; so if we buy it that increase of value will 'attach exclusively to property owned by *ourselves* as a State, or to its citizens as individuals, and *not* to that owned by the Government of the United States. . . . It is conceded everywhere . . . that Illinois surpasses every other spot of equal extent upon the face of the globe, in *fertility* of soil and in . . . the capacity of sustaining a greater amount of agricultural wealth and population than any other equal extent of territory in the world.'

To such wealth and population our Internal Improvement system 'would be a burden of no sort of consequence.' It is now alarming only because of 'our present numbers' and 'our present means.' Of consequence increased wealth and population are vital to the success of the Internal Improvement system and to the well-being of the State generally. Our chief difficulty is that 'so much of our best lands lie so remote from timber;' but if the State owned those lands, the Legislature could provide for foresting or for 'means of building and enclosure' which would not require 'the present profuse use of timber.'

As regards revenue, there are now about twenty million acres of unsold government land in Illinois which will cost us five million dollars if purchased at twenty-five cents per acre. Borrow this, sell the lands for five times as much (the present selling price), pay from the proceeds the loan and interest and we shall still have at least half of the lands left us.

Presently we shall have a heavy internal improvement debt on our hands and our public works, when completed, will not yield immediate profit, yet the interest on our debt must be paid. 'When this juncture shall arrive (as surely it will), we shall find ourselves at a point which may aptly be likened to the dead point in the steam engine, a point extremely difficult of turning, but which, when once turned, will present no further difficulty, and all will again be well. The aid that we might derive in that *particular juncture*' is the strongest reason for the State's buying the government lands. The proceeds from the sale of them will pay the interest on 'many million of our internal improvement loans' as well as all the interest on the loan for the purchase of the lands; 'and that, too, at that *particular time* when we shall have but *very small, if any* other, means of paying it.' The interest on the land loan would be but five hundred thousand dollars annually, while the sale of government lands have yielded as high as three million in a single year; and if sales hereafter are only half as large 'we still should have left one million annually, to pay interest on our internal improvement debt.'

But is there 'any *probability*' that the General Government will accept such a proposal? Lincoln thinks there is. It would relieve the Government from 'a perpetual source of expensive and vexatious legislation' and the Government would get, 'at once, and without trouble,' one third as much as she paid for the Louisiana purchase, and at a time when the Government badly needs the money. In any case 'no evil can follow the making' of the offer.

So the Committee on Finance submitted resolutions that Illinois propose to the General Government to buy the lands for twenty-five cents an acre and pledge the faith of the State 'irrevocably' to fulfil the contract if the Government accepts within two years.[1]

This was too much, it seems, even for Lincoln's steady associate, Archibald Williams, who appears to have scoffed at the proposal as merely a scheme to enrich the State, as, indeed, it was. Lincoln replied: Williams was in error. Some thought the price of lands would be raised, others thought they would be lowered. The representatives from counties where government lands lie would see to it that high prices were not charged, since that would retard settlement. But look at the lands bought up by big speculators because they were cheap. Lincoln was against low prices for lands — it would hurt the settler because speculators would buy them. If the State had all the lands the Legislature would be just to every section. As to the General Government needing the money, 'if the national debt had not been paid, the expenses of the Government would not have doubled, as they had done since the debt was paid.'[2]

Lincoln's plan appealed to the House, the Senate concurred

[1] *House Journal*, Sess. 1838–9, 223–5.   [2] *Works*, I, 93–4.

and the proposal was accordingly made.[1] So with the valor of great expectations, the Legislature enacted an extensive law actually extending the Internal Improvement act. In the numerous ballots taken on the various provisions of this bill and amendments offered, Lincoln cast no vote worthy of especial note. Throughout he merely stood by the Internal Improvement system.

Toward the close of the session an amusing debate took place on a reapportionment of the State, and Lincoln's part in it illustrates that gift of humor by which he brightened dull discussions, made everybody laugh, and kept the House friendly to him personally. He was for increasing the basis of representation and thus reducing the membership of the Legislature. 'Double' expense, 'double' time for roll-calls, 'double' the number of members 'disposed to protract business' — that was what a big legislature meant. When the House was half as numerous as now, it did its work twice as quickly.

In some fashion the number nine, as being favored by 'old women,' had been mentioned in the debate, and Lincoln seized upon this irrelevance to crack a joke. 'A few years since ... the delegation from this county were dubbed, by way of eminence, the "long nine," and, by way of further distinction, I had been called the "longest" of the nine. Now, ... if any woman, old or young, ever thought there was any peculiar charm in this distinguished specimen of number 9, I have, as yet, been so unfortunate as not to have discovered it.' This banal digression was delivered in Lincoln's inimitable fun-compelling manner, for the reporter notes that Lincoln's sally was greeted with 'loud applause.' [2]

The session came to an end with Lincoln's leadership more

[1] *House Journal*, Sess. 1838–9, 600. The Government, of course, ignored the offer.

[2] *Sangamo Journal*, Jan. 15, 1839.

Examples of Lincoln's other votes during this session are: the Legislature must not elect members or relatives to other state offices (*House Journal*, Sess. 1838–9, 121–2); against the election of school commissioners by the people (*Ib.*, 235, carried by fifty-four ayes to seventeen nays); for the mechanics lien law (*Ib.*, 350–1); both for and against betting on elections (*Ib.*, 371); twice to increase salaries of Justices of the Supreme Court (*Ib.*, 371–2; lost forty-three nays to forty-one ayes, and then carried forty-seven ayes to forty nays, Lincoln voting aye both times); against calling a Constitutional Convention (*Ib.*, 480–1, carried fifty-six ayes to twenty-six nays); against classifying railroads (*Ib.*, 510–1); for the improvement of Spoon River (*Ib.*, 594).

firmly established than ever. His good humor, friendliness, pungent stories made everybody like him and his resourcefulness, ability, and steadiness made all respect him. Cheerily and, as we shall see, with a kind of jauntiness, he went about Springfield or rode the circuit during the spring, summer, and autumn of 1839.

Stuart had beaten Douglas for Congress by a majority of only thirty-six votes in a district in which thirty-six thousand votes were polled. Douglas charged fraud, which undoubtedly had been practised,[1] challenged Stuart to submit the dispute to a new election, and Stuart had declined.[2] Douglas seriously considered contesting the election and this gave the Whigs grave anxiety.[3] Lincoln was watchful of his partner's interests. In preparation for Douglas's expected contest, he wrote a confidential letter, signed by five other prominent Whigs of Springfield [4] as well as himself, to various Whig editors in the Congressional District, among them the editor of the Whig paper in Chicago, asking them to find out and report to Stuart and Lincoln, whether any mistakes had been made in adding the votes, and whether minors, or non-residents, or unnaturalized foreigners had voted for Douglas.[5] Douglas finally dropped the idea of trying to unseat Stuart; and Lincoln hastened to advise the uneasy Congressman of the good news, albeit with misgiving,

[1] Many ballots on both sides were thrown out because of defective spelling of the candidates' names, but there is positive testimony that Douglas suffered from a systematic effort to have electors vote for him so as to have the ballots rejected. Linder testifies that a Democrat, who was vindictive because he was not nominated instead of Douglas, got the Irish workingmen on the canal to vote for John A. Douglas, James A. Douglas, and the like, for the purpose of defeating Douglas. Linder, 347.

[2] *Sangamo Journal*, May 10, 1839. The letters of Stuart and Douglas upon this election were printed in full in the Democratic paper. See *Illinois State Register*, April 5, 1839. And see *Sangamo Journal*, Sept. 8, 1838, Jan. 1, 1839; also *Illinois State Register*, Sept. 28, Dec. 21, 1838.

[3] The campaign had been hard fought on both sides. Although Douglas and Stuart travelled and spoke together all over the vast district (Stevens, 317), the party papers were unsparing in attack, unlimited in praise. *Illinois State Register*, May 11, 1838; *Sangamo Journal*, Aug. 4, 1838. When the success of Stuart was first announced, the Whigs held a barbecue at Springfield, where several speakers, including Lincoln, addressed the crowd. *Illinois State Register*, Oct. 26, 1838. The *Register* insinuated that the Whig leaders held a secret meeting to distribute Stuart's patronage. *Ib.*, Oct. 5, 1838.

[4] Joshua F. Speed, E. D. Baker, Milton Hay, and James H. Matheny. *Works*, I, 97.

[5] Lincoln *et al.* to the *Chicago Daily American*, June 24, 1839. *Works*, I, 96–8.

since, he wrote, 'you know that if we had heard Douglas say
that he had abandoned the contest, it would not be very au-
thentic.' [1]

So, attending to the firm's law business, making jokes and
telling stories on the streets, in his office, at Speed's store and
on journeys to the courts of neighboring counties, writing editorials and articles for the *Sangamo Journal* and, above all,
keeping an alert eye upon the political situation, Lincoln's days
were full of interest.

On October 19, 1839, Governor Carlin called a special session
of the Legislature to devise some method of caring for the now
appalling financial condition of the State; and December 9 the
General Assembly again convened. For the first time it met at
the new seat of government. The State House was not yet
finished and the House held its sessions in the Second Presbyterian Church, the Senate meeting in the Methodist Church,
while the Supreme Court sat in the Episcopal Church.[2]

Members were nervous, irritable, suspicious. Their state of
mind and temper indicated that the session would be what
Governor Ford afterward described it, full of 'bitterness and
personal hatred.' [3] Lincoln would not abandon his idea of lifting the burden of the internal improvement debt by the proceeds of sales of public land owned by the United States. His
scheme for buying these lands from the General Government at
one fifth the price for which they were sold to settlers having
fallen through, he renewed it from a different angle and in a
different manner.

On the second day of the session, without waiting for the
Governor's message, Archibald Williams, Lincoln's principal
lieutenant and with him on the Finance Committee, offered
resolutions that whereas the State debt now amounted to ten
million dollars with six hundred thousand dollars annual interest; that total annual revenues were not more than two hundred
thousand dollars, leaving an annual deficit of four hundred
thousand dollars, exclusive of ordinary expenses of the State
Government; that since taxes had been heavily increased,

[1] Lincoln to Stuart, Nov. 14, 1839. *Works*, I, 98–9.
[2] *Sangamo Journal*, Jan. 3, 1840.　　　　[3] Ford, 226.

further taxation would be intolerable; that the annual revenue
of the United States, exclusive of the proceeds of the sale of
public lands, was over twenty-five millions — more than enough
to run the Federal Government; therefore, in order to prevent
national extravagance and to 'protect the people of this State
from . . . ruinous taxation,' resolved that the Illinois delegation
in Congress be requested and instructed to procure a law for the
distribution among the States of the proceeds of the sales of
public lands.[1]

As we have seen, this was Lincoln's favorite idea and had been
since his first candidacy for the Legislature. But the need was
now extreme. By offering this proposal before the Democratic
Governor addressed the Legislature, it is also obvious that the
Whigs made a strategic party move of first importance. Williams' resolutions were referred to the Committee on Finance.[2]

Not to be outdone, the brilliant and resourceful Ficklin, now
a Democratic leader, offered resolutions for a Legislative investigation of the State Bank at Springfield, and of 'any charges
which may be preferred against said Bank,' which were adopted
without opposition and the Committee appointed. The House
paused long enough to elect a clerk, John Calhoun being chosen
by the Democratic majority, Lincoln voting for Andrew Johnston to whom, later, he sent some poor poetry of his own composing.[3]

Then came Carlin's message. Because of the Internal Improvement scheme an 'enormous debt' had been piled up; to
increase that debt the State's credit had been exhausted. The
situation was 'alarming;' the people were disillusioned at last,
and were against the Internal Improvement system. 'The
destiny of the State is involved.'

Let the General Assembly drop all improvement projects
which could not pay and finish only those that would pay at
least the interest on the cost of construction; and order the sale
of the remaining canal lands for carrying on that enterprise.
The State Bank, too, was again in sorry case, the Governor declared; but, after a long tirade against 'the banking system

[1] *House Journal*, Spl. Sess. 1839–40, 7.
[2] *Ib.*   [3] *Ib.*, 7, 8. And see p. 333, *infra*.

generally,' Carlin left the Bank's condition to the Legislature.[1]

For the first time since Lincoln had been a member of the House national politics were not mentioned in a Governor's message; but the approaching presidential campaign was on everybody's mind and tongue. Soon after the session opened, an extended and notable debate was held every night for a week in the church where the House met in the daytime. The country was still suffering from the desolating panic of 1837; and the Whigs lost no opportunity to impress upon the public mind that hard times were the result of Jackson's financial policies and were unduly prolonged by the Sub-treasury plan of Van Buren.

Feeling ran high. During November a joint debate had been held in the courthouse between Whig and Democratic speakers, among whom were Lincoln and Calhoun.[2] Apparently the Whigs were not satisfied with the result of that encounter, for they soon formally challenged the Democrats to another discussion of national politics, and especially of the Sub-treasury question. The Democrats promptly accepted and the debate took place between December 14 and 20, 1839. Douglas, Lamborn, and Calhoun spoke for the Administration, and Lincoln, Logan, and Baker for the Whigs.[3]

Lincoln closed for the Whigs on Friday night, December 20. His speech was to be a Whig campaign document and he had prepared with meticulous care. Interest in the debate had flagged and Lincoln's audience was small. He was embarrassed, he said, by the scant attendance, but, in spite of the 'damp upon my spirits,' he would sum up the arguments of those who had preceded him. Van Buren's Sub-treasury scheme, asserted Lincoln, would 'injuriously affect' the community through the currency. For example, the Bank, by loaning public funds to individuals, kept money 'almost constantly in circulation,' whereas if hoarded in 'iron boxes' it would be kept idle. Any-

---

[1] *House Journal*, Spl. Sess. 1839–40, 14–24.

[2] *Illinois State Register*, Nov. 30, 1839.

[3] Joshua F. Speed to Herndon, Sept. 17, 1866. Weik MSS. Logan says that Browning also spoke for the Whigs and J. B. Thomas for the Democrats. Logan's statement, no date. Weik MSS.

body could see that. How absurd to rob the people of the use of the money, which they sorely need, by letting it rust in 'iron boxes' when the Government has no need of the funds! With the skill of the natural campaigner, Lincoln pounded Van Buren's iron boxes until every voter could hear the solid sound of those treasure chests filled with gold.

Worse still, Lincoln continued, by the Sub-treasury plan the revenues would be 'collected in specie' — Van Buren had said so in his message. This would take more than half of all the gold and silver in the whole country, leaving the people 'to get along as they best can' with the remainder and whatever rags and shinplasters they may be able to put, and keep, in circulation. What a 'most glorious harvest' for office holders and public creditors, every one of whom would 'set up shaver' of shinplasters. 'Was such a system for benefiting the few at the expense of the many ever before devised?' Also by withdrawing the specie from circulation, 'distress, ruin, bankruptcy, and beggary must follow.' Who could contemplate 'without terror' that certain result? The man who buys a horse for one hundred dollars would find the animal worth only half as much, and so with every article of commerce. Of course time would adjust matters, but consider the suffering while adjustment was going on. Why invite a catastrophe so unnecessary?

Bad as all this would be for the whole country, it would be especially hard on States like Illinois where there were public lands, since the price of them would be doubled. 'Knowing, as I well do, the difficulty that poor people now encounter in procuring homes, I hesitate not to say that . . . it will be little less than impossible for them to procure those homes at all.'

Experience showed that the Bank of the United States had not contracted and expanded the currency, as the Democrats charged. Look at the long and prosperous period between the time when the Bank got fairly started and the time when Jackson began war upon it. Of course the Bank could not regulate the currency, 'either before it got into successful operation, or after it was crippled and thrown into death convulsions' by the Government. Let the Government help the Bank to supply a sound currency instead of killing the institution that had so long done well that indispensable service to the people.

Take, now, the expense of the two systems, Bank or Sub-treasury. The Bank collected and disbursed the revenues without charge and paid seventy-five thousand dollars annually for the privilege; whereas, even by the estimate of the Democratic Secretary of the Treasury, Van Buren's plan would cost at least sixty thousand dollars every year, and other competent men testified that the cost would be not less than six hundred thousand annually. Suppose these extreme estimates were wrong and the expense of the Sub-treasury midway between them, or three hundred and thirty thousand dollars per year? Add to this the sum paid by the Bank for the privilege of handling the revenues, and the result was a total outlay of over four hundred thousand dollars every year for the luxury of a Sub-treasury.

All this was 'to be thrown away once a year for nothing ... sufficient to pay the pensions of more than four thousand Revolutionary soldiers,' or to buy forty acres of land 'for each of more than eight thousand poor families.' Yet this improvidence was 'a matter entirely too small to merit their Democratic notice.'

Experience, too, proved that a National Bank is safer than a Sub-treasury. How did anybody know that anything would happen? Only by the fact it had happened before under like circumstances. Collectors of public revenue had defaulted heretofore — Lincoln named plunderers with whose defalcations the land was then ringing, and said that there had been 'some twenty-five hundred lesser lights.' Others would do the same thing if given a chance — 'most assuredly' they would.

Contrast with this forbidding chronicle the record of the Bank of the United States which, through forty years, handled nearly half a billion dollars of public funds without loss to the government of a single penny. Did this mean that bank officials were more honest than government officials? Not when the latter were 'selected with reference to their capacity and honesty,' which, alas, had not been done in recent years. Of course some men would be unfaithful, no matter how carefully chosen; even one of the disciples, 'selected by superhuman wisdom,

turned out a traitor and a devil.' Ah, yes, and 'Judas carried
the bag, was the sub-treasurer of the Saviour and his disciples.'
But the point was that the 'interest of the sub-treasurer is
against his duty, while the interest of the Bank is on the side of
its duty.' Lincoln argued this point at wearisome length, and,
at last, modestly declared that his position was not only sustained by experience, but was also 'little less than self-evident.'

The Democrats advanced the 'sweeping objection' that a
National Bank was unconstitutional, he said. A majority of the
signers of the Declaration of Independence, of the framers of the
Constitution and other 'Revolutionary patriarchs . . . have decided upon their oaths that such a bank is constitutional.' So
had Congress, time and again. Above all 'the Supreme Court,
that tribunal which the Constitution has itself established to
decide constitutional questions, has solemnly decided that such
a bank is constitutional.'

That ought to settle the matter. Moreover, every argument
against the constitutionality of the bank was equally valid
against the Sub-treasury. Lincoln here gave the familiar argument, first stated by Hamilton and elaborated by Marshall,
that Congress can pass laws which, in the words of the Constitution, are 'necessary and proper' to execute the constitutional
powers of Congress. It is plain that he had studied with great
care Marshall's opinion in McCulloch vs. Maryland and much
else on the subject, and was as much of a Nationalist as Hamilton himself.

The Whig champion took the remainder of the evening in
answering Lamborn and Douglas. He showed that Douglas was
in error as to the time of expenditures, circumstances of appropriations and the like. Lincoln marshalled his facts simply and
with effect. Voters for whom his speech was written could not
but understand the contrast he drew between Democratic extravagance and Whig economy. He would, he said, leave to the
audience to decide whether he or Douglas was 'more deserving
of the world's contempt,' either as to 'sagacity or veracity.'

Lamborn had said that while the Democrats sometimes err,
they are right in principle, whereas the Whigs are wrong in
principle; the Democrats are sound in head and heart, although

'vulnerable in the heel.' True, retorted Lincoln; the Democrats were indeed vulnerable in the heel; in fact, with their absconding officials, 'scampering away with the public money' to every foreign country 'where a villain may hope to find refuge from justice,' the Democrats were 'distressingly affected in their heels with a species of "running itch."'

Sound heads and weak heels! — yes, indeed, 'like the cork leg in the comic song,' which, the more the owner tried to stop it, the more it ran away; or like the Irish soldier who always prated of his courage in battle, but 'retreated without orders at the first charge,' and who, when questioned by his captain, explained that his heart was as brave as that of Julius Cæsar, 'but, somehow or other, whenever danger approaches, my cowardly legs will run away with it.' Lincoln made much fun of Lamborn's inept simile.

Then, in a highly colored peroration, Lincoln closed. Cowardly was the Democratic boast that in the coming election Van Buren would carry every State. 'It may be true; . . . Many free countries have lost their liberty, and ours may lose hers; but if she shall, be it my proudest plume, not that I was the last to desert, but that I never deserted her. . . . The great volcano at Washington, aroused and directed by the evil spirit that reigns there, is belching forth the lava of political corruption . . . in a current broad and deep, which is sweeping with frightful velocity over the whole length and breadth of the land, bidding fair to leave unscathed no green spot or living thing; while on its bosom are riding, like demons on the waves of hell, the imps of that evil spirit, and fiendishly taunting all those who dare resist its destroying course with the hopelessness of their effort.'

So 'all may be swept away. Broken by it I, too, may be; bow to it I never will.' Prospective defeat 'shall not deter me. If ever I feel the soul within me elevate and expand to those dimensions not wholly unworthy of its almighty Architect, it is when I contemplate the cause of my country, deserted by all the world beside, and I standing up boldly and alone, and hurling defiance at her victorious oppressors. Here, without contemplating consequences, before high heaven and in the face of the world, I swear eternal fidelity to the just cause, as I deem it, of

the land of my life, my liberty, and my love. And who that
thinks with me will not fearlessly adopt the oath that I take?
Let none falter who thinks he is right, and we may succeed. But
if, after all, we shall fail, be it so. We still shall have the proud
consolation of saying to our consciences, and to the departed
shade of our country's freedom, that the cause approved of our
judgment, and adored of our hearts, in disaster, in chains, in
torture, in death, we never faltered in defending.' [1]

Such was Lincoln's speech, prepared, be it repeated, as a
Whig campaign document in the presidential conflict of 1840
and used for that purpose. He revised it with great care for
publication even annotating it with supporting European data.[2]
The speech was printed by 'private subscription' in pamphlet
form and distributed as a party tract; [3] and is, beyond doubt,
the same in substance as that delivered by Lincoln throughout
Illinois during that strange political contest. Seemingly he had
forgotten Lovejoy, and was not, at that time, interested in the
slavery question. His crusading fervor had been aroused exclusively by Democratic financial incapacity and wickedness,
and only the campaign ahead occupied his thoughts.

Even the Democratic organ conceded that Lincoln's speech
was effective; it was, said the *State Register*, 'in the main, temperate, and argumentative,' and in pleasing contrast to the
'coarse invective, unfounded ridicule, and personal abuse'
ordinarily used by Whig orators and writers. But as to Lincoln's
speech being 'unanswerable,' as his party friends were declaring
it to be, the editor would answer it himself. This he did for two
and a half columns in the same issue of his paper which contained
his editorial praise of the speech, and gave slightly shorter
articles in each of the two succeeding issues.[4]

---

[1] *Works*, I, 100–39.   [2] *Illinois State Register*, Feb. 8, 14, 1840.

[3] Speed to Herndon, Sept. 17, 1866. Weik MSS. The title read: *Speech of Mr.
Lincoln, at a political discussion, in the Hall of the House of Representatives, December,
1839, at Springfield, Illinois*.

[4] The main points in the *Register's* long answer to Lincoln's speech were: that taxes
are collected for the specific purpose of paying the expenses of the Government and not
to be loaned to individuals, as Lincoln had contended; that the public revenue was not
'shut up in iron boxes,' since it was not collected nor disbursed all at once, but from
day to day; that the Government's balance in the Bank of the United States was,
usually, not over five or six million, which would be the most that ever could be kept

The Democratic editor could not, however, suppress his admiration for Lincoln's speech, even when answering it. Making comment on a footnote which Lincoln had added to his speech before allowing it to be printed, the editor hoped that 'the time is at hand when he [Lincoln] will be found manfully battling' for the Democratic purpose of providing 'a *sound* currency for *all* the people. We regard this declaration [that specie makes a sound currency and paper does not] as an evidence that reason is about to resume that empire over his mind that has been so long usurped by prejudice; and that he is no longer going to lend his brilliant powers to give currency to mischievous errors, but on the contrary that his powerful pen will soon be found labouring to establish those true doctrines, which heretofore it has been his object to destroy.' [1]

The joint debate over, Lincoln took up his legislative duties, first writing Stuart about the firm's business — 'a damned hawk-billed Yankee is here besetting me at every turn' about eighty dollars due a client. Lincoln also took a fling at Douglas: 'the Democratic giant is here, but he is not now worth talking about.' [2]

For once, national politics do not appear to have been discussed during the proceedings of the House throughout the ses-

---

in 'iron boxes,' instead of one hundred millions as Lincoln asserted; that business was not done only by actual cash but, also and chiefly, by the use of credits, where 'every single dollar is sufficient for doing twenty-five dollars' worth of business;' that the slight contraction of the currency caused by the Sub-treasury plan would be distributed over a period of six years. But, said the *Register*, Lincoln was so partisan that he would accept no fact if stated by Van Buren. 'If he should hear that gentleman say the sun sets in the West, doubtless he would disbelieve the evidence of his senses, rather than believe Van Buren.' *Illinois State Register*, Feb. 8, 1840.

In the *Register's* subsequent answers to Lincoln's speech the editor said that, as to the increase in the price of public lands which Lincoln had declared must be the result of the Sub-treasury plan, everybody knew that Van Buren had for years urged the policy of graduating and reducing the price of public lands — Van Buren 'is eminently the settler's friend;' that the collection of the revenue in specie would not mean good money for office-holders and bad money for the people, since paper money, 'convertible into gold and silver at the will of the holder,' is as good as specie. Surely Lincoln does not believe in 'an irredeemable paper currency,' although his argument 'would seem to imply as much;' and so did his course in the Legislature; that the Sub-treasury plan will keep more specie in circulation by compelling banks to have specie in their vaults, etc. *Ib.*, Feb. 14, 1840.

[1] *Ib.*, Feb. 14, 1840.

[2] Lincoln to Stuart, Dec. 23, 1839. *Works*, I. 139–40.

sion. Obviously the long joint debate between the Whig and Democratic champions had forestalled this customary practice; or it may be that the members were so distressed by their struggle to get the State out of the financial quicksands in which it had sunk deeply and was still sinking, that they had no time for partisan engagements.

The temper of the House was quickly shown in scathing resolutions offered by Wyatt B. Stapp, representative from Warren, Knox, and Henry Counties. They asserted that 'the present mis-named system of *Internal Improvements* was palmed upon the people without their consent or knowledge;' the facts had been kept under cover and, in order to 'clinch' the system upon the State, the people had been told that the cost would not be great. Railroads would cover 'every corner of the State' without 'one cent' of taxation; the premium on bonds and income from railroads would pay interest and also the expenses of the State government. All this had proved to be false and if the system were continued, the end would be 'ruin and desolation.' So Stapp wanted the Internal Improvement law repealed, and thirty-nine members voted with him. Thus, at the very beginning, the law was saved by only three majority, Lincoln voting against Stapp's resolutions.[1]

So began the fight which lasted throughout the session. On this subject party lines were obliterated and Lincoln's votes are of interest only as showing his somewhat confused state of mind.[2] Sometimes he did not vote at all.[3] Resolutions piled upon resolutions.[4] Debate was frequent[5] and violent in House

---

[1] The vote was forty-three ayes to forty nays on a motion to lay on the table (*House Journal*, Spl. Sess. 1839–40, 29–30), which did not, of course, kill the resolutions.

[2] *Ib.*, 128–9, 192–3, 196–7, 199–200, 201, 264–6, 275–7, 282–90, 299, etc.

[3] *Ib.*, 181–2, 188–90; etc.

[4] For example: that only one road be built (*ib.*, 34); that work be suspended on all roads except those 'in continuous lines from navigable rivers' (*ib.*, 46; also 100–1); that action on all railroads be suspended, the Board of Public Works abolished and a new Board created to conserve the State's property and untangle the condition of the

---

[5] *Ib.*, 112, 181–2, 196–7, 319–20, etc. When a legislative body goes into Committee of the whole it is for the purpose, usually, of amendment and debate, although they are not confined to this parliamentary state.

and Senate; and in the lobby the discussion was, of course, more unrestrained and acrimonious. Roll-calls came like hail storms, so many were the motions, resolutions, amendments. After five futile weeks, John Logan [1] of Jackson County moved that, since nothing had been accomplished and the House was disposed 'to break down the whole of the system at the expense and disgrace of our State,' as well as the State Banks 'before the proof is before the House of their corrupt doings;' and since 'it is better to die with short pains than long fevers,' [2] therefore the House give its immediate and exclusive attention to the subjects of banks and improvements and adjourn *sine die* February 3.[3]

This peremptory demand was not formally granted but had its effect, and the House rushed its work forward. While the meaning of some of Lincoln's votes is not entirely clear, most of them were in support of the now intensely unpopular Internal Improvement system.[4] He was pledged to maintain it, he declared to the House, and his 'limbs should be torn asunder before he would violate that pledge.' [5] He was especially anxious that the Illinois and Michigan Canal should not be abandoned, probably wrote the bill that finally passed,[6] which he reported from a select committee; and he opposed rigid requirements in the issuing of canal scrip.[7] The outcome of the long and quarrelsome discussion was the enactment of a law which abolished the

Internal Improvement system; that all State bonds sold below par and all contracts made by state agents beyond their authority be repudiated (*ib.*, 46–8); that the General Assembly decide by ballot what roads should be constructed (*ib.*, 35); that Congress donate to Illinois alternate sections of public land along lines of projected railroads (*ib.*, 107, 112); that private companies be incorporated to finish the railroads (*ib.*, 128; see also 143–4).

These few illustrations indicate the perplexity, anger, and unsettled opinions of the House.

[1] Father of John A. Logan. Linder, 343.

[2] Logan was a doctor. *Ib.*

[3] *House Journal*, Spl. Sess. 1839–40, 181.

[4] For example: Lincoln voted against the repeal bill (*ib.*, 264–5); and against suspending work on it (*ib.*, 129, 130); and for incorporating companies to finish the railroads (*ib.*, 128).

[5] *Illinois State Register*, Jan. 8, 1840. This statement was made by the Democratic organ during the next session when Lincoln, as charged, at last abandoned the Internal Improvement scheme; and since he did not deny the accusation it was undoubtedly true, for, at this period of his life, he was fertile in accusations and prompt in denials.

[6] *Laws of Illinois*, 1839–40, 79–80.

[7] *House Journal*, Spl. Sess. 1839–40, 204, 232, 235.

old and created a new Board of Public Works, and one Fund Commissioner instead of the existing funding officials.[1]

Lincoln consistently guarded the State Bank at Springfield. Early in the session he was hopeless of even preserving the Bank's charter. 'The legislature . . . has suffered the bank to forfeit its charter without benefit of clergy,' he wrote Stuart, adding that 'there seems to be little disposition to resuscitate it.' [2] But Lincoln manœuvered for the bank with skill and caution. Thus he voted that the Legislature had the right to alter or amend the charter, which proposition, however, was an amendment to another proposal legalizing the suspension of specie payments without forfeiture of the Bank's charter.[3] He voted against a resolution asserting that the charter of the Bank had been forfeited and directing the Committee on Finance to report a bill for a new charter on much severer terms than the old, which was beaten by more than four to one.[4] An amendment to the new Bank bill, making stockholders liable to the amount of stock paid in by them and exempting the State for liability for more than its 'ratable proportion,' was defeated by a heavy majority, Lincoln voting nay; [5] and another amendment, reserving to the Legislature the right 'to alter, amend or repeal' the Bank's charter as a condition of granting 'this revival of its charter,' met the same fate, as did still other amendments unfriendly to the Bank, Lincoln voting against all of them.[6]

The result of the wrangling was a decided victory for the Bank — a new law, for which Lincoln voted, that the forfeiture of the charter for refusing specie payments be 'set aside,' the charter 'revived,' and existing laws against the Bank's continuing in business be 'suspended.' [7] Lincoln's gloomy report to Stuart had been premature and without foundation.

[1] Act, Feb. 1, 1840; *Laws of Illinois*, 1839–40, 93–6.

[2] Lincoln to Stuart, Dec. 23, 1839. *Works*, I, 139. This letter was written immediately after the first contest over the bank and unpromising roll-calls. *House Journal*, Spl. Sess. 1839–40, 67–9.

[3] *Ib.*, 65–9, 80, 109, 136–7. [4] *Ib.*, 156–8. [5] *Ib.*, 230. [6] *Ib.*, 230–2.

[7] Act, Jan. 31, 1840. *Laws of Illinois*, 1839–40, 15–7. This law placed new but not burdensome restrictions on the Bank: The Bank should not make any loan on its stock; or part with its specie except for change to the amount of five dollars; or increase its circulation, while specie payments were refused, beyond its paid-in capital stock; or

The disconsolate friends of Vandalia reopened the capital fight once more, but found themselves helpless,[1] Lincoln, of course, protecting Springfield. He was a member of the select committee on the bill for the reincorporation of that town,[2] and guided it successfully through the House, a not difficult task. So was woven another strand binding Springfield more firmly to the ambitious young politician and lawyer.

Lincoln's votes on liquor legislation are of greater interest, perhaps, than any given by him at this tumultuous session. Seemingly, the so-called temperance law of the last session [3] had proved to be too drastic and was not working well; and, hardly did the House get to work, when Cheney Thomas of McLean County moved that the Judiciary Committee be instructed to inquire into the expediency of amending the law 'to permit any person without license, to vend spirituous liquors in quantities of not less than one quart, instead of one gallon.' [4]

Joseph Naper of Cook County introduced a bill for the repeal of the whole license law, while Robert McMillan of Edgar County proposed a more stringent measure.[5] On December 26, Edwin B. Webb of White County reported from the Judiciary Committee to which these bills had been referred a substitute as the license bill of the Committee.[6]

Keen and pointed debate arose. Joseph Naper of Cook County was against so high a license fee; and, besides, the Legislature had no right to interfere with men's appetites; 'public opinion ought to regulate these matters.' Look at Massachusetts 'where the Fifteen Gallon law had revolutionized the State.' Lincoln's colleague, Edward D. Baker of Sangamon

permit any single indebtedness to it above $10,000. The Bank must make monthly reports to the Governor; receive and disburse State funds without charge, etc.

[1] *House Journal*, Spl. Sess. 1839–40, 233–4, 324.

[2] *Ib.*, 252. Springfield was incorporated at this session. Act, Feb. 3, 1840; *Laws of Illinois*, 1839–40, 6–15.

[3] *Laws of Illinois*, 1838–9, 71.   [4] *House Journal*, Spl. Sess. 1839–40, 34.

[5] *Ib.*, 62. By the existing law, groceries sold liquor in quantities of less than one gallon, but the law provided no punishment for selling without license. Act, March 2, 1839. *Laws of Illinois*, 1838–9, 71–2.

By McMillan's proposed bill, a grocery could sell only in quantities more than one quart, and a fine of ten dollars was imposed for selling less than that amount without license.

[6] *House Journal*, Spl. Sess. 1839–40, 85.

County, was emphatically for the bill. He was no extremist, he said, but liquor selling must be regulated; the good of the community, not the effect on the individual, required it. Wyatt B. Stapp of Warren County wanted license money collected in towns to be paid to the town treasuries.

Lincoln agreed. 'It was but just,' he said, 'either that towns should have nothing to do with the matter [leaving the granting of licenses to County Commissioners exclusively] or, if burthened with it, that they should have the proceeds of the Licenses they granted.' Isaac P. Walker of Vermilion County dissented from Lincoln's view: if towns would support the paupers created by their groceries, he would not object to the towns keeping the 'small pittance' of the license fees; but since the counties had to keep those paupers, the license fees should help pay that expense.

Stapp withdrew his amendment and Lincoln offered another, 'giving County Commissioners the sole power over the subject.' Joseph G. Bowman of Wabash County objected; a grocery was a nuisance which towns 'should have the power of abating, if insupportable.' Groceries were an 'evil peculiarly affecting the towns where they were located.' But Lincoln's amendment was agreed to without a vote.[1]

An amendment offered by Isaac P. Walker, 'that if a majority of the qualified votes of the incorporated towns, Justice's district, or ward of any city in which said grocery is to be licensed, shall remonstrate against the granting of such license, the same shall not be granted,' was defeated by a tie vote of thirty-nine to thirty-nine, Lincoln voting nay, thus beating the amendment. He then voted to concur in the Committee's bill.[2] On the third reading of this bill William B. Archer of Clark County introduced the same amendment, and again it was beaten, Lincoln again voting against it. On final passage he voted for the bill.[3]

After all the pother of this session, not a great deal was ac-

[1] *Sangamo Journal*, Dec. 31, 1839; *House Journal*, Spl. Sess. 1839–40, 85–6. The two accounts differ in detail.

[2] *Ib.*, 86–7.

[3] *Ib.*, 162–3, 262. The vote on the final passage was fifty-two ayes to twenty-nine nays.

complished. Laws were enacted resuscitating the State Bank at Springfield,[1] forwarding work on the Illinois and Michigan Canal,[2] and for the settlement of the internal improvement debts.[3]

Lincoln could not get out of his mind his beloved land resolutions which he had induced the last Legislature to adopt. 'Will you show them to Mr. Calhoun, informing him of the fact of their passage through our Legislature,' he wrote to Stuart in Washington. 'Mr. Calhoun suggested a similar proposition last winter; and perhaps if he finds himself backed by one of the States, he may be induced to take it up again.' Lincoln reminds Stuart 'that you and the others of our delegation in Congress are instructed to go for them.' [4]

The session over Lincoln plunged into the presidential campaign of 1840, the most picturesque, perhaps, in American history. Senator White had been dropped by the Whigs as their candidate, and, solely as a matter of the politician's cherished 'availability,' the one outstanding Whig leader and statesman, Henry Clay, had been rejected for a somewhat colorless, inoffensive person who, however, had the high political assets of poverty and a military record.[5] Harrison and Tyler became the Whig candidates for President and Vice-President, against Van Buren and Johnson.

Although delighted by the defeat of Clay because he was a slave-holder, the Abolitionists, as a whole, would not support the Whig ticket and a section of them organized the Liberty party pledged to immediate emancipation, and placed its standard in the hands of James G. Birney of New York and Thomas Earle of Pennsylvania.

The Whigs adopted no platform and Harrison said no word. They agreed in nothing except hostility to Van Buren and all

---

[1] *Laws of Illinois*, 1839–40, 15–7.   [2] *Ib.*, 79–80.   [3] *Ib.*, 93–6.

[4] Lincoln to Stuart, Jan. 1, 1840. *Works*, I, 140–1.

[5] The Illinois Whig organ thus excused the desertion of Clay: 'We consent to pass by such men as Henry Clay and Daniel Webster, only because their fame is already immortal — because they shine within themselves — because the sickly light reflected from office and power, can add nothing to their splendor — because, come weal, come woe, their names will never be forgotten, so long as Cicero, Pitt and our immortal Washington shall be remembered.' *Sangamo Journal*, Nov. 3, 1838. Editorial, almost certainly written by Lincoln.

things Democratic. But fate and circumstances supplied better campaign materials than principles or policies could afford. A sneer at Harrison in a Democratic paper at Baltimore [1] gave the Whigs their campaign battle-cry. Harrison, said the contemptuous editor, would be content if somebody would give him enough money to live on in a log cabin with plenty of hard cider.

So the campaign became a volcanic eruption of volatile and unintelligent sentimentalism. Harrison was the poor man's friend, the farmer's champion, the log cabin and hard-cider candidate; Van Buren, an aristocrat who ate his meals from gold plates and drank his champagne from crystal goblets. Meetings of incredible size were held, barbecues given, monster processions formed. No other political contest produced so many popular songs, most of them without sense.[2]

June 4, 1840, a 'monster' Whig demonstration took place in Springfield. Processions paraded the streets. Hardin marched holding high a banner with the device of a dead rooster lying on its back. On its way to Springfield, the Chicago delegation had captured a Democratic emblem and hilariously displayed it on a pole in the form of a petticoat. 'While we write,' chronicles the Springfield Democratic paper, 'we are surrounded by log cabins on wheels, hard-cider barrels, canoes, brigs, and every description of painted device, which, if a sober Turk were to drop among us would induce him to believe we were a community of lunatics or men run mad. . . . We never before saw such an exhibition of humbug.' [3]

[1] *The Baltimore Republican.*

[2] For example:

> 'Oh, know ye the Farmer of Tippecanoe,
> The gallant old farmer of Tippecanoe,
> With an arm that is strong and a heart that is true,
> The man of the people is Tippecanoe.'

or

> 'No ruffled shirt, no silken hose,
> No airs, does Tip display. . . .
> Upon his board there ne'er appeared
> The costly "sparkling wine"
> But plain hard cider such as cheered
> In the days of old lang syne.'

[3] *Illinois State Register*, June 5, 1840.

Whig orators covered the State, attacking Van Buren's financial plans, but mostly appealing to passion and prejudice. The people cared for no arguments:

> 'Without a why or a wherefore
> We'll go for Harrison therefore,'

rang the refrain of a Whig campaign song. Democratic newspapers and speakers were in despair. 'We speak of the divorce of bank and state; the Whigs reply with a dissertation on the merits of hard cider. We defend the policy of the administration; the Whigs answer "log cabin."' We urge the 'honesty, sagacity, statesmanship' of Van Buren, and the unfitness of Harrison; 'the Whigs answer that Harrison is a poor man.'[1]

In this popular emotionalism one Whig speaker, at least, kept his head and appealed to his audiences with fact and reason. The Illinois Whig convention, under the perfect control of Stuart and the 'Whig Junto,' nominated Lincoln as one of the Illinois Harrison and Tyler electors, and he spoke all over the State. Thus his acquaintance and friendships broadened. No reports of his campaign speeches exist, but it is practically certain that they were substantially the same as his argument in the debate already described, modified, of course, to suit the humor of his audiences. Often he and Douglas travelled and spoke together.

Behind the storm of popular fervor, there were genuine forces — the forces of hard times, desire for a change, anger over patronage. The Whigs denounced Democratic extravagance, Democratic 'mal-administration,' Democratic 'accumulation of executive power,' the outcome of which would surely be 'an Elective Monarchy,' What the country needed, what the people demanded, was 'Reform.' Down with Van Buren with his 'English carriage, English horses, and English driver.'[2]

Lincoln did other and far more effective work for the Whigs than to make stump speeches. Long before the campaign got under way and even while the Legislature was still in session, he

---

[1] *Pennsylvanian,* 'March 25, 1840, as quoted in *History of the People of the United States:* John Bach McMaster, vi, 565.

[2] *Sangamo Journal,* Jan. 3, 1840, editorial; and Resolutions of Whig State Convention, drawn and reported by Stuart. *Ib.,* Oct. 11, 1839.

wrote instructions to picked men throughout the State; and these orders, in the form of a confidential party circular signed by the Whig committee at Springfield, were sent to every county.[1] 'We have appointed you the Central Whig Committee of your county,' began Lincoln. Watch and work; your reward will be the 'glory' of having helped to beat the Democrats, those 'corrupt powers that now control our beloved country.' The Whig candidates deserve the support of 'every true patriot who would have our country redeemed.' The whole State must be so well organized, 'that every Whig can be brought to the polls.' This cannot be done without your help.

So divide your county into 'small districts' and appoint in each a sub-committee; make a 'perfect list of all the voters,' and 'ascertain with certainty for whom they will vote.' Designate doubtful voters 'in separate lines,' indicating their probable choice. Each sub-committee must 'keep a constant watch on the doubtful voters' and 'have them talked to by those in whom they have the most confidence' — also Whig documents must be given them.

These sub-committees must report to the County Committee 'at least once a month . . . and on election days see that every Whig is brought to the polls.' Let the sub-committees be appointed 'immediately' and let them make their first report not later than the last day of April. 'On the first of each month hereafter we shall expect to hear from you;' and when 'we' have heard from all the counties 'we' will advise you of the outlook.

The Whig State Committee will get out a party [2] paper for the campaign, says Lincoln, and encloses a prospectus. 'It will be superintended by ourselves, and every Whig in the State must take it. . . . You must raise a fund and forward us for extra copies, — every county ought to send fifty or one hundred dollars, — and the copies will be forwarded to you for distribution among our political opponents. The paper will be devoted exclusively to the great cause in which we are engaged. . . .

[1] The signers of this document were, Dr. A. G. Henry, whom Adams had beaten so badly for Probate Justice, R. F. Barrett, E. D. Baker, Joshua F. Speed, and Lincoln. *Works*, I, 145.

[2] *The Old Soldier*, edited by a Whig general committee and published by Simeon Francis and Company, then publishers of the *Sangamo Journal*.

'You must inform us of results' of any election in your county 'immediately.' The next Legislature will elect a United States Senator, so 'let no local interests divide you; but select candidates that can succeed. Our plan of operations will of course be concealed from every one except our good friends.' [1]

In such practical fashion Lincoln went about the work of organizing the Whig party throughout Illinois. To Stuart he hurried off a letter asking for a 'Life of Harrison' and other campaign data — 'everything you think will be a good "war club."' He adds that he believes the Whigs will carry Illinois; 'the nomination of Harrison takes first-rate.' Large numbers of 'the grocery sort of Van Buren men [frequenters of saloons] ... are out for Harrison.' Lincoln tells Stuart of the joint debate: 'I made a big speech which is in progress of printing in pamphlet form.' [2]

Lincoln frequently wrote his partner on the political situation. 'I have never seen the prospects of our party so bright in these parts as they are now,' says Lincoln, though his own political outlook is not 'very flattering, for I think it probable I shall not be permitted to be a candidate. ... Subscriptions to the *Old Soldier* pour in without abatement.' Lincoln gives Stuart a list of Democrats who will vote for Harrison, so that Stuart can send them Whig campaign literature. [3]

Again he reports to the Illinois Whig chieftain in Washington: After all, the Whig Convention did nominate him for the House again and Baker for the Senate, but only because the delegates thought Lincoln and Baker 'necessary to make stump speeches.' He tells other local political news and adds a postscript that a prominent Springfield Democrat 'has come out for Harrison. Ain't that a caution?' [4]

As election day approached the Democrats carefully guarded the voting. 'Democrats, watch the polls,' admonished the *State Register*. 'The Federalists [Whigs] ... are not to be trusted. By fraud alone they expect to succeed. Challenge

---

[1] Jan., 1840. *Works*, I, 142–5.
[2] Lincoln to Stuart, Jan. 20, 1840. *Works*, I, 146–7.
[3] *Ib.*, March 1, 1840. *Works*, I, 148–50.
[4] *Ib.*, March 26, 1840. *Works*, I, 150–1.

every voter who is not known to be an inhabitant of the State
for the last six months. See that no one votes twice or oftener.
... "eternal vigilance is the price of liberty." [1]

In spite of seemingly insurmountable disadvantages, and in
spite of the crushing Whig victory in the nation, the Democrats
carried Illinois. This extraordinary State triumph was due to
Douglas more than to any other man. With that political dexterity and resourcefulness in which he was unequalled, Douglas
advanced two issues peculiar to Illinois and fresh in the minds of
the people. These issues were the partisan decision of the Whig
majority of the Supreme Court by which, in practical effect, the
Whig Secretary of State was given a life tenure of office, and the
Whig effort to disfranchise the so-called 'alien vote' in the
State — both questions, which, as we shall see, were to cause an
unprecedented upheaval in the next Legislature. Illinois went
for Van Buren by a heavy majority and the Legislature was
overwhelmingly Democratic. But the Whigs won in Sangamon County and Lincoln was once more a member of the
House.

On November 23, 1840, Lincoln entered the House, the last
session of that body he ever was to attend as a member. Among
the new representatives was a young lawyer from St. Clair
County, named Lyman Trumbull, who, almost immediately,
became one of the Democratic leaders. Trumbull was a native
of Connecticut where he had been well educated at Bacon
Academy, then second only to Yale, and he could read the Greek
and Latin classics in the original text. His family was one of
the most prominent in Connecticut, and Lyman was of the
seventh generation of Trumbulls in America. The boy had
started out for himself and after teaching school in Georgia,
came to Belleville, Illinois. There he studied law in the office of
Governor Reynolds and soon began the practice of his profession.[2]

Trumbull was a slender, good looking young man of medium
height, with blue eyes and intellectual face. His bearing was
quiet and cordial though dignified, his manners those of a well-

[1] *Illinois State Register*, Oct. 30, 1840.
[2] *Life of Lyman Trumbull:* Horace White. 1–7.

bred person; and his ability, integrity, and moral courage were recognized by all. He was to become a principal and distinguished actor in the drama of Lincoln's career, and for that reason his conduct and attitude during this session are of moment.

Again Lincoln received his party's vote for speaker, but was again beaten by William Lee D. Ewing.[1] In the election of Clerk of the House, party lines were obliterated, that pugnacious Democrat and vigilant friend of the Southern States, John Calhoun, receiving a majority of fifty-seven over the combined votes of his three opponents.

In his message Governor Carlin told the Legislature that the reason for calling it two weeks before the regular date was the tremendous State debt created by the Internal Improvement scheme, that offspring of 'improvident legislation.' There was no money to pay the interest falling due January 4 [1], 1841, and the General Assembly must provide funds before that time. This could be done only by selling State bonds below par, which existing law forbade. 'The future destiny of the State for weal or for woe depends upon the direction of the crisis.'[2]

In this disastrous situation every expedient was advanced that anybody could think of — even repudiation was urged. Almost at once the ancient enemies of Springfield took advantage of the mingled wrath and confusion of members; and Richard Bently of Bond County offered a joint resolution for the repeal of all laws for the removal of the State capital from Vandalia to Springfield and the return of the seat of government to Vandalia, 'until the State debt is paid.' This extraordinary resolution actually was adopted by the House, apparently without objection.[3] Seemingly the manœuver did not alarm Lincoln, who knew that the wild project would be killed in the Senate, as it promptly was.

As the end of the special session drew near indescribable excitement developed. The Bank act of the previous Legislature authorized the State Banks to continue their suspension of specie payments 'until the close of the next session of the Gen-

---

[1] Ewing forty-six, Lincoln thirty-six. *House Journal*, Sess. 1840–1, 5.
[2] *Ib.*, 18–30. [3] *Ib.*, 38.

eral Assembly;'[1] and the Banks desired to maintain as long as possible this advantageous condition. The Springfield State Bank held practically all of the State funds. It was, substantially, the public treasury. All warrants of the State Auditor were drawn on the Bank and paid in the paper of that concern. This was the case with salaries of State officers and members of the Legislature; and so the Bank held the whip-hand over the entire State Government.[2]

As has been said, the Legislature had been called to meet two weeks before the regular time for the sole purpose of providing means to pay the interest on the public debt, due January 1, 1841, and the Democrats held that the session should expire before the first Monday in December, on which day the Constitution required the regular session to begin. If, then, the present Legislature should adjourn before Monday, December 7, under the law the State Bank would have to resume specie payment on that date, or forfeit its charter and close its doors.

Under Lincoln's leadership the Whigs determined that there should be no adjournment and that the special should merge into the regular session, both sessions to be a single and continuous session. If this were done the Bank would, of course, be saved from embarrassment, perhaps collapse, at least for a season. The Democrats were equally determined that the Bank, so long favored by the Legislature, should have no further reprieve.[3]

Thus came the comic struggle in which Lincoln played so inappropriate and ludicrous a part. In response to instructions given by the House almost immediately after its organization,[4] the Judiciary Committee submitted a report on the question whether the special session was a part of the former or of the approaching session. The Committee held that the present was a special session and should adjourn *sine die* on Saturday, December 5. The Whig minority of the Committee filed a long report to the contrary, which was promptly laid on the table.[5]

In this state of affairs the Legislature assembled on Saturday

[1] Act, Jan. 31, 1840; *Laws of Illinois*, 1839–40, 15.
[2] Ford, 225.   [3] *Ib.*, 224–7.
[4] *House Journal*, Sess. 1840–1, 35–6.   [5] *Ib.*, 68–71.

morning. Seemingly the fate of the Bank was at stake. William H. Bissell of Monroe County moved a joint resolution of adjournment which, after three roll-calls was adopted and sent to the Senate for concurrence. Lincoln moved that the House adjourn; the Democratic majority refused, but adjourned only until three o'clock that afternoon,[1] when, as the Democrats expected, the Senate would concur in the House resolution and the House concur in that of the Senate, thus ending the session and blasting the hopes of the State Bank.

There was but one way to defeat the Democratic plan, and, as it was thought, save the Bank, and make the two sessions one. That way was to prevent a quorum in either Senate or House, since the Democrats had a heavy majority in both. So the Whigs absented themselves, leaving Lincoln and a few trusted lieutenants in the House to watch proceedings and demand ayes and noes, yet without a following large enough to make a quorum. By some mischance a quorum was secured in the Senate which promptly passed a joint resolution of adjournment *sine die* and sent it to the House.

In that body no quorum could be procured. The doorkeeper was sent out to gather in the recalcitrant Whigs, and returned with the doleful news that they refused to come. The doors were locked to prevent the escape of the Whigs already there. For hours the angry Democrats spoke and raged. 'The greatest excitement prevailed.' McClernand thundered denunciations, and pointed to the constitutional provision giving the House power to 'compel' attendance of members. Again the officer of the House was despatched to bring in the absentees, this time by force. The angry Whigs scorned his orders, spurned his demand. Cyrus Edwards of Madison County was found in the store of his nephew, Ninian W. Edwards, and, hand upon the cane under his arm, threatened the doorkeeper with physical resistance.

Thus matters went on until the candles were lit in the House. The watchful Lincoln was enjoying the predicament of the Democrats; but his amusement turned to consternation when suddenly the Speaker announced a quorum. Several sick Demo-

[1] *House Journal*, Sess. 1840–1, 76–7.

cratic members had reported, some of them having risen from their beds. Quickly the Senate resolution of adjournment was put to a vote. Lincoln and the other Whigs completely lost their heads and voted; [1] then 'Lincoln came under great excitement, and having attempted and failed to get out at the door, very unceremoniously *raised the window and jumped out*, followed by one or two other members.' But the Whig gymnastics were belated, for the Democratic resolution had been adopted, the slow-witted if heroic Whigs having themselves furnished the quorum by which their defeat was achieved.[2] As we shall see, Lincoln was thinking of a personal matter which, before long, incapacitated him altogether.

The Democrats were in great glee. Decidedly the joke was on Lincoln. The Democratic organ was sure that he was not hurt by his flying leap, since 'it was noticed that his *legs* reached nearly from the window to the ground.' Surely the feat would make Lincoln 'famous.' Why not raise the State House '*one story higher*, in order to have the House set in the *third story!* so as to prevent members from *jumping out of the windows?*' If that were done 'Mr. Lincoln will in the future have *to climb down the spout.*'[3]

And why, asked the Democrats, this absurd and lawless performance? 'To serve the Banks!' 'To prevent the Banks from resuming specie payments on the opening of the new session on Monday!' And that, too, in face of the fact that the State Bank at Springfield 'had informed the Legislature that she was ready at any moment to resume specie payments' and had actually done so when the disgraceful Whig manœuver failed her.[4]

The Whig organ was even harsher in its indictment of the Democrats. That party had committed an 'outrage' on the

[1] *House Journal*, Sess. 1840–1, 79–80. They voted nay, of course, but they were, therefore, recorded as being present, which was all the Democrats needed.

[2] *Illinois State Register*, Dec. 11, 1840. The writer of this account states that he 'stood inside, near the door of the House, and was an eye witness' to the proceedings. Also see *ib.*, Jan. 8, 1841, reprinting letter of William A. Munsell of Edgar County, a Whig member of the House in the *Paris Statesman*. The vote was forty-six ayes to fifteen nays. (*House Journal*, Sess. 1840–1, 80.) Had all the Whigs stayed away, or had Lincoln and his fellow Whigs present with him in the House jumped out of the windows before voting, they would have won the fight.

[3] *Illinois State Register*, Dec. 11, 1840.   [4] *Ib.*

people by the 'war it commenced against the State Bank.' The Democratic adjournment resolution was designed to ruin the Bank; by that action 'the farmer had been seriously injured,' because dealers could not buy his pork, since the Bank could not extend credit to business men. The Democrats had hurt the State Government, too, for the Bank could no longer assist it and the State must borrow from 'foreign capitalists.'[1]

As will presently appear, however, the 'rag barons,' which was the popular name for the officers and directors of the Bank,[2] had their way in the end and a new law was enacted giving the Bank greater privileges than ever.[3]

[1] *Sangamo Journal*, March 12, 1841.

[2] Ford, 227. The Democrats called the Whigs 'the ragocracy' or vassals of the Bank; the Bank's paper was called 'bank rags,' 'printed lies,' etc.

[3] The Whig position in this strange episode is well stated by Joseph Gillespie who was with Lincoln in the House guarding the Whig and Bank interest:

'Gov. Carlin convened the Legislature of 1840–41, by proclamation: two weeks earlier than it would have met under the constitution. At the previous session an act had been passed legalizing the suspension of specie payments by the Bank untill the end of the next session of the general assembly.

'On the morning of the last day of the first two weeks of the session, as we supposed, it was ascertained that the Democrats had determined to adjourn *sine die* and make those two weeks a distinct session, at the end of which the Bank would be compelled to resume specie payments or forfeit its charter. The Whigs believed that this step would be not only unfair to the Bank which had had no notice of or made any preparation for such a proceeding and that it would benefit only the Banks of other states which held the paper of our Bank by enabling them to draw its specie for its bills which they held while it could get nothing from them on their bills which it held, and that the loss of the depreciation of our Bank circulation would fall principally upon our citizens who were holders of small sums.

'The Whigs determined if possible to prevent the *sine die* adjournment knowing that the Constitution would convene the Legislature on the following Monday. It required a quorum to adjourn *sine die*. Less than a quorum could adjourn from day to day. As the constitution then stood it was necessary to have two members to call the ayes and nays to show that a quorum was not voting. If the Whigs absented themselves there would not be a quorum left, even with the two who should be deputed to call the ayes and nays.

'The Whigs immediately held a meeting and resolved that they would all stay out except Lincoln and me who were to call the ayes and nays. We appeared in the afternoon, motion to adjourn *sine die* was made and we called the ayes and nays. The Democrats discovered the game and the sergeant-at-arms was sent out to gather up the absentees.

'There was great excitement in the House, which was then held in a church in Springfield. We soon discovered that several Whigs had been caught and brought in and that the plan had been spoiled and we, Lincoln and I, determined to leave the Hall and going to the door found it locked and then raised a window and jumped out, but not untill the democrats had succeeded in adjourning. Mr. Gridley of McLean accompanied us in our exit.

'The result of this operation was just as we anticipated; the Bank resumed and paid

Hard pressed as the Legislature was by the financial plight of the State and the suffering of the people, national politics again drew the sharp attention of House, Senate, and lobby. The defeat of Van Buren and election of Harrison, who would soon take office, alarmed the Democrats for the fate of the Sub-treasury law. Might it not be repealed and the National Bank revived by the victorious Whigs? Carlin had raised the danger signal in his message: although 'the virtue and patriotism of the people' had triumphed 'over a National Bank,' let lovers of free institutions be on their guard.[1]

In the very thick of the turmoil and excitement over impending State insolvency and proposed repudiation, Democratic resolutions were offered against a National Bank, for the Independent Treasury, and in support of Van Buren. Even these were thought to be too mild, and a more ardent champion of the masses, Joseph W. Ormsbee of Scott County, instantly proposed a substitute that the National Government was now 'as simple and pure . . . and as much the Government of the people,' as it had been when created; that the Government is now 'free' from the abuses of 'the British credit system' which, if continued, 'would plunge the laboring classes . . . into hopeless poverty and misery, and make them slaves to stock-jobbers and bankers;' that public funds, once diverted from legitimate purposes and 'made the basis of bank discounts,' were now secure, the unholy alliance between the Government and banks having been sundered; that the foreign debt is now paid, excessive tariff taxation abolished, and the public domain saved 'for poor yet honest and industrious farmers to convert into freemen's homes;' and that Jackson and Van Buren had wrought these great reforms and 'deliverance for the people and their Government.'[2]

out nearly all of its specie to Banks and brokers in other states while not a cent could be obtained from them, as the Banks everywhere had been authorized to suspend specie payments. In a few weeks the folly of the course of the majority became apparent and they themselves introduced a bill again legalizing a suspension, but it was too late.' Gillespie to Herndon, Jan. 31, 1866. Weik MSS.

In this vivid account, Gillespie makes but one error. There were seven other Whigs in the House in addition to Lincoln and himself. See report of the incident, written at the time by an eye witness, *Illinois State Register*, Dec. 11, 1840.

[1] *House Journal*, Sess. 1840-1, 28-30.   [2] *Ib.*, 147-8.

The Senate acted quickly and adopted resolutions requesting and instructing the Illinois delegation to prevent the repeal of the Independent Treasury law and the reëstablishment of a National Bank.[1] Bitter partisan debate followed and speedily the Whig counter resolutions appeared. The Whigs declared that they believed the people to be entirely capable of self-government; that the recent presidential election proved that they were determined to get rid of 'the monarchical financial experiments of Martin Van Buren, with all their rich fruits of low prices and low wages, and to return to the good old republican usages;' that to dispute the verdict of the people at the polls was an 'insult' to popular intelligence and virtue; that 'as Republicans,' believing in the people, 'we acquiesce in the sentence of condemnation . . . upon Mr. Van Buren, with his Sub-Treasury and standing army projects;' and that Van Buren's misuse of Federal office-holders to defeat Harrison and elect himself, makes it necessary for Harrison to 'reform' patronage thus prostituted.[2]

By the proper parliamentary motion, Lincoln secured the ayes and noes on the Whig resolutions, which were defeated by a strict party vote, Lincoln voting for them.[3] Finally the Senate resolutions against a National Bank, for the Independent Treasury and endorsing Van Buren were concurred in, Lincoln voting against them.[4] Thus Lincoln heard and took part in another thorough if heated discussion of government financial methods and policies, as well as of the weighty constitutional questions involved in the National Bank controversy. By his thirty-first birthday, he was as fully informed on these matters as debate, conversation, and study could make him.

Although as Whig floor leader and one of those largely responsible for the disastrous predicament into which the improvement orgy had placed Illinois, Lincoln's part in the legislation on this subject does not appear except through his votes; and the meaning of these is not always clear. Sometimes, indeed,

---

[1] *House Journal*, Sess. 1840–1, 151.   [2] *Ib.*, 170–1.

[3] On a motion to table, forty-two ayes to thirty-four nays, Lincoln voting nay. *Ib.*, 171.

[4] The vote was forty-four ayes to thirty-one nays, Lincoln voting nay. *Ib.*, 167.

they are contradictory. Even before consideration was given
to the various recommendations in the Governor's message, a
storm of resolutions broke upon the House and these expressions
of the legislative mind and temper continued — resolutions of
inquiry as to what the Board of Public Works had done and was
doing, for an investigation of the 'whole proceedings' of the
Canal commissioners, for the repeal of all improvement laws, for
the immediate suspension of improvement work and the transfer
of the projects to private corporations.[1]

Lincoln voted for the repeal of the Internal Improvement
laws and against a proposition of Trumbull's that the Board of
Public Works turn over to an agent to be appointed by the
Governor, all books, papers, property, and effects 'in their possession . . . which belong to the State,' and that everybody employed on internal improvements be discharged.[2] Speeches fell
like hailstones from a Legislature prolific in oratory, sterile
in device.[3] But Lincoln did not address the House; in this
emergency the ready and resourceful talker was strangely
silent.

Rumors had spread that the State would repudiate her debts
and resolutions were offered in the House affirming the contrary;[4] but before the House acted upon them the Senate
adopted resolutions that Illinois would honor all contracts made
by her agents 'in pursuance of law . . . when the consideration
had been received.'[5] Lincoln was appointed on a joint select
committee to ascertain whether the State Bank would loan the
State enough money to pay the interest on the improvement
debt about to fall due.[6]

The bill for settling the internal improvement debt was
rushed through the House, Lincoln first voting against considering the measure and then against the bill itself, which was passed

---

[1] *House Journal,* Sess. 1840–1, 35–9.

[2] *Ib.,* 40–1. Trumbull's amendment was adopted fifty-one ayes to thirty-five nays,
Lincoln voting nay. The proposal to repeal the improvement laws was made in an
amendment offered by John J. Hardin which was laid on the table, fifty-six ayes to
thirty-one nays, Lincoln voting nay and, to that extent, for repeal.

[3] *Sangamo Journal,* Feb. 2, 5, 9, 12, 16, 1841.

[4] *House Journal,* Sess. 1840–1, 37.   [5] *Ib.,* 41.

[6] *Ib.,* 47. The loan was arranged. See Bank Act, p. 287, *infra.*

by a vote of exactly seven to one, only ten other members standing with Lincoln.[1] Yet the next day Lincoln voted against Trumbull's motion to table the bill providing for the payment of interest on the public debt.[2]

Soon thereafter Lincoln introduced a bill of his own for this purpose [3] which was referred to his Committee on Finance; but the provisions of his measure cannot be ascertained.

Quantities of State bonds had been hypothecated or sold by careless or corrupt State agents without returns to the State Treasury and from the first the harassed legislators objected to the payment of them. Trumbull offered a significant resolution against paying interest on any debt 'contracted . . . in violation of law, and when the consideration has not been received,' which was referred to the Judiciary Committee; [4] and immediately another long resolution was offered that, while it was the duty of the Legislature to 'sustain the good faith and credit of the State,' it would be 'criminal negligence . . . to rush on and pledge still deeper the faith of the State' on mere assertions as to the amount of debt and interest due on bonds for which the State had and had not received payment, and therefore that the Fund Commissioner should lay the exact facts before the House.[5]

On Lincoln's motion the bill for payment of interest on the public debt was taken up and he offered amendments that enough additional money be provided to pay freight, duty, and other charges on railroad iron received or contracted for, and to pay for the prosecution of suits by Illinois in the courts of New York; and that no interest be paid on State bonds in the hands of *original* purchasers for which the State had received no consideration. To Lincoln's last amendment, Trumbull moved to

---

[1] *House Journal*, Sess. 1840–1, 71–2. The vote was seventy-seven ayes to eleven nays, Lincoln voting nay.

[2] *Ib.*, 73–4. Trumbull's motion included amendments that hypothecated State bonds should not be forfeited for less than par and that the State should not pay more than seven per cent on borrowed money nor pay any interest on bonds 'whereon the State has not received the money originally contracted for.' *Ib.*, 73.

Trumbull's motion was adopted by a vote of sixty ayes to twenty-six nays, Lincoln voting nay. *Ib.*, 74.

[3] *Ib.*, 86.   [4] *Ib.*, 87.

[5] *Ib.*, 88–9. This resolution was adopted without roll-call.

include 'any State bonds' which have been disposed of without authority of law, and for which no consideration had been received by the State.[1]

After an elaborate report from the Fund Commissioner, calls of House and adjournments, Trumbull's amendment was adopted, Lincoln voting against it;[2] and then Lincoln's amendment as amended by Trumbull's amendment was also adopted, Lincoln opposing his own proposition when thus altered.[3] Thereupon further progress of the bill was blocked by the House's refusal to order it engrossed, a decisive parliamentary triumph for Lincoln. Lincoln quickly riveted his advantage by having the original bill, which was instantly reintroduced, referred to his Committee on Finance.[4]

Meanwhile the Senate passed an interest-paying bill and Lincoln voted against an amendment that no interest be paid on bonds sold without authority and without payment having been received by the State.[5] Then he voted for an amendment authorizing State bonds to be hypothecated in 'any amount' necessary to raise money to pay interest on the Internal Improvement debt;[6] and again voted to hold up the bill itself.[7] Yet two days later, he reversed his vote and voted to engross the bill for third reading,[8] and for the passage of the measure.[9] The Senate quickly returned the bill with amendments, which the House concurred in, Lincoln voting for them;[10] and, at last, the law was enacted.

Time and again repudiation was urged in the guise of refusing to pay interest on bonds sold without authority and without

[1] *House Journal*, Sess. 1840–1, 89–90.

[2] Forty-six ayes to thirty-nine nays, Lincoln voting nay. *Ib.*, 98.

[3] Forty-three ayes to forty-two nays, Lincoln voting nay. *Ib.*, 99.

[4] Fifty-seven nays to thirty ayes, Lincoln voting nay and Trumbull aye. *Ib.*, 99.

[5] *Ib.*, 106–7. On a motion to table this vote was thirty-nine ayes to forty-three nays, Lincoln voting aye; and on the amendment itself, the vote was forty-one ayes to forty nays, Lincoln voting nay.

[6] Defeated forty-seven nays to forty-one ayes, Lincoln voting aye. *Ib.*, 108.

[7] By refusing to order the bill to be engrossed, fifty-one nays to thirty-six ayes, Lincoln voting nay. *Ib.*, 109.

[8] Fifty-one ayes to thirty-seven nays, Lincoln voting aye. *Ib.*, 118.

[9] Fifty-two ayes to thirty-six nays, Lincoln voting aye. *Ib.*, 119.

[10] *Ib.*, 121.

consideration having been received by the State; time and again the counter proposition was offered, that this refusal should apply only to original holders of the State's obligations.[1] At every point Lincoln stood firmly for full payment when the securities were held by any except the original purchasers. So persistent were these demands that the Judiciary Committee formally protested.[2]

Finally the matter came to a head. Francis A. Olds of Macoupin County offered a remarkable resolution that 'the State of Illinois disavows all and every contract or transaction of any agent' of the State 'not warranted by expressed authority given them by law.' 'Whilst repudiating' all such illegal contracts, Illinois 'expressly declares' that she will pay 'all moneys received, and pay a just compensation for any property accepted' by the State, even though the same 'may have been acquired without legal authority.'

This last and most plausibly stated of the repudiation proposals was promptly tabled, Lincoln voting thus to dispose of it.[3] Throughout this perplexing fight over tangled questions, Lincoln again displayed that conservatism which so strongly marked his entire career in the Legislature. Another vote out of many illustrates the same disposition. An investigation of the Commissioners in charge of work upon the Illinois and Michigan Canal was ordered, but Lincoln voted against it.[4]

On Wednesday, December 16, the General Assembly elected Samuel McRoberts a Senator of the United States, the Whigs voting solidly for Cyrus Edwards, representative from Madison County. The incident is worthy of particular mention because Edwards himself, instead of casting his complimentary vote for Lincoln, voted for Edward D. Baker, State Senator from Sangamon.[5] Later in the session James Shields was elected Auditor of

---

[1] For example, *House Journal*, Sess. 1840–1, 130–1.

[2] *Ib.*, 130.

[3] Forty-one ayes to thirty-seven nays, Lincoln voting aye and Trumbull nay. *Ib.*, 146–7.

[4] There were two votes, forty-five ayes to forty-two nays and forty-four ayes to forty-two nays, Lincoln voting nay both times. *Ib.*, 119–20.

[5] McRoberts seventy-seven, Edwards fifty, Baker one. *Ib.*, 126–7.

Public Accounts, Lincoln and the Whigs voting for Levi Davis,[1] a circumstance which, within less than a year, was to result unhappily for Lincoln.

The outcome of the agitation and distress of the Legislature over the State debt and collapse of the Internal Improvement system was the enactment of two brief and peremptory laws, repealing the act for the settlement of the internal improvement debts passed at the previous session, directing the State Treasurer to take charge of all improvements and the books and papers relating thereto, and to adjust and settle accounts; and requiring the hypothecation of State bonds to raise money for the payment of interest on the improvement debt.[2] After 1841, testifies Governor Ford, no further attempt was made to pay even interest on the State debt and Illinois 'became a stench in the nostrils of the civilized world.' [3]

The 'rag barons' were more successful than ever and an act for the relief of the State Bank at Springfield was passed, setting aside the forfeiture of the Bank charter for having again suspended specie payments, authorizing the Bank to charge seven per cent interest on loans and discounts for less than six months and nine per cent for longer periods, granting the privilege of issuing for two years, one, two, and three dollar notes upon several conditions, among which was the handling of State funds without charge and the purchase at par of $200,000 of State bonds, the proceeds to be 'applied exclusively' to the redemption of hypothecated improvement bonds and payment of interest on the State's indebtedness.[4]

During the six years that Lincoln had been a member of the Legislature, no change whatever had been made in the ancient criminal code of the State, the provisions of which were as inconsistent as they were cruel; and the Attorney General, Wickliffe Kitchell, presented a succinct report pointing out the al-

[1] *House Journal*, Sess. 1840–1, 270–1. In 1835 Lincoln had written to Governor Duncan recommending the appointment of Davis as Auditor. MS. in Barrett Collection.

[2] Acts, Dec. 14, 16, 1840. *Laws of Illinois*, 1841, 166–8.

[3] Ford, 222. Ford was elected Governor in 1842 and speaks with too much feeling, perhaps, since he had the handling of this impossible situation. He was a Justice of the Supreme Court when the Democrats nominated him for Governor.

[4] Act, Feb. 27, 1841. *Laws of Illinois*, 1841, 40–2.

terations which were imperatively demanded. He made particular note of the grave defect in the liquor law of 1839 and urged that sales of intoxicants in less quantities than one quart be prohibited 'in any situation, or under any circumstances whatsoever.' [1]

Although, in his message, Governor Carlin made no mention of the liquor question, Trumbull reported a license bill from the Judiciary Committee soon after the House was organized. [2] Some ominous amendments were offered, one of which, to repeal the existing law prohibiting the granting of licenses against the majority protest of citizens, was finally adopted. [3] Richard Murphy of Cook County moved to substitute for the license bill a brief and drastic prohibition measure, forbidding the granting of any license whatever to sell 'vinous or spirituous liquors in this State' and imposing a fine of one thousand dollars upon 'any person who violates this act by selling such liquors.' Lincoln moved to lay Murphy's substitute on the table, which was done by a vote of seventy-five to eight, Lincoln voting aye. [4] When a motion to recommit the bill to the Judiciary Committee, with instructions to inquire into the constitutionality of the bill and the expediency of applying the penalties and prohibitions of the bill '*to all* persons whatsoever,' as well as to grocers, came to a vote and was defeated by a vote of fifty-eight to eighteen, Lincoln was not present. [5]

Nor did he answer to the call of his name when other important amendments to the license bill were voted on. Just before adjournment, Friday, January 1, 1841, he voted to lay on the table an amendment to the license bill the nature of which does not appear; [6] and the next day he was not present when the House rejected an amendment that money from licenses and fines should be applied to the education of 'poor children' of the township 'wherein such tipling house is established.' [7] He failed, too, to vote on an amendment fixing license fees at from five to

---

[1] *House Journal*, Sess. 1840–1, 13.

[2] *Ib.*, 98. At the beginning of the session, Trumbull had offered a resolution which was adopted, instructing the Judiciary Committee to report a bill for the punishment of every person keeping a grocery without license. *Ib.*, 32.

[3] *Ib.*, 111, 116. [4] *Ib.*, 136. [5] *Ib.*, 150. [6] *Ib.*, 172.

[7] *Ib.*, 174.

three hundred dollars, with bond of two hundred dollars; [1] nor did he vote when the bill finally was passed.[2] Near the close of the day he voted twice to adjourn.[3]

From the opening of the session November 23, 1840, until January 1, 1841, Lincoln, as the Whig floor leader, had been constant in attendance, having missed but five or six of the many roll-calls during those busy five weeks. Beginning with Friday, January 1, he showed negligence. He was present but once on that day and twice on the next, each time at the close of business. On Monday he did not appear at all, notwithstanding much business was transacted, some of particular interest to Lincoln.[4] On Tuesday he was again absent except at the opening of the House when he voted for the incorporation of Galesburg.[5] On Wednesday he voted in the morning and again just before adjournment.[6] On Thursday Lincoln answered one roll-call in the forenoon, but did not vote on two important questions immediately thereafter;[7] during the afternoon no vote was taken. From January 13 until January 21, 1841, he answered to his name only once.[8]

Thus for three weeks beginning with the new year Lincoln was present and only for short times on but four days, while he was not in the House at all during the last of the three weeks, except for a single vote on a trivial matter. For he was ill, sick in mind and, at times, sick in body. He declared that he was so miserable that he was incapable of business of any kind.[9] He had

[1] *House Journal*, Sess. 1840–1, 175. The amendment was beaten fifty-one to twenty-five.

[2] *Ib.* The vote was forty ayes to thirty-six nays. The Senate also passed a license bill (*ib.*, 394) and, finally, without further roll-calls (*ib.*, 418, 421, 423) a new law was enacted which repealed the section of the license law of 1839 prohibiting the granting of licenses when a majority of citizens affected petitioned against such license. (*Laws of Illinois*, 1838–9, 72.) But the new law reduced the quantity to be sold by groceries from less than one gallon to less than one quart. *Ib.*, 1841, 178–9.

[3] *Ib.*, 176–7.

[4] *Ib.*, 177–84. For example: The request of Lincoln's Finance Committee to be relieved from further consideration of a resolution on the Finances of the State, which was denied by a vote of thirty-eight to thirty-six.

[5] *Ib.*, 184. Again important matters were considered and important votes taken on that day, especially in relation to the Bank and the safe keeping of public funds. *Ib.*, 185–90.

[6] *Ib.*, 191, 194.   [7] *Ib.*, 196–8.

[8] A vote on the creation of a county. *Ib.*, 245.   [9] See p. 314, *infra*.

experienced a misadventure, which came near unbalancing his intellect, and from the effects of which he never entirely recovered.

By the beginning of the fourth week in January, 1841, Lincoln had so far regained his composure as again to attend regularly the sessions of the House,[1] and thereafter we find his vote recorded on nearly every roll-call. Sometimes he took active part in the proceedings, as when the amount due from citizens of Springfield on their guarantee for the building of the State House was in question,[2] upon which Lincoln spoke for his fellow-townsmen [3] and upon the passage of the State Bank bill.[4] In four or five weeks after his return, he was also once more able to amuse the House by funny stories in debate. He offered an amendment to the Canal bill that the State pay in bonds at par value for all work yet to be done and that three million dollars of bonds be issued for that purpose.[5]

Upon this proposition a lively dispute arose. Wickliffe Kitchell, Representative from Montgomery County and also Attorney General of the State, opposed Lincoln's amendment. He charged that although the State was already 'prostrated by debt,' Lincoln wanted to pile on still more; he was like the drunkard in Arkansas who 'took so much of the cretur' that he lost his reason, and knew nothing; but when he heard the word 'brandy' quickly cried out, 'that is the stuff.'

Lincoln's only reply was a counter-anecdote. Kitchell's course during the whole session reminded Lincoln of 'an eccentric old bachelor' who lived in Indiana. Like Kitchell, 'he was very famous for seeing big bugaboos in every thing. . . . One day he went out hunting. His brother heard him firing back in the field, and went out to see what was the matter. He found him loading and firing as fast as possible into the top of a tree.' His brother could see nothing in the tree and 'asked him what he was firing at.' A squirrel, exclaimed the gloomy sportsman, and

---

[1] *Illinois State Register*, Jan. 29, 1841.

[2] *House Journal*, Sess. 1840–1, 281–3.

[3] *Illinois State Register*, Feb. 5, 1841.

[4] *House Journal*, Sess. 1840–1, 482–7, 506–7.

[5] On motion of William H. Bissell, this amount was reduced to one million five hundred thousand dollars.

kept on firing. His brother looked again but could discover no squirrel. So he looked over the person of the hunter and 'found on one of his eye lashes a big louse crawling about.' So with Kitchell; 'he imagined he could see squirrels every day, when they were nothing but lice.' The press reporter records that, at this point, 'the House was convulsed with laughter.'[1] Thus Lincoln carried his amendment.[2]

The election of a Public Printer was of especial interest to Lincoln. His close political ally, Simeon Francis, owner and editor of the *Sangamo Journal*, the Whig organ of the State, wished to be chosen for that lucrative office, then held by Francis's rival, William Walters, owner and editor of the Democratic organ, the *Illinois State Register*. Scarcely had the regular session begun, when Lincoln procured the appointment of a special committee to investigate 'the very large expenditure for . . . public printing' and to report a bill for the reduction of that outlay.[3] Lincoln was made a member of the Committee of which Trumbull was Chairman. Simultaneously the *Sangamo Journal* began an attack on Walters for overcharging the State, but Walters welcomed the inquiry.[4]

After prolonged investigation Trumbull reported from the Committee that the charges of the *Journal* and Lincoln were unfounded. Lincoln filed no minority report nor did he criticise the Committee's report, a circumstance which caused the accused editor great glee. 'Mr. Lincoln has recovered from his indisposition,' sneered the *Register* on January 29, 1841, 'and has attended the House for more than a week past, during which time he made no minority report, although he attended every meeting of the committee of Investigation. Now, we ask any man of either political party, whether Mr. Lincoln is a man who would have refused to speak out, if he had had anything to tell?'[5] He was not, indeed; but during the latter part of the session Lincoln was silent on matters infinitely more important

[1] *Sangamo Journal*, March 5, 1841; reporting proceedings on Feb. 26.

[2] Forty-one ayes to thirty-two nays. *House Journal*, Sess. 1840–1, 521. The reporter seems to have been so amused that he wrote that Lincoln's amendment was lost by this vote.

[3] *Ib.*, 137.   [4] *Illinois State Register*, Jan. 2, 8, 1841.

[5] *Ib.*, Jan. 29, 1841.

than the election of a Public Printer.[1] Francis was bitter in his disappointment; but, said the *Register*, did not Francis 'procure' the investigation to be made and was it not 'conducted by his friend Mr. Lincoln?' Why then, did not the *Journal* publish the Committee's report?

When the session was more than half over, the hottest and, perhaps, the bitterest fight occurred that ever took place in the Legislature of Illinois. That contest and the outcome of it gave the Whigs of the State a rallying cry for years to come and is historic in American judicial annals. Yet, although he had sufficiently recovered from his mental and physical ills to attend the sessions of the House, and notwithstanding that he was the floor leader of his party, Lincoln took no part in that vital party conflict.

The battle arose over the announced purpose and finally successful effort of the Democratic leaders to enact a law by which the Whig majority in the Supreme Court would be converted into an overwhelming Democratic majority. Three Whigs and one Democrat then sat upon the Supreme Bench; and the Democrats proposed to create immediately five additional places in the Court and fill them by electing Democratic judges at the present session of the General Assembly.

The Whigs were angered almost to the point of physical combat. This was revolution, they cried — revolution to be thwarted at any cost, at every hazard. What! prostitute the Judiciary to partisan uses! Never, so long as a Whig could protest, so long as a Whig could struggle, so long, indeed, as honest men, regardless of party, would respond to the cry of patriotism. To the rescue then! Free institutions were in peril! In such fashion, and with exclamations more lurid, came the acrimonious party engagement in the Legislature of Illinois during the winter of 1840–41.

The significance of it in the narrative of Lincoln's life and career is his failure to take part, except by voting, in this notable and dramatic political fray — a circumstance more weighty and

---

[1] Walters was re-elected, Francis getting only the habitually regular Whig vote. *House Journal*, Sess. 1840–1, 273. On the same day, one, William S. Lincoln, received the Whig vote for State's Attorney of the Second Judicial Circuit. He was not related to Lincoln.

full of meaning than would have been the case if he had led his fellow-partisans. He was distraught, his mind clouded, his heart bleak with despair, and for the first time in his life he took no interest in anything — for the moment, even politics did not attract or concern him. Presently we shall see how he fell into this melancholy state of mind and feeling, a condition, be it repeated, out of which he was never entirely to emerge.

The cause of the political storm in the Legislature was a decision of one political case by the Supreme Court, its reported attitude upon another, and the belief of the Democrats that the Whig majority in both instances had acted as partisans and not as impartial judges. The first of these cases involved the tenure of office of the Secretary of State and the Governor's power to remove that official and appoint a successor. In 1829, Governor Edwards had appointed Alexander P. Field, then a Jackson man, who, like many others, became a Whig in a few years and an energetic and resourceful partisan. In 1838, Thomas Carlin, the first Democratic Governor to be elected since the period of partisanship began, after Field's refusal to resign, appointed John A. McClernand in his place. Field declined to give up the office and McClernand brought suit to oust him.[1] The circuit Judge, Sidney Breese, a man of ability and learning, decided in favor of McClernand, and Field appealed to the Supreme Court.[2]

At its December term, 1839, the Whig majority of that tribunal in an elaborate and extended opinion decided for Field, but the Democratic member of the Court filed a strong dissent.[3] This partisan action of the Court enraged the Democrats and they attacked the Court with ferocity.[4] Soon after the Legis-

[1] Ford, 213-4.

[2] In the Circuit Court Shields was the attorney for McClernand. His argument, which was strong and exhaustive, was published in full in the *Illinois State Register*, May 10, 1839, as was the opinion of Judge Breese which filled ten columns of that paper on May 24, 1839.

[3] Field *vs.* People *ex rel* McClernand: 2 Scammon, 79-184. One of the three Whig Justices did not sit because of relationship to Field. The case was fully argued, Douglas and Shields being of counsel for McClernand, while Justin Butterfield was the principal attorney for Field. The argument of Douglas was published in the *State Register*, Aug. 17, 1839, filling eight columns.

[4] *Illinois State Register*, Sept. 14, 1839. Editorial.

lature of 1839–40 convened, resolutions 'addressing' the Justices out of office for partisanship, ignorance, and general incompetency were offered; and even most of the Whigs, including Lincoln, voted against their indefinite postponement.[1]

The decision became a party issue in the Presidential campaign of 1840 and was one of the influences that carried Illinois for Van Buren. Again Carlin appointed McClernand Secretary of State and again Field declined to yield, the Whig Senate in both instances refusing to confirm the Governor's appointment. At the session of the Legislature of 1840–41, which was strongly Democratic in both Houses, Carlin appointed Douglas, the Senate confirmed the appointment and Field, weary of the struggle, finally gave up.[2] Undoubtedly the Whig leaders, perhaps convinced that the decision of the Supreme Court was wrong, advised the tenacious Field to stop the fight. He had been too heavy a load for them to carry in the late campaign.

The other political case involved the right of unnaturalized inhabitants to vote. The State Constitution gave the elective franchise to all free males over twenty-one years of age who had resided in the State for six months. Although both parties had striven to capture the foreign vote, the Democrats had secured most of it,[3] largely because of the skill and activity of Douglas. So the Whigs had raised the cry that the constitutional suffrage, broad as it was, did not include 'unnaturalized aliens;' and, to prevent them from voting against Harrison, had brought a fictitious suit before a Whig Judge at Galena, who promptly decided in favor of the Whigs.

To clinch this decision and make it the accepted law of the State, the case was taken to the Supreme Court; but the alarmed

[1] *House Journal*, Sess. 1839–40, 144–5. These resolutions well reflect the outraged feelings of the Democrats: the Justices had been in office too long; since the organization of the Court, the State had grown in population, wealth, intelligence, and everything else, 'with the exception of the intellectual improvement of the Justices of said [the Supreme] Court;' the majority decision in the Field case, whether 'the offspring of ignorance or . . . partizan feeling,' had violated the Constitution; and 'a vast majority of the citizens of Illinois ardently desire a change in the officers of said Court on the ground of incompetency . . . inability to discharge the duties devolving on them, and also for other and divers good and sufficient reasons.'

[2] Ford, 304. Douglas was appointed Nov. 30, 1840.

[3] The alien vote was about 10,000, of which 9,110 voted the Democratic ticket. Ford, 214–5.

Democrats took charge of the appeal. The case was argued in December, 1839, and again in June, 1840. The Democratic Justice, Theophilus W. Smith, discovered a defect in the record and told the Democratic lawyers of it. They in turn secured a postponement which carried the case over to the December term, after the presidential election. At the same time that he disclosed the flaw in the record to the Democratic lawyers, the Judge told Douglas and others that the three Whig Justices were about to decide the case against them and, indeed, that their opinions were already prepared.

Such was the source of the Democratic fury against the Supreme Court and of the Democratic assault upon it, such the origin of the memorable party conflict in the Legislature.[1] In a violent speech in the lobby, Douglas denounced the Supreme Court;[2] and a bill was quickly introduced creating five new Justices, thus making the membership of that tribunal nine in all; legislating out of office the nine circuit judges throughout the State, and assigning their duties to the Justices of the re-organized Supreme Court. Trumbull, Douglas, McClernand, and other Democratic leaders made support of this measure a test of party loyalty and standing.

To quiet the storm against it, the Supreme Court hastened its decision of the alien-voter case. The Court decided that the Democratic contention was correct; but while the opinion of Justice Smith was forthright and squarely on the main point, that of the Whig Justices was somewhat obscure and evasive.[3] The hurried action of the Court did not mollify the Democratic leaders. Neither did a written denial, signed by all the Justices including Smith, that they were about to decide the case before the election in 1840. The Democratic bill for the 'reorganiza-tion' of the Judiciary was pressed with determination and vigor. On the very day of Lincoln's permanent return to his duties in the House, this measure, until disposed of, was made the special order thenceforward for every afternoon.

The excitement was tremendous, debate virulent, personal encounters narrowly averted. Some of the speeches, however,

---

[1] Ford, 213–9.   [2] Ib., 219–20.
[3] Spragins vs. Houghton, 2 Scammon, 377–417. Judge Smith, the Democratic mem-

were very able and unspoiled by partisan rancor. Trumbull, in particular, made a notable argument against the Court for the reformation of the Judiciary.[1] For the Whigs Hardin spoke with much power, as did Cyrus Edwards.[2] So drastic was the Democratic plan, that many Democrats refused to accept it and voted with the enraged Whigs — only by a tie vote was a Whig motion to table the special order resolution defeated,[3] Lincoln voting aye. After ten days of acrimonious speeches, charge and counter charge, and many motions and roll-calls, the House passed the bill by a bare majority of two votes, Lincoln voting nay.

The Democratic managers mercilessly wielded the party whip to drive refractory members of the party into line. They were assailed and disciplined by the 'most unbounded abuse,' declared the Whig organ; they were ruled by a 'spirit of dark, vindictive and uncompromising proscription' which reduced them to 'abject terror.'[4] The desertion to the Whigs of but one more Democrat would have defeated the party measure by a tie vote.[5] 'A more perfect despotism never existed in the legislature of a free people,' said the Sangamo Journal; 'except for bloodshed, it would have resembled the General Assembly of France in the time of Robespierre and Marat.'[6]

Throughout this tumultuous and vindictive party battle, Lincoln was apathetic. He was not even present on the morning following the passage of the bill when John J. Hardin, who appears to have acted as Whig floor leader after Lincoln had ceased to take an active interest in the sessions,[7] moved that

ber of the Court, held that the inclusive words of the Constitution — 'all male inhabitants' — clearly covered those who were unnaturalized; while Lockwood and Wilson, the Whig Justices, concluded that the judges of election had no power, under the law, to investigate the question as to whether a person offering to vote had been naturalized. Again Douglas and Butterfield were the leading attorneys for the opposing sides, the arguments of both men being thorough and able.

[1] *Illinois State Register*, April 9, 1841, printing in full Trumbull's great speech which filled an entire page of that paper.

[2] The Whig organ published the speeches of Hardin and Edwards, as well as that of Senator William Gatewood, in full. *Sangamo Journal*, April 2, 9, May 21, 1841.

[3] Forty-one to forty-one. *House Journal*, Sess. 1840–1, 261.

[4] *Sangamo Journal*, March 12, 1841.

[5] The vote was forty-five ayes to forty-three nays. *House Journal*, Sess. 1840–1, 311.

[6] *Sangamo Journal*, March 12, 1841.

[7] See reports of the legislative proceedings. *Ib.*, Feb. 2 and 12, 1841.

permission be granted a member, who had been absent when the bill was passed, to record his vote. The Democrats were able to defeat the motion by only one majority.[1]

The Council of Revision disapproved the measure, the Senate again passed it over the veto [2] and sent it to the House, where again heated verbal encounters took place. After many roll-calls, Lincoln merely voting with his party, the House also passed the bill over the objections of the Council of Revision,[3] and thus, because of partisan politics in both Court and Legislature, the Supreme Court of Illinois was revolutionized. The Democrats were not without some excuse for their action. The General Assembly promptly elected five new Justices who, it must in fairness be said, were lawyers of preëminent ability, some of them of great learning, and all of them the equals, to say the very least, of the old Judges.[4]

Thirty-five Whigs, Lincoln among them, signed a strong protest, presented by Hardin and probably written by him.[5] So came to an end this aggravated party contest, thus was enacted this vitally important legislation, and such was the part taken by Lincoln in that historic matter.[6]

On March 1, 1841, the last session of the Legislature ever attended by Lincoln as a member, adjourned and he went to his law office in Springfield, 'gloom fairly dripping from him.' For more than six years he had served in the House and for the first time during that long period he left it without that happy buoyancy which his cheerful temperament and mounting fortunes had hitherto never failed to produce. We shall now pick up his daily life again and accompany him through years of discipline, vital in the development of his character and career.

---

[1] *House Journal*, Sess. 1840-1, 312.   [2] *Ib.*, 358.   [3] *Ib.*, 362-7.

[4] They were Sidney Breese, Thomas Ford, Samuel H. Treat, Walter B. Scates, and Stephen A. Douglas. It is interesting to note that Dan Stone received fourteen votes. (*Ib.*, 406.) For an impartial account of this affair see Ford, 212-22. Ford was one of the new Judges and afterward elected Governor. See also *Frontier State*: Pease, 279-81. Yet the *Sangamo Journal* charged that 'partisans the most violent' had been made Judges. *Ib.*, March 12, 1841.

Douglas's acceptance of his appointment after his bitter attacks upon the Court gave Lincoln advantage in the great debate of 1858.

[5] *House Journal*, Sess. 1840-1, 539-43.

[6] See Whig summary of the work of this Legislature in *Sangamo Journal*, Feb. 16, 1841.

CHAPTER VI
YEARS OF DISCIPLINE

Then black despair,
The shadow of a starless night, was thrown
Over the world in which I moved alone.
SHELLEY, *Revolt of Islam.*

'WHEN he first came among us, his wit and humor boiled over,'
said James H. Matheny, recalling the conduct and appearance
of Lincoln during the early period of his life in Springfield. Excepting Speed, Matheny was the most intimate unmarried
friend of Lincoln in Springfield at that time, and was his best
man when, finally, Lincoln married.[1]

Springfield was a typical western town and grew rapidly after
it became the State capital. Its population was that of a new
and raw country, vigorous, hopeful, ambitious. For the most
part manners were rough and hearty, and the general disposition was cordial though combative. Most of the people were
from Kentucky and the dominant social group was almost entirely from that State. Springfield had a well-marked small-
town aristocracy, with pretension to fashion and class distinction. The new capital became at once the social centre of
Illinois, especially when the Legislature was in session, as had
been the case with Vandalia; but in this, as in every other respect, Springfield outclassed her former rival.

Amid this lively and variegated mixture of population, Lincoln had for four years made his happy and successful way. His
quaint humor, his stories, and easy, genial companionableness
rendered him a favorite among men of all classes. He joined
with gusto in outdoor sports — foot-races, jumping and hop-
ping contests, town ball, wrestling.[2] He wrote spicy poems and
amusing papers for a select company of young associates who

---

[1] Herndon was much closer to Lincoln, personally, than anybody else; but their
partnership was not formed until seven years after Lincoln came to Springfield.

[2] James Gourley's statement, no date. Weik MSS.

had formed a private 'literary' society which met in Speed's big living-room over his store.[1]

But the place and time that Lincoln liked best were the evenings about the big log-fire in the back part of Speed's store, where men gathered informally through the long winter. These occasions were not unlike the gatherings at the country stores in Gentryville and New Salem, and the same gift for entertainment that had marked Lincoln in those places again made him the shining light in the lively company in Speed's establishment.[2] Again story and joke, wise saying, quick logic, and apt quotation amused and instructed the jolly and eager company. Douglas, who was frequently there, was no teller of stories, and could only argue and declaim; but Lincoln could do both, as well as brighten the talk with fun, anecdote, and jocund remark.

Speed had a clerk, then a youth of nineteen, 'Billy' Herndon as he was called, a keen but agreeable boy whom every one liked. He was the son of Archer G. Herndon, builder and owner of one of the first hotels in Springfield,[3] an ardent Democrat and violent anti-Abolitionist. When the killing of Lovejoy occurred at Alton the youth was in college at Jacksonville and adopted with all the heat of his enthusiastic temperament the abolition views of President Beecher and his Faculty. His father took him out of college and the boy got a job with Speed, at seven hundred dollars a year, a handsome salary at that time. By nature Billy was a hero worshipper and Lincoln became the object of his adoration. After a time the youth slept in the room over the store where his employer and Lincoln lived.[4] He heard and saw all that went on during the years we are now reviewing, and his devotion to Lincoln grew steadily. Thus fate spun another and, for Lincoln, a most fortunate thread in the many-colored fabric of his career.

Lincoln read Shakespeare, Burns, and Byron assiduously, although without steadiness or system. Indeed, at this time in his

[1] This must not be confounded with the Lyceum, where public lectures and addresses were given and which was in existence some years before Lincoln came to Springfield.

[2] Herndon, I, 187. *Reminiscences of Abraham Lincoln:* Joshua F. Speed, a Lecture, 23.

[3] Onstot, 54–5.

[4] Herndon, I, 188–9. Also Speed to Herndon, Sept. 17, 1866. Weik MSS.

life he did nothing according to plan or with any sort of regularity, except, perhaps, the practice of politics. Even the times of eating his meals, of going to bed and getting up, were determined by whim. His habits were, testifies Speed, 'regularly irregular.' But he remembered all he read and could quote more poetry than any man in town. He read Milton as well as law, and especially the newspapers; and, says Speed, he 'retained them all about as well as an ordinary man would any one of them who made only one at a time his study.' But no program or schedule of reading 'was ever checked out.' [1]

Lincoln's room-mate was amazed at his memory. 'I once remarked to him,' writes Speed, 'that his mind was a wonder to me. That impressions were easily made upon his mind and never effaced. "No, said he, you are mistaken. I am slow to learn and slow to forget that which I have learned. My mind is like a piece of steel, very hard to scratch any thing on it and almost impossible, after you get it on, to rub it out."' In short, Speed, who knew Lincoln as no other man except Herndon ever knew him, finally concluded that 'Mr. Lincoln was so unlike all the men I had ever known before or seen or known since that there is no one to whom I can compare him.' [2] His memory impressed everybody. 'Mr. Lincoln had an astonishing memory,' says Gillespie. 'I never found it at fault. He could recall every incident of his life, particularly if any thing amusing was connected with it.' [3]

Lincoln liked Byron greatly, particularly 'Childe Harold's Pilgrimage,' 'Mazeppa,' and the 'Bride of Abydos.' Speed must have sharpened his interest in Byron, for he says that Lincoln had not read Byron a great deal 'previous to my acquaintance with him.' [4] Next to Shakespeare, however, Lincoln was fondest of Burns. He constantly recited Burns's immortal satire on unction and hypocrisy, 'Holy Willie's Prayer.' That attack of the Scottish poet on religious conceit, together with his 'Address to the Unco Guid, or Rigidly Righteous,' may almost be said to have stated Lincoln's views on the religion of the times, at this

[1] Speed to Herndon, Dec. 6, 1866. Weik MSS.   [2] Ib.
[3] Gillespie to Herndon, Jan. 31, 1866. Weik MSS.
[4] Speed to Herndon, Jan. 12, 1866. Weik MSS.

period of his development.[1] For it appears that during his early years in Springfield he rejected orthodox Christianity.[2] He did not go to church, although at first, as he explained to Mary Owens, this was because he would not know how to behave himself.[3] Throughout his life he never became a member of any religious denomination, and not until a dozen years after he left the Legislature in 1841 did he become a regular attendant at church services.[4]

If Lincoln may be said to have done anything whatever continuously during these years, except to give attention to politics, it was to read newspapers and at the same time, strangely enough, to study literary style. The Springfield press printed all the State papers, as they appeared, and the speeches of leaders in Congress, especially those of Clay, Webster, Calhoun, and Benton. At the office of the *Sangamo Journal* Lincoln found the *National Intelligencer*, the great Whig organ published at Washington, as well as the more important papers of the Eastern and Southern cities. The papers of Illinois towns and cities were there, of course.

Lincoln incessantly strove to improve his method of statement and expression. His ideal, formed in boyhood, was clear-

[1] Matheny's statement, May 3, 1866. Weik MSS.

[2] 'Mr. Lincoln's Religion as I understand was of a low order — he was an infidel especially when young, Say from 1834 to 1840.' Stuart's statement, no date. Weik MSS.

'He did not believe in the orthodox theology of the day. He was a Universalist top root and all in faith and sentiment. I have talked this often and often with him commencing as early as 1834 and as late down as 1859.' Isaac Cogdale's statement, no date. Weik MSS.

'He often in conversations as late as 1850 avowed his ideas in this city [on religion] I have heard him — so has Judge Matheny, Stuart and many others.' Herndon to Weik, Feb. 11, 1887. Weik MSS.

'I have often heard Mr. Lincoln talk of the miraculous conception, inspiration, Revelation, Virgin Mary say in 1837-8-9, etc. His was the language of respect yet it was from the point of ridicule, not scoff, as I once loosely said.' Matheny's statement, no date but 1865 or '66. Weik MSS.

'I think that after he was elected President, he sought to become a believer, and to make the Bible a preceptor to his faith and a guide to his conduct.' Speed to Herndon, Jan. 12, 1866. Weik MSS.

'Mr. Matheny told me that he understood that up to the time Lincoln left Springfield, Ills., in 1860, that he was a confirmed infidel, but that after he got to Washington and associating with religious people that he [Matheny] believes that Mr. Lincoln thought he became a Christian.' Matheny's second statement, Dec. 9, 1873. Weik MSS.

[3] Lincoln to Mary Owens, May 7, 1837. *Works*, I, 53. [4] 1852.

ness and simplicity. He still indulged in that rodomontade then considered to be eloquence;[1] but the artist in him was constantly at work and in time was to make him one of the great masters of style. For, above everything else, Lincoln was by nature a literary artist. 'He was a great admirer of the style of John C. Calhoun,' testifies Speed. 'I remember reading to him one of Mr. Calhoun's speeches in reply to Mr. Clay in the Senate, in which Mr. Clay had quoted precedent. . . . Calhoun replied "that to legislate upon precedent is but to make the error of yesterday the law of to-day." Lincoln thought that was a great truth greatly uttered.'[2]

He was more than ordinarily efficient in the trial of cases before juries, and in Springfield as well as on the circuit his practice grew rapidly and steadily. But politics attracted him more than anything else and in that field his success was notable. He had lived in Springfield less than three years when he became one of the small Whig coterie directing that party. In fact, in the absence of Stuart, Lincoln was the head of the Whig 'Junto,' as this group was called. They were influential in the naming of every Whig candidate for any office, little or big; the decision of the 'Junto' as to who should be nominated by Whig conventions was usually accepted and ratified by those party representative assemblages.

A conspicuous instance of this autocratic party control was the selection of a Whig candidate from Menard County for the Legislature at the special election of 1839. Unable to decide, the Whigs of Petersburg referred the matter to 'the Springfield Junto,' Lincoln, Logan, and Baker; and this triumvirate 'at once' selected John Bennett, even over Bowling Green, Lincoln's old friend and benefactor. 'Would Mr. Lincoln be likely to urge a candidate upon the people, unless he were well assured that he would, if elected, go the whole hog with the Springfield Junto members?' asked the Democratic paper, in a stinging editorial on the 'Dictation' of the clique.[3]

---

[1] See for example Lincoln's gaudy perorations in his 'Lyceum Speech' and his 'Subtreasury Speech.'

[2] Speed to Herndon, Dec. 6, 1866.

[3] *Illinois State Register*, Nov. 16, 1839. Petersburg, county seat of Menard County,

The Bennett candidacy excited much animosity against the 'Junto.' 'I have heard a great deal said of late about Messrs. Lincoln, Baker, and Logan, bringing out Mr. Bennett,' wrote a sarcastic correspondent of the *State Register*. 'But were they not justifiable? Had not Messrs. Lincoln and Baker lost entirely the confidence of the people of Menard [County]?' So must they not satisfy 'their Whig friends' in that county? 'I am not the apologist of Messrs. Lincoln and Baker, but it does appear to me unjust to blame them for doing that which it was their interest to do.' [1]

The Democratic organ became sharply incensed at Lincoln because in one of the many Whig-Democratic debates he had called the editors of the *State Register* 'liars,' for having said that he was for Bennett when, in fact, he was, as he then claimed, for Bowling Green. In an editorial that paper attacked the audacious young Whig boss. 'Such was the language of the man selected by the Whig party to be an elector of the high office of President of the United States — language made at a time when he was shielded from being met in reply by regulations publicly proclaimed in the presence of Mr. Lincoln at the opening of the evening's discussion.' The *Register* then republished a letter from Petersburg in proof of its statement that Lincoln, Baker, and Logan did bring out Bennett. Why had Lincoln not denied the charge before? [2]

Nor was this the first time, it would seem, that such 'regular army discipline,' as Governor Ford described it, was exercised. It appears that Bowling Green wanted to run for some office in 1838 and, another being made the Whig candidate, Green rebelled, ran independently and was beaten. After the election the Whig organ printed a short editorial of regret, undoubtedly inspired by Lincoln.[3] The Junto made all party plans and devised the strategy of campaigns.

was near the site of New Salem which was abandoned for the new town about the time Lincoln went to Springfield. Menard County was cut off from Sangamon County in 1839, as were Logan and Christian Counties.

[1] *Illinois State Register*, Nov. 23, 1839.   [2] *Ib.*

[3] 'To see our old friend, Bowling Green, beaten, and to have been under the necessity of aiding in defeating him, we confess is, and has been, extremely painful to us. Under other circumstances we would have been glad to do battle for him; but as it was, he

In 1839 these young [1] Whig managers were in high feather, and they grievously irritated the Democratic leaders. The Whig paper, 'the Federal junto's organ,' as the Democrats called it,[2] published a series of anonymous letters, one of them, signed 'Madison,' assailing the editor of the Democratic paper. 'The writer is no doubt one of the Junto,' declared the *Register* in a caustic editorial, 'whose members deliberate in secret, write in secret, and work in darkness — men who dare not let the light of day in upon their acts — who seek to rule a free people by their edicts passed in midnight secrecy. . . . The *mask* is on them in all their acts.' [3]

Since neither Logan nor Baker is known ever to have written letters to the press under pseudonyms, and Lincoln had done so in the Adams controversy, the Democratic editor's reference is obviously to Lincoln. As we shall presently see, he was soon to write another unsigned letter to the *Journal* for which he was to be called to sharp account and which was to stop forever his writing of anonymous letters and personal attacks.

For four years, then, Lincoln had made rapid progress in Springfield. In law, politics, and general favor his advancement had been unchecked by a single reverse. From April, 1837, until some time in 1840, there was not a more cheery young man in Sangamon County. 'No man ever had an easier time of it in his early days . . . than Lincoln,' declares Herndon of his idol's first years in Springfield. 'He had . . . influential and financial friends to help him; they almost fought each other for the priv-

---

threw himself in the ranks of our enemies, and therefore we could do no less than we did.' *Sangamo Journal*, Aug. 11, 1838.

[1] Their respective ages were: Lincoln thirty, Baker twenty-eight, Logan thirty-nine.

[2] *Illinois State Register*, Sept. 7, 1839.

[3] *Ib.*, Nov. 9, 1839. The *Register* asks the editor of the *Journal* if he 'expects us to reply to his anonymous correspondents, whom he allows week after week to assail us under the false mask of a fictitious signature.' After ascribing the authorship of the 'Madison' letter to a member of the Junto — Lincoln, Logan, or Baker — the *Register* continues: 'For the men who compose this SECRET TRIBUNAL, we have nought but contempt. Let them disband their unholy league, throw away the "*dagger* and the *chord*," turn honest, and cease to tyrannize over their fellow men, and we may yet respect them. Till then, we must regard them as a secret band of tyrants and oppressors, whose hands are against every man who does not bow down to them.'

ilege of assisting Lincoln. . . . Lincoln was a pet . . . in this city.'
Herndon adds that 'he deserved it.' [1]

No evidence exists of gloom or despondency in his talk or conduct until December, 1840, while all the testimony of acquaintances, observers, and friends is of his gay spirits and good humor
throughout this period.[2] He was no longer the 'humble Abraham Lincoln' of New Salem. Soon that lost humility was to
be restored, but by processes of suffering and abasement.

In only one phase of life in Springfield had Lincoln not been
brilliantly successful — the social phase. He was, indeed, one of
six 'managers' of a 'Cotillion Party,' given at the American
House soon after the Legislature convened for the first time in
the new State capital; [3] but this affair was entirely political.[4]
The young Whigs were anxious that Mrs. Browning should be at
the capital; and Lincoln joined Hardin, Dawson, and Webb in
an appeal to her to come forthwith, 'bringing in your train all
ladies in general . . . and all Mr. Browning's sisters in particular.' For 'we are in great need of your society in this town of
Springfield' and will obey all your orders and those of Miss
Browning also.[5]

This whimsical petition, cast in the form of a bill in chancery,
was forwarded in a letter to Mrs. Browning, signed by Hardin
and Lincoln and, though written by Hardin, was plainly their
joint composition. Business cannot proceed in her absence they
tell her; in fact, nothing can begin while she and Hardin's wife
are away. But if Mrs. Browning will come, all will be well in the

[1] Herndon to Weik, Jan. 15, 1886. Weik MSS.

[2] The exception is Speed's and Butler's description of Lincoln's melancholy on the
day he came to Springfield, caused by his extreme poverty. See pp. 208-9, *supra*. On
the contrary, Herndon makes mention of Lincoln's 'lively humor' as one of the things
that 'imprinted his individuality' on Herndon from the beginning. Herndon, I, 181.

[3] The special session of 1839–40, which began Dec. 9, 1839. The 'Cotillion Party'
was held Dec. 16, 1839.

[4] Douglas, McClernand, Shields, and Whiteside were also 'managers,' as were Speed,
Edwards, Merryman, and others. Obviously this dance was given as a celebration of
the first meeting of the General Assembly at Springfield after the removal of the
capital, and as a welcome to the members of the Legislature and their wives.

As we have seen, the enemies of Springfield in the Legislature were alert and determined. So the managers of the ball included an equal number of leading Democratic
and Whig politicians. It had no local social significance whatever.

[5] Dawson, Lincoln, Webb, and Hardin 'To the Honorable Mrs. O. H. Browning,'
Dec. 11, 1839. MS. copy, Barrett Collection.

important matter of 'visiting, conversation, and amusement.' Butler has agreed to give her his parlor; if he fails, 'I promise as a gallant knight to give you the privilege of hanging up on a peg in my closet whenever it may seem convenient. I have been visiting the ladies this evening, they say it will be quite gay this winter, several ladies from a distance being here, with the intention of spending the winter. Mrs. Hardin will be here next week.' When Mrs. Browning arrives, her husband 'will be considered . . . as the minor party of the Quincy Delegation.'[1]

While Lincoln strove to be attractive and pleasing when he attended social gatherings, he was not in high favor with women generally. The men, however, clustered about him to listen to his boisterous stories and witty comment. Lincoln never got on well with women. Even in his boyhood he had shunned them, and in his early manhood at New Salem, his closest association with women had been with frontier matrons like Mrs. Jack Armstrong, Mrs. Bennett Abell, and Mrs. Bowling Green, each of whom cared for his needs and, in general, mothered him. Lincoln did not understand women, it appears, or, as Mary Owen put it, 'he was deficient in those little links that make up the chain of woman's happiness.' It may be that he distrusted himself and doubted his capacity to please and entertain women — seemingly standing in awe of them. At any rate he was curiously shy, ill at ease, and even perplexed in their presence. Yet, stranger still in view of this attitude, Lincoln had an eager desire for feminine company. Of the many contradictions in his complex character, no one is more striking than his attitude toward women.

At the particular time we are reviewing, the heart of the social life of Springfield and, in fact, of Illinois, was the Edwards family. Its political power was extensive, and its influence with the commercial and financial interests of the State was consider-

---

[1] Lincoln and Hardin to Mrs. Browning, Dec. 11, 1839. MS. Barrett Collection. She positively must be in Springfield by December 25 'as a living Christmas present, as large as life, twice as natural, and three times as agreeable.'

Mrs. Browning was not only powerful socially but influential in politics. Ten years later Baker wrote her intimately about his political ambitions and those of Browning — she is 'the ministering angel of his [Browning's] fortune.' Baker to Mrs. Browning, Feb. 1, 1849. MS. Barrett Collection.

able.[1] Soon after he entered the Legislature Lincoln became closely associated, as we have seen, with Ninian W. Edwards, his colleague from Sangamon County, son of Governor Edwards; and with Cyrus Edwards of Alton, the Governor's brother, a member of the State Senate from Madison County.

The wife of Ninian W. Edwards[2] was Elizabeth P. Todd, whom he had married in Kentucky, February 16, 1832, while attending Transylvania University. She was the eldest of four sisters, daughters of Eliza (Parker) and Robert Smith Todd, a prominent citizen of Kentucky and a man of considerable wealth. The second of these daughters, Frances Todd, came to Springfield to visit her sister Mrs. Edwards, and soon married[3] Dr. William S. Wallace, a leading physician of the town and a prosperous druggist as well.[4] Lincoln's partner, John T. Stuart, was a first cousin of the Todd girls, their father being the brother of Stuart's mother, Hannah Todd. Thus the Edwards, Stuart, Wallace, and Todd families were closely related by blood or marriage, and they constituted a social unit. To this aristocratic clan also belonged the families of Gershom Jayne and Charles R. Matheny.

In 1837, the year that Lincoln went to Springfield, the third of the Todd sisters, Mary Todd, came to the new capital to visit

[1] Ninian Edwards, the founder of the Edwards family, was a man of fine ability. Born in Maryland in 1775, and educated under the tutelage of William Wirt and at Dickinson College, Pennsylvania, he went to Kentucky when a youth, was elected to the Legislature before he was twenty-one years old, and became Chief Justice of the Court of Appeals before his thirty-second year.

While serving on the Bench, Madison appointed him Governor of the Territory of Illinois; and when that State was admitted to the Union, Gov. Edwards was elected to the National Senate. He resigned from the Upper House of Congress after several years of service, to become Minister to Mexico, but was recalled before reaching his post. Upon his return to Illinois he became Governor of the State from 1826 until 1830.

Governor Edwards died at Belleville, Ill., in 1833. The political organization which he had built up was not without influence for many years after his death and may be said to have been the foundation on which was built the organization of the Whig party of Illinois.

[2] Ninian Wirt Edwards was born near Frankfort, Kentucky, April 15, 1809, and was but two months younger than Lincoln. He was named after his father and also after William Wirt, his father's first preceptor.

[3] May, 1839. Statement Mrs. Jessie Palmer Weber to author, March 23, 1925.

[4] Some years afterwards another sister, Anne Maria Todd, youngest of the Todd girls, also came to Springfield and married C. M. Smith, a rich business man. 'I remember her well. She was the most quick tempered and vituperative woman (if I can use such a word), of all the sisters.' Mrs. Weber to author, March 23, 1925.

her sister Mrs. Edwards. She stayed three months and went back to Kentucky where she remained two years, finishing her education.[1] Her parents were cousins and her mother dying while Mary was a child, her father had married for his second wife, Elizabeth, daughter of Dr. Alexander Humphreys of Frankfort, Kentucky. The spirited girl quarrelled with her step-mother and her sister, Mrs. Edwards, 'wrote to Mary to come out and make our home her home.' Thus she returned to Springfield in the autumn or early winter of 1839 to live with the Edwards family.[2]

So Mary Todd was in Springfield just after Lincoln had secured the removal of the State capital to that place and probably witnessed the vociferous welcome of the 'Long Nine' by the delighted citizens. Certainly she heard the praise of Lincoln with which the town throbbed for months thereafter. She was in Springfield, too, as a permanent member of her sister's family, when the 'Cotillion Party' was held; and she undoubtedly attended that ball.

Born in Lexington, December 13, 1818, Miss Todd was then just twenty-one years of age. She was below medium stature, rotund, inclined to stoutness, weighing about one hundred and thirty pounds. Her face was round, eyes not large and bluish gray in color, mouth firm and severe, brow full and rather high, hair dark brown and abundant. She was spirited, vivacious, witty, entertaining, and fluent in conversation, with a tendency to sarcasm and quick, sharp repartee. She was well educated for the times, and accomplished.[3] Her handwriting was regular and beautiful, and her use of language accurate. She read, spoke, and wrote French, having been trained in Madame Mentelle's private school at Lexington where only French was spoken. She finished her education at a girl's academy in Lexington which was so excellent that many girls from Northern States were sent there to complete their schooling.[4]

---

[1] Mrs. Abraham Lincoln's statement, no date. Weik MSS.

[2] Mrs. Edwards's first statement. Weik MSS.

[3] Herndon to Weik, Jan. 16, 1886. Weik MSS. And see Herndon, II, 207–8.

[4] Mrs. Abraham Lincoln's statement. Waldemar de Mentelle, a royalist, fled from France in the Reign of Terror to America and settled in Lexington, Ky.

MARY TODD LINCOLN

On both sides the ancestry of Mary Todd was distinguished. Her paternal grandfather, General Levi Todd, of the Virginia family of that name, was famous as soldier and citizen in the pioneer history of Kentucky. Her father, Robert Smith Todd, was eminent in his State and President of the Bank of Kentucky when Mary came to Illinois. His first wife, the mother of his children, was the daughter of Elizabeth Porter of Pennsylvania, who married Robert Parker of Lexington, Kentucky. Mary Todd's maternal great-grandfather was General Andrew Porter of Revolutionary fame, who succeeded General Peter Muhlenberg as commander of the Pennsylvania troops in the War for Independence; and her maternal great-grandmother, the second wife of General Andrew Porter, was Elizabeth Parker, the daughter of Elizabeth Todd. Thus the Todd, Porter, and Parker families were closely united by consanguinity. All were proud of their family names and traditions, and the blood of all flowed in the veins of Mary Todd.[1]

Mary 'loved glitter, show and pomp and power,' and was abnormally ambitious for place and public distinction — 'the most ambitious woman I ever knew,' testifies her sister.[2] She 'often and often contended,' continues Mrs. Edwards, 'that she was destined to be the wife of some future President.'[3] She was nervous, sensitive, proud, and burdened with a furious temper which became ungovernable when cause for restraint was removed. But with her many accomplishments, her youth, her family connections, she at once became one of the belles of Springfield.[4]

The most prosperous young bachelor in town was Speed, a favorite in Springfield society and a frequent caller at the house of Ninian W. Edwards.[5] Speed asked Mrs. Edwards's permis-

[1] Todd genealogy. Weik MSS.

[2] Mrs. Edwards's first statement, no date; and second statement, Sept. 27, 1887.

[3] Mrs. Edwards's first statement. Weik MSS.

[4] Herndon, II, 209.

[5] Speed, too, was of Revolutionary and pioneer stock. His grandfather was James Speed of Mecklenburg Co., Virginia, a Captain in a regiment of the line; and Joshua's father, John Speed, was one of the early settlers of Kentucky. His mother was Lucy Gilmer Fry, the daughter of Joshua Fry, grandson of Joshua Fry who was associated with Dr. Thomas Walker and Peter Jefferson in surveying the southern boundary of Virginia. John Speed was a member of the Kentucky convention which brought about

sion to bring Lincoln and thus began his acquaintance with
Mary Todd.[1] Mrs. Edwards recalls that he went to see Mary
steadily during the winter of 1839–40, just after the marriage of
her sister, Frances, to Dr. Wallace; and, during the spring, summer, and autumn of 1840 Speed and Lincoln 'were frequently
at our house,' says Mrs. Edwards, Lincoln greatly enjoying the
shade of the forest trees in the Edwards's yard. 'I . . . knew he
was a rising man and nothing else modifying this, desired Mary
at first to marry L.,' confesses her sister.[2] Ninian W. Edwards
also always 'thought L[incoln] would be a great man' and jokingly made him promise that when he became President he
would give Edwards a post office. Herndon adds that 'Edwards
admits that he wanted Speed to marry Miss Edwards and Lincoln, Miss Todd.'[3] So Lincoln's attentions were welcomed and
encouraged.

The young partner of Mary's cousin was captivated. The
lively girl received him graciously but in the grand manner, and
did practically all of the talking. When Mrs. Edwards chanced
to come into the room she found her sister chatting gaily and
Lincoln listening with rapt and silent attention, as if enthralled
and under a hypnotic spell. 'He was charmed with Mary's
wit and fascinated with her quick sagacity . . . and culture,' relates Mrs. Edwards; 'Lincoln would listen and gaze on her
as if drawn by some superior power. . . . He listened — never
scarcely said a word.' But, explains Mrs. Edwards, Lincoln
'could not hold a lengthy conversation with a lady — was not
sufficiently educated and intelligent in the female line to do so.'[4]

Douglas, too, was a frequent caller on Miss Todd who flirted

the separation of that district from Virginia, while Joshua Fry was one of the first
educators of Kentucky. *Lincoln:* Speed, 3; Collins, II, 625.

At the time treated in the text, the cousin of Ninian W. Edwards, Miss Matilda
Edwards, daughter of Cyrus Edwards of Alton, was on a prolonged visit to Springfield
and Mr. and Mrs. Edwards hoped that Speed would marry her. According to her
cousin, Speed did propose and was refused, as was Douglas 'on the grounds of
his bad morals.' First statement of Mrs. Edwards and of Ninian W. Edwards, Sept.
22, 1865. Weik MSS. The same story is told of Douglas and Mary Todd. P. 311,
infra.

[1] Herndon, II, 209.

[2] Mrs. Edwards's second statement, Sept. 27, 1887. Weik MSS.

[3] Edwards's statement, Sept. 22, 1865. Weik MSS.

[4] Mrs. Edwards's first statement.

with him boldly and conspicuously. Lincoln's attentions had
been so constant that her brother-in-law, Dr. Wallace, as well
as Mr. and Mrs. Edwards, protested to Mary against her seeming partiality for Douglas.[1] Asked by her friends which suitor
she intended to marry, she answered: 'Him who has the best
prospects of being President.'[2] Although it was afterwards
given out that Douglas had proposed to Mary and was refused
because 'of his bad morals,'[3] that statement was obviously protective propaganda usual in such cases; for the shrewd, alert,
and, even then, worldly-wise Douglas never asked Miss Todd to
marry him.[4]

The course of the affair between Lincoln and Mary Todd
is confused and complicated, only the main features being clear
and well authenticated. The young woman admired the rising
politician and lawyer, as did Stuart and Edwards. Indeed,
many thought and some flatly said that Edwards planned the
whole thing.[5] But the Todd and Edwards families scorned and
detested the Hanks and Lincoln family; and Mary, especially,
'held the Hanks tribe in contempt and the Lincoln family generally — the old folks' in particular,[6] a feeling which she never
overcame.

However, an engagement to be married finally resulted. But
Lincoln soon wanted to get out of it; he was in the same frame of
mind and feeling, it seems, that had so oppressed him in the case
of Mary Owens. He wrote a long letter to his betrothed informing her of the doubtful nature of his affections and asking to be
released. We can form a good idea of what he wrote to Mary
Todd by again reading his final letter to Miss Owens.[7] Unfor-

---

[1] Herndon, II, 210–1.   [2] Mrs. Edwards's first statement.

[3] Edwards's statement, Sept. 22, 1865.

[4] 'Douglas did not solicit the hand of Miss Todd in marriage. He did pay marked
attention to her, but no more than he paid to Miss Sarah Dunlap, daughter of Col.
James Dunlap, of Jacksonville, and Miss Julia Jayne, daughter of Dr. Gershom Jayne.
During sessions of the Legislature, Springfield was a gay city, and Judge Douglas,
being fond of society, was much in company of young ladies there. Miss Julia Jayne
married Lyman Trumbull, Miss Dunlap married Gen. McClernand and, when later at
Washington, the families were the closest of friends, socially, with the Douglas's.'
Stevens, 323 n., citing letter of Dr. William Jayne, Jan. 20, 1909.

[5] Matheny's statement, May 3, 1866.

[6] Herndon to Weik, Dec. 1, 1885. Weik MSS.   [7] P. 156, supra.

tunately he showed this letter to Speed and asked him to deliver it. Speed refused and Lincoln said he would get somebody else to carry the letter. No, said Speed, don't write — that will give her an 'advantage over him [you]'; and he threw the letter in the log fire. 'If you have the courage of manhood, go see Mary yourself,' continued Speed; 'tell her, if you do not love her, the facts, and that you will not marry her;' but be quick about it, say little and leave soon.[1]

Lincoln assured Speed that he would follow his advice and started out to do so. But when he told the girl, she burst into tears, said wildly something to the effect of 'the deceiver being himself deceived,' Lincoln melted, took her in his arms and kissed her, and thus ended his attempt to sever their relations. Toward midnight Lincoln returned and told his room-mate what had happened. Speed was disgusted. Lincoln had 'not only acted the fool,' he said, but had renewed the engagement and 'in decency' could not back down again. Lincoln replied: 'Well, if I am in again, so be it. It's done, and I shall abide by it.' [2]

Finally Mary's sister and brother-in-law urged her to drop Lincoln because of their obvious and striking unfitness for each other [3] — sage counsel, since few couples have been more unsuited in temperament, manners, taste, and everything else except mutual ambition. 'She was,' says Onstot, 'entirely different from Abe in every particular.'[4]

So worried did Lincoln become about his health and mental condition that he wrote a long letter to Dr. Daniel Drake of Cincinnati, the most eminent physician in the West and head of the medical department of the College of Cincinnati. Dr. Drake had been brought up in Kentucky, was professor of *materia medica* in Transylvania University when the Lincolns moved to Indiana and, even then, had a wide reputation. Lincoln described his case and asked Dr. Drake for an opinion and course

[1] Speed's statement, Sept. 17, 1866. Herndon, II, 212.

[2] *Ib.*, 213.

[3] Mrs. Edwards's first and second statements, no date, and Sept. 27, 1887. Weik MSS.

[4] Onstot, 33.

of treatment; but the physician refused to give either without personal examination.[1]

Part of this letter Lincoln read to Speed, but he refused to read or let him see the other part. Speed, who as we shall presently see, was highly sentimental and romantic, imagined that these mysterious, hidden lines described his love for Ann Rutledge.[2] But years afterwards Lincoln told his partner, Herndon, that he thought himself affected by a bodily ailment — 'the note to Dr. Drake in part had reference to his disease and not to his crazy spell [over Ann Rutledge], as Speed supposes.'[3]

Nothing was done, the weeks wore on, and the time of the wedding was set for January 1, 1841. 'Everything was ready and prepared for the marriage, even to the supper,' relates Mrs. Edwards. But on that 'fatal' day, as Lincoln afterward called it, nothing was seen or heard of him, he took out no marriage license and, although the expectant bride was waiting, the groom did not appear — 'cause insanity,' declares the bride's sister.[4] Twice did Mrs. Edwards give Herndon the same statement about the preparations for the wedding and Lincoln's absence; and a third time she told the same story to another enquirer: 'she said arrangements for the wedding had been made — even cakes had been baked, but L. failed to appear,' Weik records in his diary.[5]

[1] Speed to Herndon, Nov. 30, 1866. Weik MSS.

Daniel Drake was the author of *Pioneer Life in Kentucky*, so frequently cited in Chap. II of this volume. He was about fifty-five years old when Lincoln wrote him, the acknowledged head of his profession and greatly admired and respected. Few men have had a more brilliant and worthy career.

Lincoln could not possibly have done better than to have gone to Cincinnati and personally consulted this wise, experienced, and highly educated physician, and it was a serious mistake that he did not do so.

[2] Speed to Herndon, Nov. 30, 1866. Weik MSS.

[3] Herndon to Weik, Jan., 1891. Weik MSS. In this confidential letter, written not long before his death, Herndon reminds Weik that he had told him this when in Greencastle, Ind., where Weik was revising the Herndon-Weik *Life of Lincoln*. Herndon says that he made a note of Lincoln's statement to him in his memorandum book, but loaned it to Lamon who never returned it. He fears that this may turn up and, in case it does, gives Weik the facts so that his literary partner can defend him.

[4] Mrs. Edwards's first statement. Weik MSS.

[5] Diary of Jesse W. Weik, Thursday, Dec. 20, 1883. MS. Weik was then pension examiner at Springfield. His diary consists of daily entries of official and other business matters. The portion of the page relating to the interview with Mrs. Edwards states: 'In the afternoon called at the home of N. W. Edwards and wife. Asked the latter as

The Edwards house did not see anything of Lincoln again for nearly two years.[1] 'The world had it that Mr. L backed out and this placed Mary in a peculiar situation,' explains Mrs. Edwards. So 'to set herself right and to free Mr Lincoln's mind, she wrote a letter to Mr L stating that she would release him from his engagements.'[2] Edwards confirms his wife's statement, adding, however, that, in releasing Lincoln, Miss Todd left 'Lincoln the privilege of renewing it if he wished.'[3] For the second time, says Mrs. Edwards, 'Mr. Edwards and myself, after the first crush of things, told Mary and Lincoln that they had better not ever marry — that their natures, mind[s], education, raising, etc. were so different they could not live happy as husband and wife — had better never think of the subject again.'[4]

Thus came about that mental and physical condition that kept him from the Legislature for a time and clothed him with apathy and gloom when finally he felt able to attend the sessions of the House. 'Lincoln . . . went as crazy as a Loon,' testifies Ninian W. Edwards, who avers that he 'did not attend the Legislature in 1841 & 2 for this reason.'[5] Speed gives the same explanation of Lincoln's absence from the House: 'In the winter of 1841 a gloom came over him till his friends were alarmed for his life. Though a member of the Legislature he rarely attended its sessions.'[6]

to marriage with Lincoln of her sister Mary Todd.' Then follows the sentence quoted in the text, and the entry continues: 'At this point Mr. Edwards cautioned his wife that she was talking to a newspaper man and she declined to say more. She had said that Mary was greatly mortified by L.'s strange conduct. Later they were reunited and finally married.' Original owned by Jesse W. Weik, Greencastle, Ind.; a photograph of the page from which the above extract is taken is in possession of the author.

[1] Forty-six years after the event, Mrs. Edwards, in her second statement to Herndon, and, obviously, to put a new and more attractive face on the matter, said that 'Lincoln's and Mary's engagement, etc. were broken off by her flirtations with Douglas.' Mrs. Edwards's second statement, Sept. 27, 1887. Weik MSS.

[2] Mrs. Edwards's first statement.

[3] Edwards's statement, Sept. 22, 1865. Weik MSS.

[4] Mrs. Edwards's first statement. Weik MSS.
Herndon assured Henry C. Whitney that 'he verified every fact as if it was in a Court proceeding and under oath;' and Whitney, who knew Herndon well, adds that 'Herndon [was] a man of the strictest honor.' Whitney to Weik, April 28, 1896. Weik MSS.

[5] Edwards's statement, Sept. 22, 1865. Weik MSS. In error Edwards places the time one year after the true one.

[6] *Lincoln: Speed*, 39.

James H. Matheny declares that Lincoln was 'crazy for a week or so, not knowing what to do.'[1] Mrs. Edwards thought that Lincoln 'went crazy . . . because he wanted to marry and doubted his ability and capacity to please and support a wife.'[2] That he was in great mental distress is certain. His friends searched for him throughout the night of January 1, but did not find him until dawn. Lincoln was in a pitiable state. So desperate was he that Speed feared he would kill himself — 'knives and razors, and every instrument that could be used for self-destruction were removed from his reach,' deposes Lincoln's room-mate.[3]

Lincoln himself bears testimony to his lamentable condition as late as three weeks after he had fled from the wedding. 'I have within the last few days, been making a most discreditable exhibition of myself in the way of hypochondriacism,' he writes Stuart who was in Washington. Lincoln urges his partner to appoint Dr. A. G. Henry postmaster at Springfield. 'You know I desired Dr. Henry to have that place when you left; I now desire it more than ever,' because 'I got an impression [on account of the 'hypochondriacism'] that Dr. Henry is necessary to my existence. Unless he gets that place he leaves Springfield. . . .

[1] Matheny's statement, May 3, 1866. Weik MSS.

[2] Mrs. Edwards's first statement.
The expressions applied to Lincoln's condition cannot be considered capable of scientific interpretation in the light of our present day knowledge of mental disorders. The evidence is too meagre for correct diagnosis and there is no proof that Lincoln was even temporarily insane. His behavior was peculiar, he suffered from marked depression — melancholia — and as is not unusual with the tender-minded, he was for some cause passing through some mental conflicts. Such depression, with accompanying mental disturbances, may easily be exaggerated, yet still exclude the idea of insanity. But Lincoln had no delusions or any of the symptoms of 'insanity.' Dr. Morton Prince writes: 'The most interesting fact brought out by you is the quality of Lincoln's mind. I mean his sensitiveness, or tender-mindedness, or whatever you choose to call it, by which his conflicts occurred and raised havoc with him. He had a conscience. The "tough-minded" have no conflicts, or if they have they are not torn by them.' Letter to author, Sept. 1, 1925.
Because of Lincoln's reticence on his mental conflicts the psychiatrist has nothing to guide him to an opinion. Dr. C. Macfie Campbell, of Boston, makes the interesting suggestion that the facts, so far as known, 'would indicate very simple depression of mood with no artistic elaboration nor flight of fantasy. . . . He is a man whose emotional reactions were apparently rather strong than complicated. He dealt with life more through the direct mechanisms of the emotions than through that of the creative imagination.' Letter to Dr. Prince, Oct. 26, 1925.

[3] Speed to Herndon, Jan. 6, 1866. Herndon, ii, 215.

My heart is very much set on it. Pardon me for not writing more; I have not sufficient composure to write a long letter.' [1]

Three days after sending this letter, Lincoln again writes Stuart in answer to a letter from his partner, 'though from the deplorable state of my mind at this time, I fear I shall give you but little satisfaction.' Still he tells Stuart briefly the political news — three Whig papers are out for Stuart's renomination and others will follow; 'our friends' met at Butler's last night, and are 'unanimously in favor of having you announced as candidate;' Stuart's reëlection 'is sure, if it be in the power of the Whigs to make it so.'

But Lincoln cannot write more, he says: 'It is not in my power to do so. I am now the most miserable man living. If what I feel were equally distributed to the whole human family, there would be not one cheerful face on the earth. Whether I shall ever be better, I cannot tell; I awfully forbode I shall not. To remain as I am is impossible; I must die or be better, it appears to me. The matter you speak of on my account you may attend to as you say, unless you shall hear of my condition forbidding it. I say this because I fear I shall be unable to attend to any business here, and a change of scene might help me. If I could be myself, I would rather remain at home with Judge Logan. I can write no more.' [2]

Such were Lincoln's feelings nearly a month after his collapse on his wedding day and, as will appear, he did not greatly improve for a long time. Even a year later, Matheny thought that Lincoln would kill himself.[3] Thus was first administered to this elemental man the stern discipline of humiliation — discipline priceless to those strong enough to survive it. Soon after Stuart received Lincoln's letters the partnership between them was

[1] Lincoln to Stuart, Jan. 20, 1841. MS. owned by Milton Hay Brown, Springfield, Ill., photostat in possession of author. Lincoln adds: 'We shall shortly forward you a petition in his [Henry's] favour signed by all or nearly all the Whig members of the Legislature as well as other Whigs. This, together with what you know of the Dr.'s position and merits, I sincerely hope will secure him the appointment.'

[2] Lincoln to Stuart, Jan. 23, 1841. *Works*, I, 157–9.

[3] During 1842 I 'thought L[incoln] would commit suicide.' Matheny's statement, May 3, 1866. Weik MSS.

dissolved; but Logan, who seems to have sympathized with Lincoln, took him into his office as partner and the firm of Logan and Lincoln was announced May 14, 1841.[1]

On the same 'fatal first of January,' 1841, Speed sold his store in Springfield to Charles R. Hurst[2] and, two or three months thereafter, went to Louisville where his family lived. He had insisted that Lincoln should come to Louisville for consolation and repose; and Lincoln writes his friend and confidant: 'I stick to my promise' to do so.[3] In the same letter he gives Speed a long account of a supposed mysterious murder which caused the 'highest . . . excitement' ever known in Springfield and describes the preliminary trial, in which Logan, Baker, and he defended the accused. Lincoln closes with this cryptic sentence: 'I have not seen Sarah since my last trip, and I am going out there as soon as I mail this letter.'[4]

Sarah Rickard was a sister-in-law of William Butler, at whose house Lincoln had boarded since he came to Springfield four years earlier. When Speed left Springfield, Lincoln went to Butler's house to live. Mrs. Butler's sister, Sarah, had made her home at the Butler's since childhood. When Lincoln first went there for his meals she was twelve years old and at once became fond of the kindly, humorous, considerate boarder, as children always were fond of Lincoln. Sarah was sixteen at the time of her hero's interrupted love affair with Miss Todd. At some time during or after his disturbance over his engagement or, perhaps, while his depression was upon him following the broken wedding arrangements, Lincoln asked Sarah Rickard to marry him. He argued that, since his name was Abraham and her name was Sarah, they plainly were meant for one another. But Sarah declined, because, as she confesses, 'I was young only 16 years old and had not thought much about matrimony. . . . He seemed

---

[1] *Sangamo Journal* of that date. Herndon, II, 264. Their office faced the public square and was on the corner of Adams and South Sixth Streets.

[2] Hurst was a young business man from Philadelphia who had come to Springfield seven years before as a clerk for the big dry goods firm of Bell and Tinsley. Power, 393. He roomed with Speed and Lincoln over Speed's store.

[3] Lincoln to Speed, June 19, 1841. *Works*, I, 168–75.

[4] *Ib*. In the *Works* the word Sarah is omitted. The originals of Lincoln's letters to Speed are in the Barrett Collection.

allmost like an older Brother being as it were one of my sisters family.'[1]

Months afterward, when he had temporarily regained his senses and old time spirits, Lincoln wrote Speed about Miss Rickard. He had returned from the trip to Louisville, upon which we are now to accompany him, and, while there, had talked to Speed about her. Writing to his confidant of other matters, he closes with these puzzling sentences: 'I have seen Sarah but once. She seemed very cheerful, and so I said nothing to her about what we spoke of.'[2] For the third time, as we shall see, Lincoln wrote to Speed of Miss Rickard, in language still more perplexing. Thus another strand of confusion is drawn into Lincoln's matrimonial tangle.

Finally about the first week in August, 1841, Lincoln went to Louisville to visit Speed and get what relief the intimate companionship of that trusted friend could afford. 'Lincoln came to see me and staid some time at my mother's in the summer and fall of 1841,' says Speed,[3] and there he continued throughout the

---

[1] Mrs. R. F. Barret [Sarah A. Rickard] to Herndon, Aug. 3, 1888. Weik MSS. And see Herndon, I, 230 n.

'Mr. Lincoln did Propose marriage to me in the winter of 1840–41.' Ib. In another letter to Herndon, undated, which because she had a 'Soar finger' was written for her by her husband, Sarah Rickard says:

'When I first met Mr Lincoln at Mr Butlers I was ten or twelve years of age. as I Grew up he use to take me to little Entertainments the first was the Babes in the woods he tooke me to the first Theatre that ever played in Springfield. when I arrived at the age of 16 he became more attentive to me. I allway liked him as a friend but you Know his peculiar manner and his General deportment would not be likely to fasinate a Young Girl just entering into the society world.' Sarah A. Barret (Rickard), no date, to Herndon. Weik MSS.

'My wife's mother, stepmother, was a Rickard. . . . She says that she has heard Mrs. Butler, a Rickard as well as her [Mrs. Herndon's] stepmother a Rickard say that Lincoln did court Sarah and that she would not have him.' Herndon to Weik, Sept. 13, 1887. Weik MSS.

'Saw John Lightfoot today: he says . . . that it was currently reported . . . that Lincoln courted Sarah Rickard — that she flung him high and dry (Rem[em]ber Speed letter about the word Sarah). . . . Lightfoot's evidence I read to my wife and that suggested to her the whole story.' Ib.

[2] Lincoln to Speed, Feb. 3, 1842. Works, I, 185–7. Again Sarah is left blank in Lincoln's published writings. Original in the Barrett Collection.

[3] Speed to Herndon, Sept. 17, 1866. Weik MSS.

'In the early summer of 1841 Mr. Lincoln came to Kentucky and spent several months at Farmington, the home of my mother, near this city [Louisville].' Lincoln: Speed, 39.

An election was held in Springfield Aug. 2, and Lincoln was present and voted. So

remainder of the summer and early autumn. He 'was kept there till he recovered finally,' inaccurately says Ninian W. Edwards.[1] These weeks are important in the change wrought in Lincoln and in the effect that change had on his personal future.

The Speed house was then one of the largest in or near Louis-ville. A red brick building, it still stands in perfect repair and is impressive for its generous proportions and the beauty of its simple lines. The house is of two stories, the family living prin-cipally in the main or second story. Some ten steps lead to the beautiful portico and doorway. A long, broad hall extends through the entire length of the house, and at the back part of this main story is a veranda looking over level and exten-sive acres to the forest a mile or more away.

The house is built on a slight elevation, at the foot of which a small brook meanders lazily. The stone foundations of some of the slave quarters may yet be seen at the usual distance from the dwelling. The Speed mansion, standing about a quarter of a mile from the main road, was about five miles from the city at the time of Lincoln's visit and a more tranquil spot it would have been hard to find.[2]

To Lincoln was given one of the pleasant bedrooms, and here his morning coffee was served to him in bed, by a slave assigned to his personal service. For the first time in his life he knew the meaning of comfort and luxury. For the first time in his life, too, he lived under the same roof with women of gentle birth. Mrs. Speed was a Southern woman, cultivated, religious, and of gracious manners. Speed's sister Mary, a young woman worthy of her mother, was also there. Speed himself was about most of the time. A joyous little girl, Eliza Davis, was of the household too. When his mood prompted, Lincoln would ride into the city, or be driven to town in the family carriage. Frequently he went to the law office of Speed's brother, James, whom he one day was to make Attorney General of the United States, and

he left for Kentucky after that date. Mr. Angle thus corrects the usual error of naming June as the time of the visit.

  Speed's father, John Speed, had died some seventeen months before — March 30, 1840.

  [1] Edwards's statement, Sept. 22, 1865. Weik MSS.

  [2] Personal inspection and *Lincoln:* Speed, 3. See *James Speed. A Personality:* James Speed (a grandson), 1914, where the house is well pictured.

there talked over politics and legal matters with that accomplished lawyer.[1]

Just at that time Speed was paying court to Miss Fanny Henning, a lovely young woman who was soon to become his wife, and this marriage was to have decisive influence on Lincoln. Speed had often written to Lincoln of his infatuation, but had not yet proposed. Fanny was an orphan and lived with her uncle, John Williamson, who had given the young merchant no opportunity to make love to his niece; for the old gentleman, a violent Whig, always insisted on talking politics when her suitor called and would never leave them alone. Speed was anxious that his friend should see the young woman and took Lincoln with him on one of his visits. With a meaning look at Speed, Lincoln, pretending to be a Democrat, engaged Fanny's uncle so heavily in a political argument that the lovers got their chance to be alone, and thus Speed proposed and was accepted.[2]

Sometimes a merry company took him with them on journeys to other towns and places of interest and on such excursions Lincoln had gay hours. Once he went with Speed to Lexington where Miss Henning had gone on a visit. He romped with Mary Speed about the house at Farmington, as the Speed plantation was called, and was cheered by other kindly and attractive women, friends and neighbors of Mrs. Speed. Writing to Mary Speed after his return to Illinois Lincoln reminds her that 'you and I were something of cronies while I was at Farmington, and that while there I was under the necessity of shutting you up in a room to prevent your committing an assault and battery upon me.'[3] He recalls the pleasant times they had together, eating 'delicious dishes of peaches and cream.' Lincoln was immensely taken with Speed's betrothed. 'Are you not convinced that she is one of the sweetest girls in the world,' he asks Mary Speed.

[1] 'I saw him daily; he sat in my office, read my books, and talked with me about his life, his reading, his studies, his aspirations.' James Speed before the Society of the Loyal Legion at Cincinnati, May 4, 1887, in response to the toast, 'Abraham Lincoln.' Speed was a native of Kentucky and, born March 11, 1812, was a few weeks more than three years younger than Lincoln.

[2] Statement of Joshua F. Speed (MS. undated) furnished the author by Joshua F. Speed, nephew of James Speed.

[3] Lincoln to Mary Speed, Sept. 27, 1841. *Works*, i, 177–80.

And 'little Siss Eliza Davis . . . kiss her "o'er and o'er again" for me,' he writes. Aunt Emma too and Mary's sisters and brothers, how nice they were! There was a Mrs. Peay also, whose 'happy face' became a 'pleasant remembrance' to Lincoln.[1] In short, everything was done to take him out of himself and dispel his disabling melancholia.

So passed the healing days and gradually Lincoln gained strength and serenity. During most of his stay, however, he was desperately sad. Sometimes 'he was so much depressed,' says Speed, 'that he almost contemplated suicide;' and once he wrote a poem on that subject and sent it to the *Sangamo Journal*.[2] Nor does it appear when he entirely recovered from his derangement, for we shall soon find him doing and saying strange and neurotic things. So 'moody and hypochondriacal' was he, that Mrs. Speed, thinking to solace and sustain him, gave him an Oxford Bible, a kindness he never forgot. Twenty years later he sent her his photograph with an inscription above his signature, recalling this gift.[3]

In mid-September Lincoln left the hospitable Speed house and family to which he owed so much and went back to Springfield. Speed accompanied him.[4] They went by way of St. Louis on the *Lebanon*, one of the great river steamboats of the time; and Lincoln was amazed to find that several slaves which, as he describes them, 'a gentleman had purchased . . . and was taking . . . to a farm in the South . . . were the most cheerful and apparently happy creatures on board' — this, although the slaves were chained together and 'were being separated forever from the scenes of their childhood, their friends, their fathers and mothers, and brothers and sisters, and many of them from their wives and children, and going into perpetual slavery, where the lash of the master is proverbially more ruthless and unrelenting than any other where. . . . One whose offence for which he had been sold was an over-fondness for his wife, played the fiddle al-

---

[1] Lincoln to Mary Speed, Sept. 27, 1841. *Works*, I, 177–80.

[2] Speed to Herndon, Feb. 9 and Sept. 13, 1866. Weik MSS. Herndon was unable to find the poem in the *Sangamo Journal*. Herndon, II, 216.

[3] Speed to Herndon, Jan. 12, Sept. 17, 1866. Weik MSS.

[4] 'I returned with him to Ills. and remained till the 1st of Jan[uar]y 1842.' Speed to Herndon, Sept. 17, 1866. Weik MSS.

most continually, and the others danced, sang, cracked jokes, and played various games with cards from day to day.'[1] Such was Lincoln's third personal contact with slavery, such his astonished comment upon the gaiety of slaves bound, as he imagined, for the dreaded plantations of the far South.

Back at Springfield once more, Lincoln plunged into the practice of the law. He started immediately on the circuit, remaining but a single day in Springfield and going to court at Bloomington the following day and thence to Charleston. His normal spirits again sparkled, as by a reaction from the depths of his despair; and he promptly wrote to Mary Speed from Bloomington, the first town visited on his circuit, the chatty and delightful letter to which reference has been made.

Even physical distress from a bungled dental operation could not prevent him from recalling the happy incidents of his Kentucky visit. He had had a toothache when at Speed's house and a Louisville dentist had tried to pull the tooth but had made 'a failure.' It began to pain him again, he tells Miss Speed, so much, indeed, that, 'about a week since I had it torn out, bringing with it a bit of the jaw-bone, the consequence of which is that my mouth is now so sore that I can neither talk nor eat. . . . I am literally "subsisting on savory remembrances."' Won't Miss Speed write him 'a line' at Charleston, Illinois? He will be there 'about the time to receive it.'[2]

By the middle of October Lincoln was again at the State capital, busy with politics. He was still a member of the Whig State Central Committee and wrote the call for the Whig State Convention to meet in Springfield in December to nominate the party candidates for Governor and Lieutenant Governor;[3] but the convention never assembled. Lincoln was not renominated for the Legislature, however, by the Sangamon County Whigs.

Speed was still in town and very blue over his approaching wedding. Lincoln's deplorable experience had had its natural effect on Speed; he had 'caught' Lincoln's neurosis and hypochondria. But he had helped Lincoln and now Lincoln would

---

[1] Lincoln to Mary Speed, Sept. 27, 1841. *Works,* I, 177–80.
[2] *Ib.*   [3] *Ib.,* I, 181.

help him. Instead of giving advice by word of mouth, Lincoln wrote to Speed, because 'were I to say it orally before we part, most likely you would forget it at the very time when it might do you some good.' Lincoln thinks it 'reasonable' that Speed will 'feel very badly' before his wedding; so let him read Lincoln's letter 'just at such a time.' For Speed is 'naturally of a nervous temperament;' the bad weather on his journey will be 'very severe on [Speed's] defective nerves;' he has nothing to do and no friends to talk to, and the 'crisis' comes on apace. If all this does not depress Speed, Lincoln will be 'most happily but most egregiously deceived.'

'What nonsense' for Speed to suppose that he does not love Fanny as he thinks he should! Why did he court her? There were 'at least twenty others' — Ann Todd for instance. There is no sense in Speed's imaginings. Lincoln argues about them like a lawyer before a jury. It was 'those heavenly black eyes' that had first attracted Speed. Suppose he should 'find her scouting and despising' him 'and giving herself up to another!' Would he have that happen for any 'earthly consideration?' Let Speed write Lincoln 'by every mail.' [1]

Speed wrote to him and Lincoln answered sympathetically. 'You well know that I do not feel my own sorrows much more keenly than I do yours.' Fanny had been seriously ill and Speed was now in distress about her health. That sentiment, says Lincoln, 'must and will forever banish those horrid doubts' which Speed had felt about his love for her. Lincoln is almost persuaded that 'the Almighty has sent your present affliction expressly for that object;' and he consoles his friend in advance. Should Miss Henning not recover, 'her religion, which you once disliked so much, I will venture you now prize most highly.' Speed 'ought to rejoice, and not sorrow, at this indubitable evidence of your undying affection for her. Why, Speed, if you did not love her, although you might not wish her death, you would most certainly be resigned to it. . . . You know the hell I have suffered on that point, and how tender I am upon it. You know I do not mean wrong. I have been quite clear of the "hypo" since you left; even better than I was along in the

[1] Lincoln to Speed, Jan. 3, 1842. *Works*, I, 182–5.

fall.' Then follows Lincoln's reference to Sarah Rickard, already noted.[1]

Miss Henning recovered, and Speed wrote that their wedding was at hand. Lincoln can advise his friend no more, he answers, since 'you will always hereafter be on ground that I have never occupied.' Lincoln hopes that Speed 'will never again need any comfort from abroad.' But if in his 'excessive pleasure,' Speed does get blue again, let him 'remember, in the depth and even agony of despondency, that very shortly you are to feel well again.' It is probable that Speed's nerves will fail him 'occasionally for a while;' if so 'avoid being idle.' So let Speed act and fear not. If he went through the wedding ceremony without making a scene he is 'safe beyond question, and in two or three months . . . will be the happiest of men.' Lincoln adds this cheering postscript: 'I have been quite a man since you left.'[2]

'Quite a man' Lincoln continued to be for several months. He took up again the part he had played in Springfield life and carried it off worthily. On February 12, 1842, Bowling Green died. He was a Mason and Springfield Lodge Number 4 of that order conducted his funeral in a grove near his cabin. Lincoln was there, and, at Mrs. Green's request, tried to say something at the grave of his old friend. Some who heard him recall that his remarks were very fine and others that he made a sorry failure.[3]

A local condition gave Lincoln new opportunity to mingle with the people and make public speeches. The temperance movement which, as we have seen, had been in progress all over the country, was now in full swing throughout Illinois; and, in Springfield and Sangamon County an extraordinary temperance agitation was in progress. The feeling against excessive drinking, which had shown itself by petitions to the Legislature, had come to a head, and fervent temperance meetings were being held in every township. Lincoln joined this crusade and made

[1] Lincoln to Speed, Feb. 3, 1842. *Works*, i, 185–7.

[2] Same to same, Feb. 13, 1842. *Works*, i, 187–9.

[3] John Barrett to Herndon, Aug. 3, 1866; A. Y. Ellis to Herndon, no date, and G. U. Miles to same, March 23, 1866. Weik MSS.

JOSHUA F. SPEED AND HIS WIFE

temperance speeches in many villages and hamlets.[1] For three or four years an address on temperance had been made, now and then, at the Lyceum. The Washingtonian Society, largely made up of reformed drunkards, had swept over the nation, and the idea of this organization strongly appealed to Lincoln. When a unit of this society was formed in Springfield,[2] he delivered a temperance address before it on Washington's birthday, 1842.

It was a great occasion. From eleven o'clock until noon a procession paraded the streets. At the head marched 'the beautiful company of Sangamo Guards under the command of Captain E. D. Baker.' An 'immense crowd' gathered at the Second Presbyterian Church where the exercises were held. Brightly shone the sun on that joyous day and loud rang the songs of temperance. So 'delighted' was the audience with the singing, that 'several pieces were a second time called for and repeated.' [3] Finally, soon after twelve o'clock, Lincoln rose and addressed the audience that packed the church.[4]

---

[1] Unsigned fragment from Pawnee, Sangamon County, no date. Weik MSS.

[2] The Springfield lodge was organized Dec. 20, 1841, with William D. Herndon as President, James H. Matheny, Corresponding Secretary, and William W. Pease, Secretary *Pro tem.* The Society held regular meetings in the 2nd Presbyterian Church. *Illinois State Register*, Dec. 31, 1841.

The first Washingtonian Society was formed in a bar room in Baltimore, April 5, 1840, by six men who had met there every night for years to drink together. At this meeting, after imbibing as usual, they resolved to stop the habit and then and there organized the Society, and wrote and signed the Washingtonian pledge.

They then went among their convivial friends 'and persuaded them in the spirit of kindness to abandon strong drink.' The Society grew rapidly and within two years had lodges all over the country. The central idea of it was that the drinker was not criminal but unfortunate and, therefore, that 'the substitution of *personal experience* for addresses and lectures' was the best method of reforming him. The Society refused to be identified with any political or religious agitation. *Foundation, etc. of the Washingtonian Society of Baltimore,* etc. By a member of the Society, Baltimore, 1842.

[3] A vest pocket song-book, the *Washingtonian Tee-Totalers' Minstrel*, contained forty-eight temperance songs, set to popular airs. Examples of those sung at temperance rallies, such as that addressed by Lincoln, are:

THE TEMPERANCE RALLY

'We have entered the field and are ready to fight
Against the rum demon from morning 'till night,' etc.

COME TO THE TEMPERANCE HALL

'Come to the Temperance Hall
The Pledge of Freedom sign —

---

[4] *Sangamo Journal*, Feb. 25, 1842.

In the sounding rhetoric of frontier oratory, he describes the progress of temperance. The cause of this quick and marvellous advance is plain. 'The warfare heretofore waged against the demon intemperance has ... been erroneous.' Speakers and tactics 'have not been the most proper. . . . Preachers, lawyers, and hired agents' are not the best advocates of temperance. 'Between these and the mass of mankind there is a want of approachability. . . . They are supposed to have no sympathy of feeling or interest with those very persons whom it is their object to convince and persuade.' How different the appeal of the reformed drunkard! 'There is a logic and an eloquence in it that few with human feelings can resist.' Not to him can be applied the objections made to preachers, lawyers, and speakers for pay — nobody can doubt his sincerity. It is 'this new class of champions' who are carrying the cause to victory.

Even 'had the old-school champions themselves been of the most wise selecting,' were their methods the 'most judicious? . . . When the dram-seller and drinker were incessantly told — not in accents of entreaty or persuasion, diffidently addressed by erring man to an erring brother, but in the thundering tones of anathema and denunciation with which the lordly judge often groups together all the crimes of the felon's life, and thrusts them in his face just ere he passes sentence of death upon him — that they were the authors of all the vice and misery and crime in the land; that they were the manufacturers and material of all the thieves and robbers and murderers that infest the earth; that their houses were the workshops of the devil; and that their

---

Come, banish Alcohol,
Rum, brandy, beer and wine,' etc.

TO PURE COLD WATER THEY COME

'What means this great commotion, motion, motion,
  The Country through?
Why 'tis the drunkards waking up
  To life anew and temperance too,
Why 'tis the drunkards waking up
  To life anew and temperance too
To pure cold water they come, come, come
  To leave their rum
To clear, cold water they come.'

persons should be shunned by all the good and virtuous, as moral pestilences — I say, when they were told all this, and in this way, it is not wonderful that they were slow, very slow, to acknowledge the truth of such denunciations, and to join the ranks of their denouncers in a hue and cry against themselves.

'To have expected them to do otherwise than they did . . . was to expect a reversal of human nature, which is God's decree and can never be reversed.'

To influence the conduct of men, 'persuasion, kind, unassuming persuasion, should ever be adopted. . . . "A drop of honey catches more flies than a gallon of gall."' So, if you would win a man to your cause, 'first convince him that you are his sincere friend.' But 'assume to dictate to his judgment, or to command his action, or to mark him as one to be shunned and despised, and he will retreat within himself, close all the avenues to his head and his heart; and though your cause be naked truth itself, transformed to the heaviest lance, harder than steel, and sharper than steel can be made, and though you throw it with more than herculean force and precision, you shall be no more able to pierce him than to penetrate the hard shell of a tortoise with a rye straw. Such is man, and so must he be understood by those who would lead him, even to his own best interests.'

Nobody knows when 'the use of intoxicating liquors commenced; nor is it important to know. It is sufficient that to all of us who now inhabit the world, the practice of drinking them is just as old as the world itself. . . . When all such of us . . . first opened our eyes upon the stage of existence, we found intoxicating liquor recognized by everybody, used by everybody, and repudiated by nobody. It commonly entered into the first draught of the infant and the last draught of the dying man.

'From the sideboard of the parson down to the ragged pocket of the houseless loafer, it was constantly found. Physicians prescribed it in this, that, and the other disease; government provided it for soldiers and sailors; and to have a rolling or raising, a husking or "hoedown," anywhere about without it was positively insufferable. So, too, it was everywhere a respectable article of manufacture and merchandise. . . .

'Wagons drew it from town to town; boats bore it from clime to clime, and the winds wafted it from nation to nation; and merchants bought and sold it, by wholesale and retail, with precisely the same feelings on the part of the seller, buyer, and bystander as are felt at the selling and buying of plows, beef, bacon, or any other of the real necessaries of life. Universal public opinion not only tolerated but recognized and adopted its use.'

Of course, 'even then,' all conceded that 'many were greatly injured by it; but none seemed to think the injury arose from the use of a bad thing, but from the abuse of a very good thing. The victims of it were to be pitied and compassionated, just as are the heirs of consumption and other hereditary diseases. Their failing was treated as a misfortune, and not as a crime, or even as a disgrace.'

The Washingtonians repudiated the idea 'of consigning the habitual drunkard to hopeless ruin. . . . They teach hope to all — despair to none. . . . "While the lamp holds out to burn, The vilest sinner may return."' Witness the result. Everywhere 'the chief of sinners' of yesterday are 'the chief apostles of the cause' to-day. Still everybody has a part to perform. 'Whether or not the world would be vastly benefited by a total and final banishment from it of all intoxicating drinks seems to me not now an open question.'

Let everybody, then, do what he or she can for the good of all. Let the total abstainer sign the pledge as an example and an encouragement to the drinker, who needs all the help he can get. Make drinking unfashionable. Would a man 'go to church some Sunday and sit during the sermon with his wife's bonnet upon his head?' Of course not. But why? It would not be 'irreligious . . . immoral . . . or uncomfortable;' but it would be 'egregiously unfashionable.' So 'let us make it as unfashionable to withhold our names from the temperance cause as for husbands to wear their wives' bonnets to church.'

For a man to refuse to join the Washingtonians, 'a reformed drunkards' society,' because to join would imply that he has been a drunkard when, in fact, he has not, is unchristian. 'In my judgment such of us as have never fallen victims have been spared more by the absence of appetite than from any mental or moral superiority over those who have.

'Indeed, I believe [that] if we take habitual drunkards as a class, their heads and their hearts will bear an advantageous comparison with those of any other class. There seems ever to have been a proneness in the brilliant and warm-blooded to fall into this vice — the demon of intemperance ever seems to have delighted in sucking the blood of genius and of generosity.'

In his peroration, Lincoln gives rein to that lurid rhetoric which spoiled his early speeches and which he was to abandon in maturer years. The temperance revolution will be greater than 'our political revolution of '76,' albeit a companion of that historic advance. On the wings of lilt and fancy he soars high and far; and, finally, pictures the march of temperance reform, 'no orphans starving, no widows weeping. . . . On and on, till every son of earth shall drink in rich fruition the sorrow-quenching draughts of perfect liberty.

'Happy day when — all appetites controlled, all poisons subdued, all matter subjected — mind, all conquering mind, shall live and move, the monarch of the world. Glorious consummation! Hail, fall of fury! Reign of reason, all hail! And when the victory shall be complete, — when there shall be neither a slave nor a drunkard on the earth, — how proud the title of that land which may truly claim to be the birthplace and the cradle of both those revolutions that shall have ended in that victory.'

Without attempting to connect date or name with his theme, Lincoln thus concludes: 'This is the . . . birthday of Washington. . . . Washington is the mightiest name of earth. . . . On that name no eulogy is expected. It cannot be. To add brightness to the sun or glory to the name of Washington is alike impossible. Let none attempt it. In solemn awe pronounce the name, and in its naked deathless splendor leave it shining on.' [1]

Lincoln's speech received various comment. Preachers, temperance speakers, and reformers generally, were angered,[2]

---

[1] *Works*, I, 193-209.

[2] 'I was at the door of the church as the people passed out,' records the faithful Herndon, 'and heard them discussing the speech. . . . "It's a shame," I heard one man say, "that he should be permitted to abuse us so in the house of the Lord." The truth was the [Washingtonian] society was composed mainly of the roughs and drunkards

Washingtonians pleased, everybody interested. The faithful Francis declared in the *Journal* that 'the address, delivered by Mr. Lincoln, in our opinion, was excellent.' [1] The Washingtonians had the speech printed; [2] it was their vindication. Lincoln was not encouraged by the public reception of his effort. When it was published he asked Speed and Fanny to read it 'as an act of charity to me; for,' Lincoln added plaintively, 'I cannot learn that anybody else has read it, or is likely to.' [3]

Three days after he made the speech he wrote to Speed in quick answer to a letter from his friend, received 'this morning,' telling of Speed's marriage. He wishes them more happiness than he can express. He is jealous of them — they will be 'so exclusively concerned for one another' that Lincoln will 'be forgotten entirely.' Speed must remind Fanny of 'that debt she owes me.' He is sorry that Speed is not coming back to Illinois. 'I shall be very lonesome without you.' What a world, how miserably arranged! 'If we have no friends, we have no pleasure; and if we have them, we are sure to lose them, and be doubly pained by the loss.' Lincoln sends 'kind remembrance' to Speed's family and others whom he had met while at Farmington — and 'ask little Eliza Davis if she will ride to town with me if I come there again.' Also 'give Fanny a double reciprocation of all the love she sent me.' [4]

By the same mail Lincoln hurried off another letter to Speed: in ten hours he had 'hardly yet . . . become calm.' The 'forebodings (for which you and I are peculiar) are the worst sort of nonsense.' It is plain that Speed is 'much happier,' or rather, 'less miserable' than he had been. 'Something indescribably horrible and alarming still haunts you?' How absurd. Speed will not say that three months hence. Let Speed's nerves get steady and 'the whole trouble will be over forever.' If Speed

of the town, who had evinced a desire to reform. Many of them were too fresh from the gutter to be taken at once into the society of such people as worshipped at the church where the speech was delivered. . . . The whole thing, I repeat, was damaging to Lincoln, and gave rise to the opposition on the part of the churches which confronted him several years afterwards when he became a candidate against the noted Peter Cartwright for Congress.' Herndon's account. Herndon, ii, 261–2.

[1] *Sangamo Journal*, Feb. 25, 1842.　　[2] *Ib.*
[3] Lincoln to Speed, March 27, 1842. *Works*, i, 214–7.
[4] Same to same, Feb. 25, 1842. *Ib.*, 210–1.

does not achieve 'Elysium' it will not be the fault of 'black eyed Fanny.' The trouble with both Speed and Lincoln is that they 'dream dreams of Elysium far exceeding all that anything earthly can realize. . . . My old father used to have a saying that "If you make a bad bargain, hug it all the tighter."' Even if in marrying Fanny he has made a bad bargain, which is unthinkable, how pleasant in her case to apply that maxim.[1]

Thus, through Speed's marriage and Lincoln's reaction to it, Fate was working out a strange pattern; and, as will appear in a moment, a deft hand was at the shuttle in Springfield. The correspondence between Lincoln and Speed was incessant, and Lincoln wrote letters such as few men have written and such as he never was to write again. He is thrilled 'with joy,' he assures Speed, 'to hear you say you are "far happier than you ever expected to be."' He got more pleasure in the moment it took him to read his friend's letter 'than the total sum of all I have enjoyed since the fatal 1st of January, 1841.'

He would have been entirely happy, since that bleak day, 'but for the never-absent idea that there is one still unhappy whom I have contributed to make so. That still kills my soul. I cannot but reproach myself for even wishing to be happy while she is otherwise.' Mary Todd had gone 'on the railroad cars' to Jacksonville with a merry company and had told people, 'so that I heard of it,' how much she enjoyed the excursion. 'God be praised for that.'

Once more Lincoln makes mysterious reference to Sarah Rickard: 'One thing I can tell you which I know you will be glad to hear, and that is that I have seen Sarah [2] and scrutinized her feelings as well as I could, and am fully convinced that she is far happier now than she has been for the last fifteen months past.'[3]

---

[1] *Works*, 210–3.

[2] Again this name is deleted in Lincoln's *Works*. Original MS. in the Barrett Collection.

[3] Lincoln to Speed, March 27, 1842. *Works*, I, 214–7.

A friend of Speed's in Louisville, one Everett, had worried Lincoln by a stream of letters about a claim which he had put into Logan and Lincoln's hands for collection; and in this letter, Lincoln asks Speed to have Everett take his business elsewhere. 'I am almost out of patience with Mr. Everett's importunity.' Besides, 'it is impossible to collect money on that or any other claim here now' — a fact of first importance in the economic distress then afflicting Illinois.

In spite of his mental distress and morbid brooding which his letters to Speed reveal, Lincoln's facility as an entertainer was not weakened. In a political journey made to capture the Democratic presidential nomination two years later Van Buren reached Illinois during June, 1842. At Rochester, a village six miles from Springfield, his party, which included James Kirke Paulding, Secretary of the Navy in Van Buren's Cabinet, stopped for the night. The leading Democrats of Springfield went to Rochester to greet the former President, taking with them various provisions which the hamlet did not afford. They induced Lincoln to go with them to amuse their distinguished guests from the East with his stories and witty talk. Everybody was in high spirits, Van Buren entering into the fun with the practised cordiality of an experienced candidate and politician. Reminiscence, story, and joke passed round the circle. As usual, Lincoln's anecdotes and quaint remarks were better than those of anybody else and 'he kept the company convulsed with laughter till the small hours of the night. Mr. Van Buren stayed some days in Springfield, and repeatedly said he never spent so agreeable a night in his life.' [1]

After this burst of humor out of sadness, Lincoln again laid bare his heart to Speed, who, it appears, had advised Lincoln to decide one way or another about again engaging himself to marry, and to stick to his decision. Right, agrees Lincoln; 'but before I resolve to do the one thing or the other, I must gain my confidence in my own ability to keep my resolves when they are made. In that ability you know I once prided myself as the only or chief gem of my character; that gem I lost — how and where you know too well.' Lincoln now believes that if Speed had understood Lincoln's 'case at the time' as well as Lincoln understood Speed's case afterward, 'by the aid you would have given me I should have sailed through clear.' But Lincoln has not yet acquired enough confidence in himself, he says, 'to begin that or the like of that again.'

As to his part in Speed's marriage, that was 'fate. . . . I always was superstitious; I believe God made me one of the instruments of bringing your Fanny and you together, which union I

[1] *Lincoln*: Speed, 36; Herndon, ii, 262–4.

have no doubt he had foreordained. Whatever he designs he will do for me yet. "Stand still, and see the salvation of the Lord" is my text just now.' [1] Thus Lincoln expressed, although in a state of tense emotionalism, that fatalism which obsessed him and which we are to behold throughout his life, even in the gravest of crises.

Tranquillity and high spirits had again left Lincoln; once more he found himself in the throes of doubt and misgiving. In his letters to Speed were reflected feelings caused by renewed relations with Mary Todd which the wildest imagination could not have forecast. As we have seen, the big, good-natured editor of the Whig newspaper at Springfield, Simeon Francis, was devoted to Lincoln. It appears that his wife, a woman well over forty and without children of her own, had made herself the motherly guardian to arrange the matrimonial destiny of young people who, as she felt, needed guidance and encouragement. She was the match-maker of Springfield, an expert in the diplomacy of managing doubtful or recalcitrant affections.

This alert and industrious lady undertook to repair the broken engagement between her husband's idol and Miss Todd. With the stealth of discretion, she managed to bring Lincoln and Mary together for a long time without the knowledge of even Mrs. Edwards — 'shrewdly got them together,' as Mary's sister puts it.[2] Not disclosing her purpose, Mrs. Francis asked the young people to come to her house at the same time; [3] and thus brought about the resumption of their relations. In this benevolent enterprise the editor's wife was effectively assisted by 'Doct. Henry who admired and loved Mr. Lincoln.' [4] Thereafter they met frequently in this somewhat clandestine fashion.

Julia Jayne, Mary's close girl friend,[5] was let into the secret,

[1] Lincoln to Speed, July 4, 1842. *Works*, I, 217–9.

[2] Mrs. Edwards's second statement, Sept. 27, 1887. Weik MSS.

[3] 'I always understood that Mrs. Francis was instrumental in bringing about the reconciliation between Mr. Lincoln and Mary Todd, by bringing them together at her house without either knowing that the other was to be there.' Trumbull to Weik, April 17, 1895. Weik MSS.

[4] Mrs. Edwards's second statement, Sept. 27, 1887. Weik MSS.

[5] 'In her young days my sister and she [Mary Todd] were very close friends.' William Jayne to Herndon, Aug. 17, 1887. Weik MSS.

Julia Jayne married Trumbull, and after he was elected to the Senate over Lincoln in 1855, Jayne says, 'Mrs. Lincoln was no longer intimate with Mrs. Trumbull.'

it appears, and sometimes was present when these meetings occurred. Finally the Edwardses learned what was going on. In
spite of our advice, 'all at once we heard that Mr. L. and Mary
had secret meetings at Mr. S. Francis',' Mrs. Edwards relates.
The girl explained the reason for concealment. 'The world —
woman, and man were uncertain and slippery,' she told her
sister; 'it was best to keep the secret courtship from all eyes and
ears.' To Lincoln she said of her letter releasing him from the
engagement, 'that she would hold the question an open one —
that is, that she had not changed her mind, but felt as always.' [1]

Such was the state of his affair of the heart, when Lincoln
wrote Speed the puzzling letters of mingled doubt, resignation,
and hesitant, changing resolve. While the patched-up courtship was in limping progress, an incident came to pass which,
naturally and inevitably, hastened a reëngagement or strengthened it if already accomplished, an incident so weighty in its
effect on Lincoln's development that it may be said to have been
an event.

In February, 1842, the State Bank of Illinois failed, 'carrying
wide-spread ruin all over the State.' Its management had been
unwise and improvident in the extreme, its loans excessive and
hazardous. Its notes scattered all over Illinois amounted to
more than three million dollars, and these State Bank bills
constituted most of the currency of the people. Though they
had been falling in value for a long time, they suddenly became
practically worthless. In June the State Bank at Shawneetown
also went under. Nearly all good money had been driven out of
the State and the people were well-nigh without any medium of
exchange. Trade almost ceased and such commerce as continued was, for a while, carried on largely by barter.[2]

How to keep the State Government itself going became a
serious and immediate problem. The State could borrow no
money because of the bursting of the internal improvement
bubble and the fear of the financial world that Illinois would
repudiate her already heavy indebtedness. The people had
nothing except State Bank bills with which to pay taxes. Obviously the collection of current revenue must be suspended

[1] Mrs. Edwards's first statement. Weik MSS.   [2] Ford, 223.

until the Legislature could devise some means of relief; but there was no law by which this could be done directly.

At the first session of the Legislature after the State Bank of Illinois at Springfield had been chartered, an act was passed anticipating exactly such an emergency as now confronted the State, and enabling the State officers to deal with it. The act 'authorized and required' the Governor, Auditor, and Treasurer, in such a case, to notify the public through the press, that bills of the Springfield institution would not be received for taxes after a specific date named in such published notice.[1] Unfortunately this law did not include the State Bank at Shawneetown; and unless a method could be devised for stopping the collection of taxes, the revenues would be paid in the worthless bills of that institution. Land speculators, in particular, would thus practically escape all taxation.

As directed by this law the three State officers published a proclamation, prohibiting the collectors from receiving the paper of the Springfield Bank, in payment of revenue, from and after the 12th of September;[2] and, still further to protect the interests of the State, collectors were admonished not to receive such notes for more than their current value, and were requested to suspend the further collection of revenue until after the meeting of the Legislature.[3] This second document was addressed to the tax collectors of the various counties and was signed, of course, by the State Auditor of Public Accounts.

James Shields then held that important office.[4] He was

[1] Act Jan. 16, 1836. *Revised Laws of Illinois*, 1839, 580. This remarkable law provided that bills of the State Bank should be received for taxes, etc.; but 'if at any time hereafter, the governor, auditor and treasurer shall be of opinion that there will be danger of loss, by receiving the bills of the State Bank as aforesaid [for taxes, etc.], they are hereby authorized and required, to cause a notice to be published in the newspaper printed by the public printer [the *Illinois State Register*], and all other newspapers printed in the state, prohibiting the further reception of said bills, after a day named in said notice, for the uses and purposes aforesaid; and after the day named in such notice, the said bills shall not be received, until otherwise directed by law.'

[2] The proclamation, dated August 5, was published in the *Sangamo Journal*, Aug. 26, 1842.

[3] Message of Gov. Carlin to the Legislature, Dec. 7, 1842. *House Journal*, Sess. 1842-3, 25.

[4] Shields was first elected by the General Assembly Auditor in 1839 and was re-elected in 1841. *House Journal*, Sess. 1840-1, 270. He received seventy-one votes to fifty-three for Levi Davis. See pp. 286-7, *supra*.

thirty-six years of age, having been born in Altmore, Tyrone County, Ireland, May 6, 1806. His ancestors were soldiers and, as a boy, he learned fencing and drilling as well as a good deal of military science from veterans of the Napoleonic wars. From one of them he also acquired French. Shields had had a stormy and picturesque life. As a youth he was a sailor and experienced a shipwreck; at Quebec he had taught fencing when nineteen years of age; and he served as a soldier in Florida, where he was wounded. He came to Illinois two years after Lincoln, studied law and taught school at Kaskaskia and, as we have seen, was quickly sent to the Legislature, although he was an outspoken Democrat and his district was strongly Whig.[1]

Shields was five feet nine inches in height, slender, active, and alert. He was a good lawyer, energetic, industrious, and very popular. He was witty, keen, determined, and courageous; but his ornate and over-ardent manners made him appear pompous. Perhaps it was for this reason that Lincoln disliked him. Whatever the cause, he detested the bustling young Irishman. As a resourceful and aggressive Democratic politician, Shields was surpassed only by Douglas, to whom from the first he was devotedly attached.[2] Although less talented than Trumbull or McClernand, he was better liked by the people and politically more successful than either. Onstot, who knew him well, testifies that Shields 'was a man of great ability . . . a grand and patriotic man;'[3] and this seems to have been the general opinion, except among the Whig group at Springfield.

Although signed by Shields only, the circular to collectors was, as stated by Governor Carlin, the expression of the judgment of the three State officers. It declared that the proclamation would have included the bills of the Shawneetown bank 'if the law had only invested us [State officers] with such powers. The object of this measure is to suspend the collection of the revenue for the current year . . . until the next Legislature may have an opportunity of acting on the subject.

'Without some such suspension act' most taxes, 'particularly that portion payable by non-resident land owners and large land companies, would be paid to collectors before the meeting of the

[1] Condon, 10–29.   [2] *Ib.*, 41, 43.   [3] Onstot, 32–3.

Legislature,' so that nothing could be done for another year and the General Assembly would be prevented 'from dissolving the degrading connexion now subsisting between the State and a bankrupt institution. . . .

'It is folly to hope for a sound circulation while the government is patronizing a worthless one. To prevent this change from operating oppressively, the Legislature will have it in its power, by the reduction of salaries and the curtailment of all expenses not absolutely indispensable to the existence of government, to make a material reduction in the taxes for the next two years.

'By this means a sound currency can be gradually, though perhaps slowly, introduced without increasing the burdens of the people. The exigency of the present crisis requires a common sacrifice, and if it be wisely and firmly made, both by the people and their agents, a few years will suffice to lift our young State out of its present prostration. Once more I take the liberty of repeating that the object and intention of the present notification is to suspend the collection of the revenue for the year 1842 until the meeting of the Legislature, at which time that body can provide for the payment of taxes in such funds as it may deem advisable, and effect such reduction in the amount of revenue as it may deem practicable.' [1]

Such was the moderate and sensible document that speedily drew upon its author vicious partisan attacks. The situation afforded an opportunity, too good to be lost, for the Whig politicians to make campaign thunder. Once more Lincoln took in hand his anonymous political pen and a letter appeared in the Whig organ purporting to be the plaint and comment of a farmer's wife, 'Rebecca.' The letter, in general, was a restatement of many of Lincoln's arguments in his Sub-treasury speech already reviewed, put in the language of the cabin and the farm. Also the discursiveness of such a character as the imaginary

---

[1] Circular letter dated Aug. 20, 1842, in *Sangamo Journal*, Aug. 26, 1842.

On the same day the *Journal* published a long editorial against the proclamation, assailing Shields particularly. The State officers, it said, were 'highly delighted with Auditor Shields' great and mighty effort, which so far eclipses Tom Carlin's, as to induce the belief . . . that Thomas Carlin and Milton Carpenter had nothing to do with it.'

Rebecca, is imitated to perfection — indeed, the first Rebecca letter comes near to being a work of art.[1]

Oh! the good old Whig days, when the girls spun and knit and sang 'about our cabin.' They are gone, 'and times are getting so hard I shall have to send you a pot of butter instead of the money' to pay for the *Journal*. Rebecca makes fun of Van Buren — 'Mattey — he was such a sweet scented gentleman.' She tells Lincoln's favorite story about the man with patent legs who couldn't stop when he got going.[2] Alas and alack! 'We han't got no national bank — we han't got no good money.' Rebecca doesn't understand such things, but she does know that 'twelve years ago we used to have U.S. Bank money, and it was better than silver.' Also 'there isn't near half as much money in circulation as there was three years ago,' and farm stuff is not worth half as much. Then follows a great deal about the tariff, and the laborer, and the farmer, and prosperity, and hard times, and Jackson's tariff letter is reproduced.

Finally Rebecca gets down to the State Bank and the Democrats. 'A pretty mess they have made of it. . . . This State Bank of Illinois will never become prosperous until the whig party are in power.' And look at the Mormons — 'Democratic pets!'[3] It was terrible. Worse still, 'we heard a few days ago, by a traveller from Quincy,[4] that the Governor was going to send instructions to collectors, not to take anything but gold and silver for taxes. He said that the office-holders wanted gold and silver; and thought that the Governor should . . . force enough out of the farmers to fill their pockets. I hope it ain't so; because we've got no gold.'[5]

The *Journal* published this screed conspicuously with extensive headlines. Soon another 'Rebecca' letter followed, en-

[1] Lincoln's carefully worded statement that he wrote but one letter 'alluding' to Shields, does not exclude the first Rebecca letter, which is plainly Lincoln's work.

[2] In Lincoln's Sub-treasury speech it was a cork leg.

[3] The relations of the Mormons in Illinois to the Democratic Party in that State, and Douglas's part in forming them, are told in Stevens, 339–43, 360–2; *Frontier State: Pease*, 345.

[4] Governor Carlin lived in Quincy.

[5] *Sangamo Journal*, Aug. 19, 1842. All the Rebecca letters purport to have been written from the 'Lost Township,' the first dated Aug. 10, 1842.

closing one from her sister 'who is a very working and reading woman, and who is married to a nice man in the upper end of the timber.' Rebecca's sister says that there is great excitement in her neighborhood, caused by the two proclamations, 'the sum and substance of which was that the People of Illinois must pay specie for their taxes after the 12th September.' When the Proclamations arrived, a 'barn raising' was going on, and a farmer made a speech from a log: 'These men [Governor, Auditor, and Treasurer of State] do not tell us in pursuance of what law, they have proceeded to make this proclamation.... There is no law for this proclamation.'

Then the imaginary farmer singles out Shields for personal attack. 'The greatest curiosity about this matter is the Proclamation of Mr. Auditor Shields.' He is against receiving State Bank paper for taxes, lest 'the State will suffer loss,' [1] and yet says that taxes can be paid in paper of the Shawneetown Bank, which is no better! [2] He says the object of the proclamation is to suspend the collection of the revenue until the Legislature meets; but at the same time gives information by which 'the large landowners and landholders' are enabled to pay their taxes in Shawneetown Bank paper, if they can do so 'before the next Legislature passes a law' against it.

'So, gentlemen, the whole operation of this measure, is to favor the rich land holders — and to grind down the poor poorer.... The whole object is to put hard money into the pockets of these office-holders at the expense of the poor people.' Look at the salaries of these State officers! 'If the scheme is successful it will fill the pockets of the public officers with specie.' Again Shields is specifically assailed and, throughout the second 'Rebecca' letter, his language and purpose are flatly misrepresented. [3]

The entire scheme, says the farmer — 'this plan of securing GOLD FOR OFFICE HOLDERS' — was a trick, undoubtedly arranged before the election; even 'the Mormon votes could not

---

[1] The exact words of the law on the subject.

[2] Shields was bound by the law, which did not apply to the Shawneetown Bank.

[3] All the 'Rebecca' letters must be read in connection with Shields's circular to the tax collectors.

have saved the party.' But now the Democrats are 'saddled on to the people;' and farmers must pay their taxes in gold or silver or 'your stock and your farms will be sold to pay them.' Rebecca's sister tells her that there is great excitement 'in the Kickapoo timber,' and 'you needn't be surprised if at the next presidential election you should see a clean vote for HENRY CLAY here.' [1]

This assault on Shields was fighting talk in that day,[2] but the outraged Auditor said nothing. The lash was to cut him still more cruelly, however. A third Rebecca letter appeared in the *Journal*, the authorship of which Lincoln finally admitted. The satire is devoted almost entirely to Shields. It purports to give a conversation between Rebecca and a neighboring Democratic farmer, 'Jeff.' This Rebecca letter begins: 'I see you printed that long letter I sent you a spell ago — I'm quite encouraged by it, and can't keep from writing again. I think the printing of my letters will be a good thing all round.... So here comes another.'

Rebecca says that she had gone to 'Jeff's' house 'to see if his wife Peggy was as well as mought be expected, and hear what they called the baby.' She found 'Jeff,' the husband, reading a paper and '"mad as the devil, Aunt Becca!" "What about?",' says I; "ain't its hair the right color? None of that nonsense, Jeff — there ain't an honester woman in the Lost Township

---

[1] Second Rebecca, Lost Township letter, *Sangamo Journal*, Sept. 9, 1842.

Lincoln's denial to Shields would seem to include this letter, although it is in the peculiar style and vein of all Lincoln's other Rebecca letters. If Lincoln did not write the second Rebecca letter, it is puzzling to speculate who did write it, since, so far as is known, nobody in Springfield was master of the distinctive style in which all the Rebecca letters, except the last, were written. See p. 348 *n.*, *infra*.

The Whigs were fanning the public irritation, which, at first, was general and severe. Even some Democratic papers, immediately after the proclamation and circular appeared, attacked them. The *Quincy Herald* thought that 'the effect upon the people of the State, and particularly, the farming community, will be ruinous.... Have our State officers calculated the injuries they may inflict upon our unoffending citizens? ... Many ... have been at considerable trouble to get State Bank paper, and lay it by on purpose to pay their taxes.' Has the State paid the Bank what she owes it? If not, 'the proclamation is unjust in the extreme,' etc. *Quincy Herald*, as quoted in *Sangamo Journal*, Sept. 9, 1842.

[2] Duels were then not infrequent. One was fought by two Springfield men, William C. Skinner and W. S. Merservy, on Bloody Island opposite St. Louis in the fall of 1837. *Sangamo Journal*, Nov. 18, 1837. Another duel occurred the year before the Lincoln-Shields affair. *Ib.*, May 29, 1841.

than ——.''' Here Jeff interrupted and said that his anger was
due to the state officer's orders to tax collectors not to take State
Bank paper; this, Jeff said, made the Bank currency which he
had toiled to get 'dead on my hands.' The imaginary farmer
fumes and rages at great length, and finally comes to Shields.

Shields's statement that the purpose of the tax proclamation
was to suspend the collection of the revenue for the current year,
is a lie. 'I say *it — is — a — lie.*' The collectors cannot suspend — their oath of office forbids. 'Is there any thing in the
law requiring them to perjure themselves at the bidding of Jas.
Shields?

'Why, Shields didn't believe that story himself — it was
never meant for the truth. . . . Its a lie, and not a well told one at
that. It grins out like a copper dollar. Shields is a fool as well as
a liar. With him truth is out of the question, and as for getting
a good, bright passable lie out of him, you might as well try to
strike fire from a cake of tallow. I stick to it, it's all an infernal
whig lie!'

It is a Democratic farmer who is talking in this imaginary
conversation; and, to Rebecca's denial that Shields is a Whig,
the Democratic farmer offers this proof that Shields is a Whig:

'Why, his very looks shows it — every thing about him shows
it — if I was deaf and blind I could tell him by the smell. I seed
him when I was down in Springfield last winter' — and the
farmer describes a fair at the Capital attended by the 'grandees'
and 'all the gals about town . . . all the handsome widows, and
married women, finickin' about, trying to look like gals, tied as
tight in the middle, and puffed out at both ends like bundles of
fodder that hadn't been stacked yet, but wanted stackin pretty
bad.' No Democrats were allowed, 'for fear they'd disgust the
ladies, or scare the little gals, or dirty the floor.'

And in this fashionable gathering of the élite of Springfield,
reports Rebecca, the Democratic farmer beheld through the
window 'this same fellow Shields floatin about on the air, without heft or earthly substance, just like a lock of cat-fur where
cats had been fightin.' The farmer then describes Shields's gal-
lantries and pompous manners, his opulent buying of knick-
knacks at the fair, his holding the hands of the girls for 'a

quarter of an hour,' his distress that he could not marry all of them — 'too well I know how much you suffer; but do, *do* remember, it is not my fault that I am *so* handsome and *so* interesting.' If Shields should act in that manner to one of the 'democratic gals in the Lost Township,' she would stick a brass pin in him 'about up to the head.' Yes, most certainly, insists the Democratic farmer, this fellow Shields must be a Whig. Rebecca's letter contains more of the same type of ridicule of the State Auditor.[1] The town roared with laughter. Still Shields said nothing.

In the same issue of the *Journal* the Whig organ printed an editorial, stating that an act of the Legislature, approved February 26, 1839, authorized the receipt for taxes of the paper of the two State banks and that this law repealed, by implication, the act of 1836 under which the State officers were acting. So, said the editorial, there was no authority for the 'pompous proclamations' of Shields and Carlin. 'Let the people turn their taxes in State Bank paper and if the collectors refuse it, let the officers sell property for taxes if they dare. . . . Verily we have a great auditor, possessing the power to make and suspend laws at pleasure.' [2] This editorial was either written or inspired by Lincoln. Still Shields took no action.

Six days later a big meeting of taxpayers was held at the Court House where the policy of the State officers was assailed by Baker and Dr. Henry, and defended by Shields and Ebenezer Peck. The State Auditor said that the purpose of the proclamation was to prevent land speculators from buying State Bank notes at twenty cents on the dollar, and to help establish a sound currency. He charged Henry with inciting rebellion against the State authorities and made 'a most glowing appeal' to his patriotism, to desist. Henry replied that the speculators could buy Shawneetown Bank paper at five cents on the dollar. Peck made 'a most heart-rending appeal' to the Whig politicians to stop their agitation. Excitement was intense. 'LET THEM TRY IT,' exclaimed the Whig paper, in denunciation of the plan of the State officers.[3]

[1] *Sangamo Journal*, Sept. 2, 1842; Herndon, II, 233–40.
[2] *Sangamo Journal*, Sept. 2, 1842.   [3] *Ib.*, Sept. 9, 1842.

In the same issue of the *Journal* containing the above account appeared a fourth Rebecca letter. It was crude and clumsy, and held Shields's physical courage up to scorn. This last Rebecca letter was the work of Mary Todd and Julia Jayne. While the anonymous assaults on the State Auditor had been appearing in the Whig paper, Lincoln was meeting the two girls at the house of the editor. They thought the Rebecca letters very funny and, with Lincoln's consent, produced the final screed of the series, in which Rebecca appears as a widow.

When Rebecca learned, runs the Todd-Jayne impertinence, that Shields was 'threatenin' to take personal satisfaction of the writer I was so skart that I tho't I should quill-wheel right where I was.' Rebecca will apologize; and as to '*personal* satisfaction, let him only come here, and he may squeeze my hand. . . . If that ain't personal satisfaction, I can only say that he is the fust man that was not satisfied with squeezin my hand.' Or Rebecca will compromise by marrying Shields, although she has long 'expected to die a widow.' Rebecca is abashed, but 'wouldn't he — maybe sorter let the old grudge drap if I was to consent to be — be — h-i-s w-i-f-e?'

Still, if Shields must fight, says Rebecca, 'Jeff tells me the way these fire-eaters do is to give the challenged party choice of weapons, etc., which bein the case I'll tell you in confidence that I never fight with any thing but broomsticks or hot water or a shovel full of coals, or some such thing; the former of which being somewhat like a shillalah, may not be very objectional to him. I will give him choice, however, in one thing, and this is whether, when we fight, I shall wear breeches or he petticoats, for I presume that change is sufficient to place us on an equality.' [1]

On the day that this effusion was printed in the *Journal*, Lincoln did so strange a thing that we cannot but connect it with his meetings with Miss Todd at the Francis house. In uncommonly clear, large and bold handwriting, he made a list of all candidates for the Legislature from the time he first ran to his last candidacy, with the votes cast at each election, showing the remarkable increase in his own strength at the polls. This state-

[1] *Sangamo Journal*, Sept. 9, 1842; also Herndon, ii, 240–2.

ment of his ever growing popularity, Lincoln had certified by Noah Matheny, Clerk of the County Commissioners Court, the Clerk's certificate attached by pink silk ribbons, tied in an attractive bow.[1] The elaborate document was undoubtedly presented to Miss Todd as a proof of Lincoln's political strength which, however, was soon to decline sharply.

When the final Rebecca insult appeared, Shields was in Quincy. He had gone there with the State Treasurer immediately after the tax meeting at Springfield to consult Governor Carlin. The result of this conference was a second proclamation which directed tax collectors to accept the paper of both State Banks 'at its specie value,' and declared that the collectors would be held responsible for any deficiency.[2]

On the day of Shields's return to Springfield, the *Journal* printed an atrocious rhyme, announcing that the State Auditor had won 'Rebecca, the widow' and that they were to be married. This jingle of eighteen lines, each worse than the other, signed 'Cathleen,' was also written by the Misses Todd and Jayne.[3] Its coarse ridicule of Shields was unworthy of notice

[1] MS., Sept. 9, 1842. Barrett Collection.

[2] This proclamation, issued Sept. 12, was not published in the *Sangamo Journal* until Sept. 23. It admitted that the act of 1839 made State Bank paper receivable for taxes, as the Whigs contended; but, said the State officers, the law of 1839 did not contemplate that the State should accept Bank paper at more than its current value. In this wise the Whigs were out-manœuvered.

[3] *Sangamo Journal*, Sept. 16, 1842. Also Herndon, II, 242–3.

> 'Ye jews-harps awake! The —— 's won —
> Rebecca the widow has gained Erin's son;
> The pride of the north from the Emerald isle
> Has been woo'd and won by a woman's sweet smile.
> The combat's relinquished, old loves all forgot:
> To the widow he's bound, Oh! bright be his lot!
> In the smiles of the conquest so lately achieved.
> Joyful be his bride, "widow'd modesty" relieved,
> The footsteps of time tread lightly on flowers —
> May the cares of this world ne'er darken their hours.
> But the pleasures of life are fickle and coy
> As the smiles of a maiden, sent off to destroy.
> Happy groom! in sadness far distant from thee
> The FAIR girls dream only of past times of glee
> Enjoyed in thy presence; whilst the *soft blarnied store*
> Will be fondly remembered as relics of yore,
> And hands that in rapture you oft would have prest,
> In prayer will be clasp'd that your lot may be blest.
>
> CATHLEEN.'

by him, but coming directly after Lincoln's savage 'Rebecca' satire and the lampoon of the tormenting girls over the same pseudonym, it unleashed his long restrained wrath.

Shields promptly sent Gen. John D. Whiteside, State Fund Commissioner, to Francis, to demand the name of his anonymous traducer. Finally the Whig editor said that Lincoln was the author of the Rebecca letters. Shields at once sought for Lincoln and learned that he had gone to Tremont to attend court there and expected to be absent several weeks on the circuit. Accompanied by Whiteside, Shields instantly started on horseback after him.[1]

When Merryman and Butler learned that Shields and Whiteside had gone to Tremont, Lincoln's two associates, knowing him to be 'unpracticed' in the weapons and 'diplomacy' of duelling, as Merryman untruthfully asserts, quickly followed, passed Shields and Whiteside during the night, reached Tremont first and told Lincoln 'what was brewing.' He said, relates Merryman, that he was 'wholly opposed to duelling, and would do anything to avoid it that might not degrade him in the estimation of himself and friends,' but would fight before he would submit to 'such *degradation*.' [2]

Unfortunate conference! If his hot-headed friends, who as their own statements make plain wanted a duel to come off, had stayed in Springfield, it is well-nigh certain that Lincoln would have made to Shields the explanation which he afterwards did make. The language of the notes signed by Lincoln is that of Merryman rather than of Lincoln. In fact Merryman appears to have been the combative, if not the malicious influence, throughout this, the most unhappy and dramatic event in Lincoln's life.[3]

---

[1] General Whiteside got his military title as commander in the Black Hawk War. The year before the Lincoln-Shields duel he had been elected Fund Commissioner by the Legislature, and so highly esteemed was he by both political parties that even the Whig organ praised him in an editorial approving his election: 'The public may rely upon his honesty, integrity and devotion to the best interests of the State.' *Sangamo Journal*, Jan. 29, 1841.

[2] E. H. Merryman to Editor *Journal*, Oct. 8, in *Sangamo Journal*, Oct. 14, 1842.

[3] Merryman was a young physician of Springfield, hot-headed, pugnacious and a violent Whig. He took keen interest in military affairs and was a fine swordsman. He was called Captain Merryman as often as he was called Dr. Merryman. Four years

Shields and Whiteside arrived Saturday afternoon, September 17, and Whiteside immediately delivered to Lincoln a note from Shields. He 'had hoped,' wrote Shields, 'to avoid any difficulty with any one in Springfield' while living there as State Auditor, and had tried to conduct himself accordingly. But 'whilst thus abstaining from giving provocation, I have become the object of slander, vituperation, and personal abuse, which, were I capable of submitting to, I would prove myself worthy of the whole of it.' On inquiry for the name of the writer of the offensive articles 'I was informed by the editor . . . that you are the author.' Shields does not know the ground of Lincoln's 'secret hostility' to him, nor will he now inquire; but he does require 'a full, positive, and absolute retraction of all offensive allusions used by you, . . . in relation to my private character and standing as a man, as an apology for the insults conveyed in them. This may prevent consequences which no one will regret more than myself.' [1]

About sundown, says Merryman, Lincoln answered that Shields had acted on Francis's statement that he had written the 'abusive' letters, 'without stopping to enquire whether I really am the author, or to point out what is offensive in them . . . and then [you] proceed to hint at consequences. Now, sir, there is in this so much assumption of facts, and so much of menace as to consequences, that I cannot submit to answer that note any further than I have, and to add, that the consequences to which I suppose you allude, would be matter of as great regret to me as it possibly could to you.' [2]

In short, let Shields go as far as he likes. Lincoln — or Merry-

after the Lincoln-Shields encounter, he removed to Chicago. *Sangamo Journal*, Feb. 10, 1848. Later, in the 50's, he went to California and thence to Costa Rica, where he engaged in mining and died of the yellow fever.

A son, James H. Merryman, was a lieutenant in the revenue service, stationed in California, and in 1863 charges were made against him. Not knowing their nature Lincoln gave a general certificate of his character: 'I only wish to say, he was raised from childhood in the town where I lived, and I remember nothing against him as boy or man. His father, now dead, was a very intimate acquaintance and friend of mine.' *Works*, VIII, 273.

Another son, William F. N. Merryman was with the Walker filibustering expedition, but returned to Springfield.

[1] Shields to Lincoln, Sept. 17, 1842. *Ib.*, I, 232–3.
[2] Lincoln to Shields, Sept. 17, 1842. *Ib.*, 233–4.

man — leaves him no alternative but to back down or fight. Promptly Shields wrote again. Since Lincoln complains that Shields has not asked him if he really did write the Rebecca letters, Shields asks him now. *Is* he the author, particularly of the one printed in the *Journal*, September 2? If not, 'your denial will be sufficient;' otherwise let Lincoln make retraction. Shields adds: 'It is not my intention to menace, but to do myself justice.' [1]

Butler had assured Whiteside, who bore Shields's second note, that Mr. Lincoln could not receive any communication from Mr. Shields unless it were a withdrawal of his first note, or a challenge; but that, if Shields would withdraw his first note, and make a 'proper and gentlemanly request for an explanation,' Butler 'had no doubt one would be given.' So Shields's second note to Lincoln was not delivered, and when, after a day's delay, on Monday morning, September 19, Whiteside brought it to Lincoln, he read it and handed it back, saying that it was not 'consistent with his honor to negotiate for peace with Mr. Shields, unless Mr. Shields would withdraw his former offensive letter.' [2]

'In a very short time Gen. Whiteside called with a note from Mr. Shields, designating Gen. Whiteside as his friend, to which Mr. Lincoln instantly replied designating me as his,' relates Merryman. The two seconds met and, upon the request of Whiteside, agreed to try to compose the quarrel, Merryman stating, however, that Shields's first note must be withdrawn before settlement was possible. This amicable proceeding was kept from the principals, Whiteside declaring that Shields would 'challenge me next, and as soon cut my throat as not,' if he learned of his second's pacific purposes. [3] So Whiteside went to Springfield, riding part of the way in Merryman's and part in Lincoln's buggy. Nothing was said about the duel during the trip. Shields's horse had gone lame and he remained in Tremont. [4]

[1] Shields to Lincoln, Sept. 17, 1842. *Ib.*, 234–5.

[2] Merryman's statement, Oct. 8, in *Sangamo Journal*, Oct. 14, 1842; Herndon, II, 248.

[3] Merryman's statement, Oct. 8, in *Sangamo Journal*, Oct. 14, 1842.

[4] Whiteside's statement, Oct. 3, in *ib.*, Oct. 7, 1842

When the party reached Springfield late Monday night, testifies Merryman, they found that 'the affair had ... got great publicity, ... and that an arrest was probable. To prevent this,' continues Lincoln's second, 'it was agreed by Mr. Lincoln and myself that he should leave early on Tuesday morning — Accordingly he prepared the following instructions for my guide, on a suggestion from Mr. Butler, that he had reason to believe that an attempt would be made by the opposite party to have the matter accommodated.' [1]

Lincoln's 'instructions' were that if Whiteside wanted to 'adjust this affair,' Merryman must say that if Shields would withdraw his first note to Lincoln and, in another note, ask Lincoln whether he wrote 'the articles of which he complains' and ask Lincoln to 'make him gentlemanly satisfaction' if Lincoln should acknowledge authorship, all 'without menace, or dictation as to what that satisfaction shall be,' — if Shields would do this, then Lincoln's second should pledge 'that the following answer shall be given:

'I did write the "Lost Townships" letter which appeared in the *Journal* of the 2d inst[ant], but had no participation in any form, in any other article alluding to you.[2] I wrote that, wholly for political effect. I had no intention of injuring your personal or private character or standing as a man or a gentleman; and I did not then think, and do not now think that that article could produce or has produced that effect against you; and had I anticipated such an effect I would have forborne to write it. And I will add that your conduct toward me, so far as I knew, had always been gentlemanly; and that I had no personal pique against you, and no cause for any.

'If this should be done, I leave it with you [Merryman] to arrange what shall and what shall not be published.

[1] Merryman's statement, Oct. 8, in *Sangamo Journal*, Oct. 14, 1842.

[2] This denial excludes the 'Rebecca' letter and 'Cathleen' jingle written by Mary Todd and Julia Jayne; strictly construed, it also excludes the second 'Rebecca' letter. It specifically admits that Lincoln wrote the third 'Rebecca' letter and, by necessary inference, the first 'Rebecca' letter. The authorship of the second letter of the series, is thus left in doubt, and, if Lincoln did not write it, the origin of it becomes an insoluble mystery. It is, of course, possible, that Lincoln was thinking only of the Todd-Jayne letter and 'poem' when he wrote this denial and overlooked the second 'Rebecca' letter.

'If nothing like this is done, the preliminaries of the fight are to be —

'*1st* WEAPONS Cavalry broad swords of the largest size precisely equal in all respects — and such as now used by the cavalry company at Jacksonville.

'*2d* POSITION A plank ten feet long, and from nine to twelve inches broad, to be firmly fixed on edge, on the ground, as the line between us which neither is to pass his foot over upon forfeit of his life. Next a line drawn on the ground on either side of said plank and parallel with it, each at the distance of the whole length of the sword and three feet additional from the plank; and the passing of his own such line by either party during the fight, shall be deemed a surrender of the contest.

'*3d* TIME On Thursday evening at 5 o'clock if you can get it so; but in no case to be at a greater distance of time than Friday evening at 5 o'clock.

'*4th* PLACE Within three miles of Alton, on the opposite side of the river, the particular spot to be agreed on by you.

'Any preliminary details coming within the above rules, you are at liberty to make at your discretion; but you are in no case to swerve from these rules, or to pass beyond their limits.' [1]

Leaving behind him these 'instructions,' Lincoln, early Tuesday morning, September 20, made off to Jacksonville, where the broadswords were to be had, and there awaited his second and friends.

Lincoln had been exercising with the broadsword for some weeks, it appears, and undoubtedly with Albert T. Bledsoe, a graduate of West Point, a practising lawyer in Springfield, and a Whig partisan.[2] 'After this affair between Lincoln and Shields,'

---

[1] Merryman's statement; also *Works*, I, 236–8.

While it is difficult to take these conditions seriously, Lincoln could not have doubted that Shields intended to fight and framed them accordingly. The second condition would provide a 'ring' about ten feet long and twelve feet wide, divided into two equal parts by the plank on edge. Should the principals stand near the outside lines they would be about twelve feet apart; but should Shields retire Lincoln could toe the plank and with his reach pink him with his sword. It may also be assumed that Lincoln expected to overcome Shields by sheer strength and weight of metal.

[2] Albert Taylor Bledsoe was a native of Kentucky and graduated at West Point in the same class with Jefferson Davis. He practised law in Springfield, Ill., having an office adjoining that of Lincoln, but became a priest in the Protestant Episcopal church and later a Methodist preacher. For some years he filled the chair of mathematics and

relates Linder, 'I met Lincoln at the Danville court, and in a walk we took together, seeing him make passes with a stick, such as are made in broadsword exercise, I was induced to ask him why he had selected that weapon with which to fight Shields. He promptly answered in that sharp, ear-splitting voice of his:

'"To tell you the truth, Linder, I did not want to kill Shields, and felt sure that I could disarm him, having had about a month to learn the broadsword exercise; and furthermore, I did not want the d—d fellow to kill me, which I rather think he would have done if we had selected pistols."' [1]

Tuesday forenoon Merryman met Whiteside who again wished to settle the difficulty. Merryman read Lincoln's terms and Shields's second declined to ask his principal to withdraw his note to Lincoln; 'he would as soon think of asking Shields to butt his brains out against a brick wall as to withdraw that paper.' But let the two seconds tell their principals that if they won't 'make the matter up they must fight us,' suggested Whiteside. Merryman refused. 'Such withdrawal [of Shields's first note] having been made indispensable by Mr. Lincoln I cut the matter short as to an adjustment, and proposed to Gen. Whiteside to accept the terms of the fight, which he refused to do until Mr. Shields arrival in town, but agreed, verbally, that Mr. Lincoln's friends should procure the broadswords and take them to the ground.

'In the afternoon,' continues Merryman, 'he came to me saying that some persons were swearing out affidavits to have us arrested, and that he intended to meet Mr. Shields immediately and proceed to the place designated, lamenting, however, that I would not delay the time that he might procure the interference of Gov[ernor] Ford and Gen[eral] Ewing, to mollify Mr. Shields. I told him that an accommodation except upon the terms I mentioned, was out of the question — that to delay the meeting was to facilitate our arrest, and as I was determined

philosophy in the University of Virginia, became assistant Secretary of War in the Confederacy, and after the war editor of the *Southern Review*.

[1] Linder, 66–7. Herndon, however, records another account of Lincoln's feelings made in his presence: 'I did not intend to hurt Shields unless I did so clearly in self-defence. If it had been necessary I could have split him from the crown of his head to the end of his backbone.' Herndon, II, 260.

not to be arrested I should leave town in fifteen minutes. I then pressed his acceptance of the preliminaries, which he disclaimed on the ground that it would interfere with his oath as Fund Commissioner.' [1]

Thus deposes Dr. Merryman. Gen. Whiteside testifies quite differently: To his 'astonishment,' he declares, in view of his 'private understanding' with Merryman that the two seconds should try to smooth out the trouble, and in view of Merryman's knowledge that Shields was still in Tremont, Lincoln's second proposed, about Tuesday noon, that the combatants meet in Missouri opposite Alton 'on the next Thursday.' This sudden proposal 'took me by surprise,' avows Whiteside, especially since it was 'known, that Mr. Shields was left at Tremont.' So Shields's second 'declined agreeing upon the terms until we should meet in Missouri,' because to do so would 'violate the laws of the State.' [2]

Violate the laws it would indeed, for by the Illinois statute duelling was a penitentiary offence.[3] Even the sending of a challenge or verbal agreement to fight, or acting as a second, or carrying a challenge, or verbally delivering a hostile message, was punishable by a heavy fine, and incapacitation to hold any public office thereafter. Shields and Whiteside then occupied two of the most important offices in the State. Technically, neither had yet broken these sweeping laws, although Lincoln and his friends had ignored them. In view of Lincoln's public appeal for observance of law, the fact that he was the offender and his insistence on fighting rather than apologizing unless Shields would withdraw his demand for retraction, it is not easy to determine his state of mind at this time.

Whiteside withdrew the 'pledge of honor' between himself and Merryman to strive for peaceable adjustment, and started for Shields whom he met twenty miles from Springfield. When they reached town they 'learned that Dr. Merryman had left for Missouri. . . . The time and place made it necessary [for us]

---

[1] Merryman's statement.   [2] Whiteside's statement.

[3] Constitution 1818, Sec. 11, Schedule. The Criminal Code (Act July 1, 1833, sec. 43) provided that a duellist should be punished by confinement to labor in the penitentiary, for not less than one or more than five years. *Revised Statutes of Illinois*, 1839, 205.

to start at once,' says Whiteside; so they left at eleven o'clock, travelled all night, took in Gen. William Lee D. Ewing at Hillsborough Wednesday morning and reached Alton Thursday.[1] Merryman, Butler, and Bledsoe had joined him near midnight at Jacksonville, procured broadswords there Wednesday morning, and, at eleven o'clock Thursday forenoon, reached Alton, where Shields and his friends were awaiting them. Lincoln and his party crossed the Mississippi to the duelling ground and Shields and his party 'soon followed.' [2]

John J. Hardin had been attending court at Carrollton, and hearing of the impending duel hastened to Alton with Dr. R. W. English, to stop the fight. These two men now appeared at the Missouri place of combat 'as the mutual personal friends of Messrs. Shields and Lincoln, but without authority from either,' and strove to reconcile the antagonists, by proposing that they submit their differences to four men selected by Hardin and English. At this point the accounts of the two seconds vary as to which of their principals was first to give in, Merryman and Whiteside each obviously wishing to save the face of his principal and his own too. But the upshot was that, without Shields's knowledge, his friends withdrew his note to Lincoln, whose friends then read Lincoln's apology, the duel was called off, and everybody went home.[3]

To prevent misrepresentation of the affair Whiteside published his account of it; whereupon Merryman published his version, in the latter part of which he flagrantly insulted Whiteside. Butler also had said something offensive about Shields, who promptly sent Whiteside 'as his friend' to Butler. Butler construed the action as a challenge and through Merryman, named sunrise next morning as the time, rifles as the weapons, one hundred yards as the distance, Butler's second to give the

---

[1] Whiteside's statement.

[2] Merryman's statement. Rev. George J. Barrett, a Methodist minister of Hillsborough, says that he met Lincoln and several others on the road going to the duelling ground, and that Lincoln helped a farmer, whose wagon had mired, get it out of the mud. Barrett's statement, no date. Weik MSS. The Rev. Mr. Barrett was the father of Oliver R. Barrett of Chicago, collector of Lincolniana.

[3] Statements of Whiteside and Merryman. Shields's friends afterwards claimed that he withdrew his challenge when he learned that Mary Todd and Julia Jayne were the authors of the most offensive of the 'Rebecca' letters. Condon, 49.

word to fire and 'the parties to stand with their right side towards each other,' Butler being left handed. Such a note was criminal and the terms unfair; but Whiteside agreed except as to the place, insisting on Missouri because of the Illinois law.

That night Shields was at a party at the house of Ninian W. Edwards. When he heard of Butler's terms and Whiteside's answer, he wrote to Butler agreeing to all his terms, including time and place; but Butler refused to receive Shields's letter on the ground that 'the matter was closed.' In this interchange, through a note carried by Lincoln, Merryman again insulted Whiteside who asked him to meet him in St. Louis, where a duel could be arranged without violating the Illinois law. Merryman refused, but said he would go to Louisiana, Missouri, 'the most suitable point out of the State.'

Lincoln bore this message to Whiteside who, at first, refused to accept it, because he had business in St. Louis which was as accessible as the place named by Merryman. When Lincoln tried to tell him the contents of Merryman's note, Whiteside thought that his antagonist had named the State of Louisiana. At this Merryman 'hooted,' and the rumor spread that Shields and Whiteside had 'backed out.' So Whiteside sent word that he would accept Merryman's note, agree to his terms including Louisiana, Missouri; but Merryman declined to send his note again, 'because he looked upon the matter as closed.' [1]

Thus ended the most lurid personal incident in Lincoln's entire life, the significance of which in his development is vital. He had received his second lesson in humility. At last his habit, formed in boyhood, of ridiculing other persons through offensive, anonymous writing, had been sternly checked. He had needlessly and heedlessly assailed a brave and honorable man, and the insulted Shields had resented it in the terms and manner of the times. Never did Lincoln forget that experience. Never again did he write an anonymous letter, never again say any insulting word about any human being. From the time of the Shields duel Lincoln was infinitely circumspect and considerate in his dealings with others.

[1] Butler, Shields, Merryman, and Whiteside correspondence and Lincoln's statement. *Sangamo Journal*, Oct. 7, 14, 1842.

As a result of the incident Shields did not suffer socially or politically. Immediately after his return from Alton and while defiances were flying between him and Butler, Whiteside, and Merryman, with Lincoln as messenger, we find Shields a guest at a 'social party' given by the Edwardses; at the very next meeting of the Legislature, which convened in a few weeks, he was reelected to the office of State Auditor by a majority of more than two to one; [1] soon thereafter he was appointed by Governor Ford a Justice of the Supreme Court of Illinois to succeed Douglas, to which office he was elected by the Legislature of 1844–45; [2] and within less than three years, he was made Commissioner of the General Land Office at Washington.[3]

The meetings of Lincoln and Miss Todd, under the supervision of Mrs. Francis, were resumed.[4] Again Lincoln was the victim of doubt, desire, duty, and remorse, blended into a state of mind so hard to analyze. Speed had been married nearly eight months. The week after his affair with Shields and while Springfield was 'in a ferment, and a street fight somewhat anticipated,' Lincoln wrote to Speed, asking 'a close question, "Are you now in feeling as well as judgment glad that you are married as you are?"' . . . Please answer it quickly, as I am impatient to know.' Speed had endured 'immense sufferings' for six months before his marriage — how does he feel now after nearly eight months as 'the husband of a lovely woman?' [5]

Speed assured Lincoln that all was well with him and, thus fortified, Lincoln again proposed to Miss Todd, was accepted, and before his faltering resolution once more broke down they were hastily married, November 4, 1842. 'One thing is plainly

[1] One hundred and four for Shields to forty-four for Levi Davis. *House Journal,* Sess. 1842–3, 201. Jan. 14, 1843.

[2] Feb. 17, 1845. Condon, 50.

[3] Shields resigned the office of Justice of the Supreme Court, April 2, 1845, to take that of General Land Commissioner, Condon, 52; and he resigned from this office a year later to go to the Mexican War as Brigadier General in command of the Illinois regiments. *Ib.,* 55.

[4] Mrs. Francis twice refused to tell Herndon anything about the affair. Mrs. S. Francis to Herndon, Aug. 10, 1887, and Feb. 9, 1888. Weik MSS.

[5] Lincoln to Speed, Oct. 4, 1842. *Works,* I, 238–40. In this letter Lincoln says that Speed had 'heard of my duel with Shields' and gives a hasty summary, from the viewpoint of his friends, of the altercations then going on among Butler, Shields, Whiteside and Merryman, in part of which Lincoln acted as messenger.

JAMES SHIELDS

discernible,' testifies the loyal and devoted Speed; 'if I had not been married and happy — far more happy than I ever expected to be — he would not have married.' [1]

Miss Todd's sister and brother-in-law were taken utterly by surprise. 'The marriage of Mr. L. and Mary was quick and sudden,' says Mrs. Edwards, 'one or two hours notice.' [2] But William Jayne, brother of Julia Jayne, thinks that a few more hours elapsed before the ceremony took place: 'Mrs. Edwards knew nothing of the wedding until the morning of the day of the wedding,' he writes to Herndon.[3] Not until late afternoon did Lincoln ask James H. Matheny to act as his best man, saying, 'Jim, "I shall have to marry that girl."' [4] Beverly Powell also 'stood up' with Lincoln, while Julia Jayne and another young woman acted as bridesmaids.[5]

The Rev. Charles Dresser, minister of the Episcopal Church, performed the ceremony with ring and book — the first time that ritual had ever been observed in Springfield. 'Only a few friends were present.' [6] The groom was not cheerful. 'Lincoln looked and acted as if he were going to the slaughter,' testifies his best man.[7] While dressing at Butler's, where he still boarded, Lincoln was in distress. Butler's son, Speed Butler, seeing Lincoln in his best clothes and blacking his boots, asked where he was going and Lincoln said, 'to hell I reckon.' [8]

A comic incident enlivened the ceremony. Among the guests was 'the Falstaff of the Bench,' Justice Brown of the Supreme Court. The rough and jovial frontier Judge had never seen so formal a wedding and the clergyman in his ministerial robes reading the impressive Episcopal service, greatly interested him. When Dresser told Lincoln to repeat the words that he endowed the bride with all his worldly goods, the old Justice cried out: 'Lord Jesus Christ, God Almighty, Lincoln, the Statute

---

[1] Speed to Herndon, Nov. 30, 1866. Weik MSS.

[2] Mrs. Edwards's first statement. Weik MSS.

[3] Jayne to Herndon, 'Dear Friend,' Aug. 17, 1887. Weik MSS.

[4] Matheny's statement, May 3, 1866. Weik MSS.

[5] Jayne to Herndon, Aug. 17, 1887. Weik MSS.　　　　[6] *Ib.*

[7] Matheny's statement, May 3, 1866. Weik MSS.

[8] Statement of Col. Speed Butler to Hon. Lincoln Dubois and by him to author, June 15, 1924.

fixes all that.' Even the minister nearly broke down with laughter.[1]

Mr. and Mrs. Lincoln went immediately to the Globe Tavern in Adams Street, kept by a widow of the name of Beck, where they lived for more than a year, paying four dollars a week for board and room.[2] Thus began his continuous and life-long tutelage in humility, his instruction in patience and the practice of that supreme virtue, which was to continue without ceasing year after year and decade after decade so long as he lived. For his wife soon unchained that temper which grew more savage through the years, was exhibited in the sight and hearing of many, and which her physician, Dr. Thomas W. Dresser, son of the clergyman who married her, believed to be due to 'a cerebral disease' that finally drove her insane.[3] She speedily became a 'she-wolf,' as Herndon, long afterwards, described her to Weik,[4] without knowing that John Hay, as Secretary to the President, had used a similar but even stronger and more picturesque phrase about Mrs. Lincoln.

The marriage caused comment. In the opinion of Matheny 'it was a policy match all round.' Stuart said the same thing.[5] But Matheny also declares that 'Lincoln often told him . . . that he was driven into the marriage, said it was concocted and planned by the Edwards family;' and that 'Miss Todd . . . told Lincoln that he was in honor bound to marry her.'[6] Herndon, however, in excuse of his hero, exclaims: 'How natural that he should seek by marriage in an influential family to establish strong connections and at the same time foster his political fortunes!'[7]

[1] Judge James H. Matheny to Weik, Aug. 21, 1888. Matheny was Lincoln's best man at the wedding and gives the incident in convincing detail. He was Judge of the Sangamon County Court when he wrote this account to Weik.

One week after his marriage Lincoln wrote to Samuel Marshall: 'Nothing new here, except my marrying, which to me is matter of profound wonder.' MS. in Chicago Historical Society.

[2] Lincoln to Speed, May 18, 1843. *Works*, I, 267-9.

[3] Dresser to Weik, Jan. 3, 1889. Weik MSS. 'While the whole world was finding fault with her temper and disposition, it was clear to me that the trouble was a cerebral disease.' *Ib.*

[4] Herndon to Weik, Jan. 16, 1886. Weik MSS.   [5] Stuart's statement.

[6] Matheny's statement, May 3, 1866. Weik MSS.

[7] Herndon, II, 205.

Lincoln was now a member of the powerful Edwards-Stuart clan; but the political results of the alliance were not encouraging to him. The next step in his plans was an election to Congress. He had, at last, accepted the convention as a method of making party nominations, as a device for party management and discipline. His old New Salem friend, John Bennett, now of Petersburg, where the inhabitants of the Sangamon hamlet had gone when it expired, did not like the convention and the use of it made by the managers. In a letter to Bennett, Lincoln regrets that any Whig 'should longer be against conventions' — that matter was settled. Only 'last Wednesday' night, chosen Whigs from over the State had met at Springfield, 'fully discussed' the matter, decided for conventions, and 'appointed a committee to draft an address to the people of the State' which Bennett will see in the *Journal*. Lincoln wrote this party appeal and assures Bennett that the argument in it for conventions 'is conclusive.' [1]

This Whig address, signed by Lincoln, Logan, and Bledsoe, states the issues on which the Illinois Whigs fought the Presidential campaign of 1844, with Clay as their standard bearer. It declares for a protective tariff as 'indispensably necessary to the prosperity of the American people' and against 'direct taxation for a national revenue.' As to 'protection,' Lincoln first quotes from a letter of Jefferson, one of Jackson, and a speech of Calhoun. The revenue has been smaller than government expenses, and there have been deficits for several years, to meet which 'loan after loan . . . has been resorted to.' The result is 'a new national debt' which is growing with a 'rapidity fearful to contemplate' — like a war debt, in fact. Resort must be had either to direct or tariff taxation. Direct taxation meant collectors everywhere, 'like swarms of Egyptian locusts, devouring every blade of grass and other green thing;' whereas a tariff required 'comparatively few officers' and would be 'paid by the consumers of foreign goods.' Thus the tariff would fall on 'the wealthy and luxurious few, while the substantial and laboring many who live at home, and upon home products, go entirely free. By the direct tax system none can escape.'

[1] Lincoln to Bennett, March 7, 1843. *Works*, i, 259–61.

The Illinois Whigs had gone back to the party doctrine of a National Bank, on the constitutionality of which Lincoln repeats his arguments advanced in his Sub-treasury speech, especially 'the sanction of the Supreme Court, the most enlightened judicial tribunal in the world.' However, why argue about the Bank; 'we could not hope to improve in the least on former discussions of the subject.'

The wisdom of Clay's land bill was 'the clearest imaginable' — more than forty thousand dollars were its product even during the 'almost unparalleled' hard times and 'almost insupportable difficulties' of 1842. Objection that Clay's munificence with the proceeds of public lands would 'impoverish the national treasury' and increase the tariff, meant only that those whose pride and wealth 'prompt them to spurn the manufactures of our country, and to strut in British cloaks and coats, . . . may have to pay a few cents more on the yard for the cloth that makes them. A terrible evil, truly, to the Illinois farmer, who never wore, nor ever expects to wear, a single yard of British goods in his whole life.'

Let 'a Whig candidate for Congress be run in every district, regardless of the chances of success,' as a means of preserving party solidarity. For the same reason the Whigs must accept the 'convention system; . . . while our opponents use it, it is madness in us not to defend ourselves with it.' Experience has proved that. Whigs have fought among themselves and seen 'the spoils chucklingly borne off by the common enemy.' Think of the fable of the bundle of sticks, told by Æsop, 'that great fabulist and philosopher; . . . and he whose wisdom surpasses that of all philosophers has declared that "a house divided against itself cannot stand."' Thus Lincoln uses the words of Jesus to support a Whig party plan. Fifteen years later he applied the same quotation to slave and free States.

Whigs must cheer up. Although beaten in most States, there is no ground for the universal Whig despondency. Look at the 'mighty host' that elected Harrison and Tyler. 'Have they gone over to the enemy?' No; tens of thousands did not vote in the late elections. 'They can come forward and give us the victory again.' Why not? Their principles are as dear as ever, their policies as sound. Everybody knew that if Harrison had lived, all would have been well. His death and Tyler's desertion of Whig policies caused the country's plight and Whig disaster. 'Let us then again come forth in our might, and by a second victory accomplish that which death only prevented in the first.' They could win; 'the Whigs are always a majority of this nation. . . . Let every Whig act as though he knew the result to depend upon his action,' and 'a Whig will be elected President of the United States.' [1] Such was Lincoln's statement to the party organization of the Whig issues in the Presidential campaign of 1844.

Under the national census of 1840 Illinois was given seven representatives in Congress. The State did not define its Congressional districts until March 1, 1843,[2] and the election of representatives was carried over from 1842 to that year. A three-cornered contest arose in the seventh district, of which Springfield was the centre, among Hardin, Lincoln, and Baker. In less than six months after Lincoln's marriage, the Sangamon County Whigs selected delegates to the Congressional Convention, to be held at Pekin, Tazewell County, and to Lincoln's chagrin and disgust, they chose Baker as their candidate. Lincoln agreed to withdraw from the contest. He hastens to tell Speed of his bad luck: 'Baker beat me, and got the delegation instructed to go for him.' Worse still! 'The meeting, in spite of my attempt to decline it, appointed me one of the delegates; so that in getting Baker the nomination I shall be fixed a good deal like a fellow who is made a groomsman to a man that has cut him out and is marrying his own dear "gal."' [3]

Lincoln brooded over his political setback and, as beaten politicians are wont to do, told friends the causes of it. One of these causes grew in his mind and presently led him to make a move of no little effect upon that greater career, then so far in the future that no one could see or suspect it. He was not will-

---

[1] *Works*, I, 243–59.

[2] *Laws of Illinois*, 1843, 71; Pease to author, May 20, 1925.

[3] Domestic matters, even the most important, are now of small concern to Lincoln; for, in answer to Speed's anxious inquiry, the disappointed politician writes but a single sentence: 'About the prospects of your having a namesake at our town, can't say exactly yet.' Lincoln to Speed, March 24, 1843. *Works*, I, 261.

ing to yield to the decision of the Sangamon County Whigs for Baker. A delegate from Menard County,[1] Martin M. Morris, had written that the County was for him, and Lincoln replied that he is glad 'to learn that while the people of Sangamon have cast me off, my old friends of Menard, who have known me longest and best, stick to me.' Lincoln tells his supporter the first of the reasons for his defeat, the strongest, too, and the one that preyed most on his mind. 'It would astonish, if not amuse, the older citizens [of the vicinity of New Salem and Petersburg] to learn that I (a stranger, friendless, uneducated, penniless boy, working on a flatboat at ten dollars per month) have been put down here as the candidate of pride, wealth, and aristocratic family distinction. Yet, so, chiefly, it was.'

Then, too, Baker had all the 'Campbellites,' to whose Church he belonged. Lincoln's wife 'had some relations' with both the Presbyterian and Episcopal churches and 'wherever it would tell,' he was 'set down as either one or the other, while it was everywhere contended that no Christian ought to go for me, because I belonged to no church, was suspected of being a deist, and had talked about fighting a duel.' He does not blame Baker, nor complain of the other 'influences ... though they were very strong ... and levied a tax of considerable per cent upon my strength throughout the religious controversy.'

Morris had written Lincoln that the Menard County Whigs thought they had 'an equal right with Sangamon' in choosing a candidate for Congress. Quite correct, says Lincoln — 'in agreeing to withdraw,' if his own county rejected him, he did so only because, with 'her heavy delegation' against him, he could not be nominated. But he recognizes Menard County's right and thinks 'that if she and Mason [County] act circumspectly, they will in the convention be able so far to enforce their rights as to decide absolutely which one of the candidates shall be successful.'

Strange talk from a delegate instructed for Baker, and talk

[1] Menard County was a part of Sangamon until 1839 when it was cut off and established as a separate county. Lincoln had great influence in Menard because of his six years' residence in New Salem and his intimate acquaintance, formed when surveyor, with most of the settlers of the countryside. Sometimes, however, his candidate was badly beaten, as in the case of the Adams-Henry contest for Probate Judge.

well understood by politicians. But Lincoln takes no chances of misinterpretation, and specifically explains. Hardin, he says, will come into the convention with sixteen votes; so 'you [Menard] and Mason [Counties] having three, can give the victory to either side.'

Moreover, if Menard County instructs for Lincoln, as his friend tells him she will unless he objects, he 'certainly shall not object. That would be too pleasant a compliment for me to tread in the dust. And besides if anything should happen (which, however, is not probable) by which Baker should be thrown out of the fight, I would be at liberty to accept the nomination if I could get it.' However, as a delegate instructed for Baker, Lincoln feels 'bound not to hinder him in any way from getting the nomination. I should despise myself were I to attempt it.' Still it would be 'proper' for Menard to instruct her three delegates for some one as first choice, another as second, and a third as third choice; 'and if in those instructions I were named as the first choice, it would gratify me very much.'

Lincoln gives even more practical details: his friend must personally 'attend to and secure the vote' of Mason County as well as that of Menard, 'if you wish to hold the balance of power.' And 'you should be sure to have men appointed delegates that you know you can safely confide in. If yourself and James Short [1] were appointed from your county, all would be safe; but whether Jim's woman affair a year ago might not be in the way of his appointment is a question. . . . I know him to be as honorable a man as there is in the world. . . . Show this letter to Short; but to no one else, unless it be a very particular friend, who you know will not speak of it.' Lincoln asks Morris to write him again.[2]

Accordingly, Menard's three delegates were instructed to vote for Lincoln in the Tremont Convention. But Lincoln was nervous. He had 'heard it intimated that Baker' was trying to get one or two of Lincoln's delegates, but Lincoln cannot believe it; 'surely Baker would not do the like. As well might

---

[1] Lincoln's close friend who lived on a farm near New Salem.
[2] Lincoln to Morris, March 26, 1843. *Works*, I, 262–5.

Hardin ask me to vote for him in the convention.' And Lincoln will not tolerate popular instructions for Baker. 'Upon the same rule, why might not I fly from the decision against me in Sangamon, and get up instructions to their delegates to go for me? There are at least 1200 Whigs in the county that took no part, and yet I would as soon put my head in the fire as to attempt it.' A nomination got in such a way would destroy harmony; 'honest Whigs ... would not quietly abide such enormities.' No! the report 'cannot be true.' But Morris must let Lincoln know 'how the matter is.' He cautiously adds: 'Don't show or speak of this letter.' [1]

Unless the Menard and Mason County delegates should deadlock the convention and turn to Lincoln, the nomination of his Springfield rival was thus made very difficult and that of Hardin much easier. Lincoln hastily writes to Speed that Hardin will be chosen. So certain of this is Lincoln that he assures Hardin that Sangamon County will support him loyally at the polls, something, as Lincoln supposes, Hardin had doubted. 'We' will try hard to give you 'the very largest majority possible in our county' — because of 'honor and pride,' because 'we love the Whig cause,' because 'we like you personally,' and because 'we wish to convince you that we do not bear that hatred to Morgan county,[2] that you[r] people have so long seemed to imagine.' Already, and 'upon pain of losing a Barbecue' we are planning to 'give you twice as great a majority in this [Sangamon] county as you shall receive in your own. I got up the proposal.' [3] Though Baker had defeated Lincoln in Sangamon County, Hardin was nominated over Baker in the Congressional Convention at Pekin, and was elected to Congress in August, 1843.

Lincoln's letter to Hardin must be read in connection with the fight for the nomination one year later. Obviously he was,

[1] Lincoln to Morris, April 14, 1843. *Works*, I, 265–6.

[2] Hardin's County, of which Jacksonville was the county seat.

[3] Lincoln to Hardin, May 11, 1843. *Works*, I, 266–7.

Lincoln is still tormented by controversies about his duel with Shields, for he adds a postscript asking Hardin to 'measure one of the largest of those swords, we took to Alton, and write me the length of it, from tip of the point to tip of the hilt, in feet and inches, I have a dispute about the length.'

with good political sense, currying favor with the man who he was sure would be nominated and elected in 1843, against the day of Lincoln's need for Hardin's support in 1844. But Lincoln's prophecy and expectation were not fulfilled. Hardin refused to be a candidate to succeed himself, and Baker was made the Whig candidate for Congress and elected in 1844.[1]

Lincoln assures Speed that he will 'support the nominee . . . all will be harmony.' Absorbed in politics he also writes jokingly on family matters. Butler had written to Speed about 'coming events' in Lincoln's family, but Lincoln tells Speed that he 'had not heard one word' concerning it before he got Speed's letter. However, Lincoln has 'so much confidence in the judgment of a Butler on such a subject,' that he rather thinks 'there may be some reality in it. What day does Butler appoint?' And now about the same kind of 'events' in Speed's family.[2] Lincoln had totally forgotten that he had written to Speed six weeks earlier on this very subject.

On August 1, 1843, a son was born and named after Mrs. Lincoln's father Robert Todd. If Lincoln made mention of the event to Speed, for whom he had expected to name the child, no evidence of that mention exists.[3] Not long after the birth of Robert the Lincolns left the Globe Hotel and moved into a one-story frame house at 214 South 4th Street. Here they remained until May, 1844, when they again moved and for the last time.

After his defeat, Lincoln realized that he was growing weaker politically, and Baker stronger. One day he took Matheny for

[1] The Whig organ gave the usual partisan account of Baker's nomination: 'The Whig Congressional Convention . . . unanimously nominated EDWARD D. BAKER of Sangamon County, for Congress. . . . Public opinion has long fixed upon him as the successor of Gen. HARDIN. . . . He will . . . be elected by a large majority. Gen. HARDIN, as we announced many months since, declined a re-election to Congress, where he is now securing "golden opinions" from his constituents. He is, indeed, a most efficient and able member and a real "workey." The resolution adopted by the Convention in reference to Gen. Hardin, will meet with a full response from his Whig friends throughout the District.' *Sangamo Journal*, May 16, 1844.

[2] Lincoln to Speed, May 18, 1843. *Works*, I, 267-9.

[3] Writing on July 26, 1843, Lincoln urges Speed to come with his Fanny for a visit, adding 'Don't fail to come, we are but two as yet.' He also intimates that 'those coming events would be in the way of a visit to the Speeds.' MS. in Barrett Collection.

a stroll in the woods and 'with great emphasis' said to him, having 'reference to L.'s marriage in the Aristocracy, "Jim, I am now and always shall be the same Abe Lincoln that I always was."' [1] For the young Whigs were leaving Lincoln and going to a champion who had not 'married into the aristocracy.' One of them, however, William H. Herndon, stuck to Lincoln, and he was uncommonly strong and influential with the young men of Springfield and Sangamon County. Ardent, convivial, frank, and attractive, he was a good politician and knew everybody. He took up with all 'reforms' from woman suffrage to abolition, which, by now, was gaining appreciable voting strength in Illinois.

Moreover, Herndon had been studying law in the office of Lincoln and Logan and had now begun to practise his profession. He had married in 1840 and, to use his own language, 'had a wife to support, had to push and hustle along [and] was poor.' [2] In his twenty-fifth year, five feet six inches tall, with friendly blue eye, raven hair, and winning smile, pleasing manners, unreserved, impulsive, outspoken, and loquacious, Herndon was an engaging figure when, in the autumn of 1844,[3] Lincoln took him for junior partner in the firm of Lincoln and Herndon, attorneys at law, to be dissolved only by Lincoln's death, twenty-two years afterward. 'Lincoln had his reasons,' cryptically observes Onstot of Lincoln's taking Herndon for a partner. As a business arrangement, it suited Lincoln; as a political partnership, it was well-nigh perfect.

The partnership with the exact and methodical Logan which had lasted three and one half years had been dissolved. That admirable lawyer and excellent business man was a staunch and determined Whig and one of the 'Junto'; but he was interested in the practice of the law rather than in the management of politics. He was careful, exact, and systematic in his office, correspondence and legal work, and had to do most of the labor of the firm.[4] He was not 'popular,' in the political sense of that

---

[1] Matheny's statement, May 3, 1866. Weik MSS. The incident occurred in 1846-7.

[2] Herndon's statement to Weik, no date. Weik MSS.

[3] Lincoln stated that he was partner of Logan from the spring of 1841 to the autumn of 1844. Lincoln to Kinkead, Sept. 13, 1853. *Abraham Lincoln, Defendant:* W. H. Townsend, 21.　　　　[4] Herndon, II, 264-5.

word, while none in Illinois was more of the 'hail-fellow-well-met' variety than was 'Billy' Herndon.

He was attached to Lincoln, too, with a devotion possible only to one of his temperament. As we have seen, this hero worship had begun when, as a little boy, Herndon had with awe beheld Lincoln pilot the *Talisman* up the Sangamon. It had grown while the youth was a clerk in Speed's store and had listened with admiring wonder to Lincoln's talk before the big fireplace; and it had developed still more when Herndon was admitted to the small and select company of young men who met in his employer's bedroom upstairs where he, too, was finally allowed to sleep. So in his junior partner Lincoln had a worshipper also; and the fact that he was even more politically ambitious for his chief, if possible, than was Lincoln himself, was no disadvantage.

Lincoln and Logan had had sharp disputes, as Herndon supposed, about the rival political ambitions of the two partners, although of this there is no evidence. At any rate Herndon was not surprised, he declares, 'one morning, to see Mr. Lincoln come rushing up into my quarters and with more or less agitation tell me he had determined to sever the partnership with Logan.' But the young lawyer 'was surprised' when Lincoln invited him to become his partner. Herndon's youth and inexperience made him hesitate. 'But,' he continues, 'when he remarked in his earnest, honest way, "Billy, I can trust you, if you can trust me," I felt relieved, and accepted the generous proposal.' So the partnership began and continued without a single misunderstanding or dispute.[1]

In May, 1844, Lincoln bought for fifteen hundred dollars a house from the Rev. Charles Dresser,[2] on land on the northeast corner of Jackson and Eighth Streets.[3] There the Lincolns went to live.

In the presidential campaign of 1844, Lincoln was again made presidential elector on the Whig ticket. May 1 of that year, at

[1] Herndon, II, 265-6. While Lincoln and Herndon practised law together for the time stated, the partnership continued after Lincoln's election and until his death.

[2] The Episcopal minister who had married him.

[3] *Works*, I, 269-70. The history of this house has been told by Archie L. Bowen in *Lincoln Centennial Association Papers*, 1925, 17-73.

the Whig National Convention in Baltimore, Clay had been nominated by acclamation. Four weeks later the Democrats had named James K. Polk of Tennessee, an almost unknown man who had not been considered as a presidential possibility. This result was favored by the readoption of the rule requiring two thirds of the delegates to nominate. Van Buren had a majority of the delegates and richly deserved the nomination; but his refusal to endorse the party's demand for the annexation of Texas defeated him. Amid indescribable confusion the Convention was stampeded for the first 'dark horse' ever chosen by a political party in a national campaign.[1]

The Democratic platform declared for the annexation of Texas and the maintenance of American title to the whole of the vast territory of Oregon — in short for expansion — and this became the overshadowing issue of the campaign. The Whigs, generally, were against taking Texas into the Union. Even many of their leaders in the South questioned the wisdom of annexation, and some boldly opposed it. The Whig Convention denounced the Democratic plan, and, during the campaign, Clay shifted his position from open antagonism to mild acquiescence in the westward movement.[2] The Whigs were, at best, sullenly antagonistic to that great folk movement which made the United States a continental Republic.

For the most part the Whigs championed protection, a National Bank, and a 'sound currency;' but popular idolatry of 'Harry of the West' was their chief practical asset. Few men have so appealed to the imagination and hearts of the masses as did Henry Clay. For twenty years he had been the choice of millions, had thrice been a candidate for the Presidency, and always the foremost leader of his party. He had not received the Whig nomination in 1840, and two years before his campaign of 1844, great Whig meetings began to proclaim him as their choice. At a tremendous gathering in Philadelphia, 'there was but one feeling' as to the man to lead the nation back to prosperity and

---

[1] For a succinct and accurate account of the nomination of Polk see *Constitutional and Party Questions:* S. A. Douglas, as reported by Col. J. Madison Cutts, 149–54.

[2] For careful and thorough treatment of the position of the Southern Whigs, see *The Whig Party in the South:* Arthur Charles Cole, 109–18.

honor.[1] The Whig papers printed Clay songs and Whig Glee Clubs sang them lustily.[2]

When the campaign came on the ardor of the Whigs knew no bounds. 'Redeem the Country,' 'restore prosperity' and, louder than all else, 'hurrah for Clay,' were the war cries of the Whigs.[3] The Democratic slogans were 'Texas,' 'Oregon,' 'Manifest Destiny,' 'Forward, to the West'; and, above all, that stirring, militant demand 'Fifty-four Forty or Fight' — war rather than to yield to Great Britain any part of the vast domain below that line, every foot of which, the Democrats claimed, belonged by

[1] *Sangamo Journal*, Sept. 16, 1842.

[2] Examples of these are 'Harry of the West,' sung to the tune of 'Hero of the Thames':

> 'Then, freeman, rise and rally round
> The statesman ever true;
> And soon his name, with trumpet sound
> Shall wake the welkin blue:
>   And millions, with admiring eyes,
>   Will call him from his rest;
>   With him we'll gain new victories,
>   OUR HENRY OF THE WEST!'
> > > *Sangamo Journal*, Sept. 30, 1842.

> 'Then pass this honored name around,
>   Till echoes catch your thunder,
> The universal glad rebound,
>   Shall make the tories wonder!
>   Come one, come all,
>   Let nought appal,
> Brave boys no longer tarry,
>   But stand by him who never quail'd,
>   Our true and gallant Harry;
>   Our true and gallant Harry;
>   But stand by him who never quail'd
>   OUR TRUE AND GALLANT HARRY.'
> > > *Ib.*, Sept. 9, 1842.

[3] The temper and spirit of the Illinois Whigs are illustrated by this later appeal to attend a great Whig rally at Peoria:

'Whigs of Sangamon! Young men, old men — and that rich crop of young whigs now panting to enter the political arena — WON'T YOU BE THERE? Will you not give FOUR DAYS, even at this busy season of the year, to your country? Will you not be there to stimulate by your presence, to fire by your zeal, to warm by your devotion the whigs of other counties, to emulate your untiring, unrelaxing, never ceasing efforts, to redeem our fair State and country from the blighting curse which has followed the reign of Loco Focoism?

'Think of it, brethren! Look about you, arrange your business. Our women will pack up our food for us — our girls will follow us with their eyes and their blessings — our boys will keep shop, will plough our corn, will see to our stock — nothing shall be neglected while WE DEVOTE FOUR DAYS TO OUR COUNTRY.' *Sangamo Journal*, June 13, 1844.

right to the United States. Indeed, as a practical influence on voters, American title to the Oregon country was quite as strong a political force in the campaign of 1844 as the annexation of Texas. Already long trains of covered wagons were making their way to the far Northwest.

Perplexing cross currents entered into the campaign. The 'native American' movement, later developing into the Know-Nothing party, as it was popularly called, had become formidable. The Democrats denounced it; the Whigs silently welcomed its aid. To ecstatic praise of Clay, Democratic speakers and newspapers replied by vitriolic attacks on his habits and personal life; Clay was a drunkard, they said, a libertine, a duellist. Cartoons represented Quakers sorrowfully telling Clay that they could not vote for him because of his bad morals.

On the dominant issue of territorial expansion the Whigs were vague or silent, the Democrats clear and outspoken. Little was said by either side about slavery. But a section of the Abolitionists would consider nothing else. In August, 1843, the Liberty Party had again nominated James G. Birney for President. Although they violently opposed Texan annexation because they believed and hotly declared that project to be a scheme to extend slavery, and although by the election of Clay the extension of our territory in the Southwest would be postponed if not permanently prevented, the supporters of Birney enabled Polk to carry New York. Clay was once more defeated in his life-long fight for the Presidency, and the annexation of Texas was made certain.[1]

Such, in brief outline, was the campaign in which Lincoln spoke for his party throughout Illinois. No report of what he said exists, but he certainly spoke on the lines of the Whig circular written by him in the fall of 1843. He made three speeches in Indiana, too, one at Gentryville, where he greeted friends of his boyhood and youth and asked after old neighbors.

So came to an end this short but vital period of Lincoln's life; in such fashion began another much like it and almost as im-

[1] For a lucid and compact statement of this campaign see Channing, v, 543–6. Garrison opposed Birney and announced 'No union with slaveholders.'

portant in the evolution of his career. We shall now accompany him through these robust and, to Lincoln, disciplinary years; and, as we go, witness the unfolding of a brilliant part of the epic of the Nation.

CHAPTER VII

CONGRESS AND DECLINE

Is there not treason in the heart that can feel, and poison in the breath that can utter, such sentiments against their own country, when forced to take up arms in self-defence, to repel the invasion of a brutal and perfidious foe? DOUGLAS.

I never was much interested in the Texas question. . . . I never could very clearly see how the annexation would augment the evil of slavery. . . . I hold it to be equally clear that we should never knowingly lend ourselves . . . to prevent that slavery from dying a natural death — to find new places for it to live in, when it cannot longer exist in the old. LINCOLN.

'YOU know that my only argument is that "Turn about is fair play,"' wrote Lincoln to one of his supporters for the Whig nomination for Congress in 1846. In the multitude of letters which he showered upon the Seventh Congressional District when pushing his candidacy the practical politics of rotation in office was the dominant note. Grave issues were before the country, great events impending; but to these he gave no heed. In fact, he appears not to have been interested in them. So 'turn about is fair play,' said Lincoln and he said little else.

From the moment of his defeat by Baker in 1843–44 he worked steadily to win next time. He overlooked no detail that might help him. Upon the assumption that Hardin would not be a candidate, it was obviously political sense for Lincoln to culti-vate the friendship of the brilliant and popular young Whig leader, and this Lincoln did. He wrote to Hardin, while the latter was still in Congress, to 'correct' unfavorable impressions among his constituents. 'Old uncle Thomas Campbell of Spring Creek (Berlin P. O.),' for instance, was disgruntled because Hardin had sent him only uninteresting documents and old newspapers. And Robert W. Canfield would like some fresh documents, too. Lincoln also informed Hardin of the senti-ment of the local Democratic leaders. '*They* are for Texas anyhow,' notwithstanding Van Buren.[1] After such watchful-ness on his behalf, could Hardin do anything else than favor

[1] Lincoln to Hardin, May 21, 1844. *Works*, I, 270–1.

Lincoln when Baker's term should expire — in case he did not run himself?

Among Whig politicians Lincoln labored diligently, writing to them and as he rode the circuit seeing personally the most effective workers in each county. Seemingly all was well, when, upon Hardin's return from Washington in the summer of 1845, talk soon sprang up that he ought to be made the Whig candidate for Governor or for Congress. Lincoln heard that two party newspapers had suggested Hardin for one or the other of those offices. In alarm he wrote to B. F. James, editor of the *Tazewell Whig*, the woeful news and added: 'I wish you would let nothing appear in your paper which may operate against me. You understand.' [1] In the *Journal* Francis had published an editorial on the subject which Lincoln saw before it was printed. 'I chose to let it go as it was, lest it should be suspected that I was attempting to juggle Hardin out of a nomination for Congress by juggling him into one for governor.' Lincoln would not object, he told James, 'if you, and the other papers a little more distant from me, choose to take the same course you have [Hardin for Governor]. . . . Confidential, of course.' [2]

To 'Friend Dummer' he was more explicit. Baker had told Lincoln that 'in accordance with what had long been an understanding between him and me, the track for the next Congressional race was clear to me, so far as he was concerned; and that he would say so publicly in any manner, and at any time, I might desire.' Lincoln wished Dummer, 'if it be consistent with your feelings,' to 'set a few stakes for me.' He 'did not certainly know' but 'strongly suspected' that Hardin wished to run again. He knew of 'no argument to give me a preference over him, unless it be "Turn about is fair play."' Dummer was to see that the Beardstown paper takes no stand that would injure Lincoln's chance, 'unless the conductor really prefers Genl. Hardin, in which case, I suppose it would be fair.' Again, this was 'confidential' and 'please write me in a few days.' [3]

---

[1] Lincoln to James, Nov. 17, 1845. *Works*, I, 278.

[2] Same to same, Nov. 24, 1845. *Ib.*, 278–80.

[3] Lincoln to Dummer, Nov. 18, 1845. MS., Chicago Historical Society. The *Beardstown Gazette* was edited by Sylvester Emmons, a bitter opponent of Mormonism.

Finally, Lincoln's misgivings were justified — Hardin announced his candidacy for Congress. 'All has happened as I then told you I expected it would,' wrote Lincoln to an influential party worker, Dr. Robert Boal. For the sake of peace, Lincoln would 'give way' to Hardin 'if *neither* of us had been to Congress, or, if we *both* had.' But Hardin had had his turn, Baker had had his turn, and now it was Lincoln's turn. 'You know that my only argument is that "turn about is fair play."' Lincoln relied on Boal, he said, for a 'fair shake' in Boal's county, and asked him for the names and addresses of other Whigs to whom Lincoln could write; otherwise 'Hardin, with his old franking list, will have the advantage of me.' [1]

After Hardin became a candidate, letters like this flowed in ever swelling streams from Lincoln's anxious pen. The few that still exist disclose the mind of the vigilant and sensible country politician intent on the practical task of securing delegates. In a doubtful county, he wrote to 'three or four of the most active Whigs in each precinct;' he made a quiet trip through parts of the district; he urged trustworthy friends to be up and doing — 'let no opportunity of making a mark escape.' [2]

The fight for delegates became so spirited and factional feeling so strong that, about the middle of January, 1846, Hardin proposed to Lincoln that they submit the choice of a candidate to the Whig voters at a party election to be held on the same day in each precinct of the District, both Lincoln and Hardin to make a public pledge that neither would go into any county but his own 'to electioneer,' or allow his friends to do so. 'The object of this being to prevent excitement . . . and leave voters . . . to their unbiased choice.' [3]

[1] Lincoln to Boal, Jan. 7, 1846. *Works*, I, 280–1.

[2] Lincoln to James, Jan. 14, 1846. *Ib.*, 282–4. And see Lincoln to John Bennett, Jan. 15, 16, 1846. *Ib.*, 284–5.

[3] *Sangamo Journal*, Feb. 26, 1846. Hardin's plan, a limited primary, was simple. A handbill printed and circulated by a Whig Central Committee at Springfield, and paid for by the winner, was to inform Whigs of the time and places of voting; the party voters in each precinct were to meet on the day of balloting and select judges of the election and these judges were to send the Central Committee a written statement of the votes cast for each candidate; the Central Committee was to publish the result as soon as all returns were in; 'whoever gets most votes in a county shall be entitled to the vote in that county in the general result made out by the Central Committee.' In determining this 'general result' each County was to have 'the same number [of dele-

Lincoln refused. 'I am entirely satisfied with the old system under which you and Baker were successively nominated and elected to Congress,' he wrote. Nor would he agree that each candidate should stay in his own county. That, said Lincoln, would give Hardin a 'decided advantage,' because he had been in Congress and his name was well known throughout the District.[1]

As soon as he received Hardin's proposal, Lincoln wrote to a friendly Whig editor that the plan would hurt him and was meant to hurt him: so 'let nothing prevent' the immediate publication of 'an article . . . taking strong ground for the old system . . . without seeming to know or suspect that any one desires to change it.'[2] Constantly Lincoln struck the chord of rotation in office — Hardin 'has had a turn and my argument is "Turn about is fair play."'[3] With the effective skill of suggestion, sometimes the more persuasive because indirect, he gave his strongest supporter detailed directions — the date and place of holding the convention, the manner of choosing delegates, who must be instructed and vote as county units, and the like. You understand. Other particulars I leave to you.'[4]

In disgust Hardin at last withdrew from the contest. He gave his reasons in an open letter to the Whigs of the District. Word had got out, he said, that he would run for Governor, but that report was untrue. Equally false was the statement and invalid the argument which had been industriously peddled about, that he had agreed with Baker not to oppose him in 1844 and that, therefore, he ought now to treat Lincoln the same way. 'I deem it an act of justice to myself,' wrote Hardin, 'to state that this report is utterly without foundation. I never made any bargain, or had any understanding, directly or indirectly, with Mr.

gates] allowed in the two last Conventions.' Thus the county strength would be preserved in the selection of a candidate and a heavy majority in any one or two counties would not overcome other counties.

[1] Lincoln to Hardin, Jan. 19, 1846. *Works*, I, 271–4. In Lincoln's *Works* the date of this letter is incorrectly given as Jan. 19, 1845. Hardin's proposal to which it was an answer was not made until the middle of Jan., 1846.

[2] Lincoln did not tell James that Hardin was the author of the plan, saying only that such a 'movement' was 'on foot.' Lincoln to James, Jan. 16, 1846. *Ib.*, 285–6.

[3] Lincoln to N. J. Rockwell, Jan. 21, 1846. *Ib.*, 286.

[4] Lincoln to James, Jan. 27, 1846. *Ib.*, 286–8.

Baker, or any other person, respecting either the last or any future canvass for Congress. Neither Mr. Baker nor any other voter of the District knew I would not be a candidate for reelection [in 1844], until I stated that fact publicly after my election.' [1]

Because of these rumors, declared Hardin, many of his friends had become 'compromitted' [pledged to Lincoln]. Moreover, it was distasteful to go on under the old system and to 'use the activity' employed 'to obtain a nomination in this District.' Also the contest had become such as to arouse 'dissatisfaction which it would be difficult to heal.' With this letter of withdrawal Hardin published his proposal to Lincoln to let the voters select the candidate and Lincoln's refusal.[2]

The Whig organ at Springfield, in an editorial familiar in such party situations, salved the feelings of Hardin and his friends. Hardin had been and still is 'a great favorite with the Whigs in the District;' but many did not expect him to be a candidate. If the situation were reversed, Lincoln's most ardent advocates 'would have supported Gen. Hardin quite as warmly.'

On May 1, 1846, the Whig Convention met at Petersburg, as Lincoln had suggested. Herndon was made Secretary and, on motion of Logan, Lincoln was nominated by acclamation. To the smallest item it was Lincoln's convention. The platform declared for the existing protective tariff, condemned the proposed Democratic reduction of it, 'utterly disapproved' the Sub-treasury, urged Whig unity, and declared that Lincoln's ability, integrity, and party services entitled him to the 'cordial and active support' of all Whigs 'in the approaching election.' [3] Such was the political program upon which Lincoln entered the congressional campaign of 1846. Texas, Oregon, expansion, slavery, all vital issues, were carefully avoided.

The Democratic organ sneered at Lincoln's convention. Only

[1] This avowal of Hardin and a like assertion by Logan to Herndon (Logan's first statement, no date. Weik MSS.) dispose of the statement which has persisted to this day, that Hardin, Baker, Lincoln, and Logan entered into an agreement or understanding that each, in turn, should go to Congress.

[2] Hardin, 'To the Voters of the 7th Congressional District, Feb. 16, 1846.' *Sangamo Journal*, Feb. 26, 1846.

[3] *Ib.*, May 7, 1846.

half the counties in the District were represented, declared the *State Register*. And Lincoln! 'Is Lincoln for 54–40, or is he for "compromising" away our Oregon territory to England, as his brother Whigs in Congress . . . appear to be determined on. . . . No shuffling, Mr. Lincoln! Come out, square!'[1] And during the campaign he did 'come out square,' but afterwards was silent. Lincoln had been nominated by 'the rotary system,' said the *State Register* with truth; 'the very worst system for the people, that was ever practiced;' and under that system Logan was to succeed him. Alas! for the Seventh District.[2] Lincoln made the same public statement which Hardin had made, that he would not be a candidate to succeed himself, and, like Hardin, afterward regretted it.

While these trivial incidents of an ordinary contest for a congressional nomination were in progress, black and heavy clouds, which for years had been rolling up from the Southwest, overspread the whole country. War with Mexico was impending and inevitable. In a final effort to adjust peaceable differences between the two countries, President Polk had sent a representative to Mexico, John Slidell, with authority to negotiate an amicable settlement. The government then in power in that country, one of many that rose after the frequent revolutions, refused to receive or listen to him. On hearing of the rebuff to Slidell American troops were sent to the Rio Grande for the protection of the newly annexed State of Texas, and faced a Mexican army on the opposite bank of that river. News of a necessary military manœuver which appeared to be an American retreat disturbed the Whig organ at Springfield. 'We do not like the appearance of Gen. Taylor moving from under the guns of the Mexicans,' exclaimed the *Sangamo Journal* a week before the Whig Convention met and nominated Lincoln for Congress; 'Surely fear could not have induced him to abandon his position.'[3]

In the same issue, this oracle of Illinois Whiggery demanded the adoption of a sterner course toward Mexico than President Polk had pursued. Because of his intimate relations with the

[1] *Illinois State Register*, May 8, 1846.
[2] *Ib.*, May 29, 1846.   [3] *Sangamo Journal*, April 23, 1846.

Sangamo Journal, with which he was always in perfect accord on political matters, its editorial statement is of high importance as showing Lincoln's opinion, at that time, of our trouble with Mexico. The Springfield Whig paper savagely denounced the President's attempt to conciliate Mexico. 'We think that the Mexican authorities have insulted our government, and robbed our people sufficiently, to call for some other policy than that of suing at their feet for our just rights. Nothing but pusillanimity on our part will continue our present policy with Mexico.'[1]

Ten days after Lincoln's nomination the storm broke. Hostilities had already begun and on May 11, 1846, Polk advised Congress of the situation. Immediately Congress declared the existence of a state of war 'by the act of Mexico,' voted ten million dollars and authorized a call for fifty thousand volunteers.[2] Three hundred thousand men responded. 'Mexico or Death,' read placards in New York; a colossal war meeting was held in Philadelphia; the South and West were on fire with eagerness for the conflict. 'For Mexico; fall in!' were the words on a recruiting banner which Lew Wallace displayed in Indianapolis.[3]

Illinois blazed with martial spirit. Her quota was three regiments, each of a thousand men;[4] they were instantly provided[5] and, in addition, thousands begged to be taken.[6] Hardin was

---

[1] *Sangamo Journal*, April 23, 1846. The *Journal* in another editorial continued: 'If she [Mexico] is to keep up a half-war on our frontier; if she is to rob our merchants on the highway of nations, acknowledge her robberies and refuse redress; if these things are to be longer done with impunity, we shall cease to respect ourselves and will most certainly be regarded with contempt by the world. We are disposed to ask of Mexico nothing which is wrong, and if we recognize a just national pride, and design to sustain a high national character, we shall exact of her what is right.'

[2] *Cong. Globe*, 29th Cong. 1st Sess., xv, 791–5; 795–804, May 11–12, 1846.

[3] *The War with Mexico:* Justin H. Smith, I, 194–5. Wallace's company was quickly filled. *Ib.*

[4] *Sangamo Journal*, June 11, 1846.

[5] Among the young men who enlisted and who afterward had notable careers were John A. Logan and Richard J. Oglesby. *Illinois — Historical and Statistical:* John Moses, I, 498.

Indiana was equally enthusiastic and more men volunteered than could be accepted. *Indiana in the Mexican War:* Oran Perry, 30–9.

[6] *Sangamo Journal*, June 25, 1846; Moses, I, 490. The Illinois Whig organ sharply assailed the Governor for refusing to take these eager volunteers. 'They flew to arms at their country's call.' *Sangamo Journal*, July 2, 1846.

the first to enlist, and was made Colonel both by election and appointment. William H. Bissell, who had also served with Lincoln in the Legislature, was placed in command of the Second Illinois Volunteers.[1] Both regiments quickly left for the front.[2] James Shields quitted his office of General Land Commissioner at Washington, was appointed Brigadier-General in charge of the Illinois troops, and was soon at Alton, the military rendezvous of his State.[3]

Without resigning his seat in Congress, Baker implored to be permitted to raise a fourth regiment in Illinois, and was finally allowed to do so. More than enough men to fill it were awaiting him when he reached Springfield;[4] and, with drums rolling and fifes shrilling, he marched out of the State capital at the head of his command, through flag-bedecked streets crowded with cheering thousands, amid the weeping farewells of women, the encouraging God-speeds of men.[5] In overwhelming numbers and with great enthusiasm, the people of Illinois were for the war when it began. Only here and there an Abolitionist shook his head, or a dour old Whig grumbled in his beard. Generally speaking, the opposition of the national Whig leaders to the conflict, which we shall presently review, had not yet penetrated the masses of their party in the youthful, rugged prairie State.

The seeds of ardor for Texas and hatred of Mexico had been sown widely and on fertile soil ten years before the clash of arms on the Rio Grande in 1846. The beginning of the Texan war of Independence in 1836 had been marked by deeds that thrilled all America. Tales of heroism and atrocity were told in every household in the United States; and these inspiring and revolting stories were true. When the call finally came, not a young man flew to the colors, who had not heard in boyhood the dramatic stories of the Alamo, Goliad, San Jacinto.

No explanation is possible of the popular fervor and stirring

---

[1] Moses, I, 490–1.   [2] July 22. *Sangamo Journal*, July 23, 1846.

[3] Moses, I, 490.

[4] *Ib.* Baker made the journey from Washington to Springfield in the unprecedentedly short space of six days. *Sangamo Journal*, June 11, 1846.

[5] *Illinois State Register*, July 3, 1846. In June, 1846, William Walters ceased to be editor of the *State Register*, having volunteered for the war, and Charles H. Lanphier succeeded him

scenes in which Lincoln found himself when a candidate for Congress, unless we bring to mind once more acts in the drama of early Texas and behold again the tragedies fresh in the eyes of American youth who took the field to defend the new State, which, at last, had been made a part of the American Republic.

After a siege of some length, at the Alamo, March 6, 1836, just before dawn, Mexican bugles suddenly blew 'no quarter' and about twenty-four hundred Mexican soldiers stormed the futile walls of the ancient monastery. Within the inadequate defences one hundred and eighty-eight Texans fought silently. In less than thirty minutes all were killed. 'In this war there are no prisoners,' said the Mexican commander, Santa Anna, to one of his officers as he ordered the assault.

Colonel William Barret Travis was among the first to fall. During the siege he had sent through the Mexican cordon an appeal, Homeric in its dauntless spirit. David Crockett, who, throughout desperate days, had cheered his fellow defenders by dropping his rifle now and then and playing his violin, died fighting surrounded by the bodies of assailants he had slain. Col. James Bowie, wounded and in bed with pneumonia, was killed.

A few days after the massacre of the Alamo occurred a tragedy even more terrible. About three hundred and fifty-eight Texan soldiers who had surrendered as prisoners of war were held at Goliad. Many of them were young men from the United States who had gone to Texas to help in her fight for freedom. On a Sunday morning they were taken out of prison with their knapsacks on their backs. Some laughed and sang, for they thought they were going home. Instead, they were lined up on the prairie and shot almost to a man.[1]

Then came San Jacinto. Towards the last of April, 1836, among the oaks, rhododendrons, and giant magnolias on the bluffs of the San Jacinto River, seven hundred or more Texans, under Sam Houston, had gathered. Before them was a force of twelve hundred men under Santa Anna, and other troops of the Mexican Dictator were hastening to reinforce him. When they

[1] *History of Texas:* H. Yoakum, ii, 98–100; *The United States and Mexico,* 1821–1848: George Lockhart Rives, i, 332–5. The day was Palm Sunday, 1836.

should arrive the assault would be ordered and another Alamo and another Goliad added to Santa Anna's reeking laurels. But at three o'clock on a fragrant, sunny afternoon, there sounded from the trees and flowering bushes that hid Houston's men the notes of a single fife, playing 'Will you come to the bower I have shaded for you,' the Texans emerged in a long line, and, shouting 'Remember the Alamo!' 'Remember Goliad!' charged the enemy. The Mexicans, expecting no such promptitude and daring, making camp and cooking food, were taken by surprise. The Texans shot them as they ran. Hundreds were killed, hundreds made prisoner.[1]

Santa Anna was captured. The vengeance maddened Texans demanded his life. Houston refused. The Mexican Dictator was, at that critical and historic hour, not only supreme commander of the Mexican army, but the official and actual head of the centralized military despotism then ruling Mexico with ruthless and bloody hand. He was, in reality and in truth, the Government of Mexico. His army at hand annihilated and himself a prisoner, Santa Anna accepted the situation and signed a compact which was also signed by the President and chief officers of the Republic of Texas.

This document is vital to an understanding of the party conflict in Congress which we are about to witness and the part in it which Lincoln finally took, when he became a member of the national House of Representatives. Santa Anna agreed to withdraw all Mexican soldiers beyond the Rio Grande, and not again to invade the soil of the new-born Republic,[2] and, without intention of fulfilling his promise, in a secret agreement pledged his influence to secure an acknowledgement of the independence of Texas.

Such were the picturesque and thrilling events, lurid descriptions of which all over the United States aroused the passionate sympathy of the American people ten years before the war with Mexico broke out. Every newspaper in the country printed accounts of horror and heroism. In the Vandalia and Springfield papers Lincoln had read these chronicles of disaster and tri-

[1] Rives, I, 346-8; *Texas and the Mexican War:* Stephenson, 83-6.
[2] Yoakum, II, 155-6; Rives, I, 357-8.

umph.[1] Throughout the nation, from Boston to New Orleans, great public meetings were held, money subscribed, volunteers offered [2] in support of Americans battling to free themselves from a tyranny far heavier and infinitely more brutal and unjust than that against which the founders of the American Nation had rebelled. Sympathy for Texas was well-nigh universal, the ardor of Northern States equalling that of Southern States; only in parts of New England was there coolness and in Louisiana outspoken opposition.[3]

Here, then, were the sources of that outburst of martial feeling which Lincoln witnessed with curious and speculative eye, as he began his campaign for election to Congress. The thousands of young men whom he saw march away to distant battlefields and the thousands more who clamored to go, were not the riffraff of cities, nor yet emotional enthusiasts. They were, as Col. Bissell described them, the best Illinois or the country had to offer.[4] That, since childhood, these young volunteers had favored Texan independence; that they sympathized with men

[1] Long narratives of what was happening in Texas were published in the capital of Illinois. *Illinois State Register*, May 6, 1836.

Revolting but accurate accounts of the Alamo were published. *Ib.*, April 22, 1836.

When the news of San Jacinto came, Vandalia was splendidly illuminated for the 'American' victory 'over the tyrant Santa Anna and his mercenary hordes.' A big meeting was held at the State House, speeches made, resolutions adopted. *Ib.*, May 27, 1836.

At Vandalia editorials and petitions from all over the country for recognition of Texan independence by the United States were printed in the *Illinois State Register*, May 27, 1836.

[2] After the Alamo, Kentucky offered more men than were wanted. J. E. Winston, *Proc. Miss. Vall. Hist. Socy.*, VIII, 165. Cincinnati contributed two four-pounders — these were the guns of San Jacinto. Stephenson, 75. Every large city in the North sent men and money. Louisiana gave $7000 and raised two companies; Georgia, two, and Mississippi and Kentucky each sent one company. Rives, I, 364.

The Texans, in their struggle 'against inhuman oppression and tyranny, . . . are entitled to our warmest sympathies, our best wishes, nay more, to our private contributions;' but no troops, no breaking of treaties. *New Orleans Commercial Bulletin*, March 31, 1836, as quoted in Winston.

[3] Winston, 168–9. Whatever backwardness was shown by Louisiana was due to commercial considerations. In New Orleans centered the larger part of the trade with Mexico which the Texan uprising endangered. On the other hand an active Texas committee in that city proved the existence of sympathy for Texas.

[4] 'They were chiefly the well taught youths of our farming communities and our quiet, moral country towns.' Bissell's speech at Belleville, on the return of his regiment, July 28, 1847. Bissell stoutly maintained that they fought for 'the rights and honor' of their country. *Belleville Advocate*, Aug. 12, 1847.

and women of their own blood, who, for a decade, had been fighting to establish and maintain a government like that of their kindred in the United States; that Texas having formally been made part of the American Republic, these youthful soldiers believed that they were upholding American rights and defending American soil; and, above all, that they were taking part, at last, in the conflict of which, as children, they had heard such glowing tales; that they were to avenge the Alamo and Goliad and repeat the glory of San Jacinto — these influences amply account for the dash and spirit of the Illinois volunteers of 1846.

So Lincoln's campaign for Congress began, continued, and was ended, while the war was new and patriotic enthusiasm ran high. Even before the call for troops, news came of battles and victories, of Palo Alto and Resaca de la Palma. As spring ripened into summer, the waiting people heard that Kearny had started on his march to Santa Fé, that American marines had occupied Monterey, California, that Taylor had advanced into Mexico itself.[1] In the Seventh Congressional District of Illinois, as elsewhere throughout the country, the only talk was of the war.

Lincoln's antagonist for Congress was Peter Cartwright, the celebrated Methodist circuit-rider, whom the Democrats had nominated as their candidate soon after the nomination of Lincoln by the Whigs. The *State Register* praised Cartwright as 'a sterling democrat and honest man . . . of upright moral character on which the breath of slander has never been blown.'[2]

While the newspapers of neither party contain any account of speeches by Cartwright or Lincoln, we know that both supported the war and made the appeals usually made by candidates for office in war time. At a great war meeting held in the State House early in June, Lincoln, Governor Ford, Dr. Merryman, and other speakers made 'warm, thrilling and effective' war speeches.[3] No faintest hint did the Whigs of the Seventh

[1] 'News from the Seat of War,' *Sangamo Journal*, May 21; 'Glorious News from the Army,' May 28; 'Letter from an Officer of the Army,' July 9, 1846, etc.

[2] *Illinois State Register*, May 29, 1846.

[3] *Sangamo Journal*, June 4, 1846.

Illinois District, or their candidate, or their newspaper organ then give that they thought the war wrongfully begun.

It is clear, too, that Lincoln and Cartwright were silent on slavery, since their views were identical. Neither believed it to be a sin, but both held it to be an evil; [1] and in Illinois the Whig and Democratic parties alike took no position whatever on the question.

As to Oregon, it is reasonably certain that during the campaign, Lincoln took the extreme Democratic expansionist position. By treaty with Great Britain, Polk had settled the controversy over the title to the immense domain called 'Oregon,' yielding to that power territory upon the retention of which by the United States his party had so militantly insisted during the Presidential contest; and, while Lincoln's campaign for Congress was going on, the Whig organ repeatedly attacked the Administration for that surrender. [2] It was a telling campaign argument, and we may be sure that Lincoln who, it cannot be repeated too often, always was of the same mind with the *Journal*, many of whose editorials he wrote, said on the stump what the newspaper said in its columns — a fact which partly explains the great numbers of Democratic voters who shifted to the Whig candidate. Moreover, in the House Douglas made a brilliant speech on expansion which the Democratic papers published four weeks before the election, [3] and an issue was thus presented which no candidate in the West would have found it wholesome to combat.

In the main, however, the contest was one of personal popularity and party organization, in both of which Lincoln had an immense advantage over the truculent, old Methodist preacher. Many Democrats thought that a minister ought not to run

---

[1] As late as 1856 Cartwright wrote of the anti-slavery agitation: 'This unholy warfare of crimination and recrimination has been carried on with unjustifiable violence, until we are almost brought to a civil war.' *Autobiography: Peter Cartwright*, 414.

[2] Polk no sooner became President, 'than he proposed to give away half of our territory in that quarter [Oregon].' *Sangamo Journal*, July 9, 1846.

The Whig organ declared that many Americans had gone to Oregon under the belief that the United States would maintain 54° 40' as our boundary. *Ib.*, July 23, 1846.

[3] *Illinois State Register*, June 26, 1846. 'There is treason in impeding the march of liberty. Its course is onward.' *Ib.*, July 10.

for political office,[1] the Democratic workers were indifferent, and the organization loose and inefficient. Indeed early in the campaign, the Democratic leaders gave up the contest,[2] and that party cast only forty-two per cent of the total vote.[3]

On the other hand, Lincoln had overcome the opposition to him that sprang up after his marriage, Herndon had again brought into line the young Whigs who had not been able to go to the front,[4] the district was heavily Whig, and the discipline of that party almost perfect. Although many religious Whigs objected to Lincoln because of his reputed infidelity and his irreverent temperance speech, he was elected on August 3, 1846, by the unprecedented majority of fifteen hundred and eleven votes.[5]

The campaign ended, Lincoln resumed his ordinary routine of life, riding the circuit, mingling with the people, telling stories, sometimes writing poetry. More than once after a successful political contest he indulged in the making of verses. Lincoln did this when Hardin withdrew from the fight for the congressional nomination, and again when he had beaten Cartwright at the polls. Andrew Johnston, Whig candidate for Clerk of the House in 1839, was one of Lincoln's co-laborers in the fields of rhyme and three of his compositions, sent to Johnston, have been preserved.

Lincoln had never read Poe's 'Raven,' and when Johnston sent him a parody of that poem, in which experience with a polecat took the place of Poe's melancholy conversation with the dismal bird, Lincoln admitted his ignorance of the original, but declared that there was 'enough in the polecat, self-considered, to afford one several hearty laughs.' Certain stanzas he found 'decidedly funny, particularly where Jeremiah "scrubbed and

---

[1] Herndon, ii, 273.

[2] Statement of Turner R. King to Herndon, no date. Weik MSS. Lincoln afterward had King appointed Register of the Land Office at Springfield.

[3] *Illinois Election Returns:* Pease, 159.

[4] Herndon was exceedingly active for his partner in this campaign. Herndon, ii, 273.

[5] *Ib.*; Pease, 159. Three years earlier, Aug. 7, 1843, Hardin's majority was only 873, and the following year, Aug. 5, 1844, Baker won by but 710 votes. *Ib.*, 141, 148. In Douglas's district the result of the election in 1846 was almost exactly the reverse of that in Lincoln's district — Douglas won by 2765. *Ib.*, 157.

washed, and prayed and fasted.'" Lincoln had sent Johnston a poem, undoubtedly Knox's doleful and commonplace observations on 'Mortality,' better known by its first line and dominant query, 'Oh why should the spirit of mortal be proud?'

Johnston asked who wrote the poem, intimating that Lincoln was the author. No, said Lincoln, he was not. 'I would give all I am worth, and go in debt, to be able to write so fine a piece as I think that is. Neither do I know who is the author. I met it in a straggling form in a newspaper last summer [1845], and I remember to have seen it once before, about fifteen years ago, and this is all I know about it.' Such is Lincoln's account of his acquaintance with the rhyme on resignation in which his thought and feeling were so perfectly expressed that he recited it more frequently than all else combined.[1]

He sent Johnston a poem of his own, inspired by his trip to Gentryville, Indiana, in the Clay campaign. It consists of ten verses on the ancient topics of death, decay, and the comforts of memory; and it was only one of four cantos. Perhaps the best of the verses in this canto, is:

> 'Oh Memory! thou midway world
> 'Twixt earth and paradise,
> Where things decayed and loved ones lost
> In dreamy shadows rise.' [2]

Fortunately, the remaining cantos of this production appear to have been lost.

Soon after his election to Congress, Lincoln again sent Johnston a poem, also the sorry fruit of his campaign visit to Spencer County, Indiana. It relates the paroxysms of madness with which Matthew Gentry, a schoolmate of Lincoln, was seized when a youth, his furious struggles, his lapse into harmless insanity, his crooning of a crazed and mournful song, his imbecile age. By far the most meritorious of these eleven verses on mental dissolution is the last:

> 'Oh death! thou awe-inspiring prince
> That keepst the world in fear,

---

[1] A copy of 'Mortality' in Lincoln's writing is in the Barrett Collection.
[2] Lincoln to Johnston, April 18, 1846. *Works*, I, 288–92.

Why dost thou tear more blest ones hence,
And leave him lingering here?' [1]

Lincoln intimated that he would send Johnston another product of his poetic pen entitled, 'A Bear Hunt,' and in due course he did so. It contains twenty-two verses, describing in minute detail the pursuit, by men and dogs, of a bear which had killed a hog — a common but lively incident in the Indiana wilderness when Lincoln lived on Pigeon Creek. Typical of all and better than most of the verses are the opening lines:

'A wild bear chase didst never see?
Then hast thou lived in vain —
Thy richest bump of glorious glee
Liest desert in thy brain.

When first my father settled here,
'Twas then the frontier line;
The panther's scream filled night with fear
And bears preyed on the swine.' [2]

Lincoln was thirty-seven years old when he wrote these 'poems.' Nearly twenty years were to elapse before he produced the Second Inaugural.

After months of mutual silence, Lincoln bethought himself of Speed and wrote his old friend. 'Being elected to Congress, though I am very grateful to our friends for having done it, has not pleased me as much as I expected,' he confessed. It had not, indeed. More than a year was still to elapse before he could take his seat and control patronage; and there were few offices to be distributed among many claimants. Lincoln told Speed about the birth of his second son now eight months old,[3] and also made interesting comment on his first born: 'He is very much such a

[1] Lincoln to Johnston, Sept. 6, 1846. *Works*, 294–7.

[2] *Atlantic Monthly*, cxxxv, 277–9. MS. in J. P. Morgan Library, New York, and letters of Andrew Johnston to Thomas H. Wynne, August 11, 1869, and R. A. Brock to the New York Co-operative Society, March 28, 1905, and to George S. Hellman, Nov. 7, 1905, in support of the genuineness of the MS.

[3] Lincoln to Speed, Oct. 22, 1846. *Works*, I, 297–8.
This child was born March 10, 1846, and christened Edward Baker, after the Congressman. Again Speed was left without the hoped for 'namesake' in Springfield; but he had been in Kentucky for six years and Baker was at hand.

child as Bob was at his age, rather of a longer order. Bob is "short and low," and I expect always will be. He talks very plainly — almost as plainly as anybody. He is quite smart enough. I sometimes fear that he is one of the little rare-ripe sort that are smarter at about five than ever after.'

So the months wore away, the autumn and winter of 1846, and the following spring and early summer. But one unwelcome incident marred Lincoln's contentment: on December 14, the Legislature elected Douglas, then thirty-three years old, a Senator of the United States.[1] Early in July, 1847, Lincoln made his first visit to Chicago.[2] He wore a 'short-waisted, thin swallow-tail coat; a short vest of same material; thin pantaloons, scarcely coming down to his ankles; a straw hat; and a pair of brogans with woolen socks.'[3] He went by the regular stage through the boundless prairies. For four or five miles before the city was reached, the roads were filled by an endless procession of great wagons laden with wheat, each drawn by two yoke of oxen.[4] Sixteen thousand people then lived in Chicago and the bustle of the infant city gave promise of its future dominance.

On July 5, 1847, twenty thousand men from Illinois and other states had assembled there.[5] They had come to attend the great River and Harbor Convention called to protest against President Polk's veto of a bill making appropriation for rivers and harbors,[6] and to strengthen the cause of internal improvements by the national government. It was, said Horace Greeley, the largest meeting that ever had gathered in America. The

---

[1] *House Journal*, Sess. 1846–7, 37. Douglas had made a remarkably brilliant record in the House and his elevation to the Senate marked him as the undisputed leader of his party in Illinois.

[2] *Chicago Daily Journal*, July 6, 1847, as quoted in Fergus Hist. Series No. 18, *Chicago River and Harbor Convention*, 138.

[3] E. B. Washburne in *Reminiscences of Abraham Lincoln*, ed. by Allen Thorndike Rice, 16.

[4] Thurlow Weed in *Albany Journal*, July 14, 1847, Fergus Hist. Series No. 18, 153–4.

[5] Greeley's report in New York *Tribune*, July 17, 1847. *Ib.*, 139. All statements in the text concerning this convention are from the official proceedings and newspaper accounts assembled by Mr. Fergus in his *Chicago River and Harbor Convention*, Fergus Historical Series No. 18. This compilation presents a full and minute account of the origin and proceedings of the convention, as well as all letters and newspaper reports.

[6] Polk's Message, Aug. 3, 1846. *Messages:* Richardson, IV, 460–6.

Eastern men were overwhelmed by the 'vastness of the West,' its 'grandeur,' and the 'ultimate destiny of this continent.' Three or four States each sent over two hundred delegates. Northern Illinois attended 'en masse.' The hotels overflowed and the visitors were lodged in private residences. Great numbers slept and ate on the big steamboats that brought them to Chicago, each of which had quarters for several hundred. Thousands were delegates and nearly all were Whigs. Lincoln was one of three delegates from Sangamon County.

The larger newspapers of the North and West had correspondents on the ground. Greeley himself reported the proceedings for his New York *Tribune*. So did Thurlow Weed, the most adroit politician of his time, for his paper, the *Albany Evening Journal*. Both were delegates to the Convention; and it is to the vivid accounts which these two trained journalists sent to their papers that we are indebted for much of our knowledge of that assemblage, for no stenographers were present.

Before the Convention formally met, a big parade marched through the streets. Despite intense heat, the delegates were in line, those of each State wearing badges of a distinct color or combination of colors. Cannon roared, drums rolled, bands played, flags waved. Military companies, cavalry, artillery, marines, gave brilliancy and spirit to the procession. Chicago's fire department made a prodigious impression. Greeley and Weed were particularly enthusiastic about it. The demonstration was 'a noble, a soul-inspiring spectacle . . . such as the West has never before beheld,' declared the Chicago *Daily Journal*.[1] It was, wrote Greeley, 'truly magnificent.'

On the appointed hour, the Convention assembled beneath a great tent in a public square. Men of national reputation were there. Letters to the Convention from numbers of the leading statesmen of the country were read to the vast throng. Those of Webster and Benton were long and able. Senator Thomas Corwin of Ohio, 'fairly lifted from his seat,' spoke and was greeted with storms of cheers. Edward Bates of St. Louis, who, fourteen years later, was to become Lincoln's first Attorney General, was made chairman of the Convention and closed its proceedings

[1] July 6, 1847.

with a speech of surprising eloquence. Schuyler Colfax of Indiana was one of the secretaries.

David Dudley Field of New York mildly criticised one enthusiastic resolution as too broad, and Lincoln answered in some brief remarks to which nobody seems to have paid much attention. Weed and correspondents of other papers said nothing at all about it, while Greeley merely observed that: 'Hon. Abraham Lincoln, a tall specimen of an Illinoian, just elected to Congress from the only Whig District in the State, was called out, and spoke briefly and happily in reply to Mr. Field.' Long and well-reasoned resolutions were printed in pamphlet form and sent broadcast throughout the Union. Two or three times the project of a railroad to the Pacific was urged, but passed over for the more immediate object of getting from Congress appropriations for river and harbor improvements.

In that colossal assemblage, Lincoln first realized the spirit of the North and West. For the first time in his life, also, he came into contact with the great world and saw and heard, in public assembly, some of the foremost men in the nation. Nothing was said about slavery, and only slight mention was made of the war then raging; but all were for internal improvements, and every man was intent on the need of his state or section for transportation and commerce. The Convention was wholly absorbed in economic problems. Democratic opposition to internal improvements was an important element in the defeat of that party in 1848 which we shall presently consider and which has been ascribed, almost entirely, to popular revulsion against our war with Mexico.

Of this practical effort to advance the material development of the country, Lincoln was not only an interested observer but an active participant. Moreover he heard at the Convention all the arguments for the expediency as well as the constitutionality of internal improvements as a national policy. He often had read those arguments, often had made them; but he listened to them afresh in Chicago during that first week in July, 1847, and witnessed the endorsement of them by tumultuous applause of cheering thousands, as the newspapers described it.

Meanwhile the war continued, but the ardor of Illinois showed signs of cooling. Immediately after the Legislature convened in the winter of 1846–47, stirring resolutions in support of the war were passed by the House without roll-call, apparently by a unanimous vote.[1] Some of the Whigs, however, could not stomach the preamble which asserted that Mexico had begun the war; and thirty-one of them voted against it.[2] But tidings from the front of American advance were unbroken. In March, 1847, the news arrived of the battle of Buena Vista, the desperate fighting, the heavy mortality, the heroic stand of the Mississippi Rifles, commanded by one Jefferson Davis, against a seemingly irresistible charge of masses of Mexican cavalry,[3] the fall of Hardin, instantly killed while withstanding the last desperate onslaught of the Mexican reserves, the reports of the cool and sagacious intrepidity of the Illinois officer.[4]

By July, 1847, the Illinois troops, their terms of enlistment having expired, were returning to their homes after a year of hard marching, hard living, and hard fighting. They met a tumultuous greeting — meetings, bands, speeches, the huzzas of great crowds, the glad welcome of relatives and friends. On July 4, five thousand people gathered at Springfield to cele-

[1] The resolutions declared that the national administration was right in sending American troops 'into our territory on the Rio Grande, when the intolerable braggadocio of the insolent Mexicans, and their concentration of forces for the invasion of our soil, rendered a war inevitable;' the strength of our government had been demonstrated by 'the rush of volunteers from every portion of our extended territory; ... the noble sons of Illinois "had" hurried in crowds to enlist,' and would continue to do so without complaint, 'unless they may complain as they have already done, that many of them are left behind.' *House Journal*, 1st Sess., 1846–7, 25–7.

[2] *Ib.*, 28. The preamble declared that the war had 'been brought on by the most unparalleled system of insult and aggression' by Mexico; that Mexico had refused to discuss the boundary dispute; and that she had wrongfully 'entered our territory and murdered our citizens,' etc., etc. *Ib.*, 25. After having voted for the resolutions which made 'substantially the same statements, it was somewhat' inept for the obstinate Whigs to oppose the preamble — a false move for which they were to pay heavily thereafter.

Two other war resolutions were passed by the House at this session, both urging the Illinois delegation to provide for the money and men requested by the President. *Ib.*, 275.

[3] Davis married a daughter of General Taylor. He was highly praised for refusing to be a candidate for Governor of Mississippi, or for any other office, so long as he was in the military service. *Illinois State Register*, May 14, 1847.

[4] Moses, I, 496. The Democratic organ paid tribute to Hardin's worth. 'Beloved by all who knew him, and without a personal enemy on earth, his fate will cast a gloom, not only over this whole State but throughout the nation.' *Illinois State Register*, April 2, 1847.

brate the day and receive the young veterans.[1] When Bissell's regiment arrived in Belleville, it was met by 'a vast concourse of people.' There was 'martial music, firing of cannon, burning eloquence . . . and tears of gratitude.' [2]

Hardin's men brought back with them the body of their beloved commander which was buried with military honors at Jacksonville,[3] his regimental bugles sounding taps and a squad of his soldiers firing the last salute above his grave. The Constitutional Convention of 1847, then in session at the Capitol, adjourned to attend Hardin's funeral, and for thirty days the members wore crape arm-bands in his memory.[4]

Now for the first time in Illinois hostility to the war was voiced. The pastor of the Second Presbyterian Church at Springfield, Rev. Albert Hale, was one of the clergymen who, in turn, opened with prayer the daily sessions of the Convention. He highly disapproved of the conduct of the returning veterans and in two sermons declared that the young volunteer had become 'a moral pest to society,' denouncing the war as demoralizing and unjust. Next day a resolution was offered in the Constitutional Convention rebuking the preacher and dispensing with his services. It was hastily tabled, another offered, a substitute presented.

For the moment the matter was dropped largely through the skill of a young member of remarkable ability, a war Democrat, who was to become one of the founders of the Republican party and a brilliant Union general in the Civil War, John M.

[1] *Illinois State Register*, July 9, 1847.

[2] *Belleville Advocate*, July 29, 1847.
This meeting was typical of all such assemblages in Illinois. 'Yesterday was one of the proudest days Old St. Clair [County] ever enjoyed. . . . At half past ten, thirteen salutes were fired from the grove, at which time the officers and privates of the 2nd Regiment of Illinois Volunteers, formed in procession, in the public square.' The parade included a brass band, the soldiers, 'the ladies, the Old Settlers, and then in the rear the people en masse,' and all moved under 'the Triumphal Arch' to the grove where a barbecue was given.
Judge Gustave Koerner delivered the speech of welcome and Colonels Bissell and Morrison, 'both men of rare talents . . . and brave as Cæsar,' responded. 'They come home crowned with honor, they and their regiment, and have received the warmest evidences of affection from a grateful people.'
At night the town was 'splendidly illuminated and a balloon was sent off. The streets were filled with people, promenading at a late hour.'

[3] Moses, I, 496.   [4] *Constitutional Debates of 1847*: Arthur Charles Cole, xxviii.

Palmer.[1] When the preacher next appeared in the Convention, however, he was 'grossly insulted and menaced with bodily injury' and the custom of opening the sessions with prayer was discontinued, not to be resumed for several days.[2]

Hale had expressed the views of those, mostly Whigs, as yet in a small minority in Illinois, who were beginning to turn openly against the war; but the real sentiment and spirit of the State were shown when, soon afterwards, the call came for two additional regiments. Again more men responded than could be taken. Many of the soldiers who had returned reënlisted and thousands of volunteers flocked to the colors. Illinois was still for the war.

Despatches from Mexico continued to be ever more encouraging. In the autumn accounts arrived of the taking of Vera Cruz, the advance on the Mexican capital, the battle of Cerro Gordo, where Shields was shot through the lungs when charging a battery. At first the Springfield newspapers announced Shields's death,[3] but later, that, though desperately hurt, he still lived.[4] Battle succeeded battle, victory trod hot upon the heels of victory. Official reports made mention of the feats of minor officers, of the sagacity, composure, and courage of a young captain in the Regular Army, Robert E. Lee, and of a lieutenant, a certain Ulysses S. Grant. A boyish subaltern of twenty, just out of West Point, George B. McClellan, was brevetted as a

---

[1] Palmer offered, as a substitute to the resolutions against Hale, a resolution declaring that freedom of speech and worship were guaranteed by the national Constitution; and that this fact prevented censure of the offending clergyman. The principle was sustained by a vote of one hundred and two to nine; but Hale escaped by the narrow vote of sixty to fifty-four. *Ib.*

[2] *Constitutional Debates:* Cole, 387–9, 457–8, 519.

[3] 'The news of General Shields's death is confirmed. He received his death wound from a grape shot while gallantly leading his brigade to storm the enemy's battery.' *Sangamo Journal,* May 20, 1847.

The Democratic paper had a long editorial account of the supposed death of Shields. The grape shot went through his lungs and came out near the spine. Shields's brigade consisted of the 3rd and 4th Illinois and two Tennessee regiments. *Illinois State Register,* May 14, 1847.

Col. E. D. Baker, of the 4th Ills. Volunteers, immediately took Shields's place as commander of the brigade. The American loss at that point of the battlefield was very heavy. Baker showed great coolness and gallantry. *Sangamo Journal,* May 20, 1847; Moses, I, 498.

[4] *Illinois State Register,* May 21, 1847.

first Lieutenant for gallantry in battle and again as Captain in another desperate encounter.[1]

Lincoln rode the circuit, as usual, that fall; and at Charleston helped to try a case of historical importance. It is of especial interest since he was, at that time, Representative-elect in Congress, was soon to take his seat in the House and to cast confusing votes on the question of slavery — a subject which was then arousing fiery controversy in the National Legislature and throughout the country.

In 1843 Robert Matson of Bourbon County, Kentucky, a young, unmarried man of good family, had bought a large farm in the northeastern part of Coles County, Illinois. He cultivated this farm by slaves brought from Kentucky for that purpose. Each fall, after the crops were gathered and stored, he sent the slaves back to Kentucky, and early in the following spring, replaced them with another lot. This was done to keep within the law that slaves not permanently domiciled in the State, but merely passing through with their owner, could not acquire rights of freedom.

But Matson kept one slave, Anthony Bryant, continually on his farm to act as foreman or overseer. Thus Bryant was in law a free man. He learned to read the Bible and became an exhorter or local preacher in the Methodist Church. In the spring of 1847 Matson, as usual, brought his company of slaves from Kentucky to do the farm labor for that year. Among them was Jane, the wife of Anthony Bryant. She was a bright mulatto and was the reputed daughter of Matson's brother. Her six children accompanied her. Three of them were obviously of white paternity, one girl having blue eyes and long red hair. Only one was certainly the child of Anthony. All were slaves, like their mother, and all but one had no surnames.

Before the time for the return of the slaves to Kentucky in the autumn, Matson's housekeeper, Mary Corbin, became enraged at Jane Bryant and declared that she would have Matson

---

[1] *Mexican War Diary of Gen. George B. McClellan*: William Starr Myers, 4. McClellan declined the captaincy because it would make him out-rank his superior officer. The diary contains remarkably able comment, solid and practical, about the proper transportation of troops and other military problems.

instantly send the slave and her children back to Kentucky to be sold for labor on the plantations in the far South.

In terror Anthony, the husband, went to the near-by village of Oakland and told friends of the desperate situation. Gideon M. Ashmore, who kept the village inn, and a young doctor, Hiram Rutherford, heard Anthony's story, and told him to bring his wife and children that night to Ashmore's tavern. This Anthony did, arriving about midnight. Rutherford and Ashmore had quietly notified other anti-slavery men to be on hand in case of pursuit by Matson.

For several days the owner tried to induce the slaves to return. Finally he made affidavit as required by the law of Illinois and, under a writ by William Gilman, Justice of the Peace, the slaves were taken to Charleston and lodged in jail.[1] A trial lasting two days was held before Gilman, Usher F. Linder appearing for Matson and Orlando B. Ficklin for the negroes. Both lawyers had served with Lincoln in the Legislature. Gilman decided that he had no jurisdiction but that, since the negroes were in Illinois without letters of freedom, they must be turned over to the sheriff to be kept, advertised and disposed of as required by the statute.[2]

The slaves were confined in jail for nearly two months. The

[1] The affidavit, dated Aug. 17, 1847, avers that Matson brought the slaves from Kentucky to Illinois 'by the request of said negroes, or a part thereof ... on a temporary sojourn with the intention of returning to ... Kentucky,' but that said slaves refused to 'return to said lawful service in the said state.' Photostat of original affidavit in possession of author.

[2] This statute was a part of the famous 'Black Laws' of Illinois. It provided that no negro or mulatto should remain in the State without a lawful certificate of freedom; that even with this document, the colored person must give bond for $1,000 that he or she would not become a charge on the county 'as a poor person'; that anyone who should 'harbor' a negro without certificate of freedom and bond should be fined $500; that, if no one claimed the negro, the sheriff should advertise the fact, and sell the labor of the slave for the cost of their keep. *Acts of Illinois.* See p. 163, *supra.*

This order reads:

'State of Illinois, Coles County

'To the Sherrif of Coles county this is to authorise you to take charge of Jane Catharine Mary June Sally Ann and Noah Colored persons which was Brought before me on A charge of being Runway [Runaway] slaves and the propperty of Rob[er]t Matson of Bourbon county Kentucky and After hearing the Evidnc in the caus they ar adjudged as Runway Slaves. According to the Law in Relation to the Runaway Law of the State of Illinois and Safly Keep them untill discharged by A due course of Law. Given under my hand and Seal this 20 day of August 1847. WILLIAM GILMAN *J. P.*' Photostat of original in possession of author.

sheriff filed a claim against Matson for the expense of keeping the negroes. From the beginning excitement was high and as the affair proceeded feeling became dangerously heated. Matson was arrested and convicted for living with Mary Corbin as his mistress. Ashmore and Rutherford applied to the Circuit Court for the release of the slaves on a writ of *habeas corpus.* In retaliation, Matson sued Rutherford for two thousand five hundred dollars damages for having taken his slaves from him.

At this point in the tangled litigation Lincoln comes upon the scene. The time arrived for holding the Circuit Court at Charleston and Lincoln came with the Judges. The litigation had attracted wide and keen interest and Justice Wilson of the Supreme Court accompanied Justice Treat from Springfield to sit with him in the trial. Linder secured Lincoln to assist in prosecuting Matson's case against Rutherford, and Lincoln attested the bond for costs given by friends of Matson in that case.[1]

Dr. Rutherford, who knew Lincoln well, rode to the county seat to employ him in his defence. Their views on slavery were in accord, and besides his friends advised him to secure Lincoln as his lawyer.

'I found him at the tavern sitting on the veranda,' Rutherford relates, 'his chair tilted back against one of the wooden pillars entertaining the bystanders and loungers gathered about the place with one of his irresistible and highly-flavored stories. My head was full of the impending lawsuit and I found it a great test of my patience to await the end of the chapter then in process of narration. Before he could begin another I interrupted and called him aside.

'I told in detail the story of my troubles, reminded him that we had always agreed on the questions of the day, and asked him to represent me at the trial of my case in court.' But Lincoln hesitated. 'He listened attentively,' testifies Rutherford, 'as I recited the facts leading up to the controversy with Matson but I noticed that a peculiarly troubled look came over his face now and then, his eyes appeared to be fixed in the distance be-

[1] Photostat of original in possession of author.

yond me and he shook his head several times as if debating with himself some question of grave import.'

Lincoln replied 'with apparent reluctance,' that he could not defend him, 'because he had already been counseled with in Matson's interest and was therefore under professional obligations to represent the latter unless released.'

Rutherford was angry and said things to Lincoln in a 'bitter tone.' Lincoln tried 'in his plausible way to reconcile me,' narrates the doctor, who, however, would not be appeased. Some hours later Rutherford received word from Lincoln that 'he had sent for the man who had approached him in Matson's behalf [1] and if they came to no more decisive terms than at first he would probably be able to represent me.' Soon another message came from Lincoln, that 'he could now easily and consistently free himself from Matson and was therefore in a position, if I employed him, to conduct my defense.'

But it was too late. The irate young doctor would now have nothing more to do with Lincoln and, instead, employed Charles H. Constable. So Lincoln agreed to appear for Matson as associate of Linder, Matson's original attorney.[2] Ficklin represented Ashmore.

The whole litigation — Matson's suit for damages, the sheriff's claim for the cost of keeping the negroes, the freedom of the slaves — depended upon the decision of the court in the *habeas corpus* proceedings. The courtroom was crowded with spectators. Linder insisted that under the Constitution the owners of slaves 'as well as of other chattels' must be protected in the possession of their property. Ficklin said that the slaves were made free in Illinois by virtue of the Ordinance of 1787 and the Constitution of the State; but the defence relied chiefly upon the holdings of the English Courts. Curiously enough neither Ficklin nor Constable cited the decision of the State Supreme Court in which Lincoln, nearly ten years earlier, had secured the liberty of a girl who had illegally been sold as a slave.[3]

[1] Undoubtedly Linder.

[2] Constable was a native of Maryland and Ficklin of Kentucky. Both were pro-slavery men, yet, in this case, they vigorously defended the slaves and secured their freedom.

[3] This case, David Bailey *vs.* William Cromwell, was tried in the Tazewell Circuit

Lincoln argued weakly, declared hearers, that the sole question was whether the slaves were *in transitu* or were meant to remain permanently on Matson's farm. 'Mr. Lincoln was pitiably weak and half-hearted' in making his argument, recalls a friendly and apologetic listener. And one of the lawyers in the case testifies: 'I remember well how he presented his side of the case. "This then," he explained, "is the point on which the whole case turns; Were these negroes passing over and crossing the State and thus, as the law contemplates, *in transitu* or were they actually located by consent of their master? If only crossing the State that act did not free them but if located even indefinitely by the consent of their owner and master their emancipation logically followed. It is therefore of the highest importance to ascertain the true purpose and intent of Matson in placing these negroes on the Black Grove farm."' [1]

Besides Matson, only one witness, Joseph Dean, a friend of Matson's, had testified that the slave owner did not intend to keep the negroes in Illinois; and Dean, 'an ignorant, worthless fellow,' as he is branded in the narrative from which this sketch is taken, 'was easily and ruthlessly impeached.' But, said Lincoln, when Matson brought the slaves to his farm, 'he declared publicly . . . [that] the settlement was not permanent and no counter statement had ever been made publicly or privately by him.'

All thought that Lincoln's speech was fatal to his client. Seemingly Lincoln thought so too. 'I shall never forget,' relates Ficklin, 'how Lincoln winced when Constable quoted from

Court in the September term, 1839, before Judge William Thomas. A promissory note was given by Bailey for the purchase of a negro girl, sold by Cromwell to Bailey, and represented, at the time of purchase, to be a slave and servant. Cromwell was to produce the necessary papers and indenture proving the girl a slave, bound to servitude under the laws of Illinois, but the papers were never produced. The girl asserted her freedom and remained with Bailey only some six months. Suit was brought on the promissory note. The lower court decided against Bailey and the case was carried to the Supreme Court, Lincoln representing Bailey, and Logan the administrators of Cromwell's estate. It was argued in the July term, 1841.

Judge Breese wrote the opinion of the Court which stated that the 'girl being free, and asserting her freedom in the only modes she could . . . could not be the subject of a sale, and no right to her services would pass by such sale.' The note, therefore, was illegal and no recovery could be had upon it. 3 Scammon Ill. Repts., 71-3.

[1] The name of the region where Matson's farm was situated.

Curran's defense of Rowan.[1] . . . Even Linder's trenchant wit and fervid eloquence — and no man more completely moved others by his language than Usher F. Linder — failed to keep the court from drifting around to [our] position. Our triumph was complete.'

The slaves were released and the court ordered 'that they shall be and remain free and discharged from all servitude whatever to any person or persons from henceforward and forever.' Rutherford says that on Saturday night, when the decision was announced, Matson hurriedly left the State for Kentucky, crossed the Wabash, evaded his creditors and never paid Lincoln his fee. Next morning 'after a wholesome breakfast,' Lincoln unconcernedly threw his saddle-bags across the back of 'his old gray mare,' and rode on to the next county seat where court was to be held.[2]

[1] In his narrative Ficklin here quotes this celebrated passage:

"'I speak in the spirit of the British law, which makes liberty commensurate with and inseparable from, the British soil; which proclaims, even to the stranger and the sojourner, the moment he sets his foot upon British earth, that the ground on which he treads is holy, and consecrated by the genius of universal emancipation. No matter in what language his doom may have been pronounced, no matter what complexion, incompatible with freedom, an Indian or an African sun may have burnt upon him; no matter in what disastrous battle his liberty may have been cloven down; no matter with what solemnities he may have been devoted upon the altar of slavery; the first moment he touches the sacred soil of Britain, the altar and the god sink together in the dust; his soul walks abroad in her own majesty; his body swells beyond the measure of his chains, that burst from around him, and he stands redeemed, regenerated, and disenthralled, by the irresistible genius of universal emancipation."' *Speeches of John Philpot Curran*, Dublin, 1868, 169.

It was from this speech of Curran that Lundy took the name of his abolition sheet — *The Genius of Universal Emancipation.*

[2] Lincoln and the Matson Negroes; A Tale of Fugitive Slave Days by Rev. John Wood, MS. Weik MSS. Ashmore raised money at Oakland and took the negroes in a wagon to the Mississippi River. He stopped at Springfield, Jacksonville, and other towns, where money was given to help the Bryants. 'Strange enough one of the donors at Springfield was Lincoln's law-partner, William H. Herndon.' At Quincy Ashmore left the negroes, who floated down the Mississippi to New Orleans. They then went to Liberia.

Obviously the American Colonization Society had taken charge of them, since the work of that organization was to assist negroes who had been freed to return to Africa.

Wood had his account of this incident soon after the trial and directly from Ashmore, Rutherford, and others, who were his personal friends. He also interviewed Ficklin, Constable, and Lincoln, and made 'laborious search among the [court] records.' His statement is probably the most accurate. He was later chaplain of the 5th Illinois cavalry for three years.

Another account of the Matson trial was prepared by D. T. McIntyre of Mattoon, Ill. He says that Matson was heavily involved in debt and brought the slaves from

Then came the time for Lincoln to go to Washington and take his seat as Representative in Congress of the Seventh District of Illinois. Mrs. Lincoln and their son Robert, now in his sixth year, accompanied him. They went by way of St. Louis, up the Ohio on a steamboat to Pittsburgh and thence, by rail to Baltimore and Washington.[1] The station at Washington was a frail and ugly building of wood, scarcely more than a shed, at Pennsylvania Avenue and Second Street. Roughs, loafers, and idle boys gathered there in offensive crowds when the two daily trains came in from Baltimore; [2] and such an assemblage was the first thing Lincoln saw when he arrived at the Nation's capital. Even more annoying and clamorous were the many drivers of hackney-cabs, who rushed to the trains with reckless speed and loudly demanded the patronage of travellers.[3]

The Lincolns went to the boarding house of Mrs. Spriggs on Capitol Hill where Stuart, Hardin, and Baker had lived when they were in Congress. Spriggs' boarding house 'was the fourth of a row of houses known as "Carroll Row,"' which stood on the site of the present Library of Congress.[4] Mrs. Lincoln and Robert remained for perhaps three months. At the boarding house she never appeared except at meals, but the boy, who 'seemed to have his own way,' was conspicuous.[5]

Kentucky in 1845 to prevent the sale of them; that in 1847, he determined to take the Bryant family back to Kentucky; that, by accident, Anthony happened on Ashmore to whom he told his trouble; and that the trial was over the impending sale of the slaves for sheriff's charges.

According to McIntyre, the mother of Jane Bryant was a concubine and Jane's father was James Matson, an elder brother of Robert Matson. 'Jane shared the condition of her mother,' continues McIntyre; and he describes the appearance of the children as stated in the text. History of the Matson Slave Trial by D. T. McIntyre, MS. I am indebted to Mr. Donald B. Craig of Mattoon, Ill., for this MS.

A story of the Matson case appeared in the Sunday Sun, Mattoon, Ill., Aug. 24, 1884.

[1] A regular stage carried passengers from Springfield to St. Louis. Sangamo Journal, Dec. 13, 1848. The other route to Washington was by the Lakes to Buffalo, thence by rail to New York and Washington; but Mrs. Lincoln says that they did not take that route. See infra.

[2] History of the National Capital: Wilhelmus Bogart Bryan, II, 357–61.

[3] Bryan to author, May 4, 1925. There were no omnibuses, no street railway, and the hackney-cabs were the only means of public conveyance. The rates were twenty-five cents for trips of not over one and one-half miles between daybreak time and eight o'clock P.M., and fifty per cent additional after that hour; and twelve and one-half cents for every fifteen minutes that the cab was detained by a passenger. Cong. Directory, 1848, 54.

[4] Personal Reminiscences: Samuel Clagett Busey, 25–6.   [5] Busey, 28.

In 1848 the white population of Washington was a little less than thirty thousand. There were also more than eight thousand free colored persons and over two thousand slaves. Some six thousand three hundred dwellings of all kinds and a slightly larger number of families of every condition comprised the city. Georgetown, hard by, had about six thousand white men, women, and children, seven hundred and twenty-five slaves, and nearly sixteen hundred free negroes.[1]

The capital looked like 'an ill-contrived, ill-arranged, rambling, scrambling village.'[2] Its houses were far apart, with privies, pigsties, cow-sheds and geese-pens in the back yards. In alleys and streets were piles of garbage, about which pigs, geese, and cows wandered at will; they were scavengers and anybody who disturbed them was liable to a fine.[3] Wells with pumps were the only sources of water for all houses.[4] Fine dwellings and shanties stood side by side,[5] 'a strange jumble of magnificence and squalor.'[6] Only two streets in the whole city were paved, and these poorly and in part; while with one exception, the few sidewalks were of gravel and ashes, ridged in the centre.[7]

Pennsylvania Avenue was laid with big cobble-stones so unevenly placed that, to avoid intolerable jolting, carriages were seldom driven over them. When covered with snow, however, the avenue was thronged with dashing sleighs, drawn by spirited horses, and filled with gay and richly dressed people. Great throngs watched the merry display.[8] On the north side of the avenue a brick sidewalk extended from the foot of Capitol Hill for more than a mile and in good weather was the one great promenade of the city, crowded with the beauty, fashion, and celebrity of Washington when Congress was in session.[9] At

---

[1] *Census*, 1850.

[2] *As I Remember:* Marian Gouverneur, 170; *Washington, the Capital City:* Rufus Rockwell Wilson, II, 66.

[3] Busey, 64–5.

[4] Bryan, II, 303–5. Water from springs was piped to the Capitol, the Executive Mansion, and the Department buildings.

[5] Gouverneur, 173.

[6] Wilson, II, 66.   [7] Busey, 64.

[8] *Ib.*, 91.   [9] *Ib.*, 87.

other times, that thoroughfare was 'like Jerusalem the day after it was sacked by Titus.' [1]

Neither wing of the Capitol had been begun and above the central portion still rose the old wooden dome.[2] Only the front part of the present Treasury building was erected and in use, and in this structure the office of the Attorney General was also housed. The State Department occupied a two-story brick edifice on the site of the north front of the Treasury. The War and Navy Departments were in separate brick houses, each of two stories which stood near each other on the ground where the building now occupied by those Departments and the State Department stands.[3] The foundations of the Smithsonian Institution had just been laid and work on its walls was in languid progress during Lincoln's term.[4] The Department of the Interior was established while he was in Congress.[5]

Washington had held a good share of the domestic slave trade since 1802, and in 1834 a thousand slaves a year were shipped thence to the South. Coffles of slaves — gangs of negroes in chains — were a common sight in the streets and the repulsive spectacle furnished the Abolitionists with some of their most telling tales of the evils of slavery. In 1854, in his address at Peoria, Lincoln speaks of the clamor of the North for the abolition of 'a peculiar species of slave trade in the District of Columbia,' a 'sort of negro livery-stable, where droves of negroes were collected, temporarily kept, and finally taken to Southern markets, precisely like droves of horses,' which had been openly maintained for fifty years in view from the windows of the Capitol.[6]

So many were the visitors during sessions of Congress that the four hotels along the avenue could scarcely find room for them. On the avenue, too, were clustered most of the shops and stores,

[1] *National Intelligencer*, Sept. 23, 1842, as quoted in Bryan, II, 275.

[2] *Indiana Historical Collections*, XI, 87–8.

[3] Bryan to author, May 4, 1925. The War building was so small that many bureaus were in private houses. *Ib.*, 39.

[4] R. R. Wilson, II, 49.

[5] *Ib.*, 68. Lincoln voted for the bill creating the Department. *House Journal*, 30th Cong. 2nd Sess., 455–6. The bill passed by a majority of thirty-four votes, seventy-eight members voting against it.

[6] *Works*, II, 202.

none extensive or richly equipped, however, since the more important shopping was done in Baltimore, which could be reached by rail in only two hours and fifteen minutes. Saloons abounded, gambling places were frequent, and all were thronged during congressional sessions.[1] Every hostelry but one, Beers' Temperance Hotel,[2] was heavily stocked with all kinds of liquors.

Liquors were served at meals in all houses as well as at hotels, however, the favorite drink of most public men being brandy or gin, without water. The principal market, just off and adjacent to Pennsylvania Avenue, midway between the Capitol and the Executive Mansion,[3] was supplied from Maryland. Provisions were brought in two-wheeled carts; and slaves, wearing patched clothes, were both drivers and vendors. Buyers attended by slaves came in high hung coaches or on horseback.[4]

The streets were not lighted, except a part of Pennsylvania Avenue which was dimly illuminated by smoky oil lamps, and this was only during sessions of Congress. Fires were extinguished by volunteer companies, the 'firemen' pulling their engines.[5] Fifteen policemen with one captain, sufficed to maintain order at night, for no police were on duty in day-time.[6] The Maryland and Virginia laws of 1802 prevailed in the District.[7] The city was notably religious, having thirty-seven church buildings belonging to eight denominations and with a seating capacity of more than twenty-five thousand;[8] but Lincoln was not a communicant, nor is mention made that he ever went to church during his term.

The national organs of the Whig and Democratic parties, the *National Intelligencer* and the *Washington Union*,[9] each with a large circulation, were published at the capital; while an

[1] *Cong. Directory*, 1848, 53. There were many shops, where 'cheap, ready-made clothing' was sold. Busey, 88-9.

[2] On the west side of 3rd Street.

[3] There were four lesser markets.   [4] Busey, 92-3.

[5] Bryan, ii, 295-7; Busey, 75.

[6] Bryan, ii, 274.   [7] Force, 28.

[8] *Census*, 1850. Of these churches, thirteen were Methodist, six Baptist, five Presbyterian, five Episcopal, four Catholic, two Lutheran, one Quaker, and one Unitarian.

[9] The editor of the *Union* was the celebrated Thomas Ritchie, founder and for many years editor of the *Richmond Enquirer*. He was over seventy years of age and was

abolition paper, the *National Era*, fiercely attacked slavery.[1]
Several other papers and periodicals of less note supplied variegated tastes. A publication, *The Huntress*, was edited by a
woman, Mrs. Anne Royall, whose comments on those she disliked had caused her to be fined as a 'common scold' and led
John Quincy Adams to call her 'the virago-errant in enchanted
armor.'[2] All told, more than eleven million copies of journals
and magazines were printed annually in Washington, during
the period under review.[3] When Lincoln was in Congress one
mail from the West arrived every day, while there were two
mails from New York, Philadelphia, and Baltimore, a well-nigh
miraculous achievement, as it was then considered, of expedition and efficiency.[4]

The social life was merry, if somewhat rural. In warm
weather women visited bare-headed and on foot, and everybody sat and gossiped on doorsteps and porches.[5] Capitol Hill,
where Mrs. Spriggs' boarding house was situated, was occupied
by residences of quiet 'church-going' people who made no
pretension to fashion. There were two or three groceries, several
drug stores, a shop where needles and ribbons were sold, two
dram shops, and a taffy dealer 'who spat on his hands' to make
his candy brittle. Boys were kept busy driving pigs and geese
from the gardens.[6] The instability of Washington society impressed foreigners — a town of officials, place-hunters, and legislators from the various and differing parts of the nation. Few
members of Congress were accompanied by their wives and in
hotel and boarding house the absence of women was noticeable.

thought, by the younger newspaper men, to be behind the times — 'the most genteel
old fogy who ever wore nankeen trousers, high shirt-collars, and broad-brimmed straw
hats.' John W. Forney as quoted in R. R. Wilson, ii, 41.

[1] The editor of the *National Era* was Gamaliel Bailey, Jr., a native of New Jersey.
The paper was the official organ of the American and Foreign Anti-Slavery Society.
Among the contributors were Theodore Parker, Bayard Taylor, Grace Greenwood,
Gail Hamilton [Mary Abigail Dodge], Mrs. E. D. N. Southworth and Harriet Beecher
Stowe. R. R. Wilson, ii, 46. *Uncle Tom's Cabin* first appeared in its columns as a
serial. The office of the *National Era* was mobbed during the first session of Congress
which Lincoln attended. *Ib.*, 45.

[2] *Social Life in the Early Republic:* Anne Hollingsworth Wharton, 291–2.

[3] *Census*, 1850.   [4] *Cong. Directory*, 1848. 53.

[5] R. R. Wilson, ii, 66.   [6] Busey, 83.

But the social life of the capital in the 40's had its features, and balls, parties, receptions, and outings were many. William W. Corcoran, the banker, entertained liberally, cultivating relations with the foreign diplomats, members of the Cabinet and of Congress, and making an impression by his setting. 'I have never seen such gorgeous furniture in Washington,' wrote Senator Fairfield of Maine, 'nor have I seen such a splendid dinner served up.'[1] Under Polk the levees at the White House took on an austerity that repelled — no dancing or refreshment of any kind. 'I had rather be whipped than go,' groaned Fairfield, but he went from policy and a sense of duty. Buchanan, a bachelor and Secretary of State, gave large affairs at the caterer's, gathering on one occasion as many as fifteen hundred guests.

Officials entertained rather than members of Congress. In the first session of the thirtieth Congress only five Senators occupied houses — Benton, Bright, Dix, Johnson, and Webster — and only four representatives — Adams, Dixon, McLane, and Winthrop. The others were crowded into hotels and boarding houses. Fairfield had a room about fourteen feet square, furnished after a fashion, for which he paid nine dollars a week, which was 'tolerably reasonable,' he thought.[2]

The social centres were not far from the Capitol, near C and Fourth Streets, northwest, and on Lafayette Square, in face of the White House. The dining hour was half past five or earlier, and tea was taken about seven o'clock. At the British minister's dinner was at six, notable for its servants in livery and its rich, massive service of silver. The guests remained at the table about two hours, after which strong coffee was brought. The widow of President Madison, sprightly in spite of her age, wearing her ancient dresses because of her poverty, still held receptions in her house on Lafayette Square, and Mrs. Alexander Hamilton, 'a tiny little woman,' who was very old, was still active.

Wealth had no influence whatever on the society of the capital, which was exclusive and based on manners, family, distinction, and charm. Of the young women in this social

---

[1] *Letters of John Fairfield:* Staples, 370.   [2] *Ib.,* 311.

set, the most admired and the leader, was Adele Cutts, 'a dark-haired beauty with skin like the petals of a water-lily,' who married Douglas a few years later.[1]

The White House grounds were open to the public; and there, on the grass as well as on board gravelled walks, the élite, Senators and Representatives often among them, gathered Wednesday and Saturday afternoons to listen to concerts by the Marine Band — a custom established by the Tylers. Webster was often there and, in his swallow-tailed coat of blue broadcloth with brass buttons, figured waistcoat and frilled shirt of fine linen, was a conspicuous and attractive figure.[2]

Such in rough outline, were the city, people, and customs, when Lincoln first went to Washington; and there was little change in his life. While in Congress he sometimes joined the throng in front of the Capitol terrace when concerts were given; but he was afforded no opportunity to enter the higher social life of the capital, even if he had cared to do so. His principal diversion was bowling, for which sport there was an alley near Mrs. Spriggs' boarding house. He was a very 'awkward bowler,' but so great was his good humor and so amusing his comment and anecdotes, that a crowd of men and boys always gathered at the hour when he played.[3]

Members of Congress living in boarding houses, formed groups, each of which was called a 'mess.' With Lincoln at Mrs. Spriggs' during his first session, were nine other members of the House, all of them Whigs.[4] There were other boarders too, one of them a young doctor, Samuel Clagett Busey, whose reminiscences are the chief source of our small knowledge of Lincoln's personal life while he was in Congress. Lincoln was the best liked man in the mess, because of his good nature, his incessant stories, 'some of which were very broad,' and his conciliatory disposition. When a dispute arose at the table he would smooth

---

[1] Wharton, 314–5. The marriage occurred Nov. 20, 1856. Miss Cutts was Douglas's second wife. She was the daughter of J. Madison Cutts, Second Comptroller of the Treasury. Miss Cutts was the most popular woman in Washington society; and, after her marriage to Douglas, his home was thronged with visitors. Stevens, 648.

[2] Wharton, 287–8.   [3] Busey, 27.

[4] Joshua R. Giddings of Ohio, Elisha Embree of Indiana, Patrick W. Tompkins of Mississippi, and the following five of Pennsylvania: John Blanchard, John Dickey, John Strohm, James Pollock, Abraham R. McIlvaine. *Cong. Directory*, 1848, 32.

it out by an anecdote that made everybody laugh and forget differences. He was always 'neatly but very plainly dressed, very simple and approachable in manner, and unpretentious,' testifies Dr. Busey, who greatly admired Lincoln for his kindness of heart, unassuming manners, wit, stories, and jokes.[1]

Lincoln was prompt and constant in his attendance on the meetings of the House.[2] He was assigned to the Committee on Post Offices and Post Roads and to that on Expenditures in the War Department [3] — fairly good places for a new member. Out of scores of votes, Lincoln missed only seven during the long and turbulent session, and those seven were on unimportant matters.[4] He made two reports from his Committee on Post Offices and Post Roads and spoke three or four times on mails, bounties, and other subjects. In making his initial effort he wrote Herndon that he was as badly scared but no more than when he spoke in court in Springfield.[5] He did things far more conspicuous, however, than offer Committee reports and make incidental comment on them. Indeed, few new members of Congress, during a first term, have been so active as Lincoln was; but he made practically no impression on anybody, and such impression as he did make was not favorable.

His seat, Number 191, one of the poorest in the chamber, was on the Whig side of the House, in the centre of the back row of the section to the left of the Speaker. In the row in front of him and four seats to the right, sat George Ashmun of Massachusetts, who, twelve years later, was to preside over the National Republican Convention that nominated Lincoln for the Presidency. Ashmun was forty-four years old, a graduate of Yale and an experienced legislator. On the same row with Ashmun, but far to the right, was the seat of Joshua R. Giddings of Ohio, Lincoln's messmate, a man of fifty-three, a violent antislavery man, bold, rash, and voluble.

---

[1] Busey, 25–7.   [2] Ib., 27.   [3] Cong. Directory, 36, 39.

[4] An amendment to the Wisconsin Statehood bill (*House Journal*, 30th Cong. 1st Sess., 787–8); adjournment (*ib.*, 836–7 and 884–5, 1181–2); suspension of rules to pass resolution to adjourn (*ib.*, 844–5); tabling memorial on post road bill (*ib.*, 880–1); and an amendment to the Judiciary bill (*ib.*, 1191–3).

[5] Lincoln to Herndon, Jan. 8, 1848. *Works*, I, 325–6. On Dec. 13 he had written Herndon: 'As you are all so anxious for me to distinguish myself, I have concluded to do so before long.' *Ib.*, 317.

Directly in front of Lincoln's place but in the exact middle of the Whig part of the House, sat a frail, thin man, thirty-six years old, of brilliant talents and compelling eloquence, Alexander H. Stephens of Georgia, who was to become Vice President of the Southern Confederacy. The graduate of a small college, sincere, courageous, highly intellectual, the story of his early disadvantages and struggles appealed to Lincoln, who liked and admired Stephens more than he did any other member of the House. Near him sat his colleague, Robert Toombs, who was to become Secretary of State in the Confederate Government and a Brigadier General in the Confederate army. He was in his thirty-eighth year, a college man, robust, full faced and florid, fearless, upright, and capable.

Two seats to the left of Toombs, was the desk of Caleb B. Smith of Indiana, forty years old, an anti-slavery Whig, stern in his devotion to principle. He was to become Secretary of the Interior in Lincoln's cabinet. Behind Smith sat John G. Palfrey of Massachusetts, of the same age as Giddings, a graduate of Harvard, a Unitarian minister, Professor of Sacred Literature in his Alma Mater, and uncompromisingly against slavery.

One of the best seats in the House was that of the most conspicuous and picturesque member, former President John Quincy Adams, then in his eighty-second year but still vigorous and alert. Highly educated and accomplished, with longer and wider experience than any other man in public life, he was relentless in his opposition to the slave power and its most effective foe. Within six weeks of Lincoln's entrance into the House, Adams was to be fatally stricken in his seat. In the Speaker's chair was Robert C. Winthrop of Massachusetts, another Harvard man, a law student and follower of Daniel Webster, whom he was soon to succeed in the Senate. He was of the historic Winthrop family of New England, a man of distinguished ability, moderate, kindly, and just.

All these men were Whigs and Lincoln's fellow partisans. Far to Lincoln's left and on the back row of the Democratic side of the House sat a blond, nervous man of uncommonly youthful appearance, with precise manners and clear musical voice,

David Wilmot of Pennsylvania,[1] a 'regular' Democrat, whose
name had already become well known throughout the country
through the amendment he had introduced to a bill in the closing hours of the last Congress. Fifteen years later Lincoln was
to appoint him a member of the Court of Claims. Two rows in
front and to the left of Wilmot was the desk of a member
whose appearance caught and held the eye. Six feet tall, slender
and erect, with a fine head and bearded face, Robert Barnwell
Rhett of South Carolina had, to an extraordinary degree, an air
of breeding and distinction. He was outspoken, brilliant and
passionate, singularly clear and logical;[2] and, by his dominant
personality, he had already driven Calhoun into acceptance of
the doctrine of extreme state rights. He had answered John
Quincy Adams' threat of disunion with a counter threat more
earnest. He was soon to leave the House for the Senate in
succession to Calhoun, and to do more to excite the Southern
States to secession than any other one man, except perhaps
Yancey.

Here and there in the Departments, were men who were to be
conspicuous actors in the long tragedy which events were preparing and in which Lincoln was to be the principal character.
One of them, Gideon Welles of Connecticut, an energetic man of
forty-eight, the editor of a newspaper in Hartford and a staunch
Democrat, was Chief of the Bureau of Provisions and Clothing
in the Navy Department.[3] He was to be Lincoln's Secretary of
the Navy.

In the Senate were Webster, Calhoun, Cass, Benton, Douglas, Crittenden, Simon Cameron of Pennsylvania, Reverdy
Johnson of Maryland, John Bell of Tennessee, Robert M. T.
Hunter of Virginia, John P. Hale of New Hampshire, and David
R. Atchison of Missouri. Some of these men were to take prominent parts in the events that led to the climax of Lincoln's
career and of American history. And another Senator was sent
to Washington by his State almost at the very time that Lincoln
was making his first long speech in Congress. The Legislature

---

[1] *David Wilmot, Free Soiler:* Charles Buxton Going, 68.

[2] *Frank Leslie's Illustrated Newspaper*, Feb. 9, 1861.

[3] *Cong. Directory*, 1848, 22–8.

of Mississippi, by acclamation, elected Jefferson Davis to the
United States Senate, amid the ringing cheers of the great
throng that crowded the State House at Jackson.[1]

Such were the more notable of the Senators and of Lincoln's
fellow-members of the House when, on December 6, 1847, he
took the oath of a Representative in Congress. His first official
act was to vote for Robert C. Winthrop for Speaker, elected on
the third ballot.[2] Then came the message of President Polk.
He briefly reviewed our efforts to avoid war by peaceable discussion; the Mexican refusal 'even to hear the terms of adjustment;' the beginning of hostilities by Mexico's 'striking the
first blow, and shedding the blood of our citizens on our own
soil;' the declaration of war by Congress; 'the rapid and brilliant successes' of the American troops; the renewed energy of
our Government in prosecuting the war; the capture of the
Mexican capital; the indispensability of territorial indemnity
if any indemnity at all was to be required, since Mexico had no
money and could not get any; the value of California, its natural place as a part of American territory, and the probability
of its seizure by a foreign power if we relinquished it; the equal
likelihood that, if our forces were withdrawn, without concluding a treaty of peace, Mexico itself, in order to avert anarchy,
might welcome European intervention; the necessity of pushing the war with greater vigor than ever, and therefore of the
authorization by Congress for the enlistment of new troops, appropriations to meet expenses already incurred and, in general,
hearty support of the prosecution of the war.[3]

At once the fight against the Administration began. The assault was largely partisan, somewhat factional, and inspired
by the tangled motives of opposition to territorial expansion,
antagonism to slavery and its spread into new territory, resentment of Polk's opposition to internal improvements,[4] desire

---

[1] *Washington Union*, Jan. 22, 1848.

[2] Winthrop was the regular Whig candidate and the slavery Whigs of the South, like
Stephens, Toombs, and Clingman, voted for him, as did Adams and Whigs of the North
like Ashmun. Palfrey, however, did not vote for him. *House Journal*, 30th Cong. 1st
Sess., 8–14.

[3] *Messages:* Richardson, IV, 533–49.

[4] On Dec. 21, John Wentworth, an anti-slavery Democrat from Chicago, offered an

for a high protective tariff, all involved in the very practical and immediate party manœuvering for the impending Presidential campaign. But the subject of loudest Whig complaint was the origin of the war; that the President had begun the conflict was the smallest of the practical motives which really inspired the opposition.

In view of the part which Lincoln took in this political mêlée and the prompt and long continued effect of his conduct upon him in Illinois, it is necessary to give a brief summary of events leading up to the Mexican War and the attitude of men and political parties in Congress toward it. Without such a review, the war resolution introduced and the war speech made by Lincoln have no meaning; nor can the revulsion of public sentiment against him in Illinois be understood or even realized. Although nobody in Washington paid any attention to what he said, the people in his own State did; and, as will appear, his 'war record' in Congress in 1848 was urged against him effectively until his campaign for the Presidency in 1860, and even in that historic contest use of it was still made.

The immediate cause of dispute between the American and Mexican governments was the conflicting boundary claims. By statute Texas asserted that the Rio Grande was her southern and western boundary,[1] but by the resolution of annexation the determination of the question was to be open to negotiation between the United States and Mexico. Texas having become a State of the Union, her soil was American soil. Mexico denied that the Rio Grande was the boundary and claimed sovereignty even over all Texas. The Mexican Government repudiated Santa Anna's recognition of Texan independence on the ground that the promise had been made under force, and openly

internal improvement resolution which was adopted by a vote of one hundred and thirty-eight ayes to fifty-four nays, Lincoln of course voting aye. *House Journal*, 30th Cong. 1st Sess. 142–3. This was the first direct rebuke of the Administration.

[1] Act, Dec. 19, 1836. At the beginning of the Texan revolution, a strong sentiment appeared in the United States that, since Texas was being 'rapidly . . . settled by our own people,' it would inevitably come into the Union, and that the Rio Grande must be made the boundary. *New York Courier*, clipped in *Richmond Enquirer*, July 17, 1835. Winston, *Proc. Miss. Vall. Hist. Socy.*, VIII, 167.

'Let its bounds be extended to the Rio Grande.' *New Orleans Bee*, March 19, 1836. *Ib.*, 168.

threatened to make war upon us if Texas was annexed to the United States. But before 1841 Great Britain, France, and the United States had recognized the Republic of Texas as a separate and independent nation.[1] When our war with Mexico broke out, Texas had been governing herself for ten years.[2] In many ways our Government had tried to appease Mexico and, in order to avert war, had 'yielded to the verge of ignominy.'[3]

Texas accepted annexation by a unanimous vote of her Congress,[4] and the President ordered a part of the small American army to the Rio Grande to protect the new State from invasion.[5] On the west side of that river was a Mexican army of six thousand regulars. The American force commanded by General Zachary Taylor, was less than half as many. In addition the Mexicans had large numbers of irregular troops. The Mexican commander peremptorily ordered Taylor to withdraw, declaring that the very presence of American soldiers on the Rio Grande was in itself the commencement of hostilities. An American reconnoitring party was attacked on the east side of the river and all were killed or captured. Thus the war began.[6]

The total strength of the regular army of the United States

[1] The United States in 1837, France in 1839, and Great Britain in 1840.

[2] In 1850, the population of Texas was 154,034 whites, 58,161 slaves and 397 free colored. Of these 43,281 had been born in the State, 92,657 were from the United States and the remainder from foreign countries. U.S. *Census*, 1850.

If these figures are reduced by one-third, we have a fair approximation of the statistics of Texas, at the beginning of the Mexican War.

[3] Channing, v, 551.   [4] Rives, i, 716–7.

[5] In anticipation of Texan acceptance of annexation, and to be prepared to protect the new State, Polk had directed a moderate number of troops to a convenient station near the Mexican boundary. Of this manœuver, which then was and since has been vituperatively assailed, Channing wisely remarks: 'In view of the probability of Mexican attack on Texas while the consideration of the annexation plan was proceeding, the strengthening of the American army . . . was perfectly justifiable, if the annexation of Texas was.' Channing, 552.

[6] For a clear and highly condensed account of the Mexican War see Channing v, ch. xvii. The latest treatments of the subject are by Rives, Smith, and Stephenson. The works of Rives and Smith are thorough and exhaustive, written from sources only. They demolish the old Whig and abolition theory of the Mexican War which, until recent years, was accepted by writers — the theory that it was a war of conquest, instigated by 'the slave power,' begun and waged by a powerful and grasping nation against a small and weak country for the purpose of seizing territory to extend the domain of slavery. For a brief and interesting account see Prof. Nathaniel W. Stephenson's *Texas and the Mexican War.*

at that time was less than seven thousand five hundred officers and men, including all branches of the service.[1] The precise number of the regular army of Mexico is unknown, but it was many times greater. The Mexican Government believed that the Northern States would not support a war in defence of Texas, that we would go to war with Great Britain over Oregon, that, in any case, Mexico would have the sympathy if not the active support of European powers.[2]

Our first claim to all the territory north of the Rio Grande and from that river westward was based on the 'Louisiana Purchase.' In the treaty with Spain of 1819 by which our title to Florida was established, President Monroe relinquished all the territory in the 'Louisiana Purchase' west of the Sabine River, now forming a part of the western boundary of the State of Louisiana.[3] Soon afterwards Moses Austin, born in Connecticut but long residing in Missouri, obtained from Spain, an extensive land grant in Texas to be settled by American families. Other like grants were made and in a few years thousands of immigrants from the United States had made their homes in this fertile frontier region.

When Spain was ousted from Mexico by a successful revolution, the new government succeeded to the Spanish title. After a second revolution, in 1824, a Mexican constitution, modeled on that of the United States, was adopted. This provided for local self-government by the various Mexican States, of which Texas and Coahuila formed one, and, in pursuance of this liberal constitution, laws were passed by the Mexican Congress, inviting immigration and guaranteeing to settlers protection of their rights and privileges, but requiring them to become members of the Roman Catholic church — a requirement not wholly fulfilled by the settlers.

Under this constitution and these laws the volume of immigration from the United States to Texas greatly increased. Even John Quincy Adams, who had desired to purchase to the

---

[1] Records War Dept. The exact number was 7,365.

[2] Smith, 114-5.

[3] Marshall (*History of the Western Boundary of the Louisiana Purchase*, 58-9) shows that Adams, then Secretary of State, failing to be supported on Texas, sought for compensation in the Oregon country.

Rio Grande in 1819 and 1827, saw in 1832 that 'the increasing settlements in Texas were all from this country, and that the inhabitants would prefer to belong to the United States.'[1] At that time and for four years afterward, the brilliant and pugnacious old statesman had never a thought that slavery was involved in the Texan question.

Revolutions were frequent in Mexico; and, in 1829, during one brief reign, slavery was 'abolished' by forms of words, a mere gesture, since peonage, Indians who were practically held in serfdom, still existed. The chief difference between peonage and slavery was that nobody looked after and cared for the peons when they became too old to work. The Mexican politicians expected abolition to have a favorable effect in Europe, especially in England, the leading anti-slavery nation, to which country Mexico was heavily indebted. Formal and ostensible 'abolition of slavery by the Mexican Republic' was a good phrase to be used later, when abolitionism developed into a political movement in the United States. Many American settlers in Texas were from adjacent Southern States, and these immigrants had taken with them a number of slaves.[2] These Texan slave-owners protested against the formal abolition declared by the Mexican authorities and Texas was excepted from the operation of the abolition decree.

Again the Mexican Government was overthrown by a fresh revolt, led by an artillery officer at Vera Cruz, Antonio Lopez de Santa Anna, who, later, perpetrated the infamies in Texas already described. He speedily became Dictator, though retaining the title of President. Santa Anna was head of a distinctive military caste,[3] which was the only organized, coherent force in the country; and his government was an armed despotism. He abolished the liberal Constitution of 1824, and established a centralized tyranny. Resistance in one state, Zacatecas,

---

[1] *Memoirs:* John Quincy Adams, VIII, 465, Jan. 31, 1832.

[2] In Texas the peonage system did not exist and the only possible substitute was negro slavery. *Annexation of Texas:* Justin H. Smith, 9.

[3] The Mexican officers were also a social order, but their low morale and ignorance were marked, though they were professional military men. The privates, on the other hand, were not 'bad material,' but the cavalry and artillery were not efficient. Smith, I, 8, 10–1.

was ruthlessly crushed.[1] Deprived of every right and privilege guaranteed to them, forbidden even to maintain a militia or bear arms,[2] and thus placed at the mercy of hostile Indians, the American settlers in Texas rebelled against Santa Anna's dictatorship.

It was to subdue this rebellion against his autocracy, that Santa Anna swept into Texas in 1836 with a well equipped army six times as numerous as any which the scattered Texans could possibly gather. So came the Alamo, Goliad, and San Jacinto. So came, too, the compact by which Santa Anna agreed to withdraw all Mexican forces beyond the Rio Grande.

Up to this time nobody prominent in public life had suggested that the Texan conflict with the Mexican despot was a scheme to extend American slave territory; and, in fact, it was not. Many of the leading men of Texas and a large number of the settlers were from the Northern States; Texan immigration was a part of the great folk movement that had peopled the whole country west of the Alleghanies and beyond the Mississippi, and, even then, was sweeping across the plains to the Pacific.[3]

Benjamin Lundy, editor of the *Genius of Universal Emancipation*, had visited Texas three times to obtain a grant of land for a proposed colony. His last and successful visit was in 1835 and he returned to the United States confirmed in an opinion held by him since 1829, that the struggle for Texan independence was part of a plot against freedom by slave owners of the States, made still more infamous by a conspiracy of land speculators. It was, he said, a war of slave-holders and land grabbers against an inoffensive Mexico where slavery had been abolished. The people of Texas and of the State of Zacatecas were, he asserted, merely 'nullifiers' like those of South Carolina; and the Texan revolution was inspired by the same treasonable spirit toward the Mexican Government that had been shown by the rebels at Charleston in 1832. Moreover the Texans were, he passionately asserted, ruffians, thieves, and murderers.[4] Many

---

[1] Adams wrote in his diary: 'In 1833 Santa Anna broke up the federal constitution, and with the aid of his bayonets was elected President.' Adams, XI, 367, April 21,1843.

[2] Smith, I, 47. [3] *Annexation of Texas:* Smith, 29–30.

[4] 'The *slave-holders, slave-breeders,* and *politicians* of the United States' plot to in-

Northern papers that had championed the Texan cause changed their attitude.[1]

At once the Abolitionists took up Lundy's outcry against Texas.[2] John Quincy Adams eagerly accepted Lundy's stories. Henceforth he was the ardent foe of Texas, as persistent and merciless as he was able and sincere, and Massachusetts supported him. When the new and feeble Republic asked for annexation to the United States in 1838, Adams spoke against it in the House in the morning hour every day for three weeks.[3] He even introduced a resolution that 'it would be the right and the duty of the free people of the Union to resist and annul' any treaty or act of Congress for the annexation of Texas.[4] Answering an objection to the admission of Iowa 'while Northern fanatics are pouring in petitions against the annexation . . . of the great and glorious republic of Texas,' Adams said that that glory 'consisted of having made of a land of freemen a land of slaves.'[5]

Thus began the assault in Congress and throughout the country upon the Texan struggle for independence and upon the movement for the reunion of the Texan people with their kindred in the United States. Thus, too, began the American championship of the Mexican cause as that of a wronged and helpless country despoiled of its territory by wicked, avaricious, bloodthirsty men — an assault and a championship which, as the slavery question grew more acute, had increasing effect

crease the power of the slave-holding States. The Yazoo frauds were 'child's play' compared to Texan land frauds. The men shot at Goliad were pirates. 'The marauders who are engaged in the Texas insurrection.' *The War in Texas. A Citizen of the United States:* Benj. Lundy, 9, 40, 46.

[1] For instance, the *New York Evening Post*, June 17, 18, July 1, 5, Dec. 13, 1836, as contrasted with same Nov. 6, 1835; the *National Gazette* (Philadelphia, Pa.) throughout 1835, as contrasted with the same the following year. Winston in *Proc. Miss. Vall. Hist. Socy.*, VIII, 169–71.

[2] 'Setting aside the Abolitionists there would be no opposition to the admission of Texas to the Union.' *New York Courier and Enquirer*, Dec. 29, 1836. *Proc. Miss. Vall. Hist. Soc'y.*, VIII, 172.

The *Boston Atlas* was sure that Austin meant to introduce slavery. *Ib.*, 174.

The *National Intelligencer*, which was against anything with which Jackson sympathized, declared, Aug. 13, 1836: 'The Rubicon is passed, a war entered upon without the shadow of justification . . . from the Mexican people.'

[3] June 16 to July 7, 1838. Adams, x, 20–30.

[4] *Ib.*, 20, June 15, 1838.   [5] *Ib.*, 11–2, June 6, 1838.

upon public opinion and even gave direction to the writing of history.[1]

As Texan annexation became more probable, Adams looked forward to it with alarm and anguish. He saw in everything that happened, no matter how disconnected and remote, 'parts of one great system, looking to a war for conquest and plunder from Mexico.'[2] His conviction was strengthened by a letter from Calhoun, then Secretary of State, to the British Minister. Part of it was singularly inept to be penned by an experienced politician and an able man. After properly asserting that slavery in the United States was no affair of any foreign power, Calhoun argued that the 'institution' was a blessing to the slaves and to society.[3] Sometimes, however, Adams came nearer the mark. 'The appetite for Texas was from the first a Western passion,' he declared in one of his innumerable comments on the subject; but, he added 'the inflexible perseverance of rapacity of our South and West ... to plunder and dismember' Mexico was 'under the spur of slavery.'[4] When Tyler sent the annexation treaty to the Senate, Adams writhed in despair: 'with it went the freedom of the human race,' he wrote in his diary; but he soon felt better and thought that, after all, it was no more than 'the immediate crisis of a great struggle between slavery and freedom throughout the world.'[5]

Adams' burning words accurately reflected the sentiments of anti-slavery men generally at the time Polk became President.

Then, too, the Democratic party was in power, and, as we have seen, Texan annexation was a Democratic policy, territorial expansion a Democratic doctrine. The Whig party had taken the opposite ground; and, while few in Congress had the courage to vote against the war declaration and war measures

---

[1] Stephenson, 109.

[2] Adams, xi, 346–7, 353, March 25, and April 4, 1843.

[3] Calhoun to Pakenham, April 18, 1844. Calhoun's *Works:* Richard K. Crallé (1855), v, 333–9. The publication of Calhoun's letter infuriated the Abolitionists and angered anti-slavery men of both political parties, and it resulted in the defeat of the treaty of annexation then pending in the Senate. Texas was afterward admitted to the Union by a joint resolution of Congress and the acceptance of the Texan Congress.

[4] Adams, xi, 348–9, 351, March 29, April 1, 1843.

[5] *Ib.*, xii, 13–4, 22, April 22, May 4, 1844.

after hostilities had begun, all were sullen and resentful.[1] This feeling had grown stronger when Congress met in the winter of 1846–47, and became stridently vocal as soon as the two Houses convened in that vituperative session.

Also a large number of Democrats had been against the admission of Texas, and they had not been mollified. To these elements of antagonism to the President, another, less conspicuous but fully as practical, must be added — the tariff. Protected manufacturers were distressed lest, through new states into which Texas could be divided and still others to be formed out of territory that might be acquired from Mexico, the South and West would be able to lower the tariff and reduce it even to a revenue basis.

Such were the incongruous forces which made common cause against the Administration when Congress met after the war had been in progress seven months. Indeed the opposition had shown its teeth when war had been declared at the preceding session. Garrett Davis of Kentucky, an aggressive Whig, asserted that hostilities had been begun, not by Mexico, but by Polk, because the Nueces River and not the Rio Grande was the true boundary between Texas and Mexico; and that when the President ordered troops to the Rio Grande he invaded Mexican soil. 'It is our own President who began this war,' said Davis amid calls for 'order,' 'order!'; but he voted for the bill which meant war.[2]

Others were not so meek. Columbus Delano of Ohio, a fighting Abolitionist though still a Whig, one of the fourteen who voted against the declaration of war, in a furious speech denounced the war as 'unholy, unrighteous, and damnable.' Up rose Douglas to whom the pleasure of answering the Whig assaults had been given, his great voice steady but charged with passion. 'Is there not treason in the heart that can feel, and poison in the breath that can utter, such sentiments against their own country, when forced to take up arms in self-

[1] On final passage only fourteen voted against the declaration of war; but on an amendment to the bill which asserted that Mexico began the war, authorized a call for 50,000 volunteers, and appropriated $10,000,000, sixty-seven Whigs voted nay. *Cong. Globe*, 29th Cong. 1st Sess., xv, 793–5, May 11, 1846.

[2] *Ib.*, 794.

defence, to repel the invasion of a brutal and perfidious foe,' he thundered in the course of one of the ablest speeches he ever made.[1]

But at the following session, 1846–47, the Whigs were bolder. Baker had hurried to Washington with despatches from the front; he was still a member of the House, and, in full uniform, he made an affecting appeal for money and men. He 'entreated' partisans to cease their 'mutual crimination and recrimination.' What mattered differences of opinion about the origin of the war? Send our soldiers 'aid, comfort, succor, and support. . . . ACTION! ACTION!! ACTION!!!' [2] Two days later he resigned as a Representative and returned to the field where glory awaited him.[3]

But in spite of Baker's dramatic appearance and passionate plea for unity in support of the war, the Whig leaders were acrimonious and defiant. 'This war is a nondescript,' shouted Robert Toombs of Georgia; 'we charge the President with usurping the war-making power . . . with seizing a country . . . which had been for centuries, and was then in the possession of the Mexicans. . . . Let us put a check upon this lust of dominion. We had territory enough, Heaven knew.' [4] Caleb B. Smith of Indiana rejoiced that the Whigs were the party opposed to the war; Polk had invaded territory 'to which we had no man-

---

[1] *Cong. Globe*, 29th Cong. 1st Sess., xvi, Appendix, 903–8. The Illinois Democrats were delighted with Douglas's speech. *Illinois State Register*, June 26, 1846.

In this speech Douglas had several passages with Adams who detested the youthful Representative. Of one of Douglas's early speeches in the House on an election case, Adams said in his diary: 'Douglas . . . now raved out his hour in abusive invectives. . . . His face was convulsed, his gesticulation frantic, and he lashed himself into such a heat that if his body had been made of combustible matter it would have burnt out. In the midst of his roaring, to save himself from choking, he stripped off and cast away his cravat, unbuttoned his waistcoat, and had the air and the aspect of a half-naked pugilist. And this man comes from a judicial bench, and passes for an eloquent orator!' Adams, xi, 510–1, Feb. 14, 1844.

Of an expansionist speech by Douglas, Adams said: 'Douglas . . . raved an hour about democracy and Anglophobia and universal empire.' *Ib.*, 159, Jan. 31, 1845.

[2] *Cong. Globe*, 29th Cong. 2nd Sess., xvii, 91–4, Dec. 28, 1846.

Baker's resolution was immediately adopted under suspension of the rules unanimously agreed to. It authorized the Secretary of War to deliver to commanding officers of volunteer regiments clothing for the men, etc. *Ib.*, 94.

The *Sangamo Journal* printed Baker's 'great speech' in full, Jan. 21, 1847.

[3] Baker resigned Dec. 30, 1846. Records Office, Ill. Sec. State.

[4] *Cong. Globe*, 29th Cong. 2nd Sess., xvii. Appendix. 140–3, Jan. 8, 1847.

ner of claim whatsoever,' since Texas 'never had owned one inch
of territory beyond the Nueces.' [1]

With characteristic bitterness Giddings declared that our
army had 'planted itself in the midst of Mexican cornfields' and
'unarmed peasants had been murdered;' our troops had slaugh-
tered 'women, children, and helpless age, . . . stabbed unarmed
Mexicans in their houses,' outraged virgins. It was a terrible
speech.[2] Charles Hudson of Massachusetts, who had been a
Universalist preacher, insisted that Texas had no pretence of
title beyond where her authority extended; the war was for conquest 'in order to give the South a perpetual preponderance in
the councils of the nation.' [3] In the Senate Thomas Corwin of
Ohio reached the climax of Whig invective: Texas could not
'claim one inch beyond the spot where she exercised jurisdiction. This desolating war arose' from American invasion. 'Sir,
. . . if I were a Mexican I would tell you, "Have you not room
in your own country to bury your dead men? If you come into
mine, we will greet you with bloody hands, and welcome you to
hospitable graves."' [4]

Nor were the Whigs the only dissatisfied element; anti-slavery
Democrats were scarcely less virulent. Moreover, the President's surrender to Great Britain of a large part of Oregon
which in the presidential campaign the Democrats had declared
we must keep, even at the hazard of war — '54–40 or fight' —
had angered Northern men. They felt that they had been
tricked. Those of the Northwest especially believed that the
Southern politicians had outwitted them by parting with territory from which free states would be made, while acquiring
Texas and an immense area where slavery would naturally and
probably go. So when the President asked Congress to give him
two million dollars to be used in an effort to make peace with
Mexico, the Northern men took the alarm and resolved to re-
taliate upon the South by excluding slavery from any territory
which might be acquired from Mexico.

Thus came the famous 'Wilmot Proviso,' which was a resolu-

[1] *Cong. Globe*, 29th Cong. 2nd Sess., xvii, 122–4, Jan. 6, 1847.
[2] *Ib.*, 34–6, Dec. 15, 1846.
[3] *Ib.*, Appendix, 370, Feb. 13, 1847.   [4] *Ib.*, 211–8, Feb. 11, 1847.

tion devised by a number of Representatives from Northern and Northwestern States. The authorship of this brief, historic paper is disputed;[1] but it was offered by David Wilmot of Pennsylvania as an amendment to the bill appropriating the two million dollars requested by the President in order to make peace with Mexico. The 'Proviso,' attached to the bill, asserted as a 'fundamental condition' to the acquisition of territory from Mexico, that slavery should be prohibited therein. It passed the House late Saturday night, August 8, 1846, by the standing vote of eighty-three to sixty-four, the ayes and noes not being recorded.[2] Congress was to adjourn at noon, the following Monday. In the Senate on that day, Dixon H. Lewis, of Alabama, moved to strike the Proviso from the bill; whereupon John Davis of Massachusetts took and held the floor until twelve o'clock, thus killing the two million dollar bill as well as the Proviso.[3]

So the Twenty-ninth Congress adjourned in unprecedented bitterness, both parties split into factions, the Administration rebuked and humiliated. The Whigs, however, kept the better alignment, since those from South and North alike were against Polk and the war. From the first the President had been surprised and bewildered by the Whig antagonism to the war, by the injection of slavery into the discussion of it, by the defection of members of his own party. He had not foreseen that his desire for territorial expansion would result in war; he had not wanted the war and had only done the plainest of plain duty in sending troops to protect Texas after that State entered the Union. What had slavery to do with the question of territory to be acquired from Mexico, he querulously asked of his diary.[4]

[1] The 'Bargain of 1844' as the Origin of the Wilmot Proviso: Clark E. Persinger, *Rept. Am. Hist. Assn.*, 1911, I, 189–95. Going, 117–41, where is reproduced the original MS. of the Proviso in Wilmot's writing, which is still attached to the appropriation bill, in the Library of Congress.

[2] *Cong. Globe*, 29th Cong. 1st Sess., xv, 1217.

[3] *Ib.*, 1220–1. At the next session, Wilmot promised Polk to vote for the appropriation without any slavery restriction, and agreed not to offer his proviso again. Polk's *Diary*, II, 288–90. There must have been a misunderstanding, as Wilmot re-introduced his amendment in the following session.

[4] Polk's *Diary*, II, 288–90, Dec. 23, 1846. Polk told Wilmot that he 'did not desire to extend slavery;' that in New Mexico and California 'slavery could probably never

Such in rough outline, was the political situation when **Lincoln** entered the Thirtieth Congress. The temper of the national Whig leaders was hotter than ever. The war had been going on for twenty months, the usual reaction had, at last, set in throughout the country,[1] and of this war-weariness, indicated by a 'sudden revulsion' of the Whig press, the Whigs took prompt advantage. 'They desire,' exclaimed the Illinois Democratic organ, 'for mere political effect, to make the whole Mexican war a farce.' [2] So from the beginning of the session the Whig leaders were on the aggressive, and Lincoln resolved to take part in the assault upon the Administration.

Up to December 22, 1847, he had said nothing publicly on Texas and had taken no stand against the war. As we have seen, he upheld it in his campaign for election to Congress; and the *Sangamo Journal*, now the *Illinois Journal*,[3] which usually ex-

exist, and the great probability was that the question would never arise in the future organization of . . . Governments in these territories.'

Again and again Polk deplored the bringing of the slavery question into the discussion of the war legislation: 'The slavery question is assuming a fearful . . . aspect. . . . It has, and can have no legitimate connection with the War with Mexico, or the terms of a peace which may be concluded with that country. It is a domestic and not a foreign question, and to connect it with the appropriations for prosecuting the war . . . must divide the country by a sectional line and lead to the worst consequences. . . . Such an agitation is not only unwise, but wicked. . . . The slavery question . . . has nothing to do with the practical business before them [Congress]. . . . I will do my duty and leave the rest to God and my country.' *Ib.*, 304–6, Jan. 4, 1847.

'A majority of one branch of Congress [House] is opposed to my administration; they have falsely charged that the war was brought on and is continued by me with a view to the conquest of Mexico.' *Ib.*, III, 348.

One of the resolutions prepared by Clay for his Lexington meeting of November, 1847, read: 'We do positively and emphatically disclaim and disavow any wish or desire on our part to acquire any foreign territory whatever for the purpose of propagating slavery, or of introducing slaves from the United States into such foreign territory.'

[1] 'The fact is, there is no enthusiasm among the people, at this time, in favor of the war. The feeling which pervaded the public mind, growing out of the splendid victories gained by our brave troops in Mexico, has almost entirely subsided. The questions which men now ask among themselves are — What is the object of this war? — How long is it to continue? — Is our country to derive any practical benefit from its prosecution?'

Even war news, 'which formerly drew multitudes of excited . . . men around the printing offices, has almost ceased of its attractions.' Farmers, especially, are listless and indifferent. 'The war is already becoming distasteful to the public mind.' *Quincy* (Ill.) *Whig*, Jan. 12, 1848.

[2] *Illinois State Register*, Nov. 12, 1847. 'It cannot now be doubted' that the people want peace. They are 'by this time well cured of their delusion.' *Rockford Forum*, March 22, 1848.

[3] Its name changed with the issue of Sept. 23, 1847.

pressed Lincoln's views, had scourged Polk for his pacific course toward Mexico. That is as far as our knowledge goes of Lincoln's opinions on the Mexican War before he came in contact with the national Whig leaders at Washington in the winter of 1847–48.

He had, indeed, before his nomination as the Whig candidate for Congress, stated his conclusions as to the annexation of Texas, and the effect of it on slavery; but he made that statement in a private letter to a friend and political supporter who was an Abolitionist or 'Liberty man.' This letter gives all the light we have upon Lincoln's views as to Texas and slavery up to the time he entered Congress.

'I never was much interested in the Texas question,' he wrote. 'I never could see much good to come of annexation, inasmuch as they were already a free republican people on our own model. On the other hand, I never could very clearly see how the annexation would augment the evil of slavery. It always seemed to me that slaves would be taken there in about equal numbers, with or without annexation. And if more *were* taken because of annexation, still there would be just so many the fewer left where they were taken from. It is possibly true to some extent, that, with annexation, some slaves may be sent to Texas and continued in slavery that otherwise might have been liberated. To whatever extent this may be true, I think annexation an evil.

'I hold it to be a paramount duty of us in the free States,' Lincoln continued, 'due to the Union of the States, and perhaps to liberty itself (paradox though it may seem), to let the slavery of the other States alone; while, on the other hand, I hold it to be equally clear that we should never knowingly lend ourselves, directly or indirectly, to prevent that slavery from dying a natural death — to find new places for it to live in, when it can not longer exist in the old.

'Of course I am not now considering what would be our duty in cases of insurrection among the slaves' — the very thing which the Southern people charged the Abolitionists with trying to incite. 'To recur to the Texas question, I understand the

Liberty men to have viewed annexation as a much greater evil than ever I did.' [1]

A little more than two weeks after he entered the House, however, Lincoln introduced resolutions which were to cause him sharp annoyance for many years to come. The preamble quoted the repeated statements of the President that the Mexicans had started the war by invading our territory and shedding 'the blood of our fellow-citizens on *our own* soil;' and the resolution requested the President to inform the House, 'whether the spot on which the blood of our citizens was shed ... was or was not within the territory of Spain, at least ... until the Mexican revolution; whether that spot is or is not within the territory which was wrested from Spain by the revolutionary Government of Mexico; whether that spot is or is not within a settlement of people, which settlement has existed ever since long before the Texas revolution, and until its inhabitants fled before the approach of the United States army;' whether the people of that isolated settlement had ever submitted to the authority of Texas or the United States in any way; whether those people did not 'flee from the approach of the United States army ... *before* the blood was shed,' and whether the first bloodshed did not occur in the 'enclosure of one of the people who had thus fled from it; whether our *citizens*, whose blood was shed,' were not then officers and soldiers of our army ordered into the settlement by the President; and whether that order was not given after Taylor had 'more than once intimated to the War Department that ... no such movement was necessary to the defence or protection of Texas.' [2]

This belligerent action of a new member hardly warm in his seat, aroused the languid curiosity of the press correspondents in Washington. One of them wrote to his paper that Lincoln's enquiries 'stick to the *spot* in Mexico, where the first blood of

[1] Lincoln to Williamson Durley, Oct. 3, 1845. *Works*, I, 275–8.

[2] *Cong. Globe*, 30th Cong. 1st Sess., XVIII, 64, Dec. 22, 1847. Also *Works*, I, 318–20. It must be remembered that Henry Clay, whom Lincoln so greatly admired, referring to the President's statement that 'war existed by the act of Mexico,' had said in a public address at Lexington, Nov. 13, 1847, 'no earthly consideration would ever have tempted or provoked him to vote for a bill with a palpable falsehood stamped upon its face.' At this time and until 1849, Clay was not in Congress.

the war was shed, with all the tightness that characterized the fabled shirt of the fabled Nissus (*sic*). Evidently there is music in that very tall Mr. Lincoln.' [1] The Democratic paper in Springfield was swift in condemnation — little did his constituents expect Lincoln to oppose the war, in which so many of them had fought and some had died.[2] But this was only a faint intimation of the storm that was soon to burst upon him.

In House and Senate the Whigs grew ever more combative. They lost no opportunity to attack the Administration and were fertile in expedients to embarrass peace negotiations. The President had asked for ten regiments; authority to raise them was provokingly delayed, and, at last, confirmed grudgingly. Hudson of Massachusetts offered a resolution that our army be withdrawn 'to the east bank of the Rio Grande,' that no indemnity be claimed, that the boundary 'be established at or near the desert between the Nueces and the Rio Grande.' Forty-one of the most aggressive Whigs actually voted for Hudson's resolution; but Lincoln and the more moderate Whigs joined the Democrats in voting against it, and thus defeated it by more than three to one.[3] The national Whig organ, in a vicious editorial covering nearly an entire page, and double leaded, assailed the Administration and the war.[4]

Other obstructive Whig resolutions were presented; and when one of thanks to General Taylor (a purely partisan manœuver for the approaching presidential campaign) was offered, Ashmun took advantage of an inept Democratic amendment by proposing an addition to it, which declared that the war was 'unnecessarily and unconstitutionally begun by the President of the United States.' Ashmun's resolution was adopted by a strict party division, Lincoln voting for it, as did Stephens, Toombs,

---

[1] *Baltimore Patriot*, as quoted in *Rockford* (Ill.) *Forum*, Jan. 19, 1848.

[2] *Illinois State Register*, Jan. 7, 1848.

[3] *Cong. Globe*, 30th Cong. 1st Sess., XVIII, 93–4. The vote was forty-one ayes, including J. Q. Adams, Ashmun, and Giddings, to one hundred and thirty-seven nays including Lincoln, Stephens, and Toombs. *Ib.*, 94. Some days later a regular Democrat offered a resolution that the Ashmun declaration was 'untrue in fact' which was tabled by a vote of one hundred and five ayes to ninety-five nays, Lincoln voting aye. *Ib.*, 401–3.

[4] *National Intelligencer*, Jan. 16, 1848; and Feb. 5, 1848.

and all Southern Whigs.[1] 'What will these gallant heroes' from the Seventh District say when they learn that their Representative in Congress has voted that the war is 'infamous and wicked,' asked the *Illinois State Register*.[2]

In this state of the party conflict, Lincoln, the only Whig member from Illinois, rose from his seat in the back part of the House on January 12, 1848, and made the speech which was to prove his immediate political undoing. He said nothing new. Indeed Hudson, Giddings, and others had used almost the same language. Lincoln's speech was merely a restatement of the Whig position on the war, as modified by the party leaders, for the coming fight for the Presidency.

Lincoln said that he had remained 'silent' until he took his seat in the House; and that he would have continued to be silent, if the President had allowed it to be so. But Polk continually insisted that 'every silent vote given for supplies' was an endorsement of his course. In all his messages the President had insisted that 'the soil was ours,' on which the Mexicans had attacked us. That fact was vital; it was, said Lincoln, 'the very point upon which he should be justified, or condemned.'

Like a lawyer in court attacking the sufficiency of a legal document, Lincoln examined that part of Polk's message which set out the American title to territory north and east of the Rio Grande. It was, he said, 'from beginning to end the sheerest deception.' Why? Because the President had assumed that either the Nueces River or the Rio Grande was the boundary of Texas, whereas 'the boundary is somewhere between the two [rivers], and not actually at either.'

The President had said that the Rio Grande was the boundary of Louisiana when purchased from France in 1803, yet had admitted that in 1819 'we sold to Spain the whole country from the Rio Grande eastward to the Sabine.' So 'what, under heaven,' had the original boundary of the Louisiana purchase to do 'with the present boundary between us and Mexico?' When

[1] The vote was eighty-two ayes to eighty-one nays. *Cong. Globe*, 30th Cong. 1st Sess., XVIII, 94–5, Jan. 3, 1848.

[2] Jan. 21, 1848.

ABRAHAM LINCOLN ABOUT 1848
From a photograph of the daguerreotype formerly owned
by Robert T. Lincoln

a man sold his land to his neighbor, how could the line that once divided them 'still be the boundary' between them?

Suppose that Texas did claim the Rio Grande as her boundary — had 'not Mexico always claimed the contrary? So . . . there is but claim against claim,' avowed Lincoln. Suppose Texas did form 'congressional districts, counties, etc.,' extending to the Rio Grande? 'All of this is but naked claim. . . . If I should claim your land by word of mouth, that certainly would not make it mine; and if I were to claim it by a deed which I had made myself, and with which you had nothing to do, the claim would be quite the same in substance — or rather, in utter nothingness.'

What if Santa Anna did make a treaty recognizing 'the Rio Grande as the western boundary of Texas. . . . Santa Anna while a prisoner of war, a captive, could not bind Mexico by a treaty.' A treaty! Nobody had ever called it that for a decade after it was signed. Polk was the first person to call 'that little thing . . . by that big name,' and he had done so 'in his extremity . . . to wring something from it in justification of himself in connection with the Mexican war.' Lincoln vigorously assailed the Santa Anna-Texan compact. That agreement settled nothing, he said.

Here Lincoln came perilously near to pettifogging. The agreement, he asserted, provided that 'to prevent collisions' between the armies, the Texan 'army should not approach nearer than within five leagues' — of what? 'Clearly . . . of the Rio Grande.' So if that river were the Texan boundary, here was a stipulation 'that Texas shall not go within five leagues of her own boundary.' Yet it was obvious and not denied by anybody, that this part of the treaty meant that the Texan forces should approach within five leagues of the retreating Mexican army.

But what was decisive, Lincoln contended, was the extent of either Texan or American jurisdiction beyond the Nueces. On that critical point the President was vague. 'He tells us it went beyond the Nueces, but he does not tell us it went to the Rio Grande.' Merely crossing one river did not mean that you went all the way to the next. Lincoln himself exercised 'jurisdiction' over his lot in Springfield which was between the Mississippi and Wabash Rivers, but did that ownership give him jurisdiction of all other land from one river to the other? Or could he annex the lot of his neighbor across the street 'by merely standing on his own side of the street and claiming it, or even sitting down and writing a deed for it?'

What was 'the true rule' for ascertaining the boundary between Texas and Mexico? 'Whatever separated the actual exercise of jurisdiction of the one from that of the other was the true boundary between them.' Since Texas occupied the western bank of the Nueces and Mexico the eastern bank of the Rio Grande 'neither river was the boundary; but the uninhabited country between the two was. The extent of our territory in that region depended . . . on revolution' alone.

Then Lincoln made a declaration of general principles which was not necessary to his special pleading and which was to be used against him when he became the supreme figure in the greatest crisis of our history. His love of the academic overcame, for a moment, his habitual caution and his devotion to the practical and the immediate.

'Any people anywhere being inclined and having the power have the right to rise up and shake off the existing government, and form a new one that suits them better. This is a most valuable, a most sacred right — a right which we hope and believe is to liberate the world.

'Nor is this right confined to cases in which the whole people of an existing government may choose to exercise it. Any portion of such people that can may revolutionize and make their own of so much of the territory as they inhabit.

'More than this, a majority of any portion of such people may revolutionize, putting down a minority, intermingled with or near about them, who may oppose this movement. Such minority was precisely the case of the Tories of our own revolution.

'It is a quality of revolutions not to go by old lines or old laws; but to break up both, and make new ones.'

Thus Texas had 'revolutionized against Mexico,' and 'just so far as she carried her revolution by obtaining the actual, willing or unwilling, submission of the people, so far the country was hers, and no farther.'

To settle that point, let the President answer the questions put to him in Lincoln's resolutions — let him point out 'the spot,' on American soil where the first blood was shed. Thereupon Lincoln burst into fiery rhetoric. If the President could not or would not answer, Lincoln would be convinced of what he more than suspected already, 'that he [the President] is deeply conscious of being in the wrong; that he feels the blood of this war, like the blood of Abel, is crying to Heaven against him; that originally having some strong motive . . . to involve the two countries in a war, and trusting to escape scrutiny by fixing the public gaze upon the exceeding brightness of military glory — that attractive rainbow that arises in showers of blood — that serpent's eye that charms to destroy — he plunged into it and has swept on and on till, disappointed in his calculation of the ease with which Mexico might be subdued, he now finds himself he knows not where.

'How like the half-insane mumbling of a fever dream is the whole war part of his late message!' exclaimed Lincoln, who went on at great length to point out the President's inconsistencies. 'His mind, taxed beyond its power, is running hither and thither, like some tortured creature on a burning surface, finding no position on which it can settle down and be at ease.' And when would peace come? Polk did not say. The war had gone on for about twenty months and the President did not have 'even an imaginary conception' of when it would end. No wonder he was 'a miserably perplexed man. God grant he may be able to show there is not something about his conscience more painful than all his mental perplexity.' [1]

In less than two weeks after Lincoln made his attack on the Administration, the treaty of peace was signed and, as soon as the despatch bearer reached Washington, the President laid it before the Senate.[2]

Before news of the treaty arrived, and a week after Lincoln's

---

[1] *Works,* I, 327–45; *Cong. Globe,* 30th Cong. 1st Sess., XVIII, 154–6.

[2] The treaty was signed at Guadalupe Hidalgo, Feb. 2, 1848, the messenger delivered it to the President, Feb. 19, and he transmitted it to the Senate, Feb. 22. Polk's *Diary,* III, 345; *Messages:* Richardson, IV, 573–4.

The treaty, amended in unimportant particulars, was ratified by the Senate May 30, 1848.

anti-war speech, John Jameson of Missouri, a great wag, in a political tirade in the House lashed out for an instant, at the lone Whig member from Illinois. 'Strange position before the American Congress for such a Representative,' the representative of a district which sent Hardin who fell at Buena Vista, and Baker who, 'in the bloody battle, and at Cerro Gordo commanded when the noble Shields fell with a grape [shot] through his lungs.' [1]

With this exception, no notice whatever was taken in Washington of Lincoln's speech. Neither the Whig nor Democratic papers at the capital made mention of it, except as a part of the routine report of proceedings in Congress. Lincoln's colleagues from Illinois did not speak of it in their letters to party friends about the political situation. McClernand frequently advised the editor of the Democratic paper at Springfield of developments in Congress, but he made no reference to Lincoln.[2] Neither did Winthrop, nor Ashmun, nor Giddings, nor Toombs, nor Stephens, nor any of the Whig leaders, whether from the North or the South.[3]

The correspondents of newspapers, except those of Springfield, did not give Lincoln's speech a single line or word. Most curious of all, the peevish and distraught but abnormally alert President put down nothing in his diary about Lincoln, then or thereafter — that voluminous and incredibly minute chronicle which Polk wrote every night about everything that happened from breakfast to bedtime.

But Herndon was distressed. He had taken alarm at Lincoln's vote on Ashmun's resolution and wrote Lincoln in earnest protest. 'Would you have voted what you felt and knew to be a lie? I know you would not,' said Lincoln to 'Dear William,' in reply. He took much pains to satisfy his partner — partner even more in politics than in law; for he knew that Herndon was in intimate contact with the people.[4] 'I do not mean this letter for the

[1] *Cong. Globe*, 30th Cong. 1st Sess., xviii, 190. Jan. 18, 1848.

[2] Lanphier MSS.

[3] Existing papers of no member of Congress while Lincoln was in the House make any mention of Lincoln's speech or, indeed, of Lincoln himself, so far as the author has seen them.

[4] 'It is a fact which has been frequently remarked by the newspaper press, that

public, but for you,' he cautioned his partner. 'Yours forever, A. LINCOLN.' [1]

His anxiety to reassure Herndon was well-nigh emotional. The day after his long explanatory letter, he wrote another about a speech in the House just made by 'a little, slim, pale-faced consumptive man,' Alexander H. Stephens of Georgia. It was 'the very best speech of an hour's length I ever heard. My old withered dry eyes are full of tears yet.' Lincoln would send 'our people' copies of it. [2]

Herndon did not wait for Lincoln's letter, but again wrote that his partner was wrong in assuming that the President could not, in a defensive war, invade the enemy country. Lincoln answered sharply and at length. Why did the Constitution give to Congress exclusively the power to declare war? So that no one man could plunge the country into war, as Kings had done. [3]

In his own district the reaction against Lincoln was immediate and vociferous. The Democratic paper at Springfield promptly published his 'spot' resolutions. Little did his constituents, it stated, many of whom had 'immortalized themselves' on bloody battle-fields, expect Lincoln to oppose the war.

---

nearly all the Whigs who have returned from Mexico are against their party on the war question.' *Illinois State Register*, Nov. 26, 1847, commenting on the position of the *Tazewell Whig*.

[1] Lincoln to Herndon, Feb. 1, 1848. *Works*, I, 351–4.

[2] Same to same, Feb. 2, 1848. *Ib.*, 354–5. Stephens' speech was delivered Feb. 2, 1848. He was the most eloquent of the Southern Whigs and assailed the war vigorously: Polk began it; the boundary of Texas did not extend to the Rio Grande, but 'just so far as her revolution successfully extended, and no further. . . . Her limits were marked by her sword.'

National honor — 'the brightest gem in the chaplet of a nation's glory' — did not justify the making of war 'against a neighboring people to compel them to sell their country. . . . If the last funeral pile of liberty were lighted, I would mount it and expire in its flames before I would be coerced by any power, however great and strong, to sell or surrender the land of my home, the place of my nativity, and the graves of my sires!'

Honor! 'Shall it be said that American honor aims at nothing higher than land? . . . Tell it not to the world.' Such honor was 'a loathsome, beastly thing.'

Taylor, that grand old Whig, was the hero of the war. Think of Buena Vista, 'one of the greatest achievements ever won by the valor of arms,' in which so many gallant officers died, among them Hardin — 'I never knew a truer, firmer and nobler man.' Did these men give their lives for nothing but land, 'gross, vile dirt'? *Cong. Globe*, 30th Cong. 1st Sess., XIX, Appendix, 159–63.

Presumably it was at one of these passages that Lincoln wept, since the remainder of Stephens' speech was devoted to unemotional argument.

[3] Lincoln to Herndon, Feb. 15, 1848. *Works*, II. 1–3.

And what would be said by the thousand volunteers from Lincoln's district when they learned of Lincoln's conduct? An editorial under the caption 'OUT DAMNED SPOT,' said that Lincoln had made his '*début* in Congress,' by an attack on the war.[1]

The Whig paper in Springfield published Lincoln's speech and challenged the Democratic editor to publish it also — did he 'fear to have it go to his readers?' [2] The Democratic organ replied with volleys of denunciation and defiance. A Washington correspondent of a Louisville paper had heard Jameson's castigation of Lincoln in the House, and wrote a short account of it. The *Register* printed his comment:

'I think Lincoln will find that he had better remained quiet. He will . . . regret that he voted that' Illinois officers [naming them] 'fell while leading brave Illinoisans to ROBBERY AND DISHONOR . . . "IN AID OF A WAR OF RAPINE AND MURDER". . . ; that he has thrown upon the escutcheon of Illinois the stain of having sent six thousand men to Mexico "to record their infamy and shame in the blood of poor, innocent, inoffending people, whose only crime was weakness". . . ; that he has declared by his vote that the "God of Heaven has forgotten to defend the weak and innocent, and permitted the strong band of murderers and demons from hell to kill men, women, and children, and lay waste and pillage the land of the just."' [3]

Obviously Lincoln had been unrestrained while delivering his speech; and, when he came to write out his remarks for the *Congressional Globe*, had left out the violent part which so incensed the newspaper correspondent.[4]

Next the Illinois Democratic organ published a lengthy 'SPEECH Not delivered in the House of Representatives in reply to Mr. Lincoln of Illinois.' The imaginary assailant said that

[1] *Illinois State Register*, Jan. 7, 21, 28, 1848.

[2] *Illinois Journal*, Feb. 10, 1848.

[3] *Illinois State Register*, clipped in *Belleville Advocate*, March 2, 1848.

[4] The version by the newspaper correspondent resembles the language of Giddings and Corwin. The reporter's account was from memory of what he heard Lincoln say, and not from the speech as it afterward appeared in the *Globe*.

Speeches published in the Appendix of the *Cong. Globe* were always written out, either before or after delivery. Lincoln made reference to this practice in his description of Stephens' speech: 'If he writes it out anything like he delivered it,' etc. *Works*, I, 355. Often speeches as delivered differed widely from the printed version in the *Globe*.

Lincoln's attack on the President was 'imbecile and silly.' Moreover his speech was a mere rehash and a poor one. Everybody had read 'in the most obscure' Whig paper the same kind of speeches, though far abler. Doubtless many loyal men had voted for Lincoln. 'Sir, will they allow him to go unrebuked who pleads here in their name, but without their authority, the cause of the guerilla bandit [Santa Anna], that draws his weapon reeking with the blood of our assassinated countrymen?' [1]

Again the *State Register* discharged a battery, and one of the heaviest calibre. About three weeks after Lincoln made his speech in the House, Douglas rose in his place in the Senate, his desk piled with books, and with volumes on the floor about him, to defend the American cause; and, with Douglas, defence always meant attack. 'I shall state no fact for the accuracy of which I have not the most conclusive authority in the books before me,' he began; and he made the ablest argument in support of the war that had been made. Yours the iniquity, the treason, the robbery, he thundered, in denunciation of the Whig championship of Mexico. [2] Delighted with this effort of the Democratic champion, the *State Register* published Douglas's speech and dared the Whig organ to print it — the *Register* offered to publish Lincoln's speech 'in full' if the *Journal* would publish Douglas's speech 'in full.' [3] The Whig paper ignored the Democratic proposal.

In such fashion began the Democratic attack upon Lincoln in Illinois. Soon public meetings were held attended by furious partisans. At one in Morgan County resolutions were adopted in fervent support of the war and in wrathful denunciation of the 'treasonable assaults of guerillas at home; party demagogues;' slanderers of the President, defenders of the butchery at the Alamo, traducers of the heroism at San Jacinto.

[1] *Illinois State Register*, Feb. 18, 1858.

[2] *Cong. Globe*, 30th Cong. 1st Sess., xix, Appendix, 221–7.

[3] *Illinois State Register*, Feb. 18, 1848. Some Washington correspondents were deeply impressed by Douglas's speech: it 'was a splendid affair ... original, bold, complete.' Washington correspondent *Louisville Democrat*, clipped in *Illinois State Register*, Feb. 25, 1848.

'Mr. Douglas spoke to a crowded auditory and was listened to with profound attention.' Senator Rusk of Texas afterward declined to speak because Douglas had said all that could be said.

And Lincoln! 'His base, dastardly and treasonable assault upon President Polk,' and 'the resolutions offered by him against his own government' were infamous. Never until now had the Seventh Congressional District 'known disgrace, so black. . . . Such black odium and infamy heaped upon the living brave and illustrious dead can but excite the indignation of every true Illinoian.'. . . Henceforth will this Benedict Arnold of our district be known here only as the Ranchero Spotty of one term.'

The *Register* published this frantic outburst as 'Another "spot" for Lincoln.' [1] Speedily other party meetings adopted similar 'spot resolutions.' [2] The name stuck, 'spotty Lincoln' was heard from Democratic lips throughout the State,[3] and he was frequently compared to the typical American traitor — he was, asserted the *Peoria Democratic Press* 'a second Benedict Arnold.' [4] Another influential paper declared that Lincoln's 'course in denouncing his country, has called forth a stern rebuke from many of his constituents, and will yet be more signally condemned.' [5]

Lincoln was aggrieved, irritated, depressed; but, except to Herndon, he made but one known defence of his course. The Rev. J. M. Peck delivered an oration at Belleville upon the first anniversary of the battle of Buena Vista. Peck sent to Lincoln a copy of the newspaper containing his speech which was a justification of the American cause. Lincoln wrote Peck a long explanatory letter, merely repeating the main points in his speech.[6]

In despair, Herndon wrote his partner again and again that his political career was ended.[7] Fortunate for Lincoln that he

---

[1] *Illinois State Register*, March 10, 1848.

[2] For example, at a Clark County meeting 'held without distinction of party': '*Resolved*, that Abe Lincoln, the author of the "Spotty" resolutions in Congress against his own country, may they be long remembered by his constituents, but may they cease to remember him, except to rebuke him — they have done much for him, but he has done nothing for them, save the stain he inflicted on their proud name of patriotism and glory, in the part they have taken in their country's cause.' *Belleville Advocate*, March 2, 1848; *Illinois State Register*, Feb. 11, 1848.

[3] *Ib.*, Feb. 25, 1848.   [4] May 26, 1848.

[5] *Belleville Advocate*, March 2, 1848.

[6] Lincoln to Peck, May 21, 1848. *Works*, II, 23–6.

[7] 'In 1847–9 I saw that Lincoln would ruin himself about the Mexican war and his

had publicly announced that he would not be a candidate to succeed himself. Like Hardin, he wanted another term,[1] but Herndon's melancholy reports extinguished his hope, and he soon devoted his practised talents as a politician to help secure the nomination of Taylor for President.

Apparently Lincoln's closest associates in the House were Southern Whigs like Stephens and Toombs. Early in the session a congressional club was formed to promote the candidacy of Taylor, the popular soldier. At first this club consisted of seven members, all but two from the South and advocates of slavery, and most of those who joined afterward were also Southern men. Of this political organization, called 'The Young Indians,' Lincoln was one of the organizers.[2] With these active and resourceful party comrades he exerted himself in the advancement of the fortunes of their candidate; and we shall now accompany Lincoln through the remainder of his congressional career in which national politics was his chief concern, and witness the next discipline that Fate administered to him.

opposition to it, and . . . I tried to prevent Lincoln's destruction. I wrote to him on the subject again and again.' Herndon to Weik, Feb. 11, 1887; and Oct. 28, 1885. Weik MSS.

[1] 'He wanted to run for Congress again, but it was no use to try.' *Ib.*

[2] *Recollections of Alexander H. Stephens*, edited by Myrta Lockett Avary, 21–2. The first members of 'The Young Indians' were Stephens and Toombs of Georgia, William B. Preston, Thomas S. Flournoy, and John S. Pendleton of Virginia, Truman Smith of Connecticut, and Lincoln. Edward C. Cabell of Florida and Henry W. Hilliard of Alabama joined later. *Ib.*

CHAPTER VIII
NATIONAL POLITICS AND COLLAPSE

Opposition to the slave-power . . . is now for the first time the leading principle of a broad, resolute, and national organization. . . . We found now a new party. Its cornerstone is freedom, its broad, all-sustaining arches are truth, justice, and humanity. SUMNER in Free Soil Ratification Meeting in Faneuil Hall, Aug. 22, 1848.

The first and indispensable step . . . is to be united among yourselves on this great and most vital question. . . . The North will not believe that you are in earnest in opposition to your encroachments, and they will continue to follow, one after another, until the work of abolition is finished. CALHOUN, Address of the Southern Delegates in Congress, Jan., 1849.

I am in favor of leaving the people of any territory which may be hereafter acquired the right to regulate it [slavery] themselves, under the general principles of the Constitution. LINCOLN, in Congress, July 27, 1848.

WHILE gloomy letters from Herndon were arriving by wellnigh every mail and confirmation of his partner's forebodings were beginning to appear in Illinois newspapers, a tragic incident in the House took Lincoln's mind, for a brief moment, from the thought of politics. Lucien B. Chase of Tennessee offered resolutions of thanks to various general officers, among them G. J. Pillow, Franklin Pierce, and James Shields, for their gallant services in the war. The Whigs objected and fifty-four of them, including Lincoln, Toombs, and John Quincy Adams, voted against suspending the rules so that the resolution could be considered.[1] After some bickering the main question was ordered, most Whigs voting against it.[2] John Quincy Adams was the first to answer to the call of his name. 'Nay,' he replied, in an 'uncommonly emphatic tone of voice.'[3] It was the last vote he ever cast.

Soon after the roll-call, the venerable statesman sank from his seat to the floor, fatally stricken. The House hastily adjourned and the dying man was carried to the rotunda for air and then to the Speaker's room, alarmed and grieving members gathering

[1] The rules were suspended by one hundred and ten ayes to fifty-four nays. *Cong. Globe*, 30th Cong. 1st Sess., XVIII, 300–1, Feb. 21, 1848.

[2] The vote was ninety-eight ayes to eighty-six nays, Lincoln, Stephens, and Toombs voting nay. *Ib.*, 381.

[3] *Life of John Quincy Adams:* W. H. Seward, 333.

about him.[1] There he lay for two days and died on Wednesday, February 23.[2]

Lincoln was appointed on the committee of arrangements for the funeral, consisting of thirty Representatives, one from each State, chosen without regard to party affiliations; but this large number was found to be cumbersome and delegated its authority to a sub-committee of which Lincoln was not a member.[3] On Saturday, February 26, the funeral services were conducted in the House which was draped in black; and, preceded by military companies, a band, and the chaplains of both Houses, a procession consisting of the House Committee, pall-bearers,[4] Adams' family, the Massachusetts delegation, the House, the Senate, the President and his Cabinet, the Supreme Court, the Diplomatic corps and other official bodies, marched to the Congressional Burying Ground.[5] Thus Lincoln witnessed the death-stroke of one of the preëminent men of the nation, an outstanding figure in American history.[6]

Soon after the death of Adams Lincoln cast his second vote of historical interest. On February 28, 1848, Harvey Putnam of New York offered a resolution which was, in effect, the Wilmot Proviso revived. It declared that slavery should be prohibited in any territory acquired from Mexico as the result of the war. On a motion to table this resolution Lincoln voted nay.[7] This

[1] *Cong. Globe*, 30th Cong. 1st Sess., XVIII, 381; Seward, 346-50; R. R. Wilson, II, 58-9.

[2] Seward, 336-7.

[3] Lincoln to Rev. Henry Slicer, June 1, 1848. *Uncollected Letters of Abraham Lincoln:* Gilbert A. Tracy, 30-1. Slicer wrote Lincoln complaining that he had been 'excluded' from the conduct of the funeral services. Lincoln answered that he knew nothing about it, since he was not on the sub-committee which had charge of the details.

'By an unfortunate omission, no seats were reserved for the Clergy; but as a number of them arrived, . . . they were conducted . . . to favorable positions.' *National Intelligencer*, quoted in *Cong. Globe*, 30th Cong. 1st Sess., XVIII, 389.

[4] Calhoun, Benton, Chief Justice Taney, and Justice McLean of the Supreme Court were among the pall-bearers.

[5] *House Journal*, 30th Cong. 1st Sess., 446-7.

[6] The news of Adams' death was not published in Springfield until nine days afterward. *Sangamo Journal*, March 2; *Illinois State Register*, March 3, 1848.

Adams' body was taken to Boston accompanied by a Congressional Committee, of which John Wentworth was the representative from Illinois. *Cong. Globe*, 30th Cong. 1st Sess., XVIII, 387.

A committee of the Legislature of Massachusetts took charge of the ceremonies at Fanueil Hall and of the burial at Quincy, Massachusetts, Adams' home. Seward, 352.

[7] It was tabled by a vote of one hundred and five ayes to ninety-three nays, all anti-

was the only time during the session that the principle of the Wilmot Proviso came directly to a vote.

Lincoln's votes on slavery in the District of Columbia are confusing. Early in the session he voted against tabling a petition of eighteen citizens of the District praying the repeal of all laws authorizing the slave trade in the District.[1] On May 29 he voted with the pro-slavery men against suspending the rules to allow a resolution to be introduced directing reports on petitions for the abolition of slavery in the District of Columbia which had been referred to various committees.[2] This curious shifting of ground we shall see repeated at the next session.

Lincoln voted for the war loan of $18,500,000, as did all members except fourteen, among whom were most of the Massachusetts delegation.[3] He also voted against tabling an army appropriation bill.[4] On a bill to raise an additional military force

slavery men, without regard to party, voting nay. *House Journal*, 30th Cong. 1st Sess., 453–4.

[1] *Cong. Globe*, 30th Cong. 1st Sess., xviii, 60, Dec. 21, 1847. The motion to table was beaten by the deciding vote of Speaker Winthrop who voted nay, because he thought that all petitions should be given 'respectful consideration.' The House stood ninety-seven to ninety-seven.

[2] *House Journal*, 30th Cong. 1st Sess., xviii, 839–41. May 29, 1848.

The vote was fifty-four ayes to ninety nays. The resolution introduced by Amos Tuck of New Hampshire declared that since citizens 'in great numbers,' including citizens of the District of Columbia, had memorialized Congress to abolish slavery in the District and that these petitions had been tabled, even without reading, or referred to various committees which had ignored them, such committees be directed 'to report thereon at the earliest practicable period.'

All strong anti-slavery men, including the whole Massachusetts delegation, voted to permit Tuck's resolution to be introduced, while Southern representatives of all parties, with all regular Northern Democrats and a few Northern Whigs, Lincoln among them, voted against allowing the resolution to be introduced.

This appears to have been all that was accomplished during the session on slavery in the District. On June 19, a bill was introduced to repeal that section of the act of 1801, 'and all other acts or parts of acts that in any manner interfere with, regulate, or sustain the institution of slavery in said District,' but nothing came of it. *Cong. Globe*, 30th Cong. 1st Sess., xviii, 352.

[3] The bill passed by a vote of one hundred and ninety-two ayes to fourteen nays. *House Journal*, 30th Cong. 1st Sess., 426–8. Six of the ten members from Massachusetts voted against it.

This loan was successfully negotiated by William W. Corcoran.

[4] *Ib.*, 1158–9.

One of these votes was curious. It was against an amendment to the Army appropriation bill providing for the payment of the expenses of Frémont and Stockton in California and for Stockton's government in that territory after taking possession. *Ib.*, 1251–2.

his votes were contradictory, against it when first presented, for it three weeks later, and, still later, against its consideration.[1] Another vote, given early in the session, is still more enigmatic. Wilmot offered a resolution for raising five million dollars annually, 'to be assessed on personal *and other* property, stocks, and money at interest,' while the war lasted and until the public debt was paid. This would have taxed the slaves of the South and financial investments in the North alike, and it was beaten by a tremendous majority, Lincoln voting against it.[2] On internal improvements and the tariff, however, Lincoln's votes are consistent and emphatic;[3] and he supported a bill which Douglas had engineered through the Senate in aid of the Illinois Central Railroad.[4] Among the petitions which Lincoln presented was one by Uriah Brown for 'further testing of his discovery of "liquid fire"' to be used in national defence.[5]

With incident and event and the routine work of the House, the months passed and time restored Lincoln's normal spirits, depressed as they had been by unhappy political news from home, by Adams' dramatic ending, by Herndon's predictions of political disaster. Mrs. Lincoln and Robert had gone to Lexington, Kentucky, on a visit to her father, and she and Lincoln often wrote to each other. In a letter to 'Dear Mary,' written April 16, he bemoans the monotonous drudgery of his office: 'In this troublesome world, we are never quite satisfied. When you were here, I thought you hindered me some in attending to business; but now, having nothing but business — no variety — it has grown exceedingly tasteless to me. I hate to sit down and direct documents, and I hate to stay in this old room by myself.

'You know I told you in last Sunday's letter [April 9], I was going to make a little speech during the week; but the week has passed away without my getting a chance to do so; and now my interest in the subject has passed away too. Your second and

---

[1] *House Journal*, 30th Cong. 1st Sess., 613–4, 693, 765–6. This bill did not pass. The Whigs voted against it as a party manœuver.

[2] *Ib.*, 347–8. The vote was forty-seven ayes to one hundred and thirty-nine nays, anti-slavery men like John Quincy Adams joining pro-slavery men like Robert Toombs against what, at that time, was believed to be a radical economic proposal.

[3] *Ib.*, 696–7, 983–7, 917–9. [4] *Ib.*, 1268–71.

[5] *Ib.*, 273, Jan. 21, 1884.

third letters have been received since I wrote before. Dear Eddy thinks father is "*gone tapilo*" [capital].[1] Has any further discovery been made as to the breaking into your grand-mother's house? If I were she I would not remain there alone.'

Mrs. Lincoln had written him to get some plain stockings for Eddie, but he cannot find a pair in Washington, he tells her, although he has inquired in all the stores. In fact he has been able to discover 'only one plain pair of any sort' that he thought 'would fit "Eddy's dear little feet."'

Lincoln is anxious lest his wife offend her father by her attention to persons he disliked. 'I wish you to enjoy yourself in every possible way, but is there no danger of wounding the feelings of your good father, by being openly intimate with the Wickliff family?' While on the point of her deportment, Lincoln adds: 'All the house [seemingly Mrs. Spriggs'], or rather all with whom you were on decided good terms, send their love to you. The others say nothing.'

He is careful to tell his wife, who was economical to the point of parsimony, that his purchases for personal adornment made in her absence have not been extravagant. 'Very soon after you went away, I got what I think a very pretty set of shirt bosom studs — modest little ones, jet set in gold, only costing 50 cents a piece or 1.50 for the whole.'

Lincoln wishes she would not write his name ostentatiously on envelopes. 'Suppose you do not prefix the "Hon." to the address on your letters to me any more. I like the letters very much, but I would rather they should not have that upon them. It is not necessary as I suppose you have thought, to have them come free.'

He is glad that his wife is relieved from a persistent headache and he makes a joke about it. 'And you are entirely free from headache? That is good, considering it is the first spring you have been free from it since we were acquainted. I am afraid you will get so well and fat and young as to be wanting to marry again. Tell Louisa I want her to watch you a little for me. Get weighed and write me how much you weigh.'

A dream concerning their oldest son worried Lincoln. 'I did

---

[1] The word is doubtful and may have been a household word without meaning.

not get rid of the impression of that foolish dream about dear Bobby, till I got your letter written the same day. What did he and Eddy think of the little letters father sent them? Don't let the blessed little fellows forget father. Most Affectionately . . . A. LINCOLN.' [1]

On the day Lincoln wrote this letter to his wife, nearly eighty slaves all from Georgetown were taken on board the *Pearl*, Captain Edward Sayres, which had been chartered for the purpose by a militant abolitionist, Daniel Drayton. His purpose was to take the slaves to a free state. The boat was pursued and captured and the slaves put in prison together with the crew.[2] Giddings offered resolutions of inquiry, the preamble being a statement of abolition views. Instantly the House was in confusion and, on objection, the resolution was not received.[3]

Wrathful excitement reigned in the city. Was law to be broken with impunity, authority to be flouted, insurrection instigated? This was the poison-fruit of abolition preaching and practise. Down with the incendiary press which, at bottom, was responsible. Gravely alarmed, the editor of the *National Era* published a disavowal that it had been 'concerned, either directly or indirectly,' with the attempted escape of the slaves. The denial availed nothing; on two nights a mob gathered before the rickety printing office, which was saved only by the prompt action of the police and city government.[4]

In the House next day Palfrey offered a resolution of inquiry and a violent debate sprang up which raged for nearly a week. Amendments were offered and finally 'the whole subject was laid on the table,' Lincoln voting thus to dispose of it.[5] What he

---

[1] Lincoln to his wife, April 16, 1848. MS. Barrett Collection.

[2] *Washington:* George Alfred Townsend, 595. Drayton was heavily fined and sentenced to prison. He was pardoned, Aug. 12, 1852. Philip Barton Key, son of Francis Scott Key, author of the Star Spangled Banner, prosecuted Drayton and Sayres; and Horace Mann and James M. Carlisle, defended them. They had broken the law, but Abolitionists boldly took the ground that a bad law ought to be broken.

[3] *Cong. Globe*, 30th Cong. 1st Sess., xviii, 641, April 18, 1848.

[4] *Recollections*, L. A. Gobright, 87–91; Bryan, ii, 186–7.

[5] *Cong. Globe*, 30th Cong. 1st Sess., xviii, 649–73, April 20–25, 1848. The vote was one hundred and thirty ayes to forty-two nays, Lincoln voting aye, as did many anti-slavery men.

Three months earlier, inspired by the alleged seizure of a colored waiter in a boarding house by three slave-traders, Giddings had offered a resolution for the repeal

thought about the affair, if anything, is unknown, for he said nothing during the debate and was silent thereafter.

Sometime during May Mrs. Lincoln answered her husband's letter. It was one of her 'peculiarities,' she said, that she could never remember the day of the month and so could not date her letters; she was so tired, however, that she knew she was writing on a Saturday night and that 'our babies are asleep.' She told Lincoln of some trivial thing, seemingly in relation to clothes for the little boys. 'It takes so many changes to do children, particularly in summer.' Mrs. Lincoln informed her husband of the news from home — 'Springfield . . . as dull as usual;' related an incident about 'Boby,' Eddie, and 'a little kitten, your hobby;' said that her step-mother was very kind, but that 'if she thought any of us, were on her hands again . . . she would be worse than ever.'

Mrs. Lincoln wrote that 'Uncle James Parker of Miss. . . . and his family' were going to Philadelphia 'to take their oldest daughter there to school,' and Mrs. Lincoln wanted to 'pack up and accompany them. You know I am so fond of sight seeing, and I did not get to New York or Boston, or travel the lake route [when the Lincolns went to Washington]. . . . How much, I wish, instead of writing, we were together this evening, I feel very sad away from you.' After some small talk, Mrs. Lincoln assured her husband that the children remembered him — 'even E— eyes brighten at the mention of your name. My love to all, Truly yours, M. L.' [1]

But Lincoln did not respond to this tender plea to let his wife come East on her longed for 'sight-seeing' expedition. The national conventions were at hand and he was engrossed in politics. At Baltimore the last of May, the Democrats nominated Lewis Cass of Michigan for President and William O. Butler of Kentucky for Vice President; and the Whigs were to hold their Convention at Philadelphia the second week in June. General

---

of the slave trade in the District of Columbia, or the removal of the capital to a free state. A motion to table was beaten by a vote of eighty-five ayes to eighty-six nays, Lincoln voting nay; but a second motion to table was carried by a vote of ninety-four ayes to eighty-eight nays, Lincoln again voting nay. *Ib.*, 179–80, Jan. 17, 1848.

[1] Mrs. Lincoln to Lincoln, 'Lexington, May, — '48.' MS. owned by Mrs. George McNutt, Springfield, Ill. Published in *Cleveland Plain Dealer*, Feb. 11, 1924.

Zachary Taylor was preëminently the candidate of the Southern Whigs, of Toombs, and Stephens, and Crittenden; and Lincoln was as feverishly anxious as they that the military hero of the hour should be made the standard bearer of the Whig party. Indeed Stephens declared that the 'Young Indians' organized the Taylor movement which resulted in his nomination. [1] Although Lincoln's former idol, Henry Clay, was again a candidate, as were Webster and General Scott, Lincoln urged his friends in Illinois to get delegates for 'Old Rough and Ready.' [2]

Linder, then a Whig, wanted to support Taylor for President and yet sustain Polk. Lincoln thought that such an attitude was bad politics. 'In law, it is good policy to never plead what you need not, lest you oblige yourself to prove what you cannot;' so if Linder went for Taylor 'because he could take some Democrats and lose no Whigs' and also uphold Polk 'on the origin and mode of prosecuting the war,' Linder would 'still take some Democrats, but . . . lose more Whigs,' and 'in the sum of the operation . . . be the loser.' If Linder would 'look around' he would find this to be true among his own neighbors.[3] But Linder was right; like Herndon he was on the ground, and knew the public temper in Illinois at that time.

Lincoln wrote Archibald Williams, that 'Mr. Clay's chance for an election is just no chance at all. . . . We can elect nobody but General Taylor; and we cannot elect him without a nomination.' [4] In answer to an inquiry from Elihu B. Washburne, a brisk and efficient young Whig politician of Galena, Lincoln said that nobody could tell who would be nominated. However,

[1] Osborn H. Oldroyd, in *Lincoln Memorial*, 241.
'It was I . . . who made him [Taylor] President. Soon after the first battles of the war . . . I urged on the anti-War party that Taylor was our man; I got his nomination in a Whig convention in Georgia in 1847. . . . We [The Young Indians] . . . opened an extensive correspondence and put the ball in motion.' *Recollections of Alexander H. Stephens*, Avary, 21–2.

[2] Toombs thus explains the abandonment of Clay by the Southern Whigs: 'He has sold himself body and soul to the Northern Anti-slavery Whigs. . . . There are not ten Southern representatives who would not support Gen[era]l Taylor against him if he were nominated. The real truth is Clay was put up and pushed by Corwin, and McLean, Greeley & Co. to break down Taylor in the South. . . . I am a Taylor man without a second choice.' Toombs to James Thomas, Washington, D.C., April 16, 1848. *Rept. Am. Hist. Assn.*, 1911, II, 103–4.

[3] Lincoln to Linder, Feb. 20, 1848. *Works*, II, 3–4.

[4] Lincoln to Williams, April 30, 1848. *Ib.*, 17.

Washburne must 'let nothing discourage or baffle' him, but 'in spite of every difficulty . . . send us a good Taylor delegate from your circuit. Make Baker . . . help about it. He is a good hand to raise a breeze.' [1]

Thus active and vocal in presidential politics, Lincoln went to Philadelphia in early June to do what he could for Taylor at the national Whig Convention. The contest between the Clay Whigs and the Taylor men was 'bitter and fierce,' testifies Stephens.[2] Vigorously Lincoln strove to get votes for 'Old Zach,' protesting earnestly against the seating of alternates from Illinois who were Clay men.[3] Arguments that the ignorant old officer was unfit fell before the single argument that he was available. Taylor could not speak or write correctly, was a large slave-holder, had no knowledge of public business, was densely ignorant of foreign affairs; nobody knew where he stood on any question of the hour and he did not know himself. Moreover he was then and during the campaign the favorite of the big slave-holders throughout the slave belt of the South. Indeed, that circumstance was the strongest concrete factor in his support.[4]

So the 'war hero' was nominated to the outspoken disgust of many delegates. Millard Fillmore of New York was named for Vice President. Foremost leaders of the party, like Webster, were affronted and rebellious. Clay was heart-broken, his friends furious and threatening vengeance. Even practical Whig

---

[1] Lincoln to Washburne, April 30, 1848. *Ib.*, 16.   [2] Avary, 22.

[3] 'Lisle Smith [of Chicago], too, was a Clay delegate at Philadelphia, and against my most earnest entreaties took the lead in filling two vacancies from my own district with Clay men.' Justin Butterfield of Chicago was also a Clay delegate from Illinois and 'fought for Mr. Clay against General Taylor to the bitter end,' to the disgust and anger of Lincoln. Lincoln to J. M. Lucas, April 25, 1849. *Works*, II, 114.

[4] *The Whig Party in the South:* Cole, 133. Cole goes so far as to say that Taylor's nomination was 'a southern Whig triumph.'

At the election the biggest Democratic gains in the South were in regions where slaves were in the minority; the Whigs almost held their own in the 'black belt,' although losing slightly even in those Whig strongholds. *Ib.*, 116.

Crittenden and Clayton seem to have been the principal managers of Taylor's campaign. Whig politicians reported to the Kentucky leader from all over the country. Crittenden MSS. Library of Congress.

Writing to Clayton from Frankfort, Ky., Crittenden said: 'The election of General Taylor is to be the event — the great event — of our time. If we fail in that our Government is but a wreck and we are given over to proscription. The crisis demands all our energies and all our wisdom.' The Whigs, said Crittenden, must concentrate on states which they could carry. Crittenden to Clayton, Aug. 30. 1848. *Ib.*

politicians were alarmed; but the more astute manipulators of public sentiment, like Weed and Lincoln, were delighted and confident.

The nominations of Taylor and Fillmore were made without any declaration of party principles or policies. This was too much even for the apostles of expediency, and, as an afterthought, resolutions were adopted by a Whig ratification meeting held at Philadelphia just after the Convention adjourned. These resolutions served as the Whig platform. A more shifty and evasive pronouncement never was made by a political party. 'The principles of the Constitution' were indorsed, Taylor declared a Whig 'at heart,' assurance given that his administration would be 'conducive of peace, prosperity, and union' because Taylor would 'make Washington's administration his model,' and Taylor's military career was grandiloquently lauded at great length. Not a word was said on any issue, small or great, before the country. Nobody was offended, and, by implication, everybody was promised everything.[1]

Within two weeks, the Free Soilers were to hold their Convention at Utica, New York, and it was well known that they would nominate Van Buren for President on an anti-slavery platform.[2] The Free Soilers drew their following from that faction of the

---

[1] *National Conventions and Platforms:* Thomas Hudson McKee, 63–5.

[2] The Convention of the Free Soil party was held at Utica, N.Y., June 22, 1848, and Van Buren was nominated for President and Henry Dodge of Wis. for Vice President. Afterwards Dodge declined, and a second and much larger Free Soil Convention was held at Buffalo, N.Y., August 9, of which Charles Francis Adams of Mass., son of John Quincy Adams, was Chairman. He was nominated for Vice President with Van Buren, who was again named for President. A little more than twelve years afterward, Lincoln appointed Adams Minister to England, where he rendered more important services to the United States than any other American diplomatic representative to the Court of St. James's ever has rendered.

The Free Soil platform asserted 'the rights of free labor against the aggressions of the slave power,' denounced the Democratic national Convention for having 'stifled the voice of a great constituency,' and the Whig national Convention for 'abandoning its distinctive principles for mere availability.' It declared against the extension of slave territory — 'let the soil of our extensive domains be kept free for the hardy pioneers' — endorsed internal improvements by the National Government, advocated cheap postage and 'free grants' of land to actual settlers.

'We inscribe upon our banner "Free Soil, Free Speech, Free Labor, and Free Men," and under it will fight on, and fight ever, until a triumphant victory shall reward our exertions.' *Ib.*, 66–9.

The Whigs rejoiced over the nomination of Van Buren because it 'split the Democrats.' *Illinois Journal*, Aug. 16, 1848,

Democrats called Barn-burners.[1] The Native Americans, fore-
runners of the Know-Nothing party, had not yet decided to hold
a convention.[2]

Lincoln was jubilant. 'We shall have a most overwhelming,
glorious triumph,' he assured Archibald Williams in answer to a
letter which he found 'in a mass of others' upon his return to
Washington from attending the nomination of 'Old Rough.'
It was true, that 'by many, and often, it had been said that they
would not abide the nomination of Taylor;[3] but since the deed
has been done, they are fast falling in. . . . One unmistakable
sign is that all the odds and ends are with us — Barn-burners,
Native Americans, Tyler men, disappointed office-seeking
Locofocos, and the Lord knows what.'[4]

That curious union of discordant groups showed 'which way
the wind blows,' said Lincoln. Some 'sanguine men' thought
that Taylor would carry every State but Illinois, and had set
that State down as doubtful. 'Cannot something be done even
in Illinois?' What admirable strategy was Taylor's nomination!
It 'takes the Locos on the blind side. It turns the war thunder
against them. The war is now to them the gallows of Haman,
which they built for us, and on which they are doomed to be
hanged themselves. Excuse this short letter. I have so many to
write that I cannot devote much time to any one.'[5]

In such exultant frame of mind, the Whig members of Congress held a caucus and 'scanned the whole field of the nation in
high hope and confidence' — even Illinois was not abandoned.
From this rosy dream Lincoln was awakened by another 'dis-

---

[1] From a popular story about a farmer who proposed to burn his barn to get rid of
rats which infested it.

[2] This anti-foreign and anti-Catholic group did hold a Convention in the autumn of
1847 at Philadelphia, and nominated Henry A. S. Dearborn for Vice President and
'recommended' Taylor for President. It adopted no platform. McKee, 69.

[3] Many Whig meetings of protest against Clay's defeat were held. Some of them
were violent. At one in New York, June 17, where Greeley spoke, the stage was broken
down and shouts arose for Clay, for Cass, and some for Taylor. The national Whig
organ, in its report of this meeting said that the supporters of Clay were 'so sorely
disappointed . . . that they could not very readily get over it,' but that they would
gradually, come to the support of the party ticket. National Intelligencer, June 19, 1848.

[4] The Free Soil or Liberty party hurt the Democrats even more than it hurt the
Whigs. Anti-slavery Democrats went over to it in great numbers.

[5] Lincoln to Williams, June 12, 1848. Works, II, 26–7.

couraging letter' from Herndon, who told him that in Sangamon County the Whigs had lost votes and gained none. In answer Lincoln explained that the reason for the Whig decline was that Sangamon County had an increased population and yet 'only half the sort of offices which are sought by men of the speaking sort of talent.' That was the chief cause for Whig defection, so far as Lincoln could see.

Herndon had complained that the young men could not lead; and he was right, for so close and exclusive had been the Springfield 'Whig Junto' that young Whigs had not been trained in party management. But, Lincoln replied, 'you must not wait to be brought forward by the older men. For instance, do you suppose that I should ever have got into notice if I had waited to be hunted up and pushed forward by older men?'

Lincoln gave his junior partner specific directions: 'You young men get together and form a "Rough and Ready Club," and have regular meetings and speeches. Take in everybody you can get.' Lincoln named several who would 'do to begin the thing; but as you go along gather up all the shrewd, wild boys about town, whether just of age or a little under age,' and Lincoln gave names as examples of 'hundreds such.' That was the way to do it. 'Let every one play the part he can play best — some speak, some sing, and all "holler."' Everybody would go to their meetings, and thus they would not only help to elect 'Old Zach,' but have fun and improve their minds. 'Don't fail to do this.' [1]

Herndon obeyed, though with no heart in his task. He gathered 'all the shrewd, wild boys about town,' of the kind to whom Lincoln was so partial throughout his life, organized a 'Rough and Ready Club,' [2] as he had been ordered to do, and soon the streets of Springfield rang with a rousing Whig campaign song:

'Come fall in, boys, eyes right and steady,
And raise the shout for Rough and Ready,
He licked Old Peg-leg with his Pass
And now he'll use up Lewis Cass.

---

[1] Lincoln to Herndon, June 22, 1848. *Works*, II, 49–53.

[2] *Illinois Journal*, July 13, 1848. Herndon, Jayne, and Matheny spoke at the first meeting of the Club.

Chorus: 'Then go it, boys, strong and steady
           And raise the shout for Rough and Ready.'[1]

But the 'shrewd, wild boys' could not enliven a Whig ratification meeting, although it was so big that the court room could not hold the crowd, and the proceedings were held in the courthouse yard. Stuart, Herndon, and J. Vincent Browne, the committee on resolutions, reported some grandiloquent language about Taylor, that 'war-worn veteran wearing the laurels of many glorious and bloody fields . . . who never surrenders.' With astonishing boldness, the resolutions asserted that 'the will of the people' ought to be 'carried out by the President.' Swallowing his wrath, Herndon agreed to an indirect attack on the war as one for 'illegal and unlawful conquest.'

Logan who had been nominated for Congress, made a solid Whig speech denouncing 'the rottenness of the convention system,' which produced platforms devised by 'a few crafty, designing wire workers,' and condemning Polk's encroachments on the Constitution in beginning the war.[2] Obviously Logan had been in correspondence with Lincoln,[3] for Lincoln made many of Logan's points in his stump speech in Congress which we shall presently review. In such spiritless fashion, the Whig campaign began in Springfield.[4] The Whig State Central Committee issued an 'Address' to the people, signed among others by Herndon, and it was as vapid and colorless as the Philadelphia resolutions, which obviously were its model.[5]

---

[1] *Illinois Journal*, July 6, 1848. 'Peg-leg' meant Santa Anna.
Another favorite Whig campaign song in Illinois was:

    'Rough and Ready is the man
    That all good Whigs delight in;
    He's just the sort for President,
    And "a" the man for fightin!
      Then raise the song, the States along
      From Maine to Louisiana.
      We've got the "coon" that sealed the doom
      Of Polk and Santa Anna.'

                                    Ib., July 27, 1848.

[2] *Illinois Journal*, June 29, 1848.

[3] None of the historically invaluable letters of Logan and Lincoln exist. Before his death Logan destroyed all of them. Statement of Logan Hay, Springfield, Ill., to author, Feb., 1925.

[4] A big advertisement appeared in the Democratic paper, asking all Democrats to attend this meeting and hear Logan's speech. *Illinois State Register*. June 23, 1848.

[5] *Illinois Journal*, July 27, 1848.

Herndon asked Lincoln for speeches 'about "Old Zach," the war, etc.' What a request! Lincoln was irritated, for he had sent Herndon the *Congressional Globe* and Appendix which contained all the speeches made on every subject during the session. 'Can I send any more? Can I send speeches that nobody has made?' But the Whig papers in the district had not published Whig speeches, or even so much as excerpts from them. Only two had printed his own speech, Lincoln complained. Yet he had sent the *Globe* and Appendix to them all. The *State Register* had given its readers 'more of Locofoco speeches in a month than all the Whig paper of the district has done of Whig speeches during the session.'

Lincoln was impatient that Herndon did not yet understand why Whigs had voted for the war resolution and still were against the war; but he explained the seeming paradox once more, notwithstanding the fact that Herndon had had 'at least twenty speeches' on the subject. As soon as campaign materials about Taylor were printed, Lincoln promised to 'send them to everybody.'[1]

Immediately after Taylor's nomination, a big public dinner was given to John J. Crittenden, who resigned from the Senate to become the Whig candidate for Governor of Kentucky. The invitations were issued under the names of thirty-four Senators, among them Webster, Calhoun, Corwin, and Davis, and sixty-five Representatives, among them Toombs and Ashmun, Stephens and Lincoln. Every Senator and scores of members of the House attended the banquet. Many speeches, customary on such occasions, were made, one of them by Lincoln,[2] and another, on request, by Jefferson Davis, in honor of the American army.[3]

But such non-partisan matters did not interest Lincoln. He

---

[1] Lincoln to Herndon, June 22, 1848. *Works,* II, 49–53.

[2] *National Intelligencer,* June 15, 1848; *Life of John J. Crittenden:* Mrs. Chapman Coleman, I, 303.

[3] 'Colonel Jefferson Davis, the gallant Senator from Mississippi, who distinguished himself so commendably at the battles of Monterey and Buena Vista, was called on by the company to respond to a toast given in honor of the Army of the United States.' *Battery,* Sept. 7, 1848.

The Whigs seem to have treated Davis with much consideration throughout the campaign. Although he was a Democrat, he was a 'war hero' like Taylor, and the son-in-law of the Whig presidential candidate.

was absorbed in the impending party struggle, and was keenly alert to every phase of the political situation. 'Do you know any democrats who will vote for Taylor? and if so, what are their names?' he inquired of a Whig politician in Illinois. 'Do you know any Whigs who will not vote for him? and if so, what are their names? and for whom will they vote?' Answer immediately.[1]

Party policy concerned him almost as much as specific votes likely to be cast. The Democrats must not outwit the Whigs in appeals to the people. The supporters of Taylor were in a quandary whether, in their campaign attack upon the war, they should say that the boundary between Texas and Mexico was the Nueces River, or some unfixed line in the 'desert' between that stream and the Rio Grande. Lincoln thought this matter highly important and wrote Horace Greeley to correct the editorial position of the New York *Tribune* on that serious point of party strategy.

'Friend Greeley,' as Lincoln addressed the New York editor, was wrong in saying in his paper that 'all Whigs and many Democrats' had always maintained that American territory 'stopped at the Nueces.' That, said Lincoln, was 'a mistake' which he disliked 'to see go uncorrected in a leading Whig paper.' For the Whigs to claim the Nueces as the boundary would give 'the Democrats an advantage of us.' 'On this very point,' Lincoln asked Greeley to read his speech which he sent the editor.[2]

A Whig campaign paper, the *Battery*, was started at Washington, identical, in purpose and plan, with the *Old Soldier* which Lincoln and other Whigs had maintained at Springfield in the Harrison campaign. Whig speakers were supplied with this source of stump inspiration and oratory; and Lincoln wrote a party campaigner that he could 'think of no better way of fitting you out, than by sending you the *Battery*. . . . Get as many subscribers as you can and send them on.' Lincoln would pay the subscription himself 'if you are not satisfied with it.'[3]

[1] Lincoln to Richard S. Thomas, June 19, 1848. Tracy, 33.
[2] Lincoln to Greeley, June 27, 1848. *Works*, II, 53–4.
[3] Lincoln to S. A. Hurlbut, July 10, 1848. *Works*, II, 58.
'The Whig Executive Committee' heartily endorsed this paper: 'If generally circu-

Towards the close of the session Lincoln became extraordinarily active in the work of the national Whig Committee.[1] He was constantly at the party headquarters sending out campaign 'literature,' and writing to Whig leaders all over the country. 'I am remaining here for two weeks to frank documents,' he informed the editor of the *Boston Atlas*, several days before adjournment.[2] But he stayed in Washington a month. Although Lincoln was not a member of the 'Whig Executive Committee of Congress,'[3] it is clear that he was attached to it, or was working under its direction. This circumstance fully explains many things otherwise unaccountable, that happened during the next few months — political letters written him from various states, his trip to Massachusetts, his conference with Weed in Albany, his statement at Worcester of his peculiar opportunity for special knowledge of the trend of the campaign. It explains, too, Lincoln's astute suggestions as to what Taylor ought to say in his campaign letter as the Whig candidate for President.

Do not bring up again the question of a national bank, he wrote. It 'is at rest' and 'were I President, I should not urge its reagitation upon Congress;' if Congress should pass a bank act

lated, [it] will contribute powerfully to the desired change in the administration of the Government.' *Battery*, July 6, 1848. This Committee pronouncement was kept in the paper throughout the campaign.

The subscription was one copy, fifty cents, twelve copies, five dollars, and twenty-five copies, ten dollars. Each issue of the *Battery* had sixteen pages. It contained speeches, long editorials, a great deal of Taylor's correspondence, reports, etc., and many Whig campaign songs. It teemed with abuse of Cass, praise of Taylor, with an occasional lashing of the Free Soilers.

The songs placed emphasis on the General's fighting qualities, his 'heroism,' firmness, patriotism, victories. The war note was incessantly sounded — Taylor had whipped the Mexicans, etc. No mention was made of any issue of the campaign, or of any public question.

[1] Much Whig politics is seen in the motions and roll-calls at the end of the session; and in these Lincoln appears actively. He voted to suspend the rules to permit a resolution censuring the President for opposing internal improvements and beginning a war of conquest (*House Journal*, 30th Cong. 1st Sess., 1135–6); for suspension of rules to permit a resolution of inquiry into Cass's expenses as Governor of Michigan (*ib.*, 1166–7); moved to suspend the rules for a report on the extra pay of Cass and Taylor (*ib.*, 1285–6); voted for printing the attack on Polk by the American Treaty Commissioner (*ib.*, 1218–21). All these were purely Whig political manœuvers, for use in the Presidential campaign.

[2] Lincoln to William Schouler, Aug. 8, 1848. Tracy, 34.

[3] This Committee consisted of Truman Smith of Conn., Dudley S. Gregory of N.J., Caleb B. Smith of Ind., Charles S. Morehead of Ky., T. Butler King of Ga., William Ballard Preston of Va., and Hugh White of N.Y. *Battery*, July 6, 1848.

'I should not arrest it by the veto.' The war debt made 'a modification of the existing tariff indispensable . . . with a due reference to the protection of our home industry.' As to the war, advocate a 'defensive line [of] policy,' as the best way to end it. Of course we should be 'under a sort of necessity of taking some territory' when peace should be made, but none 'so far south as to enlarge and aggravate the distracting question of slavery.'[1] Legislation ought to be the exclusive business of Congress, 'uninfluenced by the executive in its origin and progress, and undisturbed by the veto unless in very special and clear cases.'[2]

Thus occupied in Washington with the practical direction of national politics, Lincoln was annoyed by the renewed complaints of Herndon that, at Springfield, young men were being kept back in politics. The subject was 'exceedingly painful' to him, wrote Lincoln; he was 'now one of the old men,' he supposed, and nothing would please him more than to learn that his 'young friends at home' were 'doing battle in the contest,' and rising higher in the love and admiration of the people than Lincoln ever had risen. He had been 'young once' and never had been 'ungenerously thrust back.' Self improvement, unweakened by jealousy or suspicion, was the only way to succeed. Herndon had been 'a laborious, studious young man, . . . far better informed on almost all subjects' than Lincoln had been.[3] With this fatherly admonition he again reminded his junior partner that he had the war speeches by Lincoln and other Whigs.

In a curious mingling of irritation and fun Lincoln wrote his 'Dear Wife,' who was still at Lexington, Kentucky. He had sent her a draft at that place for a hundred dollars, he said. A store had 'dunned' him for $5.38 and another for $8.50 'for goods which they say you bought.' What about it? 'Mrs.

---

[1] This was the position of such Southern Whigs as Stephens, Toombs, and Crittenden, who wished to quiet the slavery agitation.

[2] Lincoln's draft of campaign letter for Taylor, 1848. *Works*, ii, 55–6. The date vaguely given in the editions of Lincoln's *Works* is sometime in July; but this is a bad guess, since peace had been made in May. Lincoln wrote his suggestions to Taylor long before his nomination.

[3] Lincoln to Herndon, Washington, July 10, 1848. *Works*, ii, 56–8.

Richardson [wife of a Democratic member of the House from Illinois [1]] is still here, and what is more has a baby — so Richardson says, and he ought to know.' Lincoln comforts his wife for being away from Washington — she is not missing much. 'The music in the Capitol ground on Saturday, or, rather the interest in it, is dwindling down to nothing. Yesterday evening the attendance was rather thin.'

Mrs. Lincoln was without a domestic servant, a chronic trouble with her. 'By the way,' Lincoln casually inquires, 'you do not intend to do without a girl, because the one you had has left you? Get another as soon as you can to take charge of the dear little codger. Father expected to see you all sooner, but let it pass, stay as long as you please and come when you please. Kiss and love the dear rascals. Affectionately, A. LINCOLN.'

Lincoln then regales his wife with a bit of gossip. 'Our two girls, whom you remember seeing first at Carusi's at the Exhibition of the Ethiopian Serenaders and whose peculiarities were the wearing of black fur bonnets, and never being in close company with other ladies, were at the music yesterday. One of them was attended by their brother, and the other had a member of Congress in tow. He went home with her, and if I were to guess I would say, he went away a somewhat altered man — most likely in his pockets and in some other particular. The fellow looked conscious of guilt, although I believe he was unconscious that anybody around knew who it was that had caught him.' [2]

Another letter to Herndon reveals Lincoln's state of mind at this time. Seemingly he felt that he had been too hard on his despondent partner. 'Go it while you're young,' he advised Herndon, who had said something in one of his letters about 'kissing the girls.' As to that diversion, said Lincoln, 'I know a very pretty one, but I'm afraid she won't let me kiss her.' [3]

Toward the end of the session the question of territorial governments for Oregon, New Mexico, and California came to a de-

[1] William Alexander Richardson, who was elected in 1863 United States Senator from Illinois to fill the vacancy caused by the death of Douglas.

[2] Lincoln to his wife, July 2, 1848. MS. owned by Alexander W. Hannah, Chicago, Ill.

[3] Lincoln to Herndon, July 11, 1848. MS. Barrett Collection.

cision. Lincoln voted against an amendment to strike from the Oregon bill the provision placing that territory under the famous Ordinance of 1787.[1] Among the Senate amendments to the House Oregon bill, was one extending the line of the Missouri Compromise to the Pacific Ocean. Lincoln voted against it as did all anti-slavery men.[2] Thus, by implication, Lincoln may be said to have voted three times, in indirect fashion, on the idea of the Wilmot Proviso during his first session in Congress.

While Lincoln was engaged in party manœuvring and in the daily grind of the House, with occasional interest in family affairs, and a flash of humor now and then, he spoke briefly on unimportant matters [3] and wrote two long set speeches. Both were for use in the campaign. With characteristic political astuteness, he seized upon the subject that would be most fruitful of votes. The River and Harbor Convention at Chicago had shown him the direction of popular interest. This fact and the savage reception of his anti-war speech in Illinois were more than enough to make the sensitive and practical politician realize the advisability of minimizing such talk thereafter. Instead, internal improvements were what voters really wanted — especially in the Northwest and, indeed, throughout the North generally. So Lincoln resolved to speak on that concrete and immediate issue.

His speech was delivered as a part of the debate upon the Civil and Diplomatic Appropriation bill. Lincoln knew that he was not in order because his speech was not germane to the subject before the House; and he naïvely asked the Speaker if he would be out of order. Winthrop dryly said that he could not

---

[1] *House Journal*, 30th Cong. 1st Sess., 1153–4, Aug. 2, 1848.

This amendment was defeated by a vote of eighty-eight ayes to one hundred and fourteen nays, all anti-slavery men voting against it.

The Ordinance of 1787 provided, among other things, that slavery should never exist in the territory north of the Ohio River.

For the Oregon bill as enacted, see *Acts*, 30th Cong. 1st Sess., 192–203; and for this anti-slavery section, *House Journal*, 30th Cong. 1st Sess., 1153.

[2] *Ib.*, 1245–6, Aug. 11, 1848. This Senate amendment was beaten by a vote of eighty-two ayes to one hundred and twenty-one nays.

On the day before this vote the House rejected a Senate amendment to the Civil and Diplomatic bill providing for the continuance and completion of John C. Frémont's survey of Oregon and California to find a route for railways to the Pacific, Lincoln voting against it. The vote was twenty-eight ayes to one hundred and twenty-eight nays. *Ib.*, 1233–4.

[3] *Cong. Globe*, 30th Cong. 1st Sess., XVIII, 571, 727, 797, 878, 928, 1027, 1049, 1081.

tell in advance what Lincoln would say; he might go on and, if anybody raised a point of order, the Speaker would decide it. So Lincoln made his speech and nobody objected.

The Democrats, he said, were against internal improvements. The sum of their opposition was 'Do nothing at all, lest you do something wrong.' He gave the usual arguments upon the subject, although in a dull fashion, wholly unlike·himself. Some illustrations were curiously far fetched. 'The driving of a pirate from the track of commerce on the broad ocean, and the removing a snag from its more narrow path in the Mississippi River, cannot, I think, be distinguished in principle;' or (as showing that projects for the general good should not be rejected because of the local benefits they might confer), the national Capitol was helpful 'to the property-holders and business people of Washington.' Once he used the method and language of the stump. 'An honest laborer digs coal at about seventy cents a day, while the President digs abstractions at about seventy dollars a day. . . . What a monstrous inequality in the prices!'

Lincoln confessed his incompetency to discuss the constitutional power of Congress to provide for internal improvements. 'In any attempt at an original constitutional argument, I . . . ought not to be listened to patiently. The ablest and the best of men have gone over the whole ground long ago.' So he confined himself to quotations from the *Commentaries on American Law*, by Chancellor James Kent of New York, 'one of the ablest and most learned lawyers of his age, or of any age.' At this point, Lincoln suddenly rose to lofty heights — for a moment the great Lincoln appeared, the Lincoln of coming years. He spoke briefly on the general proposition of amending the Constitution. 'As a general rule, I think we would much better let it alone. No slight occasion should tempt us to touch it. Better not take the first step, which may lead to a habit of altering it. Better, rather, habituate ourselves to think of it as unalterable. It can scarcely be made better than it is. New provisions would introduce new difficulties, and thus create and increase appetite for further change.[1] No, sir; let it stand as it is. New hands have

---

[1] On March 13, 1848, Jacob Thompson of Mississippi offered a resolution to amend the Constitution so that judges of the Supreme Court should serve only for a term of

never touched it. The men who made it have done their work, and have passed away. Who shall improve on what *they* did?' [1]

It was not necessary, he continued, to amend the Constitution to give Congress express power to appropriate money for internal improvements. 'Determine that the thing can and shall be done, and then we shall find the way. . . . How to do something, and still not do too much, is the desideratum.'

Lincoln's custom of carefully revising his speeches before permitting the publication of them is well illustrated in the case of this one. 'As soon as I can get it written out and printed,' he wrote Herndon two days after he had delivered the speech, 'I shall send [it] home' — and he added dejectedly, that he supposed nobody would read it.[2]

Before he made his next campaign speech in the House, a notable and brilliant ceremony, in which Lincoln participated, took place in the national capital. Nothing like it ever had been seen in the city. At daybreak all the bells of the churches began to ring; at sunrise, artillery thundered from the navy yard and arsenal; sections of a vast procession, soon to be formed, hurried to their stations. 'Great multitudes rushed' into Washington. Streets and open spaces were thronged — carriages, horsemen, thousands on foot. Among the crowd slowly moved negroes with baskets of food and fruit on turbaned heads, 'suspicious looking stone bottles' in their hands, selling to the hungry and thirsty. The discharge of guns and pistols, the noise of firecrackers, the songs of children, the huzzas of men mingled in continuous waves of sound.

Finally the parade was in line. It was a mile and a half long. The color, solidity, and distinction of it were 'indescribable.' At its head was a carriage containing the President with his Secretary of State, James Buchanan, followed by other carriages with the remainder of the Cabinet. The Grand Marshal of the day came next. Then, surrounded by his gorgeous staff, Major

years instead of for life. Lincoln voted against it by voting to lay it on the table. The resolution was thus killed by a vote of eighty-three ayes to sixty-eight nays. *House Journal*, 30th Cong. 1st Sess., 554–5.

[1] *Works*, ii, 28–48, June 20, 1848. The speech was printed in the Springfield **Whig** paper. *Illinois Journal*, July 20, 1848.

[2] Lincoln to Herndon, June 22, 1848. *Works*, ii, 49–53.

General John Anthony Quitman of the United States army, who had won fame in the Mexican war, rode at the head of the military — masses of infantry, artillery, cavalry, marines, their officers with plumed hats and drawn swords. Among them on a magnificent black horse was the popular hero of the hour, a soldierly young man of thirty-one with long, heavy, spreading whiskers, Captain Charles Augustus May, whose dashing exploits in Mexico were household tales throughout the land.

Military companies from Baltimore, from Richmond, from cities as distant as Boston, marched in their finest uniforms. Congress in a solid body came next, Lincoln noticeable for his great height but, at that time, distinguished for nothing else. Every organization of the capital was in line — Fire Department, Temperance Societies, school children, the Odd Fellows, the Red Men. Most conspicuous of all were the Free Masons — for they felt that it was peculiarly their day — led by their national Grand Master and Grand Chaplain. At last came the carriage of the orator of the day, Robert C. Winthrop, Speaker of the House.

It was July 4, 1848, and on that day the cornerstone of the monument to George Washington was laid with Masonic ceremonies. On the Speaker's stand sat two very old ladies, Mrs. Alexander Hamilton and Mrs. James Madison. All about were the beauty, the fashion, and the culture of many States as well as of the District.

Winthrop's address was a model of eloquence, restrained, clear, simple, lofty. The orator pleaded for 'national brotherhood,' as against the 'many marked and mourned centrifugal tendencies' then threatening to dismember the Union. These lines in closing illustrate the temper and sense of this masterpiece of eulogy: 'This wide-spread Republic is the true monument to Washington. Maintain its Independence. Uphold its Constitution. Preserve its Union. Defend its Liberty.'[1]

If the occasion and the noble address of the Speaker of the House made any impression on Lincoln, that impression did not affect his next, and his last, speech in Congress. Indeed this speech is worthy of note solely because it is the only example we

[1] *Addresses and Speeches:* Winthrop, IV, 525., *National Intelligencer*, July 6, 1848.

have of his method and manner as a stump speaker before the time, still six years in the future, when his style, matter, and delivery totally changed. For his performance in the national House of Representatives, July 27, 1848, was purely a stump speech; and, if we will imagine him delivering it before crowds in a rough and tumble political contest instead of in Congress, we shall have a fairly accurate picture of Lincoln as a campaigner at this period and during the earlier years of his life.

His theme was the sound statement, written by the Whig managers for their candidate and given out under Taylor's name, that the Presidential veto should never be used 'except in cases of clear violation of the Constitution, or manifest haste and want of consideration by Congress' — a point which, as we have seen, Lincoln had suggested Taylor should make in his campaign manifesto. This the Democrats had assailed, and Lincoln began his speech by showing that Taylor's position was 'exactly' like that of Jefferson and all early American statesmen.

In answer to the charge that Taylor had no 'principles,' or even opinions on public affairs, Lincoln declared that there was not the least doubt as to what he would do on the 'prominent questions;' and, anyway, the views of the Whig candidate were no more obscure than those of the Democratic candidate for President. But Taylor was not vague and general. Had he not said that on the tariff, currency, and internal improvements 'the will of the people' as expressed in acts of Congress, would govern him. What could be clearer, what more specific!

Principle! Taylor's position was the very essence of principle, — 'the principle of allowing the people to do as they please with their own business.' The Constitution gave the President the veto power; but to enable him to control all legislation by means of party platforms 'and other appliances' was what the Whigs and Taylor opposed. That was the broad distinction between the Whigs and Democrats.

See how laws and policies had been foisted on the country. A party was committed on several familiar questions; a new question to which a large portion of the party objected, was included in a party platform; 'the whole was strung together;' party voters had to 'take all, or reject all;' so they were forced to 'shut their eyes, and gulp the whole.'

That 'process' was wrong; the Whigs wanted a President who would 'allow the people to have their own way, regardless of his private opinions.' Taylor 'would force nothing on them which they don't want' and would not prevent them from getting what they did want — internal improvements, for instance. That was the kind of President the country needed, one who would not interfere with Congress.

Lincoln admitted that he did not know what Taylor would do on the Wilmot Proviso; he hoped that Taylor would not veto it, but he did not 'know it. Yet if I knew he would, I still would vote for him.' Why? 'Because . . . his election alone can defeat General Cass.' If Cass should be elected and 'slavery thereby go to the territory we now have,' we would have that evil 'and, in addition a course of policy leading to new wars, new acquisitions of territory, and still further extensions of slavery. One of the two is to be President. Which is preferable?'

Having thus touched upon slavery just enough to disturb the anti-slavery Democrats and not enough to arouse the pro-slavery Whigs, Lincoln quickly veered to internal improvements. On this subject he merely pointed out Democratic inconsistencies. Cass had voted for internal improvement bills and yet approved Polk's veto of them; he was for the policy and yet endorsed the Democratic platform which opposed it. Lincoln closed this branch of the subject by restating the Whig campaign position: The Democrats were for 'laying down in advance a platform — a set of party positions — as a unit, and then of forcing the people, by every sort of appliance, to ratify them, however unpalatable some of them may be;' the Whigs were for 'making presidential elections, and the legislation of the country distinct matters; so that the people can elect whom they please, and afterward legislate just as they please, without any hindrance,' except, of course, to guard against hasty and unconstitutional measures. That was the 'true Republican position. In leaving the people's business in their hands, we cannot be wrong.'

After this exposition of the difference, 'clear as noon-day,' thought Lincoln, between the Whig and Democratic view of the purpose of elections in a free government, after this demonstration of the wickedness of party platforms, and after the assertion that a President should be elected without reference to laws to be enacted during his Administration, Lincoln took the bridle from his ridicule and indulged frankly in those antics of the buffoon, then so beloved by partisan campaign audiences.

He was 'struck blind,' he said, by the speech of a Democratic member and felt with his fingers to see if he was still alive — 'a little of the bone was left, and I gradually revived.' The Democrats had accused the Whigs of having 'turned Henry Clay out, like an old horse, to root;' but were Whigs the only party 'who sometimes turn old horses out to root?' Look at Van Buren — he had been turned out to root and was now 'rooting' to the 'discomfort' of the regular, old-line Democrats. Between Van Buren and his old admirers a 'war of extermination' was being waged. Not that Lincoln cared. 'I say, "Devil take the hindmost" — and the foremost.'

The Democrats charged the Whigs with hiding 'under General Taylor's military coat-tail.' But what about General Jackson's coat-tail. The Democrats had 'run the five last presidential races under that coat-tail, and . . . are now running the sixth under the same cover.' Jackson's coat-tail had been used, not only for himself, but every Democratic candidate since who had 'clung to [it] with the grip of death. . . . Like a horde of hungry ticks you have stuck to the tail of the Hermitage lion to the end of his life; and you are still sticking to it, and drawing a loathsome sustenance from it, after he is dead.' The Democrats were like the man who advertised that he had invented a material by which he 'could make a new man out of an old one, and have enough of the stuff left to make a little yellow dog.'

Lincoln said that he would not have spoken of old horses and military coat-tails if the Democratic member had not first made mention of them; but since he had, Lincoln flung this counter challenge in discomfited Democratic faces. 'If you have any more old horses, trot them out; any more tails, just cock them and come at us.' Let the Democrats understand that to us 'degrading figures [of speech]' were not a one-sided game. (Cries:

'We give it up!'). 'Aye,' exclaimed Lincoln in triumph, 'give it up,' not because the Democrats had been outdone in unseemly metaphors, but because of the truthfulness of Lincoln's use of them.

The interruption had nearly caused him to forget another aspect of the coat-tail issue, he said — 'I mean the military tail you Democrats are now engaged in dovetailing into the great Michigander [General Cass]. Yes, sir; all his biographers (and they are legion) have him in hand, tying him to a military tail, like so many mischievous boys tying a dog to a bladder of beans.' With gusto Lincoln lampooned Cass's military record. 'He *in*vaded Canada without resistance, and *out*vaded it without pursuit,' which was 'a large part of the tail.'

Lincoln then made comparison of the military records of General Cass and himself. He, too, was a military hero, he whimsically declared. 'Yes, sir; in the days of the Black Hawk war I fought, bled, and came away. . . . I was about as near it [Stillman's defeat] as Cass was to Hull's surrender; and, like him, I saw the place very soon afterward.' Lincoln did not break his sword,[1] he said, for he had none; but he bent a musket 'by accident.' 'If General Cass went in advance of me in picking huckleberries, I guess I surpassed him in charges upon the wild onions. If he saw any live, fighting Indians, it was more than I did; but I had a good many bloody struggles with the mosquitoes, and although I never fainted from the loss of blood, I can truly say I was often very hungry.'

Lincoln then assailed Cass for his changed attitude on the Wilmot Proviso. He read from a speech by Cass and from his famous letter in which the Democratic candidate had laid down the policy of local self-government — a policy that, when advanced by Douglas a few years later, was to call upon him execrations as the author of all villainy.

Congress, wrote Cass, should have nothing to do with slavery in the territories — that subject should be 'left to the people . . . in their respective local governments. . . . I am opposed to the

---

[1] This reference is to the incident of General Cass's having broken his sword in anger and disgust, when he heard of the surrender of Detroit by General Hull in our second war with Great Britain.

exercise of any jurisdiction by Congress over this matter; and I am in favor of leaving the people of any territory which may be hereafter acquired the right to regulate it themselves, under the general principles of the Constitution, . . . leaving to the inhabitants all the right compatible with the relations they bear to the confederation.' [1]

There, declared Lincoln, was 'a true index to the whole man' — for the Wilmot Proviso in 1846; still for it in March, 1847, 'but not just then;' wholly against it in December of that year. Cass obeyed the party 'ox-goad,' went back when ordered, stood still when ordered, and would do 'whatever the party exigency for the time being' required.

And consider the 'charges' of General Cass — 'not upon the public enemy, but upon the public treasury.' Lincoln went minutely and at tiresome length into Cass's financial accounts as Governor of Michigan Territory for seventeen years. What a worker! Cass's expenditures showed 'that he not only did the labor of several men at the same time, but that he often did it at several places, many hundreds of miles apart, at the same time.' And how Cass ate! For eight months 'he eat ten rations a day in Michigan, ten rations a day here in Washington, and near five dollars' worth a day on the road between the two places!'

Talk about the old story of the 'animal standing in doubt between two stacks of hay and starving to death.' Cass would never do that. 'Place the stacks a thousand miles apart, he would stand stock-still midway between them, and eat them both at once, and the green grass along the line would be apt to suffer some, too, at the same time.'

Finally Lincoln touched gingerly on the war. Taylor was '*par excellence*,' the hero of the Mexican War, yet the Whigs said that the conflict was 'unnecessarily and unconstitutionally' brought on by the President. What inconsistency was there in that? After 'the war had begun and had become the cause of the country,' the Whigs gave their money and blood as well as the Democrats. 'Clay and Webster each gave a son, never to be returned.' Illinois had sent her most eminent Whigs. 'All fought,

[1] Cass to Nicholson, Dec. 24, 1847. Lincoln did not give the exact language used by Cass. *Lewis Cass:* William T. Young, 323.

and one [Hardin] fell, and in the fall of that one we lost our best Whig man.' Four of the five high officers killed at Buena Vista were Whigs. To be sure, Democrats had done as much elsewhere. 'I think of all those brave men as Americans, in whose proud fame, as an American, I too have a share.'

Lincoln wished he had time to speak about the disturbance in the Whig party at which the Democrats sneered. 'I would like to say a word to our dissenters.' [1] But did not the Democrats also have dissenters? If what was reported about Democratic division in New York [2] was true, it reminded Lincoln of what 'a drunken fellow once said when he heard the reading of an indictment for hog stealing,' in which the charge was that ten boars, ten sows, ten shoats, and ten pigs had been stolen; upon hearing which the drunkard observed: '"Well, by golly, that is the most equally divided gang of hogs I ever did hear of!"' So, 'if there is any other gang of hogs more equally divided than the Democrats of New York are about this time, I have not heard of it.' [3]

Such was the speech prepared for the campaign,[4] which Lincoln made during the presidential contest of 1848; but he did not make it in Illinois except, perhaps, once or twice at the close of the presidential campaign. In the Seventh District Logan ran on Lincoln's record and was badly beaten.[5] Lincoln could not — at least, he did not — go to Logan's assistance; the congressional election was on August 7, and Congress did not adjourn until August 14.

Moreover, Lincoln was busy with party national manage-

---

[1] He was soon to say that word in his New England stump speeches.

[2] Where Free Soil Democrats had joined Free Soil Whigs and nominated Van Buren for President on an anti-slavery platform.

[3] Works, ii, 59–88.

[4] History of Abraham Lincoln and the Overthrow of Slavery: Isaac N. Arnold (1867), 82. 'It was designed as a campaign document.'

[5] The majority of Thomas L. Harris, the Democratic candidate, was 106, while the Whig majority in 1846 was 1,511. The voting was very heavy. 2,934 more votes were cast than when Lincoln was elected. Records Ill. Sec. St. Office. This is explained by the absence of the volunteers in August, 1846, and the presence of the veterans at the polls in 1848. It is plain that most of them voted against the Whig candidate, who lost ground in every county.

The Illinois State Register declared that Logan was defeated because of his stand on the Mexican War. Aug. 11, 1848.

ment. Then, too, he would have hurt Logan had he taken the stump for him at that time; for, as Herndon had so often warned him would be the case, Lincoln's popularity at home had been seriously impaired, if indeed it were not for the moment destroyed. The people were against Logan, said the Democratic organ during the campaign, because he 'unblushingly endorses the vote cast by Abraham Lincoln in Congress, denouncing the war as "unconstitutional and unnecessary."' [1]

While attending the Whig National Convention at Philadelphia, Lincoln had met many Whig politicians from over the country and, apparently, had made careful note of each of them. In any case, when the presidential campaign opened in September, he sent letters to Whig politicians in various States, asking for their estimate of the political situation. 'You probably remember seeing me at the Philadelphia Convention — introduced to you as the lone Whig star of Illinois,' he wrote to a vigorous politician in Pennsylvania, Thaddeus Stevens, who was to become so influential although violent a factor in Lincoln's administration.

'Since the adjournment,' continued Lincoln, 'I have remained here, so long, in the Whig document room. I am now about to start for home; and I desire the undisguised opinion of some experienced and sagacious Pennsylvania politician, as to how the vote of that state, for governor and president, is likely to go. In casting about for such a man I have settled upon you; and I shall be obliged if you will write me at Springfield, Illinois. The news we are receiving here now, by letters from all quarters, is steadily on the rise; we have none lately of a discouraging character. This is the sum without giving particulars.' [2]

Stevens answered promptly and at length. It was 'extremely difficult' to forecast the result in Pennsylvania, and he gave Lincoln a clear and detailed analysis of the peculiar conditions in that State. 'I have some, but not strong, hopes of Penn.,' wrote Stevens, and he asked Lincoln for his opinion of the outlook in other States. [3]

---

[1] *Illinois State Register*, June 23, 1848.
[2] Lincoln to Stevens, Sept. 3, 1848. MS. Library of Congress.
[3] Stevens to Lincoln, Sept. 7, 1848. Weik MSS.

Senator John Bell of Tennessee, who in 1860 was to be the presidential candidate of the Constitutional Union Party, wrote Lincoln that he was 'glad to learn [from Lincoln] that all the late accounts received by the Whig [National] Central Com[mittee] were favorable.' Tennessee would be 'certainly Whig,' Bell said; indeed the whole South would go for Taylor except Alabama, Mississippi, Arkansas, and Missouri. But what about Illinois and the Northwest, he inquired of Lincoln.[1]

But Lincoln did not go to Illinois as he told Stevens, Bell, and others he would do. Instead he went to Massachusetts. Early in August he had written 'Friend Schooler' [Schouler], editor of the leading Whig paper in Boston, for his 'undisguised opinion as to what New England generally and Massachusetts particularly' would do at the election. Schouler had told Lincoln, apparently at the Philadelphia Convention, that Taylor would be nominated and this circumstance, said Lincoln, gave him 'confidence in your predictions.'[2] The Boston editor answered after the vague fashion of party enthusiasts, that all was going well; and Lincoln thanked him for the 'encouraging news.' Advice 'from all parts is on the lookup,' he wrote Schouler in reply. From Ohio, a doubtful State, the letters were encouraging.

But Lincoln 'would rather not be put upon explaining how Logan was defeated in my district.' He had not heard from home and did not know whether there had been a full turn out at the polls.[3] Many Whigs were against Logan, he knew. Then, too, Thomas L. Harris, the Democratic candidate against Logan, 'was a Major of the war and fought at Cerro Gordo, where several Whigs of the district fought with him.' But Lincoln's district would be all right in November. He had written to every county and had been told that the chances were more than twenty to one in favor of the Whig national ticket.[4]

---

[1] Bell to Lincoln, Sept. 17, 1848. Weik MSS.

[2] Lincoln to William Schouler, Aug. 8, 1848. Tracy, 34. The *Atlas*, of which Schouler was editor, supported the Whig ticket with extreme ardor and was extremely abusive of Whigs who left the party and became Free Soilers.

[3] The vote had been nearly 3,000 more than when Lincoln was elected. Records, Ill. Sec. St. Office.

[4] Lincoln to Schouler, Aug. 28, 1848. Tracy, 35–6. Taylor carried the Seventh District by 673 majority, although Logan had lost it by 106 three months before.

The sunny estimate of conditions in Massachusetts given by
the optimistic Boston Whig editor appeared to be the reverse of
reports received by the Whig Central Committee at Washington. It is reasonably certain that, in response to his inquiries,
Lincoln had received letters from Whig politicians of that State
as from other States, and that these answers informed him of the
desperate Whig prospects in that traditional Whig stronghold in
New England. For a formidable revolt against Taylor's nomination and the cowardly and evasive Whig 'platform,' was
working in Massachusetts.

Thousands of Whigs were flocking to the new Free Soil party.
The younger Whigs were especially militant in opposition to the
old and moribund organization. Charles Francis Adams, the
firm, resourceful, and fearless son of John Quincy Adams, had
helped to form the new party, had presided over the Free Soil
National Convention at Buffalo, and was the Free Soil candidate for Vice President.

But among the leaders of the Free Soil party in Massachusetts
was a young man of thirty-seven, highly educated, widely travelled and well known in England for his learning and social talents. He was a graduate of Harvard and was already recognized
as an eminent jurist. He was almost as tall as Lincoln, slender,
erect, and graceful. Thick masses of dark hair covered his fine
head, his brow was broad and high, eyes blue, large and alert
yet steady, nose straight and long, mouth wide and generous,
chin and jaw firm and uncompromising. His features, taken together, were intellectual and would have been beautiful but for
their force and austerity. He was to become one of the powerful
and historic figures in the Senate of the United States. Now, in
1848, Charles Sumner was of the most active and influential of
those determined men who formed a new political organization
devoted solely to the cause of freedom. He was imperious, direct, intolerant of opposition, and went forward to his objective
on straight and simple lines. Many of the Southern leaders were
of the same temper, but Lincoln was of another and antipathetic
class. By instinct as well as mind, he understood and responded
to the sinuosities, twists, and contradictions through which a
democracy expresses itself.

Sumner had zealously adopted the abolition view of the Mexican War and had bitterly opposed it. Even before it began he had delivered his notable oration against all war, 'The True Grandeur of Nations.' Indifferent to politics which he thought not worth while, he had, nevertheless, thrown himself heart and soul into the Free Soil movement after Taylor's nomination; and was one of those who called the famous Free Soil State Convention at Worcester, June 28, 1848.[1]

At that gathering Sumner thus answered the principal and abusive argument of the old-line Whigs — the argument which, in a moment, we shall hear Lincoln repeat in the very town where Sumner spoke. 'But it is said that we shall throw away our votes, and that our opposition will fail. Fail, sir! No honest, earnest effort in a good cause can fail. It may not be crowned with the applause of men; . . . But it is not lost; it helps . . . to animate all with devotion to duty, which in the end conquers all. Fail! Did the martyrs fail when with their precious blood they sowed the seed of the Church? Did the discomfited champions of Freedom fail who have left those names in history that can never die? Did the three hundred Spartans fail when in the narrow pass they did not fear to brave the innumerable Persian hosts, whose very arrows darkened the sun? Overborne by numbers, crushed to earth, they left an example greater far than any victory. And this is the least we can do. Our example will be the mainspring of triumph hereafter. It will not be the first time in history that the hosts of Slavery have outnumbered the champions of Freedom. But where is it written that Slavery finally prevailed?'[2]

At a Free Soil ratification meeting in Fanueil Hall Sumner was chairman and in a short and thrilling speech declared: 'Opposition to the slave-power . . . is now for the first time the leading principle of a broad, resolute, and national organiza-

[1] Of that gathering Sumner afterwards wrote: 'This was the beginning of the separate Free Soil organization in Massachusetts, which afterwards grew into the Republican party. . . . No great movement ever showed at the beginning more character and power. It began true and strong. All the speakers united in renouncing old party ties. None did this better than C[harles] F[rancis] Adams.' *Memoir and Letters of Charles Sumner:* Edward L. Pierce, III, 166.

[2] Pierce, III, 167.

tion. . . . We found now a new party. Its corner-stone is freedom, its broad, all-sustaining arches are truth, justice, and
humanity.' [1]

Such were the spirit and purpose of the men of New England
who left the Whig party in 1848. And the quality of the 'dissenters,' as Lincoln called them, was correspondingly high and
resolute. With Sumner and Charles Francis Adams was a young
man of thirty, John A. Andrew, who was to become the 'war
governor' of Massachusetts while Lincoln was President. Another of twenty-eight, Anson Burlingame, was to be appointed
by Lincoln Minister to China. A third, one year younger than
Sumner, Henry Wilson, was to become Sumner's colleague in
the Senate and chairman of the Senate Committee on military
affairs during Lincoln's administration.[2] Richard Henry Dana,
E. Rockwood Hoar, his brother George Frisbie Hoar, and many
others of like character and stature were of this faction.

Nearly all men of letters in Massachusetts supported the new
party — Whittier, Longfellow, Lowell. In his Biglow Papers
Lowell had already made effective use of his gift of satire and
ridicule in castigating the Whig abandonment of principle,
Taylor's unfitness for the Presidency, the wrong of slavery.
Conspicuous among New England Free Soilers because of his
age, learning, public services, and literary achievements, was
Palfrey, still in Congress and one of the directing minds of the
Free Soil agitation in his State.[3]

[1] Pierce, III, 170–1. Of this meeting the Whig campaign organ in Washington said:
'The Barnburners of Massachusetts, for so we may now call the Anti-Cass and Taylor
men of that State, held an adjourned meeting at the Temple in Boston last week. . . . The
speakers . . . devoted themselves to arguments against slavery, and to statements that
its extension can only be prevented by opposition to the two parties which now enrol
almost all the voters of the country.

'How they propose to accomplish any good result, or any result whatever, they do
not inform us. But of course they lauded each other very much for their devotion to
liberty, and denounced all Cass-and-Taylor men as "false to freedom."

'The result will be, that the Third party will be gradually thinned out until there remains nothing of it but Abolitionism and Barnburnerism proper.' *Battery*, July 13, 1848.

[2] Wilson was one of the most practically effective men in either House or in the government during the Civil War. Although a Senator, he raised a regiment in Massachusetts in 1861 and served as its Colonel until Congress convened. In 1872 Wilson was
elected Vice President on the Republican ticket with Grant. It is worthy of note that
he was a delegate to the Philadelphia Convention that nominated Taylor in 1848 and
then and there openly declared that he would not support the nominee.

[3] Garrison, Phillips, and other thorough-going Abolitionists would not join the Free

In such manner and by such men began the movement that ended in the formation of the Republican party eight years later, a movement of which Lincoln was finally to become the standard bearer, supported most ardently by the very persons whose motives he now so vigorously assailed. For it was to help crush this rebellion in the Whig party that Lincoln hastened to Massachusetts toward the middle of September, 1848.

The Whig leaders were even more virulent toward the Free Soilers than they were toward the Democrats. 'The Third party in the Northern States, under the lead of Van Buren, Giddings, Garrison, Adams, Palfrey, Wilson, and others of that kidney, is running as fast as it may into abolitionism,' exclaimed the *Battery*.[1] What could be worse!

The Free Soil upheaval was not the only danger, real or fancied, to Whig prospects in Massachusetts. The old party was well-nigh paralyzed there by the disgust and apathy of those who remained members of it. Every Whig Representative in Congress from that State, except Winthrop and Hudson, had declined to be a candidate for reëlection.[2] Webster held Taylor in infinite contempt, despised the politician's creed of availability by which he had been nominated, and did not announce his support of the Whig candidate until two weeks before the Whig

Soilers because they did not go far enough. The position of the Abolitionists was that there must be immediate and unconditional emancipation. Opposition to extending slave territory and respecting the Constitution were inconsistent, they declared, with the principle of human freedom.

Emerson is the one man of distinction in Massachusetts at that time, who seems not to have been greatly concerned about the acquisition of territory. Indeed Emerson rather favored expansion as inevitable and, on the whole, desirable.

[1] *Battery*, July 13, 1848. As the campaign progressed the Whig campaign organ became ever more bitter. The Massachusetts and Ohio Whigs who bolted the Philadelphia convention were 'mal-contents and traitors,' said the *Battery*. They were 'among the tagrag and bobtail of parties.' They were 'traitors from the start,' etc. *Ib.*, Aug. 24, 1848. Giddings, especially, was denounced by the Whig paper as the father of lies. *Ib.*, Nov. 2, 1848.

Garrison should not have been mentioned save as an influence, for he would not himself vote.

[2] In his speech at the Whig State Convention, Sept. 13, Winthrop named each of the Massachusetts delegation, accorded them the usual praise and said: 'They are about to fling away ambition. They have already signified, almost to a man, their desire and their design to be relieved from further service in the offices which they have held.' *National Intelligencer*, Sept. 23, 1848.

In the election Hudson, who had come out in support of Taylor 'as a choice of evils,' was beaten by Charles Allen, Free Soiler, and Palfrey was defeated. Of the ten Massa-

State convention. Then, at his Marshfield farm, he reluctantly broke his public silence in a half-hearted effort to check the exodus from his party.[1] Nowhere in the whole discontented North was the Whig outlook so forbidding as it was in Massachusetts.

Apparently Lincoln went to that field of party peril, as a kind of campaign inspector from the Whig national headquarters in Washington — if not, it is hard to see why he took the journey. No invitation to him to take part in the campaign on the stump has been discovered, although painstaking search for such a request has been made.[2] The Speaker of the House, Robert C. Winthrop, had not been impressed by Lincoln's work in Congress,[3] and certainly did not ask him to come. He had no engagements to speak anywhere in the State. It would appear, indeed, that Lincoln's services on the stump were not in demand

chusetts members of the House in the 30th Congress four were retired and in place of one Free Soiler (Palfrey) two (Allen and Fowler) were elected to the 31st Congress. Winthrop declined to run, because of ill-health, but was persuaded by his friends and the Whig politicians to reconsider. One of them wrote that Winthrop's refusal to be a candidate might cause the Whigs to lose the State. Letters to Winthrop, July, 1848: MSS. Winthrop Papers, Mass. Hist. Socy.

[1] Webster made his Marshfield speech, Sept. 1, 1848. Massachusetts Whigs, he said, did not favor Taylor's nomination principally because he was 'a military man merely' — the only one in our history that ever had been proposed for office. That was the main reason that the Whigs of Massachusetts, 'and I among them,' were dissatisfied, although there were other reasons 'of less importance.'

But Taylor was the Whig candidate, and a good man personally. No matter how he had been nominated, it had been done honestly and in the regular way. Pro-slavery men had not nominated him, as some seemed to think. He was chosen solely because it was thought he could win. 'That was the whole of it. That *sagacious, wise, farseeing doctrine of availability* lies at the bottom of the whole matter' — and Webster denounced availability as 'wholly unwise,' 'short-sighted,' and 'not suited to the Whig character.' Italics Webster's.

However, the real questions before the country were that there should be no more 'wars of ambition and conquest,' that slavery should not be extended, and that there should be a protective tariff. On these matters Taylor was safer than Cass. If 'a considerable number of Whigs secede' and go for Van Buren, the result would be Whig defeat.

Webster's speech tended to check the Whig revolt against Taylor in Massachusetts and throughout the North. It was widely published in the Whig press of the country and the Whig national organ printed it in full. *National Intelligencer*, Sept. 21, 1848.

[2] 'I have been unable to determine at whose solicitation he made the trip to Massachusetts.' Arthur P. Rugg in *Pro'd'gs. Worcester Socy. An't'y.* xxv, 228.

'I have wondered how Mr. Lincoln happened to come in 1848.' E. L. Pierce to Herndon, 1891. Weik MSS. The surmise that Hudson invited Lincoln is not supported by proof of any kind.

[3] 'Mr. Lincoln in Congress did not make much impression on Mr. Winthrop.' E. L.

anywhere during this campaign. Even at Georgetown he was not one of the speakers at a Whig ratification meeting where several Whig Representatives spoke;[1] nor did he appear at any of a large number of similar party gatherings in towns near Washington. Neither the *National Intelligencer* nor the *Battery* makes mention of him, although they printed speeches and letters by men so inconspicuous that their identity cannot now be determined without careful research.

Lincoln arrived in Worcester sometime during the day before the Whig State Convention which was held at that place September 13, 1848. Nobody knew that he was in town. The local Rough and Ready Club had arranged for a Whig meeting at the City Hall[2] the night before the Convention assembled; and Alexander H. Bullock, chairman of the local Whig Committee and a member of the Whig State Central Committee, had asked several men of prominence to speak at the City Hall gathering. None of them accepted, however, and Bullock was in distress until he heard that a Whig Congressman from Illinois, had arrived and was stopping at the hotel. The perturbed chairman sought him out and asked him to address the meeting, warning him of the excessive political bitterness then prevailing in the Worcester district.[3]

So it came about that Lincoln spoke at Worcester. The correspondents of two Boston papers,[4] both ardently Whig, were on hand for the State Convention next day, and sent reports of his remarks to their papers. Thus the Worcester speech was the only one of Lincoln's addresses reported during the campaign; and the account of it is of no value except as showing the matter which Lincoln, when delivering the speech in the House, said he had to leave out on account of time.

He was introduced as 'a representative of *Free Soil*,' a state-

Pierce to Herndon, no date. Weik MSS. In Winthrop's correspondence (Mass. Hist. Socy.) no mention of Lincoln is made at this time nor for many years afterward.

[1] *Battery*, Aug. 3, 1848.

[2] Arthur P. Rugg to Weik, June 25, 1909. Weik MSS. Mechanics Hall, where it has been said Lincoln made the Worcester speech, was not built until 1857. Rugg, 231, 233.

[3] *Ib.*, 229.

[4] *Boston Advertiser* and *Boston Atlas*. These papers were 'inordinately abusive of the Free Soilers.' Pierce, III, 177-9.

ment which he did not correct; to have done so would have spoiled the effect on the Free Soilers in the audience, whose desertion of the Whig party Lincoln wished to check. He wore a long linen duster,[1] and the reporter described him as 'a very tall and thin' person with an 'intellectual face, showing a searching mind, and a cool judgment.' He spoke eloquently for an hour and a half, 'only interrupted by warm and frequent applause.'

There was nothing new in Lincoln's speech at Worcester and other places in New England, except his brief mention of the slavery question and his argument that Free Soilers and Abolitionists ought to vote for Taylor. 'The people of Illinois agreed entirely with the people of Massachusetts' on slavery, he said, 'except perhaps that they did not keep so constantly thinking about it. All agreed that slavery was an evil, but that we were not responsible for it and cannot affect it in States of this Union where we do not live.' But we could control the '*extension*' of slavery into new territories.

In that respect the 'Free Soil' party was far behind the Whigs, Lincoln argued, because 'the new party had no principle except this opposition' to the enlargement of slave territory. 'If their platform held any other, it was in such a general way that it was like the pair of pantaloons the Yankee peddler offered for sale, "large enough for any man, small enough for any boy."' So the new party was 'working for the election of either Gen. Cass or Gen. Taylor,' for everybody knew that it could not elect its own candidate, Van Buren. The election of Cass meant the probable extension of slavery. So the Free Soilers ought to vote for Taylor.

The Democrats had annexed the new territory, and how absurd of the Liberty men to 'unite' with them for the purpose of preventing the extension of slavery in that very territory! Yet, in practical effect, that was what the Free Soilers would do, if they voted for Van Buren. A vote for the Free Soil, anti-slavery candidate would be half a vote for the Democratic candidate. Even if the Free Soil candidate should be elected President, he could not '*prevent*' the extension of slavery; and

[1] Rugg, 235.

Lincoln was confident that Taylor 'would not encourage it,' nor yet 'prohibit its restriction.' But if Cass were elected 'the plans of farther extension of territory would be encouraged, and those of the extension of slavery would meet no check.'

The use of the name 'Free Soil' by the new party was dishonest, since it implied that the Whigs 'were *not* Free Soil men.' The slogan of the Free Soilers that they would 'do their duty and leave the consequences to God,' was a poor 'excuse for taking a course they were not able to maintain by a fair and full argument.' What was the 'duty' of the Free Soilers, about which they talked so much? Merely to shout the word duty, did not explain it; 'if it did we should have no use for judgment we might as well be made without intellect.'

Unless divine or human law directed us what to do, duty could be determined only by the use of 'our most intelligent judgment of the consequences' of any act. But was there 'divine law, or human law for voting for Martin Van Buren?' or did 'first reasoning' show that voting for him would produce the results which the Free Soilers 'pretended to wish'? If so Lincoln would give up the argument. All that the Free Soilers were doing was to help elect Cass; and so, 'they were behind the Whigs in their advocacy of the freedom of the soil.'

After this foggy attempt to show that the Free Soilers did not know what the word 'duty' meant and had no real 'principle' as to slavery, Lincoln proceeded to show that the new party 'had *less* of principle than any other' party. Look at the ridiculous Free Soil Convention at Buffalo! Notwithstanding the denunciation of the Mexican War by former Whigs who had turned Free Soilers, their platform was silent on that subject. Why? 'Because the Van Burens [Free Soil Democrats] had been known to have supported it.' Where was 'principle' in that evasion? Did the Free Soilers still think that the two old parties were 'dissolved,' as the Free Soil platform asserted? If so, what about the recent Whig triumph in Vermont?

Lincoln assured his audience that 'he had opportunities [as one of the Whig campaign managers in Washington] of hearing from almost every part of the Union from reliable sources, and had not heard of a country [county?] in which we [Whigs] had not accessions from other parties.'[1] So let 'true Whigs come forward' and victory was certain. Let all who believed in 'keeping our fences where they are and cultivating our present possession,' all who believed in 'improving the morals and education of the people, . . . all real Whigs, friends of good honest government' vote for Taylor, and 'the race is ours.'

What a candidate Taylor was! 'Just the man to whom the interest, principles, and prosperity of the country might be safely intrusted,' a man who always did his duty asking neither praise nor reward, a man who never failed in anything he undertook no matter how hard, how seemingly impossible, a man whose character was so noble that Lincoln 'could not eulogize it if he would.'

The motive of Lincoln's speech was the folly and evil of the Free Soil party, its certain failure, its waste of Whig votes — the precise points which the old line Whigs had been making with vituperation and abuse against the Whig opponents of Taylor and his platform, and which Sumner, in the burst of lofty eloquence we have read, had answered six weeks before in that same town of Worcester.

During his speech Lincoln 'repeated anecdotes, told stories admirable in humor and in point, interspersed with bursts of true eloquence, which constantly brought down the house,' relates one of the audience. 'His sarcasm of Cass, Van Buren, and the Democratic party was inimitable, and whenever he attempted to stop, the shouts of "Go on! go on!" were deafening.'[2]

The correspondent of the Boston Whig paper which reported Lincoln's speech, described the conclusion of the meeting thus: 'At the close of this truly masterly and convincing speech, the audience gave three enthusiastic cheers for Illinois, and three

---

[1] This otherwise curious statement is explained by the fact that Lincoln was helping to direct the Whig national campaign; but he had received letters that were far from optimistic.

[2] Henry J. Gardner to Herndon, in Rugg, 230. Gardner's statement, though obviously subject to the defects of all narratives given forty years after the incident described, fixes the identity of the Worcester speech with the stump speech Lincoln had made in Congress not long before. Gardner was to be the Know-Nothing governor of Massachusetts.

more cheers for the eloquent Whig member from that state.'[1]
The Worcester papers made little mention of the meeting or of
Lincoln's speech. One said only that he spoke.[2] Another was
laudatory, though brief: 'For sound, conclusive reasoning and
ready wit it [Lincoln's speech] is unsurpassed in the campaign.
It was listened to by the crowded audience with an untiring
interest, applauded during its delivery, and enthusiastically
cheered at its close.'[3]

But Lincoln said one thing which the Whig papers did not
report. At Worcester, testifies E. L. Pierce, who was present,
'he gave offence by saying "I have heard you have abolitionists
here. We have a few in Illinois and we shot one the other day."[4]
The Free Soil papers criticised the passage and he did not repeat
it.' But, on the whole, Lincoln 'was greatly liked,' continues
Pierce; his 'was a style new to our people, and there was a general call for him as a speaker.'[5] Next morning Lincoln and several others spoke briefly to a crowd of delegates and citizens
near the railway station.[6]

At the Convention, Winthrop, Choate, Hudson, and other
Whig chieftains, following the lead of Webster, begged Whigs
to stand by their disrupted party. A platform was adopted far
in advance of any Whig party avowal that had been made.
Protection, sound money, internal improvements, were briefly
endorsed; but resistance to slavery was the dominant feature.
'We stand . . . on the *platform of free labor, a free press, and free
soil.* The whigs of the North, and especially the whigs of Massachusetts, may rightfully claim the appellation of the *free soil
party.*' The Massachusetts delegation in Congress had opposed
slavery for a quarter of a century, maintained the right of
petition, upheld the liberty of the press.[7]

[1] *Boston Advertiser*, Sept. 14, 1848, reporting Lincoln's Worcester speech, Sept. 12;
Works, II, 89–96.

[2] *Worcester Palladium*, as quoted in Rugg, 232.

[3] *National Ægis*, Rugg, 232–3.

[4] This reference was to the killing of Lovejoy.

[5] E. L. Pierce to Herndon, no date; Rugg, 234.

[6] *Worcester Spy*, in *ib.*, 233.

[7] Address adopted by the Whig State Convention at Worcester, Sept. 13, 1848.
Italics in original. The Platform was long; but the part given in the text was the rallying
cry to all Whigs opposed to slavery.

Throughout the proceedings Lincoln was a silent listener.[1] No attention whatever seems to have been paid to him;[2] but he was present at a political and social function that night. The venerable Levi Lincoln, former Governor of Massachusetts, lived in Worcester. He was a rich man, lived in a fine house, and always gave a dinner when any notable assemblage was held in that town; and he did so on the occasion of the Whig State Convention of 1848 which named him as presidential elector at large.[3]

His guests were Choate, Ashmun, and several others, including the Illinois orator of the preceding evening. Nearly forty years afterward, one who was present and who recalled with remarkable accuracy that 'the dining-room and table arrangements were superb, the dinner exquisite, the wines abundant, rare, and of the first quality,' also distinctly remembered the jokes between the aged and the younger Lincoln about their 'presumed relationship.' A remark of Lincoln's thus treasured was: 'I *hope* we belong, as the Scotch say, to the same clan; but I *know* one thing, and that is, that we are both good Whigs.'[4]

Lincoln himself seems to have been more deeply impressed with this social affair than with any incident of his visit; for when President, he is said to have described the occasion with photographic minuteness. 'I had been chosen to Congress then from the Wild West,' he is reported to have recounted, 'and with hayseed in my hair I went to Massachusetts, the most cultured State in the Union, to take a few lessons in deportment. That was a grand dinner — a superb dinner; by far the finest I ever saw in my life. And the great men who were there too! Why I can tell you just how they were arranged at table.' And we are assured that Lincoln then proved his remarkable memory.[5]

---

[1] The speeches of Winthrop and Choate were fervent pleas for Whigs not to leave their party. *National Intelligencer*, Sept. 23, 26, 1848.

[2] 'The member from Illinois . . . was that day and in that body unknown and unheard.' A. H. Bullock, as quoted by Rugg, 229.

[3] *Boston Advertiser*, Sept. 14, 1848.

[4] Henry J. Gardner to Herndon. 1890; Rugg, 229–30.

[5] Same to same, in *ib.*, 230.

After his success at Worcester, Lincoln was asked to speak at Chelsea, Dedham, Cambridge, and Lowell.[1] He made the same speech everywhere and with uniform success. The City Hall at Lowell was 'filled to its utmost capacity,' and the Whig paper loyally declared that the orator from Illinois showed 'beyond a peradventure, that it is the first duty of Whigs to stand united' and beat the Democrats who had hurt the country so badly. Lincoln's speech was 'frequently interrupted by bursts of warm applause;' and the meeting closed with 'cheer after cheer for Taylor and Fillmore.'[2]

Finally on September 22, 1848, Lincoln spoke in Boston. This meeting was held in Tremont Temple.[3] The principal speaker, William H. Seward, was a man of singularly calm and gentle manner, grave but cordial, with a face of marked intellectuality, and the restrained eloquence of the great orator. He had been Governor of New York for four years and was then the personage upon whom the anti-slavery forces of that State had, by common consent, united for the United States Senate the following year. Determined, suave, and fertile in resource, he was the most promising of the rising statesmen of the day. Eight years older than Lincoln, Seward was the outstanding leader of the movement that was to create the Republican party. He had come to Massachusetts because of the bold declarations in the Whig platform adopted at Worcester.

For the first time, on the stump in a political campaign, Lincoln heard a speaker of the highest rank. He was, Seward began, of Cicero's mind when the alternative was Cæsar or Pompey. 'He knew whom he ought to avoid, but had some hesitation whom he ought to follow.' However he was 'a disciple of the Whig doctrines promulgated by the Whigs of Massachusetts;' and, considering that either Cass or Taylor

[1] Pierce to Herndon, no date. Weik MSS.

[2] *Lowell Journal and Courier*, Sept. 18, 1848.

It is worthy of note that Taylor fell short, by 12,000 votes, of a majority in Massachusetts over Cass and Van Buren, and that the Legislature chose the presidential electors of that State. *National Intelligencer*, Nov. 9, 1848.

[3] The meeting was to have been held in Court Square, but, because of rain, it was held in Tremont Temple. The Secretary of the meeting was Ezra Lincoln. *Boston Advertiser*, Sept. 22, 1848. Advt.

would be elected, he was for the Whig ticket. But the dominant
note of Seward's speech was resistance to slavery and to the
South. 'The time would come,' he said, and that, too, in his
day, 'when the free people would free the slaves in this country.
This is to be accomplished by moral force, . . . without injustice . . . by paying a full remuneration for so great a blessing.'
Of the Whig and Democratic parties, one had 'its foundations
in South Carolina, the other on the Rock of Plymouth.' If the
third party should 'draw off all the advocates of Liberty, . . .
we shall have left the two great parties, ready to bow before the
aristocracy of the South.'[1]

We can only conjecture the effect of Seward's method and
manner on the speaking of Lincoln; but when we again listen
to him on the stump, we find him making speeches so unlike
those of the party-politician phase of his life now drawing to
a close, that another and entirely different man seems to be
delivering them. Next day Lincoln said to Seward: 'I have been
thinking about what you said in your speech. I reckon you are
right. We have got to deal with this slavery question, and got to
give much more attention to it hereafter than we have been
doing.'[2] One of the greatest qualities of Lincoln, if, indeed, not
the very greatest, was his eagerness to learn, his capacity to
grow.

Lincoln returned to Illinois by way of Albany, Buffalo, and
the Lakes, and somewhere on the journey Mrs. Lincoln joined
him. If he made a speech on the way there is no record of the
circumstance. As has been said, the national Whig organ at
Washington published accounts of meetings and addresses at
widely separated parts of the country;[3] but not a line of any
speech by Lincoln. At Albany he called on Thurlow Weed and
talked over the political situation with that skilful politician.
While at Buffalo he saw Niagara Falls and, afterward, expressed

---

[1] *Boston Atlas*, Sept. 23, 1848.

[2] Memoirs of Seward: 79–80 *n.*

[3] For example, Winthrop's and Choate's speeches at the Mass. Whig Convention
(*National Intelligencer*, Sept. 23, 26); Corwin at Carthage, Ohio, and at Cincinnati (*ib.*,
Oct. 10, 17); Rives at Richmond, Choate at Salem, Mass.; Bell at Murfreesborough,
Tenn., Chilton Allen at Winchester, Ky. (*ib.*, Oct. 12); Baker at St. Louis (*ib.*, Sept. 2);
Stephens, Toombs, and Berrien in Georgia (*ib.*, Sept. 22).

his wonder at where so much water came from.[1] He reached
Chicago on October 5, went to the Sherman House, and notice
appeared the next day in the *Chicago Daily Journal* of a Whig
rally that night at the Court House, with Lincoln as the principal speaker. 'We trust to see a spontaneous rally this evening,'
said that journal. 'The notice is short, but "Old Zack's" soldiers are all minute men.' Although called on six hours' notice
the attendance was so large as to force an adjournment to the
Public Square, where Lincoln spoke for two hours, giving the
same facts and arguments he had used in Massachusetts. He
was 'listened to throughout with great attention' and the favorable *Journal* described his speech as 'one of the very best we
have heard or read, since the opening of the campaign.'[2]

Finally he reached home, but no mention of his arrival was
made in any paper. What further part he took in the campaign
in Illinois does not appear, except that at one meeting in a small
town in Sangamon County, just before the Presidential election,
the crowd was unfriendly and a Democratic speaker handled
him roughly. As we have seen, Logan had been overwhelmed in
the August elections.[3] The result of Lincoln's first session in
Congress had been a political revolution among his constituents,[4] and, again going by the way of St. Louis and the Ohio,[5] he
returned to Washington a dispirited man. In spite of Illinois,
Taylor had been elected just as Harrison had won eight years
before, and by identical campaign methods; [6] the Democrats

[1] Herndon, II, 297.   [2] *Chicago Daily Journal*, Oct. 6, 7, 1848.

[3] In Menard County all the county officers who were elected had been in the war.
Illinois State Register, Aug. 13, 1847.

[4] The Democrats conducted the campaign on the ground that the Whigs, by moral
support, had given 'aid and comfort to the enemy.' *Ib.*, Sept. 24, 1847.

[5] Lincoln to C. R. Welles, Feb. 20, 1849. Tracy, 37-8.

[6] Of the States which went for Polk in 1844, New York, Pennsylvania, Georgia and
Louisiana gave their electoral vote to Taylor in 1848. Ohio changed from Whig in 1844
to Democratic in 1848. Of the States admitted between these years, Wisconsin, Iowa,
and Texas went for Cass and Florida for Taylor.

In the Northern States, the unpopularity of Polk was a powerful factor in the Democratic defeat: 'There is an intense desire to put down the Administration and to defeat
Gen'l. Cass.' Edward Everett to Winthrop, Cambridge, Mass., July 1, 1848. MS.
Winthrop Papers, Mass. Hist. Socy. The tariff, internal improvements, and national
finances, as well as bad distribution of patronage, had more to do with Taylor's success
in the North than the reaction against the war.

The change of popular votes in the Southern States was strongly favorable to the

were out, the Whigs in, and there was much patronage to be distributed.

Personal troubles added to Lincoln's political distress. His father had never struggled out of the morass of poverty in which he had floundered all his life — seemingly he made little effort to do so; and, when attending court at Charleston, Lincoln had sometimes given him little sums of cash, or assigned to him small notes of clients for fees. Lincoln's step-brother, John D. Johnston, too, was as thriftless as Thomas Lincoln himself, and both of them often begged Lincoln for money. One of these appeals came to him soon after he reached Washington.

His father wrote by the hand of Johnston that he must have twenty dollars at once, or lose his land; he had collected two or three small notes given him by Lincoln, but could not raise another dollar. He had hoped that his son would have come to see his parents on his way to Washington, but since he did not, 'Father' must write. On the same sheet John D. Johnston wrote a long letter, pleading, dejected, pathetic, and revealing. Johnston owed seventy or eighty dollars, he said, and could not pay, had neither cash nor property. 'I am dund and doged to death So I am most tired of living and I would all most Swop my Place in *Heaven* for that much money. I now you will think little of this for you never had the Tryal, but Abe, I would drother Live on bread and wotter than to have men allways duning me.'

Johnston would pay 'any' interest, he assured Lincoln, and

Whigs: Virginia, 5,893 majority for Polk and only 1,453 for Cass; Mississippi 5,920 for Polk and but 615 for Cass; Alabama 11,656 for Polk and a mere 881 for Cass; Louisiana 699 for Polk and 2847 for Taylor; Arkansas 4,042 for Polk to 1,712 for Cass. Tennessee gave Clay a majority of 113, while it went for Taylor by a majority of 6,286; Kentucky 9,267 for Clay and 17,421 for Taylor; North Carolina 3,955 for Clay and 8,681 for Taylor.

In Illinois the Whig gain was even greater, Cass carrying the State by only 3,523 while Polk had 12,392 majority in 1844. Birney had received 3,570 votes in Illinois in 1844, and Van Buren 15,774 in 1848. That the Democrats saved Illinois in 1848 was due solely to the exertions of Douglas.

In Massachusetts the Democrats were even more divided than the Whigs. Taylor received 61,070 votes, Cass, 35,281 and Van Buren, 38,058. Evidently the Free Soilers drew more heavily from the Democrats than from the Whigs.

As the total vote for Taylor was 1,360,099, for Cass, 1,220,544 and for Van Buren, 291,263, the importance of the third party movement in influencing the result can hardly be overestimated.

'Father will make you a Deed for all his land when you Come in the spring.' If Lincoln would send one hundred dollars, he should have all the land when Father dies.

Johnston said that he thought he could 'rays' that much money for Lincoln in three years. 'I could rayse a calf and Pig of my owen for *Tom* and *Abe* [Johnston's children] can now Doe nearly as much work in a crop as a man. I candadley would Drother never own a foot of land than to not pay my debts, nor lave any to my childern Indeed I would drother give possession now than to live here and have men a watching me to see if I hadent something the law would take to sit a man wonst behind hand in this Country and no other way to make a Living only by hiz laber it will take his Life Time to get out and pay the Cash if he has a large family.' [1]

Lincoln responded to his father's request, but frankly stated his doubt of the truthfulness of the old man's plea. 'I very cheerfully send you the twenty dollars, which sum you say is necessary to save your land from sale. It is singular that you should have forgotten a judgment against you; and it is more singular that the plaintiff should have let you forget it so long, particularly as I suppose you always had property enough to satisfy a judgment of that amount. Before you pay it, it would be well to be sure you have not paid it, or at least that you cannot prove that you have paid it.' [2]

The letter of his step-brother Lincoln ignored. With these fresh reminders of the wretched poverty of his relatives in Coles County, with the squalid spectre of his childhood and youth again rising before him, and with the conviction that his political ambitions, so dear to his heart, never again could be gratified, it was a disconsolate Lincoln who, on December 7, 1848, took his seat in the House for the short session of the thirtieth Congress. This time his wife did not accompany him to the capital, nor did she come on for the inauguration of Taylor.

Except for brief remarks on a bill granting lands to states for

[1] Thomas Lincoln and John D. Johnston to Lincoln, Coles Co., Dec. 7, 1848. MS. owned by Mr. Alexander W. Hannah, Chicago, Ill. The same hand, presumably Johnston's, wrote the two letters.

[2] Lincoln to his father, Dec. 24, 1848. *Works*, ii, 96. It took fifteen days for the letters of Lincoln's father and step-brother to go from Charleston, Ill., to Washington.

the building of railroads and canals, Lincoln said nothing during the whole session. At an early day the Wilmot Proviso, or rather the idea which it expressed that slavery should be excluded from territories acquired from Mexico, twice came to a vote; and Lincoln supported it both times.[1] Thus during his term in Congress he voted five times for the principle of the Wilmot Proviso.[2] While most of these votes were indirect, the issue was distinctly presented, and Lincoln's record was as clear and positive as any number of votes could have made it.[3] He voted, too, against extending over California and New Mexico the Constitution and laws of the United States, as did most anti-slavery men of all parties.[4]

More than ever slavery was the supreme object of discussion and debate.[5] Reference was made to the capture and imprisonment of the Georgetown slaves during the last session, and abolition of the slave-trade in the District of Columbia was again advocated with fiery vehemence. With this extreme measure Lincoln was not sympathetic, going so far as to vote, with all Southern members and in opposition to most Northern members, against permitting Palfrey to introduce a bill to repeal all laws 'establishing or maintaining slavery or the slave trade in the District of Columbia.'[6]

[1] Dec. 13, 1848. Joseph M. Root of Ohio offered a resolution for a bill for territorial government in New Mexico and California 'and excluding slavery therefrom.' A motion to table was beaten by a vote of eighty ayes to one hundred and six nays, Lincoln and all anti-slavery men voting nay. *House Journal*, 30th Cong. 2nd Sess., 98–9.

Five days later a motion to reconsider was beaten by practically the same vote, Lincoln again voting nay. *Ib.*, 105–6.

[2] Three times during the 1st and twice during the 2nd session.

[3] Lincoln's statement in 1854 that he had voted for the Wilmot Proviso forty times while in Congress, was merely a campaign exaggeration in which all stump-speakers then indulged.

[4] *House Journal*, 30th Cong. 2nd Sess., 600–2.

[5] Early in the first session, many petitions to abolish slavery in the District of Columbia were tabled, Lincoln always voting nay on such motions. *House Journal*, 30th Cong. 1st Sess., 139–40, 160–1; against extinction of slavery throughout the Union, 167–8; 251–3 (Giddings' resolution to investigate a slave kidnapping in D.C.); 324–5 (Giddings' resolutions to inquire about slave-trade in D.C.). Anti-slavery petitions from Illinois were introduced by Amos Tuck of New Hampshire. *Ib.*, 887. Tuck also introduced Illinois petitions to end the war, and to extend the Ordinance of 1787 over Oregon and Turner of Illinois, over all territory acquired from Mexico. *Ib.*, 887, 1037.

[6] *Cong. Globe*, 30th Cong. 2nd Sess., xx, 30–8, Dec. 13, 1848. Andrew Johnson also

Speaking on a claims bill providing for payment for a slave, Giddings made a ferocious attack on slavery — robbery or piracy were 'crimes of small importance compared with' slavery. The slave States might keep their 'foul contagion,' but they could not make 'slave dealers . . . traders in humanity' of other States.[1] Excitement was tense, subdued, dangerous. In Illinois a wave of negro kidnappings, as well as of the capture of fugitive slaves, had started and was sweeping over the State.[2] In this temper of the House, which had grown more serious in the three days since Giddings' defiance, and in this condition of his State, Lincoln rose on January 10, 1849, and read an amendment which he said he would make to a resolution to instruct the Committee on the District of Columbia to report a bill abolishing slavery in the District.

He proposed to direct the Committee to bring in a bill providing that slavery in the District should be confined to the slaves then living in the District; that they should not 'be held in slavery within the limits of said District,' except that Government officials who owned slaves might bring in and take out 'the necessary servants of themselves and their families,' when such officials were in Washington 'on public business'; that 'children born of slave mothers within said District' after January 1, 1850, should be free and supported and educated by the owners of the slave mothers, but should serve as apprentices until a fixed age when they should 'be entirely free'; that negroes now slaves in the District should continue as such 'at the

voted nay on this historic ballot. So did men like Rhett and Cobb. Greeley, Giddings, Palfrey, and all strong anti-slavery men voted aye.

Noteworthy, too, was the resolution offered, December 21, 1848, by Daniel Gott of New York, reciting that 'Whereas the traffic now prosecuted in this metropolis of the Republic in human beings, as chattels, is contrary to natural justice and the fundamental principles of our political system, and is notoriously a reproach to our country throughout Christendom, and a serious hindrance to the progress of republican liberty among the nations of the earth;' a bill should be reported, as soon as practicable, prohibiting the slave-trade in the District of Columbia. On a motion to lay the resolution on the table there were eighty-one ayes and eighty-five nays, Lincoln voting aye. On taking the main question there were one hundred and thirteen ayes and sixty-three nays, Lincoln voting nay. The resolution was then adopted by ninety-eight ayes and eighty-eight nays, Lincoln voting nay. *Ib.*, 83–4.

[1] *Cong. Globe*, 30th Cong. 2nd Sess., xx, 174–7.

[2] *Gem of the Prairie*, Oct. 7, 1848; *Chicago Democrat*, Sept. 26, 1848; *Quincy Whig*, May 1, July 10, 1849; *Western Citizen*, Sept. 25, Dec. 4, 1849.

will of their owners,' but that, if any owner wished to free a
slave he should be paid out of the national treasury the value
of the slave, which value should be determined by a slave-valua-
tion board composed of the President, Secretary of State, and
Secretary of the Treasury, to meet once a month for that purpose; and that this board should issue 'a certificate of freedom'
to any slave thus paid for.

To this scheme Lincoln attached a section which infuriated
Abolitionists and which gave Wendell Phillips the excuse to
denounce Lincoln as 'that slave hound from Illinois' when,
years afterward, he became a figure in national politics. 'The
municipal authorities of Washington and Georgetown, within
their respective jurisdictional limits, are hereby empowered and
required to provide active and efficient means to arrest and deliver up to their owners all fugitive slaves escaping into said District.'

Finally Lincoln's bill provided for an election at which 'every
free white male citizen' of the District who was twenty-one
years old and had lived there for one year or more, should vote
for or against the project; the President to 'canvass said votes
immediately' and, if a majority were for the bill, to 'forthwith
issue his proclamation giving notice of the fact,' after which the
law should 'be in full force and effect.' [1]

When he had finished reading his bill, Lincoln made a curious
and confusing statement: 'he was authorized to say' that the
bill had been approved by 'about fifteen of the leading citizens
of the District of Columbia to whom this proposition had been
submitted.' Perhaps they might not vote for it at an election,
but 'he had authority to say that every one of them desired
that some proposition like this should pass.' [2]

'Who are they? Give us their names,' cried several members.
But Lincoln made no answer, and the business of the House

[1] *Works*, II, 96–100. *Cong. Globe*, 30th Cong. 2nd Sess., xx, 212. In all editions of
Lincoln's Works, the date of the introduction of this measure is given as Jan. 16. The
amendment was never formally introduced. Lincoln read it to the House Jan. 10, as
stated in the text; on Jan. 16, he gave notice of a motion for leave to introduce it as
a bill (*ib.*, 244); but the record does not show that he did so.

[2] *Ib.*, 212, Jan. 10, 1849. This was practically the number of citizens whose petition
against the slave-trade in the District was presented by Giddings at the first session.
Undoubtedly they were the same persons to whom Lincoln so mysteriously referred.

went on.[1] That business was a motion to reconsider the vote by which the Committee on the District of Columbia had been instructed to bring in a bill against slavery in the District. The Abolitionists and opponents of slavery in both parties, did not want reconsideration and moved to table the motion. This was beaten by the crushing majority of forty votes, Lincoln voting against them, as did such Northern men as Caleb B. Smith and Richard W. Thompson of Indiana, together with all Southern members and those unsympathetic with abolition.[2] By practically the same vote given by the same men, reconsideration was ordered; whereupon Caleb B. Smith offered an amendment against the slave-trade in the District and John M. Botts of Virginia moved 'to lay the whole subject on the table,' which was defeated, Lincoln voting against it, as did all anti-slavery men of every shade of opinion.[3]

Three days later Lincoln gave notice that he would formally introduce his District slavery bill;[4] but, except for flashes of debate now and then, nothing more was done on the subject for nearly three weeks. On January 31, 1849, the District Committee reported its slave bill, which merely prohibited the slave-trade in the District. A motion to table the bill was beaten by a majority of forty-five votes, Lincoln voting nay.[5] Spirited debate sprang up in which the wrong of slavery, the encouragement by Abolitionists of slave uprisings, the danger of disunion, and every phase of the slavery question was passionately discussed. In this debate Lincoln took no part.

Throughout the session Southern members had been in a state of despair and desperation. During 1848 the price of cotton had fallen to ruinous depths; for years the Abolitionists had been growing bolder; at each new session of Congress bills of one kind and another against slavery received ever stronger support; and now the prospect was that slavery would be ex-

---

[1] *Cong. Globe*, 30th Cong. 2nd Sess., xx, 212. Very few persons in Washington were opposed to slavery. Jesse E. Dow received scarcely any votes for Mayor because he declared for a public school for free colored children. Bryan, II, 388–9.

[2] *Ib.* The vote was eighty to one hundred and twenty.

[3] *Ib.*, 216.

[4] *Ib.*, 244.

[5] *Ib.*, 415–6. The vote was seventy-two ayes, one hundred and seventeen nays.

cluded from the territory acquired from Mexico. Turn in whatever direction they would, dark prospects confronted the Southern people.[1]

In this situation members of Congress from the South held a conference.[2] After long discussion, all except Stephens, Toombs, and a few others agreed that they should make to their constituents a public statement of the situation. Calhoun was chosen to write it.

Since reference must be made to this address hereafter, only a hasty outline of it can be given at this place. Lincoln's District slave bill was a moving cause of Calhoun's indictment of the North, it was issued while Lincoln was in Congress, and it became the principal subject of talk among his fellow-members toward the close of his term.

Called 'The Address of the Southern Delegates in Congress, to their Constituents,' it set out in simple language the Southern point of view — the wrongs of the South, the rights of the South, the plight of the South. The Constitution had been flagrantly violated; although the North had forced the Missouri Compromise on the South, the North ignored it; Abolitionists despised the fundamental law of the nation and were fast undermining the vital idea of the Federal Government; bills at the present session, especially that of 'a member from Illinois,' spelled disaster — social, political, economic catastrophe — for the South.

Then Calhoun came to the real issue. Deeper, far deeper, than the wanton infractions of the Constitution, was the racial question. 'To destroy the existing relation between the free and servile races at the South would lead to consequences unparalleled in history. They cannot be separated, and cannot live together in peace, or harmony, or to their mutual advantage, except in their present relation. Under any other, wretchedness, and misery, and desolation would overspread the whole South.'

Emancipation 'can . . . only be effected by the prostration of the white race;' and this can only be brought about by the Federal Government controlled by the 'dominant power of the Northern States . . . against the resistance and struggle of the

[1] Channing, VI, 67-8.   [2] Dec. 23, 1848. Stephens was chairman.

Southern.' And what would follow emancipation? Would the North stop there? Certainly not — the former slaves would be given 'the right of voting and holding public offices under the Federal Government.'

Negroes vote and hold office! That would mean 'to raise them to a political and social equality with their former owners.' And then what? 'They [negroes] would become the fast political associates of the North, acting and voting with them on all questions, and by this political union between them, holding the white race at the South in complete subjection. The blacks, and the profligate whites that might unite with them, would become the principal recipients of federal offices and patronage, and would, in consequence, be raised above the whites of the South in the political and social scale.

'We would, in a word, change conditions with them — a degradation greater than has ever fallen to the lot of a free and enlightened people, and one from which we could not escape, should emancipation take place (which it certainly will if not prevented), but by fleeing the houses of ourselves and ancestors, and by abandoning our country to our former slaves, to become the permanent abode of disorder, anarchy, poverty, misery, and wretchedness.'

What must the South do to avert that impending doom? 'The first and indispensable step, without which nothing can be done, and with which everything may be, is to be united among yourselves on this great and most vital question.' Without Southern unity in the matter of the dominance of the white race 'the North will not believe that you are in earnest in opposition to their encroachments, and they will continue to follow, one after another, until the work of abolition is finished.' But 'if you become united, and prove yourselves in earnest, the North will be brought to a pause, and to a calculation of consequences.' Thus a change of measures might be brought about which would 'quietly and peaceably terminate this long conflict between the two sections.

'If it should not, nothing would remain for you but to stand up immovably in defense of rights, involving your all — your property, prosperity, equality, liberty, and safety.

'As the assailed, you would be justified by all laws, human and divine, in repelling a blow so dangerous, without looking to consequences, and to resort to all means necessary for that purpose.'[1]

Through the remainder of the session the debate raged on; but Lincoln took no further part. As we have seen, he did not introduce his District slave bill and, when early Sunday morning, March 4, 1849, the thirtieth Congress expired, nothing had been done on that subject. The House sat all night. Winthrop made a short and admirable speech of appreciation of his treatment by the House as its Speaker; and at seven o'clock, that body adjourned *sine die*.[2]

[1] Calhoun, VI, 290–313.

Stephens had little sympathy with the objects of the conference. Both he and Toombs looked upon them as intended to divide the Whigs of the South and so weaken the President-elect as to oblige him to turn to the Southern Democrats for support. 'The Southern Democracy are perfectly desperate,' wrote Toombs. 'Their Northern allies, they clearly see, will unite with the Freesoilers; and even now the peace is broken between them forever. Almost every man of the Southern Democrats have joined Calhoun's movement. After mature consideration, we concluded to go into the meeting in order to control and crush it; it has been a delicate business, but so far we have succeeded well and I think will be able to overthrow it completely, on the 15th inst.' He later wrote that 'we have completely foiled Calhoun in his miserable attempt to form a Southern party.' Calhoun's paper was recommitted by a vote of forty-two to forty-four, was 'whittled down to a weak milk and water address to the whole Union, and in that form received only forty-eight signatures, of which two were Whigs. Some Democrats refused to sign.' Toombs to Crittenden, Jan. 3 and 22, 1849. *Rept. Am. Hist. Assn.*, 1911, II, 139–41.

The effect of the 'Address' at the time was rather to divide the Southern Democrats. Cobb and Lumpkin of Georgia and Boyd and Clarke of Kentucky issued to their constituents an address in reply, and Cobb wrote to his wife of the 'erratic call of the madcap South Carolinian.' *Ib.*, 145. Writing to Buchanan he directed attention to Calhoun's purpose of 'organizing a *Southern sectional party* to supplant in the South the *Democratic party*,' and called Calhoun 'our evil genius.' *Ib.*, 164. Later the importance of the Address was recognized.

[2] *House Journal*, 30th Cong. 2nd Sess., XX, 672–3. An extract from his brief address of farewell throws a clear light on the times and reveals the deep concern of moderate men for the preservation of the Union:

'Let us rejoice that while the powers of the earth have almost everywhere else been shaken, that, while more than one of the mightiest monarchies and stateliest empires of Europe have tottered or have fallen, our own American republic has stood firm.

'Let us rejoice at the evidence which has thus been furnished to the friends of liberty throughout the world, of the inherent stability of institutions which are founded on the rock of a written Constitution, and which are sustained by the will of a free and intelligent people.

'And let us hope and trust — as I, for one, most fervently and confidently do — that, by the blessing of God upon prudent, conciliatory, and patriotic counsels, every cause of domestic dissension and fraternal discord may be speedily done away, and that the

In such fashion Lincoln's services in Congress came to an end. He saw Taylor inaugurated, on a cold, gusty day, filled with flurries of rain and snow, went with friends and other members to one of the three inaugural balls, witnessed the hilarity of the gleeful Whigs. But there was no merriment in Lincoln's heart. Measured by any standard, his term in Congress had been a failure. Illinois remained Democratic and, calamity of calamities, his own district, the one Whig stronghold in the State, had been captured by the enemy. Unless he could get some appointment he must go back to the practice of the law and to that alone; for, as he and Herndon, his gloomy wife, and everybody else who thought about the matter at all, then saw it, Lincoln had no political future.

Moreover, the Whig party was beginning to dissolve before his very eyes — nobody but the blindest partisan could fail to see that it could not survive for many more years. The 'most overwhelming, glorious triumph,' which Lincoln had predicted so joyously after Taylor's nomination, had indeed been achieved, so far as that presidential election was concerned; but that 'victory' was the last national success the Whigs ever were to win, the final flare of the burned out candle.

Still greater humiliation for Lincoln than the loss of his district and the eclipse of his popularity was just ahead. The Administration, which he had done his utmost to create, was not only to refuse to give him an office which he wanted badly, but was to fill it with another man against his vigorous and well-nigh angry protest. Midway in the short session of Congress, he had mildly advocated by means of newspaper comment, the appointment of Baker as a member of Taylor's Cabinet,[1] but nothing came of it. At Lincoln's request Speed had asked Crittenden to support Baker, but that powerful Whig declined, saying, however, that he thought well of Lincoln, for some good

States and the people, whose Representatives we are, may be bound together forever in a firm, cordial, and indissoluble union.'

[1] Lincoln to William Schouler, Feb. 2, 1849. *Works*, II, 100–1. 'The Englishman, Baker, who came from the Rio Grande to draw pay, mileage, and a year's stationery, as a member of Congress, is here, with recommendations from legislatures for the post of Secretary of War. What would General Taylor say to such impudent dictation and indelicate solicitation?' Jefferson Davis to John J. Crittenden, Jan. 30, 1849. Crittenden, I, 340. George W. Crawford of Georgia was appointed Secretary of War.

appointment. Lincoln wrote Speed that he could not expect any 'first-class office, and a second-class one would not compensate' his 'being sneered at by others who want it for themselves.' He said that the Whigs in Congress would support him for appointment as Commissioner of the Land Office, but that four of his friends in his own State wanted it, and, what was worse, although he 'could easily take it' for himself, he would have hard work to get it for 'any other man in Illinois.' [1]

There, for the moment, the matter rested and, when Lincoln reached Springfield early in April,[2] he gave attention to the distribution of local patronage. Before he left Washington he had asked that he and Baker,[3] as the 'only Whig members of Congress from Illinois,' should be consulted when any citizen of that State was to be appointed to any office 'either in or out of the State;'[4] and he had sent in several applications for the office of United States Marshal, one of them from a man in 'every way worthy of the office' and supported by 'about two hundred good citizens,' including nearly all Whig members of the Illinois Legislature as well as many Democrats — but, he added, another of the applicants 'would be the better.'[5]

At home again, Lincoln recommended the appointment of Whigs to various offices held by Democrats, saying, however, that he could not complain that the officials had 'failed in the proper discharge of any of the duties' of their respective offices, but that they were active partisans and had worked against the election of Taylor.[6]

Learning that charges had been made against one of the persons he had recommended he acted in characteristic manner. 'I write this to request that, if in this, or any other case, charges shall be sent against persons I have recommended, you will suspend action, and notify me. I will take pains to avoid im-

[1] Lincoln to Speed, Feb. 20, 1849. *Works*, II, 104–5.

[2] April 1. *Illinois State Register*, April 5, 1849.

[3] Baker had been elected from Galena at the same time that Logan had been beaten in the Seventh District.

[4] Lincoln to the Secretary of the Treasury, March 9, 1849. *Works*, II, 105–6. He undoubtedly wrote an identical letter to each member of the Cabinet.

[5] Lincoln to the Secretary of State, March 10, 1849. *Ib.*, 106–7.

[6] Lincoln to Cabinet officers, April 7, 1849. *Works*, II, 107–10.

posing any unworthy man on the Department.' In the special
case at hand, he said he was making particular inquiry. 'I am
not the less anxious in this matter because of knowing the principal object of the fault-findings to be to stab me.' [1]

Lincoln had been thinking of the General Land Office for himself even before he wrote to Speed that he could get it. But he
had promised to support Cyrus Edwards for the place. So when
certain of Lincoln's friends wrote him that they were for him,
he answered that 'if the office could be secured to Illinois only
by my consent to accept it, and not otherwise, I give that consent;' but since he was pledged to Edwards, he 'must not only
be chaste, but above suspicion;' he must be 'permitted to say
"Give it to Mr. Edwards . . . and I decline it; if not, I accept."'
So let his friends go ahead 'with this understanding' and he
would 'feel complimented.' [2]

In this tangle of candidacies, Lincoln heard that Justin Butterfield of Chicago was being considered for the place. Butterfield had supported Clay for the presidential nomination, and
the aged statesman loyally recommended the appointment of
his adherent. Webster, too, urged the appointment of Butterfield, who had been born in New Hampshire and knew Webster
well.[3] Lincoln was, at first, displeased, then angered, then
furious. Although, he wrote, Butterfield 'is my personal friend
and is qualified to do the duties of the office,' he had 'less claims'
than any of a hundred Whigs in Illinois who were equally well
qualified. Offices 'should be so given as to gratify our friends,
and to stimulate them to future [party] exertions.' Butterfield
had 'fought for Mr. Clay and against General Taylor to the
bitter end;' and now his appointment was being urged to the
most important office likely to be given to Illinois. It was too
much. 'It will now mortify me deeply if General Taylor's administration shall trample all my wishes in the dust merely to
gratify these men.' [4]

[1] Lincoln to the Secretary of Home [Interior] Department, April 26, 1849. Original
in the possession of Emanuel Hertz, of New York.

[2] Lincoln to W. B. Warren and others, April 7, 1849. *Works*, II, 110–2.

[3] Elizabeth Sawyer (Butterfield's daughter) to Weik, Oct. 12, 1888; Herndon, II,
301n.

[4] Lincoln to J. M. Lucas, April 25, 1849. *Works*, II, 114–5.

To Duff Green, in Washington, Lincoln protested wrathfully against Butterfield's prospective appointment. 'This ought not to be,' he wrote. Taylor's friends in Illinois 'would quite as lief see it go east of the Alleghanies, or west of the Rocky Mountains, as into that man's hands.' They were already 'sore' about 'old drones,' especially Butterfield, always getting 'all the valuable offices.' Let Green tell the President how matters stand. One Cabinet member would favor Green, but beat Butterfield, using Edwards or Lincoln himself, 'whichever you can to the best advantage.'[1]

Crittenden could 'control the matter,' Lincoln informed Gillespie — so let Gillespie write him or, still better, write 'directly to old Zach,' who still 'hangs fire.' Hurry. Butterfield will be appointed 'unless prevented by strong and speedy efforts. . . . Not a moment's time is to be lost. Let this be confidential except with Mr. Edwards and a few other' trusted friends.[2]

'I give you my word,' he assured Elisha Embree, a Whig member of Congress from Indiana, that Butterfield's appointment would be 'an egregious political blunder. It will give offense to the whole Whig party here.' Would not Embree 'write to General Taylor at once' that either Lincoln or the man he recommended should be appointed, 'if anyone from Illinois shall be.'[3]

Scattering behind him requests for endorsement[4] for his own appointment as Land Commissioner, Lincoln set out for Washington. But he was too late. Indeed it would appear that he never had a chance. The Illinois endorsements of Butterfield on file in the Interior Department were as strong as those for Lincoln; and some of the men he had ,asked for recommendations, notably Nathaniel Pope, Judge of the United States Court at Springfield, had merely written that the appointment of either Butterfield or Lincoln would give general satisfaction.[5]

---

[1] Lincoln to Green, May 18, 1849. *Ib.*, 118–9.

[2] Lincoln to Gillespie, May 19, 1849. *Ib.*, 119–20.

[3] Lincoln to Embree, May 25, 1849. *Ib.*, 121.

[4] For examples of these letters see *ib.*, 123–4.

[5] Pope to Thos. Ewing, Sec. Interior, June 8, 1849. MS. Interior Dept. Records, Judge Pope's letter read: 'It is said that the respective friends of my most valued friends, Justin Butterfield and Abraham Lincoln Esquires, are presented to the President for

While N. J. Henry, Chairman of the Illinois Whig State Committee, wrote that Butterfield's appointment would ruin the party, a petition was sent the Department by 'the Whig mechanics of the City of Springfield' opposing Lincoln because of his course in Congress, and requesting the appointment of Butterfield.[1]

But he wrote to Gillespie that he 'could have had the office any time before the Department was committed to Mr. Butterfield,' the President and Secretary of the Interior told him. And why had he not pressed his claims earlier? 'Chiefly for Mr. [Cyrus] Edwards' sake — losing the office that he might gain it,' Lincoln despairingly explained to Gillespie. For Edwards was angry with Lincoln who, Edwards believed, had deserted him in order to get the office for himself. Edwards even wrote to the Department at Washington against Lincoln. Yet he had been one of his 'most cherished' friends, Lincoln lamented.[2] In despair Lincoln asked the Department for 'the papers . . . recommending me for Commissioner of [the] General Land office.' [3]

As a kind of farewell to politics, Lincoln, upon his return to Springfield, gave some sound practical advice to the head of Taylor's Cabinet. It was one of the cleverest political letters he ever wrote, and it reveals, in a half-flash, the masterful Lincoln of a sterner day. In view of the treatment he had received from the Administration, it might be supposed to have been written

the office of Commissioner of the Land Department. Allow me Sir to bear my testimony in favor of both. They are just such men as should be selected for the office. They are honest and capable. The appointment of either will, I think, give general satisfaction.'

[1] MS. Interior Dept. Records. 'The Undersig[n]ed Whig mechanics of the City of Springfield, Illinois, . . . are dissatisfied with the course of Abraham Lincoln as a member of Congress from this Congressional district. Your petitioners recommend Mr. Justin Butterfield as a suitable person to occupy the office of Commissioner of the general Land Office.'

Twenty-eight names are signed to this document, all in different handwriting with the possible exception of three signatures.

[2] Lincoln to Gillespie, July 13, 1849. *Works*, II, 124–7. This letter of Edwards against Lincoln and several others have disappeared from the files of the Interior Dept. E. C. Finney, First Ass't. Sec'y., to author, June 22, 1925.

But a long letter from Edwards to Butterfield, June 11, 1849, is in the files. It gives Butterfield a full account of Edwards' candidacy 'as it forms no part of my character to sail under false colors.' From Edwards' detailed narrative the very worst that can be said is that Lincoln did not push Edwards' application with much vigor because Baker was for Don Morrison and, unless one would withdraw, Illinois would lose the office.

[3] Lincoln to Thomas Ewing, June 22, 1849. Tracy, 39.

in resentment; but the Whigs, especially those of the South, were fearful lest Taylor should fail as President. Voicing this feeling, Stephens had written Crittenden from Washington that 'every one of the Young Indians must do his duty,' [1] and undoubtedly had made that appeal to Lincoln at the capital. So Lincoln wrote John M. Clayton, Secretary of State, that Taylor must correct an unfavorable sentiment which was spreading among the people.

The public report that the President had shifted 'responsibility of the appointments upon the respective Departments' was hurting Taylor. 'It is fixing for the President the unjust and ruinous character of being a mere man of straw. This must be arrested, or it will damn us all inevitably. It is said Gen. Taylor and his officers held a council of war, at Palo Alto (I believe); and that he then fought the battle against unanimous opinion of those officers. This fact (no matter whether rightfully or wrongfully) gives him more popularity than ten thousand submissions, however really wise and magnanimous those submissions may be.

'The appointments need be no better than they have been, but the public must be brought to understand, that they are the *President's* appointments. He must occasionally say, or seem to say, "by the Eternal," "I take the responsibility." Those phrases were the "Samson's locks" of Gen. Jackson, and we dare not disregard the lessons of experience.' [2]

Loss of other friends besides Edwards depressed Lincoln,[3] and still another matter embarrassed him. John Addison wrote that Lincoln ought to be appointed Governor of Oregon, suggesting, however, that the writer himself would like to be made Secretary of the Territory. Lincoln answered that he could not accept the place if offered and that, as to the Secretaryship, while he had 'an ever abiding wish to serve' Addison, he had 'already recommended our friend Simeon Francis, of the "*Journal*."' [4] Lincoln did want to be Governor of Oregon, but

[1] Stephens to Crittenden, Feb. 6, 1849. *Rept. Am. Hist. Assn.*, 1911, II, 146.
[2] Lincoln to Clayton, July 28, 1849. Tracy, 39–40.
[3] Lincoln to ———, Dec. 15, 1849. *Works*, II, 133–4.
[4] Lincoln to John Addison, Sept. 27, 1849. *Works*, II, 129–30.

the place was never offered to him [1] and, when the matter was suggested, his wife flatly refused to go to that far western wilderness, even if her husband could get the place.[2] Lincoln was appointed Secretary of Oregon, however, but he promptly declined.[3] This position was the measure of the Whig Administration's estimate of Lincoln's political importance in the autumn of 1849.

Thus Lincoln received the invaluable discipline of defeat. He thought his political fortunes were ended forever,[4] and so did his wife, that 'most ambitious woman I ever saw,' as her sister described her. More humiliating still, Douglas was mounting high on swift and powerful wings; and Baker, McClernand, and all his associates were making headway in brilliant careers and in public regard. Worse still in Lincoln's eyes, the Legislature of Illinois had elected Shields to the Senate of the United States.[5]

Only Lincoln had failed; and, for five desolate years, he was to go into a political retirement which seemed permanent — a period of waiting, thought, and growth which, as a preparation for the doing of the colossal work before him, Lincoln needed quite as much as the hard schooling he already had received in humility and in respect for other men. Through these years of hopeless gloom as Lincoln felt them to be, we shall now accompany him and behold him emerge from them, freed of narrow partisanship and small purposes, with the foundations of greatness firmly established and visible even to hostile eyes.

[1] No record exists in the State Department of a tender of the place to Lincoln. Frank B. Kellogg, Secretary of State, to author, June 2, 1925.

[2] In a very hasty and disconnected memorandum of a talk with Stuart, Herndon jotted down a statement that Fillmore offered Lincoln the Governorship of Oregon; that friends urged him to accept; that he consented provided his wife would agree, but that she refused. Stuart assured Lincoln that he would soon come to the Senate from Oregon. Weik MSS. no date. Note on back 'Jno. T. Stuart's statement.'

[3] Lincoln to J. M. Clayton, Secretary of State, Sept. 27, 1849. *Works*, II, 130.

[4] Herndon to Weik, Oct. 28, 1885. Weik MSS.

[5] *House Journal*, 1849, 90. Shields was elected by a majority of nearly three to one, receiving seventy votes to twenty-six for two other candidates.

CHAPTER IX

LAW: LIFE: GROWTH

Melancholy dripped from him as he walked. HERNDON.

Strange mingling of mirth and tears, of the tragic and grotesque, of cap and crown, of Socrates and Rabelais, of Æsop and Marcus Aurelius — Lincoln, the gentlest memory of the world. INGERSOLL.

LINCOLN took up again his life in Springfield and began once more to ride the immense circuit from which he had been absent for nearly two years. At first he did not meet a hearty welcome. It was a different Springfield from the jubilant town which had greeted him so joyously a dozen years earlier, a different Springfield from the friendly little city from which he had set out for Washington in November, 1847 — a questioning, a doubting Springfield. But personal contact soon restored general favor, although many continued to be resentful for a long time. From the moment of his return, however, the old line Whigs stood by him faithfully.

The capital of Illinois now boasted a population of four thousand five hundred and thirty-three. Of these one hundred and seventy-one were free persons of color. In all Sangamon County only one other town, Mechanicsburg, with two hundred and one inhabitants, was large enough to be listed in the Census.[1] Springfield had passed Alton, where only three thousand five hundred and eighty-five persons lived, fewer than a decade earlier; but was behind Peoria with a population of over five thousand. The phenomenal growth of Chicago was marked by an enumeration of well-nigh thirty thousand.

Immigration had poured into the West in such volume that more than 850,000 men, women, and children lived in Illinois when Lincoln returned from Washington in 1849. The State was almost entirely agricultural.[2] The wealth in land and live

---

[1] *Census*, 1850.

[2] *Ib.* Some idea may be had of the state of the western country at the time, from the population of other cities and towns of that section. For example, Milwaukee had a trifle more than 20,000, Detroit a little over 21,000, Indianapolis slightly in excess of 8,000, and Fort Wayne 4,282.

About 17,000 people lived in Cleveland and a few hundred more in Columbus, while

stock was very large in proportion to the population. There were but ten incorporated towns in the whole State, and most of these had been little more than villages ten years earlier.[1] Here and there, on the scattered farms, frame houses were being built; but the log cabin was still the favorite habitation. The wooden plough, however, had given place to iron and steel shares; and reapers, drawn by horses, were fast supplanting the cradle and the scythe. The men wore blue jeans, usually patched, and brogans;[2] and the older women still smoked pipes.[3] The common food was corn-bread and salted smoked pork; but toward the end of the decade wheat bread, buckwheat cakes and fresh meat appeared on the tables of the more prosperous.[4]

Travel, even for short distances, was mostly by horseback; there were but few buggies until the latter part of the decade;[5] and farmers with their families attended political rallies or went to town for court week, in big, stout wagons. For four or five years after Lincoln came back from Washington, the stage-coach was the sole means of public conveyance. The roads, tolerable in late spring, early summer, autumn, or when snow made them smooth for sleds, were at other times often almost impassable. In rainy seasons long stretches were mere quagmires, and seemingly bottomless mudholes were frequent. The wheels of any kind of vehicle would sink deep in these sloughs and even horses would flounder and struggle painfully to get through them.[6]

Sangamon County had a little more than nineteen thousand people. Of these over two thousand adults could not read or write. In the whole County there were eighty-six schools and as many teachers and three thousand two hundred and twenty

Dayton had about 11,000. The big cities of that part of the country were St. Louis, with over 77,000 and Cincinnati, with more than 115,000.

[1] Besides Chicago, Alton, Springfield, and Peoria, the incorporated towns were Bloomington, Galena, Pekin, Quincy, Beardstown, and Rock Island. *Era of the Civil War:* Arthur C. Cole, 1.

[2] *Illinois in the Fifties:* Charles B. Johnson, 11, 23–5.

[3] Caton, 87.   [4] Johnson, 18–9.

[5] *Ib.,* 138. Women always rode on side-saddles.

[6] This condition of Illinois highways continued almost to the end of the century. Even today a community, here and there, is practically marooned in wet weather

pupils.[1] This was a large number, for schools were still maintained by subscription, still held, for the most part, in log cabins. At that time school conditions throughout Illinois were shocking; but a great movement for better educational facilities took place between 1850 to 1860.[2] In this movement Lincoln appears to have shown no interest.

Springfield had striven to keep pace with the growth and activity of other towns more favorably situated. Six flouring mills ground fifteen hundred bushels of wheat every twelve hours.[3] The two newspapers had from weeklies become dailies, and a public library contained more than nineteen thousand volumes.[4] But the streets were still unlighted and unpaved, sidewalks were few and inadequate, hogs wallowed in mudholes before houses, fed on offal in the streets, rubbed against fences, and disputed passageway with truculent obstinacy.[5] There was no drainage, and manure, old clothes, ashes, and other refuse were dumped into the streets.[6]

The square about the state house was in a peculiarly bad condition, and the Springfield papers wrathfully denounced it.[7] Indeed throughout this period the streets of Springfield were famed for wretchedness and squalor.[8] One of the first cases Lincoln had after his return from Congress was a suit by O. H. Browning against the city for the breaking of his leg by a fall caused by an unrepaired street.[9]

No such protection from flies and mosquitoes as screens ex-

---

[1] Of these 800 were white men and 1,166 white women. *Census*, 1850. Almost all of the free negroes were wholly illiterate.

There were 4,193 pupils 'as returned by families,' but this was nearly 1,000 more than actually went to school.

[2] *Era:* Cole, 230–8. [3] *Illinois State Register*, May 3, 1849.

[4] *Census*, 1850. In large numbers of houses the only books were the Bible and an almanac. Johnson, 117–8.

[5] *Illinois State Register*, March 24, 1855. This was true even of the larger cities.

[6] *Era:* Cole, 3.

[7] For instance, *Illinois State Register*, March 17 and *Illinois Journal*, Sept. 13, 1853.

[8] *Era:* Cole, 6.

[9] Browning *vs.* City of Springfield: 17 Ill. 143. Lincoln won this case for his friend. It was argued with much care and thoroughness. The unanimous opinion of the Supreme Court, delivered by Chief Justice Scates, is comprehensive and full of citations. The decision became a leading authority on municipal law and has been extensively cited by the Supreme Courts of other States.

isted,[1] and insects flew, unhindered, from repasts on offal without to kitchens and tables, from which, at meal time, they were sometimes brushed by leafy branches. In that day no one imagined that disease was spread by insects. The country, too, was full of malaria, and advertisements of patent medicines, guaranteed to cure such ailments, burdened the newspapers. The standard remedies, however, were quinine, calomel, and whisky, all consumed frequently and in large quantities; and doctors bled patients on the slightest pretext, cutting a vein with a septic and sometimes rusty lancet.[2] Baths were seldom indulged in; but, when cleansing the body was thought necessary, it was done in a wooden tub. Yet the City Hotel advertised that it had sumptuous 'Bathing Rooms.' [3]

Stores had increased in number and groceries were larger and more numerous; but there were no banks and merchants kept the trivial accounts of opulent customers.[4] Saturdays continued to be the time for farmers and their families to come to town for purchases, gossip, and a good time, and enterprising merchants sought customers by many devices. Among these allurements to trade, was an open barrel of whisky at the back of such stores as sold groceries. A tin cup was fastened by a chain to this barrel, and anybody who bought a certain amount of goods, was entitled to drink freely as much as he or she wanted.[5]

Lincoln had no law practice when he returned from Congress; but Herndon had, by hard work, kept up the business of the firm. Lincoln thought that it was unjust for him to share the

[1] Johnson, 53.

[2] *Ib.*, 127–9. Dosing with the drugs named and 'bleeding' were practised generally in the Mississippi Valley until as late as 1880.

[3] *Illinois Journal*, June 22, 1848.

[4] *Era:* Cole, 94. After the failure of the State Bank the first bank in Springfield was the Springfield Fire & Marine Insurance Company organized in 1851; under the name of the Marine Bank it is still in existence.

[5] Statement of William L. Patton of Springfield to author, April 27, 1925, from the account given him by his father and by James M. Garland of Springfield, both of whom personally saw this practice in operation.

These gentlemen remembered particularly the barrel of whisky with tin cup attached, which Jacob Bunn, the wholesale and retail grocer, and later the banker, one of Lincoln's clients, kept in the rear of his store. Mr. Garland says that good whisky at that time cost twenty-five cents a gallon.

proceeds of Herndon's labors and wanted to withdraw. He then had no hope of political resuscitation and thus one strong reason for the firm's existence was removed; but of this he said nothing to Herndon. The junior partner, however, insisted that he remain and so the two began once more to practise as partners under the old name of Lincoln and Herndon.[1] Grant Goodrich, a lawyer with a good practice in Chicago, proposed that Lincoln go into partnership with him; but Lincoln declined because, as he said, 'he tended to consumption, That if he went to Chicago that he would have to sit down and study hard, That it would kill him, That he would rather go round the circuit . . . than to sit down and die in Chicago.'[2]

Since the law office of Lincoln and Herndon remained unchanged throughout the decade we are now considering, at this point in the narrative description of it may be of interest. The office consisted of one 'medium sized' room, at the rear end of a dark hall on the second floor of a brick building on the public square, across the street from the Court House. It was the building Speed had occupied as a store, associated with Lincoln's coming to Springfield.[3] Two unwashed windows looked out upon the litter in the yard of a store below. The upper half of the door to the office had in it a broad pane of glass, covered by a calico curtain which was pulled down when either of the lawyers wished nobody to look into the office.

In the centre of the room stood a long table with a shorter one at the end, both 'covered with green baize.' In one corner was a desk with drawers and pigeonholes, and in this desk were kept the law papers of the firm. Against a wall was a bookcase containing 'about 200 volumes of law as well as miscellaneous books.' In one corner near the window was a lounge or sofa raised at one end. In cold weather warmth was furnished by a wood fire in a tall, round, unblackened stove, red and gray

---

[1] Statement of Judge Davis, Sept. 20, 1866. Weik MSS.; Herndon, II, 307.

[2] Davis's statement; Herndon's notes, Sept. 20, 1866. Weik MSS. When Goodrich advised Herndon not to write the life of Lincoln because his legal training unfitted him for such a literary undertaking, Herndon, in answer, wrote that Lincoln always treated Goodrich 'as an exceedingly weak headed brother. The more he kicked you the closer you clung to him.' Herndon to Goodrich, Dec. 10, 1866. Weik MSS.

[3] The building was on the present South 5th Street, one door south of Washington Street. J. C. Thompson to author.

with rust and dirt. The floor was never swept except when an uncommonly energetic law student decided to clean up. One such bustling youth who came to the firm a year or two after Lincoln's return from Congress found such piles of dirt in the corners that seeds were sprouting in them; and he swept the room, to the amazement of Milton Hay, the partner of Logan, whose offices were on the same floor at the front of the building.[1]

Here Lincoln saw his Sangamon County clients, farmers for the most part; here he talked politics, told innumerable stories,[2] read newspapers and poetry aloud to Herndon's great annoyance,[3] fell into fits of unseeing, unhearing abstraction and despondency, to his partner's mystification and alarm. Usually he arrived at the office about nine o'clock in the morning and the first thing he did was to lie down on the sofa, one leg on a chair and read the newspapers — always reading aloud.[4] In this office, too, he wrote an incredible number of letters.[5] The fragments of essays that have been retrieved and the commonplace lectures, as well as most of his immortal speeches, were put on paper in this dingy, dirt-covered office. Many of his briefs were produced in the library of the Supreme Court in the State House across the street; but most of the other legal documents were prepared in the office of the firm.

The neglect which Lincoln gave to his personal business was

[1] John H. Littlefield (the student), in *Brooklyn Eagle*, Oct. 16, 1887, as quoted in Herndon, II, 316–7.

Henry B. Rankin to Weik, May 17, 1916. Weik MSS. Rankin was for a very brief time another student in Lincoln and Herndon's office.

Gibson W. Harris, the first law student in the office of Lincoln and Herndon (*The Real Lincoln:* Weik, 106–7), describes the office in 1845. It never improved in appearance. The only change was an increase in books after Lincoln returned from Congress, undoubtedly volumes of the *Congressional Globe* and government publications. Harris says that in 1845, the office contained only 'Blackstone, Kent's Commentaries, Chitty's Pleadings (*sic*), and a few other books.'

[2] 'In our office I have known him to consume the whole forenoon relating stories.' Herndon, II, 333.

[3] 'It annoyed me more or less, and I sometimes left the room under pretense of a call elsewhere.' Herndon as quoted by Weik, 105.

[4] Herndon, II, 332.

[5] The many that have been found contain references to a far greater number that were lost or destroyed.

Letters were merely folded and sealed with wax or wafer. Postage, which ran from twelve and one-half cents to fifty cents, according to distance, was paid by the recipient. Johnson, 63.

amazing, unless the story, already related, of his paying his New Salem debts is entirely fictitious. On the records of the Circuit Court at Springfield during the whole of his career at the bar two judgments against him in favor of New Salem creditors remained unsatisfied; and, so far as the records show, they are still unsatisfied. On April 26, 1834, William Watkins secured in the Circuit Court affirmation of a judgment rendered by a Justice of the Peace against Lincoln and Berry for fifty-seven dollars and eighty-six cents and costs, from which judgment Lincoln and Berry had appealed; [1] and on November 19, 1834, judgment was awarded by the Circuit Court to Peter Van Bergen against the same defendants for one hundred and fifty-four dollars and costs.[2] Neither of these judgments ever was satisfied, a fact strange in itself, but all the more curious in view of Lincoln's severe admonition to his father concerning the old man's negligence in not examining a judgment against him in Coles County.[3]

It is still more extraordinary because another judgment against Lincoln and Nelson Alley rendered by the Sangamon Circuit Court September 13, 1833, in favor of James D. Henry for the use of James McCandless and Henry Emmerson, was 'satisfied in full March 17, 1834, as per Shff return.'[4] Since one judgment was satisfied by the sheriff's return, it is difficult to understand how there could have been an execution sale of Lincoln's horse, bridle, saddle, and surveying instruments to pay Van Bergen's judgment, as pathetically related by 'Uncle Jimmy Short.' But assuming, as seemingly we must, that these debts were paid, the fact that Lincoln failed to have the judgment satisfied of record, would appear to indicate his carelessness in business matters.

[1] Record B, 308. Circuit Court, Sangamon County, Judgment Docket, April 26, 1834.

[2] Ib., 412. This case was by agreement of the parties 'tried by the Court without pleading'; Lincoln and Berry were made 'parties to the judgment rendered at the last term against said Wm. Green,' which was reduced by credits to the sum named in the text.

[3] See p. 479, supra.

[4] Judgment Docket A, Circuit Court, Record B, 225. I am indebted to Mr. William L. Patton, Springfield, Ill., for these data. Mr. Patton called my attention to it, searched the records and sent certified transcript of the entries cited.

The family still lived in the small house of a story and a half which he had bought not long after his marriage. There were a kitchen, living room, and two bedrooms on the first floor and two low rooms beneath the roof. In the back yard was a privy, a woodpile, and a rough stable for Lincoln's horse, Old Buck, an 'indifferent, raw-boned specimen,' as an eyewitness described the animal.[1] A ramshackle, one-horse buggy, made by a Springfield backsmith, stood near the stable. There was, too, a cow, which grazed upon the common or grassy spots along the streets. Lincoln curried and fed his horse, milked the cow, cut and brought in the wood.[2]

Two or three cats added interest to the household, but there was no dog. A single shade tree was in front of the house, no fruit-trees in the back yard, no flowers anywhere about. Those who lived next door or near by, declare that Lincoln did not care for such things, although James Gourley, a close neighbor and friend of the Lincolns for a number of years and a trustworthy source of information, admits that Lincoln once set out some rose-bushes.[3] Mrs. Lincoln's sister, the wife of Dr. William Wallace, is emphatic on the same indifference to nature, although she blames Mrs. Lincoln more than the husband. Neither 'Mr nor Mrs Lincoln loved the beautiful,' she says. 'I have planted flowers in their front yard myself, to hide the nakedness, ugliness, etc., etc.' Apparently these sisterly offices were not appreciated, for Mrs. Wallace continues: I 'have done this often and often, . . . Mr. L[incoln] never planted trees, [or] roses, never made a garden, at least not more than once or twice.'[4] Gourley confirms Mrs. Wallace's testimony and adds more specifically, that 'for a year or so,' Lincoln 'had a garden and worked in it.'[5] But Harriet Hanks says: 'I never knew him to make a garden. Yet,' she continues defensively, 'no one loved flowers better than he did.'[6]

The one shade tree in front of the house was cut down by Mrs.

[1] Whitney, 30.
[2] *Ib.*, 26; Gourley's statement. Weik MSS.
[3] Gourley's statement. Weik MSS.
[4] Mrs. Wallace's statement. Weik MSS.
[5] Gourley's statement. Weik MSS.
[6] Harriet A. Chapman to Herndon, Dec. 10, [1866]. Weik MSS.

Lincoln's orders to facilitate making some repairs on the house. The workman hesitated and consulted Lincoln. 'Have you seen Mrs. L[incoln],' he asked. 'Yes,' said the man. 'Then in God's name cut it down clean to the roots,' Lincoln quickly responded.[1]

When he came from the office, he would take off his coat and shoes, lie down on the floor with head and shoulders propped against a pillow placed upon the back of a chair turned upside down, and read aloud any book or paper that took his fancy; thus he would lie and read for hours at a time.[2] He liked especially anything humorous and would read with relish all jokes and funny stories.[3] But newspapers were his comfort and delight; he would read them 'often very late at night.' Next to newspapers Lincoln liked poetry, Harriet Hanks informs us.[4]

His manners and habits distressed his wife. Even Herndon, when giving Weik material for the writing of their biography, confides to his associate that 'I have always sympathized with Mrs. Lincoln. . . . Mrs. Lincoln was not a . . . wildcat without cause.'[5] If anyone knocked at the door, Lincoln would answer in sock-feet, coatless, and without the stock which he removed from his neck as soon as he came home. Sometimes in this state of undress, except that he wore flapping carpet slippers, he went to Gourley's to borrow a table necessity, and Gourley particularly observed that but one suspender held up his trousers.[6] This single 'gallis,' as he called it, was a strange peculiarity of Lincoln's which the most credible of friendly witnesses made note of when he was on the circuit and at other times.

While at Washington, Lincoln conformed to the prevailing style in dress, and continued to wear the same attire after he returned to Illinois. A tall brown hat, the nap roughened or worn off; ill-fitting, swallow-tailed coat of broadcloth, rusty and seldom brushed; trousers always too short; boots, never black-

---

[1] Statement of P. P. Enos, no date, but 1866. Weik MSS.

[2] Harriet A. Chapman to Herndon, Nov. 21, 1866, and Dec. 10, [1866]. Weik MSS.

[3] Mrs. Wallace's statement. Weik MSS.

[4] Mrs. Chapman to Herndon, Nov. 21, 1866. 'I fancy I see him now lying full length in the Hall of his old home reading.'

[5] Herndon to Weik, Jan. 16, 1886. Weik MSS.

[6] Gourley's statement, *supra*. 'He used to come to our house with slippers on, one suspender and an old pair of pants.'

ened or greased; and about his neck a high stock, seldom renewed — such, in general, was his apparel. When on the circuit
he carried a dilapidated, striped carpet-bag, and a big stout
umbrella 'of faded green, well-worn, the knob gone, and the
name "A. Lincoln" cut out of white muslin, and sewed in the
inside;' a string tied about the middle kept the umbrella from
flapping open. In chill weather he wore 'a short circular blue
cloak, which he got in Washington in 1849, and kept for ten
years.' Lincoln had become totally indifferent to his appearance. 'Whether they [his clothes] fitted or looked well was
entirely above, or beneath, his comprehension.'[1] In warm
weather he wore a long linen duster and would start over the
circuit without any other coat. At Urbana in the fall of 1857,
a photographer, Sam Alschuler, wanted to take his photograph
and for the purpose, had to lend Lincoln a black coat with a
velvet collar.[2] Papers and letters were carried in his hat.[3]

Henry C. Whitney came to Urbana in 1854 when he was
twenty-one years old and opened a law office in that town. He
soon met Lincoln, became warmly attached to him, and for
several years was in close and frequent contact with him.[4] It is
probable that Whitney was associated with Lincoln in more
litigation than was any other lawyer except Herndon and, possibly, Leonard Swett. To Whitney, more than to any other
man except Herndon, we owe most of our knowledge of Lincoln
during his last six years in Illinois, and he describes his hero as
he looked when Whitney first met him and thereafter until, as
President, he left Springfield for Washington:

'He was six feet and four inches in height, his legs and arms
were disproportionately long, his feet and hands were abnormally large, he was awkward in his gait and actions. His skin

[1] Whitney, 32; Herndon, II, 346–7.   [2] Whitney, 50.

[3] *Ib.*, 42; Herndon, II, 314–5. The practice of carrying papers, letters, etc., in hats
was general. Even constables and sheriffs thus carried official papers to be served.
Johnson, 26.

[4] 'When he struck our end of the Circuit I was with him continuously till he left it;
after I moved to Chicago and went in with Gen[eral] Wallace he [Lincoln] made our
office his headquarters.' Whitney to Weik, Aug. 27, 1887. Weik MSS.

'My memory is good and I took to Lincoln on the Circuit from the start and happened to have . . . more intimacy with him than ordinary,' although 'Davis and Swett
were more intimate.' Whitney's statement. Weik MSS.

was a dark, sallow color, his features were coarse: — his expression kind and amiable: — his eyes were indicative of deep reflection, and, in times of repose, of deep sorrow as well. His head was high, but not large: his forehead was broad at the base, but retreated. . . . He wore a hat measuring seven and one-eighth. His ears were large; his hair, coarse, black and bushy, which stood out all over his head, with no appearance of ever having been combed.'[1] Lincoln's chest was thin, shoulders narrow, he walked with a stoop and had the look of a consumptive. When sitting he appeared of only average height.[2]

On the circuit, Whitney, who often occupied the same bed with Lincoln, observed that he slept 'in a home made, yellow flannel undershirt;'[3] and Herndon describes the same garment as reaching 'halfway between his knees and ankles.' A young lawyer who saw him thus attired for bed, declared afterwards that Lincoln 'was the ungodliest figure I ever saw.'[4] A photographer of Springfield who was an ardent political adherent of Lincoln thus describes him when he first saw him in 1855: 'I saw a tall, lank, awkward man, who wore a tall hat, a short Raglan coat, short top-boots, with one leg of the trousers stuck in the top, walking with a stoop and carrying one hand behind him.' The youth asked 'who that gawk was.'[5]

While Lincoln dressed better during his campaign with Douglas in 1858,[6] the above is a faithful picture of his attire and appearance from the time of his return from Congress until after his election to the Presidency. The numerous trustworthy descriptions of him during that decade vary so slightly that the differences are negligible.

Lincoln's voice was as peculiar and distinctive as his clothes and manner, and friends and observers made as much note of it as they did of his appearance or characteristics. All agree that it was high pitched and thin, but that it had remarkable carrying

[1] Whitney, 31–2. Lincoln's hat was six and seven-eighths, or by stretching seven. Measurements of hat in the Chicago Historical Society, taken by Oliver R. Barrett and author, March 30, 1927. The hat is flexible and not shrunken.

[2] Herndon's Lecture on Lincoln: Weik, 110, 114.

[3] Whitney to Weik, Aug. 27, 1887. Weik MSS.　　　　[4] Herndon, ii, 347.

[5] J. G. Stewart of Bloomington, in High School *Ægis*, Feb., 1906, 71–3.

[6] Whitney, 32.

power. Judge Drummond describes it as 'by no means pleasant, and, indeed, when excited, in its shrill tones, sometimes almost disagreeable.'[1] Herndon, in a long and detailed description of Lincoln when addressing a jury or a political assemblage, testifies that his 'voice was, when he first began speaking, shrill, squeaking, piping, unpleasant,' but adds that the tones became fuller as he proceeded.[2]

On February 1, 1850, Lincoln's second son, Edward, then four years old, died. The funeral services were conducted by Rev. James Smith, pastor of the First Presbyterian Church, and this circumstance is said to have led Mrs. Lincoln to join his congregation.[3] On December 21, 1850, another son was born and named for the husband of Mrs. Lincoln's sister, William Wallace; and twenty-eight months later still another son, Thomas, came to the Lincoln household.[4]

As the children grew up Lincoln delighted to play with them.[5] Sometimes he would take the boys walking 'way out in the country [and] . . . explain things carefully,' says Gourley; 'he was kind, tender and affectionate to his children, very, very.'[6] 'He was,' declares Harriet Hanks, 'all that a Husband Father and Neighbor should be. . . . Never did I hear him utter an unkind word to enny one.'[7] Mrs. Wallace adds her testimony that Lincoln 'was the very best kindest . . . father I ever saw.'[8]

He let the boys do whatever they pleased. 'They litterally ran over him,' declares Gillespie,[9] and this fact is attested by all

[1] Whitney, 257. Drummond was Judge of the United States Court for the Northern District of Illinois in which Lincoln frequently appeared.

[2] Herndon to Bartlett, July 19, 1887. MS. Mass. Hist. Socy.

[3] Mrs. Lincoln did not join the Presbyterian Church at Springfield, until April 13, 1852, and her husband never joined, although he sometimes attended the services with her. In the sermon delivered at the funeral of Mrs. Lincoln, Springfield, July 20, 1882, Rev. James A. Reed states that 'Mrs. Lincoln and her husband and family regularly attended church from that time [April, 1852] till they went to Washington City.' As to Lincoln, the statement is not borne out by the disinterested testimony of others.

[4] Thomas was the boy called 'Tad,' born April 4, 1853.

[5] Mrs. Chapman to Herndon, Nov. 21, 1866. Weik MSS.

[6] Gourley's statement. Weik MSS.

[7] Mrs. Chapman to Herndon, Nov. 21, 1866. Weik MSS. Miss Hanks married Col. A. H. Chapman of Charleston, Ill. She lived several months with the Lincolns while she attended school in Springfield.

[8] Mrs. William Wallace's statement. Weik MSS.

[9] Gillespie to Herndon, Jan. 31, 1866. Weik MSS. 'He was the most indulgent parent

who describe the family as it was at that time. Testimony of friends and observers is unanimous that Lincoln so adored his children that he was blind and deaf to their faults. 'He restrained them in nothing,' testifies a friendly observer.[1] Indeed he submitted to indignities from his eldest son, without realizing the boy's rudeness. For instance, once in his office when playing chess with Justice Treat of the Supreme Court, Bob came and told his father that it was time for dinner. Lincoln said he would come right away, but forgot and played on. He was very fond of chess [2] and, when playing, was absorbed in the game. Again the boy came with the same message, and again his father said he would come and again forgot. A third time Bob arrived with the summons, a third time Lincoln gave assurance, but played on. Then the boy deliberately kicked the chess-board from the knees of the players, scattering the pawns over the floor; and the father rose with a laugh and, without a word of protest or reproof, accompanied his impatient son.[3]

Herndon relates that Lincoln's boys would come to the office, throw papers here and there, pull books from shelves, blunt pens on the stove and do other irritating things; and that their father would not punish, scold, or even restrain them.[4] It would seem, indeed, that they were privileged characters in Springfield. One of their amusements was to hide behind a hedge and, with a lath, knock off hats of passers-by. They once thus knocked off Lincoln's hat; he mildly admonished them that the next man might not be so easy with them.[5]

In his house Lincoln was given to those curious spells of abstraction which all who knew him agree to have been his outstanding characteristic during the decade under review. His sister-in-law, Mrs. Edwards, testifies that she was often at the

I ever knew. His children litterally ran over him and he was powerless to withstand their importunities.'

[1] Weik, 101.   [2] Harris to Weik, *ib.*, 107.

[3] Treat's account to Weik, *ib.*, 102–3.

[4] Herndon to Weik, Jan. 8, 1866. Weik MSS.

When the children came to the office, Lincoln would turn them loose 'and they soon gutted the room, gutted the shelves of books, rifled the drawers and riddled boxes, battered the points of my gold pen . . . turned over the inkstands on the papers, scattered letters over the office and danced over them and the like.' *Ib.*

[5] Joseph P. Kent's statement, Nov. 21, 1916. Weik MSS.

Lincoln house at meal-time, and that he would sit at the table looking with unseeing eyes straight ahead, unconscious of the food before him and oblivious of his surroundings.[1] Mrs. Wallace relates that she frequently walked over to her sister's house where 'Lincoln would lean back, his head against the tip of a rocking chair, sit abstracted that way for . . . 20 or 30 minutes, and all at once burst out in a joke, though his thoughts were not on a joke.'[2] Sometimes Lincoln's spell would be broken by a quotation from a favorite poem like 'Mortality,' 'The Last Leaf,' or 'The burrial of Sir Tom [John] Moore.'[3] He would take the children for a ride in a little wagon which Lincoln pulled along the uneven sidewalk; a child would fall off crying; but Lincoln would go on hauling the wagon, his eyes bent downward.[4]

Mrs. Lincoln was irritable and high tempered. Her loud shrill voice could be heard across the street, and her incessant outbursts of wrath were audible to all who lived near the house. Frequently her anger was displayed by other means than words, and accounts of her violence are numerous and unimpeachable. Malicious gossip, which is over-plentiful and acrid, must be disregarded; but the clear though reluctant testimony of not unfriendly witnesses cannot be ignored.[5] For domestic conditions are the largest part of the personal life of any married person. Lincoln paid little or no attention to his wife's out-

[1] 'I have seen him sit down at the table and never unless recalled to his senses, would he think of food.' Mrs. Edwards's statement. Weik MSS.

[2] Mrs. Wallace's statement. Weik MSS.

[3] Mrs. Chapman to Herndon, Nov. 21, 1866. Weik MSS.

[4] Weik, quoting Herndon. Weik, 101.

[5] For instance, the father of Mrs. Hillary A. Gobin was pastor of the Methodist Church in Springfield between 1855–60, and lived near Lincoln's house. Mrs. Gobin says: 'Lincoln and my father were warm friends. I heard my mother say, "they [the Lincolns] were very unhappy in their domestic life, and she was seen frequently to drive him from the house with a broomstick."' Mrs. Gobin to author, May 17, 1923. Quoted by permission.

Mrs. Gobin is the widow of the late Dr. Hillary A. Gobin, formerly President of DePauw University, Greencastle, Ind., and emeritus Professor of Greek in that institution.

In the same class of credible evidence are the statements of Matheny, King, Bradford, Gourley, Enos, Herndon, and others. The swarm of stinging tales from less acceptable sources are omitted from the text and have had no influence on the narrative or the tone of it.

bursts,[1] which were inflicted upon others who displeased her as well as upon himself.[2]

Sometimes Lincoln would spend the night at the house of a friend.[3] During sessions of the Supreme Court, Lincoln often spent his evenings in the library or office of the Clerk of that tribunal, preparing for his arguments and amusing his fellow lawyers with stories and jokes. When the Legislature met, Lincoln was with members of that body, if not in the Supreme Court library. At other times when in Springfield, says Whitney, he usually would 'pass the evening in some grocery store, or other citizens' *rendez-vous*, engaged in his usual avocation of telling stories; or, perhaps, wandering alone, aimlessly, in the unfrequented streets,' brooding or thinking.[4] It would appear, in short, that Lincoln was at his house but very little, since he was away on the circuit for half the year, and when not on circuit was down town on most evenings. Mrs. Wallace asserts, however, that he was 'a domestic man' and frequently at home.[5]

Yet Lincoln was considerate of his wife, and would go home to comfort her when a thunder-storm arose, for such storms always terrified her.[6] After prolonged philosophizing about the influence of women on the great, Whitney declares with peculiar emphasis: 'Lincoln thoroughly loved his wife. I had many reasons to know this in my intimacy with him, and she therefore wrought a great influence over him.'[7]

Mrs. Lincoln had difficulty in keeping a hired girl. She quarrelled incessantly and acquired a bad name with those who went into domestic service. Lincoln usually took the side of the maid of all work, though he did so covertly and without the know-

[1] Gourley's statement. Weik MSS.

[2] Matheny's statement, May 3, 1866. Weik MSS.

[3] Lincoln once went to the house of A. Y. Ellis, who was appointed postmaster on his recommendation. He had lingered at the post-office telling stories until after eleven o'clock and then said: 'Well I hate to go home.' Ellis asked Lincoln to 'come down to my house and stay all night,' and he did so. Statement of P. P. Enos, no date. Weik MSS.

Some acquaintances are terribly severe on Mrs. Lincoln: 'Lincoln's wife was a hellion, a she devil, vexed and harrassed the soul out of that good man, wouldn't cook for him, drove him from home . . . often and often.' Statement of Turner R. King, no date, but 1866. Weik MSS. King was one of Lincoln's strongest political supporters.

[4] Whitney, 568.   [5] Mrs. Wallace's statement. Weik MSS.

[6] Weik, 108.   [7] Whitney, 94–7.

ledge of his wife. He induced one to remain by secretly paying
her a dollar a week extra; and said to her privately, after one
of Mrs. Lincoln's scoldings: 'Stay with her, Maria; stay with
her.'[1] 'If Mr. Lincoln should happen to die,' said Mrs. Lincoln
impulsively to friends when grievously tried by a quarrel with
a servant, 'his spirit will never find me living outside the boundaries of a slave State.'[2]

About 1853 a daughter of Dennis Hanks, Harriet, of whom
Lincoln was very fond, came from Coles County to live at his
house while she attended school in Springfield. She was a girl of
spirit, sense, and pleasing disposition. Mrs. Lincoln tried to
make a household drudge of her and at this Lincoln rebelled.
So far as is known Harriet Hanks is the only relative of Lincoln
who ever so much as visited his house. Neither his father nor
step-mother ever went to Springfield, although they lived but
seventy miles away, and Herndon thought that Mrs. Lincoln would not have admitted them if they had come to her
house.[3]

In the winter of 1850–51, Lincoln's father became very ill,
grew steadily worse, and it finally appeared to those in his
dreary cabin in Coles County that he would not recover. John
D. Johnston wrote Lincoln of his father's condition, but Lincoln
did not answer. Again Johnston wrote and again Lincoln
ignored the letter. At last Harriet Hanks wrote, and in response Lincoln sent Johnston a strange letter, which is made
intelligible only by recalling the mutual dislike between father
and son, displayed during Lincoln's boyhood in Indiana.

Lincoln tells Johnston that he received the two letters his
step-brother had written him; he had not answered them, 'because it appeared to me that I could write nothing which would
do any good. You already know I desire that neither father nor
mother shall be in want of any comfort, either in health or sickness, while they live; and I feel sure you have not failed to use
my name, if necessary, to procure a doctor, or anything else for
father in his present sickness.'

[1] Weik, 100.   [2] Statement John S. Bradford to Weik, Weik, 99.

[3] Herndon to Weik, Dec. 1, 1885. Weik MSS. 'While the young lady was here Mrs.
Lincoln tried to make a servant — a slave — of her' and 'This created . . . a fuss between Lincoln and his wife.'

But Lincoln cannot come. 'My business is such that I could hardly leave home now, [even] if it was not as it is, that my own wife is sick-a-bed. (It is a case of baby-sickness, and I suppose is not dangerous.) I sincerely hope father may recover his health; but if not, let him put his trust in God. At all events, tell him to remember to call upon and confide in our great and good and merciful Maker, who will not turn away from him in any extremity. He notes the fall of a sparrow, and numbers the hairs of our heads, and He will not forget the dying man who puts his trust in Him.'

Here was language that Thomas Lincoln could understand; time and time again he had heard such words from itinerant preachers in the backwoods of Indiana, often Lincoln had repeated them when a boy. But among these familiar phrases of unction, Lincoln manages to hint at the life-long antagonism, albeit he quickly turns to words deeply graven on his father's mind:

'Say to him that if we could meet now it is doubtful whether it would not be more painful than pleasant, but that if it be his lot to go now, he will soon have a joyous meeting with many loved ones gone before, and where the rest of us, through the help of God, hope ere long to join them.' [1]

Five days later, January 17, 1851, the old man died [2] and was buried near his Coles County cabin, his wife, the Johnstons, the Hankses and, possibly, the families of one or two farmers in the desolate neighborhood shivering beside that wintry grave.

Lincoln and his wife lived in reasonable harmony, considering their temperaments and the provocations which, by reason of

[1] Lincoln to Johnston, Jan. 12, 1851. *Works*, II, 147–9.

Lincoln had in the autumn of 1851 paid to Thomas Lincoln two hundred dollars, for the land in Coles County occupied by him. On Oct. 25, 1851, he entered into a bond to convey the tract to John D. Johnston or his heirs, on the death of Thomas Lincoln and his wife, and on payment of two hundred dollars, without interest, if paid on that event.

The land is described as the 'North East quarter of the South East quarter of Section twenty one in Township Eleven North of Range Nine East.' This would be about the center of the township and west of Embarrass [Ambraise] River. Circuit Court, Coles Co. Records, Mortgages, Book 1, 43. Aug. 31, 1851, Lincoln sent Johnston a 'deed for the land,' though the step-mother was still living, but it appears to have covered only a part of the plat. *Works*, II, 149–51.

[2] Lincoln to Jesse Lincoln, April 1, 1854. *Ib.*, 180–2.

their antipathetic natures, each gave the other.[1] Lincoln never asked his friends to dinner; and Judge David Davis who, as we shall see, was as intimate with Lincoln as any other man except Herndon, declares that he was never invited to his house at all.[2] O. H. Browning relates that, when in Springfield, he called upon the Lincolns five times, twice at Mrs. Lincoln's parties which she occasionally had, as was the fashion in Springfield, and that once or twice he spent the evening with them. Isaac N. Arnold of Chicago says that he made similar visits. But neither Browning nor Arnold makes mention of having been asked to come.

The Lincoln table was scantily supplied,[3] but what was saved through such economy was more than spent by Mrs. Lincoln on dresses and apparel for herself and the children.[4] Yet she entertained friends, and at such times made shift to have servants in evidence.[5] She 'put on plenty of style but [was] stingy,' says a friend of the family.[6] At these parties she would dress up the boys, bring them before the company, make them dance, speak, quote poetry, and show off generally. Then the

[1] Gourley's statement. Weik MSS.
They 'got along tolerably well, unless Mrs. L[incoln] got the devil in her. Lincoln . . . would pick up one of his children and walked off — would laugh at her — pay no earthly attention.' *Ib.*

[2] 'Judge Davis told me that Lincoln never invited him to his house and [I] have heard many others of Lincoln's best friends say the same thing.' Herndon to Weik, Feb. 5, 1887. Weik MSS.
Also Davis's statement to Weik, Weik, 90–1. 'He told me . . . that often as he had been in Springfield Lincoln had never entertained him, nor, so far as he could learn, any other visiting lawyer at his home.'

[3] Harriet A. Chapman to Herndon, Dec. 10 [1866]. Weik MSS. 'His table at home was usually set very sparingly. Mrs. Lincoln was very economical. So much so that by some she might have been pronounced Stingy.' *Ib.*
'His table at home generally was economized to the smallest amount. He never dared as a general thing to invite his friends to his house. Mrs. Lincoln was a very stingy woman and yet she would occasionally have parties.' Herndon to Weik, Feb. 5, 1887. Weik MSS.

[4] Weik, 94. 'Mrs. Lincoln was not only economical, but close; but in order that she might gratify her passion for the ornamental her economy and self-denial ended at the kitchen.' Statement of 'a lady relative' to Weik.
'Mrs. Lincoln was the cause of his poor tables: She economised here to swell otherwise.' Herndon to Weik, Feb. 5, 1887. Weik MSS.

[5] Weik, 94. 'As a rule servants were conspicuous about her household only when she entertained.' Statement of 'a lady relative' to Weik.

[6] Kent's statement, Nov. 21, 1916. Weik MSS.

proud mother would rhapsodize over the excellence and accomplishments of her offspring. If Lincoln happened to be present on such occasions he would observe dryly that 'these children may be something sometime, if they are not merely rareripes, rotten ripes — hothouse plants. I have always noticed that a rareripe child quickly matures, but rots as quickly.'[1] She often bought perfumery at Diller's drug store and then sent it back, declaring that it was not good; which so impressed the druggist that his son remembered half a century later that 'Mrs. L[incoln was] very hard to deal with.'[2]

Sometimes Lincoln would come to the office in the morning, unwrap from a newspaper some cheese, crackers, and bologna sausage and make his breakfast from these provisions. Now and then he would bring Bob with him and, sitting on the sofa, father and son would silently eat their uninviting meal. At such times, says Herndon, he was so sad that he would not greet his partner, who took it for granted that Lincoln had been 'driven from home.' So 'I would let down the curtain [over the glass in the office door] . . . go out and lock the door behind me taking the Key out and with me.'[3] But Lincoln was 'a hearty eater,' being especially fond of corn-cakes which, he insisted, he could devour as fast as two women could make them.[4]

Lincoln spent at least six months of every year away from Springfield riding the circuit, and he was the only lawyer that attended the courts in every county seat. His prolonged absences irritated his wife, who often confided to their next door neighbor that 'if her husband staid at home as he ought to she could love him better.'[5] Court was held in the various counties from the middle of March to the middle of June, and again

[1] Herndon to Weik, Jan. 8, 1886. Weik MSS.

[2] Statement of J. R. Diller to Weik, Nov. 21, 1916. Weik MSS. In the *Springfield Directory*, 1855–6, the firm is given as Corneau and Diller, 5 E S Public Square.

[3] Herndon to Weik, Jan. 16, 1886. Weik MSS. Herndon says that he would return at intervals to see if Lincoln had recovered from his spell of gloom. Such awakening was always made known by Lincoln's speaking to Herndon, almost invariably followed by a funny story.

[4] Mrs. Chapman to Herndon, Dec. 10 [1866]. Weik MSS.

[5] Gourley's statement.

from early September until the first of December.[1] For more than three years after his Congressional term the Eighth Circuit comprised fourteen counties, Sangamon, Tazewell, Woodford, McLean, Logan, De Witt, Champaign, Vermilion, Piatt, Edgar, Shelby, Moultrie, Macon, and Christian. It was nearly one hundred and forty miles long by almost a hundred and ten miles broad,[2] nearly one-fifth of the entire area of the State.[3] In 1853 the Circuit was reduced to eight counties, the last six named being transferred to other districts; and four years later Sangamon, Woodford, and Tazewell were attached to the Seventh District.[4]

The Judge of the Eighth Circuit was David Davis, who had been elected to that office in 1848 when thirty-three years of age. He continued on the bench by reëlection until 1862 when Lincoln appointed him a Justice of the Supreme Court of the United States. He was over six feet tall, weighed about three hundred and twenty pounds, was ruddy of face and forthright, positive, and hearty in speech and manner. A short beard that circled from ear to ear and under the chin added to the rugged appearance of his powerful features. He was personally acquainted with almost every man, woman, and child in Central Illinois, and was liked and trusted by everybody regardless of party. Notwithstanding his sternness, he was a skilful and effective politician. No other one man did so much to bring about Lincoln's nomination for the Presidency as Judge Davis. In the Republican National Convention of 1860 we shall see this burly Judge of the biggest Illinois judicial circuit appealing directly for Lincoln to the farmer delegates from States west of the Alleghanies, and no man better understood them than he or knew so well how to approach them. He was one of the three men whom Lincoln took with him on his journey to Washington in 1861.[5]

[1] Angle to author, no date; Swett: Rice, 455–6, gives other times for the court sessions.

[2] Whitney, 40. Also *Lincoln the Lawyer:* Frederic Trevor Hill, 167.

[3] Statement George P. Davis (son of David Davis), no date. Weik MSS.

[4] Weik, 145.

[5] Justice Davis, in the Legal Tender Cases, was one of the Justices who upheld the constitutionality of the acts making treasury notes a legal tender; he was an opponent

Judge Davis was a native of Cecil County, Maryland, a graduate of Kenyon College, Ohio, had studied law in Massachusetts and in the law school of Yale. He came to Bloomington, Illinois, when he was twenty years of age and was admitted to the bar as soon as he was twenty-one. In a few years he was elected to the Legislature, then to the Constitutional Convention of 1847 and, while still a member of that body, was elected Judge of the Circuit made famous by Lincoln's practice throughout its wide extent for a dozen years. Not only was Davis a good lawyer and judge, but an excellent man of affairs as well; and, largely through the purchase of fine land at low prices, he amassed what for those days was a very great fortune. Lincoln had unbounded confidence in his business sagacity, and so close were their relations that Davis was designated administrator of his estate.

The Judge used his power to the utmost to advance the fortunes of those he liked, and of all the lawyers who practised in the Eighth Circuit Lincoln was his favorite. Perhaps no other man had greater influence on Lincoln, and, until sometime after he became President, that influence was conservative and restraining. It is a curious fact and, possibly, one full of meaning, that the two men who were in most intimate and frequent contact with Lincoln, personally, politically, and professionally during the years between 1850 and 1860, strove to draw him in opposite directions. Herndon, the partner, was radical in the extreme, constantly urging Lincoln to take advanced ground against slavery, while Davis, the Judge, as steadily counselled patience and caution with respect to that vital question and especially the avoidance of anything offensive to the Southern States.

Such was the Judge before whom Lincoln practised for many years, such the man with whom he rode the circuit and upon

of Grant's Administration, and in 1872 accepted the nomination for President by the National Labor Reform Party. After serving on the Supreme Bench for fifteen years, Justice Davis resigned in order to accept the office of United States Senator, to which he was elected in 1877 in succession to John A. Logan, who was defeated by the votes of independents and Democrats in the Legislature. As a Justice of the Supreme Court he delivered the opinion of the Court in *Ex parte* Milligan (4 Wallace, 107), an opinion which deserves to stand within the class of Marshall's pronouncements on constitutional law.

DAVID DAVIS

whom he leaned heavily for guidance and comfort, such the friend who was so partial to him and alert to promote his interests. The statements of Judge Davis, always reserved and cautious, as to Lincoln's conduct and characteristics, are conclusive.

'Lincoln was with me all round the circuit . . . out 6 mo[nths of] each year,' says Davis.[1] Until the middle fifties, when railroads began to appear, these series of journeys from county seat to county seat were made in buggies or wagons, over the wretched dirt roads described and across streams often bridgeless. The Judge started on his prolonged judicial pilgrimage as soon as the roads were passable.[2] It was slow going. As late as 1857 an entire day was required for the bench and bar of the Eighth Circuit to go in a livery 'rig' from Urbana to Danville, a distance of thirty-six miles.[3] Some years earlier Chief Justice Caton, after his appointment to the Supreme Court, journeyed in a buggy with his wife and child from Ottawa to Springfield in four days.[4] It took Washburne three days, 'travelling incessantly' to go by stage from Galena to Springfield.[5] Lincoln usually went over the circuit in his buggy, driving Old Buck, sometimes taking with him another lawyer, but often going alone over the long miles of the vast prairies. It required two horses to draw the buggy of Judge Davis.[6]

Among his circuit-riding companions in a few of the counties of the Eighth Circuit was a young lawyer, Leonard Swett, a native of Maine who was in his twenty-fourth year when Lincoln again took up practice upon his return from Congress. He was the best trial lawyer in the circuit and, next to Lincoln, was the favorite of Judge Davis. He, too, was immensely popular. Indeed Davis, Lincoln, and Swett were known among the members of the bar as 'the great triumvirate.'[7] While he contributes little that is trustworthy to our information about Lincoln, Swett is not a negligible thread in the fabric of Lincoln's

---

[1] Judge Davis's statement, Sept. 19, 1866; Herndon, II, 337.
[2] Lawrence Weldon to Hill: Hill, 170.
[3] Whitney's statement, no date. Weik MSS.   [4] Caton, 153.
[5] Elihu B. Washburne: Rice, 12–3.   [6] Geo. P. Davis's statement.
[7] Whitney, 67–70.

destiny because of the assistance he gave to Davis in securing Lincoln's nomination for President in 1860.[1]

As we have seen, one of Lincoln's best liked and trusted colleagues in the Legislature was Joseph Gillespie; and this excellent lawyer and skilful politician was one of the five or six men with whom Lincoln may be said ever to have been intimate. While always championing his leader, Gillespie's account is of only less value than the data supplied by Herndon, Davis, and Matheny.

It is worthy of repetition that Lincoln was the only lawyer who travelled the whole circuit. Other members of the bar would attend courts in an adjoining county and then return home, always in time to spend Sunday with their families.[2] Lincoln, however, remained at the town where the court happened to be on Saturday and occupied his time with friends at the village inn. 'As a general rule,' says Judge Davis, 'when all the lawyers of a Saturday evening would go home and see their families and friends, . . . Lincoln would refuse to go home.'[3]

Whitney describes the county seats as 'small and primitive villages' with 'unkempt court-rooms, where, ten months in the year, the town boys played at marbles or rudimentary circus.'[4] Swett says that, in 1850, these towns each had from five hundred to a thousand people and that the court-houses and jails were of logs.[5]

The offices of the travelling lawyers of the Eighth Circuit were on the sunny side of the court-house, or under a tree, or in the street — wherever client and attorney could talk.[6] When

---

[1] Leonard Swett was born near Turner, Maine, Aug. 11, 1825. He had a remarkably successful career at the bar, but was disappointed in his political ambitions.

'Poor Swett! He got less from the public according to his deserts of any man in America.' Whitney to Weik, Aug. 23, 1891. Weik MSS.

[2] Geo. P. Davis's statement, no date.

[3] Judge Davis's statement, Sept. 20, 1866. Weik MSS.; Davis's account to Weik, Weik, 90. Courts were held on Saturdays and Mondays.   [4] Whitney, 41.

[5] Swett: Rice, 455-6. The Court-House at Urbana, built in 1848, was a small brick building of two stories in the upper of which was the court room. The structure cost $2,744. Here Lincoln delivered some of his most important political speeches. *Hist. Champaign Co.*: J. O. Cunningham, 731.

The jail was of logs, and so insecure that prisoners escaped frequently. 'It might answer for the imprisonment of infants or of men who are badly crippled, but will not do for the retention of rascals.' *Urbana Union*, Jan. 11, 1855, as quoted in Cunningham, 735.   [6] Whitney, 41.

the small tavern had but one bedroom, it was given to the Judge and his friends, other lawyers sleeping on sofa, tables, or floor.[1] Everybody, from prisoners to Judge, washed in the same tin basin and dried hands and faces on the same towel.[2]

When the county-seat towns were large enough, local attorneys, nearly always very young men, came there to live, and they employed older riders of the circuit to conduct the litigation they secured. These country lawyers prepared the cases, and their experienced circuit-riding partners tried them.[3] From these county-seat attorneys, Lincoln received most of his employments, as well in the Supreme Courts as on the circuit.[4] Now and then local partnerships were formed, the better known itinerant lawyer as the head of the firm, an arrangement which advertised the junior.[5]

One such county partnership is notable in Lincoln's life, that with Ward Hill Lamon at Danville. This local arrangement was made in 1853, when young Lamon was about twenty-five years of age. He had heard of Lincoln's reputation for 'originality, oddity, wit, ability, and eloquence,' and was very curious about him. Stuart introduced him to Lincoln, the partnership was formed, and the two rode together to courts of adjacent counties.[6] Thus began a friendship which nothing ever impaired.[7]

In his earlier years in circuit practice, however, Lincoln and

[1] Hill, 172.   [2] Caton, 77.

[3] *History of Logan County:* Lawrence B. Stringer, 317.   [4] Hill, 200.

[5] For example, Leonard Swett had Whitney for his partner at Urbana. Whitney, 71.

[6] *Recollections of Abraham Lincoln:* Lamon, edited by his daughter, Dorothy Lamon Treillard, 14–5. These connecting counties were Champaign and McLean with Urbana and Bloomington, respectively, the county seats.

[7] It was Lamon whom Lincoln chose over an army officer to go with him on the supposedly hazardous trip from Baltimore to Washington on his journey to the capital to be inaugurated; and Lincoln at once appointed his associate to be Marshal of the District of Columbia, an office which, at that particular time, was of great importance. Lamon seems to have been pompous and showy and thus to have given offence to many. Also imprudent action in attempting to raise a military force during the war led to a congressional investigation and rebuke.

Lamon was subjected to virulent attacks, not wholly justified, because of statements in a *Life of Lincoln* which appeared in 1872. It was written by Chauncy Black, the son of Jeremiah S. Black, Attorney General in Buchanan's cabinet. Black used the Herndon MSS.; but he personally disliked Lincoln and while most of his statements are correct, a few are not, and the temper of the book was unfriendly to the subject of it.

Because of the ferocious assaults on Lamon on account of this volume, he has been discredited, perhaps unduly. Certain it is that Lincoln's fondness for and confidence in Lamon continued as long as Lincoln lived.

other travelling attorneys were employed by clients as soon as
the Judge and his legal retinue arrived. 'The lawyer would,
perhaps, scarcely alight from his horse when he would be surrounded by two or three clients requiring his services,' says
Justice Caton. A bill in chancery, an answer, a demurrer, special
pleas, and the like would have to be determined and prepared
'before the opening of the court the next morning.' Thus quick
and accurate thinking and exact knowledge were necessary.[1]
Such speed was the one thing in which Lincoln was at a disadvantage: he himself declared, and all of his associates assert,
that his mind worked slowly and that he required plenty of time
for preparation.

At every county seat Lincoln was the most popular man. The
capital of Logan county was named Lincoln in his honor. In
1853 when this site was laid off, Lincoln was attorney for the
promoters of the new town. What name do you give the town?
he asked of his clients, when writing the paper in which the name
had to be stated. After considering several names, the donor of
the site suggested that the town be called Lincoln. 'You'd
better not do that, for I never knew anything named Lincoln
that amounted to much,' said the attorney. But his name was
agreed upon, and inserted in the papers and the town was finally
incorporated as Lincoln, Logan County, Illinois.[2]

Except that at Springfield there were no law libraries in the
county seats of the Eighth Circuit, and lawyers carried few, if
any, books with them.[3] It does not appear that Lincoln took a
single legal volume when, twice a year, he started on his long
journeys, each lasting for three months. But he took other
books which he thought more useful, and still others which he
found more entertaining. Soon after his marriage, Lincoln
began to carry Euclid with him on the circuit;[4] and to the mas-
tering of this work he applied himself with vigor when he again

---

[1] Caton, 51; Whitney, 42.

[2] Stringer, 565–9, gives a detailed account of the establishment of Lincoln.

Once when asked if the town of Lincoln had not been named after him, he dryly remarked: 'Well, yes, I believe it was named after I was.' Whitney, 117. This is often
cited as a fine example of Lincoln's ready wit.

[3] Justice Caton says that Blackstone and *Coke upon Littleton*, were the two authorities most relied on. Caton, 219.   [4] Stuart's statement, no date. Weik MSS.

took up the practice of law after his term in Congress.[1] He studied algebra [2] too, when on the circuit and pored over a treatise on astronomy. 'I have seen him myself, upon the circuit, with "a geometry," or "an astronomy" . . . working out propositions in moments of leisure,' says Swett.[3]

Whitney confirms Herndon's testimony that Lincoln read nothing thoroughly.[4] 'His reading was more desultory and less profound than that of any man of his own time, or if not, indeed, of any time,' is Whitney's sweeping conclusion.[5] *Flush Times in Alabama* was a favorite with him and he would read from it to his companions what he considered a superlatively fine story about an earthquake.[6] Yet Herndon is positive that, for the first five or six years after Lincoln's return from Congress, he was 'a hard student,' especially of mathematics, and that he 'read much in the political world.' [7]

When at Springfield Lincoln was interested chiefly in works on science. One day Herndon, who always was buying new books, brought to the office a small volume, the *Annual of Science*,[8] one of a series on that subject. Lincoln was keenly interested in the book, and told his partner that he 'must buy the whole set, started out and got them.' When he came back he said to Herndon: 'I have wanted such a book for years, because I sometimes make experiments and have thoughts about the physical world that I do not know to be true or false. I may, by this book, correct my errors and save time and expense. I can see where scientists and philosophers have failed . . . or can see the means of their success and take advantage of their brains, toil,

[1] Herndon to Weik, Feb. 11, 1887. Weik MSS.

'He [Lincoln] studied and nearly mastered the six books of Euclid since he was a member of Congress.' Autobiography, *Works*, VI, 28.

[2] Whitney, 49.

[3] Swett: Rice, 467. Also Gillespie to Herndon, Dec. 8, 1866. Weik MSS. 'He was fond of astronomy.' *Ib.* Herndon thought that Lincoln studied Euclid and Shakespeare to supply his lack of education. Herndon, II, 319.

[4] *Ib.*, 320. 'He never in his life sat down and read a book through.'

[5] Whitney, 109. While Whitney's statement seems extravagant, it is supported by Harris (Weik, 107), by Herndon, and by all others who were with Lincoln often and for long periods of time.

[6] Whitney, 185. It is in the chapter on 'Cave Burton, Esq., of Kentucky' in Joseph G. Baldwin's volume.

[7] Herndon to Weik, Feb. 11, 1887. Weik MSS.

[8] *Annual of Scientific Discovery*, edited by David Ames Wells, 1850–71.

and knowledge. Men are greedy to publish the successes of [their] efforts, but meanly shy as to publishing the failures of men. Men are ruined by this one sided practice of concealment of blunders and failures.' [1]

It appears that he cared principally for science, mathematics, and poetry. Lincoln read history sparingly and with caution, for he doubted the accuracy or rather the impartiality of it, believing that books of the kind did not give all sides of any event or tell the whole truth. 'Indeed he thought that history as generally written was altogether too unreliable,' testifies Gillespie,[2] a statement which Stuart confirms.[3] Biography he refused to read at all, because it was merely eulogistic. On this point he was emphatic and unyielding. 'Biographies as written are false and misleading,' he told Herndon, when his partner, who was a devotee of books, was urging Lincoln to read a Life of Burke [4] which Herndon had bought: 'The author of the life of his hero paints him as a perfect man — magnifies his perfections and suppresses his imperfections — describes the success of his hero in glowing terms, never once hinting at his failures and his blunders. Why do not book merchants and sellers have blank biographies on their shelves always ready for sale, so that when a man dies, if his heirs — children and friends — wish to perpetuate the memory of the dead, they can purchase one already written, *but with blanks* which they can fill up eloquently and grandly at pleasure thus commemorating a lie; an injury to the living and to the name of the dead.' [5]

But 'the source and developement of language' attracted him strongly, he told Gillespie, and added that he was 'surprised to find his investigations in that direction so interesting and in-

---

[1] Herndon to Weik, Dec. 15, 1886. Weik MSS. 'This he said substantially to me with much feeling. . . . The last . . . he spoke . . . in glowing terms.'

[2] Gillespie to Herndon, Dec. 8, 1866. Weik MSS.
'Mr. Lincoln never I think studied history except in connection with politics with the exception of the history of the Netherlands and of the revolutions of 1640 and 1688 in England and of our revolutionary struggle he regarded it as of trifling value as teaching by example.'

[3] Stuart's statement, no date. Weik MSS.

[4] Probably James Prior's *Memoir of Burke*, first published in 1826.

[5] Herndon to Weik, Feb., 1887. Weik MSS. 'This, Mr. Lincoln said to me in substance just as I have written it.' *Cf.* version of this opinion in Herndon, III, 437 *n.*

structive.' He even prepared a lecture on the origin and growth of speech.[1]

We are now well within the period when accounts of Lincoln are given by men of trained minds, lawyers for the most part, who were with him much of the time and who made their statements not many years after the happening of the incidents they relate. Their testimony is, therefore, more trustworthy than the recollections on which we have had to rely, of very old persons concerning things that took place many decades before the narration of them and obviously colored by the desire to be associated with Lincoln's fame. Yet even those who rode the circuit and practised law with him were so influenced by the atmosphere of adulation which surrounded them when they gave their descriptions, that their accounts must be received with caution. Indeed, some of these men appear to have been under a sort of intimidation. Swett, for instance, wrote a letter to Herndon which renders valueless parts of his published reminiscences. He admonished Herndon that the truth must not be told, because, at that time, the public would disbelieve and resent it.[2]

Bearing in mind the conditions under which Lincoln's associates gave their recollections of him, his outstanding characteristics upon which all agree are the more impressive. Of these characteristics the most striking was Lincoln's melancholy. Everybody observed his abysmal sadness. His gloom was not periodical and succeeded by weeks of brightness, but was made manifest every day, yet interwoven with hours of abnormal gayety — black despondency and boisterous humor following one another like cloud and sunshine in a day of doubtful storm.

Sometimes his depression was shown in strange ways. When on the circuit, Judge Davis and two other lawyers often slept in the same room, Davis in one bed, and the other two together in another bed. Once at Danville, where this arrangement always was made, Whitney, who was sleeping with Lincoln that night,

---

[1] Gillespie to Herndon, Dec. 8, 1866. Weik MSS. Lincoln never delivered this lecture, nor has the MS. of it been found.

[2] Swett to Herndon, Aug. 30, 1887. Weik MSS. 'You will note that I have stricken out all allusion to Mr. Lincoln's swearing, and reading the Bible. . . . The public would believe I lied about it. . . . The heroes of the world are its standards, and in time . . . they become clothed with imaginary virtues.'

was awakened early in the morning by the sound of a voice. It came from Lincoln who was sitting on the side of the bed talking incoherently to himself. The weather was cold and he finally got up, put wood on the fire, and sat before it staring into the blaze and mumbling now and then, seemingly profoundly sad. When Judge Davis and Whitney arose at the usual hour, Lincoln had not moved. They said nothing to him about the circumstance for, testifies Whitney, 'we knew this trait: it was not remarkable for Lincoln.' [1]

Time and again Herndon had experiences of the same nature. Lincoln would sit opposite his partner at the table in their office; for a long time he would look with vacant eyes steadily at the wall, without a sound or a motion, unconscious of Herndon's presence; suddenly he would spring to his feet, burst into wild laughter and rush from the room, through the hallway and down the stairs. Anxious and mystified, Herndon would go after Lincoln to learn the cause and outcome of his seizure. But out on the street, he would be normal again, amusing acquaintances with story or jest as if nothing had happened.[2] Joseph Gillespie testifies that 'Mr. Lincoln appeared to be either extremely mirthful or extremely sad.' [3]

So intermingled were Lincoln's melancholy and abstraction that some of his friends and admirers could not tell whether he was lost in thought or gloom. Judge Lawrence Weldon, then a young lawyer, literally adored Lincoln and is one of the most

---

[1] Whitney, 47–8. Judge Davis occupied 'a three-quarter bed, and Lincoln and I occupying the other one, jointly. . . . One morning, I was awakened early — before daylight — by my companion sitting up in bed, his figure dimly visible by the ghostly firelight, and talking the wildest and most incoherent nonsense all to himself.

'A stranger to Lincoln would have supposed that he had suddenly gone insane. Of course I knew Lincoln and his idiosyncrasies, and felt no alarm, so I listened and laughed.

'After he had gone on in this way for, say, five minutes, while I was awake, and I know not how long *before* I was awake, he sprang out of bed, hurriedly washed, and jumped into his clothes, put some wood on the fire, and then sat in front of it, moodily, dejectedly, in a most sombre and gloomy spell, till the breakfast bell rang, when he started, as if from sleep, and went with us to breakfast.

'Neither Davis nor I spoke to him; we knew this trait; it was not remarkable for Lincoln, although this time to which I refer was a radical manifestation of it, a proof that "True wit to madness, sure, is oft allied."'

[2] Herndon to Weik. Weik MSS.

[3] Gillespie to Herndon, Dec. 8, 1866. Weik MSS.

credible witnesses as to his appearance and conduct during Lincoln's last six years on the circuit. He relates that Lincoln 'would frequently lapse into reverie and remain lost in thought long after the rest of us had retired for the night, and more than once I remember waking up early in the morning to find him sitting before the fire, his mind apparently concentrated on some subject, and with the saddest expression I have ever seen in a human being's eyes.' [1] When thus gazing into dying flames, says Weldon, he would often recite 'Mortality.' [2]

As trustworthy as testimony can be in the account of his observation and experiences with Lincoln is the narrative of Jonathan Birch, which was found among his papers after his death. Birch, when a youth, studied law in his brother's office at Bloomington, Illinois, and, as we shall presently see, Lincoln arranged for his admission to the bar. Like young Weldon, he loved and admired Lincoln and almost worshipped his memory. He relates that, when attending court at Bloomington, Lincoln would keep hearers in court-room, office, or on the street convulsed with laughter at one hour and the next hour be so deeply submerged in speculation or despair that no one dared arouse him. He would, says Birch, sit in a chair tilted against the wall, his feet on the lower rung, legs drawn up and knees level with his chin, hat tipped forward, hands clasped about knees, eyes infinitely sad, 'the very picture of dejection and gloom. Thus absorbed I have seen him sit for hours at a time defying the interruption of even his closest friends.' [3]

Whatever the quality of the witnesses who give various accounts of Lincoln at the bar, all concur upon his extreme depression throughout this decade. 'Melancholy dripped from him as

---

[1] Weldon in Hill, 190–1.

[2] Weldon to Herndon, Feb. 10, 1866, as quoted in Herndon, II, 319.

[3] Paper on Lincoln by Jonathan Birch of Greencastle, Ind. Weik MSS. Mr. Birch enlisted in the Union Army at the outbreak of the Civil War and served throughout that conflict. After the war was over he settled at Greencastle. He was regarded, by members of his profession and by all who knew him, as a man of a remarkable devotion to truth and a curious insistence upon accuracy of statement, even in the smallest details.

The value of Birch's narrative is enhanced by the fact that it was written for his own satisfaction and not for publication. The author, when in college, knew Captain Birch, then a very old man. See Weik, 133.

he walked,' says Herndon; [1] and his face 'when in repose . . . was
. . . prevaded by a look of dejection as painful as it was prominent.' [2] Often when on the street, he was so abstracted that he
took no notice of those who met and spoke to him.[3] He would
look directly at some one for a long time without seeing him.[4]
Whitney testifies that Lincoln would shake hands with him without knowing it; [5] even when in court he would act as if he were
in a solitude. In the thick of busy scenes, declares his circuit
companion, Lincoln would be 'entirely oblivious of all that was
passing before his very eyes.' Whitney felt that Lincoln's despondency was 'mysterious,' a term frequently used by other
observers in their futile efforts to describe his sombre state of
mind. So intense and conspicuous was his gloom that people
felt sorry for him.[6]

Weik thought that accounts of Lincoln's sadness must be exaggerated, and, when gathering materials for his book, pointedly
asked those most closely associated with Lincoln the truth of the
matter — Stuart, Matheny, Judge Treat, Judge Davis, Swett,
Whitney, and others. 'My inquiry on this subject among Lincoln's close friends,' declares Weik, 'convinced me that men who
never saw him could scarcely realize this tendency to melancholy.' [7] This brooding was strongly colored by apprehension of
personal disaster. 'Billy, I fear that I shall meet with some terrible end,' he said to his partner upon coming out of one of these
fits of dejection.[8]

As we have seen, Lincoln quoted poetry a great deal, but the
poems he repeated oftenest were those that expressed hopelessness, woe, and foreboding.[9] 'Oh, why should the spirit of mortal

[1] Weik, 113. [2] Herndon's Lecture. *Ib.*, 113–4.

[3] Herndon to Weik, Feb. 11, 1887. Weik MSS.

[4] J. H. Burnham of Bloomington, in High School *Ægis*, Feb., 1906, 70–1. Burnham
says that he, personally, had this experience with Lincoln.

[5] Whitney, 111. 'I can recollect of two distinct occasions when he saw me plainly,
and shook hands with me, rather mechanically, yet with apparent intelligence, and
notwithstanding this, he repeated the same performance, but with zeal and enthusiasm,
within one hour thereafter, assuring me that I was mistaken, that he had not spoken to
me before, that day.' See also *ib.*, 113, 139.

[6] 'His sad countenance aroused universal sympathy.' Whitney, 107.

[7] Weik, 112.

[8] Herndon to Bartlett, Aug. 16, 1887. MS. Mass. Hist. Soc'y.

[9] Herndon, II, 320.

be proud,' he would begin, and recite the whole of that rhyme on futility; or Holmes's 'Last Leaf,' or Poe's 'Raven,' or poems of resignation.[1] Once when walking along a street in Springfield, he heard a young woman in a house singing 'The Enquiry.' At Lincoln's request she sent him the lines and he read them over and over, 'charmed' with them, as Herndon expresses it. This poem, too, was on earthly despair.[2] One day in Whitney's office at Urbana he surprised his youthful colleague by picking up a copy of Byron — 'which no boy's library at that time was without' — and reading impressively and sadly from the third canto of Childe Harold's verses about the desolation of greatness.[3] Whatever the cause, the bleak fact remains that the dominant quality in Lincoln's life, from 1849 to the end, was a sadness so profound that the depths of it cannot be sounded or estimated by normal minds.[4]

Certainly political disappointment had something to do with his despondency. As we shall see he was deeply engaged in politics during practically the whole time covered by descriptions of him as a lawyer given by his associates at the bar; and he suffered two big defeats, each of which, as we are told by those closest to him at the time, he regarded as fatal to his political career.[5] That career was the thing he cared most about.

[1] Stuart's statement, *supra;* Weldon: Rice, 213; Herndon, II, 320. Poe's 'Raven' first appeared in the *Whig Review,* 1845.

[2] Herndon, II, 320–2, where the verses are printed. This poem, written by Charles Mackay, ranges the universe with the enquiry as to where surcease can be found; winds, sea, moon, answer that happiness does not exist on earth; but, finally, the 'secret soul' of man reassures him that balm and blessing are to be experienced only in heaven.

[3] Whitney, 141.

[4] *Ib.,* 140. He was 'naturally' disposed to be pessimistic. Gillespie to Herndon, Jan. 31, 1866. Weik MSS.

Stuart attributed his depression to a sluggish liver, and after Lincoln's election to the Presidency, advised him to take blue-mass pills. He did so for awhile, but had no relief from them and stopped using them. Whitney, 139.

Domestic unhappiness was the theory of Judge Davis: 'It seemed to me that L[incoln] was not domestically happy.' Judge Davis gave this as a reason for Lincoln's refusal to go home Saturdays, when on the Circuit. Davis's statement, Sept. 20, 1866. Weik MSS.

Herndon and many others thought that political disappointment and Mrs. Lincoln's temper combined were the causes which produced Lincoln's sadness; although his partner also included derangement of secretions.

[5] In 1855 and 1858, both for the Senate.

Writing to his collaborator, when their book was in process of making, Herndon assured Weik that 'at this time he despaired of ever rising again in the political world; he was very sad and terribly gloomy.' [1] Seemingly, Weik was anxious to put emphasis on his eminence in the law, for Herndon asks his literary partner: 'How are you going to make a *great* lawyer out of Lincoln? His soul was afire with its own ambition and that was not law.' Indeed, continues Herndon, he did not care much about law, but thought constantly of politics.[2] And even the alertly partial Gillespie concedes that 'he was unquestionably ambitious for official distinction,' but hastens to reassure us. 'He only desired place to enable him to do good and serve his country and his kind.' [3]

Interwoven with Lincoln's black moods was a vein of superstition; [4] he 'believed more or less in dreams, . . . had apparitions and tried to solve them,' Herndon confides to Bartlett the sculptor.[5] Running, like a thread of changing colors through the fabric of contradictions that made up Lincoln's character was a freakish credulity in strange antagonism to the general attitude of his inquiring and doubting mind. For instance, he believed in the 'mad-stone' and Mrs. Wallace relates that once, when Bob was bitten by a dog, Lincoln took the boy to Terre Haute to have that remedy applied.[6] The reason of his faith in mad-stones, he explained to Gillespie, was that 'he found the People in the neighborhood of these stones fully impressed with the belief in their virtues from actual experiment.' [7] Yet Lincoln had developed a sort of fatalism; [8] what was to be would be, he thought, modified somewhat, but not much, by personal exertions.

[1] Herndon to Weik, Oct. 28, 1885. Weik MSS.
[2] *Ib.*, Dec. 9, 1886. Weik MSS.
[3] Gillespie to Herndon, Dec. 8, 1866. Weik MSS.
[4] Same to same, Jan. 31 and Dec. 8, 1866. Weik MSS.
[5] Herndon to Bartlett, Aug. 16, 1887. MS. Mass. Hist. Soc'y.
[6] Mrs. Wallace's statement. Weik MSS.
[7] Gillespie to Herndon, Jan. 31, 1866. Weik MSS.
[8] Whitney, 140–1, 149.
'Closely allied with this sad trait was an inherent belief in his destiny; perhaps the specific destiny was not very clearly indicated, but that, somehow . . . Destiny, had touched him with her wand, and marked him for her own.'

From his talk and actions, Herndon became saturated with the conviction that his partner was a votary of the idea of a fixed destiny, whose chosen child Herndon firmly believed Lincoln to be; and he spins endless cobwebs of speculation in his effort to analyze and explain this curious element of Lincoln's character.[1] Gillespie was puzzled, too, though he bravely struggles to reconcile his friend's fatalism with orthodox religious views. 'I do not think that he was what I would term, a blind believer in fate or destiny, but that he considered the means foreordained as well as the end, and therefore he was extremely diligent in the use of the means.' [2]

He was particularly obliging and helpful to young lawyers.[3] Lincoln always paid marked attention to all young men; nor did he discriminate against those whose habits were bad. In fact, as will presently appear, he showed great fondness for their company.[4] For there was not a trace of the Pharisee about Lincoln. But he especially cultivated the younger members of the bar and law students, and they in turn were devoted to Lincoln.[5] 'It seemed,' writes Whitney, 'as if he wooed me to close intimacy and familiarity, at once' — this out of sheer kindness of heart.[6] He never was too busy to give advice to a young attorney, never too occupied to help him solve a knotty legal problem.[7] 'Lincoln was so good natured, and so willing to give advice, that young lawyers went to him a great deal.' [8]

One of the best descriptions of Lincoln on the circuit is given by Judge Weldon when telling of Lincoln's hearty willingness to

[1] Herndon to Weik, Feb. 26, 1891, on 'Lincoln's philosophy'; Herndon undated MS. Weik MSS.

[2] Gillespie to Herndon, Dec. 8, 1866. Weik MSS.; Whitney, 267–8.

[3] Weldon: Rice, 200.

[4] For accounts of these dissolute associates of Lincoln see Weik, 215–6. Judge Davis says that Lincoln's love of jokes made him take up with low vulgar and unscrupulous men; but that 'he used such men as a tool.' Sept. 20, 1866. Weik MSS.
'Lincoln and George Lawrence, a worthless, drunken lawyer, used to play billiards together: one played about as well as the other.' Whitney to Weik, Aug. 27, 1887. Weik MSS.

[5] Washburne: Rice, 16–7.

[6] Whitney, 31.

[7] *Ib.*, 111–2. Whitney says that Lincoln would thus help any lawyer, old as well as young.

[8] Whitney to Herndon, Aug. 27, 1887. Weik MSS.

assist him soon after Weldon began to practise. He went to the older lawyer in the court-room at Bloomington and asked what he ought to do in a confused matter. Lincoln was without coat or vest and a button for his suspenders had come off his trousers.

'"Wait until I fix this plug for my 'gallis,'" said Lincoln, "and I will pitch into that like a dog at a root." While speaking,' continues Judge Weldon, 'he was busily engaged in trying to connect his suspender with his pants by making a "plug" perform the function of a button.' [1]

Young lawyers at county seats would get Lincoln to help them try difficult cases. In Tazewell County a youthful attorney thus employed him to defend a man indicted for obstructing the public road. 'I want you to open the case,' said Lincoln, 'and when you are doing it talk to the jury as though your client's fate depends on every word you utter. Forget that you have any one to fall back upon, and you will do justice to yourself and your client.' James Haines, who relates this incident, gives it as 'a fair sample of the way he [Lincoln] treated younger members of the bar.' [2]

Young Birch wanted to be admitted to the bar, but could not get a license because of a rule in that examining district which required that the applicant should have studied at least two years in the office of a practising lawyer. Lincoln heard of the youth's predicament, sent for him, told him that there was no such rule in the Springfield district, suggested that he go to that town and from there make the proper application to the Supreme Court, asking the appointment of a special committee to examine him. Birch did so and Lincoln was designated as examiner. 'I remember,' narrates Birch, 'his first question was: "What books have you read?" When I had told him he said: "Well, that is more than I had read before I was admitted to the practice."' Then Lincoln told a story of his encounter with a college-bred lawyer whose learning impressed the bench and bar, but whose erudition was all lost on the jury; 'and they,' said Lincoln, 'were the fellows I was aiming at.' Suddenly he re-

[1] Weldon: Rice, 200–1.

[2] Haines to Hill: Hill, 186–7. The case was People vs. Gideon Hawley; there were thirty-two counts in the indictment.

sumed the examination, rapidly asking questions to test Birch's memory, although 'they bore but a faint relation to the practice of law.' Stopping abruptly Lincoln remarked: 'Well, I reckon I've asked you enough,' wrote a certificate recommending the license, told Birch what books to study thereafter, and the young man's ordeal was over.[1]

If Lincoln was ever happy after his breakdown in 1841, it was when riding the old Eighth Circuit or when trying a case in some little county seat court-house. 'In my opinion,' says Judge Davis, 'Mr. Lincoln was happy, as happy as *he* could be, when on this Circuit, and happy in no other place. This was his place of enjoyment.'[2] The life led by lawyers in those rural courts and at country taverns was care-free and merry. Usually they went in companies from town to town. Never less than a day was required for these journeys, and often two and even three days were necessary. The seasons were the best for travel, and in spring and early summer the prairies were grandly beautiful. Wild flowers filled with color the waving grass which, interspersed with delightful groves, stretched into the far distance. Travellers who saw the Illinois prairies at that time wrote wellnigh ecstatic descriptions of the loveliness and magnificence of the spectacle.

The country was still thinly settled,[3] and in some parts of the Eighth Circuit no house, no field, no sign of human occupation appeared for a score of miles.[4] 'The wild Illinois prairies . . . [were] then[5] quite as desolate and almost as solitary as at Creation's dawn,' asserts Whitney.[6] When the building of the Illinois Central Railroad began in 1853, the country for more than a hundred miles south of Chicago 'was an almost unbroken prairie, inhabited only by deer, wolves, and other wild animals, with no settlement in view.'[7] In 1854, when Champaign County was twenty years old, 'vast, undulating prairies were seen on every hand. . . . Within all its borders not twenty

---

[1] Birch's narrative. The Supreme Court at once issued the license on Lincoln's recommendation.

[2] Judge Davis's statement, Sept. 20, 1886. Weik MSS.

[3] Swett: Rice, 455–6.   [4] Caton, 101, 220.

[5] 1854–57.   [6] Whitney, 40.

[7] *Illinois Central Railroad:* W. K. Ackerman, 83–4.

houses were to be found one mile from the protection and convenience of a grove or belt of timber. . . . Probably two-thirds of the lands of the county were owned by the Government, and the solitude and stillness of nature was almost universal.'[1]

Along the country roads, through and across these far-flung miles of grass and flowers and scattered clumps of trees, went the Illinois circuit-riding lawyers of the fifties. 'The itinerant lawyer was as sure to come as the trees to bud or the leaves to fall,' declares one of them.[2] Remarkable men they were, of uncommon ability and excellent lawyers.[3]

Sometimes several lawyers rode with the Judge in a wagon; more often they went in groups of two, or three, or four. They told stories, argued, talked politics and philosophy, and, led by Lincoln's Danville partner, Ward Lamon, sang negro melodies.[4] At the tavern when the county seat was reached at night-fall, mirth and jollity reigned among them. Indeed all of court time at these country towns was full of activity and varied interest for bench and bar — in court all day, at the tavern all night, every waking hour 'replete with bustle, business, energy, hilarity, novelty, irony, sarcasm, excitement, and eloquence,' as the lawyer-historian of the old Eighth Circuit describes the life.[5] Of these happy, fun-loving, fun-making companies Lincoln was always the centre and inspiration.

For his exuberant humor was almost as pronounced as his melancholy and abstraction. The absurd anywhere always caught his watchful eye: a showman's advertisement of a 'grate

---

[1] Cunningham, 745. Writing to the Chicago *Daily Democratic Press*, April 25, 1854, a land investigator describes thirty miles of country in Champaign County as 'a wild, rich, boundless, and almost unsettled prairie.' In ten miles there was 'not a house or improvement.' Urbana had 'a few small stores and residences.' *Ib.*, and see Whitney, 41.

[2] Weldon: Rice, 200.

[3] Whitney, 265. After naming the members of the bar of the Eighth Circuit, Whitney says: 'These were great men, . . . three of them were, at times, Supreme [Court] Judges, four of them have been Congressmen, three U.S. Senators and one a governor. Two or three of them were among the best lawyers in the State, or any other state.'
Speaking of the leaders of the bar during Lincoln's first years as a lawyer, Chief Justice Caton says: 'All of these men would have ranked high at any bar, and were thoroughly read in the fundamental principles of the law.' Caton, 52. Caton names Logan, Stuart, Browning, Ford, Hardin, all from the South; and Breese, Baker, and himself, from the East.

[4] Whitney, 49.   [5] *Ib.*, 42.

sho of snaix' amused him vastly.[1] His stories were incessant, inexhaustible. 'It was as a humorist that he towered above all other men it was ever my lot to meet,' Gillespie wrote to Herndon. Although 'Illinois was conspicuous for the number of its story-tellers . . . when Mr. Lincoln was about I never knew a man who would pretend to vie with him in entertaining a crowd.' [2] Judge Davis sometimes stopped court to listen to Lincoln's stories.[3] 'O Lord wasn't he funny?' exclaimed Linder.[4] Any remark, any incident brought from him an appropriate tale. The fact that these stories were frequently broad and sometime indecent did not detract from the boisterous enjoyment of them.[5] Lincoln laughed at his own jokes as uproariously as any who heard him. He insisted that country folk, and especially farmer boys, were the originators of nearly all good stories; and he declared that it was from this source that he got the best of those he told.[6]

Such a return to the grass roots was merely a phase of Lincoln's belief in the people as the origin of all that is wise, right, and attractive. One of the first cases that Herndon laid before Lincoln upon his return from Congress, related to the narrowing of suffrage. Lincoln refused to join his partner, who had become city attorney, in the argument. 'I am opposed,' he said, 'to lessening the right of suffrage; and I am in favor of its extension and enlargement. . . . I don't intend by any act of mine to crush or contract suffrage ' [7]

Although he professed to get his stories from the people, Lincoln himself would construct a tale from anything unusual. At Postville, when it was the capital of Logan County, a man came to the inn at midnight, aroused the landlord, and awakened everybody else, with a demand for whisky. There chanced to be none in the tavern and every place in the hamlet where a drink

[1] Whitney, 183.   [2] Gillespie to Herndon, Dec. 8, 1866. Weik MSS.

[3] Whitney's statement.

[4] Linder to Gillespie, Aug. 8, 1867. MS. Chicago Hist. Socy.

[5] Whitney, 45. 'The pity is that his funniest stories don't circulate in polite society or get embalmed in type.'

[6] 'He always maintained stoutly that the best stories originated with Country boys and in the rural districts.' Gillespie to Herndon, Jan. 31, 1866. Weik MSS.

[7] Herndon MS. no date. Weik MSS.

could be had was closed for the night. 'Great Heavens! Give
me an ear of corn and a tin cup and I'll make it myself,' cried the
thirsty visitor. Lincoln who was in the hostelry, thought the incident funny in the extreme and made from it one of his most
popular stories.[1] Yet he could not analyze his gift. 'He used to
say that the attempt to ascertain wherein wit consisted baffled
him more than any other undertaking of the kind. That the first
impression would be that the thing was of easy solution, but the
varieties of wit were so great that what would explain one case
would be wholly inapplicable to another.' [2]

When on the circuit, everybody — Judge Davis, the lawyers,
court officials, witnesses, plaintiffs, and defendants in law suits,
even those indicted for offences — ate at the same long table in
the village tavern.[3] Here Lincoln was as indifferent to food as he
was in Springfield. Others complained, and often swore: Lincoln
accepted with good humor everything set before him. 'Well, in
the absence of anything to eat I will pitch into this cabbage,'
was a remark that Judge Davis remembered for a dozen years.[4]
Whitney and Herndon were convinced that Lincoln did not
know whether food was well or badly cooked — did not, indeed,
realize what he was eating, just as he had no idea whether or not
his clothes fitted.[5] Gillespie testifies that Lincoln cared nothing
whatever about the kind or quality of the food he ate; [6] and
he was equally indifferent as to where or with whom he slept.[7]
Herndon confirms these accounts. 'Lincoln had a good appetite and good digestion, ate mechanically . . . he filled up and
that is all: he never complained of bad food nor praised the
food.' [8]

During terms of court in county seats, each of which terms
lasted from three days to a fortnight or more,[9] a select company
of lawyers gathered at night in the room of Judge Davis. When
court was held in their own and near-by counties, Swett, Whit-

[1] Stringer, 216.   [2] Gillespie to Herndon, Dec. 8, 1866. Weik MSS.
[3] Whitney, 42; Caton, 115. Judge Caton says there were a number of tables.
[4] Davis's statement, Sept. 20, 1866. Weik MSS.
[5] Whitney, 52, 111.
[6] Gillespie to Herndon, Jan. 31, 1866.
[7] Whitney's statement, no date. Weik MSS.
[8] Herndon to Weik, Feb. 5, 1887. Weik MSS.   [9] Linder, 183.

ney, and Lamon were among those who gathered in the Judge's
room, at the country hotels, 'the scenes of our revelries;'[1] but
Lincoln was always there in every county seat of the district.
The leading men of the town were present too, merchants, the
local banker, doctors, and farmers, who were attending court.
If any one came whom Davis disliked, he was 'frozen out.'[2] It
was these assemblages which continued far into the night, jollity
and argument concealing the flight of the hours. Often lawyers
were tried and fined for some impropriety — talking too loud or
long to a jury, charging too small or too big a fee, and the like —
before an 'orgmathorial' court, as Davis called it, held in his
room; and the merrymakers would display as much ingenuity
and eloquence in these contests as they did in the court
room.[3]

Liquor was plentiful at some of these gatherings and at other
times when lawyers assembled, but Lincoln never joined in the
drinking. When he was with the 'coterie,'[4] Ward Lamon, Lincoln's local partner at Danville, was usually expected to provide
a pitcher of whisky.[5] 'Things were free and easy in Urbana and
Danville,' says Whitney. 'There was a hard crowd used to meet
us in the latter town. Lincoln was not as gloomy at that end of
the Circuit as in yours.'[6] Lincoln never objected to anyone else
drinking, although he did not, himself, drink. Nor did he use
tobacco. 'He was a remarkably temperate man,' testified Gillespie, 'eschewing every indulgence not so much, as it seemed to
me, from principle as from want of appetites. I never heard him
declaim against the use of tobacco or other stimulants although
he never indulged in them.'[7] When Douglas offered Lincoln a

[1] Whitney, 47.

[2] *Ib.*, 45, 62. It would seem that the only test was whether a man was personally
agreeable. Once a defendant on trial for perjury, spent the evening with 'the coterie'
in Davis's room. *Ib.*, 52.
'Davis would freeze out of our charmed circle any disagreeable persons.' Whitney's
statement, no date. Weik MSS.

[3] Whitney, 46-7.

[4] Davis, Swett, Whitney, Lamon, and Lincoln. Whitney, 47.

[5] *Ib.*, 50-1. Also Whitney's statement, no date. Weik MSS. 'Lamon would have
whisky in his office for the drinking ones.'

[6] Whitney to Herndon, Aug. 27, 1887. Weik MSS.

[7] Gillespie to Herndon, Jan. 31, 1866. Weik MSS.

drink at Bloomington in 1854, he answered: 'I do not drink anything, and have not done so for a very many years.' [1]

Swett says that Lincoln told him that he 'never tasted liquor in his life.' [2] But Herndon in his lecture on Lincoln quotes his partner as saying: 'I am entitled to little credit for not drinking, because I hate the stuff. It is unpleasant and always leaves me flabby and undone.' [3] And Herndon assured Weik that Lincoln 'did sometimes take a horn . . . when he thought it would do him good.' [4] Whitney says that Lincoln 'did not drink at all;' [5] but relates that 'once I remember several of us drove out to the residence of Reason Hooten, near Danville, where we were treated to several varieties of home-made wine. A mere sip of each affected Lincoln, and he said comically: "Fellers, I'm getting drunk." That was the nearest approach to inebriety I ever saw in him.' [6]

Far into the night — sometimes all night long — they told stories, cracked jokes, talked of the state of the country, discussed the progress or decline of man.[7] Wit sparkled in the ill-furnished room of the country tavern and laughter rang. 'All were young men,' relates Chief Justice Caton, 'and after the pressure of the first few days of the court was over, they spent their evenings, and I may say nights, in hilarity, which was at times . . . boisterous.' [8] There were wisdom too, and sound sense, and searching comment. In all this merriment and solid conversation Lincoln was the leader. 'Ah! what glorious fun we had sometimes!' exclaims Linder with reminiscent regret.[9] Small wonder that bright pictures of these gay nights did not fade from the recollection of these jolly circuit-riders of the bar, for 'the good cheer and conviviality were exuberant,' especially

---

[1] Weldon: Rice, 198. Judge Weldon says that he saw and heard this incident.

[2] Swett: Rice, 462-3.

[3] Weik, 111; Herndon to Weik, Feb. 5, 1887. Weik MSS.

[4] *Ib.*, and same to same, Nov. 17, 1885. Weik MSS.

[5] Whitney's statement. Weik MSS.

[6] Whitney, 157.

[7] *Ib.*, 45. 'We frequently talked philosophy, politics, political economy, metaphysics and men; . . . our subjects of conversation ranged through the universe of thought and experience.'

[8] Caton, 52.

[9] Linder, 183.

when the docket was light.[1] Lincoln was, asserts the adoring
Lamon, 'the life and light of the court.' [2]

Yet — inexplicable mingling of incongruous characteristics —
Lincoln was singularly aloof. He was undemonstrative, even
cold, seemingly without emotion.[3] He permitted no familiarity,
such as slapping on the shoulder or back, and never indulged in
it himself.[4] He called by their first names jurors and acquaintances among farmers and the 'common people,' but, grotesque
inconsistency, he spoke to all but two of his close friends and
associates at the bar by the family name, rarely by the Christian
name, as Whitney instead of Henry, Logan, not Stephen, Swett,
not Leonard; and he was similarly addressed as Lincoln, not as
Abe nor as Mr. Lincoln.[5] Once when a street urchin shouted
'Abe' at Lincoln, he was astonished although amused.[6] When
speaking of Lincoln, however, although not in his presence, he
was generally referred to as 'Uncle Abe.' [7] He was often spoken
of as 'Old Abe' and 'Honest Old Abe,' in the correspondence
of friendly newspapers during his political contests.[8] Lincoln
called a few by their first names, as Lamon, whom Lincoln called
'Hill,' [9] and Herndon whom he usually called 'William,' and
sometimes 'Billy.'

If there was a show of any kind in town, Lincoln never failed
to go. At Danville, one night, he was absent from the usual
gathering in Judge Davis's room. After Davis and Whitney had
gone to bed Lincoln came in and told them he had been to an
entertainment where he saw a 'magic lantern' by which 'wonderful sights, and transformations' were shown. There were an
'electrical machine,' too, and other marvels. Lincoln described

---

[1] Whitney, 41.   [2] *Recollections:* Lamon, 16.

[3] Gillespie to Herndon, Jan. 31, 1866, Weik MSS. 'Mr. Lincoln was undemonstrative ... so he was sometimes misunderstood. He was by some considered cold hearted
or at least indifferent towards his friends.' Gillespie to Herndon, Dec. 8, 1866. Weik
MSS.

[4] Hill, 174–5.   [5] Whitney, 53; Judge Weldon to Hill: Hill, 175.

[6] Hill, 175.   [7] Whitney, 53.

[8] For example, *Chicago Tribune*, Sept. 14, 1858: 'Old Abe in Montgomery County.'
The *Tribune* published Lincoln's biography in 1860 under the title of 'HONEST OLD
ABE, PEOPLES CANDIDATE.' *Ib.*, May 19, 1860. That paper announced the Republican
victory as 'HONEST OLD ABE ELECTED.' *Ib.*, Nov. 7, 1860.

[9] Whitney, 53.

all the features of 'that primitive show,' relates Whitney, 'with as much zest and enthusiasm as a school-boy would have done.' The next night he went again to witness 'an entire change of programme.' [1]

Negro minstrels were his especial delight. When trying the 'sand bar' case in Chicago, in 1860, he went with Whitney to a performance of Rumsey and Newcomb's Minstrels and heard 'Dixie,' then sung for the first time in that city. Lincoln, pleased with and applauding everything at the show, was enthusiastic over 'Dixie' and loudly called for a repetition of it.[2] Thus began his fondness for the Southern song which we shall see him manifest in significant fashion at a dramatic and critical hour.[3]

Lincoln preferred going alone to shows. Once at Bloomington, for instance, when he, Stuart, and Whitney were together at the hotel, Lincoln went by himself, although Stuart also was in the audience.[4] A company of singers, calling themselves 'the Newhall Family,' regularly visited several towns in the Eighth Circuit, and Lincoln always attended their concerts.[5] He greatly liked one of the troupe, Mrs. Lois E. Hillis, and wrote out and gave her the poem 'Mortality' which he had recited for her at the hotel on the previous evening. Mrs. Hillis, he declared, was 'the only woman that ever appreciated me enough to pay me a compliment.'[6]

Not only were his stories funnier and more pointed than those told by the others, his wit keener, his remarks shrewder, but he was the best liked of all the company.[7] There was little envy or jealousy in Lincoln, and he generously praised his rivals.[8] It is

[1] Whitney, 132.

[2] *Ib.*, 87–8. It was 'the most extravagant minstrel performance I ever saw. Lincoln was perfectly "taken" with it; and clapped his great hands, demanding an *encore*, louder than anyone. I never saw him so enthusiastic.'

[3] In April, 1865. Whitney, 89.

[4] *Ib.*, 51; Whitney's statement, no date. Weik MSS.

[5] 'If they struck a town where Lincoln happened to be, he would invariably arrange his affairs so that he could be at the church or town hall in time to attend their entertainment. No trial, consultation or business engagement of any kind was allowed to interfere.' Whitney's statement to Weik. Weik, 76; Whitney to Weik, Aug. 27, 1887. Weik MSS.

[6] Whitney, 51; Whitney to Herndon, Aug. 27, 1887. Weik MSS.

[7] Washburne: Rice, 14; Weldon: *ib.*, 197.

[8] Whitney's statement. Weik MSS.

impossible for us to realize the spell he exercised by sheer personal presence, impossible to realize the irresistible quality of his stories, or the pungency of his humor, or the depth of his philosophy. When read, the tales he told appear to be commonplace and sometimes repellent, his humor flat, his comment neither unusual nor profound; but when vitalized and lighted by his presence and personality, all he said had compelling effect upon his companions, a sort of wizardry, not to be understood nor even apprehended by those who never saw nor heard him. Yet Herndon assures us that other lawyers in Springfield were jealous of Lincoln as his practice grew.[1]

Even to his friends Lincoln's irruptions of humor were as incomprehensible as his long and abysmal periods of despair. Both his glee and melancholy were colossal, like cataclysms of nature, vast, without restraint, wholly abnormal and wholly fascinating. Those who were oftenest with him, disagree in their attempts to analyze his mind and character. Judge O. T. Reeves of Bloomington, who met Lincoln frequently from March, 1855, until his nomination for the presidency and often tried cases with him, says that Lincoln's personality was 'complex and not easy of solution.' [2]

Whitney thought that Lincoln was hugely 'uneven,' 'eccentric,' without balance or proportion.[3] Gillespie, on the contrary, was sure that no element of his nature was preponderant, but that having all the qualities of the average man and in the average proportion, in Lincoln those qualities were magnified tremendously.[4] The mystical Herndon found the miraculous in his inexplicable partner.[5] But none of them understood Lincoln,

[1] Herndon, II, 356.

[2] Judge O. T. Reeves in *Bloomington Pantagraph*, March 13, 1909.

[3] Whitney, 147–8. 'I repeat that his was one of the most uneven eccentric and heterogeneous characters. . . . One of the most obvious of Mr. Lincoln's peculiarities was his dissimilitude of qualities, or inequality of conduct, his dignity of deportment and action, interspersed with freaks of frivolity and inanity; his high aspiration and achievement, and his descent into the most primitive vales of listlessness, and the most ridiculous buffoonery.'

[4] Gillespie to Herndon, Jan. 31, 1866. Weik MSS.

[5] Herndon's lecture: Weik 104–5. 'To me he was ever imperturbable and mysterious.' 'Lincoln was a curious, mysterious, quite an incomprehensible man.' Herndon to Bartlett, Feb. 27, 1891. MS. Mass. Hist. Socy. This letter is one of the last Herndon ever wrote. He died a fortnight afterwards. Note by Bartlett on top of MS.

none really knew him. Perhaps no one ever understood him, or ever will understand him. After decades of that contact which is possible only between trusted partners and after twenty-two years of reflection succeeding that partnership, Herndon's puzzled and hopeless conclusion was that 'Lincoln is unknown and possibly always will be.' [1]

For he was secretive, reserved, infinitely cautious. 'He was a hidden man and wished to keep his own secrets,' asserts Herndon. When on the circuit, and indeed, in Springfield also, he was singularly taciturn about his own affairs. 'This terribly reticent, secretive, shut-mouth man never talked much about his history, plans, designs, purposes, intents, and when a man tells you this or that about what Lincoln said, believe what you *must* and no more,' was the information and advice Herndon gave Bartlett when gathering data for his volume on Lincoln.[2] 'I knew the man so well: he was the most reticent, secretive man I ever saw or expect to see,' said Davis to Herndon.[3] These qualities we shall see strikingly displayed while Lincoln was President. For historical purposes they are more important than his humor or his gloom. There was no dash in him, no gallantry of spirit. In the ordinary affairs of life he took no chances, hazarded nothing. Yet, as we shall see, at the greatest crisis of our history, this seemingly hesitant and overly sure-footed man made tremendous decisions and risked mightily.

He would not commit himself in casual talk as to his views on important questions. Particularly silent was he when the subject of religion was broached. Even to those most familiar with him and oftenest and most intimately in his company, he made no slightest mention of his religious opinions. Lincoln never spoke about such matters to Davis, or Whitney, or Swett, or Fell.[4] 'I never heard him mention religion at all,' asserts

[1] Herndon to Bartlett, Sept. 22, 1887. MS. Mass. Hist. Socy.

[2] Same to same, Aug. 22, Sept. 22, 1887. MS. Mass. Hist. Socy.

[3] Davis's statement, Sept. 20, 1866. Weik MSS.
'I watched the man closely for 30 years — 20 of which were just across this table, 10 × 3 ft. .... He was incommunicative, silent, reticent, secretive.' Herndon to Bartlett, Oct., 1887. MS. Mass. Hist. Socy.

[4] For other notices of his opinions on religion, see p. 301, *supra*.

Whitney.[1] Jesse Fell of Normal, Illinois, whose personal relations with Lincoln make his testimony convincing, notes that 'Mr. Lincoln seldom communicated to any one his views on this subject.' [2]

Judge Davis declares: 'I don't know anything about Lincoln's Religion — don't think anybody knew.' [3] His neighbor in Springfield, James Gourley, to whom Lincoln talked as familiarly and with as little reticence as he talked to any one except Herndon, was of like opinion. 'Had he ever had a change of heart, religiously speaking, he would have told me about it,' insists Gourley; 'he couldn't have avoided it.' [4] G. O. Brown who often talked to Lincoln says that he 'never heard Lincoln say anything about his religious views — or religion in any aspect.' [5]

The only exception is that related by Father Chiniquy, of Kankakee County, 'a recusant Catholic priest,' as Whitney calls him. This loquacious clerical, who was always in trouble with somebody and was expelled from the priesthood, asserts that Lincoln confided to him, in the most unreserved fashion, his deep religious faith. The occasion for this revelation of Lincoln's views which he kept from everyone else, was a theatrical trial in which Lincoln was one of the attorneys for the bustling and pugnacious priest. In a part of Kankakee County was a settlement of French Catholics of which Chiniquy was pastor. He was also the 'proprietor' of a village called St. Anne's. One of his flock, Peter Spink, whom Whitney describes as 'a French gentleman of high honor and chivalric disposition,' and who certainly was a man of substance and standing, was 'proprietor' of another village, L'Erable in Iroquois County. In a sermon at this hamlet Chiniquy denounced Spink as a perjurer. The enraged Spink sued the priest for slander, and Chiniquy took a change of venue to Champaign County.

Picturesque was the sight in and about Urbana when the case came on for trial. The French inhabitants of St. Anne's and

---

[1] Whitney's statement. Weik MSS.
[2] Fell to Lamon, Sept. 22, 1870. Weik MSS.
[3] Davis's statement, Sept. 20, 1866. Weik MSS.
[4] Gourley's statement, no date. Weik MSS.
[5] Brown's statement, no date, but 1866. Weik MSS.

L'Erable attended en masse. Taverns were crowded, and families camped near the town. Spink had the best three lawyers in Champaign County and Chiniquy had four, Swett and Lincoln among them. The testimony, given in French, was translated by a young attorney from Kankakee, named Brosseau. When the lengthy trial was nearly over, word was brought that a juror's child was dying, the jury was dismissed and the case set for the next term. Again came the throng, again 'the camp-outfits, musicians, parrots, pet dogs and all.' But after the jury was chosen, Lincoln effected a compromise, which consisted in Chiniquy's retracting his charge against Spink and making the written apology entered in the court records.[1]

From this association Chiniquy boasted of intimate friendship with Lincoln. After Lincoln's death, in the first blaze of his fame, Chiniquy wrote an account of revelations about his destiny which he claimed Lincoln confided to his client. Whitney fairly snorted with angry disgust when told of it. It was, he said, mere 'sickly sentimentality. . . . That was not like Lincoln and I doubt if it ever happened.'[2] Judge Davis, before whom the whole proceedings were held, is positive and emphatic. The idea that he told his religious views to any one was absurd.[3]

During the term of court at each county seat the people came in from every township. Court week in spring and autumn was the gala season for the farmers and their families. At such times the whole country bought provisions for the next six months.[4] They came to town in big wagons filled with women and children. At these gatherings, everything of interest was talked about — the merits of this case and of that, who was the best lawyer, who the best pleader. But above all else, politics was the subject of conversation, argument, and dispute. Lawyers everywhere in Illinois during court week made political speeches for their respective parties after court had adjourned for the day.[5]

Usually there was a speech by a Democrat and one by a Whig, or a Republican after 1856, a form of joint debate. Lincoln was

---

[1] Whitney, 53–5; Weik, 162.
[2] Whitney's statement, no date, but in Whitney's handwriting. Weik MSS.
[3] Davis's statement, Sept. 20, 1866. Weik MSS.
[4] Whitney, 42.   [5] Linder, 248.

always in demand and always in readiness. His humor, logic, droll stories and information, simple statement and apt illustration captivated the crowds of farmers.[1] In such fashion, and entirely aside from his frequent political debates on the stump during campaigns, Lincoln had a thorough schooling in this kind of public controversy, for, first and last, he rode the circuit for more than twenty years.

Thus Lincoln came to know, personally, more men, women, and children in Central Illinois than any other man, or with the possible exception of Judge Davis, than any dozen men combined. He called hundreds by their first names; [2] and he usually was acquainted with most and sometimes with each member of every jury before which he tried a case, and he always knew the leading men.[3] The advantage given Lincoln by this personal acquaintance and friendship with nearly every man who could be empanelled annoyed opposing counsel, but they never could overcome that advantage. Once when examining a jury a hostile lawyer tried to exclude one of them because of this circumstance, and Lincoln retorted sharply and with quick wit.

'Do you know Lincoln?' the lawyer asked of the juror. The court said that that inquiry was improper.

When his turn came to question the jury, Lincoln asked if the man knew the opposing attorney, and again the Judge admonished that such a fact was no disqualification.

'No, your Honor,' Lincoln replied mildly: 'but I am afraid some of the gentlemen may *not* know him, which would place me at a disadvantage.' [4]

The people believed what Lincoln said — or, rather, believed that he was sincere. This fact is often stated in political letters to the newspapers at that time. 'Such has become the established integrity of Lincoln with us,' writes the local correspondent of the *Chicago Tribune* in his account of a political meeting addressed by Lincoln at Danville, 'that let a jury be empanelled from any part of our populous county, to try a cause, and they will take his exposition of the law and the facts

---

[1] James S. Ewing's Recollections, in Bloomington High School *Ægis*, Feb., 1906, 69.
[2] Stringer, 212.   [3] Weldon: Rice, 200.
[4] Judge Weldon to Hill: Hill, 214-5.

of a case without a scruple; for they know that as Lincoln has never misconstrued the law, nor perverted the evidence, they can follow him and do no wrong. And when a man brings that kind of a reputation on the hustings, his power with the people is almost omnipotent.'[1]

The opinion of Judges and lawyers as to Lincoln's honesty was as high as that of juries. Lincoln was 'the fairest lawyer I ever knew,' declares Justice Sidney Breese of the Supreme Court.[2] Whether arguing to the Bench, speaking to juries, or addressing audiences, he was so just that all who heard him made note of it.[3] 'I have often listened to him when I thought he would certainly state his case out of court,' relates Gillespie; and cites an instance where Lincoln abandoned a case in which Gillespie was opposed to him, rather than 'attempt to bolster up a false position.'[4] John Dean Caton, Chief Justice of the Supreme Court of Illinois during much of the time that Lincoln practised before that tribunal, testifies that 'he seemed entirely ignorant of the art of deception or of dissimulation. His frankness and candor were two great elements in his character which contributed to his professional success.'[5]

These formal tributes to Lincoln prepared for the public are sustained by the more robust words in a private letter of Herndon. 'He was all honor — full of manly integrity ... truly a noble man.'[6]

Judge S. C. Parks of Lincoln, Illinois, who practised for many years in some of the same courts with Lincoln, avers that he never saw so honest a man; and he adds that this was true of Lincoln as a politician as well as a lawyer.[7] Judge W. W.

---

[1] *Chicago Tribune*, Sept. 27, 1858. Lincoln 'was a marvel of fairness in debate both in the courts and in the political arena and he never desired to obtain an unfair advantage.' Gillespie to Herndon, Dec. 8, 1866. Weik MSS.

[2] Illinois Supreme Court *Memorial*, May 3, 1865; Hill, 315.

[3] T. R. King's statement, no date. Weik MSS.

[4] Gillespie to Herndon, Jan. 31, 1866. Weik MSS.
The case was Buckmaster for the use of Denham *vs.* Beems and Arthur in the Supreme Court. 'Another gentleman less fastidious took Mr. Lincoln's place and gained the case.'

[5] Ill. Supreme Court *Memorial*. Hill, 314.

[6] Herndon to Bartlett, July 8, 1887. MS. Mass. Hist. Socy.

[7] Parks to Herndon, March 25, 1866. Weik MSS.

Thomas, in whose Court Lincoln appeared in several counties, says that he was positively distinguished for his fairness and candor.[1] Judge Drummond of the United States District Court, declares that Lincoln 'never intentionally misrepresented the evidence of a witness or the argument of an opponent,' nor 'misstated the law, according to his own intelligent views of it.' [2] Whitney, who was associated with him in many cases, states that 'Lincoln's honesty was excellent stock-in-trade to him, and brought success and victory often.' [3]

To be sure, the uprightness of any reputable lawyer may be taken for granted, and, as a general thing, the introduction of character witnesses is unnecessary. But all who knew and worked with Lincoln place such emphasis on this quality, that particular note of it must be made in any attempt to portray his character. While not so dramatic as the melancholy which clung to him day and night like a black and evil spirit, his integrity was of such a peculiar nature that associates and observers, without exception, go out of their way to speak of it — speak strongly and at length. Quotations of the kind would fill a fair sized volume.

Judge Davis, who was as good a business man as he was a fine lawyer and a great Judge, sometimes left the bench for several days to attend to personal affairs, and he would ask some informed and trusted attorney to take his place on the bench.[4] Thus he would have Lincoln act as Judge during his absences. Whitney's first motion in Court as a very young lawyer was heard before Lincoln when acting as Judge in Davis's place.[5] Trials were frequently held before him; but he never would preside unless the lawyers for both sides requested him to do so.[6] Of course such substitution of a member of the bar for the elected Judge upon his mere request, was not legal, and reversals were secured on that ground in two cases thus heard by Lincoln.[7]

It is related that once when an argument to the jury was being made in a case tried before him, Lincoln left the bench, went

[1] Thomas to Herndon, Nov. 1, 1866. Weik MSS.
[2] Whitney, 257.   [3] *Ib.*, 263.
[4] *Ib.*, 63–4.   [5] *Ib.*, 31.
[6] Weldon in Hill: Hill, 188–9.   [7] Whitney, 263.

to the back of the court-room where he told funny stories to the auditors who promptly gathered about him. Sometimes Davis would get Lincoln to take his place for an hour, sometimes for a day and, at times, for an entire term.[1] He once held court for Davis at Urbana for a period of ten days. A case of much local importance was pending,[2] involving the payment of notes given by well-to-do citizens for the establishment of a newspaper, and transferred to innocent holders by the journalistic promoter who then fled the country. There was no defence, and the debtors employed the youngest attorneys to do the best they could; they tried to postpone the trial and succeeded up to the hour for final adjournment of court for that term, the plaintiff all the while pressing for judgment.

At last Lincoln said he would hear the case at 'candle light.' He did so, and, finding no defence wrote the order giving judgment: 'Ordered by the Court: Plea in abatement [filed that day] by . . . a defendant not served . . . be stricken from the files by order of Court. Demurrer to declaration, if ever there was one, overruled.[3] Defendants, who are served now, at 8 o'clock P.M. of the last day of the term, ask to plead to the merits, which is denied by the Court, on the ground that the offer comes too late, and therefore, as by *nil dicit*, judgment is rendered for plaintiff. Clerk assess damages.'

'How can we get this up to the Supreme Court?' asked Whitney.

'You all have been so smart about this case that you can find out for yourselves how to carry it up,' Lincoln retorted and adjourned court.[4]

Lincoln's honesty was so striking that those who came in contact with him were impressed by it in an unaccountable fashion — unaccountable because many other men were as honest as he. But the manifestation of that quality in Lincoln was so unlike the same characteristic in others, that everybody who knew him felt called upon to assert it particularly and with

---

[1] Whitney, 263.   [2] Chaddon *vs*. Beasly *et al*.

[3] Whitney, who was one of the youthful attorneys, had said while Lincoln was writing the order of court, that a demurrer *had* been filed.

[4] Whitney, 263–4.

emphasis. And it should be said again that the esteem in which he was held for truthfulness and integrity was a priceless possession in that political career to which the remainder of this work will be devoted — a career without precedent or parallel in our history.

Only once was Lincoln's trustworthiness ever challenged, and he was quick and hot in his response. Robert Todd, the father of Mrs. Lincoln, died in 1849, and in 1853 his estate was finally settled. That part of the proceeds which went to his daughters in Springfield [1] was paid to their lawyer in Kentucky, George B. Kinkead. Todd had been a member of the firm of Oldham, Todd and Company, manufacturers of cotton goods. Before Kinkead paid Mrs. Lincoln her share of her father's estate, the remaining partners, Oldham and Hemingway, sued Lincoln in the Circuit Court of Fayette County, Kentucky, for nearly five hundred dollars, the amount, as they alleged, of claims that the firm had sent Lincoln for collection and which he had collected and kept.[2]

Lincoln was attending court at Danville, 'a hundred and thirty miles from home,' when his brother-in-law, Ninian W. Edwards, sent him a copy of a letter from Kinkead telling the Todd heirs at Springfield of this suit against Lincoln. Instantly Lincoln wrote the Kentucky lawyer: 'I find it difficult to suppress my indignation towards those who have got up this claim against me.' How was Hemingway 'induced to *swear* he *believed* the claim to be just!' Lincoln enclosed his answer and demanded that a bill of particulars be filed 'stating *names* and *residences*,' so that he could 'absolutely disprove the claim. . . . If they will name any living accessible man, as one of whom I have received their money, I will *by that man* disprove the charge. I know it is for *them* to prove their claim, rather than for *me* to disprove it; but I am unwilling to trust the oath of any man, who either *made* or prompted the oath to the Petition.' [3]

Oldham and Hemingway making no reply, Lincoln again wrote Kinkead. Still nothing was done and a third time Lincoln

---

[1] Mrs. Lincoln, Mrs. Wallace, Mrs. Edwards, and Mrs. Smith.

[2] *Litigant:* Townsend, 107, and more fully in *Abraham Lincoln, Defendant,* by the same writer.

[3] Lincoln to Kinkead, May 27, 1853. *Litigant:* Townsend, 108–9.

enquired of his Kentucky lawyer: 'This matter harasses my feelings a good deal;' won't Kinkead answer 'immediately.' Kinkead wrote Lincoln that his brother-in-law, Levi Todd, had said, and would so state in court, that Lincoln had told him that he owed the amount for which Robert Todd's partners had sued him — an assertion which astounded Lincoln. Finally the items were filed, Lincoln took depositions at Springfield, Shelbyville, and Beardstown, and disproved every claim made, and in 1854, Oldham and Hemingway had their complaint dismissed.[1]

Such was the single instance that has been discovered where Lincoln's integrity was so much as questioned in his quarter of a century at the bar, and such was his prompt and crushing defence of his reputation. While unblemished honor is a pre-eminent element of his character, undue effort has been made, perhaps, to extend his peculiar reputation over every incident of his life as a lawyer; and he is represented to us as a sort of heavenly agent of justice, succoring the unfortunate in earthly courts and scourging the unworthy. 'I was attorney for the Illinois Central Railway from Iroquois county to Effingham,' relates Whitney, 'and . . . in Davis's circuit I employed Lincoln when I needed aid; . . . and I never found any difficulty in Lincoln's appearing for a "great soulless corporation" (as was always urged against us) and making the best of the case — for they always were in tort, and were for alleged carelessness of our employes, therefore, always doubtful. In such cases he always stood manfully by me, and I always, of course, tried to win. He was not therefore a milk-sop, nor did he peer unnecessarily into a case in order to find some reason to act out of the usual line; but he had the same animus ordinarily as any lawyer, as a rule.' [2]

In short, Lincoln's treatment of clients and associate lawyers was like that of most high-minded and honorable attorneys. He sometimes refused employment in a case that he might have won, but the winning of which would have hurt innocent persons, just as thousands of other humane lawyers have rejected the proffer of like employment.[3] 'In a clear case of dishonesty,'

---

[1] Lincoln to Kinkead, Sept. 13, 1853. *Litigant:* Townsend, 110–2.

[2] Whitney, 261–2.

[3] The only basis for the touching story of Lincoln's rejecting a case which he could

says Whitney, Lincoln 'would hedge . . . so as to not, himself, partake of the dishonesty. In a doubtful case of dishonesty, he would give his client the benefit of the doubt, and in an ordinary case he would try the case . . . like any other lawyer.' [1]

Once or twice Lincoln withdrew from a trial when he found that his client had deceived him or that the case, though legally valid, was immoral — an experience not uncommon to scrupulous lawyers everywhere and in all times. But he was no knight-errant of the law seeking out the poor and distressed in order to lift up and relieve them, scorning the service of powerful and rich that he might be free to assail them. He accepted what came to him, provided it was not morally bad, and did his best for his client.[2]

He once brought suit for a client to collect an account. At the trial the defendant produced a receipt in full; Lincoln left the court room; the Judge called for him; he was found in the tavern washing his hands and refused to return. 'Tell the Judge that I can't come — *my hands are dirty and I came over to clean them.*' [3] From this incident that trial became locally famous as 'The Dirty Hands Case' and strengthened Lincoln's repute for honesty throughout Logan County.[4] In no other case, however, does it appear that Lincoln took such peremptory action. Generally speaking, he did not retire from a case when in the course of the trial he found himself in the wrong, did not desert associates, did not give up fees, did not try both sides in the interest of justice.[5]

For instance, a murder case in Champaign County [6] was celebrated, and the best available lawyers were employed to assist the prosecuting attorney. The accused, a saloon keeper, had rich relatives and friends, and Swett, Whitney, and Lincoln were retained to defend him. The trial was held before Judge Davis.

have won and unctuously lecturing the man who offered to employ him, is an unsigned, undated fragment without names, but in Herndon's handwriting. It is in the Weik collection. Yet this incident, thus casually and vaguely described, has become imbedded in the mass of untrustworthy Lincolniana. The original version, signed 'Lord' and of a date about 1866, is in Herndon, II, 345 *n.*

[1] Whitney, 263.   [2] *Ib.*, 262–3.

[3] S. C. Parks to Herndon, March 25, 1866. Weik MSS.

[4] Stringer, 217.   [5] Whitney, 262–3.   [6] People *vs.* Patterson.

Lincoln became convinced that his client was guilty. Indeed, 'we all thought so,' says Whitney. Lincoln said to his principal colleague: 'The man was guilty. Swett you defend him. I can't.' [1] But he did not abandon the case. 'Lincoln made the closing speech,' declares Whitney, 'and I can to this day repeat almost verbatim a part of his speech.' [2] Patterson was convicted, and Lincoln accepted his share of one third of the fee.[3]

Lincoln appeared in cases of directly opposite characters, and strove as vigorously in one as the other. For instance at the trial of several women, indicted in Clinton County for having knocked in the head of a whisky barrel and spilled the contents, he was asked to say a word in their defence. Although not employed in the case, he did so; and it is recalled that he told the jury that the indictment should read 'The State vs. Mr. Whiskey instead of The State vs. The Ladies,' and inveighed dramatically against the evils of strong drink.[4]

On the other hand, Lincoln made an exhaustive argument in the Supreme Court in defence of a saloon keeper, one Patrick Sullivan, who had been indicted, convicted, and fined ten dollars in the Macon Circuit Court, for selling liquor without license. The case involved the construction of the liquor laws of 1845, 1851, and 1853. From the unanimous opinion of the Court, which decided every point against Lincoln's contentions, the case appears to have been uncommonly clear; but the abstract of Lincoln's argument in the report of the case indicates that he did his utmost to have the laws so construed that a person could not be fined for selling intoxicants without license.[5]

This case is the most curious and, seemingly, inexplicable, that Lincoln ever had. The amount involved was only ten dollars and the mere costs of appeal exceeded that sum. Lincoln appeared alone for Sullivan. The facts of record strongly indicate that the wholesale grocers of Springfield, the most pro-

---

[1] Judge Davis's statement, Sept. 19, 1866. Weik MSS.   [2] Whitney, 130–2.

[3] Davis's statement, Sept. 19, 1866. Weik MSS.; Whitney, 262.

[4] Herndon, ii, 343.

[5] Sullivan vs. The People: 15 Ill., 233–5. In the course of the opinion the Court says: 'It was the design [of the Legislature] not only to restore the authority to grant licenses, but the power to inflict punishments for retailing liquors without license. . . . A different view of the case would impeach the wisdom of the Legislature.'

fitable part of whose business was the sale of liquor to saloon keepers in Central Illinois, were back of the appeal by Sullivan to the Supreme Court. As we have seen, Jacob Bunn, Lincoln's client and personal friend, was one of these wholesale liquor dealers.

In trials in Circuit Courts Lincoln depended but little on precedents; he argued largely from first principles.[1] When speaking to juries he took great pains to make himself understood.[2] He spoke directly and exclusively to them.[3] His statements were very clear, very simple, his sentences short, compact, and distinct, his words plain and familiar. In brief, he spoke the language of the jurymen, the speech of the people.[4] And he centred attention upon the one crucial point in the case — he 'never let it escape the jury,' declares an associate who heard Lincoln try more than a hundred cases.[5] He took pains that the jury never should be confused, never required to have in mind too many points.

Lincoln was skilful in the questioning of witnesses and uncommonly clever in the difficult and dangerous art of cross-examination. He never made notes of testimony, but remembered every word of it.[6] He never asked an unnecessary question,[7] never brow-beat witnesses, never attempted to confuse or distract or alarm them. Instead he tried in a gentle and friendly fashion to assist the witness to tell the facts — provided he thought that the witness was honest and truthful. But if he believed that the witness was lying or trying to dodge his questions, or to impose on the jury in any way, he became severe and merciless.[8] Yet in the conduct of the most exciting case Lincoln never displayed emotion; perfectly calm, he appeared to be without either enthusiasm or apprehension.[9]

[1] This was true generally. 'Causes were tried on principle rather than precedent.' Judge R. M. Benjamin, in *Bloomington Pantagraph*, Feb. 23, 1909.

[2] 'If Mr. Lincoln studied any one thing more than another and for effect it was to make himself understood by all classes.' Gillespie to Herndon, Dec. 8, 1866. Weik MSS.

[3] Whitney, 260.   [4] Weldon: Rice, 203.

[5] E. M. Prince of Bloomington in Hill; Hill, 211-2.

[6] Whitney, 250.   [7] James S. Ewing to Hill: Hill, 222.

[8] Weldon in Hill: Hill, 222.

[9] Whitney, 253.

Most lawyers are stronger in the conduct of cases when they feel that they are in the right, and this was so conspicuously true of Lincoln that judges, lawyers, juries, and auditors particularly observed it. Some go so far as to say that he could not do well unless he felt that he was on the side of justice. Judge Davis states that Lincoln was 'great in court anywhere if he thought he was right.'[1] When he felt that a client was oppressed, his denunciation of the wrongdoer is described by hearers as 'terrible' and 'terrific.' He once scourged the slanderer of a woman school-teacher in Petersburg in such fashion that his philippic was remembered for a generation.[2]

Even a judge did not escape Lincoln's wrath whose rulings he thought unjust and personally prejudiced. Herndon wrote Weik two long pages in the attempt to describe Lincoln's castigation of the court for a vital decision on a point in the hard fought Quinn Harrison murder case. It 'was terrible, blasting, crushing, withering,' says Herndon. 'I shall never forget the scene. Lincoln had the crowd, the Jury, the Bar in perfect sympathy and accord.' Yet in the whirlwind of his anger, Lincoln kept 'just inside the walls of the law — did not do or say anything . . . that would be a contempt of Court.'[3]

This trial is cited as an example of Lincoln's influence over juries. 'Peachy' Harrison, as he was known, was the grandson of Peter Cartwright, Lincoln's opponent for Congress in 1846. In a fight at a country village the youth had fatally stabbed another young man, Greek Crafton. Harrison's father, a rich man, employed four lawyers, among them Lincoln, to defend his son. At a dramatic moment Lincoln put the aged Cartwright on the stand and drew from him a story of his visit to the dying youth. Crafton had told him, said Cartwright, that he forgave his assailant and prayed that Harrison would not be held responsible for his death. How Lincoln ever induced the court to admit such evidence does not appear; but, exclusively upon this pathetic recital, he made the appeal that cleared 'Peachy' Harrison.

---

[1] Judge Davis's statement, Sept. 19, 1866. Weik MSS. 'When he thought he was wrong he was the weakest lawyer I ever saw.' S. C. Parks to Herndon, March 25, 1866. Weik MSS.

[2] S. C. Parks to Herndon, March 25, 1866. Weik MSS.

[3] Herndon to Weik, Nov. 20, 1883. Weik MSS.

Lincoln pleaded with the jury to act in the magnanimous spirit of the deceased, and not to burden with woe the last days of the tottering, white-haired minister.[1]

Lincoln would turn cheap and insincere appeal to juries upon the lawyer who made them. When, with Whitney, he was defending a railroad company in a damage suit, the plaintiff's attorney said the usual things about the client's having a soul and the corporation none. As reported by Whitney, Lincoln replied thus: 'Counsel avers that his client has a *soul*. This is possible, of course; but from the way he has testified under oath in this case, to gain, or hope to gain, a few paltry dollars he would sell, nay, has already sold, his little soul very low. But our client is but a conventional name for thousands of widows and orphans whose husbands' and parents' hard earnings are represented by this defendant, and who possess souls which they would not swear away as the plaintiff has done for ten million times as much as is at stake here.'[2]

Ridicule was a favorite weapon of Lincoln, and in its use he was not delicate, but chose words and illustrations that appealed to the juries of that time and place. But he knew when to stop; for that gifted, natural actor never overdid his part, and by that means he often won a seemingly hopeless case.

Thus, throughout the fifties, went Lincoln over the circuit, thus he tried cases, thus he appeared in Springfield, strange, contradictory, inexplicable, engaging; and we shall now hear him as he defends 'Duff' Armstrong, witness his rough treatment by eminent lawyers, examine his celebrated suit for his biggest fee, behold him as the champion of Chicago and the great railway interests, and review his work as the most successful lawyer in Illinois before the Supreme Court of that State.

[1] Herndon to Weik, November 20, 1883. Weik MSS. Also Hill, 236–7. The case was tried in the Circuit Court of Sangamon County at Springfield, in 1859. J. B. White, John M. Palmer, N. M. Broadwell, and Isaac Cogdale were for the prosecution. Besides Lincoln for the defence, were Herndon, Logan, and Shelby M. Cullom, then just beginning to practice. The case aroused wide attention and was fully reported in the *Illinois State Journal*, Sept. 1, 2, 3, and 5, 1859.

[2] Whitney, 258–9.

CHAPTER X

LAST YEARS AT THE BAR

'Such has become the established integrity of Lincoln with us, that let a jury be empanelled from any part of our populous county, to try a cause, and they will take his exposition of the law and the facts of a case without a scruple.' Campaign correspondence from Danville, Ill., *Chicago Tribune*, Sept. 27, 1858.

MANY lawyers and judges in Illinois became rich men during the period before the Civil War; but their wealth was not acquired by practising law or administering justice. It was obtained, chiefly, through wise and far-seeing investments,[1] for professional earnings were moderate.

Fees of lawyers and doctors were on a scale with wages, salaries, prices, and the cost of living. From 1850 to 1860 laborers were paid from seventy-five cents to a dollar and five cents for a day of eleven or twelve hours.[2] The price of land throughout the decade varied from a dollar and twenty-five cents — or even lower — for virgin tracts to five dollars an acre for improved farms.[3] Charges at country taverns were·trifling. E. M. Prince relates that for supper, lodging, and breakfast for Lincoln and himself, as well as the feed and stabling of two horses, the entire bill was seventy-five cents.[4] Twenty dollars for a suit of ready-made clothing was considered high. Once, when holding court for Davis, Lincoln decided that twenty-eight dollars was excessive for a suit bought on credit by the son of a prosperous farmer. 'I have very rarely in my life worn a suit of clothes costing $28,' he declared from the bench.[5]

---

[1] Thus Justice Caton, Judge Davis, and several lawyers like Stephen T. Logan, became wealthy men.

[2] *Era of the Civil War:* Arthur Charles Cole, 202.

[3] A little earlier, improved farm land in Central Illinois sold for five dollars per acre. *Personal Recollections of John M. Palmer*, 38-9.

[4] Statement of E. M. Prince, no date. Weik MSS.

[5] Swett to Herndon, Jan. 15, 1866. Weik MSS.
The case was heard by Lincoln at Clinton, DeWitt County. A merchant sold the clothes to the minor son of a 'fair farmer who owned a good farm.' The father had not authorized the purchase, refused to pay, and the merchant sued him. Swett says that 'the question was whether they were necessaries and suited to his condition in life. . . . I happened in court, just as Lincoln was giving his decision.'

Attorney fees ranged from fifty cents to a thousand dollars; and, as we shall see, Lincoln once received five times the larger sum, and in three other cases scarcely smaller amounts. He tried as hard as any other lawyer to get employment. He 'always displayed a commendable zeal and alacrity to obtain business,' testifies his faithful champion, Gillespie.[1] But he did not invest his earnings, as other alert lawyers about him did. He said that he did not know how to do it, and had no taste for speculation. He merely saved his fees and held what he got. Whitney states that Lincoln had 'no method, system or order in his ... affairs; ... had no commonplace book, ... no diary.' [2] When in 1850 and 1855 Congress granted 'bounty lands' to soldiers in all our wars,[3] Lincoln belatedly took out warrants for two parcels of land which he located in Iowa; and he kept that farm as long as he lived.[4] But, with the exception of his lot in Springfield and a lot in Lincoln, the county seat of Logan County, the Iowa farm is the only real estate he ever owned.[5]

[1] Gillespie to Herndon, Dec. 8, 1866. Weik MSS.

[2] Herndon, II, 346. Gillespie to Herndon, Jan. 31, 1866. Weik MSS. 'He was not a good business man, as the world understands that term.' Whitney, 110, 118.

[3] An attorney of Quincy, Ill., E. S. Greene, advertised that honorably discharged soldiers 'in *any* war' were, each, entitled to one hundred and sixty acres. *Quincy Whig*, March 17, 1855.

[4] Lincoln's land warrant under the Act of 1850, was No. 52076 for forty acres, issued April 16, 1852. The land was located July 21, 1854, by Lincoln's attorney John P. Davies, at Dubuque, Iowa, on the N.W. Quarter of S.W. Quarter of Sec. 20, Township 84 N. of Range 15 West. The patent to this tract, signed by Franklin Pierce, was issued to Lincoln, June 1, 1855.

The warrant under the Act of 1855 was No. 68645 for one hundred and twenty acres issued April 22, 1856, and located by Lincoln himself at Springfield, Dec. 27, 1859, on the E. half of the N.E. quarter and N.W. quarter of N.E. quarter of Sec. 18, Township 84 N. of Range 39 W. The patents to these tracts, signed by James Buchanan, were issued to Lincoln Sept. 10, 1860, in the midst of his campaign for the Presidency, and they were sent to the Register of the Land Office at Springfield for delivery to Lincoln Oct. 30, a week before his election. Records Gen. Land Office, Interior Dept., Washington.

Lincoln owned this Iowa land when he was assassinated; it descended to his heirs, and on March 22, 1892, was sold by Robert T. Lincoln, the only surviving heir, for $13,000, to Henry Edwards. Records Recorder's Office, Crawford County, Iowa.

[5] The lot in Lincoln came to him by accident. It was owned by James Primm, the most prominent citizen of Logan County. By overspeculation in lands Primm had become heavily indebted and, in 1857, he went to New York to raise money. Lincoln, who was also in New York at the time, endorsed Primm's note for four hundred dollars. When it fell due the maker could not pay and Lincoln took up the note. In turn, Primm on March 11, 1858, deeded the lot to his endorser, who kept it as long as he lived. Stringer, 221–2. The lot was No. 3, Block 19.

Exhaustive pains have been taken to exhume every possible instance of low charges made by him, his refusal of fees, his rendering of gratuitous services. The first fee he ever earned on the circuit, he refused, we are told, and when pressed to accept it, he gave it to his father.[1] 'You must think I am a high-priced man,' Lincoln wrote a client for whom he had secured a lease, and who had sent him a fee of twenty-five dollars. 'You are too liberal with your money. Fifteen dollars is enough for the job. I . . . return to you a ten dollar bill.'[2] He charged but two hundred dollars for winning a case involving a disputed title to a farm, when the opposing lawyer, who had lost, charged three hundred dollars, thinking that sum very small.[3] 'Don't you think I have honestly earned twenty-five dollars?' asked Lincoln of opposing counsel, after securing a verdict of six hundred dollars in a slander suit — four hundred dollars of which his client remitted on Lincoln's advice, the defendant to pay his fee. The trial, which was hotly contested, had lasted for two days, and the defeated lawyer thought that a hundred dollars was the smallest fee that Lincoln ought to charge, especially since his client had to pay it.[4]

Consideration of all trustworthy data, however, shows that Lincoln's fees were normal, except that his meticulous honesty would not permit him to overcharge. But his fees were by no means trifling. Even when in partnership with Stuart, that firm charged one fee of five hundred dollars and took notes for it, secured by mortgage on the client's farm.[5] He was as prompt and keen as anyone in collecting what he had earned. 'We *win* our . . . case,' he wrote to a client; 'as the Dutch justice said when he

[1] Statement of George B. Balch of Janesville, Ill., no date. Weik MSS.

[2] Lincoln to Geo. P. Floyd, Feb. 21, 1856. *Litigant:* Townsend, 4–5.

[3] John W. Bunn, quoted in Weik, 164–5.

[4] Dungey *vs.* Spencer. DeWitt Circuit Court, Clinton, 1855. Judge Weldon, quoted in Weik, 162–3.

This case is described as an example of Lincoln's cleverness in jury trials. Dungey was a swarthy, almost black, Portuguese and Spencer had said of him: 'Black Bill, is a negro and it will be easily proved if called for.'

One of Spencer's attorneys was C. H. Moore. In Lincoln's speech to the jury, Lincoln is reported to have exclaimed: 'My client is not a Negro. His skin may not be as white as ours, but I say he is not a Negro, though he may be a Moor.'

[5] Stringer, 213.

married folks, "Now vere ish my hundred tollars."' [1] Moreover
Lincoln and his partners sued clients for fees just as other lawyers sued their clients.[2] Yet Herndon assures us that Lincoln
was indifferent to the firm's finances, 'usually leaving all such to
me.' After his return from Congress, he never made an entry in
the account book of the partnership; and when a fee was paid to
him, he divided it with Herndon.[3]

Most fees were from ten to fifty dollars; nor did the nature of
the general run of cases and the work required in the conduct of
them deserve larger compensation.[4] Clients usually gave notes
for fees, and these were easily sold at a moderate discount by the
lawyers to merchants or tavern keepers in the county seat.[5]
Such fee notes constituted a kind of medium of exchange, a sort
of 'legal tender,' as Dennis Hanks said of coonskins and venison
hams in Indiana during Lincoln's boyhood and youth. In this
wise, enterprising lawyers often gathered considerable earnings.

[1] Lincoln to Andrew McCallen, July 4, 1851. *Litigant:* Townsend, 6.

[2] Lincoln *vs.* Spencer and William Turner, DeWitt Circuit Court, Clinton, 1841, on
fee note. *Ib.*, 7–8.

Logan & Lincoln *vs.* James D. Smith, Executor, will of William Trailor, deceased,
for $100, for defending Trailor against an indictment for murder. Sangamon Circuit
Court, Springfield, July term, 1845. *Ib.*, 8.

Same *vs.* John Atchison, same court, July 29, 1845, for fee of $200; verdict for $100.
Ib., 19.

Lincoln & Herndon *vs.* John B. Moffett, same Court, March term 1850 for $150 fee;
judgment for $75 and costs. *Ib.*, 20.

Lincoln *vs.* Samuel Brown, Justice of the Peace Court, for fee for defending Brown
against an indictment for shooting. *Ib.*, 20–1.

Lincoln *vs.* Samuel Sidner, Sangamon Circuit Court, Aug., 1854, on fee note and foreclosure. Judgment, Nov. 21, 1854, for $594.80. Lincoln bought property at foreclosure
sale, Feb. 5, 1855. *Ib.*, 21.

[3] Herndon, II, 333.

[4] 'It is strange to contemplate that in these comparatively recent, but primitive days,
Mr. Lincoln's whole attention should have been engrossed in petty controversies or
acrimonious disputes between neighbors about trifles; that he should have puzzled his
great mind in attempting to decipher who was the owner of a litter of pigs, or which
party was to blame for the loss of a flock of sheep, by foot-rot; or whether some irascible
spirit was justified in charging that his enemy had committed perjury; yet I have known
him to give as earnest attention to such matters, as, later, he gave to affairs of State.'
Whitney, 41.

A collection of cases on the circuit and in Justices of the Peace Courts which are
above the trivial may be found in Weik, 146–75. In their books, Hill and John T.
Richards, *Abraham Lincoln: The Lawyer Statesman*, also make mention of several cases
in the trial courts. All cases to which Lincoln was a party are set out in Mr. Townsend's
two books, *Lincoln Defendant*, and *Lincoln the Litigant*.

[5] Judge Caton says that, as a rule, a fee was a little cash and notes for the balance.

Chief Justice Caton relates that, at a single session of one court, when a very young lawyer, he accumulated a hundred and fifty dollars in 'good notes' and as much more in cash.[1] The notes of successful farmers or of others with substantial amounts of property had a steadier value than the bank paper in circulation.[2] So variable and untrustworthy was such currency that a little pamphlet, called a *Counterfeit Detector*, was indispensable to those who handled such money in even moderate quantities.[3]

Of the instances of Lincoln's championship of the needy without compensation, the most dramatic is the Wright case. A pension agent by the name of Wright had charged the widow of a Revolutionary soldier half her pension of four hundred dollars for getting her claim allowed. The old woman, 'crippled and bent with age,' went to Lincoln and Herndon with the story of her wrongs. Lincoln demanded of the agent the return of the money; he refused and Lincoln and Herndon sued him to compel a refund. At the trial the only witness Lincoln introduced was the widow who, weeping, told what Wright had done. In his speech to the jury Lincoln explained the causes of the Revolution, recounted the horrors of Valley Forge, extolled the suffering and heroism of the patriot soldiers, and then launched

---

Sometimes a horse or colt was brought in to be given as a fee and the lawyer led the animal home or sold it in the village. Where the title of land was in litigation the lawyer might make a contract with the client for half the land. Caton, 52, 80.

[1] Caton, 77.

[2] Very little metallic money was in circulation in Illinois during the 50's. The coinage was gold twenty-dollar, ten-dollar, and five-dollar pieces; silver one-dollar, fifty, twenty-five, and five-cent pieces; copper one and two-cent pieces. Two Mexican coins also circulated, the 'picayune,' or Spanish half-real of six and a quarter cents, and the 'bit,' or real of twelve and a half cents. Twenty-five cents was called '2 bits' and fifty cents '4 bits.' Johnson, 61–3.

In 1849 Speed directed Herndon to remit a collection either by 'Kentucky money or drafts on New York, Philadelphia, Baltimore, or Boston. Speed to Herndon ('Dear Bill'), July 24, 1849. Weik MSS.

[3] Counterfeiting was general throughout the decade. *Illinois State Register*, Nov. 21, 1850; *Ottawa Weekly Republican*, Jan. 23, 1858. Three dollar bills were altered to five dollar bills. *Quincy Whig*, April 24, 1854. The two dollar bills of the Grayville Bank were changed to ten dollars. *Alton Daily Courier*, March 26, 1859. Bogus half dollars were widely circulated. *Illinois State Journal*, Nov. 9, 1855. In 1855 counterfeiting became such a menace and a burden that the business men of Chicago held meetings to discuss means of avoiding it. *Chicago Daily Democrat*, Jan. 9, 1855. 'Wild Cat' currency was the commercial bane of the times. *Rockford Forum*, Dec. 15, 1852; *Illinois Journal*, Dec. 15, 1852; *Illinois State Register*, Dec. 23, 1852, and Jan. 6, 1853.

into a philippic against the robbers of their widows of whom Wright was a revolting example. Judge Davis says that Lincoln was 'merciless in his castigation,' and Herndon adds that 'I never, either on the stump or on other occasions in court, saw him so wrought up.'

He had made careful preparation for his appeal to the jury: 'No contract. Not professional services. Unreasonable charge. Money retained by Def't not given by Pl'ff. Revolutionary War. Describe Valley Forge privations. Ice — Soldier's bleeding feet. Pl'ff's husband. Soldier leaving home for army. *Skin Def't. Close*' — so run Lincoln's notes for his speech. His partner reproduces his peroration — the parting at the cabin home when the young soldier left for the army, the fond farewell to the lonely wife, the kissing of the baby in its cradle and other touching incidents of the patriot's departure. 'Time rolls by; the heroes of '76 have passed away and are encamped on the other shore. The soldier has gone to rest, and now, crippled, blinded, and broken, his widow comes to you and to me, gentlemen of the jury, to right her wrongs. She was not always thus. She was once a beautiful young woman. Her step was as elastic, her face as fair, her voice as sweet as any that rang in the mountains of old Virginia. But now she is poor and defenceless. Out here on the prairies of Illinois, many hundreds of miles away from the scenes of her childhood, she appeals to us, who enjoy the privileges achieved for us by the patriots of the Revolution, for our sympathetic aid and manly protection. All I ask is, shall we befriend her?'

Of course the jury, half of whom were 'in tears,' would befriend her, and they promptly returned a verdict against Wright who cowered in his chair 'writhing' under Lincoln's terrible invective. Lincoln paid his client's hotel bill and her fare home, and, when the judgment was collected, sent the aged woman all of it and charged her nothing for his services.[1]

On the other hand, Linder recalls that Lincoln, with other Springfield lawyers, defended a woman and her paramour who were indicted for poisoning her husband.[2]

Another engaging example of services rendered by Lincoln

[1] Herndon, II, 340–2.   [2] Logan, Stuart, and Edwards. Linder, 184–5.

without pay is his refusal to charge anything for saving the farm of a young woman, one Rebecca Daimwood. She inherited the land from an uncle, Christopher Robinson, the administrator of whose estate was a man of the name of John Lane. It would appear that the girl had made her home with Lane who had occupied the farm. Miss Daimwood married a young farmer, William M. Dorman, and claimed the land. Thereupon Lane petitioned the Court at Shawneetown for the sale of the property to satisfy his claim of a little more than a thousand dollars against Robinson's estate, which claim had been allowed him by the Court some fifteen years earlier.

The young married couple resisted Lane's petition, but were beaten in the trial court. Their attorney, Samuel D. Marshall, took an appeal to the Supreme Court and retained Lincoln to conduct the case in that tribunal. Lane was represented by Lyman Trumbull. Argument on both sides was thorough and Lincoln supported his points by the citation of many authorities. The Court in a long opinion sustained Lincoln's principal contentions and reversed the decree of the trial court. It is interesting to find that that opinion was delivered by Justice James Shields, Lincoln's duelling antagonist of a year or two before he argued this case. When asked for the amount of his fee, Lincoln said that his services were his wedding present to Rebecca and William.[1]

More affecting is the story told by Lamon of the Scott case in which he was associated with Lincoln. Scott had a 'demented' sister who owned property valued at ten thousand

---

[1] Dorman *et ux. vs.* Lane; 6 Ill. 143–52. In the course of his opinion Justice Shields says that 'although no personal property of the deceased [Robinson] ever came to his [Lane's] hands, possession or knowledge, yet he suffered fifteen years to elapse before making any application for the sale of the real estate for the payment of his debt. It would be extremely hazardous for this Court to sanction such gross negligence, and particularly in a case where the same person was both administrator and creditor.'

An account of this litigation was given Herndon by F. M. Eddy of Shawneetown, which cannot be reconciled with the statement of the case by the Supreme Court. According to Eddy, Lane was the guardian of Rebecca Daimwood, an orphan, and sold her land upon false pretext that the proceeds were needed for her maintenance; she sued Lane for the recovery of the farm, married Dorman who thus became a party to the suit, won in trial court and Lane appealed to the Supreme Court. Eddy says that young Dorman was so grateful that, although a Democrat, he ever after voted for Lincoln. In this form the story sometimes appears in Lincolniana. F. M. Eddy to Herndon, March 21, 1888. Weik MSS.

dollars, and the Court appointed a 'conservator' to care for this estate. A 'designing adventurer' sought to marry her for her money, and through attorneys assuming to represent the girl moved to have the custodian of her property discharged. Scott placed the case in the hands of Lamon who was the local member of the firm of Lincoln and Lamon at Danville, agreeing to pay two hundred and fifty dollars if the motion were defeated. Lincoln won 'inside of twenty minutes,' and Scott paid Lamon the stipulated fee.

'What did you charge that man?' Lincoln asked his youthful business-getting partner. When Lamon told him the amount of their fee Lincoln sternly rebuked the young lawyer.

'Lamon, that is all wrong. The service was not worth that sum. Give him back at least half of it.' To Lamon's protestation that the fee was 'fixed in advance' and that Scott was satisfied, Lincoln exclaimed, 'with a look of distress and of undisguised displeasure:

'"That may be, but *I* am not satisfied. This is positively wrong. Go, call him back and return half the money at least, or I will not receive one cent of it as my share."'

The disgusted Lamon did so; the client was 'astonished,' but took the money; Judge Davis and the lawyers present were annoyed and resentful. Davis called Lincoln to the bench and, in a rasping whisper which could be heard all over the court room thus chided his favorite at the bar:

'Lincoln, I have been watching you and Lamon. You are impoverishing this bar by your picayune charges of fees, and the lawyers have reason to complain of you. You are now almost as poor as Lazarus, and if you don't make people pay you more for your services you will die as poor as Job's turkey.' O. L. Davis, 'the leading lawyer in that part of the State,' as Lamon describes him, joined in the Judge's rebuke but 'Mr. Lincoln was immovable.'

'That money comes out of the pocket of a poor, demented girl,' he declared sympathetically, 'and I would rather starve than swindle her in this manner.'

That night in Judge Davis's room, Lincoln was tried before the 'orgmathorial court,' found guilty and fined for his 'awful crime against the pockets of his brethren at the bar. The fine he paid with great good humor, and then kept the crowd of lawyers in uproarious laughter until after midnight.' But he would not relent. Never, he asserted, should his firm deserve the popular title of 'Catch 'em and Cheat 'em.' [1]

Although neither Davis, Whitney, Swett, Herndon, nor anyone else makes mention of this vivid example of Lincoln's generosity, it is not disputed, and it is quite as well authenticated and trustworthy as any of the similar tales about Lincoln's reduction or relinquishment of fees. That there was some basis for each of them is more than likely, and that all of them, taken together, do reflect a general truth as to Lincoln's attitude is certain. But, like so many accounts of this and that action or saying of Lincoln, these stories are mostly second-hand hearsay, searched for, discovered, and set down on paper from fifteen to forty years after the incident thus related and recorded.

In one notable case, however, Lincoln gave his services freely and with his whole heart. In the trial of that case, too, he exerted himself to the limit of his powers. Because of the nature of the case, of the persons concerned in the outcome of it, and of a dramatic circumstance during the trial, Lincoln's defence of 'Duff' Armstrong has become famous. So much has been written about it that a brief statement of the facts must be given.[2] The same is true of the other three important cases in which Lincoln appeared. As each of these legal engagements has been so extensively discussed and such clouds of speculation have gathered about them, a fairly comprehensive review cannot be avoided.

[1] *Recollections:* Lamon, 17–9. This book was written in 1911, in a final effort to counteract the effect of the attacks on Lamon's ill-starred Life of Lincoln. Its statements are to be received with caution.

[2] The review of this case in the text is from the following sources and authorities:

a. Original papers in People *vs.* Armstrong. Office Clerk Circuit Court Cass County, Beardstown, Ill. This file includes indictment, subpœnas, warrants, verdict of jury, instructions to jury, etc., etc. All personally examined by author and photostats of many in his possession.

b. Letters of J. Henry Shaw to Herndon, Sept. 5 and Aug. 22, 1866. Weik MSS. Shaw was the leading lawyer of Cass County and was employed to assist Hugh Fullerton, States Attorney, in the prosecution of Armstrong. Among other items of first-hand information, Shaw's letters contain the statement to him of Milton Logan who was foreman of the jury, etc.

c. Letters of William Walker to Herndon, June 3, Aug. 27, and Sept. 17, 1866.

In the latter part of August, 1857, a camp-meeting was held in Mason County, Illinois. On Saturday, the twenty-ninth of that month, a fight or series of fights took place near a sutler's wagon about half a mile from the camp-meeting. The wagon supplied whisky to the rough men and youths who always gathered near camp-meetings to drink, race horses, and disturb the religious gatherings. On this occasion the rowdies quarrelled among themselves and fights resulted. James H. Norris and William D. Armstrong, popularly called 'Duff,' had such an affray with a very drunken farmer by the name of James Preston Metzker, who after the fight mounted his horse with difficulty and rode to his home near Mason City. On the way he fell from his horse two or three times. Three days later he died.

At the October term of the Mason Circuit Court, Norris and Armstrong were indicted for the murder of Metzker. The indictment charged that Norris struck Metzker on the back of the head with a piece of wood three feet long, that Armstrong hit him in the right eye with a slung-shot, and that on September 1 Metzker died of the wounds thus inflicted. Norris was

Weik MSS. Walker was Armstrong's attorney in Mason County and was assisted by Lincoln in the trial at Beardstown.

d. Statement of Judge James Harriott, no date. Weik MSS. Harriott was the Judge who presided at the trials of Norris in Mason County and Armstrong in Cass County.

e. Statement of Hannah Armstrong, mother of 'Duff,' no date. Weik MSS. This statement is chiefly about Lincoln in New Salem.

f. Address of Abram Bergen before the Kansas State Bar Association. Mr. Bergen was present during the entire trial.

g. Affidavit of John Armstrong, only living brother of Duff, as to what occurred at the trial.

h. Affidavit of George T. Saunders of Beardstown, Ill., Aug. 15, 1925. Mr. Saunders was thirteen years old at the time of the trial.

I am indebted for these affidavits to Mr. Allen T. Lucas of Chandlerville, Ill., who went to much trouble to secure for me the sworn statements of Armstrong and Saunders. Mr. Lucas also procured an order of the Circuit Court of Cass County by which the original papers in the case were placed in my keeping for thirty days.

i. 'Lincoln's Defense of Duff Armstrong' by J. N. Gridley in the Journal Ill. State Hist. Socy, III, 24-44. Gridley's article contains among other things the statement of John T. Brady, one of the jurors.

The letters of Shaw and Walker, the statement of Judge Harriott and the address of Mr. Bergen are, when taken together, and in connection with the court records, well-nigh complete and conclusive.

The account in the text is from so many and so scattered statements in these sources, that separate citation of each is impracticable.

immediately tried in Mason County, convicted of manslaughter, and sentenced to the penitentiary for eight years. A change of venue was secured for Armstrong upon the ground of public prejudice against him, and Judge James Harriott transferred the case to Cass County in the same circuit.

At the November term of the Cass Circuit Court at Beardstown, the county seat, application for bail was made. At this point Lincoln appears in the case. The accused man, then twenty-four years of age, was the son of Lincoln's old comrade of New Salem days, Jack Armstrong, the leader of the Clary Grove Boys, and his wife Hannah, who during those years had befriended Lincoln. He had often rocked the cradle of the baby, who, grown to manhood, was now indicted and in jail for murder.

The mother says that she wrote to Lincoln. On receiving his answer, she went to Springfield to beg him to defend her son and Lincoln agreed to do so. In such a fashion came his famous defence of 'Duff' Armstrong.[1]

The State's Attorney for the district was Hugh Fullerton, and J. Henry Shaw of Beardstown, then the leading lawyer of Cass County, was employed to assist in the prosecution. Shaw's account discloses a cross-play of litigation, revealing two of Lincoln's characteristics, honesty and secretiveness. The Beardstown lawyer wrote to Lincoln to assist him in the defence of an important divorce case[2] at the November term of the Cass County Circuit Court. The case was tried, Shaw and Lincoln were beaten, the divorce granted and the custody of the child given to the mother; but the question of alimony went over to the May term of the court. Lincoln, who had said nothing about the Armstrong case, then moved that Duff Armstrong be admitted to bail and argued 'hotly' for his motion, which

---

[1] Mrs. Armstrong's statement, no date. Weik MSS. Hobson prints what purports to be a letter of Lincoln to Mrs. Armstrong, dated Springfield, 'Ohio,' Sept. 18, offering his services because of favors he had received from her and her husband, Jack Armstrong.

The original of this letter has not been found and, in face of the positive statement of the mother, its authenticity is doubtful, to say the very least. In his careful account of the Armstrong trial, J. N. Gridley says that her friends advised Mrs. Armstrong to get Lincoln's services and that she drove to Springfield for that purpose.

[2] Ruth A. Gill *vs.* Jonathan Gill. Shaw to Herndon, Sept. 5, 1866.

Judge Harriott promptly overruled.[1] Thus for the first time, Shaw learned that Lincoln was so much as interested in the murder case.

When Lincoln came to Beardstown at the next term of court, Shaw supposed he was there to argue the matter of alimony in the divorce case. Again he said nothing of Armstrong who was to be tried almost immediately. But he did speak about another suit brought by Shaw for specific performance, in which Lincoln represented the defendants.[2] Shaw showed his proofs to Lincoln who declared that Shaw's client 'was justly entitled to a decree, and he should so represent it to the court, that it was against his principle to contest a clear matter of right. So My client got a deed for a farm,' relates Shaw, 'which, had another Lawyer been in Mr. Lincoln's place, would have been in litigation for years, with a big pile of costs and the result probably the same.'

Still thinking that Lincoln had come to Beardstown 'more particularly to attend to the Gill and Moore cases,' Shaw was amazed at the 'immense interest he took in the Armstrong Case. He went into it like a Giant,' declares the assistant of the prosecuting attorney.

That now celebrated trial has been minutely described by several persons who took part in it or were present and their accounts do not vary greatly in the main features. Perhaps Mr. Bergen's narrative is the most trustworthy since it was the first trial he attended after his admission to the bar. He 'was seated . . . not more than four feet' from the attorneys who tried the case, 'and noticed everything with the deepest interest and most watchful scrutiny.'

The day was hot and sultry; but, says Judge Harriott, 'there was no excitement. . . . It was a common trial.'[3] Walker had

[1] Shaw makes this statement specifically. No formal motion for bail was entered of record, however (Records Cass County Circuit Court); and the tradition in the Armstrong family is that no application for bail was ever made. Allen T. Lucas of Chandlerville, Ill., to author, Aug. 15, 1925. The probability is that the entire proceeding was oral, as often was the case in such matters at that time, and that Lincoln, finding Judge Harriott determined not to grant bail, did not file a written motion.

[2] George Moore *vs.* Christina Moore and the heirs of Peter Moore. Lincoln's client lived near Springfield. Shaw to Herndon, Sept. 5, 1866.

[3] In his account of the trial Judge Harriott angrily denounces an emotional magazine

brought with him full notes which he had made of the testimony given in the trial of Norris in Mason County, and, since the evidence against Armstrong was substantially the same, Lincoln carefully studied the notes and thus learned what the witnesses would say. Walker conducted the examination for the defence, Lincoln prompting him now and then from the testimony given at the trial of Norris. Sometimes he, himself, asked questions, and young Bergen was astonished at the knowledge of anatomy which Lincoln displayed.

But most of the time, Lincoln sat motionless, staring at the wall as though unconscious of his surroundings. The State proved the attack on Metzker as charged in the indictment; and it was established that Metzker's skull was fractured in two places, the back near the base of the brain and the front near the corner of the right eye; and that either fracture was fatal, although the latter was the worse. But the chief witness for the prosecution, Charles Allen, overstated in detail, or perhaps was caught in a trap set for him by Lincoln. Allen was a friend of 'Duff' Armstrong and the Armstrong family, did not want to testify, and was at a tavern in the town of Virginia, thirteen miles from Beardstown, when the time of the trial arrived. A summons for him was issued by the State and the Sheriff served it; but he refused to attend. Thereupon a warrant was issued directing the Sheriff to seize the reluctant witness and bring him into court. The officer arrested Allen and brought him before the Judge. In such fashion the chief witness against Armstrong finally was placed upon the stand. It was largely upon Allen's testimony that Norris had been convicted in Mason County, and he told substantially the same story at the trial of Armstrong.[1]

Allen testified so clearly and frankly that the jury believed him. Judge Harriott asserts that Lincoln also believed him. He swore that he saw Norris hit Metzker on the back of the head with something that looked like a neck-yoke, and Armstrong

article that had been printed on the Armstrong case: 'The article from beginning to end is a humbug.' Harriott's statement, no date.

[1] J. N. Gridley says that Lincoln sent for Allen to prevent a continuance of the case and another long period in jail for Armstrong.

strike him in the right eye with what appeared to be a slung-shot. Casually and with seeming unconcern Lincoln asked as to the time of the attack, how far away Allen was standing, and how much light there was. The witness answered promptly that he was fifteen or twenty yards distant, that the hour was eleven o'clock at night, that the moon was shining brightly and was about as high as the sun would be at ten o'clock.[1] Curiously enough, Allen had not been asked at the trial of Norris about the position of the moon, nor had he been an unwilling witness for the State as he now was in the trial of Armstrong.

Thereupon Lincoln produced an *Almanac* for 1857, which showed that, at the hour of the murder, the moon was not in the position named by Allen, but, instead, was low in the west-ern sky — in fact within an hour of setting. The jury broke into laughter. That 'Almanac *floored* the witness,' several jurymen told Shaw long afterward. The almanac was examined by Judge Harriott, by the attorneys for the prosecution and by the jury, and Allen's testimony was thus seriously impaired. Lincoln had brought the almanac with him from Springfield, testifies Bergen, who saw him take it 'from his capacious hat,' during a recess of the court, and give it to the Sheriff, 'with the request that he would hand it to him when he called for it.' Bergen further states that Lincoln said to Judge Harriott that, although he supposed the Court would take judicial notice of an almanac, nevertheless he would introduce it in evidence.

Since he had brought the almanac with him, it would appear that Lincoln knew that Allen would give a wrong answer as to the place of the moon in the heavens at the time of the fight. Even if he sent for an almanac when Allen stated the position of the moon, the same inference may be made; but it is more probable that he learned the fact for the first time when Allen so testified. In the event he was prepared to impair Allen's whole testimony by means of the almanac. As Walker, his associate in the trial, declares, Lincoln casually pointed out to

[1] The narratives differ somewhat as to Allen's testimony on this vital point. John T. Brady, a juror, says that he swore that the moon was where the sun would be at one o'clock, while Walker and Shaw state the testimony as given in the text. Some assert that Allen testified to ten o'clock as the hour of the altercation and others that he named eleven o'clock.

the jury that if this witness was so badly mistaken on so conspicuous a fact as the position of the moon, he might be in error on other matters.

Quite as important to the defence and as damaging to the prosecution as the disparagement of Allen, was the testimony of Nelson or William Watkins. The State had produced the slung-shot, had adduced evidence that it belonged to Duff Armstrong, and that it was the same weapon with which he had struck Metzker. But the weapon had been found a long way from the scene of the murder, and Watkins swore that he was the owner of the slung-shot. He described it minutely and stated that he had made it himself; and that, the day after the fight, he had thrown it away 'at the particular place' where it was found. Lincoln made a great deal of this in his speech to the jury, cutting open the slung-shot and thus showing that it was made as Watkins had sworn it was made. Lincoln told the Armstrongs after the trial was over that Watkins' testimony was as helpful as the refutation of Allen's statement about the moon.

The defence also proved that Metzker had fallen from his horse once or twice on his way home, and struck his head on the ground. A physician and surgeon, Charles E. Parker, was then put upon the stand; [1] and, by the aid of a skull, he showed the jury that such a fall and blow on the back of the head, or the stroke by Norris, might easily have caused the fracture near the right eye from which Metzker died. Judge Harriott maintains that Dr. Parker's testimony was the strongest feature in the defence. On the other hand, the physician who was brought into court to testify for the State, Dr. B. F. Stevenson, was plainly a reluctant witness; for, like Allen, he ignored two summonses for him, and the Sheriff was ordered to take him on the same warrant issued for the arrest of Allen. Several character witnesses testified to Duff Armstrong's good reputation. [2]

Such was the evidence upon which Lincoln went to the jury. But it was not the almanac, nor Watkins' dramatic statement,

[1] Dr. Parker was summoned to appear 'instanter.' Records Cass County Circuit Court.

[2] The prosecution produced fifteen and the defence twenty-two witnesses. Two subpœnas were issued served on Allen and Stevenson, before the order of their arrest was given.

nor Dr. Parker's demonstration, nor any item of testimony for
the defence, which was decisive of the case. The verdict was
secured by Lincoln's speech to the twelve friends who held
Duff Armstrong's fate in their hands. Walker attached so little
importance to the almanac that he makes no mention of it in his
first careful and detailed account of the trial which he wrote to
Herndon, and not until Herndon asked him specifically about
the almanac, did he recall it. He is not even certain that Lincoln laid particular emphasis upon the matter: 'Mr. L. in his
Speach may have alluded to the absence of a moon' to show
that, since 'the witness was mistaken in regard to one thing,
the Jury Should receive all his testimony with caution.'

Judge Harriott was not impressed by the incident of the
almanac, but was particularly attracted by Lincoln's plan of
defence and by the testimony of a doctor in support of it. 'Lincoln's Theory was that the neck yoke killed Metz[ker] and that
it cracked the Skull in front — where Armstrong is supposed
to have struck. The Almanac may have cut a figure, but it was
Doct. Parker's testimony confirming Lincoln's Theory,' that
shook the prosecution.

Shaw, who writes with intelligence and precision, is emphatic
that 'Armstrong was not cleared by any want of testimony
against him, but by the irresistible appeal of Mr. Lincoln in his
favor.' So confident of conviction were Fullerton and Shaw
that the opening speech to the jury was almost perfunctory.
Walker made the first speech for the defence, and then came
Lincoln's appeal for Armstrong. He rose with grave impressive-
ness, took off his coat and vest and began to speak slowly,
distinctly, and without emotion. Soon he removed the stock
from his neck. As he proceeded one of his suspenders, which
were of knitted wool, fell from a shoulder, and Lincoln, not
noticing it, let it hang throughout his speech. He talked for
about an hour, and for most of that time, gave a simple analysis
of the evidence. 'He spoke slowly and carefully,' relates Walker,
'reviewed the whole testimony [and] picked it all to pieces.'

It was the last part of Lincoln's speech, however, that won
freedom for the son of Jack and Hannah Armstrong. He appealed frankly to the sympathy of the jurors. He told the story

of his own arrival at New Salem, penniless and without a friend, of the help and comfort given him by the parents of the accused, of pioneer hardships and struggles, of the recent death of the father, of the plight of the widow, and of the hopeless, desolate life that would be hers if her son should be taken from her — her poverty, disgrace, distress. Tears poured down Lincoln's wrinkled face, for he was in desperate earnest. The jury was overcome and wept with Lincoln. 'Such was the power and earnestness with which he spoke that Jury and all sat as if Entranced and when he was through found relief in a Gush of tears,' Lincoln's colleague relates; and Walker adds: 'I have never seen such Mastery exhibited over the feelings and Emotions of men as on that occasion.'

Shaw, who then and ever after firmly believed that Armstrong was guilty and that proof of his guilt was overwhelming, thus describes Lincoln's appeal to the jury and the effect of it: 'There were many witnesses, and each seemed to add one more cord that seemed to bind him down till Mr. Lincoln was something in the situation of Gulliver after his first sleep in Lilliput. But when he came to talk to the jury (that was always his forte) he resembled Gulliver again; he skilfully untied here and there a knot and loosened here and there a peg, until, getting fairly warmed up, he raised himself in full power and shook the arguments of his opponents from him as though they were cobwebs. He took the jury by storm. There were tears in Mr. Lincoln's eyes while he spoke. But they were genuine. . . . His terrible sincerity could not help but arouse the same passion in the jury. I have said it a hundred times that it was Lincoln's *speech* that saved that criminal from the Gallows.'

In vain did the prosecution, in the final speech to the jury, insist on conviction; the jury was deaf to that demand for cold and formal justice. While Shaw or Fullerton was thus closing the case for the State,[1] Lincoln, sitting at his table, prepared instructions to the jury, which Judge Harriott gave exactly as

[1] It is not stated in any of the narratives by those present, which one of these men made the opening and closing argument to the jury; but since the trial was held at Beardstown and Shaw was the foremost attorney of that place, he probably made the last speech for the prosecution.

Lincoln had written them. They were but two in number and very brief: 'The Court instructs the jury —

'That if they have any reasonable doubt as to whether Metzker came to his death by the blow on the eye, or by the blow on the back of the head, they are to find the defendant "Not guilty" unless they also believe from the evidence, beyond reasonable doubt, that *Armstrong* and *Norris acted by concert,* against Metzker, and that Norris struck the blow on the back of the head.

'That if they believe from the evidence that Norris killed Metzker, they are to acquit Armstrong, unless they also believe beyond a reasonable doubt that Armstrong acted in concert with Norris in the Killing, or purpose to Kill or hurt Metzker.' [1]

While Lincoln was pleading for the life of her son, Hannah Armstrong, her face almost hid by a 'huge' old-fashioned sun-bonnet, sobbed piteously. As the jury were filing into their room, one of them heard Lincoln assure her that 'her boy would be cleared before sundown.' Only one ballot was taken and a verdict of acquittal quickly returned into the Court. 'Mr. Lincoln shook hands with Duff Armstrong and then led him to his mother,' told him to care for and comfort her, 'and try to make as good a man as his father had been.' [2] Later Lincoln went to see Mrs. Armstrong. 'I asked him what he charged me — told him I was poor,' she relates. 'He said, "Why, Hannah, I shan't charge you a cent — never. Anything I can do for you I will do for you willingly and freely, without charge."' [3]

When leaving the court room Lincoln handed Armstrong's

[1] The original instructions in Lincoln's handwriting are among the records in the office of the Clerk of the Cass County Circuit Court at Beardstown, Ill. On the margin the word 'given' is written by Judge Harriott. Judge Harriott also gave all instructions, four in number, asked by the prosecution. Records Cass Co. Cir. Ct. Photostats in possession of author.

[2] When the Civil War came on, William Armstrong and three of his brothers enlisted in the Union Army. William fell ill in 1863, his mother appealed to Lincoln to send him home to her, the President immediately ordered that he be discharged, and the mother 'nursed him back to health.' *Works,* ix, 126.

[3] Walker's account differs from that of Mrs. Armstrong in stating that she came to see Lincoln at the hotel, 'took him by the hand and, with Streaming eye, Said God would Bless him and his Children Because he had been Kind to the widow and orphan,'

that it was an up to date almanac; this I am sure of, as it was passed up to the Judge, Jury and lawyers, who all examined it closely.' Still more convincing is Bergen's positive assertion: 'When Lincoln called for the almanac he exhibited it to the opposing lawyers, read from it and then caused it to be handed to the jury for their inspection.' They compared it with another almanac for the same year, 'and found they substantially agreed.... All this I personally saw and heard and it is as distinct in my memory as if it had occurred but yesterday.' [1]

It is hard to account for the origin of the gossip of the false almanac; hard to explain the vitality and persistence of the story. Perhaps it was started by the verdict of acquittal which, it would seem, the people thought unjust in view of the evidence against Armstrong. The story was revived in Lincoln's contest with Douglas later in the year in which the trial was held, and it appeared again in the presidential campaign two years afterward. But whatever the source of the tale and whatever the means by which it was kept alive, the incident of the almanac has been unduly magnified. Nor is the production of the almanac evidence of Lincoln's uncommon shrewdness and foresight. Any alert lawyer could not possibly have failed to do the same thing; and thousands of resourceful lawyers have devised other expedients equally skilful to impair or break down positive testimony which they knew would be adduced.[2]

[1] Jayne's *Almanac* for 1857 shows that on the night of Aug. 27, of that year, the moon set a little before midnight in the latitude of Philadelphia. No Jayne's *Almanac* of that year for the latitude of Chicago has been located; but the *Methodist Almanac* (Chicago Hist. Socy.) for 1857 shows that the moon set at midnight in the latitude of the scene of the murder.

The moon really set on that night at 12.05 A.M. (Computation for author by Observatory of Harvard University.) The whole matter is of no moment, since there was plenty of light at the time of the fight. As stated in the text the almanac was in conflict only with Allen's statement as to the position of the moon.

[2] Shaw took the almanac and kept it as long as he lived. Apparently Lincoln gave it to him along with the slung-shot. Upon Shaw's death John Huston, who had been deputy Sheriff at the time of the trial, got possession of the almanac (Saunders' affidavit). He was 'a bitter Democrat' (Barton, i, 313). Thirty or forty years after the trial he sold to Gunther of Chicago an almanac which he alleged to be the one Lincoln used at the Armstrong trial. Gunther gave it to the Chicago Hist. Socy., but within the last five years it has disappeared. It is, however, unworthy of notice since it was not Jayne's *Almanac* which Milton Logan, the foreman of the jury, declared in 1866 and George T. Saunders asserts in 1925, was the almanac in question.

In late American editions of *Ram on Facts* the index contains a reference, 'Lincoln,

The records show that in trial courts Lincoln won many more cases than he lost. But he was no phenomenon of success. He often failed. He had runs of bad luck it seems. Bunn told Whitney that Lincoln in a single year was beaten in every trial at every court held throughout the whole circuit — three months of continuous defeats.[1] Yet all testify that he was the leader of the bar in the Eighth Circuit,[2] and many assert that he was the best jury lawyer in Illinois. He was never without employment and appeared in nearly every case that was tried, usually for the defence. It is a singular fact that in cases in the Circuit Court described by the Judge or other lawyers, Lincoln seldom appeared for the plaintiff. His associates declare that in jury trials he showed little knowledge of decisions or textbooks,[3] but relied upon principle and reason.

Lincoln's mind worked slowly, he had to have plenty of time to think out courses of action and did poorly when hurried. 'I have seen him,' testifies Herndon, 'lose cases of the plainest justice, which the most inexperienced member of the bar would have gained without effort,' because he had not been given time to prepare.[4] He was willing to let the trial of cases go over to the next term; but, Weldon says, that this was because Lincoln 'was not an industrious lawyer.'[5] Gillespie admits that Lincoln was slow in his mental processes, but thinks the cause of such deliberation was that he looked carefully into every aspect of a case, and this, too, is Bergen's explanation.[6]

Lincoln once explained to his impatient partner how his mind worked: '"Give me your little pen-knife, with its short blade, and hand me that old jack-knife, lying on the table." Opening the blade of the pen-knife he said: "You see, this blade at the point travels rapidly, but only through a small portion of space till it stops; while the long blade of the jack-knife moves no faster but through a much greater space than the small one.

President Abraham, how he procured an acquittal by a fraud,' and the text gives the almanac episode on the authority of Shaw's letter in Lamon and Arnold.

[1] Whitney, 255.   [2] Weldon: Rice, 200.

[3] Whitney, 252; Weldon: Rice, 202; Bergen in Kansas Bar Assn. Address (MS.).

[4] Herndon, II, 337.   [5] Weldon: Rice, 200.

[6] Gillespie to Herndon, Jan. 31, 1866. Weik MSS.; Bergen's Kansas Bar Assn. Address.

Just so with the long, labored movements of my mind. I may not emit ideas as rapidly as others, because I am compelled by nature to speak slowly, but when I do throw off a thought it seems to me, though it comes with some effort, it has force enough to cut its own way and travel a greater distance.'" [1]

Because he knew so little of decisions [2] and required so much time to prepare, Lincoln's best work as a lawyer was in the argument of cases before the Supreme Court. For such arguments he never failed to prepare with utmost thoroughness. He examined available precedents, carefully studied the textbooks; [3] his briefs and addresses to the court were well-reasoned and strongly supported by authorities; [4] and he was usually successful. All told he had one hundred and seventy-five cases in the Supreme Court of which he won ninety-six. [5] Lincoln's conduct of cases before the Supreme Bench was, by far, his most distinguished effort at the bar. His arguments covered almost the whole range of the law and included values from a three dollar hog case [6] to a disputed liability on a note for over one hundred and thirty thousand dollars. [7] He appeared for subscribers to railroad stock who refused to pay [8] and for the railroad company to collect stock subscriptions. [9]

While he was employed more frequently by railroad companies than against them, when Lincoln did oppose them he was as vigorous as when he supported them. For instance, he re-

[1] Herndon, II, 338-9. 'This was said to me when we were alone in our office simply for illustration. It was not said boastingly.'

[2] Herndon to Weik, Oct. 22, 1885. Weik MSS.

[3] Address of R. M. Benjamin in *Bloomington Pantagraph*, Feb. 23, 1909. 'Study with Mr. Lincoln was a business, not a pleasure.' Gillespie to Herndon, Dec. 8, 1866. Weik MSS.

[4] Lincoln 'was a perfect *case* lawyer, . . . studied special cases thoroughly. . . . He remembered his special reading and applied it to other cases and so on till he got to be a No. 1 Sup[re] m[e] Court Lawyer.' Herndon to Weik, Oct. 22, 1885. Weik MSS.

'He was a case Lawyer but in a case where he felt that he had the right none could surpass him.' O. B. Ficklin to Herndon, Charleston, Jan. 25, 1865. Weik MSS.

[5] Richards, 64.   [6] Byrne *vs.* Stout, 15 Ill. 180-2.

[7] Smith *et al. vs.* Dunlap, 12 Ill. 184-94; and Dunlap *vs.* Smith *et al.*, *Ib.* 399-402. Of these cases Lincoln won the first and lost the second, in which Senator Douglas appeared.

[8] Banet *vs.* Alton & Sangamon R. R. Co., 13 Ill. 504-14; and Sprague *vs.* Ill. River R. R. Co., 19 Ill. 174-83. Lincoln lost both these cases.

[9] Klein *vs.* A. & S. R. R. Co., *Ib.* 514-6. Lincoln won this case.

sisted the efforts of the Chicago, Burlington and Quincy Railroad Company to secure condemnation of lots in Kane County for shops and a depot, but was beaten.[1] Another example is his securing of a verdict of a thousand dollars against the Chicago, Alton and St. Louis Railroad Company in Logan County for Joseph A. Dalby. A conductor had violently put Dalby and his wife off the train because they would not pay extra fare, having tendered the price of tickets which they had been unable to get at the station which was out of tickets. The company appealed to the Supreme Court and energetically opposed the instructions given by the trial judge. Lincoln as stoutly upheld them, and, in a long and careful opinion by Chief Justice Caton, the Court sustained Lincoln's contentions and established rules in such cases which remain the law to this day.[2]

But whatever the nature of the case in the Supreme Court, Lincoln conducted it with all his power and exhausted the resources of the Supreme Court Library in his effort to support his position. For in these cases Lincoln had the leisure to consider questions and form plans of procedure which was indispensable to him for informing himself on the law of a case. He did not write many briefs, however, seeming to prefer oral argument supported by notes of authorities left with the Court. But two briefs in Lincoln's handwriting have been discovered, and they are worthy of note solely because they are examples of his method of argument by means of briefs.

In a slander suit[3] the Supreme Court had decided against Lincoln and he petitioned for a rehearing. One woman had publicly charged that another was the mother of negro children. Lincoln had won in the trial court, and the Supreme Court re-

---

[1] C. B. & Q. R. R. Co. *vs.* Isaac G. Wilson, 17 Ill. 123–31. James F. Joy represented the railroad company and Lincoln with Grant Goodrich appeared against it. The company applied to the Supreme Court for a mandamus to compel Judge Wilson of the Thirteenth Circuit to appoint commissioners to condemn the land. The Judge had refused to do so. The case involved the construction of the company's charter, the necessity for condemnation, the failure of the company to show that it could not have acquired the land by purchase, etc. The Supreme Court decided in favor of the company and awarded the mandamus.

[2] Chicago, Alton & St. Louis R. R. Co. *vs.* Dalby, 19 Ill. 353–76. An account of the trial of this case is given in Stringer, 219. For Lincoln's connection with the Chicago and Alton R. R., see *Lincoln and the Railroads*: John W Starr, Jr., 80–4.

[3] Patterson *et ux. vs.* Edwards *et ux.*, 7 Ill. 720.

versed the judgment because the proof varied materially from
the allegations in the complaint. In his brief Lincoln tried to
show there was no real difference. The words alleged were:
'Mrs. Edwards has raised a family of children by a negro.' The
words proved were: 'Your mother has had children by a negro,
and all her children are negroes.'

These words, argued Lincoln, were substantially the same —
they were 'equivalent words . . . a variance to be material . . .
must be a variance in *sense*. . . . "Is there any difference *in
sense* between saying a woman has *raised* children by a negro,
and saying she *had* children by a negro?"' Even if there were a
variance, still the defendant's lawyers at the trial had made no
mention of it; and this being so, was it fair to the court below to
reverse its judgment? Besides the old rule that words to be
slanderous must '*necessarily*' amount to a shameful charge 'has
been exploded nearly or quite a hundred years,' as the new edition of *Starkie on Slander* shows; and a new rule substituted that
the words 'need only be *capable* of the meaning attached to
them.' [1]

The first litigation of great importance in which Lincoln was
retained was the famous 'Reaper Case,' McCormick *vs.* Manny
et al., in 1854–55. What happened in the course of that chancery
suit so reveals Lincoln that a sketch of it cannot be left out of
this narrative. The incidents at the hearing also had a decided
effect on his development; and it is more than probable they
were of influence at a critical time after he became President.
Nor can his experience in the 'Reaper Case' be wholly disconnected from at least two other large employments that came to
him, one a little while before and the other not long afterwards.

During the year 1834, in the beautiful little town of Lexington, Virginia, a young man of an important family of the Shenandoah Valley, Cyrus H. McCormick, invented a reaping machine. It worked well and, in a few years, he and his brothers
went to Chicago to manufacture and sell it. From time to time

---

[1] Weik, 170–4. The court promptly denied the petition.

Lincoln's other brief was in Smith *vs.* Smith, 21 Ill. 244. It is upon an election bet
which Lincoln's client tried to avoid on the ground that such a wager was gambling, as
'contrary to public policy and morality.' Weik, 174–6. The court decided that in the
absence of a statute forbidding such a bet, it was valid.

McCormick made improvements and secured patents. The business became so profitable that other companies, east and west, began to manufacture reapers, similar to that of McCormick, but differing in important features.

One of these concerns, a partnership at the head of which was John H. Manny, had a factory at Rockford, Illinois. In 1854 McCormick sued Manny and his associates in the United States Court for the Northern District of Illinois for infringement of his patents. Thomas Drummond, before whom Lincoln had practised and who knew Lincoln well, was the Judge of this court.

Rival manufacturers in the East joined the Rockford manufacturers in their fight upon McCormick, although they did not appear of record in the litigation. Both sides regarded the McCormick-Manny suit as a test case. A large fund was raised — 'there was money enough at our disposal,' relates George Harding, the chief counsel for the reaper combination, 'to do whatever we thought would conduce to success.'

The ablest patent lawyers were employed — Edward M. Dickerson of New York for McCormick and George Harding of Philadelphia for the defence. Dickerson and Harding were the outstanding patent lawyers of that day and of almost equal eminence, although Dickerson, somewhat older than Harding, had, perhaps, a little wider reputation. With Dickerson was Reverdy Johnson, then a leader of the American bar.

What happened in the conduct of the case is clearly told by Harding, who, in the spring of 1876, gave a comprehensive and detailed account to Robert H. Parkinson, a lawyer then of Cincinnati, now of Chicago. So full, frank, self-critical is this statement of Harding to Parkinson that it must be accepted as accurate and complete, and the only other trustworthy narrative supports it in all important points.[1]

[1] 'In the spring of 1876, with Harding as my senior counsel, I helped argue a case in Nashville, Tenn., before Judge Emmons, of Detroit, then U.S. Circuit Judge of the Sixth Circuit. Harding made the closing argument and, immediately upon its conclusion, a decree was entered in favor of our client.'

Parkinson took Harding and Judge Emmons for a drive in the country, and the young lawyer asked his senior counsel about the rumor that Harding had been instrumental in making Lincoln President, quoting a compliment that Lincoln was said to have paid Harding's argument in the Reaper Case.

I 'asked him [Harding] to give us the whole story,' and 'Harding, who was more

'I had been retained by a group of reaper manufacturers East and West,' Harding relates, 'to resist McCormick's charge of infringement.' Watson, who afterwards became President of the Erie Railroad, assisted in the preparation of the case, for which work 'he was especially well qualified.' Supposing that the trial would be before Judge Drummond at Chicago, it was decided to employ a local lawyer 'who understood the judge and had his confidence;' but Harding 'felt that we were not likely to find a lawyer there who would be of real assistance in arguing such a case.'

In this spirit, the astute eastern attorneys first tried to get Isaac N. Arnold as their local associate; but Arnold had 'some adverse retainer. A Springfield lawyer, whose name was given as "A. Lincoln" or "Abe Lincoln," was then suggested.' Harding was not well impressed, but his 'Illinois clients' insisted, and he sent Watson to Springfield 'to look Lincoln over with authority to retain him if he concluded it was best.' From the first Harding had wanted as his associate in the case another Pennsylvania lawyer whom he knew well, an aggressive young man of notable ability and tireless industry, Edwin M. Stanton. Harding's only thought in employing an Illinois lawyer was that he might make matters easier in the Chicago court because of local knowledge and, perhaps, influence.

Watson arrived at the capital of Illinois late in the afternoon, and found Lincoln's office closed. He sought him at his house and 'found it a small frame structure,[1] not such as would indicate that its occupant was a lawyer of such standing as we required. There was neither door-bell nor knocker.' Watson rapped on the door.

'"Who is there?" asked a woman, sticking her head out of an upper window. Watson said he wanted to see Lincoln.

'"Business or politics?" she asked.

'"Business," answered Watson.

'"Abe, here is a man who wants to see you on business,"' cried the woman in a 'modified tone.'

genial and approachable that day than I ever saw him before or after,' then gave the narrative which Parkinson carefully wrote out for the author and which is followed in the text. Parkinson to author, May 28, 1923.

[1] Lincoln's house was still a story and a half; the upper story was not raised until 1857.

Responding to his wife's summons, 'the door was opened by a tall man having on neither coat nor vest, who said he was Lincoln and was just putting up a bed.' Into 'a small, plainly furnished room,' went Watson, satisfied that Lincoln was not the man the defence wanted in that vital litigation. After talking with him awhile, however, Watson concluded that Lincoln 'might be rather effective in that community' and that, having consulted him, the defence had better employ him than to risk his possible hostility. So, to Lincoln's surprise, Watson paid him a cash retainer, 'arranged for quite a substantial fee to be paid' when the trial was over, and left Lincoln 'under the impression that he was to make an argument and [was] expected to prepare for it.'

Watson told Harding what he had done 'and why.' It was better, he advised, to 'keep Lincoln in line but, without disabusing him, quietly employ Stanton . . . and ultimately find a way for side-tracking Lincoln.' Watson's description of the uncouth aspect of the Springfield attorney 'confirmed' Harding in his first opinion, 'that it would be quite out of the question to have him take part in the argument.' The agreement that the case should be heard in Cincinnati, instead of Chicago 'removed the one object we had in employing Lincoln.'

Such was the state of mind of the chief and managing counsel for the defending reaper combination when, in September, 1855, Lincoln arrived in Cincinnati. He had prepared, with perhaps greater thoroughness than ever in his life, to argue this immensely important case, the only great case he had ever had. But Harding and Stanton, who were already on the ground, were thinking only of winning; nor did they, nor any other person anywhere, then foresee the immortality that ten years thereafter was to clothe the name of Lincoln, nor realize the blame to be visited on them for not having had superhuman prescience. So they acted as most trustworthy and competent lawyers would act in a like situation. They were responsible for the conduct of the case, and, if they had lost, their clients would have criticized them harshly and with reason for having permitted a country lawyer, with little knowledge of patent law and with no reputation whatever in that field, to make an argument on

questions so highly technical as those involved in a contest
which affected so profoundly such extensive interests.

Notwithstanding, then, the circumstance that Lincoln had
come 'to Cincinnati with his argument prepared, and without
an intimation that other arrangements had been made,' Harding and Stanton 'determined that he should be altogether dis-
pensed with.' Their decision was strengthened by the first sight
of their Illinois associate whom Harding instantly recognized
from Watson's description of him. He was at the Burnet House,
says Harding, 'standing on the platform at the head of the steps
ascending from Third Street.' He looked like 'a tall, rawly
boned, ungainly backwoodsman, with coarse, ill-fitting clothing,
his trousers hardly reaching his ankles, holding in his hands a
blue cotton umbrella with a ball on the end of the handle. I can
see distinctly that umbrella and Lincoln standing there with it.

'When introduced, we barely exchanged salutations with him,
and I proposed to Stanton that he and I go up to the court.

'"Let's go up in a gang," remarked Lincoln.

'"Let that fellow go up with his gang. We'll walk up together,"' said Stanton, aside, to Harding. And 'we did,' Harding relates.

McCormick's two lawyers had heard that Lincoln was there
for the defence, and Dickerson and Johnson wanted him to 'take
an active part.' When court opened, 'Johnson arose and in his
suave manner said: "We perceive that defendants are represented by three counsel. We are quite willing that they shall be
fully heard and shall waive objection to there being more than
two arguments on a side, merely asking that Mr. Dickerson be
permitted to speak twice, if we so desire."'

Instantly Harding and Stanton saw the trap. If they walked
into it, Dickerson could speak both before and after Harding.
Springing to his feet and 'in his pugnacious way shaking his fist,'
as Harding describes the scene, Stanton said that 'we sought no
indulgence from our opponents, and needed none; that there was
no intention of having more than two arguments on our side,
that we should not think of so violating the usage of the Court,
and that he would forego the argument he had expected to make
rather than be a party to such an impropriety.'

Stanton made 'it plain to Lincoln that we expected him to withdraw, and, upon his offering to do so, he was taken at his word instantly, and treated as no longer connected with the case.'

In spite of the affront Lincoln stayed in Cincinnati during the entire hearing which lasted about a week. He was constantly in court and, Harding says, 'was a close observer throughout.' After he found that he was not to speak he sent to Harding, 'through Watson, a roll of manuscript which he said contained the argument he had intended to deliver,' for any use Harding might care to make of it. 'I was so sure that it would be only trash on which I must waste no time,' frankly admits Harding, 'that I never glanced at it or even opened it.' Lincoln asked Watson if Harding had read his manuscript. Watson carried back the answer that it had not been read. Lincoln requested the return of it 'intimating that he wished to destroy it.' So 'it went back unopened.'

Watson was the messenger in this, the only communication Lincoln had with his associates. Although they were all at the same hotel, neither Harding nor Stanton 'ever conferred with him, ever had him at our table, or sat with him, or asked him to our rooms, or walked to or from the court with him.'

Nor was this conduct the only humiliation to which Lincoln was subjected. 'During the week Justice McLean entertained counsel on both sides at dinner in his residence at Clifton, one of the suburbs of Cincinnati. Lincoln was not invited.' When the hearing was over Harding and Stanton left the city without saying good-bye to him.

Ralph Emerson, one of Manny's partners at Rockford and a defendant in the McCormick suit, was an eager attendant of the hearings. He knew Lincoln well, and he asserts that it was he who insisted that Harding and Watson should employ Lincoln.[1] Emerson told Parkinson what he saw and heard, and, with the exception of quotations from a pamphlet written many years later, the statements here given are from his conversations with Parkinson. He observed Lincoln closely while the arguments were being made. Lincoln was as one entranced. 'The argu-

[1] *Personal Recollections*, by Mr. and Mrs. Emerson, 1909.

ment in that case was a revelation to him. He had never seen anything so finished and elaborated, and so carefully prepared. . . . It was a fine exhibition of accomplished lawyers conducting a great trial.'

Emerson told Parkinson that Lincoln was particularly captivated by Harding's address. While that talented lawyer was speaking, he 'sat behind him, following every word, and by the expression of his face and by his apparently unconscious gestures, emphasizing every point. Judge Drummond, who held Lincoln in high esteem, was watching him as closely as he was watching Harding himself, and I think Lincoln thus added considerably to the effect of Harding's argument.' Emerson relates that Lincoln was even more deeply impressed by Stanton's address. 'So intensely interested was Lincoln in this speech that . . . he stood rapt in attention, or else was walking back and forth in the court room listening intently. . . . From what Lincoln said to me when he was President I am satisfied that it was that speech which made Lincoln choose Stanton as his final Secretary of War.' [1]

Emerson declared in his account to Parkinson, as well as in his pamphlet, that the principal immediate effect upon Lincoln of his experience with Harding and Stanton and of witnessing the conduct of the case by the lawyers for both sides was to make him resolve to improve himself. He did not reproach his associates, it appears, even in his heart. 'He had not a particle of envy in his nature,' Gillespie testifies in his analysis of Lincoln's character.[2] 'It required no effort on his part to admit another man's superiority.' [3] While disappointed, he was 'quick to see the disadvantage to which lack of education and refinement exposed him.' Emerson says that he was aware of Lincoln's great ability, but he also knew his deficiencies, and he adds defensively:

[1] Emerson, 7. Emerson says that there was some talk of a compromise 'in our office,' at which Stanton 'was ablaze at once; and with gestures as though he held a sword in his hand, he exclaimed: "Compromise! I know of but one way to compromise with an enemy, and that is with a sword in your hand, and to smite, and keep smiting."' Emerson's pamphlet is not nearly so clear and trustworthy as his statement to Parkinson, which was made many years before he wrote the pamphlet.

[2] Gillespie to Herndon, Dec. 8, 1866. Weik MSS.

[3] Same to same, Jan. 31, 1866. Weik MSS.

'You can hardly imagine how primitive and coarse were the conditions under which he had grown up. . . . Lincoln had acquired a command of language effective with such audiences as he then had, was acute in his reasoning power, and apt in telling pertinent stories. . . . Some of these stories were such as a gentleman of refinement would neither tell nor wish to hear, though they were never, I think, told except for the illustration of a point.' But, as yet, he was not in the least equipped to meet such men as those whom he had heard conduct the great Reaper case before Justice McLean of the National Supreme Court and Judge Drummond of the United States Circuit Court at Cincinnati during that week of September, 1855. So, at least, Lincoln believed.

'I am going home to study law! I am going home to study law!' he exclaimed repeatedly, as he and Emerson walked from the court room down to the river when the hearing had ended. Emerson said that that was what he had been doing. 'No,' Lincoln replied, 'not as these college bred men study it. I have learned my lesson. These college bred fellows have reached Ohio, they will soon be in Illinois, and when they come, Emerson, I will be ready for them.'

From that time on, insists Emerson, who often heard Lincoln thereafter, his style and manner of speech and argument improved greatly and steadily — the result, as the old manufacturer stoutly contended throughout his long life, of Lincoln's connection with the celebrated patent case of McCormick *vs.* Manny *et al.*[1]

[1] Emerson's statement was made to Mr. Parkinson, who recounted it to the author, and afterward, at his request, put it in writing. Years after Harding had given Parkinson the account quoted, Parkinson was defending the McCormick Harvesting Machine Co. in a patent suit. 92 Fed. 167, 34 C. C. A., 280. Emerson who was deeply interested in the case financially — the real plaintiff, in fact — was present, most of the time, especially while Parkinson was cross examining the plaintiff's expert.

Emerson and Parkinson were very friendly, however, and often conversed socially. 'I knew that he had been a client of Harding's,' writes Mr. Parkinson, 'and that he had known Lincoln and his associates quite intimately before Lincoln was much known outside of Illinois. I did not then realize that he had attended the trial at Cincinnati as a party defendant in this McCormick case.'

Parkinson made mention of Harding's part in that litigation in relation to Lincoln. In this wise came Emerson's narrative as stated in the text.

'The sequence and circumstances of these conversations [with Harding and with Emerson] impressed them on my memory with unusual definiteness. Hence I have

Harding and Stanton won. In January, 1856, Justice McLean at Washington handed down a long opinion in favor of the defendants. 'The case was argued on both sides with surprising ability and clearness of demonstration,' declares the Justice.[1]

When Lincoln received a check for his fee, he 'returned it, saying he made no argument, and was entitled to no pay beyond the original retainer.' Watson, who 'disbursed the funds,' again sent the check to Lincoln, insisting that, since he had prepared his argument, 'he was as much entitled to the fee as if he had made the argument.' Lincoln then accepted.[2]

Not for years did Harding or Stanton change their minds about Lincoln. Harding thus admits the continuance of his prejudice: 'When Lincoln was named for President by the party to which I belonged, my disgust was such that I felt I could not vote for him and I did not intend to, but the situation had become so ominous by election day that I finally took a Lincoln and Hamlin ballot, closed my eyes, and with great reluctance dropped it in the box.' In the same campaign Stanton, who was an aggressive Democrat, attacked Lincoln with unbridled violence, as a person without sense, manners, or character. Yet he changed his mind, and we shall hear him tell Harding how badly both were mistaken in Lincoln and how supremely great was the man whom they had once insulted. Lincoln, too, remembered them, never for a moment with bitterness or resentment, however, but with understanding and appreciation. As President, he offered one of them the office of Commissioner of Patents [3] and, when a great day came, made the other his Secretary of War.

Some two years before the Reaper Case, Lincoln secured another employment, payment for which was not made until a

mentioned these incidents, as I otherwise would not.' Parkinson to author, May 28, 1923. Mr. Parkinson thinks Emerson's statement trustworthy and accurate.

[1] McCormick vs. Manny et al. 6 McLean, 539–57. The point in the decision was that parts of Manny's machine were different 'in form and principle,' from those in McCormick's reaper. The opinion is extremely technical. In a separate opinion, written without knowledge of McLean's conclusions, Judge Drummond concurred 'at every point.' Ib., 543.

[2] Harding's narrative; Parkinson to author, May 28, 1923. The amount of this fee is unknown.

[3] Ib.

judgment in his favor was rendered in Court nearly two years after his melancholy experience at Cincinnati. In 1853–54 he appeared for the Illinois Central Railroad Company in a suit by the corporation against McLean County to enjoin the collection of taxes. The outcome of that suit was, at that particular time, almost vital to the road's existence. Because the fee in that case was the largest he is known ever to have received, and because of conflicting and sadly confused accounts of the collection of it, overmuch has been written about it.

The original law authorizing the incorporation of the Illinois Central Railroad was passed January 18, 1836. It provided that for the first six years the company should pay to the State five per cent of its gross earnings, and thereafter seven per cent annually, in lieu of all other taxes. But no effort was made to build the road for fifteen years thereafter. On May 2, 1850, Douglas got a bill through the Senate and, on September 17, Ashmun secured its passage through the House,[1] granting to Illinois a large amount of public lands to aid in the construction of the road. With this law as a basis the Legislature gave an elaborate charter to the Illinois Central Railroad Company by which the Governor of the State was required to deed to the company all lands granted to the State, and the company was required simultaneously to transfer all its property to trustees named in the act.

The charter also provided that the Railroad Company should pay to the State, semi-annually, five per cent of its gross receipts, and exempted from taxation all the property of the company for six years; after which 'an annual tax for State purposes shall be assessed by the [State] auditor upon all the property and assets of every kind and description belonging to said corporation.'[2] Thus the interests of the State were secured until the road was completed and in operation. The deed of trust amounted to a mortgage.[3]

Under this arrangement, work on the road began in 1851. The general counsel of the company was James F. Joy of Detroit, a

---

[1] Ackerman, 15–7. Mr. Ackerman was President of the I. C. R. R. Co. when he wrote this historically valuable brochure.

[2] Charter I. C. R. R. Co., Act, Feb. 10, 1851. *Laws of Illinois*, 2nd Sess. 61–75.

[3] Separate Opinion Justice Skinner, I. C. R. R. Co. *vs.* McLean Co. *et al.* 17 Ill. 297.

leading railway lawyer in the West. It would appear that almost immediately after construction of the Illinois Central began, he retained Lincoln as the company's attorney at Springfield.[1] Joy also employed Lincoln, who was 'influential in the State House,' to help him get from the Legislature an act authorizing the Michigan Central Railroad Company to build across northern Illinois into Chicago.[2] At all events, Lincoln was very early attorney for the Illinois Central.[3] On October 14, 1853, Joy telegraphed Lincoln to act as an arbitrator between that company and the Northern Indiana Railroad Company.[4]

In May, 1853, the first section of the road between LaSalle and Bloomington was finished and put in operation.[5] After several months the officials of McLean County decided to assess the property of the road within that county for local taxes. The company refused to pay and brought suit in the Circuit Court to enjoin collection. The question involved was of first importance to the State as well as to the company; for if each of the numerous counties through which the road passed could tax the company in addition to the large amount which it paid to the State under its charter, the operation of the road would have been almost impracticable, the further building of it delayed if not prevented. Even without the additional burden of county taxation the completion of the road was achieved with the utmost difficulty.

Lincoln was acutely anxious to represent one side or the other

[1] 'On Friday morning last, Mr. Joy filed his papers, and entered his motion for a mandamus, and urged me to take up the motion as soon as possible.' Lincoln to Charles Hoyt (Atty. for the I. C. R. R. at Chicago), Jan. 11, 1851. *Works*, II, 146–7.

[2] 'Detroit Memories of Lincoln:' Joseph Greusel, *Detroit Free Press*, Feb. 12, 1911. Greusel got his information from Joy.

[3] Mr. Hill puts the date of Lincoln's employment by the I. C. R. R. Company in 1853. Hill, 202; but this is almost certainly a year later than Lincoln's first retainer by the road.

[4] Hill, 250. The dispute between these roads related either to a crossing agreement or to losses growing out of a collision. Stuyvesant Fish (Pres. I. C. R. R. Co.) to J. M. Dickinson (General Counsel) March 27, 1906. MSS. Files Legal Dept. I. C. R. R. Co., Chicago.

[5] In July, 1854, the section from Chicago to Champaign was completed, and trains were running over it. The section from Cairo to LaSalle was completed Jan. 8, 1855. The entire road, 705.5 miles in length, was finished in September, 1856. Ackerman, 84–8.

in this most important litigation, preferably the counties in which the road had property; and he was alertly active in efforts to secure employment. He could not afford, he said, to lose the chance to earn such a fee. He had discussed the question with the tax officials of at least one other county than McLean, it appears, urging the two counties to 'make common cause' against the railroad company; but neither county had retained him and Lincoln said that the road had offered 'to engage' him. In this situation and before the tax suit was begun, Lincoln wrote from Bloomington to T. R. Webber, Clerk of the Court of Champaign County:

'I find that McLean county' (of which Bloomington was the county seat) 'has assessed the land and other property of the Central Railroad for the purpose of County taxation. An effort is about to be made to get the question of the right to so tax the [Railroad] Co. before the court and ultimately before the Supreme Court, and the [Railroad] Co. are offering to engage me for them.

'As this will be the same question I have had under consideration for you, I am somewhat trammelled by what has passed between you and me, feeling that you have the first right to my services, if you choose to secure me a fee something near such as I can get from the other side.

'The question in its magnitude to the [Railroad] Co. on the one hand and the counties in which the Co. has land on the other is the largest law question that can now be got up in the State, and therefore in justice to myself, I can not afford, if I can help it, to miss a fee altogether.

'If you choose to release me, say so by return mail, and there an end. If you wish to retain me, you had better get authority from your court, come directly over (to Bloomington) in the stage and make common cause with this county.' [1]

Neither county retained Lincoln, however, and three weeks

---

[1] Lincoln to T. R. Webber, Bloomington, Sept. 12, 1853. *Litigant:* Townsend, 22–3. This letter is not in Lincoln's *Works*.

Webber wrote immediately to John B. Thomas, Judge of Champaign County, urging the employment of Lincoln, and Judge Thomas replied, Sept. 15: 'I fully concur with your opinion that no time is to be lost in securing the services of Mr. Lincoln, and hope you or Mr. Jaquith will leave immediately for Bloomington, confer with the

after he sent the above letter, he wrote to the railroad company's attorney, Mason Brayman, who appears to have been in charge of this particular matter locally. Lincoln was now attending court at Pekin and was becoming nervous, it would seem, over the prospect of being left out of the case altogether.

'Neither the County of McLean nor anyone on its behalf has yet made any engagement with me in relation to its suit with the Illinois Central Railroad on the subject of taxation,' Lincoln advised the road's attorney. So 'I am now free to make an engagement for the road, and if you think of it you may "count me in." Please write me on receipt of this. I shall be here at least ten days.'[1] Brayman then employed Lincoln and sent him a draft for two hundred and fifty dollars as a retainer.[2] It appears that there was no contest in the Circuit Court; a decree of dismissal was entered *pro forma*, and, for purposes of appeal which was immediately taken, the decree contained a stipulation 'that the only question to be made in the Supreme Court' was whether the road could be taxed by the county.[3]

Early in 1854 Joy resigned as General Counsel of the road; but the company insisted that he finish this case. Accordingly he came to Springfield for that purpose. With him in the Supreme Court were Brayman and Lincoln. McLean County was represented by Logan, Stuart, and Benjamin Edwards. The case was heard at the May term, 1854, but the Court was in such doubt that the 'cause stood over, and re-argument was ordered that full discussion and deliberate examination might remove these apparent difficulties.'[4]

The question turned on the construction of Section two, Article nine of the State Constitution of 1847. This section provided

authorities of McLean [County] and take such measures as the circumstances may suggest as to the fee to be offered Mr. Lincoln. I have only this to say, that we have no right to expect his services for a trifle and in this respect have no hesitation in giving you full authority to contract for a fee in proportion to the importance of the claim.' He suggests a retaining fee of fifty dollars ['you need not give it all if less will do'], and an additional contingent fee, 'such as may be necessary even to $500.' Starr, 60.

[1] Lincoln to Brayman, Pekin, Oct. 3, 1853. *Works*, II, 179–80.

[2] Herndon, II, 352. The original draft and Lincoln's letter accepting the retainer are owned by Jesse W. Weik, Greencastle, Ind.

[3] Statement of case. Ill. Cent. R. R. Co. *vs.* the Co. of McLean and George Park, Sheriff, etc.' 17 Ill. 291.

[4] Statement in opinion of the court, delivered by Chief Justice Scates. *Ib.*, 292.

for uniform taxation of all property in proportion to its value, 'and not otherwise;' but the Legislature could tax in any way it pleased excepted classes, specifically named, 'and persons using and exercising franchises and privileges.' [1]

The brief was written by Lincoln.[2] At either the first or second argument, the attorneys for the road took the position that the real issue was not between McLean County and the Illinois Central Railroad Company, but between the County and the State; because the action of the County in taxing the road under the general laws of the Constitutional rule of uniformity in taxation was in direct conflict with the road's charter granted by the Legislature.[3]

In a long and somewhat involved opinion, in which many authorities were cited,[4] the Court unanimously held that, under the Constitution, the Legislature could make exceptions from the rule of uniformity; that the provision in the road's charter requiring payment to the State of a percentage of its gross earnings, was such an exception; and therefore that counties could not tax the road. The decree of the McLean County Circuit Court was, accordingly, reversed.[5]

Joy's fee was twelve hundred dollars.[6] Lincoln wished, as his compensation, 'a particularly beautiful section of land belonging to the company;' and wrote Joy at Detroit to intercede for him with the officers of the company to secure this land as his fee. When in Chicago sometime thereafter Joy did so; but the officials said that they could not give Lincoln a clear warranty deed to the section because all the lands were mortgaged to the bondholders.[7] Joy so advised Lincoln who, sometime after-

---

[1] Sec. 2, Art. IX, Illinois Constitution, 1847.

[2] The original owned by Jesse W. Weik, Greencastle, Ind., in Lincoln's handwriting, was signed by Brayman, Joy, and Lincoln.

[3] 'The question ceases to be one between the railroad and the county, and becomes one, *in the light in which it has been discussed*, between the county and the State.' Chief Justice Scates in delivering the opinion of the Court. 17 Ill. 292. (Italics author's.)

[4] Among the numerous laws and decisions, the Court cited the fact that Pennsylvania and Massachusetts, at that time, exempted railroads from all taxation on the ground that they were public works. *Ib.*, 296.

[5] 17 Ill. 291–7.

[6] Greusel; *Detroit Free Press*, Feb. 12, 1911.

[7] *Ib.* Also there was the trust deed to the State.

slung-shot to Shaw, saying with his quizzical smile: 'Here, Henry, I'll give you this to remember me by.' [1]

After the trial a rumor spread that the almanac produced by Lincoln was for the year previous to the murder; and Shaw wrote Herndon that this was the general belief in Beardstown 'at that time (and I may also say at the present)' — 1866.[2] Shaw says that the story was that, when Lincoln came into court, he handed to the clerk an almanac for 1856, 'stating that he might call for one during the trial and if he did, to send him that one;' that when the witness testified that he could see plainly because the moon was nearly full and 'about in the same place that the sun would be at ten o'clock in the morning,' Lincoln called for the 'prepared' almanac and showed from it that at the time testified by the witness, 'the moon *had already set;*' that 'in the roar of laughter following, the jury and opposing counsel neglected to look at the date;' and that thus the trick succeeded. 'My own opinion is,' concludes Shaw, 'that when an almanac was called for by Mr. Lincoln, two were brought, one of the year of the murder and the other of the year previous; that Mr. Lincoln was entirely innocent of any deception in the matter.'

But Milton Logan, the foreman of the jury, told Shaw 'that the almanac was a " Jayne *Almanac*," that it was the one for the year in which the murder was committed, and that there was no trick about it, that he is willing to make an affidavit that he examined it as to its date and that it was the almanac of the year of the murder.' Although giving his account some forty years after Logan's emphatic statement, another juror, John T. Brady, supports it: 'The Almanac showed that the moon at that time was going out of sight. There has never been a question in my mind about the genuineness of the almanac,

---

[1] Shaw kept the slung-shot for many years, he assured Herndon. 'I have that same slung-shot now,' writes Shaw. 'It was made by Armstrong for the occasion. He took a common bar of pig lead, pounded it round, about the size of a large hickory nut, then cut a piece of leather out of the top of one of his boots, and with a thread and needle he sewed it into the shape of a slung-shot, and thus improvised in a few minutes a very fatal weapon.'

[2] Mr. Saunders in his affidavit says that 'while some people in this community [Beardstown] believed the almanac ... was changed and was not for the year A.D. 1857, yet the great majority believed the almanac was genuine.'

wards, sent to the company a fee bill of five thousand dollars.[1]
Seemingly the road's officials thought Lincoln's fee excessive,
in view of Joy's moderate charge, and the President, William
H. Osborne, suggested that Lincoln sue for the amount and the
company would pay the judgment.[2]

This is not unlikely, for, just at this point the road fell upon
desperate times. By the end of 1854 only three hundred miles
had been constructed, and these were in detached fragments.
The operating cost was heavy, earnings small, and all of the
road's net income was more than absorbed by the interest on a
bonded indebtedness of nearly twenty million dollars and floating obligations aggregating two and a half million more. The
crops in Illinois for that year were 'almost a total failure,' and
land sales were checked.[3] The directors of the road lived in New
York and other eastern cities. Foreclosure was threatened by
the company's bondholders and every cent that the road could
gather or save was indispensable.[4] The future of the enterprise
was an unsolved problem.

In this situation John M. Douglas who succeeded Joy as the
road's principal attorney told Lincoln that he could not give a
voucher for so large a fee, and advised him to bring suit against
the road, which would not contest it. Douglas and other officers of the company had been sharply instructed by the Board
of Directors to send every available dollar to New York in order
to prevent suits in that State for receiverships; and the General
Counsel, in advising Lincoln to sue the road, was attempting to

[1] *Works*, II, 288.

[2] Greusel, as *supra*. 'The simple truth is that the whole trouble was with Mr. James
F. Joy . . . whom Mr. Lincoln afterward despised.' Charles L. Capen to John G. Drennan, April 6, 1906. MSS. Files Legal Dept. I. C. R. R. Co.

[3] These I. C. R. R. lands were offered for sale on easy terms and long time. *Illinois
State Register*, June 1; *Chicago Daily Democrat*, Nov. 21, 1854, Feb. 12, April 4, Sept. 6,
1855; *Ottawa Free Trader*, Aug. 1, 1857, etc.

Sales revived in 1855. *Free West*, July 12, 1855. 'Yesterday Mr. Du Puy, agent of
the Illinois Central Land Department, received a letter from one of the association
[Vermont Emigrant Association] stating that about *two hundred* families were preparing to leave Vermont to settle on farming lands, located on the main trunk of the
road,.

Most of the emigration from New England and New York, etc., became Republican
and supported Lincoln in his contest with Douglas and thereafter.

[4] Ackerman, 63–4, 67.

secure a delay in the payment of so large a sum, until the financial crisis of the road had passed.[1]

Sometime during March, 1857, Lincoln went to New York,[2] undoubtedly to see the directors of the railroad company about his fee, since, so far as has been discovered, he had no other reason for taking so long and expensive a journey at that time.[3] Upon his return, he filed his complaint against the railroad company in the McLean Circuit Court at Bloomington, at the April term, stating his services and demanding judgment for five thousand dollars. The usual formal allegations in cases of debt were made, demand, refusal to pay, and the like.

When the case came on for hearing Thursday, June 18, 1857, no one appeared for the railroad company and judgment was rendered by default. But that afternoon Douglas reached Bloomington, asked that the judgment be set aside, Lincoln promptly agreed, and the case was set for trial on the following Tuesday. The only reason for this procedure was that Douglas did not want the record to show that the company had defaulted because of his absence. The trial, a mere formality, took but a few minutes. Judge Davis presided, the jury, personally selected by him, was the same before which most cases were tried semi-annually in Bloomington, and had known Lincoln for years.[4] In the court room at the time was James S. Ewing, a prominent lawyer of Bloomington, Adlai Ewing Stevenson,[5]

[1] Stuyvesant Fish to Drennan, April 6, 1906. MSS. Files Legal Dept. I. C. R. R. Co.

[2] Stringer, 221–2. The fare from St. Louis to New York was $26.85. *Alton Daily Courier*, April 29, 1853. By 1857 there were sleeping cars with staterooms on the I. C. R. R. Co. *Daily Democratic Press*, Sept. 29, 1857. Lincoln used a pass on the I. C. R. R. Co. on this journey.

[3] It was on this visit that Lincoln endorsed Primm's note for $400 and thus got the lot in Lincoln, Logan County.

Governor Matteson of Illinois was in New York at the same time. Stringer, 222.

[4] 'The selection of the jury at that time was vested by law in the Sheriff, but as a matter of fact, in McLean County at least, they were selected by Judge Davis; most of them being his intimate friends, substantial old settlers of good judgment, sound sense and integrity; the same men appearing term after term as jurors. Mr. Lincoln, who had been attending the McLean County Court for years, knew every one of them and they knew him, and it would have taken a good deal of evidence on the part of the Railroad Company to convince them that Mr. Lincoln was asking an excessive fee.' Ezra M. Prince to John G. Drennan, April 5, 1906. MSS. Files Legal Dept. I. C. R. R. Co.

[5] Vice President of the United States, 1893–97.

then a law student in that town, and Ezra M. Prince, a young attorney. The statements of these men, each of whom declares that he remembered distinctly what occurred, settle this long-controverted matter.

Clearly and briefly Lincoln told the jury the history of the case, the question involved, work done, benefits to the road. He said that Douglas had 'kindly consented that a statement which he had written out and which had been signed by some of the prominent lawyers of the State, might be read in evidence with the same effect as if the depositions of these gentlemen had been taken.' This certificate, which was not sworn to, was signed by Grant Goodrich, Norman B. Judd, Archibald Williams, Norman H. Purple, O. H. Browning, and Robert S. Blackwell. It stated that five thousand dollars was a reasonable fee for the services Lincoln had rendered. Without Douglas's consent it could not have been received as evidence.

Lincoln said that Mr. Joy thought his fee was too high and that a jury would have to decide it. 'Mr. Douglas said that Mr. Lincoln's statement was substantially correct and fair and that he himself did not think the fee charged, was too much.' A verdict was promptly returned for the full amount asked, but reduced by two hundred dollars when Douglas reminded Lincoln that the company had paid him that sum as a retainer fee, an item Lincoln had forgotten.[1]

Stevenson confirms all that Ewing states and adds: 'It appeared to me to be in the nature of an amicable suit.' [2] Prince is equally clear and specific. His understanding was that Douglas thought Lincoln's bill 'reasonable, but in deference to others, it was agreed that an amicable suit should be brought; and the proceedings certainly bear out that view.' Prince gives almost

[1] Statement of James S. Ewing, Bloomington, Ill., April 5, 1906. MSS. Files Legal Dept. I. C. R. R. Co.

Ewing says that the original statement of the lawyers that Lincoln's fee was reasonable was in his 'possession for many years. I had it framed and hanging in my office where it was destroyed in the Bloomington fire of 1900.'

Lincoln made a copy with the signatures in his handwriting; and it is this copy which has been reproduced as the original, with intimation that it never was signed by those whose names are attached to the statement.

The exact amount of the retainer was $250. See p. 587, *supra*.

[2] Adlai E. Stevenson's statement, Bloomington, Ill., April 6, 1906. MSS. Files Legal Dept. I. C. R. R. Co.

exactly the same account as Ewing, but says that 'the case was submitted without argument on either side. The entire trial lasted but a few minutes, and in the ordinary meaning of the term was not a trial at all. . . . I was present at the trial and remember it distinctly.'[1]

The company was hard pressed for funds during all this time payment of the judgment was delayed and, on August 1, a writ of execution was issued to the Sheriff.[2] Fortunately for Lincoln the crisis in the road's finances was not reached until autumn; and on August 12, 1857, four thousand eight hundred dollars, the exact amount of the judgment, was deposited to his credit in the Springfield Fire and Marine Insurance Company, in which Lincoln kept his account. On August 31 he drew out this entire sum [3] and paid half of it, in cash, to Herndon as his share of the firm's windfall.[4] A few weeks later the great panic of October, 1857, prostrated business everywhere, all New York banks but one [5] suspended specie payments, as did most financial institu-

[1] Ezra M. Prince to John G. Drennan, General Attorney I. C. R. R. Chicago, Ill., dated Bloomington, Ill., Apr. 5, 1906. MSS. Files Legal Dept. I. C. R. R. Co. Mr. Prince was Secretary of the McLean County Historical Society at the time he wrote this letter.

In a letter to Judge Drennan, Charles L. Capen, attorney of Bloomington and President of the Illinois State Bar Association, says that his former partner, Robert E. Williams, who was present at the trial, often told him about it: 'The simple truth as stated by him, is that, when Mr. Douglass asked Mr. Lincoln to set aside the judgment by default he told him [that] the Rail Road Company would not make any defence, but that it was embarrassing to him (Douglass) to have the records show how the suit had gone by default.

'At the trial, after Mr. Lincoln had made his opening statement, Mr. Douglass said that statement was fair, and that he, Douglass, thought the bill reasonable and should be paid. . . . The case was given to the jury without argument on either side. All that Mr. Douglass said at the trial, other than the above stated was to call Mr. Lincoln's attention to the fact [that] $200.00 had been paid on the bill, which Mr. Lincoln admitted, saying he had forgotten it, and remitted the amount from his claim. . . .

'The only question in the case was as to the reasonableness of the fee charged. All Mr. Lincoln had was the memorandum for use on the trial as to the facts to be proved.' Charles L. Capen to John G. Drennan, dated at Bloomington, Ill., April 5, 1906. *Ib.*

[2] *Litigant:* Townsend, 29.

[3] Depositor's Ledger C, for 1857, 438. Springfield Fire & Marine Ins. Co.

[4] Herndon, II, 352–3.

[5] The Chemical Bank. Ackerman, 65.

The panic of 1857 was very hard in Illinois. It really began in 1854 and was largely due to railroad construction, heavy issues of bank-notes, and the war in Europe.

'The failure of the People's Bank at Carmi has fallen with great severity on the people of this section of the State. Its bills comprised about one-half of our circulating medium.' *Joliet Signal*, Feb. 3, 1857.

tions throughout the country; and on October 9, the Illinois Central Railroad was also 'forced to suspend payment.'[1]

Had not the judgment been rendered in the friendly suit in June, or had the company delayed payment of it, Lincoln would not have received his fee for at least a year and probably longer, and it is doubtful whether he could have made the campaign against Douglas in 1858. Certainly, in that contest, he would have been without this important addition to his limited funds.[2]

Such are the facts in this extensively discussed and sharply controverted case. That Joy, in view of his own moderate fee, thought Lincoln's charge excessive, and that the company's officers, considering the financial plight of the road, agreed with Joy, appear to be fairly clear. In this situation it is also plain that John M. Douglas did not want to give Lincoln a voucher for so large a sum; and it is certain that all concerned agreed that the best way out of the matter would be for Lincoln to bring a suit which the company would not contest.

Throughout the disputes and negotiations over Lincoln's fee he continued to act as attorney for the railroad. Whitney, who had become the company's lawyer, in charge of local litigation such as damage suits, relates that 'we had a contract that Lincoln was to take no case against us and that I could call on him to help me when he was there;[3] and when my clients wanted help I always got Lincoln.'[4] When travelling over the road, Lincoln used a pass, as did all of the company's officers and attorneys.

'The financial pressure now prevailing in the country has no parallel in our business history.' *Chicago Democratic Press*, Sept. 30, 1857.

'Money is about as tight as it can be, for it is scarcely possible to get it on any terms.' *Ib.*, Oct. 9, 1857.

'Of the 66 banks in Illinois, only 39 are doing business — the remaining 27 having gone into liquidation.' *Central Illinois Gazette* (Champaign), Apr. 14, 1858.

[1] Notice of Directors of I. C. R. R. Co., signed by the Treasurer, J. N. Perkins. It was published in all New York newspapers.

Stuyvesant Fish says that the road made a voluntary assignment to three trustees, which was placed of record in New York but not in Illinois; and that this assignment was cancelled in the latter part of 1858. Fish to Drennan, April 6, 1906. MSS. Files Legal Dept. I. C. R. R. Co.

[2] The road was saved only by the great exertions and resourcefulness of William Henry Osborne, then President of the Company. Ackerman, 66–7.

[3] At the court where the case was tried.

[4] Whitney to Herndon, Aug. 27, 1887. Weik MSS. Also see Whitney, 261–2.

In asking in 1856 for a renewal of a similar pass on the Chicago and Alton Railroad Lincoln wrote: 'Says Tom to John: "Here's your old rotten wheelbarrow. I've broke it, usin' on it. I wish you would mend it, case I shall want to borrow it this arternoon."

'Acting on this as a precedent, I say, "Here's your old 'chalked hat' I wish you would take it, and send me a new one, case I shall want to use it the first of March."' [1]

Four months after the McLean County tax case was decided by the Supreme Court Lincoln rendered to a client a written opinion on the construction of the land grants by Congress.[2] In the year of Lincoln's suit against the company for his five thousand dollar fee, he and Whitney appeared for the road before the Supreme Court in a case which they had appealed from the Circuit Court of Champaign County where they had been beaten. This case is of interest as showing the efforts of the railroad to save money in its then desperate financial condition. The only question was how much weight would be lost by hogs kept in cars negligently delayed in transit. The jury gave a verdict for $860.25. Whitney and Lincoln moved for a new trial on the ground that such damages were excessive; the plaintiff remitted all but six hundred dollars, for which amount the Court gave judgment. From this judgment the railroad took an appeal, obviously for delay only, since the sole issue before the Supreme Court was 'whether the evidence justified a verdict for the amount for which the judgment was rendered.' The Court in a curt and almost contemptuous opinion decided against the railroad company.[3]

At the same term of the Supreme Court Lincoln and Whitney won another case for the railroad company of first importance to all common carriers by rail. The company was sued for damages to cattle by delay in transit, although the shipper had signed a written contract releasing the railroad from injury or delay in consideration of reduced rates for transporting the cat-

[1] Lincoln to R. P. Morgan, Superintendent of the Chicago and Alton R. R., Feb. 13, 1856. *Works*, II, 289.

[2] Drennan to Hill, April 10, 1906. MSS. Files Legal Dept. I. C. R. R. Co. Lincoln's opinion was rendered March 6, 1856. For this opinion see Starr, 60.

[3] I. C. R. R. Co. Appellant *vs*. Brock Hays *et al*., Appellees, 19 Ill. 166-7.

tle. The Court held unanimously that such a contract was valid
and confirmed a rule of law important to railroad interests.[1]

When Lincoln's fee controversy was coming to a head a young
man of thirty, a graduate of West Point who had served with
notable gallantry in the Mexican War and had been an observer
in the Crimea, but who had resigned from the army, Captain
George B. McClellan, was appointed Chief Engineer of the Illinois Central Railroad; and so well did he discharge his duties
that in less than a year he was made Vice-President as well as
Chief Engineer and placed in charge of the operation and conduct of the road. When the company was forced to suspend
payments during the panic of 1857, McClellan was appointed
one of the trustees to which the road was temporarily turned
over.[2]

Thus Lincoln first met McClellan. 'Mr. Lincoln was the attorney of the Illinois Central Railroad Company, to assist the
local counsel in the different counties of the circuit,' writes
Judge Weldon of an incident he personally witnessed. In De
Witt County during a session of the Court at Clinton in 1858 or
9, Lincoln and the company's local attorney wanted to postpone the trial of a case against the railroad 'and Mr. Lincoln remarked to the court:

'"We are not ready for trial."

'Judge Davis said: "Why is not the company ready to go to
trial?"

'Mr. Lincoln replied: "We are embarrassed by the absence or
rather want of information from Captain McClellan."

'The Judge said: "Who is Captain McClellan, and why is he
not here?"

'Mr. Lincoln said: "All I know of him is that he is the engi-

---

[1] I. C. R. R. Co. vs. Morrison et al., 19 Ill. 136–41. See statement of rule by Justice
Breese on 141. This suit was brought in Charleston where Ficklin resided and was local
attorney of the I. C. R. R. Co., and he, therefore, was in the case with Lincoln and
Whitney in the Supreme Court.

[2] Data on picture in office Chief Engineer, I. C. R. R. Co., Chicago; Ackerman, 93.
President Ackerman says of McClellan: 'The financial resources of the company at this
time were quite limited, so that the position [of McClellan] proved a most trying one to
fill. . . . He was courageous under difficulties, exceedingly tender-hearted, just and considerate in his treatment of those placed under him, and was beloved by all with whom
he came in contact.'

neer of the railroad, and why he is not here this deponent saith not."' [1]

At the same time that Lincoln was thus coming in contact with McClellan, another young graduate of West Point who had also won laurels in the Mexican War and who had also resigned his commission in the Regular Army, Captain Ulysses S. Grant, was without success trying to win a livelihood at Galena, Illinois. In the office of the railroad company at Chicago was a third young graduate of West Point, the inventor of a breech-loading rifle, Lieutenant Ambrose E. Burnside, who had also left the army and was now cashier of the land department and treasurer of the company.[2]

Within five years Lincoln was to make each of these men a general in the Union Army.

Seemingly the DeWitt County case was another example of the policy of delay which the company's financial plight had forced its officials to adopt. Lincoln often met McClellan in the business of the road. As Vice-President, he had charge of legislation affecting his company as well as of the grave matter of taxes. Under the road's charter the value of the company's property taxable after six years from the date of the charter was determined by the State Auditor; and from his decision no appeal was provided. In the fall of 1857 the six years expired and a dispute arose between the company and the State Auditor, Jesse K. Dubois, as to the amount of taxes due the State on the general tax, then assessed for the first time. The State threatened to sue the company, which offered the amount it believed to be due. In this situation Lincoln wrote Dubois, who was one of his closest personal and political friends, urging him to accept the money which the railroad company tendered: 'J. M. Douglas of the I. C. R. R. Co. is here and will carry this letter. He says they have a large sum (near $90,000) which they will pay into the treasury now, if they have an assurance that they shall not be sued before January, 1859 — otherwise not. I really wish that you would consent to this. Douglas says they *can not* pay more and I believe him. I do not write this as a lawyer seeking an advantage for a client; but only as a friend, only urging

[1] Weldon: Rice, 201.   [2] Ackerman, 93.

you to do what I think I would do if I were in your situation. I mean this as private and confidential only, but I feel a good deal of anxiety about it.' [1]

It appears that the State Auditor did what Lincoln asked. To settle the matter of this and like disputes, it became necessary to secure the enactment of a law giving the railroad company the right of appeal to the Supreme Court. Thus matters stood for two years, and, in February, 1859, a bill was introduced into the Legislature providing for such an appeal. While this measure was pending, an arranged case was brought in the Supreme Court by the State against the railroad company to settle the basis of valuation of the company's property; and it was agreed that if the bill passed the Legislature, there should be no appeal from the valuation of 1857 and that the question should be left to the court. The bill speedily became a law.[2]

Such was the state of affairs when, at the December term of the Supreme Court, 1859, this important case was argued before that tribunal. Lincoln and J. M. Douglas appeared for the railroad company, while Logan and Hay assisted the State's attorney. The Court did not hand down its decision until the November term 1861, when, in a clear and able opinion by Justice Sidney Breese, the Court unanimously decided in favor of the railroad company.[3]

Thus Lincoln's connection, as attorney of the Illinois Central Railroad, continued until his nomination for the Presidency. Indeed only two months before the assembling of the historic Convention in the Wigwam at Chicago he was in that city for two weeks trying a case of vital concern to the road. This was the celebrated sand bar litigation and involved the title to exten-

---

[1] Lincoln to Dubois, Dec. 21, 1857. *Works*, ii, 354.

[2] Act Feb. 21, 1859. *Laws of Illinois*, 1859, 206–7. The fifth section granting the appeal, provided that if the I. C. R. R. Co. should be dissatisfied with the valuation by the State Auditor, 'they shall be allowed an appeal from the decision of the auditor to the supreme court . . . and it shall be the duty of said supreme court, at the term next succeeding the taking of such appeal, . . . to hear and determine the aggregate value of the stock, property and assets owned by said company.'

McClellan was in Springfield during this session of the Legislature and is said to have written a vivid account of the passage of this bill and the defeat of other bills hostile to the I. C. R. R. Co.; but no such letter can now be found.

[3] St. Ill. *vs.* I. C. R. R. Co., 27 Ill. 64–70.

sive lands on the lake front. Although the railroad company did not appear of record by name, it was the real defendant and was successful. The case had been tried three times, the jury failing to agree. On the fourth trial, March 19, 1860, Lincoln appeared among the counsel for the defence. The proceedings were before Judge Drummond in the United States Court and lasted nearly two weeks. The jury returned a verdict for the defendants.[1]

Of far more effect on the development of the country, and quite as replete with legal difficulties as the reaper patent case or the railroad tax cases, was the next extensive litigation in which Lincoln appeared after he argued the suit of the Illinois Central Railroad Company against McLean County. Again he was one of three counsel for the defence and again the issue was momentous; but in this case there was no embarrassment, no affront, no dispute, or delay as to fees — only success and commendation. Also it is not unlikely that the services he rendered and the result of the trial helped to bring him strong political support in Chicago when, a year after the verdict was rendered, Lincoln took the field against Stephen A. Douglas — for the vital interests of Chicago were at stake.

About 1855, the Rock Island Railroad Company, through a subsidiary corporation, the Rock Island Bridge Company, built a railway bridge across the Mississippi from Rock Island to Davenport. Business men of St. Louis and the river steamboat interests were acutely alarmed and vigorously protested. On May 6, 1856, the steamer *Effie Afton*, Captain Hurd, started from Cincinnati and St. Louis for St. Paul. The vessel was new, well-equipped and worth about fifty thousand dollars. She was loaded with freight and carried two hundred passengers. Passing through the draw of the bridge, the boat struck one of its seven piers and was thrown against another. Stoves were up-

[1] The title of the case was William S. Johnson *vs.* William Jones and Sylvester Marsh. Counsel for the plaintiff were Buckner S. Morris, Isaac N. Arnold, and John A. Wills; for the defendants, Samuel W. Fuller, Van H. Higgins, John Van Arman, and Lincoln. Whitney, 254.

Lincoln made his headquarters at the office of Whitney, who had moved to Chicago. Whitney's statement. Weik MSS.

The records in the Federal Court at Chicago were destroyed in the great fire of 1871, and this case was not reported in the press.

set and the steamer with her cargo and machinery was burned. The draw of the bridge also burned and fell into the river.

Captain Hurd and other owners of the boat immediately sued the bridge company in the United States Circuit Court for the northern district of Illinois, alleging that the *Effie Afton* was carefully and skilfully navigated at the time, and that the boat 'was forcibly driven by the currents and eddies caused by said piers against one of them,' resulting in the 'imminent danger' of sinking and of the actual destruction of the boat and cargo by fire. The bill of complaint also averred that the bridge was a permanent obstruction to navigation. The prayer of the bill was for damages to the value of the boat and cargo, with insurance. 'The defendants pleaded not guilty to the charge made. And this is the important issue you are sworn to try,' Justice John McLean said in charging the jury.[1]

The contest, however, was really between St. Louis and other cities and towns on the Mississippi and Ohio rivers on the one side, and Chicago and inland railway centres on the other side. More broadly, it was a conflict between exclusive river transportation north and south and rail transportation east and west. In a deeper, though indirect sense, this law-suit was another of the many economic antagonisms between North and South, and in the argument to the jury disunion was hinted.

On December 16, 1856, the St. Louis Chamber of Commerce held a meeting and resolved to assist vigorously in the prosecution of the case against the bridge company; and the Chicago papers charged that the rival city was the real plaintiff.[2] The bitterest possible feeling was aroused.[3]

[1] Justice McLean's charge to jury. *Chicago Daily Democratic Press*, Sept. 25, 1857.

[2] *Ib.*, April 27 and Sept. 26, 1857; Richards, 35–6.

[3] 'Facts . . . do not warrant the incessant clamor kept up by those who insist that that magnificent and necessary structure shall be torn down. . . . We trust that . . . the outcries of the St. Louis and river press may be silenced.' *Chicago Tribune*, April 17, 1857. Editorial.

'The *St. Louis Republican* has been of late particularly notorious as the leading Border Ruffian organ in Missouri; the opponent of the Emancipation movement and as the unscrupulous enemy of the Rock Island Bridge. . . . There is a point beyond which the enemies of this structure must not go. . . . When they pile falsehood upon falsehood . . . it is time they should be rebuked as common liars.' *Davenport Gazette*, as quoted in *Chicago Tribune*, May 18, 1857.

'The Railroad Bridge at Rock Island is an intolerable nuisance. . . . It is utterly

At the trial, which began in Chicago September 8, 1857, uncommonly able lawyers appeared for Captain Hurd — Judge H. M. Wead of Peoria, the best 'river lawyer' in the State, Corydon Beckwith of Chicago, afterwards a Justice of the Supreme Court of the State and later General Counsel of the Chicago, Alton and St. Louis Railroad, and Timothy D. Lincoln of Cincinnati, an admiralty lawyer of great repute. The bridge company was represented by Norman B. Judd of Chicago, Joseph Knox of Rock Island, and Lincoln. At Chicago interest in the trial was intense, and the *Cincinnati Enquirer* declared that the case engaged 'the attention of the whole country.'[1]

Both sides had prepared with utmost thoroughness. Many depositions had been taken. Lincoln and Judd, the attorneys of the Rock Island Railroad Company, and B. B. Brayton, Sr., the 'Bridge Engineer,' had gone together to Rock Island and carefully examined the bridge and currents of the river. Lincoln was particularly minute in his inspection. Mr. Brayton's son, then a youth, who was present, relates that 'the explanations offered by the bridge master, bridge engineer, and others, did not seem to satisfy him as to the currents, etc., and approaching me, he said, "young man, are you employed here on this bridge? If so will you go with me to the head of the draw-pier and answer some questions?"' After this final inspection was made with young Brayton, Lincoln said that he 'understood the situation,' and the party returned to Chicago.[2]

Judd, who had charge of the defence, was aggressive in his opening statement: 'Every bushel of wheat that went from the West to the East would be affected — hence this nervousness on the part of the St. Louis people. . . . St. Louis had under-

---

impossible for any man not an idiot to note the disasters at Rock Island and honestly ascribe them to any other cause than the huge obstruction to navigation which the Bridge Company have built there and insist shall remain, even though lives by the score and property by the million are destroyed every year. . . . We have rarely seen such illustration of supercilious insolence, as have been presented by advocates of the bridge.' *St. Louis Republican*, as quoted in *Chicago Tribune*, May 18, 1857.

[1] Richards, 29–33.

[2] 'The Crossing of the River: The Turning Point for the Railroad and the West.' By B. B. Brayton, *Davenport Democrat and Leader*, 'Half Century Edition,' Oct. 22, 1905. Mr. Brayton's article is done with great care.

taken the keeping of the Mississippi and Missouri Rivers, and said there should be no bridge.' [1]

The *Chicago Press* reports that 'scores of witnesses were examined and depositions read. Some of the witnesses were men of eminent positions in society, and the greater part were scientific experts.' A model of the steamboat, another of the bridge, and many maps were exhibited.[2] The questions involved were complicated — currents, proper location of piers, right methods of bridge construction, skill in running steamboats, and the like. The conflict in the testimony was direct and extensive.

A committee of three from the St. Louis Chamber of Commerce watched the trial 'and gave to the looker-on the impression that Captain Hurd and other plaintiffs were mere spectators of the fight,' declared the *Chicago Daily Democratic Press;* and that paper charged that over half a million dollars had been subscribed 'under lead of the St. Louis Chamber of Commerce by the river interests between Pittsburgh and St. Paul to prosecute this suit to the bitter end,' bring still another suit and prevent the building of other bridges across the Mississippi.[3]

For the defence Judd and Knox examined the witnesses and argued most of the questions of admissibility of evidence which arose during the trial. Timothy D. Lincoln did the same on behalf of the plaintiff.[4] When Judd offered to prove the volume of business 'done over the river' in comparison with that 'done upon the river,' the plaintiff's counsel objected and a lengthy argument ensued, in which all the attorneys in the case spoke except Beckwith. Lincoln 'gave a history of the Peoria bridge case,' admitted that the bridge must not be a material obstruction, qualified, however, 'by the necessity of the bridge. The plaintiffs held that their vested interests could not be interfered with, but the decisions of our courts were conforming, as they should do, to the nature and wants of our country.'[5]

[1] *Chicago Daily Press*, Sept. 9, 1857.   [2] *Ib.*, Sept. 25, 1857.

[3] *Ib.*, Sept. 26, 1857, as quoted in Richards, 35–6.

[4] 'Mr. Judd, who managed the case on the part of the defence, and Mr. Lincoln, of Cincinnati, on the part of the plaintiff, displayed untiring industry and great ingenuity.' *Chicago Democratic Press*, Sept. 25, 1857. Editorial.

[5] *Chicago Tribune*, Sept. 21, 1857. The argument on the admissibility of this evidence indicates that counsel on both sides regarded it as crucial.

T. D. Lincoln, citing many authorities, said that all citizens had a right to the free

For about two weeks witnesses were examined, depositions were read, counsel contended. Finally both sides rested, and arguments to the jury began. Lincoln made the closing speech for the bridge company. He would not 'assail anybody,' he soothingly began, having reference to the acrimony shown throughout the trial; his earnestness must not be mistaken for ill-nature. Let us try to reconcile conflicting testimony and believe that witnesses 'are not intentionally erroneous as long as we can.' St. Louis and the steamboat interests did as others would do under like circumstances, and Lincoln had no prejudice against them. 'St. Louis as a commercial place may desire that this bridge should not stand as it is adverse to her commerce, diverting a portion of it from the river;' perhaps that city 'supposes' that, if the bridge is removed, the products of Iowa will necessarily be sent to St. Louis. Doubtless 'some prejudice has added color to the testimony' of certain witnesses because they had attended the St. Louis meetings; but that was the only connection those meetings had with the case.

Nothing could displease him more, said Lincoln, than the blocking of 'one of these great channels extending almost from where it never freezes to where it never thaws;' but the demands of travel and traffic from east to west 'are not less important. . . . It is growing larger and larger, building up new countries with a rapidity never before seen in the history of the world.' Look at Illinois, at Iowa! 'This current of travel has its rights as well as that of north and south.' Consider the business done by this

navigation of the river; 'the bridge was equally an obstruction, no matter how much business was done upon it. . . . To open such a question would lead to endless evidence upon the comparative commerce of rivers and railroads,' etc.

Knox replied that it was 'a startling doctrine, that however great the public necessities of the Union, they could not be shown, nor a river bridged.' Conflicting interests must 'harmonize' for the general good. The defence would prove that a hundred times more business was done over the bridge than on the river.

Judge Wead argued vigorously: 'According to the doctrine asked for as commerce increases across the river, the right of free navigation diminishes,' which was absurd. The only question was 'whether the bridge was a material obstruction; with that the commerce over the bridge had nothing to do.'

Justice McLean, in a very clear opinion, held that the evidence should be received 'to show that the bridge was not unnecessarily built' but 'not for the purpose of authorizing the bridge to obstruct navigation.

'These great (railway) interests must be accommodated, but so arranged as not to materially obstruct commerce. . . . Railroads cannot be cut off from passing navigable rivers, but must not materially obstruct them.'

particular railroad [1] in less than a single year! From September 8, 1856, to August 8, 1857, more than twelve thousand five hundred freight cars and more than seventy-four thousand passengers had passed over this bridge! The river is closed to navigation for well-nigh a third of the year — the bridge is serviceable at all times. 'This shows that this bridge must be treated with respect in this court and is not to be kicked about with contempt.' Judge Wead had spoken of the conflict of interests 'and even a dissolution of the union.' The only rule of safety was that of 'live and let live;' if that rule were observed, there would be an end of 'this trouble about the bridge.'

How had the steamboat men acted when the bridge was burned? 'Why there was a shouting and ringing of bells and whistling on all the boats as it fell. It was a jubilee, a greater celebration than follows an excited election.'

Lincoln reviewed the evidence as to accidents. 'The dangers of this place are tapering off and as the boatmen get cool the accidents get less. We may soon expect if this ratio is kept up that there will be no accidents at all.' The tests of the current made by the bridge engineers were accurate; the piers built at the proper angle, considering that 'the course of the river is a curve.'

'What is a material obstruction? . . . What is reasonable skill and care?' Surely more care must be taken by boatmen after a bridge has been built across a river, than before. 'When a pilot comes along it is unreasonable for him to dash on heedless of this structure which has been *legally put there*.' The pilot of the *Effie Afton* had plenty of time to examine the bridge while the boat was lying at Rock Island, and would not every juror have taken advantage of that opportunity?

Lincoln then argued at great length as to the details of the conflicting testimony about currents, the placing of piers on which the boat struck, the depth of water, the size of the vessel, and other items. While he was in the thick of his discussion court adjourned until the following day. Next morning he went into a long technical explanation of the mechanism of the boat, the effect of one wheel only in operation, the certain result of the

[1] The Rock Island.

boat's having improperly entered the draw because of her passing another boat which went in true and got through without trouble.

Apparently Judge Wead, who spoke before Lincoln, had said that tunnels should be constructed under rivers, rather than bridges be built above them; but, Lincoln replied, that is not practicable. There 'is not a tunnel that is a successful project in this world. A suspension bridge cannot be built so high but that the chimneys of the boats will grow up till they cannot pass. The steamboat men will take pains to make them grow. The cars of a railroad cannot without immense expense rise high enough to get even with a suspension bridge or go low enough to get through a tunnel; such expense is unreasonable.'

In conclusion, Lincoln reminded the jury that the burden of proof was on the plaintiffs to show that the bridge was a 'material obstruction and that they have managed their boat with reasonable care and skill.' He had much more to say, and 'many things that he could suggest,' but 'wished to close to save time.' [1]

Timothy D. Lincoln closed the argument for the plaintiffs. He spoke for more than seven hours, and even the *Chicago Press* stated that his speech was 'able, elaborate, and ingenious.' That paper prepared a 'lengthy report of it' which, however, was 'crowded out of our columns to make room for Judge McLean's charge.' In an editorial, after the verdict, describing the trial and showering praise upon the participants, the *Press* said: 'Mr. A. Lincoln in his address to the jury was very successful, so far as clear statement and close logic was concerned.' [2]

Justice McLean charged the jury at great length, summarizing the testimony clearly, compactly, and with notable fairness. The whole matter, he said in conclusion, depended on the existence of cross currents and eddies in the draw and of the care and skill with which the boat was managed. If the jury believed witnesses of plaintiffs, they must award them damages to the amount of the value of the boat including insurance; but if the jury believed that there were no currents and that the vessel was not competently navigated, they must find for the defendant.

The jury were out but a few hours and 'reported that they

---

[1] *Works*, II, 340–54.   [2] *Chicago Democratic Press*, Sept. 25, 1857.

could not agree — that they stood nine to three.'[1] The court seeing from the evident temper of the jury that it was impossible for them to agree, dismissed them.[2] Chicago and the railway interests were jubilant; St. Louis, Cincinnati, and the river interests disappointed and very bitter. For two or three years the fight was kept up through Congress and the War Department. Not until the approach of the Civil War did the defenders of river traffic give up the contest.[3]

While Lincoln was in Chicago on this case, Mrs. Lincoln had the half-story of their house made into a full second story, the whole house painted, and the rooms papered. Upon his return, when Lincoln saw this imposing change, he said to a neighbor on the street, one Stout, a grocer: 'Stranger, can you tell me where Lincoln lived? He used to live there.'

'Yes, that is his house there,' said Stout, falling into Lincoln's humor.

'No,' Lincoln answered, 'when I left here, my house was a story and a half, but that is a fine two story house.' Stout insisted that it was the same house declaring that it had grown while Lincoln was away.[4]

Lincoln continued to practise law until after his nomination as the Republican candidate for President. On June 20, 1860, the case of Dawson vs. Ennis was tried in the United States District Court at Springfield; and Lincoln, with McClernand and Isaac J. Ketcham, appeared for the plaintiff, who demanded ten thousand dollars damages, because Ennis had sold in Morgan County an improved patented double plough which he had agreed not to sell. Lincoln had written the complaint. John M. Palmer represented Ennis. The case was submitted to the Court and Lincoln made the argument for the plaintiff. On

---

[1] Seemingly nine for plaintiffs and three for defendants.

[2] *Chicago Democratic Press*, Sept. 25, 1857.   [3] *Chicago Tribune*, April 9, 1858.

[4] John W. Bunn's statement to Clinton L. Conkling, March 5, 1918. Also Gourley's statement, no date. Weik MSS. 'Mrs. Lincoln and myself formed a conspiracy to take off the roof and raise the house.'

During one of Lincoln's long absences from home about this time, his wife bought a carriage, 'a fine one.' When he came back he 'complained, but all to no purpose.' Gourley helped Mrs. Lincoln select the carriage. It appears that when she wished to drive, horses were furnished by a livery stable and driven by a youth, Joseph P. Kent. *Ib.*

March 9, 1861, five days after he was inaugurated President, the Court found 'for the defendant and judgment entered against Lincoln's client for costs.' [1]

So came to an end Lincoln's career at the bar. During the last six years that he practised law he was actively engaged in politics. Indeed he took part in political affairs almost from the moment of his return from Congress; and it cannot be said that he ever lost interest in that, to him, engaging game. From 1854 Lincoln was incessantly occupied with the vast and vital controversy which had been developing for more than twenty years, and that grew in violence and dramatic rapidity until, in the presidential election of 1860, it came to its tragic fullness.

Throughout those last six years of circuit riding he made those great speeches which expressed more accurately than was done by any one else or in any manner the moral and intellectual movement of those stirring times. He witnessed with poignant regret the dissolution of the Whig party and saw the beginning and the rise of the Republican party which he joined, albeit without haste or enthusiasm, and finally emerged as the choice of that party for the Presidency. During this period those mighty issues, which had existed for so long a time, were gradually being made plain to the people — issues, the outcome of which was the American Civil War.

Now comes the dawn of Lincoln's greatness, a lowering dawn, and, with him, we shall behold the breaking of that sullen and forbidding day. We shall witness the efforts of statesmen to avert the approaching storm; we shall see the state of mind of the Southern people which caused them, at last, to throw in the face of fate a gallant, yet desperate, challenge; we shall listen to Lincoln's calm but exalted appeals, hear his historic debate with Douglas, and see the last triumph and the swift downfall of that daring, brilliant, and powerful man.

As we proceed through these stirring years and discern the rise of Lincoln as a gigantic figure, an elemental creation of destiny to perform a tremendous task, we must ever have in mind

---

[1] Weik, 138–9. Mr. Weik points out the curious fact that Lincoln lost this, the last case he ever tried, and also lost the first case he ever had in the Supreme Court, Scammon *vs.* Cline, 3 Ill., 456.

the qualities displayed to his associates at the bar. We must think of his tall, gaunt figure, his negligent dress, his whimsical manner, his bottomless melancholy combined with a boundless humor, his profound and peculiar honor, his belief in destiny tinged with superstition, his secretiveness and caution, strongly mingled with simplicity, and, above all, his basic devotion to what he thought was right. For these, and all other characteristics which we have seen manifested, were as much a part of his political as of his professional life. Taken together, they make up the man Lincoln, who wrought the wizardry that has mystified historians of all lands.

END OF VOLUME I